This book offers a full and comprehensive account of one of the most colourful and formative reigns in French history, that of Francis I (1515–47), and is published to coincide with the 500th anniversary of his birth in September 1494.

Francis was the contemporary and rival of Henry VIII of England and of the Habsburg Emperor Charles V. He was also an outstanding patron of the arts and of learning, and the builder of world-famous châteaux such as Chambord and Fontainebleau. Professor Knecht aims to do justice to all aspects of Francis's rich cultural legacy, and takes into account much recent research on the king's administration, and financial and religious policies. The king's ambivalence towards the challenge of Protestantism also offers the historian scope for controversy, as does the overall nature of his rule: how far was Francis an absolute monarch? In the course of examining such aspects, Knecht surveys the economy and society of France during the Renaissance, as well as the political background of wars in Italy and of the rivalry between Francis I and Charles V.

This book is a completely revised version of Knecht's earlier study of the king, *Francis I*, first published in 1982 and for many years the standard work on the subject. That edition is now superseded by this substantially larger work, in which much new written and illustrative material has been included. No other English work on the subject is as up-to-date or as authoritative.

Renaissance Warrior and Patron:
The Reign of Francis I

Renaissance Warrior and Patron: The Reign of Francis I

R. J. KNECHT

Emeritus Professor of French History
University of Birmingham

CAMBRIDGE
UNIVERSITY PRESS

Published by the Press Syndicate of the University of Cambridge
The Pitt Building, Trumpington Street, Cambridge CB2 1RP
40 West 20th Street, New York, NY 10011–4211, USA
10 Stamford Road, Oakleigh, Melbourne 3166, Australia

First published 1994

Printed in Great Britain at the University Press, Cambridge

A catalogue record for this book is available from the British Library

Library of Congress cataloguing in publication data

Knecht, R. J. (Robert Jean)
Renaissance Warrior and Patron: The Reign of Francis I/R. J. Knecht.
  p. cm.
Includes bibliographical references and index.
ISBN 0 521 41796 1
1. Francis I of France, 1494–1547. 2. France – History – Francis I, 1515–1547.
3. France – Kings and rulers – Biography.
I. Title.
DC113.K58 1994
944′.028′092—dc20
[B] 93–24891 CIP

ISBN 0 521 41796 1 hardback

CE

For Maureen

Contents

List of illustrations	*page*	xi
Preface		xvii
Note on coinage		xx
List of abbreviations		xxii

1.	Childhood and youth	1
2.	France in 1515	19
3.	King of France	41
4.	Marignano and after (1515–19)	62
5.	'The Most Christian King'	88
6.	The king and his court	105
7.	Humanism and heresy	142
8.	Valois *versus* Habsburg	165
9.	The sinews of war	185
10.	Treason	200
11.	Defeat and captivity	216
12.	The king's return (1526–28)	249
13.	The 'Peace of the Ladies' (3 August 1529)	272
14.	Protestants and Turks (1529–34)	291
15.	The threat of heresy	306
16.	Montmorency's triumph (1535–38)	329
17.	Domestic issues	342
18.	Poverty and wealth	354
19.	France overseas	369
20.	Fruitless entente (1538–42)	385
21.	Madrid and Fontainebleau	398
22.	Patron of the arts	425
23.	'Father of letters'	462

24. The return to war (1542–44)   478
25. Gathering clouds (1544–47)   495
26. An absolute monarch?   519
27. Le roy est mort! Vive le roy!   541

     Epilogue   555

     Manuscript sources   561
     Select bibliography   562
     Index   586

Illustrations

Plates

1. The baptism of Francis of Angoulême. (Bibliothèque Nationale, *page* 2 Paris)
2. Louise of Savoy, the Dauphin's compass. Miniature. 5 (Bibliothèque Nationale, Paris)
3. Francis of Angoulême and his sister playing chess. Miniature. 7 (Bibliothèque Nationale, Paris)
4. Medal of Louis XII and Anne of Brittany. (British Museum, 9 London)
5. Medal of Francis of Angoulême, duc de Valois (1504). 10 (Bibliothèque Nationale: Cabinet des Médailles)
6. The Salamander amid flames. Reverse of the medal of Francis, 10 duc de Valois. 1504. (Bibliothèque Nationale, Paris: Cabinet des Médailles)
7. Medal of Marguerite d' Angoulême. (Bibliothèque Nationale: 10 Cabinet des Médailles)
8. Medal of Louise of Savoy, comtesse d'Angoulême. (Bibliothèque 10 Nationale: Cabinet des Médailles)
9. The betrothal of Francis of Angoulême and Claude de France 13 (1506). Miniature. (Bibliothèque Nationale)
10. Francis being presented to Christ by St Agnes. (Bibliothèque 14 Nationale)
11. Medal of Francis of Angoulême, duc de Valois (1512). 16 (Bibliothèque Nationale: Cabinet des Médailles)
12. Guillaume Gouffier, seigneur de Bonnivet, Admiral of France by 44 Jean Clouet. (Musée Condé, Chantilly)

13. Bas-relief of Chancellor Duprat sealing documents. (Paris: Musée   51
    des Monuments français/Photo Giraudon)

14. The Emperor Charles V. Terra cotta bust by Conrad Meit.   66
    (Gruuthusemuseum, Bruges)

15. Henry VIII. Miniature. (H.M. The Queen)   68

16. Bas-relief of the battle of Marignano by Pierre Bontemps from   71
    the tomb of Francis I. (Basilica of Saint-Denis/Photo:
    Lauros-Giraudon)

17. The battle of Marignano by the Maître de la Ratière. (Musée   74
    Condé, Chantilly/Photo Giraudon)

18. Francis I charging at Marignano. Miniature. (Bibliothèque   76
    Nationale)

19. Portrait of Francis I and profile of Julius Caesar. Miniature.   78
    (British Museum, London)

20. Francis I in conversation with Julius Caesar. Miniature.   79
    (Bibliothèque Nationale)

21. Jacques 'Galiot' de Genouillac, *grand écuyer* by Jean Clouet.   80
    (Musée Condé, Chantilly)

22. 'Horus Apollo'. Crowned lion holding a bear on a leash.   81
    Miniature. (Musée Condé, Chantilly/Photo Lauros-Giraudon)

23. Francis I about 1515. Painting by unidentified artist. (Musée   106
    Condé, Chantilly/Photo Lauros-Giraudon)

24. Francis I in 1516. Anonymous. Chalk. (Hermitage Museum,   108
    St Petersburg)

25. Francis hunting in the forest of Fontainebleau. Miniature.   110
    (Bibliothèque Nationale, Paris)

26. Françoise de Foix, comtesse de Châteaubriant. By Jean Clouet.   115
    (Musée Condé, Chantilly/Photo: Monuments historiques)

27. Charles de Maigny, captain of the gateway to the king's   119
    household. By Pierre Bontemps. (Musée du Louvre, Paris/Photo
    Lauros-Giraudon)

28. Château of Blois: Façade of the loggias. (Photo: J. Feuillie/Photo: 135
    Paris/S.P.A.D.E.M.)

29. Château of Blois: Francis I staircase. (Archives photographiques,   136
    Paris/S.P.A.D.E.M.)

30. Château of Chambord.   138

31. Château of Chambord: double-spiral staircase.   139

32. Map showing the Ile-de-la-Cité and university quarter of Paris in   143
    1552. (Musée de la Ville de Paris, Musée Carnavalet,
    Paris/Photo: Lauros-Giraudon)

33. Medal of Erasmus of Rotterdam by Quentin Matsys. (Victoria   148
    and Albert Museum, London)

34. Guillaume Budé by Jean Clouet. (Metropolitan Museum of Art, New York)   151

35. The proclamation of an edict against heretics. Woodcut by Geoffroy Tory. (Bibliothèque Nationale, Paris)   158

36. Francis I, his mother and sister at prayer. Miniature. (Bibliothèque Nationale, Paris)   160

37. The Emperor Charles V. Anonymous. (Musée Municipal, Dôle/Photo: Lauros-Giraudon)   169

38. The Field of Cloth of Gold. Bas-relief from the Hôtel Bourgtheroulde, Rouen. (Musée des Monuments Français, Paris/Photo Giraudon)   172

39. The Field of Cloth of Gold: the English temporary palace and French tents. (H.M. the Queen)   173

40. Odet de Foix, seigneur de Lautrec, marshal of France. By Jean Clouet. (Musée Condé, Chantilly)   181

41. Infantry battle by Hans Holbein the Younger. Drawing. (Kunstmuseum, Basel: Kupferstichkabinett)   183

42. Charles de Bourbon, Constable of France. Anonymous drawing. (Bibliothèque Nationale/Photo: Monuments Historiques)   202

43. Pope Clement VII by Sebastiano del Piombo (*c.* 1526). (Galleria Nazionale di Capodimonte, Naples)   217

44. The battle of Pavia, 1525. (Ashmolean Museum, Oxford)   220

45. Francis I leading a cavalry charge at the battle of Pavia. Tapestry after the design by B. van Orley. (Galleria Nazionale di Capodimonte, Naples)   223

46. The *échevins* of Amiens presenting a book to Louise of Savoy. Miniature. (Bibliothèque Nationale, Paris)   228

47. Etienne Le Blanc asks to be 'cured' by Louise of Savoy Miniature. (Bibliothèque Nationale, Paris)   230

48. Antoine Duprat, Chancellor of France, cardinal-archbishop of Sens. Terra-cotta. (Musée du Louvre, Paris/Photo: Lauros-Giraudon)   233

49. Part of a letter written by Francis I to his mother during his captivity at Pizzighettone. (Bibliothèque Nationale, Paris)   241

50. Anne de Montmorency about 1530. Drawing by Jean Clouet. (Musée Condé, Chantilly)   251

51. Medal of Pope Clement VII by Benvenuto Cellini, 1534. (Museo Nazionale del Bargello, Florence)   258

52. The entry of Cardinal Duprat into Sens. (Cathédrale Saint-Etienne, Sens/Photo: Giraudon)   262

53. Francis I presiding over a meeting of the Parlement. Woodcut. (Bibliothèque Nationale, Paris)   265

54. Golden 'bulla' used to seal the treaty of Amiens, 1527. (Public   273
     Record Office, London)
55. Francis I makes reparation for the mutilation of a statue of the   280
     Virgin. Miniature. (Musée Condé, Chantilly/Photo:
     Lauros-Giraudon)
56. Francis I and his suite receiving communion. (Amiens: Musée de   281
     Picardie/Photo: Lauros-Giraudon)
57. Francis I and Eleanor of Portugal. (H.M. The Queen)   287
58. Francis I by Jean Clouet. (Musée du Louvre, Paris/Photo: 288
     Giraudon)
59. Guillaume du Bellay, seigneur de Langey. Anonymous. (Musée   292
     de Versailles)
60. Henry VIII's departure for Calais. (H.M. The Queen)   298
61. Casket by Valerio Belli given to Francis I by Pope Clement VII,   301
     1533. (Palazzo Pitti, Florence: Museo degli argenti)
62. Marguerite d'Angoulême, queen of Navarre, sister of Francis I.   310
     By François Clouet. (Musée Condé, Chantilly/Photo: Giraudon)
63. The Placard against the Mass of October 1534, written by   314
     Antoine Marcourt and printed at Neuchâtel by Pierre de Vingle.
64. Bronze medal of the Emperor Charles V in 1537. (Bibliothèque   332
     Nationale, Paris/Photo: Giraudon)
65. Francis I in armour. Bronze bust by Louis Claude Vassé. (Musée   336
     du Louvre, Paris)
66. Charles V and Francis I. Fresco by Taddeo Zuccari, *c.* 1559.   390
     (Villa Farnese, Caprarola)
67. Château of Saint-Germain-en-Laye: elevations of the king's *logis*   406
     by J. Androuet Du Cerceau.
68. Cartouche of *Porte Dorée* and *Cour de la Fontaine c.* 1540.   409
     (Château of Fontainebleau/Photo: Giraudon)
69. The château of Fontainebleau: *Galerie François Ier.* (Château of   413
     Fontainebleau/S.P.A.D.E.M.)
70. The *Royal Elephant.* Detail of a fresco by Rosso in the *Galerie*   414
     François Ier at Fontainebleau. (Château of Fontainebleau/Photo:
     Giraudon)
71. *Venus and Cupid.* Fresco by Rosso in the *Galerie François Ier* at   415
     Fontainebleau. (Château of Fontainebleau/Photo: Lauros-Giraudon)
72. *Diana and Callisto* by Francesco Primaticcio. Drawing. (Musée   416
     du Louvre, Paris: Cabinet des Dessins)
73. *Alexander taming Bucephalus* by Francesco Primaticcio in the   418
     Chambre de la duchesse d'Etampes. (Château of
     Fontainebleau/Photo: Lauros-Giraudon)

74. Francis I as a composite deity. By Nicholas Belin. (Bibliothèque 426
    Nationale, Paris: Cabinet des Estampes/Photo: Giraudon)
75. *The death of Leonardo* by Giuseppe Cades. (Ashmoleum 428
    Museum, Oxford)
76. *The Virgin and Child with St Anne* by Leonardo da Vinci. 429
    (Musée du Louvre, Paris)
77. *Charity* by Andrea del Sarto. (Musée du Louvre, Paris/Photo: 430
    Musées Nationaux)
78. *Mars and Venus*. Drawing by Rosso. (Musée du Louvre, 433
    Paris/Photo: Musées Nationaux)
79. *Bacchus, Venus and Cupid*. By or after Rosso. (Musée du Grand 434
    Duché de Luxembourg)
80. *St Michael slaying the demon* by Raphael. (Musée du Louvre, 437
    Paris)
81. Joanna of Aragon by Raphael and Giulio Romano. (Musée du 438
    Louvre, Paris)
82. Perfume burner allegedly designed by Raphael. Engraving by 440
    Marcantonio Raimondi.
83. Michelangelo's *Hercules*. Drawing by P. P. Rubens. (Musée du 442
    Louvre: Cabinet des Dessins)
84. Francis I by Titian. (Musée du Louvre, Paris) 444
85. Pietro Aretino by Titian. (Palazzo Pitti, Florence) 446
86. Medal of Francis I by Benvenuto Cellini. (Fitzwilliam, Museum, 450
    Cambridge)
87. *Juno*. Drawing by Benvenuto Cellini. (Musée du Louvre: Cabinet 451
    des dessins/Photo: Musées Nationaux)
88. *Satyr*. Drawing by Benvenuto Cellini. (Woodner Collection, New 453
    York)
89. The Saltcellar of Francis I by Benvenuto Cellini. 454
    (Kunsthistorisches Museum, Vienna)
90. 'Panegyric of Francis I'. The author presents his book to Francis 463
    I. (Musée Condé, Chantilly/Photo: Lauros-Giraudon)
91. Clément Marot by Corneille de Lyon. (Musée du Louvre, Paris) 465
92. Antoine Macault reading to the king and his courtiers. 474
    Miniature. (Musée Condé, Chantilly/Photo: Giraudon)
93. Two bindings of books owned by Francis I. (a: Musée Condé, 476
    Chantilly/Photo: Giraudon and b: Bibliothèque Nationale)
94. The tomb of Philippe Chabot, Admiral of France, by Pierre 488
    Bontemps. (Musée du Louvre, Paris)
95. Francis I about 1540. Drawing attributed to François Clouet. 496
    (Musée du Louvre, Paris: Cabinet des Dessins)

96. Anne de Pisseleu, duchesse d'Etampes. By Corneille de Lyon.   498
    (Metropolitan Museum of Art. Bequest of Mrs H. O.
    Havemeyer, 1929. The H.O. Havemeyer Collection)
97. Francis I as Julius Caesar by Primaticcio. (Musée Condé,   523
    Chantilly/Photo: Giraudon)
98. Francis I in old age. Drawing by François Clouet. (Musée Condé,   542
    Chantilly)
99. *Gisant* of Francis I by Pierre Bontemps. (Basilica of   547
    Saint-Denis/Photo: Lauros-Giraudon)
100. Tomb of Francis I and Claude de France by Philibert de l'Orme.   548
    (Basilica of Saint-Denis/Photo: Giraudon)
101. Monument for the heart of Francis I by Pierre Bontemps.   550
    (Basilica of Saint-Denis/Photo: Lauros-Giraudon)

Figures

1. Map of France, *c.* 1515–47   20–21
2. The relative sizes of French towns according to the tax levy of   27
    1538 for the payment of the infantry. (from B. Chevalier, *Les
    bonnes villes de France*. Paris: Aubier, 1982)
3. Map of north Italy, *c.* 1515–47   64–65
4. Map of Francis I's progresses in 1532–34   126–27
5. Plan of the château of Chambord, J. Androuet Du Cerceau, *Les*   137
    plus excellents bastiments de France (1576–1607)
6. The battle of Pavia. (Sir Charles Oman, *A History of the Art of*   221
    War in the XVIth century. New York, 1937, p. 197)
7. Map of the voyages of Jacques Cartier   376–77
8. Plan of the ground floor of the château of Madrid. (J. Androuet   402
    Du Cerceau, *Les plus excellents bastiments de France*)
9. Elevation of the château of Madrid. (*ibid.*)   403
10. The château of Fontainebleau. (*ibid.*)   408
11. Plan of the second floor of the château of Saint-Germain-en-Laye   420
    showing the distribution of rooms in 1550. (Drawing by Jean
    Blécon, CRAHAM. From M. Chatenet, *Le château de Madrid au
    Bois de Boulogne*. Paris: Picard, 1987, p. 248)

Preface

The fifth centenary of the birth of Francis I will be celebrated on 12 September 1994. Few monarchs have left so rich a cultural legacy. His magnificent châteaux – Blois, Chambord and Fontainebleau – continue to attract hordes of tourists each year. The paintings he collected, including *Mona Lisa*, are among the Louvre's finest masterpieces. His books and manuscripts, many of them in finely engraved leather bindings, are among the most precious now belonging to the Bibliothèque Nationale, and the Collège de France, one of the world's most important seats of learning, traces its origins back to the royal lectureships founded by the king in 1530. Such a lasting and varied achievement surely calls for celebration.

More than ten years have elapsed since Cambridge University Press published my *Francis I* and during that time much new light has been thrown on certain aspects of his reign. In a work of great erudition and originality, Anne-Marie Lecoq has explored the corpus of literary and visual imagery that was used to portray the king, the kingdom and the nature of his rule in the years before 1520. This assumed various forms, some Christian, others pagan; they found expression in the symbolism displayed in royal entries, commemorative medals, architectural decoration, speeches, poems and in the illuminations that accompanied literary works. Two recent works have brought to life important buildings erected by Francis, which have, alas, completely vanished. Using hitherto neglected documents pertaining to the royal office of works in the seventeenth and eighteenth centuries, Jean Guillaume has reconstructed and illuminated the origins of the *Galerie d'Ulysse* at Fontainebleau. Once the longest gallery in France, it contained murals by Primaticcio, which were for a long time much admired by visiting artists, including Rubens. It was destroyed in 1739. To Monique Chatenet we are indebted for an astonishingly complete reconstruction of the little château, called Madrid, which the king erected just outside Paris after his release from captivity in Spain. Thanks to

F. Marias we can now be fairly sure that it owed its curious name to a building outside Madrid which Francis must have seen during his captivity. Madame Chatenet has also illuminated a hitherto obscure subject: namely, the use to which the rooms in the châteaux were put. If modern research has added little that is new to the political history of the reign, our understanding of its religious history has been significantly deepened by a number of scholars interested in the early stages of the Continental Reformation. In particular, we are much better acquainted with the Vaudois of the south of France who were the victims of a terrible massacre in 1545, thanks to the remarkable thesis of Gabriel Audisio. Whereas in 1982 I was persuaded to omit any mention of the synod of Chanforan, I can now allude to it with confidence. Recently, Philippe Hamon has completed the most thorough treatment to date of Francis I's fiscal system and of its personnel. He has cast doubt on the notion that the king and his ministers systematically worked to a master-plan aiming at centralization, unification and simplification. They responded to situations as they arose, and if they produced a system more efficient than the one they had inherited it was largely by a process of trial and error. The frequency of wars and ministerial vagaries militated against any long-term programme of fiscal reform. I am most grateful to Monsieur Hamon for allowing me to make use of his findings in anticipation of the publication of his research which cannot be long delayed.

A writer, who is allowed second thoughts about his work, is fortunate indeed. Now that a certain objectivity has set in, I can see that my *Francis I* was too rigorous in sacrificing chronology to analysis. Without giving chronology its head completely, I have tried to avoid disrupting the sequence of events. Thus instead of dealing with the regency of Louise of Savoy separately from her son's Spanish captivity, I show them as closely inter-related events. Material concerning the economy and society, which was originally buried in the middle of *Francis I* has been brought forward, as has the description of the French tax system, and I have added new sections on social structure and on Paris. Some reviewers of my first book criticized me for giving too much space to diplomatic exchanges. Taking their criticism to heart, I have given relatively less attention to foreign policy so as to leave space for other topics, such as patronage of letters. I include short sections on Marot and Rabelais, and also one on music.

In the past ten years I have had second thoughts about certain aspects of the reign. In spite of all the ink that has been spilt on the subject of 'absolutism', I still cannot swallow the notion of Francis as a kind of democrat *manqué*. He tended to accept constraints on his power only when he lacked the means to remove or avoid them. His authoritarianism is implicit in almost every page of Hamon's thesis, particularly the chapters dealing with the relentless prosecution of financiers. But in 1982 I was far too selective in my treatment of the political ideas of his reign and I admit that I was wrong to describe Seyssel as any kind of 'absolutist'. I hope to have made amends in the present volume which takes into account the ideas of political writers such as Chasseneuz and Du Moulin. As I have been repeatedly accused of crediting Francis I with too much power, I wish to place on record that I fully endorse David Parker's view that in early sixteenth-century France 'royal authority was both absolute and limited'. With regard to religion I have benefited from the research of Nicole Lemaitre on conditions in the French church on the eve of the Reformation. Guillaume Briçonnet was far from being the only reforming bishop. I have also tempered my interpretation of the Affair of the Placards in the light of research by David Nicholls and others. If royal policy towards dissidents hardened as a result of the affair, this change did not mark the end of Lucien Febvre's 'long period of magnificent religious anarchy'.

As I hope to have indicated, the present volume is far more than a new edition of my *Francis I*. Inevitably, some sections cover the same ground. But my work has been completely restructured, rewritten, enlarged and brought up to date, hence the change of title which represents fairly accurately Francis I's dominant interests: war and patronage of letters and the arts. His other preoccupations are not so easily encapsulated. To have added 'lover' to the title might have been accurate but not altogether fitting.

To conclude, it goes without saying that I remain indebted to all those persons named in the preface to my *Francis I*. I hope they will forgive me if I do not list them again, for the circle of my indebtedness has widened considerably in the past ten years. I am deeply grateful to Cambridge University Press and, in particular, to William Davies for giving me this opportunity to revise and improve my work. I also thank my copy-editor, Michele Ellar, for her discreet vigilance and tolerant acceptance of many afterthoughts on my part. A great source of satisfaction for me has been the recognition given to my first book by French scholars, including, Jean Jacquart, who, after being a 'rival', has become a friend. Other French scholars, who have helped me include Gabriel Audisio, Monique Chatenet, Denis Crouzet, Robert Descimon, Jean Guillaume, Philippe Hamon, Anne-Marie Lecoq, and Nicole Lemaitre. I am grateful to Raffaele Tamalio for showing me his unpublished transcripts of the letters of the young Federico Gonzaga from the French court in 1516–17, a wonderful collection shedding light on Francis's court in its beginnings which, I am happy to say, is soon to be published. Others who have helped me in various ways include Joseph Bergin, Peter Biller, Caroline Elam, Charles Giry-Deloison, Mark Greengrass, Vivienne Larminie, Robert Oresko, Elizabeth Powis, Mía Rodriguez-Salgado and Paul Spencer-Longhurst. My greatest debt is to my wife without whose encouragement and patience this book would never have been accomplished.

Note on coinage

The sums of money mentioned in this book reflect the division between the two types of money which existed side by side in early modern France. These were *money of account*, which was the measure of value, and *actual coin*, which was the medium of exchange. Thus Francis I's accounts were kept in the former and actual transactions made in the latter. With a considerable variety of coins in circulation, the need for some yardstick and standard of value was necessary. This was provided by money of account. The two systems were as follows.

Money of account

The most common money of account in sixteenth-century France was the *livre tournois*. This was subdivided into *sous* (or *sols*) and *deniers*: i.e. 1 *livre tournois* = 20 *sous*; 1 *sou* = 12 *deniers*.

It was the French equivalent of the English system of pounds, shillings and pence sterling. There were about 10 *livres tournois* in 1 pound sterling; i.e. the *livre tournois* was worth about 2 shillings English.

The *livre parisis*, worth a quarter more than the *livre tournois*, was used hardly at all under Francis. But the *mercuriales* of the Halle of Paris were expressed in *livres parisis* till 1568. In this book the word, *livre* is used, meaning *livre tournois*, unless otherwise specified.

Actual coin

Gold

Ecu au soleil. Issued from 1475. Worth 36 *sous* 3 *deniers* in 1515, 40 *sous* in 1516, 45 *sous* in 1533. Weight 3.357 gm. In 1516 it was worth about 4 English shillings. The English *crown* (introduced in 1526) was worth 44 *sous tournois* in 1533 and 1549.

Ecu à la croisette. Essentially the same as *écu au soleil.*

Demi-écu. Half the weight and value of the *écu.*

Ecu à la couronne. Older than the *écu au soleil.* Worth 51 *sous*. Weight 3.819 gm.

Silver

Teston. Issued from 1514. The first French coin to carry, like certain Italian coins, the portrait bust of the king (hence its name). Worth 10 *sous tournois* in 1515, 10 *sous* 6 *deniers* in 1533; 10 *sous* 8 *deniers* in 1541; 11 sous in 1543. Weight 9.555 gm.

It remained the principal silver coin till Henri III introduced the *franc* in 1576. A gold *franc* existed in medieval France, but it had ceased to be struck by the early fifteenth century. Thereafter the *franc* was sometimes used as a sort of money of account equivalent to the *livre tournois.*

Demi-teston. Half the weight and value of the *teston.*

Billon

This was a mixture of silver with a high proportion of copper: it was divided into '*billon blanc*' and '*billon noir*'.

Douzain. Worth 12 *deniers* (hence its name). It was very common, as it represented the *sou tournois*, the principal unit of account in the retail trade.

Dizain

Sizain

There were about a dozen types of billon coins in circulation in 1515.

In addition to royal coins, provincial and foreign coins circulated in France. Provence had its own money of account, the *florin*, and coins: the *courronal*, worth ¾ of a *denier tournois*, and the *patac.*

Two kinds of foreign coins circulated: coins struck by French kings in Italy and coins struck by foreign rulers. In March 1541 Francis authorized the circulation of thirty-three foreign coins.

Abbreviations

A. du M.	*Annales du Midi*
A.N.	Archives Nationales, Paris
A.R.	*Archiv für Reformationsgeschichte*
Arch. Stor. It.	*Archivio storico italiano*
Barrillon	*Le journal de Jean Barrillon, secrétaire du chancelier du Prat*, ed. P. de Vaissière, 2 vols. (1897–99)
B.H.R.	*Bibliothèque d'humanisme et Renaissance*
B.I.H.R.	*Bulletin of the Institute of Historical Research*
B.L.	British Library, London
B.N.	Bibliothèque Nationale, Paris
B.S.H.P.F.	*Bulletin de la Société de l'histoire du Protestantisme français*
C.A.F.,	*Catalogue des actes de François Ier*, 10 vols. (1887–1910)
Champollion-Figeac	*Captivité du Roi François Ier*, ed. A. Champollion-Figeac (1847)
C.S.P.Span.	*Calendar of State Papers, Spanish*, ed. G. A. Bergenroth, P. de Gayangos and M. A. S. Hume, 12 vols. (London, 1862–95)
C.S.P.Ven.	*Calendar of State Paper, Venetian*, ed. R. Brown, C. Bentinck and H. Brown, 9 vols. (London, 1864–98)
D.B.F.	*Dictionnaire de biographie française*
Decrue, i	Decrue, F., *Anne de Montmorency, grand maître et connétable de France à la cour, aux armées et au conseil du roi François Ier* (1885)

Decrue, ii	Decrue, F., *Anne de Montmorency, connétable et pair de France sous les rois Henri II, François II et Charles IX* (1889)
Desjardins	*Négociations diplomatiques de la France avec la Toscane*, ed. A. Desjardins, 6 vols. (1859–86)
Doucet, R.	Doucet, R., *Etude sur le gouvernment de François Ier dans ses rapports avec le Parlement de Paris*, 2 vols. (1921–6)
Doucet, *Institutions*	Doucet, R., *Les institutions de la France au XVIe siècle*, 2 vols. (1948)
du Bellay	*Mémoires de Martin et Guillaume du Bellay*, ed. V.-L. Bourrilly and F. Vindry, 4 vols. (1908–19)
Econ. H.R.	*Economic History Review*
E.S.R.	*European Studies Review*
F.H.	*French History*
F.H.S.	*French Historical Studies*
Florange	*Mémoires du Maréchal de Florange dit le jeune adventureux*, ed. R. Goubaux and P. A. Lemoisne, 2 vols. (1913–24)
G.B.A.	*Gazette des beaux arts*
Granvelle, *Papiers d'état*	*Papiers d'état du cardinal de Granvelle*, ed. C. Weiss, 9 vols. (1841–52)
Guiffrey	*Cronique du roy Françoys Premier de ce nom*, ed. G. Guiffrey (1860)
Herminjard	*Correspondance des réformateurs dans les pays de langue française*, ed. A. Herminjard, 9 vols. (Geneva, 1886–87)
H.J.	*Historical Journal*
Imbart de La Tour	Imbart de La Tour, P., *Les origines de la Réforme*, 4 vols. (1905–35)
Isambert	*Recueil général des anciennes lois françaises*, 29 vols. (1827–33)
J.B.P.	*Le journal d'un bourgeois de Paris sous le règne de François Ier (1515–36)*, ed. V.-L. Bourrilly (1910)
J.W.C.I.	*Journal of the Warburg and Courtauld Institutes*
Kaulek	*Correspondance politique de MM. de Castillon et de Marillac, ambassadeurs de France en Angleterre 1537–42*, ed. J. Kaulek (1885)
Le Glay	Le Glay, *Négociations diplomatiques entre la France et l'Autriche*, 2 vols. (1845)

L.P.	*Letters and Papers, Foreign and Domestic, of the reign of Henry VIII*, ed. J. S. Brewer, J. Gairdner and R. H. Brodie, 21 vols. (London, 1862–1910)
Michaud et Poujoulat	J.-F. Michaud and J.-J. F. Poujoulat, *Nouvelle collection de mémoires*, 1st ser., vol. v (1836)
Ordonnances	*Ordonnances des rois de France: règne de François Ier*, 9 vols. (1902–75)
R.D.B.V.P.	*Registres des délibérations du Bureau de la Ville de Paris*, 3 vols. (1883–86)
Rev. d'hist. écon. et soc.	*Revue d'histoire économique et sociale*
Rev. d'hist. mod. et contemp.	*Revue d'histoire moderne et contemporaine*
R.H.	*Revue historique*
R.H.E.F.	*Revue de l'histoire de l'église de France*
Ribier	Ribier, G., *Lettres et mémoires d'Estat des roys, princes, ambassadeurs et autres ministres sous les règnes de François Ier, Henri II et François II*, 2 vols. (1666)
R.Q.H.	*Revue des questions historiques*
St.P.	*State Papers of Henry VIII*, 11 vols. (London, 1830–52)
Versoris	*Livre de raison de M^eNicolas Versoris, avocat au Parlement de Paris 1519–1530*, ed. G. Fagniez (1885)

All references to *C.A.F.* and *L.P.* are to document numbers, not pages, unless otherwise stated.

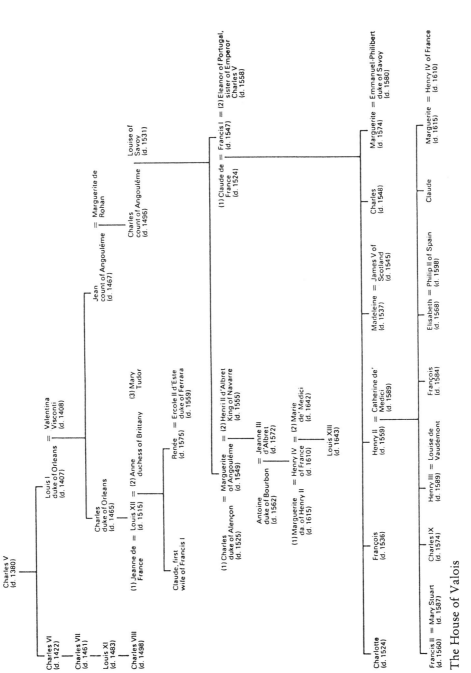

The House of Valois

Chapter one

Childhood and youth

The small town of Cognac stands on the left bank of the river Charente in the midst of a fertile and undulating countryside in western France. To most people it means only one thing, the finest brandy, but it has another claim to fame, for it was the birthplace of King Francis I, the 'knight-king' (*roi cheva-lier*) and 'father of letters' (*père des lettres*). The castle in which he was born is now the warehouse of a distillery.

Francis was a scion of the house of Angoulême, a cadet branch of the royal house of Valois, which was founded by Jean comte d'Angoulême, the second son of Louis I, duc d'Orléans, and of Valentina Visconti, daughter of the last duke of Milan of that name.

At the age of thirteen, Jean was sent as a hostage to England, where he remained for thirty-two years. In 1415 he was joined by his elder brother Charles, duc d'Orléans, the poet of the *Rondeaux*, who had been taken pris-oner at Agincourt. Jean shared his brother's literary tastes, and, after returning to France in 1445, he built up a fine library in his château at Cognac. He was not, however, a rich man, having had to sell part of his estates in order to pay his ransom.[1]

Jean was succeeded in April 1467 by his second son, Charles, who was only seven years old. In 1478 there was some question of his marrying Mary of Burgundy, but King Louis XI betrothed him instead to his two-year-old niece Louise, daughter of Philip, count of Bresse, a younger son of the duke of Savoy. Philip became duke in 1496, but died in the following year. Having lost her mother, Marguerite de Bourbon, when she was only seven, Louise was brought up by her aunt, Anne de Beaujeu, Louis XI's daughter, who shared the regency of France with her husband, Pierre, during Charles VIII's minority. Charles d'Angoulême tried to escape the matrimonial fate prescribed for him by Louis XI by taking part in an aristocratic revolt, called *la Guerre folle*, in 1487. He

---

[1] *D.B.F.*, ii. 1219–21.

Du trofne duun fins transmse.
Par la puissance innisible.
De resus qui en son eglise.
Me mst apres sa mort terrible.
Chascun doit dont estre pemble.
De mentretemr en tout liens.
Car sane foy. il est impossible.
Que on sceut estre plaisant a dieu.

1. The baptism of Francis of Angoulême. The babe, already crowned, is being held over a font shaped like a chalice. A living statue of Faith beneath it points at appropriate verses below. Miniature from B. N., ms. fr. 2275 f. 4b.

assembled an army in Saintonge, but was crushed 'like a waffle between two irons'. The price of his submission was his marriage to Louise on 16 February 1488.[2]

Though Charles was twenty-eight years old in 1488 and Louise only twelve, their marriage proved, by all accounts, reasonably happy; no harsh word was ever heard to pass between them.[3] Yet the count did have two mistresses, Antoinette de Polignac and Jeanne Comte. By the first he had two daughters, Jeanne and Madeleine, and by the second another daughter, Souveraine. In the fifteenth century, however, illegitimacy did not carry the stigma that it has since acquired. Louise apparently accepted her husband's infidelities with equanimity. She brought up his bastards along with her own children, and took Antoinette de Polignac as her companion.

Charles had two children by Louise: Marguerite, who was born on 11 April 1492, and Francis (François), who was born two years later, on 12 September.[4] The latter owed his Christian name to Francis of Paola, an Italian hermit, who had been called to France in 1482 to save the life of Louis XI. Although he failed in his mission, he was persuaded to settle in France, where he soon gained the reputation of being a miracle-worker.[5] He specialized in getting divine assistance for the production of heirs and heiresses, and boys who came into the world through his intercession were usually named after him. Louise had called on the hermit at Plessis-lez-Tours soon after her marriage and had been told by him not only that she would have a son but that he would become king of France. This showed a truly prophetic insight, since in 1494 the odds were heavily weighted against Francis ever reaching the throne. He was only the cousin of the reigning monarch, Charles VIII, the next in line of succession to the throne being Louis II, duc d'Orléans. Only if both were to die without male issue would Francis become king. Females, of course, were debarred from the throne by the Salic law.

Charles d'Angoulême never became politically significant; he was an easy-going, weak person whose chief redeeming feature was a love of literature and art. In spite of his limited means, he continued to build up the library at Cognac, and his entourage included Robinet Testard, a talented illuminator of manuscripts, Jean de Saint-Gelais, the official historian of Louis XII's reign, and his brother, Octovien, the *rhétoriqueur* poet, who translated Ovid's *Heroides* (1497) and Virgil's *Aeneid*.

On an exceptionally cold winter's day in 1495 Charles left Cognac to go to court, but he was taken ill that same night at Châteauneuf. Several doctors were called and Louise 'attended on him day and night as tenderly and

[2] *Ibid.*, ii. 1202–3.   [3] P. Paris, *Etudes sur François Premier* (1885), i. 28.
[4] Michaud et Poujoulat, v. 87.
[5] G. Roberti, *Francesco di Paola* (Rome, 1915); A. Renaudet, *Préréforme et humanisme à Paris pendant les premières guerres d'Italie, 1494–1517* (1953), pp. 171–2.

humanely as the poorest wife might nurse her husband'.[6] Her devotion, however, proved unavailing: on 1 January 1496 the count died, leaving a will in which he appointed Louise as the guardian of his children.[7] But, as she was only nineteen and the minimum legal age for guardianship was twenty-five, Louis d'Orléans, the children's nearest male kinsman, claimed the guardianship. Louise, however, opposed him by invoking a custom of Angoumois, which fixed the age of guardianship at fourteen. The dispute was submitted to the *Grand Conseil* and a compromise reached: Louise was allowed to retain custody of her children, while Orléans was appointed their honorary guardian. This meant that Louise could not transact any important business without the duke's prior knowledge and consent. He was to get full custody of the children in the event of Louise remarrying.[8]

Charles VIII died childless on 8 April 1498 and was succeeded by Louis d'Orléans, who thus became King Louis XII. As he too was childless, Francis became heir presumptive to the throne. Louis granted him an annuity of 8,000 *livres* and, in 1499, created the duchy of Valois for him out of the Orléans patrimony. He also confirmed Louise's guardianship of her children and invited her to bring them to the court at Chinon, where he received them with an almost paternal show of affection. A week later, however, he entrusted them to the custody of Pierre de Rohan, seigneur de Gié and marshal of France, who took them first to the château of Blois, then to that of Amboise. Gié was a middle-aged widower, second only in political importance to Georges d'Amboise, archbishop of Rouen. In 1503 he took as his second wife Charlotte d'Armagnac and assumed her late father's title of duc de Nemours. Being ambitious, he doubtless regarded his custody of the heir to the throne as a unique opportunity for self-advancement. As he had been appointed by word of mouth, his duties are not precisely known, but presumably he was expected to ensure Francis's safety. To this end, he purchased the captaincy of Amboise, establishing there a company of twenty-five archers under a lieutenant called Roland de Ploret. Gié also exercised some control over Louise's household. Thus he dismissed Jean de Saint-Gelais and others who had served the countess and her late husband for many years, replacing them by his own creatures. Although Gié was often at court, he did visit Amboise from time to time; he would then dine at Louise's table and accompany her son to church or on outings.

Louise deeply resented any restriction of her independence. She slept in the same room as her children, and would allow only certain ladies to be present at her *lever* and *coucher*. No gentlemen were admitted, and Ploret was only

[6] Paris, i. 27.
[7] *Procédures politiques du règne de Louis XII*, ed. R. de Maulde La Clavière (1885), pp. 716–22.
[8] *Ibid.*, pp. 723–7.

2. Louise of Savoy, dressed as a widow in black, holds the Dauphin with one hand and a giant compass, meant to evoke the circle as the most perfect shape given by God to all creation. The allegory points to the need to give the Dauphin a perfect education. The compass was a symbol commonly associated with Prudence. Miniature from B.N., ms. fr. 2285, f. 5.

allowed as far as her chamber door, when he came each morning to escort Francis to mass. One day, however, he delegated this duty to a subordinate called du Restal, who, finding the door shut, simply broke it down. Louise was understandably furious. She obtained du Restal's dismissal, but failed to get rid of Gié as well. The king ordered Francis's removal from her room at night so that Gié's men might keep watch over him at all times.[9]

It seems that Louise was allowed a free hand in her children's education and that she took her responsibilities seriously.[10] In keeping with her motto, *libris et liberis*, she commissioned books specially for them. A history book and an atlas, now at the Bibliothèque Nationale in Paris, may have been used by Francis as a child.[11] He learnt Italian and Spanish from his mother and was taught biblical history and Latin by François Demoulins (also called Roche-fort). The latter is mentioned in the accounts of the comtesse d'Angoulême from 1501 until 1508 as her son's 'schoolmaster'. He also appears in Francis's accounts for 1513. A churchman and a humanist, Demoulins was a prolific author, though only one of his works was printed. Among numerous manu-scripts ascribed to him are two concerned with examining one's conscience and confession. The first, which is dedicated to 'Monseigneur' and carries Francis's coat of arms, adheres to the main themes of Christian humanism and seeks to promote a grand style of French oratory. The same traits are present in Demoulins's *Dialogus* (1505) – a discussion between a confessor and a penitent about games of chance. We may assume that it had been commissioned by Louise to counter her son's liking for cards and dice. Another work written by Demoulins for Louise is concerned with the four cardinal virtues: Prudence, Strength, Justice and Temperance. It reveals a passionate hatred of bad priests and deceitful theologians. At the same time, it exalts the virtues of the future royal house of France.[12]

Francis may also have had lessons with Christophe de Longueil, the Flemish humanist, but the 'new learning' did not play an important part in his edu-cation. Ironically, the future 'father of letters' was a poor Latinist.[13] Guillaume Budé wrote his *L'institution du prince* in French because he knew that Francis would not read it if it were in Latin.[14] Yet contemporaries regarded the duke's education as unusually enlightened. Florange, who was brought up with Francis, believed that no prince had been better taught, and even Castiglione,

---

[9] *Ibid.*, pp. xiii–cxxxi.
[10] The presence of a few salacious books in her library hardly warrants Guizot's severe judgment that Louise gave her son 'neither principles, nor moral examples'. Paris, i. 37.
[11] B.N., mss. fr. 143, 2794, 5709.
[12] A.-M. Lecoq, *François Ier imaginaire: symbolique et politique à l'aube de la Renaissance française* (1987), pp. 77–101.
[13] Paris, i. 37; *Procédures politiques*, pp. 233–41.
[14] C. Bontems, L.-P. Raybaud, and J. P. Brancourt (eds.), *Le prince dans la France des XVIe et XVIIe siècles* (1965), p. 7.

3. Francis of Angoulême and his sister, Marguerite, playing chess. Miniature from the *Livre des échecs amoureux* by Jacques Le Grant.

author of *The Book of the Courtier (Il Cortegiano)* was favourably impressed by him when he visited Louis XII's court.[15] 'I believe', says Count Lodovico in *The Book of the Courtier*, 'that for all of us the true and principal adornment of the mind is letters; although the French, I know, recognize only the nobility of arms and think nothing of all the rest; and so they not only do not appreciate learning but detest it, regarding men of letters as basely inferior and thinking it a great insult to call anyone a scholar.' To which the Magnifico Giuliano replies: 'You are right in saying that this error has prevailed among the French for a long time now; but if good fortune has it that Monsieur d'Angoulême, as it is hoped, succeeds to the throne, then I believe that, just as the glory of arms flourishes and shines in France, so also with the greatest brilliance must that of letters. For when I was at that Court not so long ago, I set eyes on this prince … and among other things I was told that he greatly loved and esteemed learning and respected all men of letters, and that he condemned the French themselves for being so hostile to this profession.'[16]

'Nobility of arms', however, was not overlooked in Francis's education. Florange's memoirs contain a vivid account of Francis and his young companions at Amboise disporting themselves in the open air. They played an Italian game called *l'escaigne*, in which a large inflated ball was hit by a bat shaped like a stool with legs filled with lead. Francis excelled in archery and in hunting deer and other animals with nets. He and Florange used to fire darts from a small gun or *serpentine* at a target fixed to a door. Another Italian game was played in pairs: Francis and Anne de Montmorency *versus* Florange and Philippe Chabot de Brion. A ball 'as large as a barrel and filled with air' was hit with a piece of tin lined with felt and strapped to the forearm. Being tall and strong for his age, Francis was particularly successful in this game, which required both skill and strength. He and his friends also used to besiege and defend model forts; and, as they grew up, they wore armour and took part in jousts and tournaments.[17] Inevitably, there were accidents. On 25 January 1502 Francis was carried off by a horse given to him by marshal Gié. Louise's anguish found expression in her *Journal*.[18] Francis's survival was interpreted as miraculous, particularly as the incident happened on the anniversary of St

---

[15] Michaud et Poujoulat, v. 7.

[16] B. Castiglione, *The Book of the Courtier*, tr. G. Bull (Harmondsworth, 1967), p. 88. The passage in question may not have been disinterested, for Francis had some involvement in the creation of the *Courtier*. About late 1515 or early 1516 Castiglione interpolated in the first draft of his work the claim that Alfonso Ariosto at the behest of the king had urged him to continue working on it. This claim was dropped from a later draft, which served as the basis for the first printed text (1528). For a full discussion see C. H. Clough, 'Francis I and the Courtiers of Castiglione's *Courtier*', *E.S.R.*, viii (1978), 23–70.

[17] Michaud et Poujoulat, v. 6–7.

[18] H. Hauser has shown (*Revue historique* vol. 86, pp. 280–303) that Louise's *Journal* probably had an astrological purpose. It was compiled at the end of 1522 probably by François Demoulins from rapid notes taken day-by-day by Louise. A.-M. Lecoq, *François Ier imaginaire*, p. 100.

4. Bronze medal of Louis XII and Anne of Brittany by Nicolas Le Clerc, Jean de Saint Priest and Jean Lepère (1500).

Paul's fall from his horse and conversion on the road to Damascus. It was doubtless for the same reason that 25 January 1515 was eventually chosen as the date for Francis's coronation.[19]

In January 1499 Louis XII, having divorced his first wife, Jeanne de France, married Charles VIII's widow, Anne, duchess of Brittany. This was, of course, a matter of grave concern for the house of Angoulême, for Anne, who was only twenty-two years old, could reasonably be expected to produce a son, who would inevitably displace Francis as heir to the throne. Her first child by Louis, however, was a daughter, Claude, born at Romorantin on 13 October 1499, who was for eleven years the only child in the royal nursery and the pivot of Louis XII's matrimonial diplomacy. Though plain, she was a desirable match because her dowry comprised the Orléans patrimony, the duchy of Brittany and the French claims to Asti, Milan, Genoa and Naples. If the kingdom were to remain united, it was essential that she should marry the heir to the throne. Consequently, in April 1500, her father made a secret declaration nullifying in advance any other match.[20] In the following year, however, the Archduke Philip the Fair, son of the Emperor Maximilian, requested Claude's hand for his infant son, Charles of Luxemburg, and Louis granted his request in the hope that Maximilian would, in return, give him the investiture of Milan. Anne of Britanny welcomed the marriage as a means of preserving her duchy's

---

[19] At Fontevrault, on 6 August 1508, Francis was struck on the forehead by a stone. Such accidents were to punctuate much of his life. *Ibid.*, v. 88; Lecoq, *François Ier imaginaire*, p. 144.
[20] *Procédures politiques*, p. 135.

5. Medal of Francis of Angoulême, duc de Valois (1504).
6. Reverse of the medal of Francis duc de Valois (1504) showing his emblem of the salamander amidst flames. The device: 'Notrisco al buono, stingo el reo' means: 'I feed on the good fire and extinguish the bad'.

7. Medal of Marguerite d'Angoulême, sister of Francis I.
8. Medal of Louise of Savoy, countess of Angoulême, mother of Francis I.

independence of France. A marriage treaty was accordingly signed on 10 August, and soon afterwards the archduke and his wife came to Blois to see their prospective daughter-in-law. It was on this occasion that Francis made his first official appearance as heir to the throne.[21] In September 1504 he celebrated his tenth birthday, and his mother had a medal struck for the occasion. This shows, on one side, the boy's head in profile, wearing a bonnet, and, on the other, a salamander in the midst of flames with the motto (in archaic Italian) *Notrisco al buono, stingo el reo*. Every visitor to the châteaux of the Loire

21 J. S. C. Bridge, *History of France from the Death of Louis XI* (Oxford, 1921–36), iii. 208–14.

knows Francis I's salamander, which adorns so many fireplaces, chimney-stacks and other architectural features; fewer, one may safely assume, are familiar with the origin of that emblem or its significance. The fallacy that a salamander can go through fire unscathed, extinguishing it at the same time, can be traced back to the works of Aristotle and other scholars of antiquity. Contrary to popular belief, Francis may not have been the first member of his family to use the salamander as an emblem; it was apparently used by his grandfather, Jean, during festivities in 1461. Jean was renowned for his wisdom and kindness; indeed, an attempt was made in 1515 to have him canonized. Thus the choice of the salamander in 1504 may have been intended to recall the good life of Francis's ancestor. Neoplatonists saw fire as both good and bad: it ignited the hearts of believers while consuming the souls of the damned; hence the meaning of the motto *Nutrisco et extinguo*. In its complete form (as on the medal of 1504) it can be translated as: 'I feed upon the good (fire) and put out the evil one' (i.e. 'I am burning with lawful zeal, faith, a desire for peace and love, and I put out guilty zeal, harmful and destructive passions, unjust war and lust'). The salamander, which was often amusingly represented in the ceremonial entries of Francis I, was seen either swallowing fire or spitting water. Its third attribute – that of being able to live through fire – made it also a symbol of endurance.[22]

Louis XII fell seriously ill in 1504, and in the absence of his chief minister, the cardinal of Amboise, who had gone to Rome, the government passed into the hands of Marshal Gié, Francis's governor, whose views on Breton independence were in direct opposition to the queen's. He feared that, if the king died, Anne would return to her duchy, as she had done after the death of her first husband; only this time she would take her daughter Claude with her so as to frustrate any chance of the latter marrying Francis. Whether Gié tried to prevent such an eventuality is uncertain; what is clear is that, after Louis had recovered his health, Gié was accused by Pierre de Pontbriant, a servant of Louise of Savoy, of having attempted a *coup d'état* during the king's illness. Somewhat reluctantly, the king ordered an enquiry during which Louis confirmed all Pontbriant's allegations. Gié, she claimed, had planned to carry her son off to the castle at Angers, he had talked of the need to collect boats on the Loire, he had pressed her to allow his son to sleep in the same room as Francis, and had recommended some of his servants to him. Eventually, Gié was sent for trial on more than a hundred charges. He admitted that he had always wanted the marriage of Claude and Francis, but denied all the other charges. Pontbriant's allegations, he claimed, were lies inspired by Louise, who wanted to be avenged for certain measures he had taken by order of the king. In February 1506 Gié was acquitted of high treason but found guilty of 'certain

[22] A.-M. Lecoq, *François Ier imaginaire*, pp. 35–52.

excesses and faults'. He was suspended as marshal of France, fined and banished from court.[23] He was also replaced as Francis's governor by Artus Gouffier, seigneur de Boisy, whose younger brother Guillaume, seigneur de Bonnivet, now joined Francis's circle of friends.[24]

In April 1505 Louis XII again fell ill and on 31 May, made his will. He ordered Claude and Francis to be married as soon as possible, notwithstanding his obligations to Philip the Fair; appointed a council of regency, which included the queen and Louise of Savoy; and bequeathed to Claude the Orléans patrimony, including Blois, Genoa and Milan. He also forbade her to leave the kingdom on any pretext whatever. Queen Anne showed her disapproval of these arrangements by retiring to her duchy after the king's recovery. Louis, in the meantime, visited Amboise and took Francis with him to Plessis-lez-Tours. His council took steps to ensure that the king's will would be properly executed. Thus the captains of the *gendarmerie* had to promise in writing that they would serve Francis and Claude 'without excepting anyone here or outside the kingdom'. On 8 October, the cardinal of Amboise was entrusted with the 'total administration' of Francis, duc de Valois, until his majority.[25]

Before Francis and Claude could be married, however, it was necessary to repudiate the treaty of Blois, in which she had been promised to Charles of Luxemburg. This Louis did not mind doing, since he had now been given the investiture of Milan. But, under the treaty, Burgundy, Milan and Asti were to be forfeited to Charles if his marriage to Claude were broken off by Louis, Anne or Claude herself. The king overcame this difficulty by shifting the responsibility for his breach of faith on to his subjects. In April 1506 an Assembly of Notables, including representatives of the 'good towns' (*bonnes villes*) and universities were summoned to Tours. The deputies were received by Louis XII on 14 May and their spokesman, Thomas Bricot, made a speech. He began by acclaiming Louis as 'Father of the people' on account of the stable peace and sound justice which he had given them. Then as the deputies fell upon their knees, Bricot came to the point. 'Sire', he said, 'we are come here to proffer a request for the general welfare of your kingdom. Your humble subjects beg that it may please you to give your only daughter in marriage to my Lord Francis here present, who is France's son [*tout français*].' The king, apparently much moved by these words, promised to consider them carefully. Five days later the delegates were told that he had granted their request. They were asked to swear in return that they would see the marriage carried out when the children came of age, and to recognize Francis as their sovereign lord should Louis die without male issue. Before returning home they witnessed the

[23] *Procédures politiques.*   [24] Paris, i. 36; Barrillon, i. 5.
[25] C. Terrasse, *François Ier: le roi et le règne* (1945–70), i. 39–40.

Ce prire romaine come restet seure
hystonographes et orateurs soloient dire
que en regardant les ymages honorables
et arez de triuple de seurs predecesseurs avoit

9. The betrothal of Francis duc de Valois and Claude de France before the estates of Tours (1506). On the left stand the nobles, on the right, the town representatives. Cardinal Georges d'Amboise blesses the young couple. Anne of Brittany (crowned) and Louise of Savoy look on. All are smiling (though Anne strongly opposed the match). Miniature from B.N., ms. 5083, f. 1vº.

10. Francis, duc de Valois, being presented to Christ by St Agnes. The miniature (from B.N., ms. lat. 8396, f.1) seems to refer to the saint's feast day, 21 January 1512, when Anne of Brittany's son was still-born, thereby clearing Francis's way to the throne. The portrayal of the pope belongs to the anti-papal polemic that was virulent in France at the time.

betrothal of the royal children.[26] This was performed by the cardinal of Amboise on 21 May in the great hall of the château of Plessis-lez-Tours, the marriage contract being signed on the following day.[27]

On 3 August 1508 Francis left his mother to settle permanently at court.[28] He was nearly fourteen years old, the age at which in France a youth was traditionally deemed capable of assuming the full responsibility of kingship. But he

[26] J. Russell Major, *Representative Institutions in Renaissance France, 1421–1559* (Madison, WI, 1960), pp. 122–4.
[27] J. d'Auton, *Chronique de Louis XII*, ed, R. de Maulde La Clavière (1889–95), iv. 44ff; *Procédures politiques*, pp. 221–2.
[28] Michaud et Poujoulat, v. 88.

could not yet be certain of reaching the throne. In April 1510 Queen Anne became pregnant for the seventh time. The king prayed for a son, but on 25 October he was given a second daughter, called Renée.[29] In 1512 Anne did produce a son, but he died almost immediately. Louise, who set great store by the unimpeded advancement of her son, expressed her relief in her *Journal.* 'Anne, queen of France', she wrote, 'gave birth to a son on 21 January, the feast of St Agnes; but he was unable to prevent the exaltation of my Caesar, for he was still-born.' The king now abandoned hope of perpetuating his line, and Francis became popularly known as 'Monsieur le Dauphin'. He was admitted to the king's council and appointed captain of a hundred *lances.*[30] In September 1512 he was given command of the army of Guyenne, but being too young and inexperienced to be left in charge of operations, he was accompanied by Odet de Foix, seigneur de Lautrec, who bore the title of *lieutenant-général.* The task facing the army was the reconquest of Navarre, the small Pyrenean kingdom which Ferdinand of Aragon had recently overrun. The ensuing campaign, however, was a fiasco. The French, after trying unsuccessfully to prevent the duke of Alba from retreating to Pampluna, laid siege to the town as winter closed in upon them. Francis was only marginally involved in these operations, his responsibility being to cover Bayonne. Nor did he see the campaign through to the end: early in November, after leading an unsuccessful diversionary attack on San Sebastian, he disbanded his troops and returned to court. Later that month, the French raised the siege of Pampluna and retreated northwards, leaving behind their sick and wounded and even their precious artillery. Francis's experience of real warfare had been anything but glorious. Even so, a beautiful bronze medal was struck bearing his effigy in profile, crowned with laurels, and bearing the inscription: *Maximus Franciscus Francorum Dux, 1512.*[31]

In June 1513 the French in north Italy suffered a crushing defeat at Novara at the hands of the Swiss. In September, after they had been driven out of the peninsula, the Swiss swept into Burgundy as far as the walls of Dijon. The local commander, La Tremoïlle, had to sign a humiliating treaty, which Louis subsequently refused to implement. Meanwhile, the king of England, Henry VIII, and his ally, the Emperor Maximilian, invaded Picardy and laid siege to Thérouanne. A force of French cavalry was routed at Guinegatte as it tried to bring supplies to the beleaguered garrison. The action became known as the 'Battle of the Spurs' because the French fled from the field so fast. Louis XII, who was at Amiens at the time, sent out another force under Francis and the duc de

---

[29] In 1528 she married Ercole d'Este, who became duke of Ferrara in 1534. She became a patron of the Reformation. See C. J. Blaisdell, In *A.R.*, lxiii (1972), 196–226.
[30] *Procédures politiques*, p. 314.
[31] P. Boissonnade, *Histoire de la réunion de la Navarre à la Castille* (1893), pp. 379ff; A.-M. Lecoq, *François Ier imaginaire*, pp. 120–1.

11. Bronze medal of Francis, duc de Valois (1512). This is the first French example of an effigy in the classical style, hatless and crowned with laurels. Although Francis was heir presumptive to the throne, he was not the king's son, and therefore not entitled to call himself Dauphin: hence, the curious inscription: *Dux Francorum*.

Bourbon, but it could not save Thérouanne, which capitulated on 23 August. A month later the much more important town of Tournai also fell into English hands.

On 9 January 1514 Anne of Brittany died, leaving the way to the throne clear for Francis.[32] It was still possible, of course, for Louis XII to remarry but Francis was fairly confident on this score. 'Even if the king should be foolish enough to marry again', he said, 'he will not live long; any son he might have would be a child. This would necessitate a regency and in accordance with the constitution I would be the regent.'[33]

Although Francis was not yet allowed any share of policy-making, he became politically significant as people began to regard him as Louis XII's likely successor. Foreign ambassadors tried to win his friendship. On 13 March

[32] Florange, i. 146–9; *Procédures politiques*, pp. 338–40.   [33] *Ibid.*, pp. 353–4.

he signed a truce with Ferdinand of Aragon at Louis's request.[34] Ferdinand was anxious to follow this up with a marriage between his grandson and Princess Renée, hoping that her dowry would include Milan and Naples. This was acceptable to Louis, but not to Pope Leo X, who did not wish to see Ferdinand more powerful in Italy. His envoy to France decided to enlist Francis's help. 'I have spent a long time with him', he wrote, 'pointing out the dangers and explaining that he would be the chief sufferer, having regard to the position for which God intends him. With suitable arguments I have convinced him that the affair should not be allowed to go on. His views are sound and he has done some good. I am especially commissioned by him to tell His Holiness that his one desire is to do him service, and that, if he ever attain the station to which he may peradventure be called, he will give an unequivocal manifestation of his respect for and devotion to Holy Church.'[35]

The death of Anne of Brittany also facilitated the marriage of her daughter, Claude, with the heir to the throne. This was celebrated at Saint-Germain-en-Laye on 18 May. The ceremony was extremely simple, as the court was still in mourning for the queen. Francis came from Paris, bringing with him only a bed, bolster and blanket, while Claude arrived from Blois with bed hangings of white damask. Both wore mourning at the nuptial service, which few guests attended: even Louise of Savoy was absent.[36] She would probably have preferred a more attractive daughter-in-law, for Claude was 'very small and strangely corpulent'. She also had a bad limp. But she was all sweetness, affability and piety. An ambassador remarked that her 'grace in speaking greatly made up for her want of beauty'. Whether or not Francis valued these qualities, he had reason to rejoice in his marriage: it enabled him to assume the title of duke of Brittany, and, on 20 May, he seemed like a changed man to the Venetian ambassador. 'Henceforth', Francis declared, 'I shall be kept informed of everything; and nothing but good will come of this; I promise to speak frankly to the king as I have not dared to do so far.'[37]

In May 1514 Francis expected soon to be king. Louis XII's health had been failing for some time, and now that the queen was dead the chance of his acquiring a son and heir must have seemed remote. On 7 August, however, the king signed two treaties with Henry VIII: the first left Thérouanne and Tournai in English hands and provided for the resumption of Henry's French pension, while the second laid down that Louis would marry Henry's sister, Mary. Public opinion was shocked that a girl of eighteen, universally acclaimed for her looks, should be married off to a gouty dotard of fifty-three, but Mary apparently accepted her fate with composure, having been assured by her

---

[34] *Ibid.*, p. 342.   [35] Desjardins, ii. 601–6.
[36] *Procédures politiques*, p. 358; Florange, i. 151–3; du Bellay, i. 39–40.
[37] *Procédures politiques*, p. 360.

brother that she would be free to choose her next husband. She was, moreover, prepared to put up with a great deal to be queen of France.[38]

Louis and Mary were married at Abbeville on 9 October, and, after their first night together, the old king 'seemed very jovial and merry and in love', boasting that 'he had performed marvels'.[39] But Francis had doubts about Louis's virility. Two days after the wedding he said to Florange: 'I am happier and more at ease than I have been for years, for I am certain, unless I have been told lies, that the king and queen cannot possibly have a child.'[40] Soon Louis began to show signs of wear and tear. The clerks of the *Basoche*, who specialized in ridiculing the 'establishment', put on a play in which Louis was shown being carried off to Heaven or Hell by a filly given to him by the king of England.[41] His health certainly collapsed under the strain of being a *gentil compaignon* to Mary. Soon after Christmas he fell seriously ill and was confined to his room at the palace of the Tournelles in Paris. 'He sent for Monsieur d'Angoulême', writes Florange, 'and told him that he was very ill and would not survive, whereupon the said lord comforted him as best he could ... and, after fighting hard against death, he died on New Year's Day, and the weather that day was worse than had ever been seen ... The king being dead, Monsieur d'Angoulême put on mourning as the nearest person to the crown, and coming to the palace in haste, informed all the princes and ladies of the kingdom, especially his mother, Madame Louise. It was, I must say, a splendid New Year's gift, for he was not the king's son, and for your information the said seigneur d'Angoulême was born on New Year's Day and acquired the kingdom of France on New Year's Day.'[42]

Florange was wrong about Francis's birthday, but his insistence on 1 January as a memorable date in the annals of the house of Angoulême is echoed in Louise of Savoy's *Journal*. 'On the first day of January', she writes, 'I lost my husband and on the first day of January my son became king of France.'[43]

---

[38] C.S.P. Ven., ii. 196; L.P., i (pt.2), pp. 1343, 1351.
[39] C.S.P. Ven., ii. 207–11; Florange, i. 154–9.
[40] Florange, i. 160.
[41] *Ibid.*, i. 163. *Basoche* was a name given to the Palais de Justice. Its clerks were ill-disciplined young men, whose farces and morality plays provided the only comic element in the French theatre during the Renaissance. For an account of the activities of the *Basoche* and of measures taken to restrict them under Francis I see H. G. Harvey, *The Theatre of the Basoche: The Contribution of the Law Societies to French Mediaeval Comedy* (Cambridge, MA, 1941), pp. 228–31.
[42] Florange, i. 163–4.
[43] It has been argued, not very convincingly, that Louis XII died on 31 December 1514, not 1 January 1515. See H. Hauser, 'Sur la date exacte de la mort de Louis XII et de l'avènement de François Ier', *Rev. d'hist. mod. et contemp.*, v (1903–04), 172–82. For the argument in favour of 1 January see Bridge, *History of France*, iv. 267–83.

Chapter two

France in 1515

France in 1515 was still at a comparatively early stage of her national development. A national consciousness can be found in the writings of humanists like
Robert Gaguin and Valéran de Varennes and also at a more popular level, yet
France still lacked well-defined frontiers, a common language and a unified
legal system. Her eastern border was so blurred in places that some villagers
did not know to which nation they belonged and exploited this confusion to
evade taxes and the law. In so far as this frontier existed at all, it followed
roughly the rivers Scheldt, Meuse, Saône and Rhône from the North Sea to the
Mediterranean. People who lived west of this line were vassals of the French
king; those to the east owed allegiance to the Holy Roman Emperor. French
suzerainty over Artois and Flanders, however, was purely nominal, effective
control of these areas having passed to the house of Burgundy. Further east, the
frontier cut across the duchy of Bar so that its ruler, the duke of Lorraine, did
homage for one half to the king of France and for the other to the Emperor. In
the south, Dauphiné and Provence were still not regarded as integral parts of
the kingdom, because they were situated east of the Rhône: the king was
obeyed as Dauphin in the one and as count in the other. The south-west border
of France more or less followed the Pyrenees, avoiding Roussillon, which
belonged to Aragon, and the small kingdom of Navarre, ruled by the house of
Albret. Within France, there were three foreign enclaves: Calais belonged to
England, the Comtat-Venaissin to the papacy and the principality of Orange to
the house of Chalon. A few great fiefs also survived, notably the duchy of
Brittany, which did not become officially part of France till 1532, and the large
Bourbon domain in central France.[1]

France at the close of the Middle Ages still lacked linguistic unity. Modern
French is descended from *langue d'oil*, a dialect spoken in northern France

---

[1] G. Zeller, *Les institutions de la France au XVIe siècle* (1948), pp. 1–9; H. Stein and L. Legrand, *La
frontière d'Argonne* (1905).

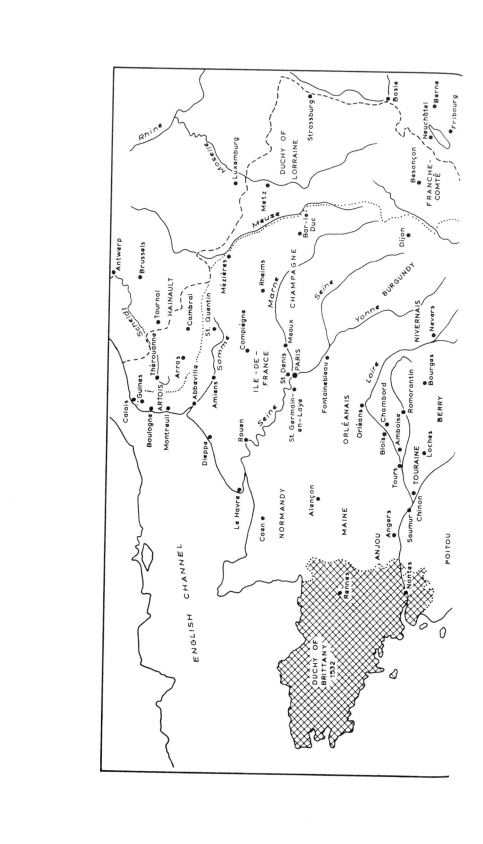

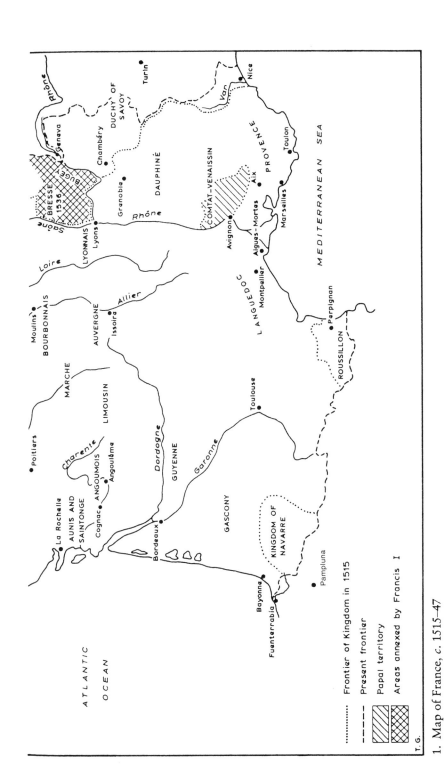

1. Map of France, c. 1515–47

ATLANTIC OCEAN

Poitiers

La Rochelle

AUNIS AND SAINTONGE

Cognac Charente

ANGOUMOIS Angoulême

MARCHE

BOURBONNAIS Moulins

LIMOUSIN

AUVERGNE Issoire Allier

Loire

Rhône Sâone BRESSE BUGEY 1536 Geneva

Turin

DUCHY OF SAVOY

Chambéry

LYONNAIS Lyons

Grenoble

DAUPHINÉ

Rhône

Var

Nice

COMTAT-VENAISSIN Avignon Aix

PROVENCE

Toulon

Marseilles

Aigues-Mortes

MEDITERRANEAN SEA

LANGUEDOC Montpellier

Perpignan

ROUSSILLON

GUYENNE Dordogne

GASCONY Garonne

Toulouse

Bordeaux

Bayonne

Fuenterrabia

KINGDOM OF NAVARRE

Pampluna

Frontier of Kingdom in 1515
Present frontier
Papal territory
Areas annexed by Francis I

T. G.

during the medieval period; in the south, *langue d'oc* (also called *occitan*) was used. The linguistic frontier ran from the Bec d'Ambès in the west to the col du Lautaret in the east, passing through Limoges, the Cantal and Annonay. South of this line, even educated people used the local idiom or Latin; French was spoken by feudal magnates only when addressing the king. After 1450, as the French monarchy asserted its authority following the expulsion of the English, the *langue d'oil* began to make deep inroads in the south-west. The parlements of Toulouse, Bordeaux and Aix used it, and noblemen from the south who took up offices at court adopted it. They continued to speak it when they returned home and passed the habit to their servants. By 1515 the expansion of the *langue d'oil* southwards was in full swing, at least in so far as upper-class usage was concerned. But the linguistic unity of France still had a long way to go.[2] As Fernand Braudel has written: 'What we think of as civilization (the way people are born, live, love, marry, think, believe, laugh, eat, dress, build houses, lay out fields or behave towards each other) was practically never the same in the south (where the word for yes was *oc*) as in the north, (where it was *oil* later *oui*) There always has been and always will be "another" France in the south.' Nor should we imagine that the divide was simply between north and south. Within each linguistic half there were 'whole families of provincial patois, themselves sub-divided almost to infinity', not to mention the more or less foreign languages on the outer periphery of the kingdom, such as Basque, Breton or Flemish.[3]

Another area where unification was far from complete was the law. During the Middle Ages each province, each *pays* and often each locality had its own set of customs. Broadly speaking, Roman law prevailed in the south while customary law held sway in the north, but patches of customary law existed in the south and Roman law penetrated the north to a limited extent. For a long time customs were fixed only by practice, and were, therefore, subject to continual change; this made for flexibility, but also uncertainty. So, from the twelfth century onwards charters were drawn up listing the customs of individual lordships or towns. The first serious attempt at codification was made by Charles VII, but no real progress was made till Charles VIII set up a commission in 1495. It was under Louis XII, however, that codification really got under way. The king appointed two commissioners for each area, one of them being Antoine Duprat, the future Chancellor, who was chosen to codify the customs of Auvergne. In each *pays coutumier* an assembly of representatives of the three estates was asked to draw up a code for scrutiny by the commissioners. Those parts of the code which were generally approved were promul-

---

[2] A. Brun, *Recherches historiques sur l'introduction du français dans les provinces du Midi* (1923); E. Le Roy Ladurie, *Carnival: A People's Uprising at Romans, 1579–80*, tr. M. Feeney (London, 1980), p. 46.

[3] F. Braudel, *The Identity of France*, vol. I (London, 1989), 85–92, 116.

gated at once, while the rest were referred to a decision by the appropriate *parlement*. Within a few years many customs were printed, and the process was to continue under Francis.[4]

The surface area of France in 1515 was far smaller than it is today: 459,000 square kilometres as against 550,986. Yet it must have seemed enormous to people living at the time, given the relative slowness of their communications system. It has been estimated that fifteenth-century Burgundy in terms of travelling time was ten or twelve times as large as the whole of France to-day. To contemporaries France must have seemed 'a territory so vast as to be difficult to cross, difficult to supervise and difficult to control'.[5] The speed of road travel may be assessed by consulting the guidebook published by Charles Estienne in 1553.[6] One could cover fifteen to sixteen leagues in a day when the terrain was flat, fourteen when it rose gently and only eleven to thirteen where it rose steeply. Thus it would have taken normally two days to travel from Paris to Amiens, six from Paris to Limoges, seven and a half from Paris to Bordeaux, six to eight from Paris to Lyons and ten to fourteen from Paris to Marseilles. These figures, however, are theoretical optima. 'In the sixteenth century all timetables were completely dependent on the weather. Irregularity was the rule.'[7]

The social and cultural implications of distance were far-reaching. Braudel has suggested that it made for a fragmented society in which villages, towns, *pays*, even provinces 'existed in sheltered cocoons, having almost no contact with one another'. Each community was a small world. 'The vast majority of French people', Dupâquier has written, 'were able to put a name to every face they met; and they in turn were known and recognized.'[8] This may have been true of the peasantry in general, but the immobility of French life should not be exaggerated. In spite of the distances there was a continual movement of people in and out of towns. 'We would be wrong to imagine', writes Chevalier, 'our ancestors as immobile beings, riveted to their fields or workshops.'[9]

The population

France about 1515 was largely rid of the misfortunes that had devastated her between 1340 and 1450. They did not disappear completely, but were more

[4] J. H. Shennan, *The Parlement of Paris*, (London, 1968), pp. 50–3; A. Buisson, *Le chancelier Antoine Duprat* (1935), pp. 70–96.
[5] F. Braudel, *The Identity of France*, tr. S. Reynolds (1989), Vol. I, p. 112.
[6] C. Estienne, *Le guide des chemins de France de 1553*, ed. J. Bonnerot, 2 vols. (1936); R. Mousnier, *Etudes sur la France de 1494 à 1559* (Cours de Sorbonne, 1964), pp. 9–13.
[7] F. Braudel, *The Mediterranean and the Mediterranean World in the Age of Philip II*, tr. S. Reynolds (London, 1972–3), i. 360.
[8] Braudel, *Identity of France*, i. 115; J. Dupâquier, *La population rurale du Bassin Parisien à l'époque de Louis XIV* (1979), p. 204.
[9] B. Chevalier, *Les bonnes villes de France du XIVe au XVIe siècle* (1982) p. 34.

widely spaced and generally less severe. Outbreaks of plague still occurred
from time to time, but there were no pandemics of the kind that had swept
across the kingdom between 1348 and 1440. Epidemics were limited now to
one or two provinces at most, and destructive ones were less frequent. Another
scourge from which the kingdom was largely freed after 1450 was war. Except
for certain border areas, little fighting took place within France between the
Hundred Years War and the Wars of Religion. True, large companies of disbanded troops and brigands did terrorize certain areas from time to time, but,
in general, the fear and uncertainty that had discouraged agricultural enterprise
before 1450 were removed. Another stimulus to rural prosperity was the
absence of any major grain famine between 1440 and 1520.

Fewer epidemics, famines and wars served to foster a rise in the population
of France after 1450. No precise figures can be given because of the paucity of
documentary evidence: there is no general census for this period, and relatively
few parish registers survive. These relate mainly to Provence and north-west
France, and are often in poor condition: they do not provide complete baptis-
mal lists, seldom record burials and mention marriages only occasionally. The
population of France is unlikely to have exceeded 15 million around 1500, yet
it was growing. Having been cut by a half between 1330 and 1450, it seems to
have doubled between 1450 and 1560. The rise was not uniform across the
kingdom: some villages, even regions, maintained a high annual growth rate
over a long period, while others made more modest advances. In Languedoc
and Provence, the rise began later than in northern France, reaching its peak in
the early sixteenth century, when the rise in the north slowed down. Even
within a province there could be sharp local differences; nor was the rise necessarily continuous. Yet, despite such variations, the population of France had
by 1560 returned to the same level as before the Black Death, though its distribution was not necessarily identical.[10]

The countryside

The need to feed more mouths stimulated a rise in agricultural production
after 1450. This was achieved as a consequence of land clearance and reclamation rather than improved agricultural techniques. In areas, such as Cambrésis, where long-term fallow was an anomaly, attention was concentrated on
hitherto neglected marginal lands. But, in most cases, the agricultural revival
took the form of a reclamation of arable that had been allowed to go to waste.
The reconstruction began in earnest about 1470 and continued till about 1540.

---

[10] P. Goubert, 'Recent Theories and Research on French Population between 1500–1700', in D. V.
Glass and D. E. C. Eversley (eds.), *Population in History* (London, 1965), pp. 456–73; F. Braudel,
The Identity of France, vol. II (London, 1991), pp. 170–3.

It was left to the initiative of individual seigneurs, who had to overcome huge difficulties. On countless estates nothing was visible except 'thorns, thickets and other encumbrances'; the old boundaries had disappeared and people no longer knew where their patrimonies lay. The task of compiling new *censiers* and terriers was expensive and time-consuming. There was also an acute short-age of labour in the early stages, and lords had to offer substantial concessions to attract settlers to their lands.

The process of reclaiming arable, like the resettlement of the countryside, was subject to many regional variations. It began sooner, for example, in the Paris region and the south-west than in the Midi. Even in the north there were local differences: whereas in the Paris region most land had been reclaimed by 1500, in some areas of thin or heavy soil the process continued till about 1520. In Provence and Languedoc it took up virtually the entire first quarter of the sixteenth century. Reclamation was not accomplished without some damage to pastoral farming. Many village communities, anxious to maximize their arable, tried to limit grazing. Access was restricted to transhumant animals, and peasants were forbidden to own more than a fixed number of animals; but the need for manure precluded a complete ban on livestock. In certain areas, moreover, such as mountains, where arable farming was less significant, steps were taken to protect pastures from excessive land-clearance. Thus, in spite of demographic pressure and resulting land-hunger, pastoral farming held its own.[11]

The towns

The rise of France's population after 1450 was reflected in the growth of her towns. Although evidence for this is often selective (e.g. tax returns) or incomplete (e.g. parish registers) all of it points in the same upward direction.[12] Thus at Périgueux the population rose gently between 1450 and 1480 and then steeply, reaching a peak in 1490. Using the base index of 100 for the number of known families, this had fallen to 29 in 1450, before rising to 87 in 1490 and levelling off at 79 in 1500.[13] Paris, which was by far the largest town in France, more than recovered its population (*c.* 200,000) of before the Black Death and the Hundred Years War. Navagero estimated it as 400,000 in 1528 and Cavalli

---

[11] M. Bloch, *French Rural History* (London, 1966), pp. 21–63, 112–49; G. Duby and A. Wallon (eds.), *Histoire de la France rurale*, ii (1975); E. Le Roy Ladurie and M. Morineau, *Histoire écono-mique et sociale de la France*, i (1450–1660), pt. 2, *Paysannerie et croissance* (1977), pp. 483–689.

[12] The difficulty of using hearth tax records in respect of urban population is fully discussed by Che-valier, *Les bonnes villes*, pp. 22–4. 'Let us resign ourselves;', he writes, 'it is impossible to know, even very roughly, the number of inhabitants of a town in early modern times'. The main trouble is that tax records omit the poor and the exempt, even sometimes the rich and powerful.

[13] Chevalier, *Les bonnes villes*, p. 28.

as 500,000 in 1546. The latest estimate, based on the city's annual grain consumption, is a maximum of 300,000 in 1565.[14]

A royal document of 1538 distributing the cost of 20,000 infantry among the cities in accordance with their presumed ability to pay enables us to rank them in order of size. Immediately below Paris were four provincial towns (Rouen, Lyons, Toulouse and Orléans) of between 40,000 and 70,000 inhabitants, then perhaps a score of towns of between 10,000 and 30,000 inhabitants, then another forty or so of between 5,000 and 10,000. Finally, there were many more small towns with fewer than 5,000 inhabitants. The document shows the relative importance in 1538 of towns, like Orléans, Troyes and Dieppe, which would subsequently decline relatively. In all, it lists 246 localities which may not be the totality of communities deserving to be called towns. The line distinguishing a small town from a large village was difficult to draw. A town, it seems, was usually walled. It also possessed certain privileges and comprised a wider variety of occupational and social types than a village.[15]

A comparison of the tax roll of 1538 with a document of 1330 listing the 226 towns where the mendicant orders established houses shows a remarkable change in the pattern of urbanization in France. In 1330 the main towns were concentrated in two areas: the southern crescent between Lyons and La Rochelle, and Outre-Seine. In 1538, except for the high mountains and the *bocages* of western France, each *pays* seemed to be organized around a middling or small town.[16]

The character of each town was determined by its main activity. Trade was important to all of them, but some were administrative, intellectual and ecclesiastical centres as well. Eight (Paris, Toulouse, Grenoble, Bordeaux, Dijon, Rouen, Aix and Rennes) had parlements, about ninety were capitals of *bailliages* and *sénéchaussées*, fifteen (Paris, Toulouse, Montpellier, Orléans, Cahors, Angers, Aix, Poitiers, Valence, Caen, Nantes, Bourges, Bordeaux, Angoulême and Issoire) had universities, and about 110 were archiepiscopal or episcopal sees. Virtually the only industrial towns were Amiens, where the manufacture of cloth kept half the population employed, and Tours, where silk was important.[17]

By the end of the fifteenth century the walled towns, commonly described as *bonnes villes* to distinguish them from the large villages or *villes champêtres*,

---

[14] J. Jacquart, 'Le poids démographique de Paris et de l'Ile-de-France au XVIe siècle', *Annales de démographie historique* (1980), 93–4. J.-P. Babelon, *Nouvelle histoire de Paris: Paris au XVIe siècle* (1986), pp. 159–66 gives an estimate of more than 350,000 residents in 1555. But see B. B. Diefendorf, *Beneath the Cross: Catholics and Huguenots in Sixteenth-Century Paris* (Oxford, 1991), pp. 9, 183 n.7.

[15] *Crisis and Social Change in Early Modern France*, ed. P. Benedict (London, 1989), pp. 24–5.

[16] Chevalier, *Les bonnes villes*, p. 40.

[17] P. Chaunu and R. Gascon, *Histoire économique et sociale de la France*, i (1450–1660), pt.i, *L'état et la ville* (1977), pp. 404–6.

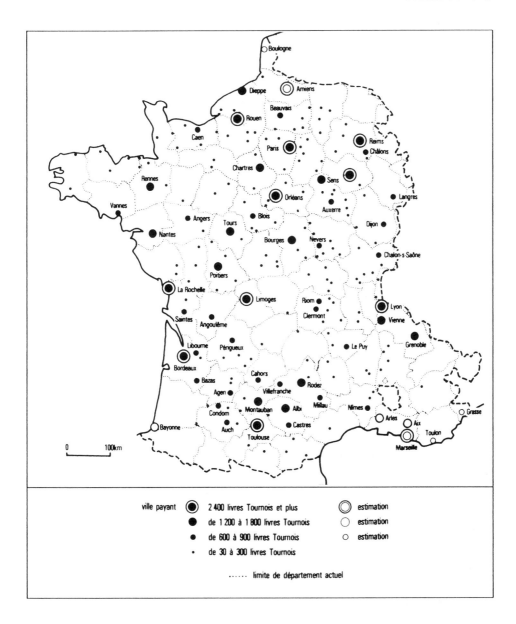

Boulogne
Dieppe   Amiens
Beauvais
Rouen
Caen
Paris   Reims
Châlons
Chartres
Rennes   Sens
Vannes   Orléans   Langres
Angers   Blois   Auxerre
Tours   Dijon
Nantes   Bourges   Nevers
                    Chalon-s-Saône
Poitiers
La Rochelle   Limoges   Riom   Lyon
Saintes   Clermont   Vienne
Angoulême
Libourne   Périgueux   Le Puy   Grenoble
Bordeaux
Bazas   Cahors
Agen   Villefranche   Rodez
Condom   Montauban   Albi   Millau   Nîmes
Auch   Castres   Arles   Aix   Grasse
Bayonne   Toulouse   Marseille   Toulon

0   100km

ville payant   ● 2 400 livres Tournois et plus   ◎ estimation

● de 1 200 à 1 800 livres Tournois   ◯ estimation

• de 600 à 900 livres Tournois   ○ estimation

· de 30 à 300 livres Tournois

...... limite de département actuel

2. The relative sizes of French towns according to the tax levy of 1538 for the payment of the infantry (from B. Chevalier, *Les bonnes villes de France*. Paris: Aubier, 1982)

were playing an active role in the political life of the kingdom. In 1482 Louis XI asked the people of Amiens to endorse a treaty, giving as his reason 'the need to secure the consent and ratification of the men of the estates and communities of the *bonnes villes* of our kingdom'. The towns have been described as a fourth power in the kingdom along with the king, the church and the nobility. The crown and the towns worked together as allies, but watched each other closely.

The walls of many towns had fallen into disrepair by the thirteenth century. As a result many had fallen prey to English armies in the Hundred Years War. To protect themselves many had repaired their walls at their own expense and the process was still going on as the sixteenth century began. In 1513, when France was threatened with invasion, there was hardly a town anywhere that did not repair its walls, dig moats and renew its artillery. To be a *bonne ville* it seems that a town needed not only a wall but also the human and material resources necessary to defend itself. Thus Seyssel, writing in 1510, stated: 'a *bonne ville* or *place forte* that is well supplied, well equipped with guns and with all things necessary to sustain a siege and nourish a garrison and relief force is the safeguard of an entire kingdom'. A recent survey has traced the remains of 1700 *places-fortes* in France dating back to before 1500.[18]

Trade and industry

The rise in population, the growth of urbanization and a general rise in the standard of living were mainly responsible for an economic boom which began in the 1460s and lasted till about 1520. France was fortunate in being largely self-sufficient in respect of basic necessities, such as grain, wine, salt and textiles. Grain was her most important produce. Foreign grain was sometimes imported in times of famine, but normally France produced enough for her needs and exported the surplus. Paris drew its supplies from a large area comprising Beauce, Brie, the Ile-de-France, Picardy and Vexin. In difficult years it made demands on more remote provinces, such as Champagne. Lyons's main supplier was Burgundy, but in times of dearth it turned to Languedoc, Provence, Xaintois, Lorraine, the Ile-de-France, Picardy and Beauce.[19]

Wine consumption increased enormously during the sixteenth century, as is shown by the rapid expansion of vineyards around Paris, Orléans, Rheims and Lyons, the yield from duties on wine and the multiplication of taverns. Then, as now, wine was produced not only for the home market, but also for export. Thus several major vineyards were developed along the Atlantic coast, around Bordeaux, La Rochelle and in the Basse-Loire. England and the Netherlands were the best customers.[20]

---

[18] Chevalier, *Les bonnes villes*, pp. 13, 46–7.   [19] Chaunu and Gascon, i. 256–60.
[20] *Ibid.*, pp. 260–1; R. Boutruche, *Bordeaux de 1453 à 1715* (Bordeaux, 1966), p. 101.

Salt, like wine, was produced for the home and foreign markets. Salt from marshes along the Mediterranean coast was sent up the Rhône and Saône to south-east France, Burgundy and ultimately to the Swiss cantons and Savoy. Another group of salt marshes along the Atlantic coast supplied a much wider area. Their salt travelled up the Loire to Orléans and Chartres or by sea to Rouen and the towns of northern France. England, the Netherlands and the Baltic states all imported French salt, mainly from Nantes and La Rochelle.[21]

Metalware, especially of iron or steel, was not widely used in early sixteenth-century France. Agricultural and industrial tools were still largely made of wood. Apart from a few basic iron pots, the greatest demand was for nails and pins. For non-ferruginous metals, France depended largely on foreign imports: copper, brass and tinplate from Germany, pewter and lead from England and steel from Italy.[22]

As trade developed in France towards the close of the Middle Ages, a widespread demand arose for the establishment of markets and fairs under royal licence: no fewer than 344 were set up between 1483 and 1500. When a fair was established it was given privileges designed to attract merchants: foreign money was allowed to circulate freely, the goods of aliens were guaranteed against seizure and distraint, and the *droit d'aubaine*, whereby an alien's inheritance was liable to forfeiture by the crown, was set aside. Some fairs were exempt from entry or exit dues and sometimes special judges were appointed to hear the suits of merchants, thereby sparing them the delays of ordinary justice.

By 1515 most big towns and many smaller ones had fairs.[23] The four annual fairs of Lyons attracted many foreigners, especially Italians, Germans and Swiss. They were also important for the development of banking. Though banks had existed in France since the thirteenth century, if not earlier, it was only in the fifteenth that they became important as agencies of credit and exchange. They fixed themselves at Lyons because of the large amount of business transacted there, and threw out branches in other trading centres. Use of the bill of exchange almost eliminated the need to transport large amounts of cash, and the Lyons fairs became a regular clearing-house for the settlement of accounts. At the same time, bankers took money on deposit, lent it at interest and negotiated letters of credit. The crown was one of their best customers.[24]

No statistics exist for the volume of French overseas trade in 1515, but it had certainly recovered from its stagnation during the Hundred Years War. The

[21] Chaunu and Gascon, pp. 263–4.   [22] *Ibid.*, pp. 264–5.
[23] J. S. C. Bridge, *History of France from the death of Louis XI* (Oxford, 1921–36), v. 261–8.
[24] R. Doucet, 'La banque en France au XVIe siècle', *Rev. d'hist. écon. et soc.* 29 (1951), 115–23; M. Brésard, *Les foires à Lyon au XVe et au XVIe siècles* (Lyons, 1914), pp. 238–93; M. Vigne, *La banque à Lyon du XVe au XVIIIe siècle* (Lyons, 1903); R. Gascon, *Grand commerce et vie urbaine au XVIe siècle: Lyon et ses marchands* (1971), i. 240–63.

annexation of Provence in 1481 was an event of major significance for French trade in the Mediterranean. Though Marseilles was unable to wrest the monopoly of the Levantine trade from Venice, it established useful links with the ports of the Ligurian coast, Tuscany, Catalonia, Sicily, Rhodes and the Barbary coast. With a single exception, its chief merchants were Italians who turned to the Lyons bankers for capital.[25] The French Atlantic and Channel ports also recovered in the late fifteenth century and carried on an active trade with England, Spain, the Netherlands and Scandinavia.[26] Land communications being so poor, harbours developed, not only along the west coast, but along navigable rivers, even far inland. As many as 200 ships might be seen at any time along the quays at Rouen. By far the most important port of the south-west was Bordeaux, which was visited each year by the English wine fleet.[27]

The expansion of trade was related to industrial growth. The most important French industry was cloth-making, which was centred in the north but was also becoming entrenched in other areas, notably Languedoc. Although usually called after towns, the various kinds of cloth were mainly produced in the countryside, the towns being merely centres from which the cloth merchants operated. Generally speaking, French cloth was of ordinary quality and cheap; it served the day-to-day needs of the lower orders of society. Even the best French cloth (from Rouen and Paris) could not compete with certain foreign imports, such as Florentine serges. The finest wool also had to be imported from Spain, England, the Barbary coast and the Levant. An important development, apart from the introduction of the fulling-mill, which facilitated the production of cheaper cloth, was the establishment of a luxury cloth industry, first at Tours, then at Lyons. But France alone could not satisfy the increasingly sophisticated taste at court and among the nobility. For the finest linen she looked to the Netherlands and South Germany, and for silks to Italy. These comprised velvet from Genoa, damask and satin from Florence and Lucca, and cloth of gold from Milan.[28]

A major new industry which was fast developing in France in the early sixteenth century was printing. After it had been imported to Paris from its birthplace in Germany in 1470, it spread to Lyons in 1473, Albi in 1475 and Toulouse and Angers in 1476. By 1500 there were 75 presses in Paris alone. As yet France lagged far behind Italy in terms of book-production. The capital of printing was Venice, but Paris and Lyons were catching up fast. The statistics speak for themselves: between 1480 and 1482 Venice produced 156 editions, and Paris 35; between 1495 and 1497 Venice produced 447, Paris 181 and

[25] R. Collier and J. Billioud, *Histoire du commerce de Marseille* iii (1480–1599) (1951), 3–165.
[26] E. Trocmé and M. Delafosse, *Le commerce rochelois de la fin du XVe au début du XVIIe siècle* (1952).
[27] R. Boutruche, *Bordeaux de 1453 à 1715* (Bordeaux, 1966), pp. 113–38.
[28] Chaunu and Gascon, i. 251–53.

Lyons 95. Whereas in 1480 only nine French towns had printing presses, by 1500 the number had risen to 40. Although the earliest French printers addressed themselves to an academic clientèle, they very soon branched out in pursuit of high profits. Their output was far from limited to classical or humanistic texts. They also published religious works of various kinds (missals, breviaries, books of hours, manuals for confessors), and works of secular literature, such as tales of chivalry. Apart from university teachers and students, the rich clergy of the cathedral towns were good customers, as were the magistrates and lawyers attached to the parlements. This was why many printers set up businesses near lawcourts.[29]

Social structure

The vast majority of French people lived in the countryside and most of them were peasants living in one of the kingdom's 30,000 villages. A village was largely self-contained: if it looked outwards at all, it was only to the surrounding parishes or to the nearest *bourg* with its market and lawcourt. Yet some peasants did venture further afield. Each year, for example, thousands of Auvergnats took up seasonal work in Spain. Teams of Norman peasants helped to bring in the grain harvest in Beauce and the Ile-de-France, and stonemasons from Limousin went wherever building was undertaken. Some peasants might also go to Italy in the king's army. Yet most stayed in or near their birth places.[30]

Each village had its hierarchy at the top of which was the seigneur, who was commonly but not necessarily a nobleman, for a *seigneurie* could be bought like any other piece of property. It consisted of a landed estate, which could vary enormously in size, and of a judicial area. The *seigneurie* usually fell into two parts: the demesne which comprised the seigneur's house and tribunal, and the lands and woods which he cultivated himself, and the *censives* or *tenures* – lands he had entrusted in the past to peasants so that they might cultivate them more or less freely in return for numerous obligations (*redevances*), the main one being the *cens*. This was an annual rent, often quite light, which was paid on a fixed day. Usually the seigneur retained the mill, the wine-press and the oven and expected payment for their use. He took a proportion of any land sold, exchanged or inherited by a *censitaire*, and exacted the *champart*, a kind of seigneurial tithe, at harvest-time. The seigneur also had judicial rights over his tenants. Usually he had surrendered his criminal jurisdiction to the royal courts; but he still acted in civil matters through his *bailli* and other officials.

[29] L. Febvre and H.-J. Martin, *The Coming of the Book: The Impact of Printing* (London, 1986), pp. 170–7, 181–6.
[30] J. Jacquart, *François Ier*, (1981), pp. 54–5.

His court adjudicated in quarrels among the *censitaires* but also between them and himself. Inevitably, in a country as varied as France, *seigneuries* were not omnipresent: in the centre and the south there were many allodial lands (*alleux*) totally free of seigneurial dominance. By contrast Brittany and Burgundy were oppressively seigneurial.[31]

Socially, the start of the sixteenth century saw the culmination of two important trends in the countryside: a reduction in the wealth and authority of the *seigneur*, and the rise of a village aristocracy. During the agricultural renaissance, the *seigneur* had been forced to make concessions to his tenants: new leases had laid down precisely, and in writing, the services they owed, thereby protecting them from arbitrary exactions in future. By 1500 serfdom had virtually disappeared. In the sixteenth century, however, as the demographic rise created land-hunger, the *seigneur* tried to backtrack on concessions. Sometimes he was successful, but usually he failed. New customs were already held to be 'immemorial', and, even when the law decided in the *seigneur*'s favour, it could not always be enforced. His authority, moreover, was being eroded by the crown. A long series of royal enactments dating back to Charles VII rode roughshod over local customs. The king's judges heard appeals from decisions taken in the seigneurial courts, and, in cases involving bloodshed, pardons were frequently granted by the crown. Another blow to seigneurial prestige was the responsibility assigned by the crown to most village communities to allocate and collect the main direct tax, the *taille*. The *seigneur* also suffered a loss of income. He had been forced in the fifteenth century to accept a reduction of the *cens* and to convert dues in kind into cash payments. As these were fixed by custom, they were inevitably devalued by the sixteenth-century price rise. In these circumstances, the *seigneur* relied for the bulk of his income on his demesne; he tried to increase the rent paid by his tenant farmers. Yet if he lost something of his wealth and authority, he retained his social pre-eminence in the countryside.[32]

Historians have sometimes assumed that the decline of the *seigneur* in the fifteenth century continued into the following century. They have depicted him as uninterested in running his estates and lured into an extravagance he could ill afford by attending the royal court, serving in the king's armies in Italy or engaging in a sophisticated Renaissance life-style. The effects of his profligacy, it has been alleged, were exacerbated by a rise in prices that eroded the real value of his income as fixed by custom. Some *seigneurs* may well have succumbed to the urban middle class, keen to invest its profits in land and to achieve at least a semblance of nobility through ownership of a *seigneurie*. But the decline of the *seigneur* should not be exaggerated. Although there undoubtedly was an invasion of the *seigneurie* by the urban middle class, especially royal office-

[31] P. Goubert, *L'Ancien régime* (1969), i. 81–5.   [32] Duby and Wallon, ii. 108–20, 134–47.

holders, in the early sixteenth century, all noble *seigneurs* did not necessarily experience terminal decline. Like the *nouveaux-riches*, many noble *seigneurs* adapted to new circumstances. They were not all uninterested in their estates or extravagant. Relatively few went to court. Many managed their estates with care. Some reconstituted their demesne and leased it in the form of *métairies*. Since the contracts placed on the share-cropper (*métayer*) many of the obligations formerly owed by tenants, the *seigneurs* were able to restore their revenues.[33]

The peasantry, too, underwent a significant social transformation in the century after 1450. At the top of the social scale were the *fermiers* or *coqs de village*, who frequently acted as intermediaries between the *seigneur* and the rest of the peasantry. With at least thirty hectares at his disposal, the *fermier* could produce more in a year than he needed to feed his family and pay the seigneurial dues. The surplus enabled him to set up as a grain-merchant or cattle-breeder. He lent tools, seed and money to less fortunate peasants and offered them seasonal work and artisanal commissions. At the same time, *fermiers* collected leases, levied seigneurial dues and monopolized positions of influence in the village or parish. The rise of this village aristocracy did not affect the whole of France or even the majority of communities. The west was hardly touched by it. It was none the less a development of great significance for the future.[34]

Urban society was far more varied, open and mobile than rural society. For one thing it was continually being renewed, as the death rate in towns was far higher than in the countryside. This was mainly the result of overcrowding coupled with very low standards of hygiene. Even a mild epidemic could be devastating in a town and a regular flow of immigrants was needed to maintain and increase the population. Such immigrants comprised apprentices and journeymen, domestic servants and wetnurses, students and clerics. They would converge on a town each day from the rural hinterland looking for a better life and, possibly, social advancement. Beggars came expecting more efficient alms-giving, and the rural poor looking for work, when the population rise reduced their chances of employment on the land. The number of immigrants could be enormous. Thus at Nantes at the end of the fifteenth century the population might in a year of crisis rise from 20,000 to 30,000. This shows how difficult it is for the demographic historian to estimate urban population precisely at this time.[35] Most immigrants swelled the ranks of the urban proletariat which remained highly susceptible to any famine.

Contemporaries tended to divide urban society into two groups: the *aisés* or well-to-do, and the *menu peuple* or proletariat. The reality, however, was

[33] J. H. M. Salmon, *Society in Crisis: France in the Sixteenth Century* (London, 1975), pp. 41–4.
[34] Duby and Wallon, ii. 147–51.   [35] Chevalier, *Les bonnes villes*, pp. 35–6.

more complex. Apart from the nobility and the clergy, which were not specifically urban categories (they were exempt from urban taxes and service in the
militia), the upper end of the social scale comprised merchants and office-
holders. In towns, like Bordeaux and Toulouse, which had a parlement yet
were important in international trade, the two groups were fairly evenly balanced, but in others like Lyons, where trade was all-important, the merchants
were pre-eminent. They owned comfortable town houses and added to the
profits of their trade revenues from their estates in the neighbouring countryside. In towns which were primarily administrative centres, office-holders were
dominant. They were often as rich as the merchants, from whose ranks many
of them had risen. The core of urban society consisted of artisans and small to
middling merchants. They worked for themselves, served in the urban militia,
paid taxes, participated in general assemblies of the commune and owned
enough property to guarantee their future security. Although not immune to
the indirect effects of food shortages, they could count on having their own
daily bread at least. Artisans were mainly of two types: those who employed
large numbers of workmen and those who employed no labour other than their
own families.

The lower stratum of urban society – the *menu peuple* – consisted of manual
workers, who were excluded from any share in local government and lived in
constant fear of hunger. They included journeymen, who were paid in money
or money and kind, *manoeuvres* (paid by the day) and *gagne-deniers* (paid by
the piece). Typical of the *menu-peuple* was the building worker, who in Paris
received 35 *deniers* per working day (there were about 260 such days in a year,
the rest being feast days). This had to pay for his daily food, rent, clothing and
fuel. If he had a large family, his resources were stretched to the limit. A sudden
rise in the cost of living, sickness, an accident or unemployment could easily
drive him into poverty.[36]

Paris

The topography of Paris in the sixteenth century was determined, as it
always has been, by the river Seine flowing through the middle. The city fell
accordingly into three parts: the *Cité*, on the island in the middle of the river;
the *Ville* on the right bank; and the *Université* on the left bank. Paris was
encircled by medieval walls; but only the left bank remained within the twelfth-
century wall of Philip Augustus; the right bank had long since outstripped it,
and was now hemmed in by a fourteenth-century wall. Beyond the walls lay
the suburbs or *faubourgs*, the most important having grown around the old
abbey of Saint Germain-des-Prés.

[36] *Cities and Social Change*, pp. 11–17; Jacquart, *François Ier*, pp. 62–6.

The surface area within the walls was small and densely built up. Its inhabitants were crammed into narrow houses two or three storeys high. All the streets, except a few axial thoroughfares, were narrow and virtually impassable to wheeled traffic. They also stank because of the ordure which was thrown into them. Among the few open spaces in the city were the Cemetery of the Innocents and the Place de Grève, both of them on the right bank. Two bridges linked the *Ville* to the *Cité*: the Pont au Change, a wooden bridge built in 1296 which was lined with shops owned by goldsmiths, jewellers and money-changers, and the Pont Notre-Dame, which had been rebuilt following the collapse in 1499 of an earlier bridge. The two bridges linking the *Cité* with the left bank – the Petit-Pont and Pont-Saint-Michel – were in poor condition.

The *Cité* was the oldest part of Paris and could be considered the heart of the kingdom. In addition to being a thriving business community, it was also a religious and judicial centre. At the eastern end of the island stood the cathedral of Notre-Dame, the national sanctuary, where *Te Deums* were sung and entries and princely marriages celebrated. Close by were the fortified episcopal palace and the gated close containing the houses of thirty-seven canons. At the opposite end of the island stood the *Palais* or old royal palace, now occupied by the Parlement, the highest court of law, and other sovereign courts. Its business attracted a vast number of councillors, barristers, procurators, solicitors, ushers etc. in addition to all the litigants, many of whom came from afar, and the people who came to shop at the many stalls erected by tradesmen within the palace. Also on the island was the Hôtel-Dieu, the city's main hospital. The *Ville* was the business quarter. It contained the markets of the Halles, expensive shops in the rue Saint-Denis and mixed commerce around the rue Saint-Martin. Many of the streets were organized by trades. The Place de Grève, in addition to serving as a port, was a gathering place for the militia and a site for civic ceremonies and public executions. On the square's east side stood the seat of the municipal government or Hôtel de Ville. Other important secular buildings in the *Ville* were the Louvre, a medieval fortress that had outlived its defensive purpose, and the Châtelet, headquarters of the *prévôté* of Paris. The palace of the Tournelles was the only royal residence in the capital still used by the king in 1515, but it lacked the unity of style and grandeur expected of a Renaissance monarch. The University of Paris, which had been founded in the twelfth century and was best known for its faculties of theology and arts, occupied the left bank of the Seine. It also had faculties of canon law and medicine. In the fifteenth century it had declined in reputation and attracted fewer students from abroad than in the past. While the faculties conferred degrees, teaching was done in the fifty or so colleges, the most famous being the Sorbonne and colleges of Navarre, Cardinal Lemoine, Sainte-Barbe and Montaigu. Not all the students lived in them; many lodged in 'digs', some of them run by their tutors. For physical exercise they could use the Pré aux Clercs, a large meadow just outside the Porte de Nesle.[37]

The book-trade was, of course, well represented on the left bank by printers, booksellers and bookbinders. Paris had long been an important centre for the production of manuscripts, and the printed book was easily assimilated to an existing network of distribution. Thus Antoine Vérard ordered an illustrated *Decameron* from the printer, Jean du Pré, while continuing to supply hand-illuminated manuscripts to rich clients. Printing produced a special kind of capitalist, like Jean Petit, who between 1493 and 1530 published several thousand books. He acquired a large fortune and became one of the principal promoters of humanist thought. Among talented printers he recruited was Josse Bade, a Fleming, who, after working for Trechsel in Lyons, set up his own press in the rue Saint-Jacques. Erasmus turned to Bade for the publication of some of his works. Among other prominent Parisian printers around the turn of the century were Simon de Colines and Henri Estienne.[38]

Paris needed an extensive hinterland to feed its large and growing population. Fortunately it lay within a fertile grain belt, and a network of rivers in northern France made the transportation of bulky goods (e.g. grain, timber and wine) to the capital relatively simple. They were unloaded from boats at the Place de Grève. But, as a Venetian noted in 1546, the capital could not stock supplies for more than a week; this meant that certain items had to be brought in daily. In the winter, when the Seine iced over, scarcity ensued. Parisian merchants shared in France's export trade. They shipped abroad grain, wine, building-stone, coarse woollens, paper and eau-de-vie, while sharing in the profits from the sale of more distant produce, such as pastel from Toulouse or salt from the Atlantic marshes. Luxury goods for which Paris was famous (e.g. haberdashery, books and jewellery) were a relatively small, yet valuable, part of their trade. Parisians were consumers as well as producers of luxury goods: they imported exotic goods like furs, spices, sugar and Italian silks. While French and foreign merchants came to Paris in large numbers, especially during the annual fair of Saint-Germain, Parisian merchants travelled quite far with their wares, Rouen and Lyons being their main outlets. The presence in Paris of the Parlement and other sovereign courts helped to stimulate trade; by spending lavishly on their homes, clothing and entertainment, their personnel helped to sustain the capital's large population of skilled craftsmen. They were organized in closed corporations (*métiers*), headed by the *Six-Corps*: the drapers, grocers, hosiers, mercers, furriers and jewellers. Such artisans were

---

[37] Diefendorf, *Beneath the Cross*, pp. 10–27; J.-P. Babelon, *Paris au XVIe siècle*, pp. 50–5, 79–90, 111–19, 198–9, 215–61.
[38] *Ibid.*, pp. 100–4.

subject to strict rules of admission to and practice of a trade. The nature and quality of their products were closely supervised by guild wardens.[39]

Keeping order in Paris was subject to several authorities – the governor, the *prévôt*, the Parlement, and the *Bureau de la Ville* – whose jurisdictions sometimes overlapped. The responsibility for defending Paris rested with the governor, who was always a nobleman appointed by the king. In February 1515 Francis appointed Charles de Bourbon, duc de Vendôme, to that office.[40] Like the governor, the Parlement transmitted royal commands to the city. Its magistrates intervened on their own authority in various matters touching the capital's security and welfare. But being ill-equipped to carry out policies, they often acted through the *prévôté* and *Bureau de la Ville*.

The municipal government of Paris originated in the medieval corporation responsible for water traffic on the Seine (hence Paris's emblem of a ship). Over time it had enlarged its public responsibilities and been rewarded with privileges and royal recognition. By the sixteenth century the *Bureau* comprised a mayor (*prévôt des marchands*) and four aldermen (*échevins*) who were co-opted to serve for two years from a narrow local élite. Along with their subordinates, they engaged in a wide variety of public services. They were assisted in their deliberations by twenty-four councillors and in their daily tasks by sixteen *quarteniers*, one for each district. Both positions were held for life and recruitment was again restricted to the bourgeois élite. The local officers (*dizainiers, cinquanteniers*) who reported to the *quarteniers* were mainly drawn from among the craftsmen. One of the *Bureau*'s duties was to organize the local militia and night watch. All heads of households were expected to serve in the militia, which was organized by trade, but several found servants to act for them. The night watch guarded the city gates. The *Bureau* also disposed of some 200 professional troops, and there was also a royal partol of sixty men.

The officers of the *Bureau de la Ville* rarely initiated public projects. They nearly always acted in response to some directive from above – either from the Parlement, *prévôté* or king and council. Yet they did assert themselves occasionally: for example, when the king asked for a forced loan which they regarded as excessive. According to a mid sixteenth-century writer, Paris was a ship and the *prévôt des marchands* her captain, but the king was the wind that moved her sails.[41]

The three estates

Whereas we tend to divide society into groups according to place of residence, occupation or wealth, sixteenth-century Frenchmen used quite different

---

[39] Diefendorf, pp. 15–19.   [40] C.A.F., i. 86.   [41] Diefendorf, pp. 22–27.

criteria. They classified people, great and small, rich and poor, into one of three estates – clergy, nobility and third estate – which were regarded as divinely ordained and permanently fixed. Each estate had its distinctive function, life-style and privileges, which were acknowledged in both law and custom. Social peace rested on respect for this sacred hierarchy, yet the possibility was admitted that merit and wealth might enable an individual or a family to move from one to another.

Of the three estates, the clergy was the most clearly defined since its members had to be ordained or at least to have taken minor orders. It had its own code of discipline and its own hierarchy. At the top were the archbishops, bishops and abbots. Then came the canons of cathedrals and collegiate churches, and below them the great mass of parish priests, unbeneficed clergy, monks, friars and nuns. In terms of wealth, the gulf between a prelate and a humble parish priest was immense. The bishop often disposed of large temporal revenues. Thus the bishop of Langres was also a duke. He was *seigneur* of 100 villages and owned seven châteaux.[42] *Seigneuries* were also held by cathedral chapters and collegiate churches. By contrast the humble *curé* was often desperately poor: the *dime* paid to him by his parishioners was so meagre that he might be forced to run a small business on the side or to serve as the *seigneur*'s agent in order to make ends meet. Theoretically, under the constitution, called the Pragmatic Sanction of Bourges (1438), bishops and abbots were elected by their chapters, but in practice the church had difficulty resisting the demands of royal patronage. When the crown did not directly dispose of major benefices, elections were often disputed and the crown had to act as arbiter. Many smaller benefices were in the gift of a patron, ecclesiastical or lay.[43]

It is difficult to give a precise global estimate of the numbers of clergy about 1515. There were about 100 ordinary bishops, many suffragan bishops, a large number of canons, about 30,000 parish priests, and a huge crowd of unbeneficed clergy. The total may have reached 100,000. In addition there was an unquantifiable number of regular clergy. The monastic establishment included 600 Benedictine abbeys, 400 mendicant houses, more than 100 commanderies of St John and sixty charterhouses. Even if the number of inmates had fallen of late, these figures imply a sizeable cloistered population.[44]

Although the nobility was the second estate, it was nevertheless the one that was widely envied for its prestige and life-style. The noble condition was identified with perfection, while juridically and politically it implied a special status enjoyed by certain individuals, or rather, lineages. For heredity was essential to the concept. A nobleman was born rather than made, hence the

---

[42] Doucet, *Institutions*, p. 726.   [43] Salmon, *Society in Crisis*, pp. 79–83.
[44] Jacquart, *François Ier*, p. 67.

phrase 'nobility of race'.[45] Although many ancient lineages had died out by the end of the Middle Ages, many nobles at court and elsewhere flaunted pedigrees going back to 'times immemorial'. The Lévis even claimed to be cousins of the Virgin Mary. Yet it was possible for a nobleman to be created. The king had the right of rewarding someone who had served him well by ennobling him. Once the royal letters of ennoblement had been registered by the sovereign courts, the recipient and his heirs were integrated into the second estate. This was originally an exceptional favour, but in the fifteenth century holders of certain state offices (e.g. notaries and secretaries of the king's household and chancery) were automatically ennobled and the practice soon spread to some other public offices. It was accompanied by the widespread acquisition of *seigneuries* by office-holders. Some nobles, of course, simply usurped their status. This could be done by 'living nobly' (that is to say, avoiding any business activity), holding a public office, fighting for the king, owning a fief or *seigneurie*, and living in a house large enough to be a manor. But a spurious nobleman had to ensure that his name was dropped from the rolls of the *taille* over a long period. If his claim to tax exemption was challenged, he would call witnesses, who would testify that his family had 'lived nobly' for as long as anyone could remember. He could usually find an obliging lawyer to fake documentary evidence in support of his case and would call himself after some landed estate. However, becoming a nobleman tended to be a slow process, not easily pinpointed in time. There were also provincial differences affecting the nobility. In some areas nobles were comparatively few, whereas in others (e.g. Brittany) they were plentiful. For these reasons it is impossible to be precise about the numerical strength of the second estate. It may have been between 120,000 and 200,000.[46]

The bulk of France's population was represented by the third estate. It comprised people of widely different fortunes and occupations. A huge gulf, for example, separated the peasant from the *parlementaire* who aspired to become a nobleman. Although a small provincial nobleman (*hobereau*) was as far removed in terms of wealth from an aristocratic courtier, yet the two men shared the same values and outlook on life, and could understand each other. This was not true of the peasant and the *parlementaire* who belonged to different worlds in spite of being members of the third estate. Seyssel in his *La Monarchie de France* (1519) made a useful distinction between the middling people (*peuple moyen*) and the lesser folk (*peuple menu*). The former, he explained, were merchants as well as officers of finance and justice. France, according to Seyssel, had 'more officers of justice, primary and accessory –

---

[45] Arlette Jouanna, *Ordre social: mythes et hiérarchies dans la France du XVIe siècle* (1977), pp. 9–10, 39–48, 54–72.

[46] Jacquart, *François Ier*, pp. 67–9; Salmon, *Society in Crisis*, pp. 92–113. See also D. Potter, *War and Government in the French Provinces: Picardy, 1470–1560* (Cambridge, 1993), pp. 113–54.

advocates, procurators, clerks and so forth – than the whole rest of Christendom taken together. The *peuple menu* were principally engaged in 'the cultivation of the land, the mechanical arts and other inferior crafts'. Seyssel believed that such people should not be 'in too great liberty or immeasurably rich and especially not generally trained in the use of arms'. Otherwise they might be tempted to rise against their betters.[47] The third estate had its own hierarchy, defined by custom and expressed in certain honorific titles (e.g. *noble homme* or *honorable homme*) in notarial documents. But many Frenchmen did not even qualify for such titles. In the words of Jacquart, 'four fifths of Francis I's subjects fell into anonymity'.[48]

Sixteenth-century people generally believed that social distinctions reflected God's will. They saw inequality among humans as an exact reflexion of the inequalities visible in the animal kingdom. A nobleman was held to have inherited the virtue without which his status counted for nothing. If he failed to live up to it, some doubt was cast on his social origins. Thus Noël du Fail faced with a nobleman who maltreated his dog, explained this lapse by supposing that his mother had once slept with a butcher.[49] Yet the possibility of social movement, both upwards and downwards, was not discounted. Otherwise there would have been little point in education. A nobleman needed to be trained to love the virtue that he had been born with. Likewise it might be possible (though the question was hotly debated) for a bourgeois to achieve nobility through education. Generally speaking, however, everyone had his divinely allotted place in society and ought to accept the fact with resignation.

---

[47] C. de Seyssel, *The Monarchy of France*, ed. D. R. Kelley (New Haven, CT, 1981), pp. 60–2.
[48] Jacquart, *François ler*, p. 70.
[49] Jouanna, *Ordre Social*, p. 46.

Chapter three

King of France

'Kingship is the dignity, not the property, of the prince.' These words, spoken by Philippe Pot at the Estates General of 1484, embody the theory of royal succession in France at the close of the Middle Ages. The king was not free to dispose of the crown as if it were a piece of private property; whatever his own wishes might be, he was bound to be succeeded by his nearest male kinsman. 'The crown is not strictly hereditary', wrote the jurist Charles Du Moulin, 'for the new king is not the heir of his predecessor, and does not succeed him in the possession of his goods or in the heritage abandoned by the deceased, but he succeeds to the crown by right of blood in accordance with the Salic law.'[1] It was on the basis of this principle that Francis of Angoulême secured the throne on the death of Louis XII. His right to do so was unimpeachable, yet his accession has been described as 'in a certain measure a *coup d'état*', because he proclaimed himself king regardless of the fact that Mary Tudor might still produce a son by the late king.[2] But it was a clearly established principle that 'the king never dies'; he was to be followed immediately by his eldest son or nearest male kinsman. This ruled out the possibility of an interregnum, so that Francis's accession cannot be regarded as unconstitutional. It would have been so only if Mary had given birth to a son and Francis had refused to stand down.

While preparations were being made for the funeral of Louis XII, which took place at Saint-Denis on 12 January 1515, Francis had to attend to much urgent business. In theory, he was not obliged to honour any of his predecessors' obligations: he was not bound to settle Louis's debts or to recognize officials he had appointed or the liberties and privileges he had conceded to towns and corporations. In practice, however, a new king usually confirmed

---

[1] Doucet, *Institutions*, i. 81.
[2] H. Hauser, 'Sur la date exacte de la mort de Louis XII et de l'avènement de François 1er', *Rev. d'hist. mod. et contemp.*, 5 (1903–04), 179.

former grants of offices, privileges and the like in return for appropriate fees. Thus, on 2 January Francis confirmed members of the Parlement of Paris and of the other 'sovereign courts'. Five days later he did the same in respect of members of the provincial parlements and *chambres des comptes*. Among distinguished members of the old régime who were kept in office were Charles de Rohan, comte de Guise and *Grand échanson de France*; Louis de La Tremoïlle, the king's lieutenant-general in Burgundy; and above all, Florimond Robertet, who has been fairly described as 'the father of the secretaries of state'.[3] 'He governed the entire kingdom', wrote Florange, 'for since the death of the legate of Amboise he was the man closest to his master ... he was undoubtedly one of the most intelligent and able men I have ever seen and it is to his credit that, as long as he was in charge of the affairs of France, they fared marvellously.'[4]

Continuity, however, was not all that was required of the new king; the administration also needed an infusion of new blood. On 7 January Francis appointed Antoine Duprat to the office of Chancellor of France, which had been vacant since 1512. The Chancellor was the head of the judicial administration and also had vast administrative responsibilities.[5] Like so many successful Frenchmen of his day, Duprat hailed from Auvergne. The son of a merchant of Issoire, he had entered the legal profession and had worked his way up from the parlement of Toulouse to that of Paris, becoming its First president. He had won the favour of Anne of Brittany by his prosecution of Marshal Gié and, after her death, had entered the service of Louise of Savoy. It was doubtless with her backing that he now obtained the chancellorship at the age of fifty-two.[6] Duprat was hard-working and shrewd, but also ruthless and grasping. He became universally unpopular.

Another office that was vacant when Francis came to the throne was the constableship of France. The Constable, who, like the Chancellor, was appointed for life, was considered the most important of the 'great officers' of the crown. His duties were exclusively military and included the enforcement of discipline among the troops, the supervision of army supplies, the appointment of commissioners of musters, the authorization of military expenditure and the allocation of troops to garrison towns. In wartime it was customary for the Constable to command the army in the king's absence and the vanguard in his presence. On ceremonial occasions, it was his privilege to carry the king's

[3] Barrillon, i. 2–4; C.A.F., i. 17, 26; v. 5675.
[4] Florange, i. 152; C.A.F., v. 15674–5. For the development of the office of secretary of state see N. M. Sutherland, *The French Secretaries of State in the Age of Catherine de Medici* (London, 1962). See also C. A. Mayer and D. Bentley-Cranch, *Florimond Robertet, homme d'état français* (Geneva, 1994).
[5] See below pp. 51–2.
[6] Barrillon, i. 7–9; *Ordonnances*, i. no. 4; A. Buisson, *Le chancelier Antoine Duprat* (1935), pp 17–68.

naked sword. On 12 January 1515 Francis appointed Charles III, duc de Bourbon, his most powerful vassal, to the office.[7] He was twenty-five years old, handsome, and could already boast of a distinguished military record, having fought bravely against the Venetians at Agnadello in 1509 and against the Swiss in 1513.[8] In addition to being Constable, Bourbon was governor of Languedoc and *Grand chambrier de France.*

The marshals of France, though subordinate to the Constable, were on a par with dukes and peers and were entitled to call the king 'my cousin'. At Francis's accession, they numbered only two: Stuart d'Aubigny and Gian-Giacomo Trivulzio, a member of an old Milanese family who had entered the service of the French crown in 1495.[9] Francis soon created two new marshals: Odet de Foix, seigneur de Lautrec, who belonged to a cadet branch of the house of Foix, and Jacques de Chabannes, seigneur de Lapalisse, a veteran of the Italian wars.[10] On being appointed marshal, Lapalisse relinquished the office of Grand Master (*Grand maître*) of France, which was given to Artus Gouffier, seigneur de Boisy, Francis's former governor.[11]

Francis did not forget his relatives and friends in distributing favours. Jean Barrillon, whose diary is an important source for the early part of the reign, states that the king handed over to his mother the proceeds from the confirmation of office-holders. Her county of Angoulême was raised to ducal status in February 1515 and she was also given the duchy of Anjou, the counties of Maine and Beaufort-en-Vallée and the barony of Amboise.[12] Her half-brother, René, who was usually called 'the great bastard of Savoy', was appointed *Grand Sénéchal* and governor of Provence. Francis's brother-in-law, Charles, duc d'Alençon, was officially recognized as 'the second person in the kingdom' and made governor of Normandy. The house of Bourbon also benefited from the king's largesse. The *vicomté* of Châtellerault, which belonged to François de Bourbon, the Constable's brother, was turned into a duchy, and the county of Vendôme, belonging to Charles de Bourbon, was raised to the same level.[13] Guillaume Gouffier, seigneur de Bonnivet, who had been one of Francis's companions at Amboise, received an annuity of 1,000 *écus*.[14] On 31 December 1517 he was made Admiral of France. This gave him supreme jurisdiction over all maritime affairs and entitled him to sizeable revenues, such as a share of wreckage and prizes.[15]

[7] *Ordonnances*, i. no. 13; Doucet, *Institutions*, i. 112–13.
[8] A. Lebey, *Le connétable de Bourbon* (1904), pp. 31–43; Barrillon, i. 15–16.
[9] C.A.F., v. 15664.
[10] Barrillon, i. 4; B. de Chantérac, *Odet de Foix, vicomte de Lautrec* (1930), pp. 13–25.
[11] C.A.F., i. 13; Doucet, *Institutions*, i. 122–3.   [12] Barrillon, i. 4, 16; *Ordonnances*, i. nos. 20, 21.
[13] C.A.F., i. 106, 108; v. 15661; *Ordonnances*, i. nos. 28, 31, 32. This Charles de Bourbon was not the Constable.
[14] C.A.F., v. 15669.   [15] C.A.F., i. 762; Doucet, *Institutions*, i. 120–2.

12. Guillaume Gouffier, seigneur de Bonnivet and Admiral of France. He was Francis I's favourite until he was killed at Pavia in 1525. This drawing is one of a notable series depicting members of the king's entourage drawn by Jean Clouet.

The *sacre* at Rheims

By the sixteenth century, the coronation or *sacre* at Rheims was no longer considered by jurists as essential to the exercise of kingship. The king ruled from the moment he succeeded to the throne and his regnal years were reckoned accordingly, yet the *sacre* remained important as a symbol of the supernatural quality of kingship and of the close alliance that existed between church and state. An essential element of the mythology of French kingship was the legend of the Holy Ampulla. This was given concrete form by Hincmar, archbishop of Rheims, in the ninth century, but it did not make an impact on the coronation ceremony till the thirteenth. According to Hincmar, as Saint Rémi (or Remigius) was about to baptize the Frankish king, Clovis, in AD 496 a dove brought down from heaven a vessel containing a sacred chrism thereby demonstrating God's special regard for France. The chrism continued to be used from this time onwards to consecrate her kings. This made them spiritually superior to all other Christian monarchs.[16]

Francis left Paris for Rheims on 18 January accompanied by his mother, the Princes of the Blood and a host of lords and dignitaries. The queen, however, had to stay behind as she was pregnant.[17] The royal cortège arrived at Rheims on 24 January and was received by the archbishop, Robert de Lenoncourt, and other prelates. It was customary for the king to spend the evening before his consecration on a vigil, not unlike that of a candidate for initiation into knighthood.[18] He attended vespers and said prayers at the cathedral before retiring to bed in the archbishop's palace. The next morning he was awakened by the bishops of Laon and Beauvais who assisted his *lever* and led him to the cathedral, where the nobility of the kingdom had already gathered. Wearing a gown of white damask over a shirt and tunic of white silk, he advanced along the nave, which had been adorned with gorgeous tapestries. He took his seat in the choir opposite the archbishop's throne, and the peers of the realm disposed themselves on either side of him. The archbishop then went to the cathedral porch and received the Holy Ampulla. This was normally kept at the abbey of Saint-Rémi, in Rheims. Some people believed that it was filled miraculously before each coronation; others, that the level of oil remained constant or registered fluctuations in the health of the reigning monarch.[19]

The coronation service began with the oath. This fell into two parts: the ecclesiastical oath and the oath of the kingdom. In the first the king promised

---

[16] *Ibid.*, i. 87–8; R. A. Jackson, *Vive le Roi! A History of the French Coronation from Charles V to Charles X* (Chapel Hill, 1984), pp. 31–3.

[17] T. Godefroy, *Le cérémonial françois* (1649), i. 245–53; M. Sanuto, *Diarii* (Venice, 1887), xx. cols. 22–34; Barrillon, i. 17.

[18] R. A. Jackson, pp. 134–5.   [19] M. Bloch, *Les rois thaumaturges*, (1961), p. 224.

to protect the church's privileges and to defend each bishop and his church to the best of his ability. In the second the king, standing over the Gospels, promised to promote peace in Christendom, to protect Christians against injuries and iniquities, to dispense justice fairly and mercifully and to expel heretics from his dominions.[20] Although many contemporary authorities claimed that the king of France promised at his coronation not to alienate his domain, there is no evidence of such an oath in the coronation records. The doctrine of inalienability, it seems, derived from canon and Roman law rather than from a specific coronation pronouncement.[21]

The oath was followed by the anointing, the most important part of the whole ceremony. Thrusting his hand through specially contrived openings in the king's tunic and shirt, the archbishop anointed his body with the sacred chrism. This conferred on him an almost sacerdotal character. Although no French king ever claimed the right to celebrate Mass, he did take communion in both kinds, a privilege otherwise enjoyed only by priests.[22]

Francis next discarded his garments and put on his coronation robes: a blue gown embroidered with gold fleurs-de-lis and a great cloak or *soccus*. According to a fourteenth-century treatise by Jean Golein, this part of the ceremony signified the king's rejection of the 'wordly estate' and his adoption of the 'royal religion'. Golein attributed to the *sacre* the same regenerative force as baptism.[23] The king also received from the archbishop the royal insignia: the sword, the ring, the sceptre and the hand of justice. The sword, which symbolized the king's military power, was blessed by the archbishop. Francis then placed it on the altar before handing it to the duc de Bourbon, who carried it upright during the rest of the ceremony.

The scene was now set for the coronation proper. At a call from the chancellor, the peers gathered round the king and helped the archbishop place the heavy crown of Charlemagne upon his head. They stretched out their hands as if to uphold the crown, a gesture that can be interpreted as pledging support to the crowned monarch. They then escorted him to a throne raised on a platform above the screen. Removing his mitre, the archbishop made a low bow, embraced the king, and cried out three times: 'Vivat Rex in aeternum!' After the peers had also acclaimed him, the trumpets blared out, the organ roared and the entire congregation shouted: 'Vive le roi!' This was followed by the singing of the *Te Deum* and by high mass. At the offertory, the king made the customary presentation of a silver loaf, a silver pitcher filled with wine and thirteen pieces of gold. His crown was removed and replaced by a smaller one,

---

[20] R. A. Jackson, pp. 57–9. See also below p. 161.   [21] *Ibid.*, pp. 68–93.
[22] M. Bloch, p. 194.
[23] *Ibid.*, pp. 197–8; R. A. Jackson, p. 215.

and his robes, too, were taken from him. He then returned in procession to the archbishop's palace, in whose great hall he dined with the peers.[24]

From Rheims, Francis went to the shrine of Saint-Marcoul at the priory of Corbeny in the Aisne valley.[25] The pilgrimage was closely connected with his thaumaturgical powers. Early in the Middle Ages the idea had developed that the king of France was endowed with the miraculous power of healing the sick. The only other Christian ruler to claim this power was the king of England. In time, it became restricted to the curing of scrofula, a disease more repulsive than dangerous and subject to periods of remission. Originally it was assumed that the king derived his power of healing from his anointing, but about the twelfth century an obscure Norman saint, called Saint-Marcoul, posthumously acquired the reputation of curing scrofula, presumably as a result of a pun on his name (*mar* = bad; *cou* = neck). By the late Middle Ages it had become customary for kings of France to visit his shrine immediately after their coronation in order to boost their own thaumaturgical powers through his intercession. This soon led to the idea that the king owed his power of healing to the saint, not to his anointing.[26]

The royal pilgrimage to Corbeny was a well-regulated affair. The monks went in procession to meet the king, who received the saint's skull from the prior. Then, after carrying the relic to the church and praying before the shrine, the king retired to the *pavillon royal*, a part of the monastery reserved for his use. Next day he healed a number of victims of scrofula: touching their sores and tumours with his bare hands, he made the sign of the cross over each one, saying: 'The king touches you and God cures you.' Each then received two small silver coins.[27]

From Corbeny Francis visited the shrine of the Black Virgin at Notre-Dame de Liesse. Then, after spending a few days at Compiègne, he went to Saint-Denis, burial place of his royal predecessors, where he confirmed the abbey's privileges and underwent another, less elaborate, coronation. Finally, he made his entry into Paris.

The Parisian entry of 1515

By the early sixteenth century a royal entry into the capital consisted of two elements: first, a procession of the various corporations, both civil and religious, within the city followed by that of the king and his court; secondly, various *apparati* such as theatrical side-shows, fountains flowing with wine or street decorations. For some time, too, small books, some of them illustrated,

[24] B. L. Harley Ms. 3462 contains a long account of Francis I's coronation (fols. 202b–214b). I owe this reference to the kindness of Professor John Shearman.
[25] Barrillon, i. 23.   [26] M. Bloch, pp. 261–6; Florange, i. 169–70.   [27] M. Bloch, p. 281.

recorded these entries in detail. Yet, curiously, no such booklet was produced for Francis's entry into Paris in 1515. The only detailed description that exists appeared three years later in *La Mer des hystoires* and this deals only with the procession, omitting all mention of *apparati*. Yet we know that Jean Marchand, carpenter, and Pierre Gringore, historian and *facteur*, were paid 115 *livres* by the *prévôté* of Paris for a 'mystery' which was staged during the entry outside the 'Porte de Paris', which was probably the Porte Saint-Denis. Are we to deduce that this was the only show put on for this entry? Though not conclusive, the evidence points that way. A possible explanation is that the Parisians had only recently given a splendid and expensive entry to Mary Tudor and could hardly be expected to put on a repeat performance so soon afterwards. Yet, with or without *apparati*, Francis's entry was enthusiastically acclaimed by Parisian observers. The Bourgeois de Paris describes it as 'the most beautiful entry that was ever seen' and the register of the *Bureau de la Ville* also praises the magnificence of the procession.[28]

On 15 February the mayor (*prévôt des marchands*) and aldermen (*échevins*), the representatives of the seventeen trade guilds, and the members of the Parlement and other sovereign courts met the king at La Chapelle-Saint-Denis and escorted him back to a crowded and jubilant capital. First to enter the city were the *gens de ville*. Then came the *gens du roi*, some wearing the late king's badge of the crowned porcupine, others Francis's salamander and motto. They were followed by the four marshals of France and the Grand Master, all of them resplendent in suits of cloth of silver and gold, and by the gentlemen pensioners and others wearing the king's colours. The obese figure of Chancellor Duprat appeared next, preceded by his staff; a horse carried the Great Seal in a blue velvet coffer. After a flurry of pages, musicians and heralds came four gentlemen carrying respectively the king's hat, cloak, sword and helmet. These were followed by members of the royal household. Only then did Francis appear, radiant in a suit of silver cloth and a white hat with flashing jewels. As he bounded forward on his horse, regardless of the canopy beneath which he was meant to ride, he threw fistfuls of gold and silver pieces into the crowd lining the processional route. No sharper contrast could have been drawn with the reign of Francis's elderly and sick predecessor. Behind the king rode the princes of the blood and other nobles, gorgeously attired and bejewelled. Among the many precious stones on display was the great diamond of the house of Dunois, worn by the duc de Longueville. The anonymous author of the description in *La Mer des hystoires* gives particular notice to the devices, combining images with mottoes, worn by the nobles. The growing impact of classicism was reflected in the frequent use of Latin in the mottoes.

[28] A.-M. Lecoq, *François Ier imaginaire: symbolique et politique à l'aube de la Renaissance française* (1987), pp. 171–2.

The Constable of Bourbon bore the cryptic motto, *A toujours mais*, written 'in large Greek letters'. The rear of the procession was made up by two companies of the *Cent-gentilshommes* and by 400 archers.

The procession led to Notre-Dame, where the king attended a solemn service of thanksgiving. Traditionally, kings had crossed the river Seine by using the old Pont au Change, but this had become rickety, and Francis caused another stir by using the Pont Notre-Dame. This had been recently built on strictly symmetrical lines by the Veronese architect and engineer, Fra Giocondo. It had six arches, sixty-eight neatly aligned and identical houses, and four turrets. By choosing it instead of the old bridge, Francis may have had an eye to more than safety. He may have wished to demonstrate his taste for modern architecture and thereby add another symbol of renewal to his entry. The service at Notre-Dame was followed by a splendid banquet at the royal palace, and the day ended with dancing and an entertainment staged by the clerks of the *Basoche*. Thereafter jousts and tournaments were held for several days in the rue Saint-Antoine. On 11 March the *Bureau de la Ville* gave Francis a statue in solid gold of his patron saint.[29]

The government of the realm

From the start of his reign Francis was strongly authoritarian in his acts and pronouncements. He did not consider himself bound by tradition and believed that he had the right to depart from existing ordinances, institutions and methods of government. On several occasions he rejected the parallel, which the Parlement liked to draw, between itself and the Senate in ancient Rome. The king was supported in his authoritarianism by Chancellor Duprat, who denied that the Parlement had any right to oppose the king's wishes. 'We owe obedience to the king', he declared, 'and it is not for us to question his commands.' All authority, he explained, including the Parlement's came from the king; otherwise the kingdom would be an aristocracy, not a monarchy.[30] But how far could the king implement his wishes? What kind of machinery of government did he have at his disposal?

Among the various organs of central government in early sixteenth-century France, four stand out as particularly important: the king's council or *conseil étroit*, the chancery, the *Grand Conseil* and the Parlement of Paris. Originally they had all been part of the Curia Regis and were still closely related in theory. Yet they were separate bodies performing essentially different functions.

---

[29] *Ibid.*, pp. 173–6; *R.D.B.V.P.*, i. 221–2; M. Félibien, *Histoire de la ville de Paris* (1725), ii. 933–4; Godefroy, i. 266–78.
[30] Doucet, i. 49.

The development of the king's council in the period between 1483 and 1526 is difficult to trace owing to the absence of proper minutes. The attendance of members has to be reconstructed partly from extant acts, ordinances and letters bearing the signatures of councillors; partly from stray *procès verbaux*. According to Jean du Tillet, who wrote in the 1560s, Francis and his three immediate predecessors divided the council into three parts to deal with war and affairs of state, finance and justice respectively. But this is inaccurate. What happened in 1526 was the creation of a small inner group, called *conseil étroit*. Previously the council comprised a large membership – numbering 120 in the period from August 1484 to January 1485, but only a small proportion of these members attended with any degree of frequency. It seems likely that a core of working councillors existed within the larger body. Thus in 1502 there was a close council of only four members, three of whom belonged to the house of Amboise. Financial business seems to have been dealt with separately by experts, who nevertheless continued to attend the council when non-financial matters were being discussed. The council might also divide for administrative convenience. In 1494, for instance, part of the council followed Charles VIII to Italy, while the rest stayed at Moulins with Pierre de Bourbon. The situation has been neatly summed up by John Guy as 'one of relative informality and of response to immediate royal needs. Some councillors were specialists and the disposition of personnel in terms of location was fluid, but these were not structural arrangements within the council as an institution.'[31]

Members of the king's council fell into six categories:

(1) princes of the blood and their bastards, client and 'foreign' princes, dukes and peers, and lords of great fiefdoms;
(2) officers of state and household (e.g. the Chancellor, Keeper of the Seals, Constable, marshals, Admiral, Grand Master etc.);
(3) provincial administrators, minor officials, presidents and councillors of parlements, and lesser nobility;
(4) ecclesiastics;
(5) fiscal officials; and
(6) masters of requests and legal counsel.

There were many routes to membership of the council: birth, skill in law, diplomacy or administration, regional importance, ecclesiastical dignity and the influence of patrons and relatives. Councillors served at the king's pleasure and not for life, and membership was not hereditary. Some councillors served

---

[31] J. A. Guy, 'The French King's Council, 1483–1526', in *Kings and Nobles in the Later Middle Ages*, ed. R. A. Griffiths and J. Sherborne (New York, 1986), pp. 274–94. See also M. Harsgor, *Recherches sur le personnel du conseil du roi sous Charles VIII et Louis XII*, 4 vols. (Lille, 1980); F. Decrue, *De consilio regis Francisci I* (1885); R. Mousnier, *Le conseil du roi de Louis XII à la révolution* (1970).

13. Bas-relief from the cathedral of Saint-Etienne at Sens showing Antoine Duprat, as Chancellor of France, sealing state documents.

under all three kings from 1483 to 1526, but membership was usually for shorter periods. The council was not only a point of contact between the crown, the nobility and the local communities; it was also a tool whereby the crown tried to secure the obedience of the governing classes and to arbitrate between them.[32]

Among the king's councillors, the most important was certainly the Chancellor of France. He was invariably an eminent jurist who had previously worked in a Parlement. Sometimes he was also a high-ranking churchman. His powers and duties ranged more widely than those of any other *grand officier de la couronne*. In fact, he was a kind of prime minister. As the head of the royal chancery, he kept the Great Seal and other seals of state. All documents emanating from king and council were drawn up in the chancery and sealed in the Chancellor's presence. He had to ensure that the text of each one matched the orders received, and could refuse to seal a legally incorrect document. This power, moreover, extended to all other chanceries in the kingdom, including those of the sovereign courts. The Chancellor's authority was, therefore, nation-wide. His influence on legislation was also dominant. He exercised it not only as a councillor but also by drafting royal edicts himself. As head of the judiciary, the Chancellor was by right entitled to preside over any sovereign

[32] J. A. Guy, pp. 280–1.

court, including the Parlement. He appointed judges and received their oaths of office unless they had already sworn them before the king. He attended the king's council regularly and took the chair in the king's absence. He helped to determine policies and, if necessary, explained them to the Parlement. From time to time, the Chancellor served on major diplomatic missions. He was appointed for life by the king, but could be replaced functionally by a Keeper of the Seals, who had neither his prestige nor influence.[33]

The chancery was the nearest equivalent to a modern ministry in early sixteenth-century France. In 1500 it had a staff of 120 which became even larger as the century unfolded. Unlike the sovereign courts, it continued to follow the king on his travels. Originally all the clerks drew up documents to be sealed with the Great Seal, but in the course of the Middle Ages some began to specialize: the *clercs du secret* drafted documents that came directly from the king. In time they became known as secretaries. Under the ordinance of 1482 notaries of the chancery were effectively granted the monopoly of drawing up and signing all royal acts, chancery letters, conciliar decisions and decrees of the sovereign courts. They were automatically ennobled and enjoyed the privilege of *committimus* as well as numerous tax exemptions. Alongside them were various specialists: for example, the *audiencier*, who presented documents to the Chancellor for sealing, and the *chauffe-cire*, who applied the seal.[34] The quantity of documents thus processed was huge. It has been estimated that if the Chancellor held his regular audience twice a week, he must have sealed fifty-five to fifty-seven letters each time, not counting a few for which the fee was waived.[35]

Closely associated with the Chancellor were the *maîtres des requêtes de l'hôtel*, who, in spite of their title, were effectively his deputies. There were eight of them at the end of the fifteenth century, but their number increased rapidly thereafter. Under an edict of December 1493 they were authorized to preside at the courts of the *bailliages* and *sénéchaussées*, to receive complaints against local officers and to correct abuses. They could preside at the *Grand Conseil* and sit in the Parlement, where they ranked immediately after the presidents. The *maîtres des requêtes* were often given temporary commissions in financial and diplomatic, as well as judicial, affairs. They were the ancestors of the *intendants*, who became the principal agents of royal centralization in the seventeenth century.[36]

The *Grand Conseil* was an exclusively judicial body which had taken over part of the work formerly exercised by the king's council: it investigated complaints against royal officials, intervened in conflicts of jurisdiction between

[33] Doucet, *Institutions*, i. 104–9.   [34] *Ibid.*, i. 109–11.
[35] H. Michaud, *La Grande Chancellerie et les écritures royales au XVIe siècle* (1967), p. 340.
[36] M. Etchechoury, *Les maîtres des requêtes de l'hôtel du roi sous les derniers Valois (1553–1589)*, (1991), pp. 19–23.

other courts and could revoke enactments that the Parlement had registered. It also acted as a court of appeal and of first instance for a wide range of legal cases. Though its procedure was fairly simple and comparatively cheap, the court had one great disadvantage for suitors: like the *Conseil étroit*, it still followed the king on his travels about the kingdom. Its records had to be carried around, and suitors were obliged to change their lawyers as it moved from place to place. Because of its proximity to the king, the *Grand Conseil* was more susceptible to his influence than was the Parlement, and he often used it to bend the law in his own interest.[37]

The Parlement of Paris, which had 'gone out of court' in the thirteenth century, was permanently housed in the royal palace on the Ile-de-la-Cité. It comprised several chambers, the most important being the *Grand' Chambre*. Originally the Parlement's *ressort* or area of jurisdiction had been the whole kingdom, but as the latter had been enlarged a number of provincial parlements were added. By 1515 they numbered six: Toulouse, Grenoble, Bordeaux, Dijon, Rouen and Aix-en-Provence. Yet the Parlement of Paris retained control of two-thirds of the kingdom: it was responsible for the whole of France, excluding Normandy, as far south as the Lyonnais and Upper Auvergne. Within this area it judged in the first instance all *cas royaux* (i.e. offences against the king's person, rights and demesne), ranging from treason and *lèse-majesté* to rape and highway robbery. At the same time, it was a court of appeal from lesser royal and seigneurial tribunals.[38]

But the Parlement was much more than a court of law. It issued decrees regulating such matters as public hygiene or the upkeep of roads, bridges and quays; it ensured that Paris received enough corn and fuel; it controlled the quality, weight and price of bread; fixed wages and hours of work; penalized shoddy workmanship; and intervened in academic affairs. As printing came into its own, the Parlement began to intervene in the book trade. The first successful application for a privilege came in June 1507 when a bookseller, called Eustace de Brie, sought to protect two books from being copied by competitors.[39] Not even the church escaped the Parlement's vigilance: no papal bull could be applied in France if it had not been registered by the Parlement. The court also kept an eye on the conduct of royal officials in the provinces.

Finally, the Parlement played a significant role politically in ratifying royal legislation. If it found an enactment satisfactory, this was registered and published forthwith; if not, the Parlement submitted a petition (*remontrances*)

[37] Monique Pelletier, 'Le Grand Conseil de Charles VIII à François 1er (1483–1547)'. Thesis summarized in *Ecole nationale des chartes. Positions des thèses ...* (1960), pp. 85–90.
[38] E. Maugis, *Histoire du Parlement de Paris*, 3 vols. (1913–16); J. H. Shennan, *The Parlement of Paris* (London, 1968).
[39] E. Armstrong, *Before Copyright: The French Book-Privilege System (1498–1526)* (Cambridge, 1990), p. 37.

to the king, either verbally or in writing, whereupon he would either modify the enactment or issue a command (*lettre de jussion*), ordering the court to register it as it stood without further delay. Such a move might lead to more remonstrances and more *lettres de jussion*. In the end, if the Parlement remained obdurate, the king would come to the court and personally supervise registration of the enactment. This ceremony, called a *lit de justice*, implied a temporary resumption by the king of the authority he had delegated to the Parlement.[40] Only the *Grand' Chambre* could register royal enactments or issue decrees (*arrêts*). Though its official head was the Chancellor of France, its effective head was the First President (*Premier président*), who was assisted by three other presidents and about thirty lay and clerical councillors.

Local government

Local government in early sixteenth-century France was far from neat and precise. There were eleven provincial governorships (*gouvernements*), but they did not cover the whole of France: large areas of the centre and west were excluded, presumably because they ranked as royal appanages. Nor were the boundaries of the *bailliages* and *sénéchaussées* clearly defined; a running battle was still going on between the king's officials and the agents of the various *seigneurs*. Yet, in spite of tax and other anomalies, a system of local government did exist, and it played an essential role in exercising royal authority.

At the head of the hierarchy of local officials was the provincial governor, who was always a high-ranking nobleman, enjoying royal favour and commanding a large clientèle among the aristocracy of his province. Though never more than a commissioner appointed by the king and revocable at his pleasure, he was commonly accorded quasi-regalian honours – for example, a canopy when he entered a town in his province for the first time. A governor was so often at court or fighting for the king that he seldom resided in his province. His local duties were performed by a lieutenant – usually a lesser nobleman or prelate – who was often appointed by the king. But a governor could do much for his province even at a distance. He could, for example, ensure that the demands (*doléances*) of the local estates were given a favourable hearing in the king's council.

The governor's presence at court also gave him unique opportunities of patronage which he might use to build up a powerful clientèle within his province. This comprised three elements: the *compagnies d'ordonnances*,

---

[40] Sarah Hanley has suggested in *The Lit de Justice of the Kings of France* (Princeton, NJ, 1983) that the first *lit de justice* was held by Francis on 24 July 1527 and that all previous meetings of the Parlement in the king's presence were 'royal séances'. This suggestion seems to me untenable for reasons given in my 'Francis I and the *Lit de Justice*: A "Legend" Defended', *F.H.*, 7 (1993), pp. 53–83; see also below, pp. 264–7, 526–7.

household officers and servants and local gentlemen. No law stipulated that a governor should be a captain of the royal standing army (*gendarmerie*), but he usually was. Though officially in the king's service and paid out of his treasury, the companies were tied to their captains who controlled their recruitment and promotion within their ranks. The governor would also have a large private household capable of providing jobs for members of the local nobility and education for their children. In time, their sons might serve in the governor's company. Most military offices in a province, such as captaincies of forts, castles and towns, were in his gift. It follows that a governor was potentially dangerous. He might use his personal following within a province to undermine the crown's authority. With this danger in mind, Louis XII had attempted to restrict the powers of governors, but his law had not been strictly enforced.

The terms laid down in a governor's commission were seldom clearly defined. While it was customary for his military responsibilities (e.g. the security of fortresses and frontiers, the supplying and disciplining of troops) to be stressed, the commission frequently contained a clause open to wider interpretation. In 1515, for example, Odet de Foix, governor of Guyenne, was instructed 'generally to do ... in other things all that we would see and recognize as necessary to the good of ourselves and our affairs and useful to the commonwealth'.[41] This was tantamount to a general delegation of royal authority. But the commissions issued to governors lacked uniformity: in drafting them, the king was more concerned with particular circumstances than in maintaining a functional harmony among his senior provincial representatives. A distinction needs to be drawn between a *gouverneur* and a *lieutenant-général*. Both titles were commonly given to the same person, but a *lieutenant-général* was not necessarily a *gouverneur*. The crown sometimes conferred exceptional powers on a great personage in an emergency. Such an appointment carried the title of *lieutenant-général*; it was always temporary, and the authority conveyed by it could extend over several provinces.[42]

The basic unit of local government in France was the *bailliage* or *sénéchaussée*. The term *sénéchaussée* was used mainly, though not exclusively, in the Midi. About 1500 there were eighty-six such units across the whole of the royal demesne, but their boundaries were subject to frequent changes. The average *bailliage* was probably rather smaller than a *département* in modern France. The *bailli* or *sénéchal*, however, was no longer the powerful figure he had been in the early Middle Ages; his title had become essentially honorific. This was because he was invariably a member of the nobility of sword who lacked the legal qualifications essential to perform judicial duties. He was no

[41] *Ordonnances*, i. no. 5.
[42] G. Zeller, 'Gouverneurs de provinces au XVIe siècle', *R.H.*, 185 (1939); R. R. Harding, *Anatomy of a Power Elite: The Provincial Governors of Early Modern France* (New Haven, CT and London, 1978). See also Potter, *War and Government*, pp. 65–112.

longer expected to reside in his *bailliage*, and was often at court engaged on other duties. For example, Etienne de Vesc, *sénéchal* of Beaucaire, was one of Charles VIII's most influential councillors. He consequently delegated most of his duties to a *lieutenant-général*. Originally, the lieutenant was chosen by the *bailli* at his pleasure, but by the end of the fifteenth century the crown had laid down certain rules: the lieutenant was to be chosen by the king from a list of three names submitted by the assembly of the *bailliage*; he also had to be a graduate in both civil and canon law of a 'famous' university.

There were certain powers, however, which the *bailli* by virtue of being a nobleman could not delegate. These were essentially feudal and military. Being the natural link between the king and the provincial nobility, the *bailli* kept up to date the roll of fiefs and sub-fiefs. When the king called on his vassals to render him military service, it was the *bailli* who called the *ban et arrière-ban*, passed the musters, judged claims of exemption, led the contingent of the *bailliage* to the army and often commanded it on campaign. Often he was also the captain of a castle or *place-forte*.

In all other respects, however, the *bailli*'s duties were carried out by the *lieutenant-général* who was assisted by three or four *lieutenants particuliers*, eight *gens du roi*, and an ever-increasing number of unpaid councillors, whose role was purely consultative. Each *bailliage* also had its supporting staff of *greffiers*, *huissiers*, *sergents* and the like.

The *bailli*'s competence, as exercised by his deputy, was judicial, administrative and financial. He judged cases concerning nobles or royal officials, ecclesiastical benefices, acts of fidelity and homage, and many touching the royal demesne. He also dealt with criminal cases, deemed to be *cas royaux*, that had been removed from the seigneurial courts, and with appeals from the subordinate courts of the *prévôtés*, *châtellenies* or *échevinages*. It was possible to appeal from his judgments to the Parlement. The *bailli* also had wide-ranging administrative powers. He registered and published royal ordinances as well as decrees of the parlements. They were proclaimed in the streets or squares, or read out in the main courtroom of the *bailliage*. The *bailli* issued regulations of his own, called *ordonnances*, which were enforceable in his area of jurisdiction unless amended or annulled by the Parlement. He supervised public works, the levy of tolls, the regulation of trade guilds, markets and fairs, and the taxing of essential commodities. He frequently upset the local *échevins* by intervening in municipal affairs. The *bailli* also collaborated with the crown's fiscal officials in respect of domainial revenues.[43] In short, his authority was of major significance in bringing royal authority to the people.

The most important *bailliage* was the *prévôté* and *vicomté* of Paris whose

---

[43] Doucet, *Institutions*, i. 251–64; G. Zeller, *Les institutions de la France au XVIe siècle* (1948), pp. 167–75.

area of jurisdiction covered not only the capital but a large area of the surrounding countryside. It was possibly the oldest *bailliage* and already had a large staff in the fourteenth century. Its tribunal was the Châtelet, a stronghold of which the only surviving vestige is the Tour Saint-Jacques. Paris was the largest centre of book-production and bookselling in the kingdom, and as early as the reign of Louis XII the *prévôt* was issuing book-privileges. In 1514 short-term privileges were being granted on his authority for printed accounts of current events. The policing of Paris was in the *prévôt*'s hands and he had special responsibilities for the university.[44]

The provincial parlements developed out of the courts that had existed in the great fiefs before their absorption into the kingdom. Modelled on the Paris Parlement, they exercised a similar jurisdiction within their respective areas. At Francis's accession there were five provincial parlements: Toulouse, Bordeaux, Grenoble, Dijon and Aix-en-Provence. Normandy had a high court that had developed out of the old Exchequer, but it was Francis who turned it into a parlement in February 1515. Brittany had *Grands Jours*, which met annually at fixed dates. All these parlements claimed equality of authority and jurisdiction with that of Paris, but the latter had certain privileges not shared by the rest: it could admit office-holders, judge crimes committed by princes and turn itself into a court of peers. Each parlement was sovereign within its own territory in respect of the registration and publication of royal ordinances. Thus many laws which were applied in Paris were never registered by the parlement of Toulouse and therefore not applied in Languedoc.[45]

At the provincial level, representative estates existed in a large part of France. The principal *pays d'états* were Normandy, Languedoc, Dauphiné, Burgundy, Provence and Brittany. In most of them the three estates were represented, but they were not always chosen in the same way; nor was their role identical from one province to another. The clergy sat as landowners, not as representatives of the church, so as to avoid binding it to decisions taken by the estates. The nobles represented not only themselves but the rural population in general. As for the third estate, it consisted of urban representatives only. There were numerous local variations. In Normandy, for example, a complicated electoral system gave the third estate a numerical preponderance in the general assembly; in Languedoc, a high proportion of nobles and clergy failed to attend, while the third estate represented only municipal oligarchies; in Brittany and Provence the nobility tended to dominate the estates, the upper clergy seldom attended and the third estate was again restricted to urban oligarchies. None of the estates was democratic: the majority of the people, both rural and urban, had no voice. The estates depended for their existence on the king: he

[44] *Ibid.*, p. 175; E. Armstrong, *Before Copyright*, pp. 48–9.
[45] Doucet, *Institutions*, i. 211–17; Zeller, *Institutions*, pp. 147–63.

called them, fixed the date and place of their meeting, appointed their president
and determined their agenda. His commissioners put forward his demands,
negotiated with the delegates and met some of their requests. Usually the
estates met once a year, but they could meet more often. The frequency of
meetings was determined by the crown's fiscal needs.[46]

The tax system

Francis inherited a complicated tax system and a cumbersome fiscal
administration. Broadly speaking, there were two kinds of royal revenue in
early sixteenth-century France: the 'ordinary' revenue (*finances ordinaires*),
which the king drew from his demesne, and the 'extraordinary' revenue
(*finances extraordinaires*), which he got from taxation.

The 'ordinary' revenue comprised not only feudal rents, which were fixed
and predictable, but also a wide range of variable dues owed to the king as
suzerain. Thus he inherited from bastards, from persons who died intestate and
from foreigners who died on French soil (*droit d'aubaine*); he received the
usual profits of justice and the property confiscated from criminals, such as
false coiners and traitors; he also got a share of the produce of French mines
and levied tolls on roads and rivers.

The 'extraordinary' revenue owed its name to the fact that originally it had
been levied only for a special purpose and for a limited period, usually in
wartime. By the sixteenth century, however, it consisted of regular taxes levied
in times of peace and war. There were three main kinds of tax: the *taille*, the
gabelle and the *aides*. The *taille* was the only direct tax. It was levied each year,
the amount being fixed by the king's council, and it could be supplemented by
a surtax (*crue de taille*). There were two sorts of *taille*: the *taille réelle*, a land
tax payable by all irrespective of social rank, and the *taille personnelle*, which
fell mainly on land owned by non-privileged commoners. Of the two kinds of
taille, the first was obviously the fairer, but it was found in only a few areas,
including Provence and Languedoc. The nobility and clergy were exempt from
the *taille* along with many occupational groups (e.g. royal officials, military
personnel, municipal officials, lawyers, university teachers and students). What
is more, a large number of towns (the so-called *villes-franches*), including Paris,
were exempt. Thus if the whole peasantry was *taillable*, the same was not true
of the bourgeoisie.

The *gabelle* was a tax on salt. By the late Middle Ages the salt trade had
become so important in France that the crown decided to share in its profits by

---

[46] Doucet, *Institutions*, i. 337–59; J. R. Major, *Representative Government in Early Modern France*
(New Haven, CT, 1980), pp. 58–122, 138–59.

controlling the distribution and sale of salt. But royal control was strongest in the northern and central provinces (*pays de grandes gabelles*), which had constituted the royal demesne of King Charles V. Here, the salt was taken to royal warehouses (*greniers*), where it was weighed and left to dry, usually for two years. It was then weighed again and taxed before the merchant who owned it was allowed to sell it. He was also restricted as to where he could sell and the amount of profit he could make. In order to prevent illicit trading in salt, of which there was a great deal, the crown introduced the system of *sel par impôt*, whereby every household had to purchase from a royal *grenier* enough salt for its average needs. The burden, however, was less onerous in the sixteenth century than later in the Ancien Régime. Outside the *pays de grandes gabelles* the salt tax was levied in various ways. In the west of France (*pays de quart et de quint*) it was a quarter or a fifth of the sale price, while in Languedoc it was a sort of tariff levied when the salt passed through royal warehouses situated at various points along the Mediterranean coast. The personnel responsible for the administration of the *gabelles* varied from one part of the country to another. In the *pays de grandes gabelles* each warehouse was run by a *grenetier*, assisted by a *contrôleur*; in the *pays de quart et de quint* the tax was farmed out by commissioners.

The *aides* were levied on various commodities sold regularly and in large quantities. The rate of tax was one *sou* per *livre* on all merchandise sold either wholesale or retail, except wine and other beverages, which were taxed both ways. An important *aide* was the levy on livestock raised in many towns. The *aide* on wine was called the *vingtième et huitième*. But indirect taxation was also subject to local variations. For several reasons many parts of France were exempt from the *aides*.

How were taxes collected? The usual procedure in respect of the *taille* was for the leading men of a parish to elect from among themselves an assessor and a collector. The assessment, once completed, was read out in church by the local priest; a week later the parishioners paid their taxes to the collector as they left church. The assessor and collector were not inclined to leniency, as they were liable to be imprisoned or to have their property confiscated if the sum collected fell below the anticipated amount. Indirect taxes were usually farmed by the highest bidder at an auction.[47]

The most lucrative tax was the *taille* which amounted to 2.4 million *livres* out of a total revenue of 4.9 million at the beginning of Francis's reign. It was followed by the *aides*, which brought in about a third of the *taille*. As for the

---

[47] G. Jacqueton, *Documents relatifs à l'administration financière en France de Charles VII à François 1er (1443–1523)* (1891), pp. v–ix; M. Wolfe, *The Fiscal System of Renaissance France* (New Haven, CT and London, 1972), pp. 304–65.

gabelle, it was bringing in 284,000 *livres* (about 6 per cent of the total revenue) in 1515.[48]

In the early sixteenth century the king of France had more control over the purses of his subjects than any other monarch in western Europe. This power went back to the reign of Charles VII, who in 1440 began to levy the *taille* without the consent of the Estates General. But even in the sixteenth century the king's control of taxation was not absolute, for he continued to seek the consent of local representative bodies. The most important of these were the provincial estates which survived in several areas (*pays d'états*). Consent to taxation, however, did not carry the right to refuse the *taille* or even to discuss it; only increases and surtaxes were negotiable. The main function of the estates, it seems, was to learn what was expected of them by way of additional help to the king, and even in this respect their powers were limited. What was perhaps more important to them than the amount of tax was its allocation (*répartition*) to the various provincial subdivisions; but only in Languedoc, Burgundy and Provence were they able to control this process; in other *pays d'états* it has handled by royal commissioners. Thus the amount of consultation which took place at the provincial level was not particularly important, and the same was true of town assemblies. Towns that were free of the *taille* could petition the king, but only if he asked them for a 'forced loan'.[49]

The fiscal administration

The fiscal administration at the start of Francis's reign, like the tax system, had not changed since the reign of Charles VII. It comprised two distinct branches corresponding with the two kinds of revenue. The first, called the *Trésor*, was responsible for the 'ordinary' revenues. It was headed by four *trésoriers de France*, who had wide powers. They could farm out parts of the demesne or have them managed by royal officials under their control. All royal acts concerning the demesne needed their endorsement before being put into effect. Each *trésorier* was responsible for one of four areas, called respectively Languedoïl, Languedoc, Normandy and Outre-Seine et Yonne, but these areas did not cover the whole kingdom; provinces falling outside were subject to a different régime. The *trésoriers* supervised the collection and disbursement of revenues, but did not handle them; this task was left to the *receveurs ordinaires*, each of whom was responsible for a subdivision of the *bailliages* and *sénéchaussées*. The receiver-general for all revenues from the demesne was the

[48] A. Spont, 'La taille en Languedoc, de 1450 à 1515', *A.du M.*, ii (1890), p. 369; Wolfe, pp. 99–100, 340; L. S. Van Doren, 'War Taxation, Institutional Change and Social Conflict in Provincial France – The Royal *Taille* in Dauphiné, 1494–1559', *Proceedings of the American Philosophical Society*, cxxi (Feb. 1977), 70–96.
[49] Wolfe, pp. 25–66.

Changeur du Trésor, who was based in Paris, but only a very small proportion of the revenues ever reached him; for the crown normally settled debts not included in its regular budgets by means of warrants (*assignations*) assigned on a local treasurer. This avoided the expense and risk of transporting large quantities of cash along dangerous roads, while passing on the recovery costs to the crown's creditor.

The four *généraux des finances* who were in charge of the 'extraordinary' revenues, had virtually the same powers as the *trésoriers de France*, each being responsible for an area, called a *généralité*, which was divided into *élections*. There were eighty-five *élections* at the start of the sixteenth century, but they did not cover the whole kingdom. Generally speaking, they did not exist in the *pays d'états*. The *élection* took its name from the *élu*, whose main function was to make regular tours of inspection of his district. There were usually two *élus* per *élection*.

Standing on the same hierarchical level as the *Changeur du Trésor* and performing the same duties, though in respect of the 'extraordinary' revenue, were the four *receveurs généraux des finances*, one for each *généralité*.

The two branches of the fiscal administration were not entirely separate, for the *trésoriers de France* and *généraux des finances* (known collectively as *gens des finances*) were expected to reside at court whenever they were not carrying out tours of inspection. They formed a financial committee, which met regularly and independently of the king's council, and were empowered to take certain decisions on their own. They also attended the council whenever important financial matters were discussed. But their main duty was to draw up at the start of each year a sort of national budget, called *état général par estimation*, based on the accounts from each fiscal district. The payment of expenses foreseen in the *état* required no special authorization by the king, but all other expenses did.[50]

---

[50] G. Jacqueton, *Documents*, pp. ix–xvii.

Chapter four

Marignano and after (1515–19)

Within the first year of his reign Francis invaded Italy in pursuit of a dynastic claim to the duchy of Milan which he had inherited from his great-grandmother, Valentina Visconti. His action, far from being a new departure in French foreign policy, was a continuation of the Italian wars begun by King Charles VIII in 1494. Their motivation was essentially traditional. The kings of France were not seeking to round off natural frontiers or to gain economic advantages, but to affirm territorial and dynastic rights.

Italy at the end of the fifteenth century was a tempting prey to a comparatively powerful neighbour, for it consisted of many more or less independent states, different in size and constitution, which could be played off against each other. The most important were Venice, Milan, Florence, the States of the Church and Naples. The Venetian republic, though threatened by the westward expansion of the Ottoman empire, was at the height of its power: in addition to an extensive territory on the mainland, it controlled lands along the Adriatic's eastern seaboard, in the Aegean and the eastern Mediterranean. The Venetian constitution was the most stable in Italy, being vested in an aristocratic oligarchy and exercised through a system of elected councils. To the west, in the Lombard plain, lay the duchy of Milan, created by the house of Visconti out of a collection of cities. It was now ruled by the house of Sforza, under which it continued to prosper economically. A strong Milan was regarded by other Italian powers as a necessary bulwark against foreign invasion and Venetian expansionism. Florence was theoretically ruled by a popular government, but effective authority lay in the hands of the Medici family. Although weak militarily, the republic enjoyed a considerable influence among the Italian states because of the Medici's extensive banking connexions and genius for diplomacy. The States of the Church stretched diagonally across the Italian peninsula from the Tiber to the Po, and comprised a number of virtually autonomous towns and districts. The city of Rome was continually disturbed by the rivalries of its leading families, while dreams of republican self-govern-ment still stirred among the inhabitants. A principal aim of the Renaissance popes was to establish their authority firmly throughout their territories, and to do this they often resorted to nepotism. Naples, the only feudal monarchy in the peninsula, was a land of large estates ruled by turbulent barons. It was divided into two parts: Sicily belonged to the house of Aragon, while Naples and the mainland were ruled by an illegitimate branch of the same house. Notable among the lesser states of Italy were the duchy of Savoy, sitting astride of the Alps and under the shadow of France; the republic of Genoa, which had lapsed into political insignificance as a result of domestic squabbles; and the duchy of Ferrara, serving as a buffer state between Venice and the States of the Church.

After 1454 peace was more or less maintained in Italy by a skilful policy of equilibrium among the principal states, but this was upset in 1494 by the armed intervention of Charles VIII of France, who founded his ambitions on earlier French successes in the peninsula. The house of Anjou had once reigned in Naples and that of Orléans had intermarried with the Visconti of Milan. The French invasion precipitated a revolution in Florence and the overthrow of the Medici. Naples fell into French hands, but a coalition forced Charles to return home. He narrowly escaped defeat at Fornovo, and the army he had left behind in Naples was soon wiped out by disease. In 1499, his successor, Louis XII, led another expedition across the Alps. He gained control of Milan and Genoa, but foolishly agreed to partition Naples with Ferdinand of Aragon. This led to conflict between the two occupying powers, and, in 1504, the whole of Naples passed under the Aragonese crown. Four years later Louis allowed himself to be drawn by Pope Julius II into a coalition against Venice. Once Venice had been defeated, the pope devoted all his energies to getting the French expelled from Italy. With the military assistance of the Swiss, he drove them out of the peninsula, and an attempt by Louis to stage a comeback in 1513 ended dis-astrously. The Swiss, after routing the French at Novara, swept into Burgundy and laid siege to Dijon. They withdrew after La Tremoïlle, the local comman-der, had signed a humiliating treaty, which Louis subsequently refused to ratify.

By January 1515 France had lost all her Italian territories. The house of Sforza had been restored to power in Milan in the person of Massimiliano Sforza, Genoa was an independent republic, and the whole of Naples belonged to Aragon. Thus a twofold responsibility weighed upon Francis I at the start of his reign: he had to regain the ground lost by his predecessors and avenge the military defeats recently suffered by French arms. Old commanders whose reputations had been tarnished and young noblemen, who had yet to prove their valour, looked to him for satisfaction; and he seemed to possess all the

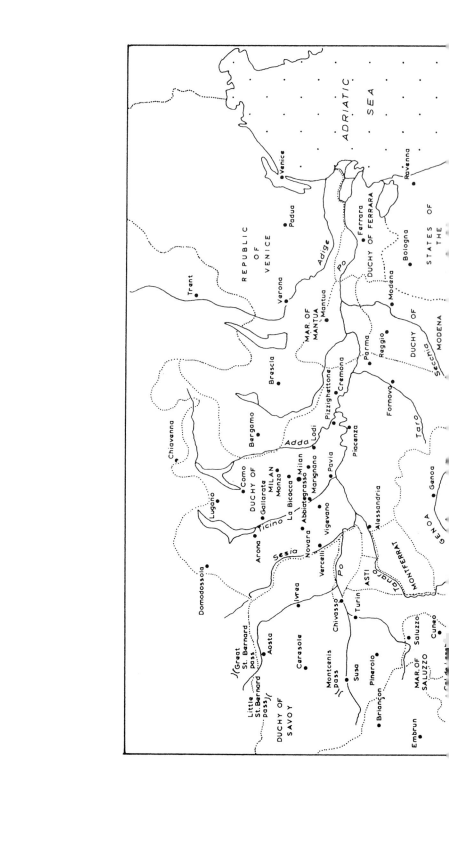

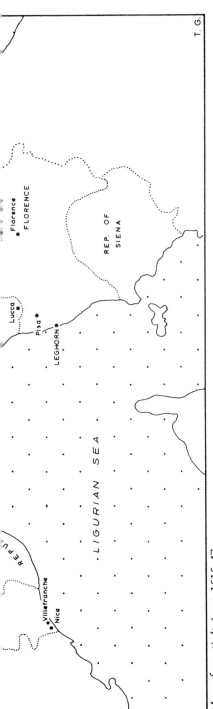

3. Map of north Italy, c. 1515–47

T. G.

14. The Emperor Charles V as a young man, modelled by the sculptor Conrad Meit.

necessary qualities for the task. His youthful spirit and powerful physique fitted him perfectly for a life of action: he had only to complete preparations begun by Louis XII.

Francis immediately set about neutralizing his more powerful neighbours. The most important was Charles of Luxemburg, a shy and unprepossessing youth of fifteen. He was the son of the Archduke Philip the Fair and the grandson of the Emperor Maximilian and Ferdinand of Aragon. On his father's death in 1506, he had inherited the territories of the house of Burgundy (Franche-Comté, the duchies of Luxemburg and Brabant and the counties of Flanders, Holland, Zeeland, Hainault and Artois) as well as a claim to the duchy of Burgundy, which France had annexed in 1477. A Burgundian by birth and upbringing, Charles grew up obsessed with the idea of rebuilding his mutilated inheritance. In 1515, however, his policy was determined by Guillaume de Croy, lord of Chièvres, the leader of the traditionally francophil Walloon aristocracy. Francis was therefore able to secure his neutrality easily. In the treaty of Paris (24 March) Charles was promised the hand of Louis XII's daughter, Renée.[1]

[1] *Ordonnances*, i. 147–72.

King Henry VIII of England was the reverse of shy and unprepossessing. Twenty-four years old, he lived 'with huge, extroverted ebullience ... revelling in spectacular living'.[2] He was an excellent sportsman, a good linguist, an accomplished musician and a competent amateur theologian, but he was also unstable, vain, jealous and cruel. He was most anxious not to be outshone by the new king of France, yet did not wish at this stage to pick a quarrel with him.[3] Having recently tasted victory on the continent, Henry was content for the present to enjoy himself and leave policy-making in the capable hands of his minister, Thomas Wolsey. His first move was to send Charles Brandon, duke of Suffolk, to congratulate Francis on his accession. The duke was also expected to gain possession of the jewels given to Mary Tudor by her late husband, Louis XII, and to take advantage of France's desire to recover Tournai, which the English had captured in 1513. The courteous exchanges between Henry and Francis concealed a web of intrigue about Mary's future. She complained to Suffolk that Francis had been importunate 'in divers matters not to her honour'. All that is known for certain is that Suffolk and Mary were married secretly in France in mid-February with Francis's encouragement. It seems that it was Mary who precipitated the marriage out of desperation, fearing that Francis or Henry would marry her off to another husband as unappetizing as Louis XII. Francis was 'eager to extract all he could from Brandon's desire for his confidence and need for his protection after the secret marriage'.[4] He agreed to pay Mary part of her dowry, but failed to return her jewels. On 5 April the treaty of London, which was soon to expire, was given a new lease of life.[5]

In Italy, French diplomacy was less successful. The Venetians agreed to help Francis militarily in return for his support against the Emperor Maximilian, and Genoa reverted to her allegiance to France in return for local concessions.[6] But the other powers were not inclined to co-operate with France. The Swiss, in particular, remembered Louis XII's refusal to ratify the treaty of Dijon; nor were they prepared to give up territories ceded to them by Sforza or the pension they received from him in return for their armed protection.[7] From the French standpoint this was unfortunate, as the Swiss had become the leading military power in Europe. Swiss pikemen were the best mercenary troops available. Their victories over the Burgundians in the 1470s had shown that wars could no longer be won by cavalry alone.

[2] J. J. Scarisbrick, *Henry VIII* (London, 1968), p. 16.
[3] See Henry's well-known conversation with the Venetian, Pasqualigo, inviting a comparison between his looks and Francis's. *C.S.P.Ven.*, ii. 1287.
[4] S. J. Gunn, *Charles Brandon, Duke of Suffolk, c. 1484–1545* (Oxford, 1988), pp. 35–8. W. C. Richardson, *Mary Tudor, the White Queen* (London, 1970), pp. 128–85. See also A. F. Pollard, *Henry VIII* (London, 1913), p. 81; *L.P.*, ii. 70, 80, 105–6; Florange, i. 164–7; Barrillon, i. 12–13, 54–5.
[5] *Ordonnances*, i. 224–47; Barrillon, i. 54.   [6] *Ordonnances*, i. 260–2; Barrillon, i. 61–2.
[7] Barrillon, i. 57.

15. Henry VIII. Miniature attributed to Lucas Horenbout. Watercolour on vellum. The inscription points to a sitting in 1527 when Henry sent his miniature as a gift to Francis I.

Sforza was also supported by Ferdinand of Aragon, who was anxious not to lose control of Naples, and by Pope Leo X, who wished to avert a repetition of the events of 1494 which had led to the overthrow of his Medici relatives in Florence. He was also anxious to retain control of Parma and Piacenza, which Sforza had ceded to him. As for the Emperor, he was at war with the Venetians and was not prepared to negotiate with France, who was their ally. On 17 July the duke of Milan, the pope, the king of Aragon and the Emperor formed a league for the defence of Italy.

The French army in 1515

One of the main tasks facing Francis in 1515 was to raise a large force of infantry. His standing army, though the largest in western Europe, consisted almost entirely of cavalry. The *compagnies d'ordonnances*, known collectively as the *gendarmerie*, were made up of aristocratic volunteers grouped into units or *lances*, each comprising a man-at-arms, two archers and a variable number of auxiliaries. The man-at-arms was heavily clad in armour, while the archers wore only light protection. Both categories fought with lances, though in 1515 some men had bows and crossbows. There were eight horses per *lance*: four for the man-at-arms and two for each archer. The usual number of *lances* in a company was fifty or sixty, and each company was commanded by a captain of high social rank or his lieutenant, for a captain might command several companies at once. A system of terminal musters kept a check on the numerical strength of the companies, and their wages were paid at the same time. The duty of providing the *gendarmerie* with fodder, billets, fuel, candles, salt and vinegar was borne by the garrison towns; other necessities had to be bought, but the troops usually preferred to pillage the countryside.

Alongside the *gendarmerie* and modelled upon it were the troops of the king's household: the Scottish archers, the *Cent gentilshommes*, consisting of two companies of a hundred men each, and three companies of French archers. In wartime, the crown could raise additional cavalry by summoning the *ban et arrière-ban* or feudal levy. Every vassal was bound to give military service to the king in proportion to the value of his fief. Thus a tenant holding a fief worth 500 *livres* a year would be expected to supply one fully equipped man-at-arms with two auxiliaries, while a lesser one might be required to supply only a single archer. A tenant who for reasons of age or health could not give personal service paid a tax related to the value of his fief. Actually, many categories of people enjoyed exemption from the *ban et arrière-ban*. Those who were liable to serve attended musters held by the *baillis* and *sénéchaux*; they were grouped into companies of fifty men-at-arms and a hundred archers, each under a captain and subordinate officers. The entire force was commanded by a captain-general. Although the *ban et arrière-ban* continued to be called from time to time in the sixteenth century, it was not of great military value: its duration of service was strictly limited and, as young noblemen joined the *compagnies d'ordonnances*, it was increasingly made up of older men with inferior horses and equipment.[8]

For infantry the king depended on volunteers, known as *aventuriers*,

[8] A. Spont, 'Marignan et l'organisation militaire sous François Ier', *R.Q.H.*, n.s. xxii (1899), 59–77; P. Contamine, *Guerre, état et société à la fin du Moyen Age* (1972), pp. 227–319. For an account of the French army in the early sixteenth century with special reference to Picardy, see Potter, *War and Government*, pp. 155–99.

recruited by captains holding a royal commission. Thus, in 1515, Francis instructed Pedro Navarro to raise a force of 8,000 Gascons, Basques and Roncalois.[9] Gascony and Picardy were the main recruiting grounds of native volunteers, who were formed into companies 500 strong under veteran captains. Wearing a leather jerkin and a light helmet, they were armed with a pike, halberd, crossbow or arquebus. During the early sixteenth century the crossbow was gradually superseded by the arquebus, whose heavy bullet was a distinct asset in spite of its limited range of barely 400 metres. The infantry was mustered on a monthly basis and paid less than the cavalry.

Foreign mercenaries were also employed by the king of France. Until 1510 he had been able to call on the Swiss, but now that they were employed by the enemy, he had to look elsewhere. In 1515 he raised 23,000 German landsknechts, including the famous 'Black band' from Guelders, comprising 12,000 pikemen, 2,000 arquebusiers, 2,000 men armed with two-handed swords and 1,000 halberdiers.[10] The landsknechts terrorized their homeland in peacetime and were prepared to fight for the Emperor's enemies in wartime. Their tactics were closely modelled on those of the Swiss, but they were less disciplined, as their captaincies went to the highest bidder, not the best soldier. Though extremely brave, they would often exploit a crisis to extort more money from an employer.

The French artillery in 1515 was second to none. From the mid fifteenth century important changes had taken place in the designing of guns: size was abandoned in favour of portability and accuracy of fire. Pioneers of this trend were the brothers Jean and Gaspard Bureau whose guns had blasted the English out of castles in Normandy and Guyenne in the 1450s. When the French invaded Italy in 1494, the Italians were surprised by their ordnance. Their guns, Guicciardini noted, were 'lighter and all cast in bronze ... [they] were drawn by horses with such dexterity that they could keep up with the marching speed of an army ... [they] shot at very short intervals ... and could be used as usefully in the field as in battering walls'. But, if the new French guns seemed highly mobile by comparison with the clumsy bombards of the early fifteenth century, they were not particularly manoeuvrable by modern standards; European field artillery had a low degree of mobility and a poor rate of fire till the mid seventeenth century. Cannon continued to be more effective against masonry than against men, and the absence of any standardization made the supply and transport of ammunition difficult and wasteful. In 1515 the French artillery comprised about sixty guns of many calibres.[11]

[9] Barrillon, i. 58–9.
[10] F. Lot, *Recherches sur les effectifs des armées françaises des guerres d'Italie aux Guerres de Religion, 1494–1562* (1962), p. 42.
[11] C. M. Cipolla, *Guns and Sails* (London, 1965), pp. 28–9; P. Contamine, 'L'artillerie royale française à la veille des guerres d'Italie', *Annales de Bretagne*, lxxi (1964), 221–61; and his 'Les industries de guerre dans la France de la Renaissance: l'exemple de l'artillerie', *R.H.*, 271 (1984), 249–80.

16. The battle of Marignano. One of twenty-seven marble bas-reliefs depicting battle scenes by Pierre Bontemps from Francis I's tomb in the Basilica of Saint-Denis.

Marignano

On 26 June 1515 Francis informed the 'good towns' of his kingdom that he was about to leave for Italy and that his mother would be regent in his absence. He also obtained from his queen the formal cession of her claim to Milan. Three days later he slipped away from Amboise before daybreak. He travelled to Lyons where a spectacular entry awaited him on 12 July. Among the tableaux performed by members of the city's leading families was one showing the king and his companions defending Peace against Sforza and the Swiss bear; another showed him as Hercules gathering fruit in the garden of the Hesperides.[12] Francis spent three weeks in Lyons completing his invasion preparations. On 15 July he appointed his mother as regent. Her authority, however, was limited by the fact that the Chancellor took the Great Seal to Italy.[13]

At the end of the month Francis joined his army at Grenoble. His enemies,

[12] J. Chartrou, *Les entrées solennelles et triomphales à la Renaissance (1484–1551)* (1928), pp. 32–3.
[13] *Ordonnances*, i. 262–8.

meanwhile, prepared to defend Italy. Between 12,000 and 15,000 Swiss troops were sent to the Milanese. On 17 July the duke of Milan, the pope, the king of Aragon and the Emperor formed a defensive league, and 1,500 papal horse under Prospero Colonna were sent to Piedmont to assist the Swiss, who had no cavalry of their own. Assuming that the French would cross the Alps either by the Mont-Genèvre or Montcenis pass, the Swiss took up positions in the Val Chisone and Val di Susa.[14] But Francis, acting on the advice of Marshal Trivulzio, chose the Col de Larche, a pass normally used only by local peasants. More than a thousand sappers were sent ahead of the army to clear obstacles and bridge torrents. On 11 August the vanguard under Bourbon began to cross the mountains. It emerged a few days later near Cuneo in the plain of Piedmont. Hearing that Colonna's cavalry was close by at Villafranca, three companies of French men-at-arms fell upon the town. Colonna was taken completely by surprise and captured along with 300 of his men.[15] The Swiss thus lost their cavalry support.

Francis, meanwhile, left Guillestre with the rest of the army. Despite the sappers, he did not find the crossing of the Alps easy. 'We are in the strangest country that any of us has ever seen', he wrote to his mother, 'but I hope to reach the plain of Piedmont with my army tomorrow. This will be a great relief to us, as we are finding it irksome to wear armour in these mountains; most of the time we have to go on foot, leading our horses by the bridle.' On the Italian side the descent was so precipitous that horses and mules slipped and fell into ravines, while guns had to be dismantled and lowered on ropes. A Venetian eye-witness thought nothing comparable had happened since Hannibal's crossing of the Alps.[16]

On reaching the plain of Piedmont, Francis advanced rapidly eastward, stopping only briefly in Turin, capital of Savoy. He imposed a strict discipline on his troops in the hope of winning the confidence of the local people. He forbade his infantry to enter towns that had opened their gates and intervened personally wherever incidents were brought to his notice. The Swiss, meanwhile, finding themselves outflanked, retreated from the Alpine passes to Lake Maggiore. Prompted by the duke of Savoy, Francis sent his uncle René to treat with them at Vercelli. He offered them a large subsidy and military help in the future if they would acquiesce in his occupation of Milan. He was even prepared to indemnify Sforza for the loss of his duchy. At first, the Swiss seemed ready to talk, but, after a treaty had been drafted, they asked for a new round

---

[14] P. Pieri, *Il Rinascimento e la crisi militare italiana* (Turin, 1952), p. 514.

[15] Barrillon, 179–80; du Bellay, i. 63–5; Florange, i. 176–80.

[16] Barrillon, i. 65–6, 78, 82–3; F. Mignet, *La rivalité de François Ier et de Charles-Quint* (1875), i. 77–8. Not all the French artillery was carried across the Col de Larche: the heavier guns were taken over the Mont-Genèvre pass.

of negotiations. This time René of Savoy was joined by Marshal Lautrec, while the duke of Savoy acted as mediator.[17]

Francis, in the meantime, pressed on eastward, crossing the Ticino on 31 August. At Bufalora a deputation from Milan offered him victuals and promised him a friendly reception in the city. The king, however, reacted cautiously to this move. He sent Trivulzio on a reconnaissance towards Milan, while he himself began a semi-circular movement to the south of the city. He aimed to make contact with the Venetian army under Bartolomeo d'Alviano which was at Lodi. Francis was right to be cautious, for the Milanese were divided into two factions: while the Ghibellines were ready to submit to him, the Guelfs wanted to resist. As Trivulzio approached Milan, the Guelfs forced him to withdraw.[18]

On 9 September Francis received the text of a new treaty negotiated with the Swiss at Gallarate. In return for a subsidy of one million *écus*, of which 150,000 were to be paid at once in cash, they agreed to give up all their Milanese territories, except Bellinzona. Sforza was to be given the duchy of Nemours as compensation for Milan along with the hand of a French princess of royal blood and a company of men-at-arms. Francis was to be allowed to raise as many troops as he liked in Switzerland in return for a subsidy to each canton. He was also to help them with cavalry and artillery, unless he needed them himself, if they went to war.[19] Stiff as these terms were, Francis was ready to accept them as the price of gaining Milan and Swiss military support in the future. Within ten hours he had collected the 150,000 *écus* from his entourage and sent them to Gallarate.[20] On 10 September he moved his camp to Marignano (now Melegnano) and sent Louis d'Ars to occupy Pavia. That evening Alviano called on Francis, who urged him to cover his rear against a possible attack by the Hispano-papal army that had gathered at Piacenza.[21]

Francis's caution was again justified, for the Swiss were as disunited as the Milanese. While the men of the cantons of Berne, Fribourg and Solothurn voted to go home, those of the eastern and central cantons refused to accept the treaty of Gallarate. They were encouraged by Matthias Schiner, cardinal-bishop of Sion, to fight on.[22] A minor skirmish outside Milan with a party of French scouts precipitated a decision. About midday the Swiss swarmed out of the city. Most of them wore no hats, shoes or armour. Their artillery consisted only of eight small guns. Schiner and 200 papal horse followed in the rear. In order to surprise the French, the Swiss carried no drums. As they marched

---

[17] Barrillon, i. 83–7, 90–3, 109.   [18] *Ibid.*, i. 87–91, 93.   [19] *Ordonnances*, i. 286–92.
[20] Barrillon, i. 108.
[21] Pieri, p. 515.
[22] For different versions of a speech delivered by Schiner to Swiss troops outside the Franciscan convent in Milan on 13 September see F. Guicciardini, *The History of Italy*, tr. A. P. Goddard (London, 1763), vi. 347–52; Barrillon, i. 114–15.

74

17. The battle of Marignano. Pen and ink drawing by the Maître de la Ratière. The action is shown from the arrival of the Swiss, led by Cardinal Schiner, to their flight. In the centre: confrontation of the Swiss pikemen with Francis's landsknechts. The appropriate standards are flying over each group. In the foreground, Francis leads a cavalry charge.

briskly and silently towards the enemy, they threw up a cloud of dust into the clear blue sky.

The French camp was situated near the village of San Giuliano, some five kilometres north of Marignano. It was flanked on the west by the road from Milan to Lodi and on the east by the river Lambro. The intervening terrain was marshy and intersected by many ditches. The camp itself was divided into three parts: the van, commanded by Bourbon, was nearest Milan. It comprised the artillery, which was protected in front by a ditch and a line of marksmen and, on its flanks and rear by 10,000 French infantry; secondly, a huge square of 10,000 landsknechts; and thirdly, 950 men-at-arms. The centre or 'battle', which was at Santa Brigida, about a kilometre further south, comprised another block of 9,000 landsknechts and the flower of the *gendarmerie* under the king. Finally, the rearguard was three kilometres further south. It comprised only cavalry and was under Francis's brother-in-law, Charles d'Alençon.[23]

The alarm was sounded in the French camp after sappers had reported a cloud of dust in the direction of Milan. Bourbon warned the king, who passed on the message to his brother-in-law. The Swiss pikemen, as usual, advanced in an échelon of three compact squares, each containing about 7,000 men. The first square encountered the French about 4 pm. It broke through the line of sharpshooters and crossed the ditch protecting the French guns. The French infantry dispersed, leaving the gunners isolated. The landsknechts now moved forward against the Swiss, and two gigantic squares of pikemen collided. Again the Swiss broke through and a French cavalry charge was thrown back. As the first Swiss square began to tire, the second moved up to give it flanking support. Although night had fallen, the moon still shed enough light for the fighting to continue. About midnight, however, it vanished, plunging the field into obscurity. The armies broke apart: as the French rallied to shrill trumpet calls, the Swiss responded to the bellowing of their huge war horns. Only a ditch separated the two camps and skirmishing went on throughout the night.

Francis used the respite to reorganize his army. The rearguard were brought forward to form a single line with the centre and the remnants of the vanguard. Meanwhile, Duprat wrote to Lautrec, instructing him not to hand over the money to the Swiss at Gallarate. He also wrote to Alviano, urging him to bring the Venetian army without delay, and to Louis d'Ars, ordering him to guard Pavia well in case Francis should need to retreat there.[24]

As dawn broke, battle was resumed. The three squares of Swiss pikemen moved alongside each other and engaged the entire French line. The French

---

[23] On the battle of Marignano see H. Harkensee, *Die Schlacht bei Marignano* (Göttingen, 1909); Pieri, pp. 516–24; G. Treccani degli Alfieri, *Storia di Milano*, viii (Milan, 1957), 181–4; F. L. Taylor, *The Art of War in Italy, 1494–1529* (Cambridge, 1921), pp. 101, 111, 123–5.
[24] Du Bellay, i. 71; Michaud et Poujoulat, v. 596; Barrillon, i. 122; Pieri, p. 518.

18. Francis I charging at Marignano. Frontispiece of a French translation by Etienne Le Blanc of Cicero's speeches (B.N., ms. 1738, f. Av⁰). The author claims the victory as greater than those of Hannibal, Scipio and Alexander and calls for another Homer or Cicero to sing its praises.

right, under Bourbon, managed to repulse the first square which had been weakened by its losses on the previous day. In the centre, the Swiss were more successful: braving the fire of the French guns, they crossed the ditch, scattered the infantry and forced back the landsknechts, but Francis and the *gendarmerie* drove them back. Meanwhile, on the left, the Swiss overwhelmed the French artillery, scattered the infantry and lunged into the landsknechts, who fought heroically. About 8 am, as the French left was about to collapse, shouts of 'San Marco! San Marco!' announced the arrival of the Venetians.[25] The French, their spirits revived, mounted a counter-attack, and by 11 am the Swiss had been routed.

Marshal Trivulzio, the veteran of seventeen battles, described Marignano as a 'battle of giants' beside which the others were but 'children's games'. The gravediggers reported that they had buried 16,500 bodies, but the exact number of losses is unknown. Both sides made absurd claims. What is certain is that many French noblemen were killed; their embalmed bodies were sent to France for burial.[26] Never again, Francis wrote, would the *gendarmerie* be called 'hares in armour'. He singled out for praise Galiot de Genouillac, Master of the artillery, whose guns had torn large gaps in the Swiss ranks.[27] Another hero was Pierre du Terrail, seigneur de Bayard. Legend has it that the king had himself knighted on the battlefield by Bayard.[28]

The immediate result of the battle was the capitulation of Milan on 16 September, but Sforza surrendered the citadel only on 4 October. He was promised a pension and settled in France where he died in May 1530.[29] Francis entered Milan in triumph on 11 October and remained there till the end of the month. Duprat was appointed Chancellor of Milan and Jean de Selve Vice-Chancellor. The senate, originally set up by Louis XII and consisting of French and Italian members, was revived. A heavy fine was imposed on the people of Milan as punishment for their 'great rebellions and acts of disobedience'. They were also required to submit hostages.[30]

Francis did not attempt to chase the Swiss out of Italy; for, in the long term, he needed their services. He thanked the cantons that had pulled out of the war and offered to mediate between them and the other cantons. He wanted to be

[25] Harkensee (pp. 97–101) attaches little significance to the Venetian intervention, but S. Frey (*Le guerre milanesi* fasc. 2, Berne, 1936) of *Storia militare svizzera* ed. R. M. Feldmann and H. G. Wirz (12 vols., Berne, 1915–36, p. 391) believes that it transformed the imminent victory of the Swiss into a defeat, a view shared by Pieri (p. 519). Although Francis failed to mention the Venetians in his official account of the battle, he nevertheless showed them his gratitude. Barrillon, i. 127.

[26] They included François de Bourbon, the comte de Sancerre, the prince de Talmont and the seigneurs de Bussy and d'Humbercourt. Lot, *Recherches sur les effectifs*, p. 44; Spont, 'Marignan', pp. 72–3; Barrillon, i. 125; M. Sanuto, *Diarii* (Venice, 1879–1903), xxi. col. 97.

[27] Michaud et Poujoulat, v. 595–7.

[28] *Le loyal serviteur*, ed. J. Roman (1878), p. 246; J. Jacquart, *Bayard* (1987), p. 236; S. Champier, *Les gestes ensemble la vie du preulx Chevalier Bayard*, ed. D. Crouzet (1992), pp. 195–6.

[29] *Ordonnances*, i. 294–300.   [30] Barrillon, i. 160–3.

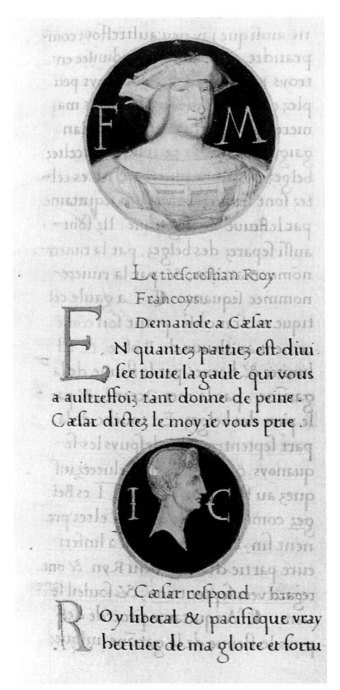

19. Francis I and Julius Caesar. Miniatures attributed to Jean Clouet and Godefroy le Batave from vol. I of the *Commentaires de la guerre gallique* (B.L., Harley Ms. 6205 f. 3). Francis's medallion is larger than Caesar's, his dress is modern and the 'F.M.' probably stands for *Franciscus Magnus*.

20. Dialogue between Francis I and Julius Caesar in front of Diana and Aurora in the forest of Fontainebleau. Miniature by Godefroy le Batave from vol. II of François Demoulins' *Commentaires de la guerre gallique* (B.N., ms. fr. 13429 f. 4b).

allowed to hire mercenaries in Switzerland and to prevent them serving others. As money was the only language the Swiss understood, he empowered his envoys to bribe them handsomely and to promise them more. On 7 November ten cantons made peace with France; the rest offered their services to the Emperor.[31]

No one was more anxious than Pope Leo X after the battle of Marignano, for he had backed the wrong horse. Fearing that Francis would follow up his victory by marching on Florence and unseating the Medici, he offered him

[31] *Ibid.*, i. 142–6, 148–59; *Ordonnances*, i. 304–12.

21. Jacques, called Galiot, de Genouillac (1465–1546), seigneur d'Assier, *sénéchal* d'Armagnac, captain-general of the artillery and *Grand écuyer*. Drawing by Jean Clouet. His guns contributed significantly to Francis's victory at Marignano.

ardues cest afin que vous puissies en
comprendre mieulx le sens

Ay donecques woulu tresnoble et
digne princesse desdier a votre subli/
mite ce petit œuure vous supliat bien
benignement repceuoir ? prendre en
gre.

Leternite.

22. A crowned lion, symbol of courage, dominates the chained Swiss bear. Miniature celebrating the king's victory at Marignano from a French translation of a Greek work by Horus Apollo. The author seeks to show that great deeds can be represented by animals, as in Egyptian hieroglyphs (Chantilly: Musée Condé Ms. 682, f. 2).

peace and friendship. Actually, Leo had nothing to fear, for Francis badly needed his friendship. The pope was more than a spiritual ruler: he controlled a sizeable territory in central Italy, he could effectively rally other powers to aid or hinder a foreign invader and could authorize a secular ruler to tax his clergy. Recent history had shown that the French could hope to establish a permanent foothold in Italy only with papal co-operation. Even after Marignano, Francis's position in the peninsula was precarious: the Swiss were intent on revenge and the Emperor and the king of England might well join them. The threat of such a coalition made it all the more urgent for Francis to gain the pope's support or at least to neutralize him. What is more, as suzerain of Naples, Leo had its investiture in his gift. Thus a treaty was speedily arranged between Francis and the pope: in exchange for Parma and Piacenza, Francis gave the duchy of Nemours and a large pension to Leo's brother Giuliano, and another pension to his nephew Lorenzo. This, however, was only a first step. The two rulers needed to settle other questions, notably the abrogation of the Pragmatic Sanction of Bourges of 1438, which the papacy had been demanding for some time. They therefore agreed to meet in December at Bologna.[32]

Francis arrived in Bologna on 11 December, three days after the pope, and was accommodated in the Palazzo Pubblico, immediately beneath Leo's apartments, an arrangment betokening mutual trust.[33] Though shrouded in secrecy, the talks are known to have focused on Italian affairs. The pope hinted at the possibility of Francis being given Naples on the death of Ferdinand of Aragon if, in return, he would support the Medici in Florence. Leo agreed to cede Reggio and Modena to the duke of Ferrara, but turned a deaf ear to Francis's intercession on behalf of the duke of Urbino who had broken his fealty to the Holy See. Agreement was reached on the need for a crusade against the Turks and Francis was allowed to levy a tenth on the French clergy towards this end. But the most important decision taken at Bologna was to substitute a Concordat for the Pragmatic Sanction of Bourges. Details of the new agreement were left to be worked out by legal experts.[34]

The conference lasted four days. On 13 December the pope celebrated Mass in the church of San Petronio. During the service Francis and his followers asked the pope for absolution which he readily conceded. Next day, Adrien Gouffier, brother of Admiral Bonnivet, was made a cardinal. On 15 December

---

[32] *Ordonnances*, i. 300–4; Barrillon, i. 141–2.

[33] Barrillon, i. 164–73; Le Glay, ii. 85–90; L. von Pastor, *The History of the Popes*, tr. F. I. Antrobus and R. F. Kerr (London, 1891–1933), vii. 134–7. See also B. L. Harley Ms. 3462, fols. 197b–199a. A detailed account of the king's entry into Bologna and his first encounter with the pope is contained in a letter of 11 December from Stazio Gadio to Francesco Gonzaga. See *Federico Gonzaga alla corte de Francesco I*, ed. R. Tamalio (forthcoming).

[34] Duprat acted for the king and the cardinals of Ancona and Santi Quattro Coronati for the pope. Pastor, vii, 141–6; Barrillon, i. 173–4.

Leo gave Francis a superb crucifix of solid gold.[35] The king then returned to Milan for Christmas and, on 7 January, presided over a meeting of the senate in the course of which he remitted the fine that had been imposed on the city, released its hostages and allowed its exiles to come home and resume their property. The citizens duly thanked the king and swore fealty to him. On 8 January Francis set off for home after appointing Bourbon as his lieutenant-general in the duchy.[36]

While Francis was still in Milan, he received several letters from his mother and sister urging him to come home. They arranged to meet him in the south of France and left Amboise on 20 October with a distinguished company. On their way south, Louise and Marguerite stopped in Lyons and fulfilled a vow to go on pilgrimage to the supposed tomb of Mary Magdalene at Saint-Maximin-la-Sainte Baume. Wherever they passed they were given the honours due to ladies of their rank. Eventually, they reached Sisteron, where they met Francis and his companions on 13 January 1516. 'And God knows', wrote Louise in her *Journal*, 'how happy I was, poor mother, to see my son safe and sound after he had suffered so much violence for the sake of the commonwealth.' On 21 January Francis also went to Saint-Maximin on pilgrimage. He then travelled to Marseilles, where a spectacular entry awaited him. He was greeted by a procession led by 2,000 children all dressed in white. Heading the clergy was bishop Claude de Seyssel on his mule. As the king entered the city, a salvo was fired by many guns ranged along the walls. Later, all the galleys in the harbour fired their own salute. There were the usual *tableaux vivants* along the processional route, including scenes from the life of St Louis of Aragon. The king and his entourage also watched dancing by people dressed as pilgrims, moors, savages, sirens, archers and giraffes. On 23 January Francis visited the royal galleys commanded by Préjent de Bidoux and took part in a battle of oranges. The queen had her own entry but was spared the gun salvoes. Young girls in white accompanied her to Notre-Dame-de-la-Garde where they prayed for her to be blessed with a son. From Marseilles Francis travelled to Aix, Salon, Arles, Tarascon and Avignon.[37] On 24 February he arrived in Lyons where he remained until 10 July except for a pilgrimage on foot, this time to the Holy Shroud at Chambéry. This took place on 28 May and the king dressed appropriately for the occasion. Wearing an elaborate party-coloured outfit (black, tawny and white), a gold coif and a large plumed hat, he carried a pilgrim's staff. He was accompanied by a large band of courtiers, all similarly dressed and equipped. The procession was led by the duc d'Alençon and a captain of

[35] The king's gifts to the pope gave less satisfaction. Pastor, vii. 138–40; Le Glay, ii. 88. See below p. 103.
[36] Barrillon, i. 177–86; Sanuto, xxi. cols. 448–9; *C.A.F.*, v. 16093.
[37] E. Baux, V.-L. Bourrilly and P. Mabilly, 'Le voyage des reines et de François Ier en Provence et dans la vallée du Rhône (décembre 1515–février 1516), *A. du M.*, vol. 16 (1904), pp. 31–64.

landsknechts carrying a two-handed sword on his shoulder. The whole of Lyons, we are told, gathered on the bridge across the Rhône to see the holy marathon on its way. After spending the summer in the Loire valley, the court returned to Paris on 4 October. Next day Francis went to the abbey of Saint-Denis and performed the ceremony of returning the relics, which had been on the high altar during the war, to the vault that was their peacetime sanctuary.[38]

Meanwhile, on 23 January 1516, King Ferdinand of Aragon died, an event which seriously altered the balance of power in Europe. Ferdinand left his kingdom, comprising Castile, Aragon and Naples, to his grandson the Archduke Charles, who already ruled the Netherlands and Franche-Comté. He became overnight France's most powerful neighbour and the ruler of territories in which she had an interest. Louis XII had ceded his claim to Naples to his niece, Germaine de Foix, Ferdinand's second wife, on condition that she had children by him. This had not happened, so that Francis felt entitled to claim Naples for himself, but, before doing so, he ordered a search of the archives of the counts of Provence for evidence of his title. The actual investiture of Naples lay in the gift of the pope, who had given Francis to understand that he might support his claim. The king now reminded Leo of this. As a goodwill gesture, he also freed Prospero Colonna, whom he had been holding prisoner since before Marignano. Colonna promised in return to assist Francis's Neapolitan designs. Another potential trouble-spot was Spanish Navarre which Ferdinand had wrested from its king, Jean d'Albret, in 1512. It had since been annexed to Castile, and Jean looked to the king of France for help in regaining it. 'My cousin', Francis wrote to him, 'the hour has come when you must exercise extreme diligence to recover your kingdom, and I for my part wish to help you in every possible way.'[39]

However, early in 1516, Charles still had to take possession of his Spanish kingdoms. There were powerful forces in Aragon and Castile favouring a return to separate rulers, and in Castile the authority of the monarch was being challenged by turbulent nobles and towns. Only Charles's speedy arrival could assure him of a trouble-free succession, and this required the co-operation of France. On 13 August Charles and Francis signed the treaty of Noyon. This substituted Francis's infant daughter, Louise, for Princess Renée as Charles's future bride and added Naples to her dowry. Pending completion of the marriage, Charles undertook to pay Francis an annual tribute for Naples of 100,000 *écus*, thereby implicitly recognizing the king's claim to that kingdom.

---

[38] Richly detailed accounts of the pilgrimage to Chambéry and of the ceremony at Saint-Denis are contained in letters written on 31 May and 5 October respectively by Stazio Gadio to the marquis of Mantua. See *Federico Gonzaga alla corte di Francesco I*, ed. R. Tamalio (forthcoming).

[39] *Ibid.*, pp. 58–64; Barrillon, i. 195.

He also promised conditionally to give satisfaction to Jean d'Albret's widow, Catherine.[40]

Meanwhile, in Austria, Cardinal Schiner, who had escaped from the field of Marignano, had been urging the Emperor to invade Milan and restore the Sforzas to power. Maximilian was assured that, given the opportunity, the Milanese people would rise against the French. He could also count on the support of the Swiss cantons that had been defeated at Marignano and on the financial help of Henry VIII of England whose jealousy had been aroused by the French victory. Early in March 1516 Maximilian invaded north Italy, relieving Brescia and forcing the French to retreat to Milan. On 24 March, however, the French garrison was reinforced by 8,000 Swiss from the cantons that had signed the treaty of Geneva. This dashed Maximilian's hope of a swift victory. After pausing two days at Marignano, he suddenly decamped, leaving his troops behind.

The Emperor's ignominious flight enabled Francis to come to terms with the Swiss. On 29 November the so-called 'Perpetual Peace' of Fribourg was signed.[41] Francis agreed to pay the Swiss a war indemnity of 700,000 *écus*. They were also promised 300,000 *écus* for the castles of Lugano and Locarno and fortresses in the Valtelline. Finally, an annual subsidy of 2,000 *écus* was promised to each canton. The Swiss, for their part, agreed not to serve anyone against the king in France or Milan. Although the treaty did not give Francis the full alliance he had hoped for, it did give him the right to hire Swiss mercenaries in the future instead of having to fight them.

On 11 March 1517 Francis, Maximilian and Charles of Spain signed a treaty at Cambrai in which they agreed to help each other if attacked and to join in a crusade. Secret clauses provided for the partition of Italy at the expense of Venice, but it is doubtful if Francis intended them seriously. He effectively nullified them on 8 October by renewing his alliance with Venice.[42] The peace of Cambrai rounded off the first phase of the Italian Wars and Francis could feel reasonably satisfied with his achievements so far: he had won a spectacular victory thereby avenging the disasters suffered by French arms in 1513, he had exploded the myth of Swiss invincibility and had acquired the monopoly of future troop recruitment in the cantons, he had restored French rule in Milan and Genoa, he had come to terms with the pope who had virtually promised him Naples, and the Emperor Maximilian had made himself ridiculous in the eyes of Europe. 'There was great peace and tranquillity in the kingdom of France', wrote Barrillon in 1517, 'and no noise or rumour of war, division or partisanship. Merchants plied their trade in perfect safety as well on land as on

---

[40] *Ordonnances*, i. 409–30.
[41] *Ibid.*, i. 477–93. The treaty remained in force until the reign of Louis XVI; hence its nickname.
[42] *Ordonnances*, i. 494–502, ii. 7–18, 164–8.

sea. Frenchmen, Englishmen, Spaniards, Germans and all other natives of Christendom traded peacefully together. This was a great favour bestowed by God on Christendom.'[43]

Peace came at a time when Christendom desperately needed to unite against the westward expansion of the Ottoman Turks. Under Mehmet II they had captured Constantinople, penetrated far into the Balkans and expelled the Venetians from Euboea. Now, under Selim the Grim, they were advancing once more: having overrun Syria in August 1516, they invaded Egypt early in 1517. 'It is time', Leo X declared, 'that we woke from sleep lest we be put to the sword unawares.'[44] In November the Sacred College proposed a new crusade to be led by the Emperor and the king of France. It was hoped that Francis would respond favourably, especially since he had been allowed to levy a tenth for the crusade. But he did so only on 23 December, when he asked to control the crusade funds and for permission to raise another tenth. The replies sent by the Emperor and the king of Spain were equally disappointing, yet Leo did not give up his plan. In March 1518 he proclaimed a five-year truce among all Christian powers and sent four cardinals to the courts of Europe to rally support for the crusade. Yet no one was really interested. Although the seriousness of the Turkish threat was generally admitted, other problems seemed more urgent to the princes of Christendom.[45]

The treaty of Noyon had become a millstone around the neck of Charles of Habsburg now that he had become king of Spain. He could not afford to pay Francis the annual tribute for Naples and showed little inclination to compensate Catherine d'Albret for her loss of Navarre.[46] In February 1518 the deputies to the Castilian Cortes offered to sacrifice their lives and property for the defence of Navarre, calling it 'the principal key to Spain'. Charles assured them that he did not intend to give it up and, in August, persuaded Ferdinand's widow, Germaine, to hand over to him her claim to Navarre. Yet, even now, Charles's authority in Spain was not sufficiently secure for him to risk an open breach with France. Thus, far from repudiating the treaty of Noyon, he assured Francis of his good intentions. He even asked for the king's daughter, Charlotte, to be substituted for her recently deceased sister, Louise as his prospective bride under the treaty.[47]

In May 1519 a conference opened at Montpellier to examine outstanding differences between Francis and Charles. The French delegation was led by the Grand Master Boisy and the Spanish one by Chièvres who was known for his francophil sentiments. Alain d'Albret, regent of Navarre, sent representatives to press the claim to the kingdom of his grandson, Henri. The conference,

---

[43] Barrillon, i. 273.   [44] L. von Pastor, vii. 218.   [45] *Ibid.*, vii. 223–54.
[46] Le Glay, ii. 147.
[47] P. Boissonnade, *Histoire de la réunion de la Navarre à la Castille* (1893), pp. 508–29.

however, got off to a bad start. Boisy fell ill on the first day, leaving his colleagues, Bishop Poncher and President Olivier to negotiate on their own. After squabbling over the agenda, the conference turned into an acrimonious debate over the lawful ownership of Navarre. The Spaniards argued that it belonged to Charles by right of inheritance and gift. They tactlessly recalled that it had been annexed by Ferdinand of Aragon after the pope had excommunicated Jean d'Albret for conniving at Louis XII's schism. This provoked a sharp rejoinder from the French. 'Never', they declared 'had the king of France ceased to be a Very Catholic and Very Christian sovereign; never had he been infected with the leprosy of schism.' A proposal from Chièvres that Henri d'Albret should be given a cash indemnity was rejected by the French.[48] Boisy's death on 10 May gave them a convenient pretext for going home. 'The said death', wrote du Bellay, 'was the cause of great wars . . . for, if they had finished their talks, Christendom would certainly have remained at peace till now; those who subsequently had charge of affairs cared less for the peace of Christendom than did the said Chièvres and the Grand Master.'[49]

[48] *Ibid.*, pp. 532–9; Le Glay, ii. 450–4.
[49] Du Bellay, i. 95. Florange believed that Boisy's death was responsible for the deaths of 200,000 men. Florange, i. 257.

Chapter five

'The Most Christian King'

Francis I bore the title of 'Most Christian King'. In the early Middle Ages this had been conferred by popes on any rulers they wished to favour; but during the twelfth and thirteenth centuries it became regularly attached to the king of France. Philip the Fair was the first to require his subjects to address him regularly as 'Most Christian King'. He exploited the title juridically to demonstrate his independence of both Emperor and pope. Royal propagandists opposed the claims of Pope Boniface VIII by maintaining that France was held of God alone and that her king recognized no superior in this world. France was 'the principal and most venerable part of Christendom'.

In the late fourteenth century the title of 'most Christian' was transformed into an ancient privilege exclusively attached to the French king and his realm. Various arguments were used to justify the privilege. Writers pointed to the kingdom's 'wealth of relics and holy bodies', to the many large abbeys and cathedrals, to the rich benefices, to the numerous clergy and to the learning they drew from the University of Paris. A long-standing tradition held that the French had had faith even before their conversion. France had given birth to many saints, martyrs and crusaders. No heretic, it was claimed, had ever lived in France. About 1300 writers began to assert that God had given France His special blessing and approval. As visible signs of His favour he had sent the Holy Ampulla, the lily and the oriflamme. The kingdom of France was equated with that of Israel; its people were described as the second Chosen People. They were the descendants of King David who would one day return to Palestine.[1]

Royal propagandists from around 1300 onwards claimed that an exemplary line of royalty, as supremely Christian as the people it ruled, had sat upon the French throne. The blood of kings was the hereditary transmitter of all that

[1] Colette Beaune, *The Birth of an Ideology: Myths and Symbols of Nation in Late-Medieval France* (Berkeley, CA, 1991), pp. 172–81.

was most Christian. This bloodline was held to be continuous, stretching through time from one king to the next. Royal blood was clear, transparent, luminous, and, in contrast to normal blood, a sombre red. According to the jurist Cosme Guimier, 'the bloodline of France is perpetual to the thousandth degree'. Thus an heir would always be guaranteed, especially since it was God who provided him.[2]

Although Francis I was only the cousin of Louis XII, his predecessor on the throne, it was clear to many that he had been chosen by God. His life had been providentially spared when, as a child, he had been carried off by his horse. The date of his accession, 1 January, was also taken as evidence of divine selection. André de la Vigne saw it as the start of a new era for the kingdom in which the great designs of Providence would be realized by a monarch chosen by God. A spokesman for the University of Paris interpreted as a good augury the fact that Francis was the first of his name and became king on the first day of the year, on the first of the month and on the first day of the week. Francis's old tutor, Demoulins, wrote that he had come to the throne by the grace of Jesus Christ, not by the action of Fortune. For both de la Vigne and Demoulins his physical qualities as well as his moral virtues were evidence of his divine election.[3]

One of the side-shows staged for Francis I's entry into Lyons in July 1515 showed God the Father on His celestial throne on an upper stage and the baptism of Clovis underneath. A motto read: 'Every excellent gift comes from above.' As the king arrived, God expressed his satisfaction at the manner in which Clovis had kept his promise and sent angels down to him bearing as gifts the Holy Ampulla, a new standard with three gold fleurs-de-lis on a blue background, the oriflamme and the gift of healing scrofula.[4] In the late Middle Ages Clovis had become an unofficial saint, the most holy founder of the French monarchy. His military actions had been ennobled. He was shown as having set aside his personal ambitions to realize God's plan for France. He had been the first recipient of the sacred oil sent down from Heaven in the Holy Ampulla. This event showed, first, how God confirmed, established and approved the creation of the kingdom; secondly, it pointed to the king's duty to be a good and faithful Christian, a defender of Holy Church and an upright wielder of the sword of justice.[5]

The canonization of Louis IX in 1270 served to confirm a widely held belief in the saintliness of French kings, which they themselves gradually assumed to be a dispensation from any sacred quality conferred from outside. Although from Charles V onwards they were knighted at their coronations, this was

[2] *Ibid.*, pp. 181–93.
[3] Anne-Marie Lecoq, *François Ier imaginaire: symbolique et politique à l'aube de le Renaissance française* (1987), pp. 139–42. See above p. 18.
[4] *Ibid.*, pp. 199–201.   [5] C. Beaune, *The Birth of an Ideology*, pp. 70–89.

sometimes considered unnecessary since they were deemed to be born as knights in the service of God. By the fifteenth century the coronation had become no more than a declaration of existing kingship: only the royal blood was essential to the succession. The king's ability to work miracles also came from his blood. As Jean de Rély said in 1484: 'The best blood, the most pious, the surest that exists in the world, is that most noble blood of the house of France.' The anointing of the king set him apart from other men; it gave him at least a quasi-sacerdotal character. The blessing of his ring was a modified form of the blessing of the episcopal ring. The similarity between bishop and king was further emphasized by the unction of the hands and the investiture with gloves after the hands were anointed.[6]

At his coronation, as we have seen, the king of France took the following oath: 'I promise to all of you [the bishops] and grant that to each of you and to the churches entrusted to you I shall protect the canonical privilege, due law, and justice, and I shall exercise defense of each bishop and of each church committed to him, as much as I am able – with God's help – just as a king ought properly to do in his kingdom.'[7]

The Concordat of Bologna

The relationship of church and state in France was one of close mutual dependence. While the king at his coronation swore to uphold the church's privileges, the church for its part deferred to his authority in various ways: no capitular election could be held without his permission and a successful candidate had to swear allegiance to him before he could be consecrated; the king was entitled to summon and preside over an assembly of French prelates; he could also intervene in diocesan affairs. But if the relationship between church and state in France was clear, the role of the papacy in that relationship was highly controversial. Did the church in France owe obedience primarily to the king or to the pope? Was the pope free to interfere in its affairs regardless of the king's wishes? These were some of the questions that had been at the root of the great struggle between King Philip IV and Pope Boniface VIII at the end of the thirteenth century. In the bull *Clericis laicos* (1296) Boniface excommunicated any ruler who taxed the clergy without papal permission; Philip retaliated by banning the export of money to Rome. In 1302 Boniface proclaimed in the bull *Unam Sanctam* that obedience to the Holy See was essential to salvation. When the king appealed to a general council of the church, Boniface excommunicated him, releasing his subjects from their allegiance to him. The

---

[6] *Ibid.*, pp. 190–3.
[7] R. A. Jackson, *Vive le Roi! A History of the French Coronation from Charles V to Charles X* (Chapel Hill, NC, 1984), pp. 57–9. I have amended the translation slightly.

pope's successors annulled the sentences passed on Philip, acknowledging that the Holy See had no authority over the king of France and no right to interfere in the government of his kingdom.

This, however, was not the end of the rivalry between the French crown and the papacy. In the late fourteenth century Christendom had to choose between two rival popes. The French church suggested that they should both resign so that another might be elected. When Benedict XIII refused, the king of France suspended his allegiance for five years; in 1407 he issued two ordinances which are commonly regarded as marking the birth of Gallicanism.[8] They pledged royal support for the maintenance of the ancient liberties of the church governing ecclesiastical appointments and forbade payments to the Holy See arising out of interference with beneficial affairs. These principles were affirmed in March 1418 and again in the famous Pragmatic Sanction of Bourges of July 1438.[9] This was a royal edict embodying decisions taken by an assembly of the French church that had met at Bourges under the presidency of King Charles VII after Pope Eugenius IV had broken off relations with the council of Basle. It asserted that a general council of the church was superior in authority to the pope, upheld the decision of the council of Basle that elections to major benefices should be restored, safeguarded the rights of those traditionally authorized to appoint to lesser benefices, severely curtailed the payment of annates to Rome and endorsed the council's disciplinary reforms.

The papacy was deeply offended by the Pragmatic Sanction – 'this thorn driven into the eye of the church' – and during the remainder of the century it continually pressed for its abrogation. The Parlement refused to give way, but Louis XI saw that he could make political capital out of the Sanction. In 1462, he revoked it to gain papal support for his policies in Italy; when the pope failed to satisfy him, he reverted to a Gallican position. Then, in 1472, he signed a Concordat with Sixtus IV, allowing him a half share of appointments to French benefices. Three years later, Louis again fell out with the pope, so the Sanction was reaffirmed by an assembly of the French church. The papacy continued to demand its revocation, and, in December 1512, supporters of the Sanction were summoned before the fifth Lateran council.[10]

In addition to manipulating the Pragmatic Sanction, the French crown put pressure on the Holy See by playing on its fear of a General Council. The doctrine that a council was superior in authority to the pope was an important element in Gallicanism. France was the cradle of conciliarism. It was at the prompting of a French cardinal that the council of Constance had issued the decree *Sacrosancta* to the effect that it derived its authority directly from Christ

[8] V. Martin, *Les origines du Gallicanisme* (1939), vol. i.
[9] N. Valois, *Histoire de la Sanction Pragmatique de Bourges sous Charles VII* (1906).
[10] R. Aubenas and R. Ricard, *L'église et la Renaissance, 1449–1517* (1951), pp. 56–7, 70–2, 78–81.

and that everyone, including the pope, should obey it. Even after the Holy See had triumphed over the conciliar movement, the theory of conciliar supremacy continued to have adherents in France. It was kept alive by a general desire for church reform and by an increase of anti-papal feeling generated by the administrative methods of Sixtus IV. In the fifteenth century 'Gallican France was the real stronghold of the strict conciliar theory and the University of Paris its citadel'.[11] In 1511 Louis XII retaliated against the anti-French policies of Julius II by calling a council. It met at Pisa and suspended the pope, but he cleverly took the wind out of its sails by calling the fifth Lateran council, which received much wider support.[12]

By the sixteenth century, then, Frenchmen were generally opposed to papal interference in the administration of their church. But what of royal interference? In theory, the church was governed according to the Pragmatic Sanction, but it lacked the cohesion necessary to withstand external pressures. Consequently, the electoral freedom of chapters often succumbed to force and bribery. In these circumstances, the crown could easily determine the outcome of elections. Louis XI freely appointed to bishoprics and abbeys from 1471 onwards: if the chapters resisted, he simply imposed his nominees on them. The scope of the *régale* was so enlarged at this time that the king was also able to appoint to many archdeaconries, canonries and prebends.[13]

The election of François d'Estaing to the see of Rodez in November 1501 may be taken as typical of the external pressures suffered by cathedral chapters at this time. D'Estaing was elected by fifteen out of sixteen canons, yet his election was challenged by Charles de Tournon, who had royal and papal backing. Three troubled years ensued during which the chapter appealed to the Parlement against the refusal of the archbishop of Bourges to confirm d'Estaing's election. The king demonstrated his support for Tournon by evoking the case to the *Grand Conseil*. Tournon, meanwhile, gained possession of the see with the backing of troops. It was only after his death in September 1504 that d'Estaing was able to take possession of his see. He had to surrender an abbey to the Tournon clan as the price of the king's grudging consent. A payment of 10,000 *livres* to Italian bankers at Lyons secured the necessary papal bulls of provision.[14]

A demand by the Estates General in 1484 that the Pragmatic Sanction be strictly observed was disregarded; by 1515 royal control of the ecclesiastical

[11] H. Jedin, *A History of the Council of Trent*, tr. E. Graf (London, 1957–61), i. 32.
[12] *Ibid.*, i. 106–12; A. Renaudet, *Le concile Gallican de Pise-Milan* (1922).
[13] Imbart de la Tour, *Les origines de la Réforme* (Melun, 1944), ii. 211; A. Renaudet, *Préréforme et humanisme pendant les premières guerres d' Italie, 1494–1517* (1953), p. 5; G. Loirette, 'La première application à Bordeaux du Concordat de 1516: Gabriel et Charles de Grammont (1529–30)' *A. du M.*, lxviii (1956), 317. For a long list of disputed elections between 1490 and 1510 see Nicole Lemaitre, *Le Rouergue flamboyant: le clergé et les fidèles du diocèse de Rodez, 1417–1563* (1988), p. 222.
[14] *Ibid.*, pp. 217–21.

hierarchy was an acknowledged fact. This is shown by the instructions given to René of Savoy when he was sent to negotiate with the Swiss: 'and if the brother of the said Massimiliano [Sforza] wishes to become a churchman, the king will obtain benefices in his kingdom for him'.[15] In March 1515 Mondot de La Marthonie acknowledged the king's control of church appointments by asking him 'to provide *gens de bien*, of good life and sufficient years, to bishoprics, archbishoprics and prelacies, and likewise good men of religion to the monasteries of his kingdom and dominions'.[16]

Any restriction of papal authority in France was a source of satisfaction to the Parlement of Paris, believing, as it did, that the king should be master in his own house. It was firmly committed to the Pragmatic Sanction and hostile to any ultramontane move by the crown. But Francis I was anxious at the start of his reign to improve his relations with the Holy See. The main objective of his foreign policy was to restore French rule in Milan and Naples. To acquire a permanent foothold south of the Alps, however, he needed papal co-operation. This had been the lesson of recent events: Louis XII had been successful in Italy only as long as he had enjoyed the support of Alexander VI and Julius II; when the latter had turned against him, he had been driven out of the peninsula. The pope was a significant temporal power: he controlled the overland route from the north to Naples, he could rally other powers to aid or hinder a foreign invader, and he could authorize a secular ruler to tax his clergy. Moreover, as suzerain of Naples, he alone could confer its investiture. Thus Francis needed Pope Leo X's friendship for several good reasons. This is what Duprat tried to make the Parlement understand in April 1515 when it was asked to ratify the powers of the papal legate, Canossa: 'It was a question', he explained, 'of gratifying the pope for good reasons and to achieve things of the utmost importance which cannot be disclosed to everyone.'[17] But the Parlement was not interested in the king's foreign ambitions and viewed with suspicion his efforts to draw nearer to Rome. It agreed to ratify Canossa's powers on condition that no harm was done to the Pragmatic Sanction or to the liberties of the French church.[18]

The Holy See, however, wanted not merely acceptance of its legate, but the complete repudiation of the Pragmatic Sanction. On this basis alone would it seriously envisage a political rapprochement with France. By winning the battle of Marignano Francis had strengthened his negotiating position, but he was still not sufficiently secure in Italy to dictate terms to the pope. His hold on Lombardy was precarious: the Swiss were bent on revenge, while the Emperor and the king of England were ready to help them. The threat of a new coalition made it all the more urgent for Francis to neutralize the pope, or, better still,

[15] Barrillon, i. 89.   [16] Renaudet, *Préréforme et humanisme*, p. 578.   [17] *Ibid.*, p. 579.
[18] Doucet, i. 71–2.

win his support. For a long time French kings had put pressure on the Holy See by either manipulating the Pragmatic Sanction or threatening a General Council. Only the first alternative was available to Francis: after the fiasco of Pisa he would only have exposed himself to ridicule by resorting to the conciliar cudgel. So the Pragmatic Sanction had to be revoked, even at the price of causing bitter resentment among his Gallican subjects. As the principle lawcourt, the Parlement of Paris favoured the existing régime, which restricted appeals to Rome, while the University of Paris had a vested interest in a system which reserved a third of vacant benefices to graduates. The king, on the other hand, had little to lose by revoking the Sanction: his effective control of church appointments was unlikely to be reduced by a restoration of papal authority in France.

The Concordat, which was approved by Leo X on 18 August 1516, consisted of three bulls: *Pastor aeternus*, which abolished the Pragmatic Sanction; *Divina providente gratia*, which promulgated the Concordat; and *Primitiva illa ecclesia*, which contained its text.[19] Bishops, abbots and priors, who in the past had been elected by chapters, were henceforth to be nominated by the king and instituted by the pope, though an exception was made of churches that had been given by the papacy the privilege of electing their superiors. Benefices vacated at the curia or which remained vacant beyond a certain time were to be filled by papal, not royal, nomination. It was laid down that nominees to lesser benefices should indicate their real value in their letters of appointment. Ostensibly, this was to check pluralism; in reality, it pointed to the resumption of annates which the Pragmatic Sanction had abolished. The Concordat was ratified by the Lateran council on 19 December, Francis being allowed six months in which to secure its registration by the parlements.

On 5 February 1517 the king came to the Parlement accompanied by high-ranking churchmen, canons of Notre-Dame and university representatives. The purpose of this exceptional meeting was to explain the Concordat. Speaking first, Chancellor Duprat, who could reasonably claim to be its architect, explained that the king had done all in his power to save the Pragmatic Sanction, but papal demands had been too powerful. Had he resisted them, his kingdom would have been placed under an interdict and its enemies would have been given a pretext to invade it and carve it up among themselves. If, on the other hand, he had given way without negotiating, the French church would have fallen under the tyranny of Rome, and the abuses that had been swept away by the council of Constance would have returned. By securing the Concordat, the king had achieved a settlement in the best interest of the kingdom and its universities. Francis intended to submit the Concordat to an assembly of the clergy and notables; it would then be sent to the Parlement for

---

[19] *Ordonnances*, i no. 91.

registration. The king then added a few words of his own. He criticized the court for defying his orders in recent lawsuits and expressed the hope that it would be more compliant in respect of the Concordat. Following a debate, Cardinal de Boisy, speaking for the clergy, asked that the Concordat be examined by an assembly of the Gallican church before it was registered. Francis retorted that, unless the clergy yielded, he would send them to Rome to discuss the Concordat with the pope. He was better pleased with the Parlement's reply, vague as it was, that it would satisfy God and the king.[20]

On 21 March another meeting was held in Paris, this time of representatives of the 'good towns'. It had been called by the king ostensibly to seek advice on how best to enrich the kingdom, but Duprat's speech to the delegates was less concerned with economic matters than with the Concordat. Clearly, the meeting was an attempt to force the Parlement's hand by mobilizing an influential section of public opinion. The Concordat, Duprat explained, was a bilateral convention aimed at preserving the régime of the Pragmatic Sanction. True, capitular elections had been abolished, but only because they had become corrupt; the king hoped eventually to restore them, in a purer form. What the delegates made of all this is not known. They were invited to send proposals in writing after consulting 'the larger and wiser part' of the inhabitants of their respective towns. When these proposals eventually reached Paris they were dropped unopened into a large leather bag and quietly forgotten.[21]

The papal bulls embodying the Concordat reached Paris at the end of April and, on 13 May, Francis ordered its execution, but the Parlement failed to respond. The king accordingly sent Duprat to remind the court of the urgent necessity to register the Concordat, but the court was not given its full text until 5 June.[22] The Parlement then appointed a committee to examine the document. On 21 June, the king ordered the court to register the Concordat forthwith. At the same time, he instructed his uncle, René of Savoy, to sit in on the Parlement's debates. This attempt to intimidate the court provoked an instant reaction. Two *parlementaires*, La Haye and Dorigny, were dispatched to Francis with excuses and a request for the rescinding of the order to René. But the king was in no mood to compromise. Some *parlementaires*, he admitted, were 'worthy men' (*gens de bien*), but others were madmen (*une bande de folz*). He intended, he said, to be obeyed like his predecessors and reminded the delegates that Louis XII, with whom he was sometimes unfairly compared, had banished two *parlementaires* for their disobedience. He was ready to do likewise. René, he insisted, would attend the Parlement's debates; as for the Concordat, it would be registered.[23]

[20] B.N., ms. fr. 10900, fol. 3a–b; Doucet, i. 84–7.   [21] Barrillon, i. 275–83, 302–4.
[22] *Ibid.*, i. 306–7.
[23] A.N., X^{1a} 1519, fols. 205r–206r; Doucet, i. 89–95.

On 13 July, the Parlement allowed René to attend its debates, but, on 24 July, it flatly refused to register the Concordat and proclaimed its loyalty to the Pragmatic Sanction. René was invited to give the king an account of all that had been said, especially concerning the 'great evils and inconveniences' that would flow from the Concordat. The Parlement also offered to send another deputation to Francis with a fuller statement of its views.[24] Though startled by the Parlement's stand, Francis agreed to receive the representatives. Three were promptly chosen, but for various reasons were detained in Paris. An angry reminder from the king, on 22 December, prompted the court to appoint two new delegates, Verjus and de Loynes. They arrived at Amboise on 13 January, and were told that the king was sorely tempted to keep them waiting as long as he had been left in suspense by the Parlement. This, however, would only have delayed further the Concordat's registration. So the two *parlementaires* were asked for a memorandum which the king might study before seeing them. They duly produced a condemnation of the Concordat on three counts: the implicit restoration of annates; the evocation of major ecclesiastical causes to the Roman curia, and the abolition of elections to benefices in favour of nominations.

The memorandum is a well-argued presentation of the case against the Concordat. All benefices, it asserts, will become liable to papal taxation once the elective system has been abolished, and gold and silver will be drained away from the kingdom. The removal of 'major causes' from the local ecclesiastical courts will open the door to large-scale papal interference in the affairs of the Gallican church. The abolition of elections will profit only the Holy See: even if royal nominations to major benefices are allowed, there are enough loopholes in the Concordat to enable the pope to advance his own creatures. He has no right to deprive the French church of its immemorial right of free election, based as it is on Scripture, the decrees of church councils and royal ordinances. The replacement of elections by nominations, far from removing abuses, will facilitate a permanent system of simoniacal annates. Here, the memorandum timidly points to the risk of royal interference in church affairs: a king may easily succumb to pressure from advisers, acting in the interest of friends.

The memorandum also challenges the legality of abolishing the Pragmatic Sanction. *Pastor Aeternus* threatens the king's subjects with confiscation, revokes the Sanction which is a royal ordinance and refers back to *Unam Sanctam* that supreme statement of papal superiority over kings. Abrogating the Sanction must entail the repudiation of the doctrine of conciliar supremacy over the pope. It cannot be valid since the French church has not been formally summoned to appear before the Lateran council; nor can the decisions of one pope override those of the councils of Constance and Basle. Two courses are

[24] A.N., X^{1a} 1519, fol. 222r; Doucet, i. 95–7.

open to the king: he can either persuade the pope to call a General Council or he can himself summon an assembly of the Gallican church. Finally, the memorandum criticizes Duprat's defence of the Concordat. The king, it asserts, has no superior *in temporalibus*; therefore, he does not need to fear that his kingdom will be delivered to his enemies. Should the pope venture on such a course, Francis has enough power to defend himself. The memorandum concludes that the Concordat is 'against the honour of God, the liberties of the church, the king's honour and the public good of his kingdom'.[25]

Francis, after reading the memorandum, asked Duprat to reply and the Chancellor eagerly grasped this opportunity to criticize the Parlement. The gist of his own memorandum is as follows: in difficult times the Parlement always says that everything is badly administered and directed. If its wages are slightly delayed out of sheer necessity, it complains that 'all is going badly and the king's treasury is being robbed'. Opposition to the Concordat is the work of churchmen with a vested interest in the old corrupt system and of men of routine who cannot face a new one. The Concordat would have been registered already if the Parlement had only examined it properly. Its criticisms are childish and its refusal to register the Concordat has struck at the roots of royal authority. The Parlement is trying to imitate the Roman Senate and make the king accountable for his actions. The kingdom, however, is not an aristocracy; it is a monarchy in which decisions are taken by a few and the rest have only to obey. The Parlement's authority derives from the king; having submitted remonstrances, its duty is to obey him once his decision is known. It is nonsense to suggest that Francis has exaggerated the perils facing his kingdom. Although he has tried to save the Pragmatic Sanction, he has been forced to choose between submission and schism; yet he has skilfully managed to persuade the papacy to swallow the substance of the Sanction in the form of a Concordat, the only major difference between them being the abolition of elections. Francis has secured an exemption for privileged churches and still hopes to bring back the old system eventually.

Duprat then takes a closer look at the elective system. The Parlement sees its abolition as in breach of the Gallican liberties; but what, he asks, are those liberties? He for one does not believe they exist. As for the elective system, it has been totally discredited by violent quarrels, legal wrangles, perjury and simony, and the unworthiness of those elected. Such an intolerable régime needs to be replaced by another, better suited to modern conditions. Elections do not have the backing of divine law: they are simply an administrative device which the pope is entitled to change, as he thinks fit. He is not bound to obey conciliar decrees, since his authority is superior; his decision has, in any case, been endorsed by the Lateran council. Leo X has also been generous: instead of

[25] B.N., ms. fr. 10900, fols. 5b–6a; n. ac. 8452, no. 133; Doucet, i. 99–106.

reserving all nominations to himself, he has given most of them to the king, while respecting the privilege of election held by certain churches. Francis will not misuse his right to nominate, as the Parlement has insinuated, nor will he allow the pope to encroach upon it. Benefices will not be left vacant long enough for the pope to intervene and the king will ensure that his nominees are not rejected by the pope on grounds of insufficiency. As for annates, Francis dislikes them as much as the Parlement does. The demand for a statement of the true value of benefices should not be seen as the first step towards their resumption: it is simply intended to facilitate the allocation of benefices.[26] Nor is the present system of ecclesiastical jurisdiction to be changed: the Concordat has, in fact, guaranteed its survival. Whatever its imperfections may be, it is surely better to live in harmony with the pope and the rest of Christendom than schismatically with the Pragmatic Sanction, which the Lateran council has condemned. Finally, Duprat sees no need to call another General Council from which the Sanction could expect no other treatment. As for an assembly of the Gallican church, it has always been the king's intention to call one, but the Concordat ought to be judged by its results; it should, therefore, be registered first by the Parlement.[27]

Duprat's memorandum was intended to provide Francis with a stock of arguments for his meeting with the Parlement's representatives. This took place on 28 February. The king began by asking Verjus and de Loynes if they wished to add anything to their memorandum. They asked to see Duprat's reply, but Francis refused. When they insisted, he vehemently attacked the Parlement. It had taken a hundred men seven months, he said, to prepare a document which his Chancellor had taken just a few days to answer. There would be only one king of France, and what had been done in Italy would not be undone in France; he would see to it that no Venetian senate was set up in his kingdom. He advised the Parlement to put its own house in order. Justice, he complained, was still as badly administered as it had been a hundred years before, and he threatened to make the Parlement 'trot after him like those of the *Grand Conseil*'. Finally, he criticized the Parlement's recruitment of new members. As the two delegates attempted to reply, Francis dismissed them: 'Go!', he said, 'Go tomorrow without fail.' After returning to their lodgings, Verjus and de Loynes were ordered to hasten their departure. They begged for a delay as the river Loire was in flood, but were warned that, if they had not left by 6 am next morning, they would be thrown into a pit and left there for six months.[28]

On 6 March 1518, six days before Verjus and de Loynes reported back to the

[26] Annates were specifically mentioned in a bull of 1 October 1516, which Francis submitted to the Parlement after the Concordat had been registered, thereby giving the lie to Duprat's statement. Doucet, i. 133.
[27] A.N., J. 942; Doucet, i. 106–15.   [28] B.N., ms. fr. 10900, fols. 6a–7b.

Parlement, Francis sent his chamberlain, La Trémoïlle, to the court. He demanded immediate registration of the Concordat under threat of certain secret measures; it was rumoured that he planned to set up a new parlement at Orléans.[29] This had the desired effect. On 7 March, the *avocat général* Le Lièvre advised the court to waive its opposition to the Concordat on two conditions: first, the words *de expresso mandato regis iteratis vicibus facto* must be added to the formula of registration as evidence of duress; secondly, it must be made plain that publication of the Concordat did not entail abrogating the Pragmatic Sanction. Although this amounted, in effect, to a total surrender, the Parlement decided to accept Le Lièvre's advice, albeit with modifications. On 18 March, it stipulated that publication of the Concordat should take the form of a royal ordinance in the presence of an important person nominated by the king. It also decided to continue judging cases in accordance with the Pragmatic Sanction. La Trémoïlle, however, insisted on immediate compliance with the king's request and again uttered vague threats. The Parlement, seeing the risk involved in further resistance, at last decided to publish the Concordat. At the same time, it secretly repudiated its responsibility for this act and affirmed its determination to abide by the Pragmatic Sanction in judging future beneficial lawsuits. The Concordat was registered on 22 March with the formula indicating duress. Two days later, the Parlement disclaimed responsibility in a second secret protestation.[30]

No sooner had the Parlement given way than the university and clergy of Paris began to agitate against the Concordat. The university was determined to uphold the Gallican principles enunciated by its teachers in the past as well as the reforms they had carried through. Despite an assurance to the contrary by the Parlement's First President, the doctors of the university feared that benefices would henceforth fall to rich courtiers rather than poor students. On 27 March, they drew up an appeal to a future General Council, rejecting the Concordat on three grounds: it had been devised by an unauthorized body; it had cancelled decisions taken by earlier church councils; and it had been published without the consent of the university and other interested parties. The appeal, which was printed and widely circulated, blamed papal greed, not the king's policy, for the Concordat. At the same time, a document, attacking the Concordat, was distributed to preachers as fuel for their Lenten sermons, posters to the same effect being put up in colleges and public places. Meanwhile, on 22 March a deputation of Parisian clergy, led by the dean of Notre-Dame went to the Parlement. It asked to see the text of the Concordat and for an assembly of the Gallican church to be called. Unless these demands were met, the clergy threatened to oppose execution of the Concordat.

[29] Barrillon, ii. 79–80.
[30] A.N., X^{1a} 1520, fols. 116–18, 120, 122, 126; B.N., ms. fr. 10900, fols. 7b–12a; Doucet, i. 118–23.

On 4 April, Francis ordered the Parlement to have the Concordat printed and to enquire into disturbances at the university. He complained of 'evil and dangerous persons who cause others to do what they themselves do not dare to do openly' and threatened to act 'in a way that would be for ever more remembered'. On 12 April, he appointed two commissioners to investigate the university. This led to trouble among the students and the Parlement ordered twelve college principals to keep better discipline. It declined, however, to register a royal edict which threatened to banish the university and suspend its privileges if it continued to meddle in state affairs. During the summer several people associated with the university's appeal to a General Council were arrested, but they were soon released and the case against them dropped. Having obtained what he wanted, Francis presumably decided not to stir up further Gallican opposition by making a martyr of the university.[31]

What was the long-term significance of the Concordat? Historians have argued that it destroyed the independence of the Gallican church and conferred so many advantages on the king of France that he was never tempted to break with Rome.[32] This claim cannot be accepted without some reservations. First, the king's effective control of ecclesiastical appointments in France was, as we have seen, considerable even before the Concordat. What this agreement achieved was an increase of royal control by giving the king the *right* to appoint to major benefices, whereas previously he had acted in defiance of the Pragmatic Sanction. Secondly, some important churches in France were allowed to continue electing their superiors.[33] They lost this privilege only in 1531 as a result of a new agreement between the king and Pope Clement VII. Thirdly, the Concordat included a number of safeguards against the abuse of royal power. The pope reserved to himself the right to set aside any royal nominee whose qualifications fell short of the canonical requirements.

The Concordat did not produce any marked change in the character of the French episcopate, which continued to be recruited mainly from the nobility, especially the nobility of the sword. Having been closely associated with the latter since childhood, Francis recruited most of his friends and advisers from it, and by exercising his rights of patronage in its favour he hoped to ensure its loyal support both at home and abroad. In 1516, out of 102 bishops, sixty were

[31] *Ibid*, i. 125–39; C.-E. du Boulay, *Historia Universitatis Parisiensis* (1665–73), vi. 88–92; Barrillon, ii. 79–84; *C.A.F.*, i. 814; v. 16782.

[32] 'The French monarchy was fated to remain Catholic. What had it to gain from going Reformist? In the all-important business of appointing to bishoprics and wealthy abbeys, the king of France, under the Concordat of 1516, was as much Head of the Church as Henry VIII of England.' J. E. Neale, *The Age of Catherine de' Medici* (London, 1943), pp. 14–15.

[33] This privilege was sometimes disregarded by the king. Thus, when the chapter of Troyes tried to hold an election in November 1518 on the strength of it, Francis compelled it to accept his nominee. Also in 1518 Jean de Magdeleine, abbot-elect of Cluny, was ousted by Aymar Gouffier, the king's protégé. J. Thomas, *Le Concordat de 1516; ses origines, son histoire au XVIe siècle* (1910), ii. 349ff; iii. 105–6; !mbart de la Tour, ii. 479–80.

drawn from the old nobility, and fourteen from recently ennobled families. Only four were commoners and sixteen were foreigners, most of them Italians. Only thirty-eight held sees in their native provinces, while the most important benefices were given to members of leading noble families in the king's entourage or to major office-holders and financiers (e.g. Briçonnet, Duprat). These trends are confirmed by 243 nominations made between 1516 and 1559. A sharp rise in the number of Italians appointed (about 20 per cent of nominations) points to the king's policy of creating a clientèle beyond the Alps. The few commoners appointed owed their sees to their reputation as humanists.[34]

Royal control of episcopal appointments did not eradicate abuses; in fact, it may have made them worse. Pluralism and absenteeism continued to flourish among some of the highest-ranking prelates. Thus under Francis I, fifty sees passed through the hands of only eight prelates. The richest pluralist was Jean de Lorraine who had nine sees and six abbeys. He was closely followed by Louis and Charles de Bourbon-Vendôme who held seven sees and numerous abbeys. The most flagrant pluralists, however, were Italian cardinals. Ippolito d'Este, for example, in 1550 was archbishop of Lyons, Arles and Narbonne and bishop of Autun and Tréguier. He also held the sees of Milan and Ferrara in Italy. Service to the crown, notably as diplomats, was the main criterion for royal nomination.[35] Consequently, many bishops (e.g. Jean du Bellay, bishop of Paris from 1532 to 1551) were almost permanently at court or abroad. Others were expected mainly to represent the king's interests in the provinces where their sees were located; evangelization was almost the last of their concerns. After taking possession of their sees, they leased the revenues to the highest bidder. Some were never ordained. They would appoint a vicar-general, who was invariably a lawyer recruited from the bishop's staff or the cathedral chapter, and he would delegate the bishop's pontifical duties (e.g. ordinations and confirmations) to a suffragan bishop, usually a regular with a degree in theology. Not all the suffragans were good preachers or pastors; some multiplied ordinations indiscriminately to augment their income.

However, Francis I's episcopal nominees were not universally unworthy. Augustin Grimaldi, bishop of Grasse, earned high praise in 1517 on account of his saintliness. Several bishops (e.g. François d'Estaing at Rodez, Guillaume Petit and Odard Hennequin at Troyes, Etienne Poncher at Paris and later at

---

[34] J. Le Goff and R. Rémond, *Histoire de la France religieuse*, vol. II, p. 188. The figures are those of M. Péronnet. But see also Marilyn M. Edelstein, 'The Social Origins of Episcopacy in the reign of Francis I' in *F.H.S.*, viii (1974), 377–92. She provides slightly different figures: 123 bishops out of 129 Frenchmen whose origins are identifiable were nobles and six were commoners. The nobles comprised nine princes of the blood, ninety-three nobles of the sword, and twenty-one nobles of the robe. At least twenty-three of the foreigners were nobles. Edelstein thinks the robe lost ground under Francis because of royal mistrust arising out of many instances of corruption in the royal administration.

[35] M. Edelstein, 'The Social Origins of the Episcopacy', pp. 381–2.

Sens, Artus Fillon at Senlis and Guillaume Briçonnet at Meaux) were notable for their zeal, piety and learning. The next generation of bishops (1530–50) also included some very worthy men, such as Pierre Palmerio, archbishop of Vienne (1528–54) or Antoine Filhol, archbishop of Aix (1533–50). Synods were frequently held between 1516 and 1559 and the statutes of 60 out of 112 dioceses were published at this time. In many dioceses, revised editions of missals, breviaries and other liturgical books were printed. Episcopal visitations were also probably more numerous than the surviving records indicate. A most conscientious visitation was carried out by François d'Estaing in the diocese of Rodez in 1524: it lasted from 4 May till 14 November and covered 282 centres of worship.[36]

The qualifications imposed on the king's episcopal nominees were the same as under the Pragmatic Sanction. A bishop, for example, had to be at least twenty-seven years of age, a doctor or licentiate in canon or civil law or a master or licentiate in theology. However, in the first draft of the Concordat the king exempted princes of the blood from these requirements, and the final text expanded the exemption from the educational requirements to members of 'great families'. Several of Francis I's nominees were below the canonical age. For example, Martin Fournier became archbishop at Tours at twenty-three, Louis de Husson bishop of Poitiers at eighteen, Gabriel le Veneur bishop of Evreux at fourteen and Charles de Guise archbishop of Rheims at nine. Nor was Francis particularly concerned about the educational qualifications of his nominees. Royal service by the nominee or a member of his family was far more important, it seems. Thus Thomas Duprat became a bishop because of the services given to the king by his brother, the Chancellor. Charles de Villiers was appointed to Limoges because he belonged to a 'great and noble house' that had served the crown well.[37] Such cases do not reflect on the Concordat, only on the strictness of its enforcement.

It is not difficult to see why the papacy connived at this state of affairs. While the Concordat undoubtedly strengthened the king's authority by legalizing and extending the scope of his ecclesiastical patronage, it was also a triumph for the papacy. The authority of the Holy See which had been so drastically undermined by the Pragmatic Sanction, was now restored to its full splendour. Conciliarism had been overthrown, and, in theory at least, the papacy once more held sway over the French church. The 'thorn' had been removed from the 'eye of the church'; annates and appeals could now reach Rome unimpeded. The Concordat, in short, was not just a feather in the king's cap; it was also a jewel returned to the papal tiara. Having gained so much from it, the pope would have been foolish to quibble over details of its applica-

[36] Le Goff and Rémond, ii. 190–3; N. Lemaitre, *Le Rouergue flamboyant*, pp. 238–40. See below, p. 155.
[37] M. Edelstein, 'The Social Origins of the Episcopacy', pp. 379, 381–2; Thomas, iii. 184–5, 204.

tion. Francis, for his part, was never inclined to repudiate it, although he did not gain as much papal support for his policies in Italy as he had hoped. Had he done so, he would have incurred the ridicule of the Gallicans and forsaken the domestic advantages he had gained from the agreement. Even if the bargain struck with the pope did not quite live up to his political expectations, it was none the less worth keeping.

The new Constantine

Leo X's parting gift to Francis at Bologna in December 1515 was a superb reliquary valued at 15,000 ducats. Shaped like a cross and containing a piece of the True Cross, it was clearly intended to remind the king of his mission to lead a crusade. Yet Francis, it seems, needed no reminder: he told the pope that a crusade had been in his heart since childhood. One of his reasons for treating with the Swiss on the eve of Marignano had been 'in order to use their men in the war which he proposes to unleash soon against the Infidels'. But the pope continued to issue reminders. Two seals, made specially for the Concordat, carried an image of the cross and the three nails along with the motto: *In hoc signo vinces* (You will vanquish by this sign). This recalled a vision seen by the Emperor Constantine on the eve of his victory over Maxentius and of his conversion to Christianity. The cross and the motto provided the leitmotiv for the crusade that was preached in France in 1517 and 1518.[38]

The absolution for the crusade given by Leo to France was published in Paris on 4 January 1517.[39] It was valid for two years during which all other absolutions and indulgences were suspended. To qualify for absolution a contributor had to give, after confession, the equivalent of what he and his family normally spent over three days. The money was to be used 'to go against the Turks'. On 16 December 1516 Francis I appointed Josse de La Garde, commissioner for the crusade in the diocese of Toulouse. He was instructed to set up a tall cross bearing the motto *In hoc signo vinces* alongside the collection box and also to prepare a banner showing the meeting between the pope and the king. Thus did Francis usurp the place traditionally filled by the emperor. This was evidently encouraged by the pope, for whom a *Coronation of Charlemagne* was painted by associates of Raphael in the Vatican palace. This shows Leo III in the likeness of Leo X and Charlemagne in that of Francis.

The moneys collected in France for the crusade did not amount to much. In March 1518 it was preached in Rome, solemn processions were held to invoke divine assistance against the Turks, and legates left for various courts, including France, to hasten preparations. These efforts, however, were all in vain. A crusade was no longer feasible within the politico-religious context of early

[38] A.-M. Lecoq, *François Ier imaginaire*, pp. 261–5.   [39] *J.B.P.*, p. 43.

sixteenth-century Europe. It may have been used by Francis to stake a claim to the Empire or merely as a fiscal expedient. His only contribution, in fact, was to assist the Knights of St John who were being besieged in Rhodes. In 1518 he sent them a kind of exploratory mission and in 1520 a small fleet which was fairly successful. However, the outbreak of war with Charles V in 1521 forced Francis to abandon Rhodes to its fate. Thereafter the crusader of 1517 became, as we shall see, the ally of the Turks.

Yet if the crusade never took place, it was the subject of a significant literary output in which Francis was portrayed as the 'new Constantine'. In 1518, for example, Jean Thenaud dedicated the second volume of his *Triumphes de Vertuz* to 'Francis, the very great and very good, king of France, future Emperor and destroyer of the Turkish empire, invincible'. The designers of royal entries frequently alluded to the crusade. Thus at Rouen in August 1517 Jupiter, dressed to look like Francis, was shown hurling his thunderbolt at the Giants. 'For the giants', a contemporary explains, 'one should understand the Turks and Infidels, or whichever enemies of the king, etc.'[40]

[40] A.-M. Lecoq, *François ler imaginaire*, pp. 265–71.

Chapter six

The king and his court

The King and his family

What kind of a man was Francis I? The English chronicler, Edward Hall, describes him as 'a goodly prince, stately of countenance, merry of chere, brown coloured, great eyes, high nosed, big lipped, fair breasted and shoulders, small legs and long feet'.[1] Less succinct, but equally vivid, is a description by Ellis Griffith, a Welshman in Henry VIII's service, who saw the king at the Field of Cloth of Gold. Francis, he writes, was six feet tall. His head was rightly proportioned for his height, the nape of his neck unusually broad, his hair brown, smooth and neatly combed, his beard of three months' growth darker in colour, his nose long, his eyes hazel and bloodshot, and his complexion the colour of watery milk. He had muscular buttocks and thighs, but his legs below the knees were thin and bandy, while his feet were long, slender and completely flat. He had an agreeable voice and, in conversation, an animated expression, marred only by the unfortunate habit of continually rolling his eyes upwards.[2] Antonio De Beatis, who visited the French court in August 1517, described Francis as follows: 'The King is very tall, well featured and has a pleasant disposition, cheerful and most engaging, though he has a large nose and in the opinion of many, including Monsignor, his legs are too thin for so big a body.'[3]

A number of early portraits of Francis bear out these descriptions. One at Chantilly shows him wearing a black cap, wide-necked shirt, slashed doublet and fur-trimmed cape. His oval face is framed by neatly combed chestnut hair, reaching down to the nape of his neck; the eyebrows are thin and the eyes hazel, almond-shaped and widely spaced; the nose is long, the mouth large

---

[1] E. Hall, *Henry VIII*, ed. C. Whibley (London, 1904), i. 200.
[2] P. Morgan, 'Un chroniqueur gallois à Calais', *Revue du Nord*, xlvii (1965), 199.
[3] *The Travel Journal of Antonio De Beatis*, ed. J. R. Hale (London, 1979), p. 108.

23. An anonymous portrait of Francis I about the time of his accession.

with full lips and the chin well-defined beneath a nascent beard. A drawing at St Petersburg clearly shows Francis's cleft chin. In the well-known half-length portrait attributed to Jean Clouet, the king is shown with a full growth of beard. His fondness for fine clothes finds expression in his suit of silk with gold embroidery and his black velvet hat with a white plume and jewels[4] (see p. 288).

Contemporaries often remarked on Francis's eloquence and charm of manner, but it seems that he was shy. 'If a man speak not to him first', wrote Sir Thomas Cheyney, 'he will not likely begin to speak to him, but when he is once entered, he is as good a man to speak to as ever I saw.'[5] There were few things he enjoyed more than a good conversation: he would talk easily on almost any subject though his knowledge was sometimes superficial; it was the form rather than the content of what he said that impressed listeners. Francis could also write well. His letters to his mother during his first Italian campaign are spontaneous and vivid; some of his poems have an emotive sincerity rare in French poetry of the early sixteenth century. The king's poetry is a subject of great complexity.[6] Many poems attributed to him are now known to have been composed by other contemporary poets. Altogether it seems that 205 poems (including *rondeaux*, *ballades*, *épîtres*, *épitaphes* and many shorter poems) can be safely attributed to him. None survives in his own hand or is dated, but most seem to date from before 1535. No collection of Francis's poems was published in his life-time or for 300 years afterwards. A number of them were set to music in his day, mainly by composers in the royal service, such as Sermisy, Janequin and Sandrin.[7]

Francis was, first and foremost, a man of action, who was happiest, it seems, when riding to hounds, tilting in a joust or performing in a masque. No joyful occasion at court was complete without such entertainments. Mock battles, reminiscent of those fought by him and his friends as children, continued to be a favourite pastime. A most elaborate one took place at Amboise in April 1518, when 600 men, led by the king and the duc d'Alençon, defended a model town, complete with moat and gun battery, against an equal number, led by the dukes of Bourbon and Vendôme. 'It was the finest battle ever seen', wrote Florange, 'and the nearest to real warfare, but the entertainment did not please everyone, for some were killed and others frightened.' At Marseilles, in January 1516, Francis threw himself with gusto into a battle of oranges staged for his entertainment. In the words of a local chronicler: 'This prince, who had so much ardour for real combats, wanted also to be a party to this one; having

---

[4] P. Mellen, *Jean Clouet* (London, 1971), pp. 49–50. This portrait was probably painted about 1530. François Clouet may have had a hand in it, since the treatment of the bust and clothing is more advanced pictorially than is consistent with the apparent age of the sitter. The only other large-scale portrait of the king is by Joos van Cleve, who was invited to the court in 1529–30. It is in the Museum of Art, Philadelphia. C. Scailliérez, *François Ier et ses artistes* (1992), pp. 42–3.
[5] *L.P.*, iii. 2050.   [6] *François Ier: Oeuvres poétiques*, ed. J. E. Kane (Geneva, 1984).
[7] See below pp. 458–61.

24. Francis I. An anonymous chalk drawing dating from about 1516.

seized a large shield, he began to shoot and scored many fine hits, having received a few himself to his head and body.'[8] Another mock siege, held at Romorantin in January 1521, almost brought the reign to an untimely end. A party of courtiers, led by the king, attacked a house occupied by the comte de Saint-Pol and friends. As Francis tried to force open the main door, one of the defenders dropped a smouldering log on his head from an upstairs window. The king was knocked senseless, and for several days his life was at risk.[9] Francis loved to show off his physical strength, as is confirmed in a letter by a Mantuan observer. The king was showing Federico Gonzaga over the château of Blois: to reach the gardens, they needed to enter a gallery. As the key was not readily available, Francis hurled himself twice against the door, breaking it open. Further on, the scene was almost repeated. 'He then wished to show him [Federico] the library, but the key-holder could not be found, so he wanted to break down the door; Monsignor told him that he would see it the next day, urging and begging him not to give himself so much trouble. His Majesty calmed down and replied that in any event he would show it to him in the morning before his departure.' Soon afterwards, at a late hour of the night, Francis led Federico to the rooms where the queen's ladies slept and threatened to break down the doors unless they opened them promptly.[10]

Francis's love of violent sport made him particularly accident-prone: in Septgember 1519, he was almost blinded when he struck a branch while hunting near Blois; in February 1523, he suffered a dangerous injury below the knee after being thrown from his horse. On 18 February, Sir Richard Wingfield, writing to Wolsey, reported that Francis had regained consciousness after being in a coma for two days, but he was paralysed on one side 'in so much that, as touching his own person, either in wit or activity for the war, he is not like to do any great feat'.[11]

Hunting was the chief pastime of the French aristocracy when it was not engaged in war. It was seen as the perfect antidote to idleness and sinning. Man's senses were kept in tune by studying the ways of wild animals and out-witting them. Hunting enabled him to maintain a range of mental and physical skills that he might soon need in battle. The hunt was also a jolly social occa-sion; it provided a setting for amorous dalliance and was a rich source of erotic imagery used in tapestries and murals of the period.[12] Hunting was mainly of

---

[8] Florange, i. 225–6; E. Baux, V.-L. Bourrilly and P. Mabilly, 'Le voyage des reines et de François Ier en Provence et dans la vallée du Rhône (décembre 1515–février 1516), *A.du M.*, vol. 16 (1904), pp. 51. See the account by S. Gadio of the mock battle at Amboise in May 1518 in E. Solmi, 'Documenti inediti sulla dimora di Leonardo da Vinci in Francia nel 1517 e 1518' in *Archivio Storico Lombardo*, IV, ser.ii (1904), pp. 398–407.

[9] Barrillon, ii. 179; Michaud et Poujoulat, v. 92.

[10] M. H. Smith, 'François Ier, l'Italie et le château de Blois', *Bulletin monumental*, vol. 147 (1989), pp. 310–11.

[11] Michaud et Poujoulat, v. 9; *L.P.*, iii. 2833, 2846.

[12] J. Cummins, *The Hound and the Hawk: The Art of Medieval Hunting* (London, 1988), pp. 1–11.

25. Francis I hunting a stag in the forest of Fontainebleau. Miniature by Godefroy le Batave from vol. II of the *Commentaires de la guerre gallique* (B.N. ms. fr. 13429, f. 1). The king is accompanied by his favourite huntsman, Perot.

two kinds: with hounds (*vénerie*) or with birds of prey (*fauconnerie*), both forms being represented in the organization of the court. Whereas Louis XII had favoured hawking, Francis preferred hunting with hounds.[13] Hawking was like a single combat between a bird and its prey; while hunting with hounds resembled a full-scale battle. The huntsmen guided and encouraged the hounds, interpreting their cries.[14] A contemporary miniature shows Francis chasing a stag, surrounded by his pack of hounds. He is accompanied by a huntsman, labelled Perot, who is blowing his horn.[15]

In April 1520 Sir Richard Wingfield sent Henry VIII the following account of a boar hunt at the French court:

> soon after three o'clock the said afternoon, he [Francis] went to hunt for the wild boar, and caused me to go with him, which boar was killed after such manner as here follows. When he came to the place in which the boar lay, there was cast off one hound only to him, the which incontinently had him at the bay, and then immediately was thrown off upon a twenty couple of hounds, with three or four brace of mastiffs let slip, all which drew to the bay, and there plucked down the poor boar, and the king, with divers others, being afoot, with their boar spears had dispatched him shortly; and then the king himself, after their fashion, cut off the right foot of the said boar, which done he mounted to horseback, and passed through the forest to have seen a flight to the heron, at the request of M. de Lautrec, unto which disport I assure Your Grace he has no more affection than Your Highness has. Notwithstanding, the said Seigneur de Lautrec with divers others, do what they can possible to fashion one appetite to be in him, which shall be hard for them to bring about, after my conceit.[16]

The appetite, it seems, had been fashioned by 1539 when the bishop of Saluzzo wrote:

> Here one thinks only of hunting. When one comes across one of these lodgings (*gîtes*) one stays there as long as there are herons and kites in the area. Numerous as they are, they do not last long as the king and the great courtiers have more than five hundred falcons between them ... One then hunts the stag twice [in a day], sometimes more often; and with nets once; then one moves on to another lodging.[17]

Francis well deserved the title of 'père des veneurs' given to him in a treatise of 1561.[18] 'He is very fond of the chase', wrote De Beatis, 'especially of hunting stag with the spear.'[19] In 1521, Francis spoke frequently of hunting to Fitzwilliam, the English ambassador, and showed him the French way of hunting deer.

[13] G. Zeller, *Les institutions de la France au XVIe siècle* (1948), p. 103.
[14] J. Cummins, *The Hound and the Hawk*, p. 9.
[15] B.N. ms. fr. 13429. 'Perot' is identifiable with Perrot de Ruthie to whom Francis gave 20,000 *livres* towards his marriage in April 1533. See C.A.F., ii. 5676, p. 382.
[16] St.P., vi. no. 27, pp. 57–8. I have modernized the spelling. See also below p. 249.
[17] A. Desjardins, *Négociations diplomatiques de la France avec la Toscane* (1859–75), iii. 16.
[18] M. Devèze, *La vie de la forêt française au XVIe siècle* (1961), ii. 57n.
[19] *Travel Journal of Ant. De Beatis*, p. 108.

'I assure your Grace', Fitzwilliam wrote to Henry VIII, 'they know their deer right well, as well by his view, feeding, and feumyshing, as also by such other tokens as a woodman should have.' On 21 February, the king spoke to the ambassador for a good hour about hunting. He promised to send Henry some wild boar each year, and advised him to empark them in the thickest ground he could find and leave them there to breed.[20] Francis extended the practice of trapping game with large nets. He also raised the number of huntsmen attached to his court. They began to specialize, some being assigned to the greyhounds, others to the white dogs and so on.[21]

In hunting, as in war, Francis showed great physical courage. At Amboise in June 1515 he was dissuaded from fighting a duel with a wild boar only by the combined entreaties of his queen and mother. The boar was pitted against dummies in the courtyard of the château, all exits having been blocked; but the boar, after tearing the dummies to pieces, battered its way up a staircase leading to a loggia where the king and the courtiers had gathered to watch the sport. As panic seized the spectators, Francis faced the boar with as much composure 'as if he had seen a damsel coming towards him'. He pierced it with his sword, whereupon the boar staggered down another staircase and dropped dead in the courtyard.[22]

As is well known, Francis was a great womanizer. Some of the stories that have been told about him are hard to swallow. For example, it has been alleged that he had a mistress at the age of ten, that his relations with his sister were incestuous, and that he built Chambord to be near one of his mistresses. Some of these tales can be traced to late sixteenth-century works by authors associated with the house of Bourbon, who wanted to blacken the king's reputation.[23] Yet Francis was undoubtedly a libertine. He was reputed to be such by contemporaries and may have contracted syphilis as early as August 1524, when he was said to be 'sick of his own French disease'.[24] About the time of his accession he was having an affair with the wife of Jacques Disomme, a prominent Parisian barrister; Mary Tudor also complained that Francis had been 'importunate with her in divers matters not to her honour'.[25] The letters which

---

[20] L.P., iii. 1160, 1176.   [21] Zeller, *Institutions*, p. 103. See below, p. 123.

[22] We owe this story to Pierre Sala, a former servant of Charles VIII and Louis XII, who was also well-versed in tales of chivalry. It is in his *Les prouesses de plusieurs roys* (BN, ms. fr. 10420 ff. 140v–143v). The encounter enabled Francis to demonstrate his *virtus* and doubtless served as a good augury for his Italian expedition. See A.-M. Lecoq, *François Ier imaginaire* (1987), pp. 207–11; P. Paris, *Etudes sur François Premier* (1885), i. 44–7.

[23] For a list of these stories and an attempted refutation of them, see Paris, i. 4–25. The legend of Francis's incestuous love for his sister originated in the eighteenth century and received support in the nineteenth from F. Génin, who misinterpreted one of Marguerite's letters, and from Jules Michelet. For its repudiation, see P. Jourda, *Marguerite d'Angoulême* (1930), i. 63–4. See also below, p. 557.

[24] L.P., iv. 606.

[25] With reference to Madame Disomme, there is an interesting correlation between a story told by Marguerite d'Angoulême in the *Heptaméron* (ed. M. François (1942), pp. 203–6) and an entry in

the young Federico Gonzaga or his secretary, Gadio, wrote to the marquis of Mantua and his wife from the French court in 1516 and 1517 suggest that the king's morals were far from irreproachable. Federico, who became a notorious libertine himself, may well have picked up some of his habits during his years at Francis's court.[26]

Three women were pre-eminent at court during the first half of Francis's reign: his mother, sister and wife. Louise of Savoy, being only in her forties and a widow, free from the normal domestic commitments of a wife, was able to devote herself entirely to her son's service. She was given a powerful voice in government and served as regent twice, in 1515 and 1524, when Francis led his armies into Italy.[27] De Beatis described her as 'an unusually tall woman, still finely complexioned, very rubicund and lively and seems to me to be about forty years old but more than good, one could say, for at least another ten. She always accompanies her son and the Queen and plays the governess without restraint.'[28] Louise's influence, particularly on foreign affairs, was considerable. Wolsey referred to her as 'the mother and nourisher of peace'.[29] In October 1521, the English ambassador advised the cardinal to write to Louise in the hope that she might persuade her son to accept a truce. 'I have seen in divers things since I came hither', he wrote, 'that when the French king would stick at some points, and speak very great words, yet my Lady would qualify the matter; and sometimes when the king is not contented he will say nay, and then my Lady must require him, and at her request he will be contented; for he is so obeissant to her that he will refuse nothing that she requireth him to do, and if it had not been for her he would have done wonders.'[30]

The king's sister, Marguerite, was intelligent, vivacious and physically quite attractive. As a child, Louis XII tried to marry her off to Arthur Prince of Wales, then to his brother, the future Henry VIII. But their father, Henry VII, was not interested in such a match, since Marguerite's brother could not be certain of succeeding to the French throne. Later he changed his mind and asked for Marguerite's hand for his younger son, then for himself. This time, it was Louis who was not interested, while Marguerite said that she hoped to find a husband without crossing the sea. On 2 December 1509 she married Charles,

---

J.B.P., pp. 14–15. For a discussion of this, see Jourda, ii. 778–9. On Mary Tudor, see A. F. Pollard, *Henry VIII* (London, 1913), p. 81.

[26] A large number of letters written from the court of France in 1516–17 by Federico Gonzaga and his servants, Stazio Gadio, Giovan Francesco Grossi and Gian Stefano Rozone survive in the Archivio di Stato, in Mantua. They have been recently transcribed and edited by Raffaele Tamalio to whom I am indebted for this information. His 'Federico Gonzaga alla corte di Francesco I di Francia nel carteggio privato con Mantova (1515–1517)' will soon be published. See also M. H. Smith, 'François Ier, l'Italie et le château de Blois' in *Bulletin monumental*, 147 (1989), 307–23.

[27] G. Jacqueton, *La politique extérieure de Louise de Savoie* (1892), pp. 3–10.

[28] *Travel Journal of Ant. De Beatis*, pp. 107–8.

[29] J. J. Scarisbrick, *Henry VIII* (London, 1968), p. 92; *L.P.*, iii. 1696.   [30] *L.P.*, iii. 1651.

duc d'Alençon, but it seems that she did not find happiness.[31] The marriage proved childless, and Marguerite began to devote herself to pious meditation and good works.[32] In June 1521 she sought the spiritual guidance of Guillaume Briçonnet, bishop of Meaux, a leading reformer within the church; she corresponded with him regularly for three years and through his teaching became acquainted with the ideas of Jacques Lefèvre d'Etaples.[33] She also began writing religious poems, which Simon du Bois published in 1531. In July 1526, Pierre Toussain, a young evangelical scholar, described Marguerite as 'so well instructed in the Lord, so well schooled in Holy Scripture, that she cannot be torn away from Christ'.[34] Even after her marriage, Marguerite was often at court. She shared her mother's interest in foreign affairs and was frequently mentioned by foreign ambassadors in their dispatches. In January 1527, less than two years after Alençon's death, she married Henri d'Albret, king of Navarre, and her court at Nérac became a place of refuge for evangelical reformers fleeing from persecution in France.[35]

As for Queen Claude, she was renowned for her sweet, charitable and pious nature. 'The Queen is young', wrote De Beatis, 'and though small in stature, plain and badly lame in both hips, is said to be very cultivated, generous and pious.' Despite his philandering, Francis appears to have been genuinely fond of her. 'It is a matter of common report', wrote De Beatis, 'that he holds his wife the Queen in such honour and respect that when in France and with her he has never failed to sleep with her each night.'[36] If Claude's looks fell short of his ideal, she gave him no cause to complain on other grounds: over a period of nine years she bore him no fewer than three sons and four daughters. Such intensive childbearing naturally precluded her from any active share in public life, yet she was allowed one brief moment of glory: her coronation at Saint-Denis on 10 May 1517 and her entry into Paris, two days later, were comparable in magnificence to the king's.[37] Claude died at Blois on 26 July 1524 after a brief illness. The king, who was absent at the time, was deeply affected: 'If I

---

[31] Jourda, i. 12–16, 31–2.

[32] L. Febvre, *Autour de l'Heptaméron: amour sacré, amour profane* (1944), p. 33.

[33] The correspondence, comprising 123 letters (59 from Marguerite) is in B.N., ms. fr. 11495. See G. Briçonnet and Marguerite d'Angoulême, *Correspondance (1521–24)*, ed. C. Martineau and M. Veissière, 2 vols. (Geneva, 1975–79). Also M. Veissière, *L'évêque Guillaume Briçonnet (1470–1534)* (Provins, 1986), pp. 187–96. Marguerite may also have been influenced by Savonarola's teaching through the French activities of Battista della Palla. On this see Polizzotto, L. and C. Elam, 'La unione de' gigli con gigli', *Rinascimento* (1991), 239–59.

[34] P. E. Hughes, *Lefèvre: pioneer of ecclesiastical renewal in France* (Grand Rapids, MI, 1984), p. 174.

[35] *Ibid.*, pp. 179–80.   [36] *Travel Journal of Ant De Beatis*, p. 107.

[37] The street theatricals for Claude's entry were prepared by Pierre Gringore, who, as *historien et facteur* had a kind of monopoly of this kind of ceremony. He had also planned Francis's entry in 1515. Two illuminated manuscripts (B.N. mss. fr. 5750 and 14116) relate to Claude's entry. 'The connecting link between all the stages was the theme of mutual love and the union of hearts: between the king and queen, between the royal couple and God, between the French people and their queen and between Christian princes.' The entry was also used by the Parisians to remind the king of the ideal of a popular and 'paternal' monarchy. Lecoq, *François Ier imaginaire*, pp. 377–91.

26. Françoise de Foix, dame de Châteaubriant, the first official mistress of Francis I. Drawing by Jean Clouet. Evidence recently come to light shows that she was already prominent at court in 1516 and noted for her elegance.

could bring her back with my life', he said, 'I would gladly do so.' Because of the war, Claude's funeral had to be postponed. Meanwhile, her body was embalmed and laid to rest in a chapel at Blois, where it allegedly performed miracles.[38]

Louise, Francis's first child, was born at Amboise on 19 August 1515, while he was in Italy. He did not rejoice, as he had been hoping for a son. In the following year, on 23 October, he was again disappointed when Claude produced a second daughter. She was called Charlotte after the king of Spain, whose ambassador held her over the font at her christening. Significantly, Francis absented himself from the ceremony.[39] In November 1517 Francis walked from Amboise to the shrine of St Martin at Tours to pray for a son, and was duly rewarded on 28 February 1518, when a Dauphin was born at Amboise. A tide of *Te Deums* swept through the cathedrals of the kingdom and a rash of bonfires erupted in the towns. So many people flocked to see the prince that Francis instructed his chamberlain to admit only members of the royal family or people with a written permit. The baptism of the Dauphin, who was called François, was deferred till Easter to allow for the preparation of 'great triumphs'. The king's second son was born at Saint-Germain-en-Laye on 31 March 1519 and christened Henri after the king of England. On 10 August 1520 Claude produced another daughter, Madeleine. Francis's third son, Charles, was born at Saint-Germain on 22 January 1522, and was followed, on 5 June 1523, by a fourth daughter, Marguerite. Of all these children only two, Henri and Marguerite, outlived their father.[40]

Two other ladies at the court of Francis I need to be singled out. They were his official mistresses, Françoise de Foix, dame de Châteaubriant and Anne de Pisseleu, dame d'Heilly. Comparatively little is known about the first: we do not know when the king met her for the first time or when he jilted her. A number of love letters and poems attributed to one or other of them are uninformative and may not even be genuine. However, Françoise, who had married Jean de Laval, sire de Châteaubriant, in 1509, is known to have been present at court as early as June 1516. She was one of Queen Claude's twelve ladies-in-waiting and evidently had some political influence. She was asked to intercede with her brother, marshal Lautrec, in an effort to stop incursions by his troops into Mantuan territory. Françoise was also noted for her elegance. The magnificent clothes she wore at a banquet held at l'Arbresle on 11 July 1516 were

[38] Jourda, i. 90; Florange, ii. 148–9; Guiffrey, p. 41.
[39] Stazio Gadio to Isabella d'Este (Amboise, 31 Oct. 1516): 'Il signor mio non se potté retrovarvi perché il Re lo menò seco fora dil castello a spasso, finché fusse fornito quel' officio.' I am grateful to Raffaele Tamalio for this citation.
[40] Barrillon, i. 86, 249; ii. 78, 122, 173; Michaud et Poujoulat, v. 89–90; *J.B.P.*, pp. 92, 101, 139; *L.P.*, iii. 289, 306.

much admired.[41] If she was already the king's mistress, as seems likely, there may be some truth after all in the tradition that she was instrumental in obtaining high military commands for her three brothers, Odet, Thomas and André. She died in 1537.[42]

In 1530, following the peace of Cambrai, Francis married Eleanor, the sister of his great rival, the Emperor Charles V, but she never won a place in his affections. She was eclipsed from the start by the king's second official mistress, Anne de Pisseleu, who became duchesse d'Etampes. For some years she had to compete with the Constable of Montmorency for influence over the king's mind. The Constable was devoted to Eleanor and wanted to bring about a rapprochement between Francis and her brother. Following Montmorency's fall from favour in 1541, which she helped to engineer, Madame d'Etampes ruled supreme.[43]

The court

The court of France was, much larger than the king's family circle: it comprised his household, the separate households of members of his family and an amorphous mass of hangers-on. Though less magnificent than the court of the dukes of Burgundy, it had nevertheless become by the fifteenth century an important political institution.[44] Whoever had the king's ear shared to some extent in his power.[45] Nobles went to court hoping to gain offices, pensions and other royal favours, a process which was boosted in the early sixteenth century as inflation began to depress the value of their revenues. The king, for his part, welcomed a trend which increased the nobility's dependence on his authority.

Kings of France had from the earliest times surrounded themselves with boon companions and servants, but it was only by degrees that their household became a well-regulated institution. In 1261 it was already divided into six departments, each with its personnel, and a distinction was drawn between services to the king's person (*bouche*) and to his entourge (*commun*). House-

---

[41] Federico Gonzaga to Francesco Gonzaga, Chambéry, 17 June 1516: 'Havendo ricercato a mada-mosella de Chiateobrian sorella di monsignor di Leutrech che volesse scriber in racommandatione dele cose di Vostra Excellentia ha scritto l'alligata, Quella la farà legere et se le parerà di mandarla la potrà inviarla con quella dil Re la qual credo satisfarà a lei, se la serrà ubedita.' Also Stazio Gadio to Isabella d'Este, L'Arbresle, 11 July 1516: 'Il Re fece quella dominica uno banchetto et festa et fece vestir quatuordeci dameselle all italiana, con riche veste che Sua Maestà portò de Italia, dodece vi erano dela Regina e due de Madame di Borbone; et tra quelle dila Regina eravi mada-moisella di Chiatobriant, sorella di monsignor di Leutrech, vestita d'una veste di veluto morello cremosino recamata tutta de catene d'oro, con tavolette di argento ben colocate nelle catene, sopra quale era scritto sponte . . . ' I owe these citations to the kindness of Raffaele Tamalio.
[42] P. Paris, i. 118–71.   [43] See below pp. 497–9.
[44] *Comptes de l'hôtel des rois de France aux XIVe et XVe siècles*, ed. L. Douët-d'Arcq (1865), pp. i–xiii.
[45] P. S. Lewis, *Later Medieval France* (London, 1968), pp. 121–4.

hold officials were paid in money, kind or both. Remuneration in kind included the right to eat at court and to receive allowances of fuel, candles and fodder. Details of these allowances were carefully regulated, usually with an eye to eliminating abuses.[46]

The evidence provided by a fragmentary series of payrolls for the court suggests a notable increase in its size from about the end of the fifteenth century. Credit for this development is usually given to Anne of Brittany, though the expansion seems to have coincided less with her marriage to Charles VIII than with his invasion of Italy in 1494.[47] In 1523, under Francis I, the *maison du roi* comprised 540 officials, more than twice as many as in 1480.[48] The sixty or so categories of officials included a confessor, almoners, chaplains, physicians, surgeons, an apothecary, barbers, stewards, gentlemen of the chamber, valets, ushers, bread-carriers, cup-bearers, carvers, squires, grooms, pages, secretaries, a librarian, quartermasters, porters, musicians, sumpters, coopers, spit-turners, sauce-makers, pastry-cooks, tapestry-makers and laundresses.[49]

This large and variegated staff was distributed across a number of departments, each responsible for a particular court function. The three main departments were the chapel, the chamber and the *hôtel*. The chapel, under the Grand Almoner (*Grand aumônier*), attended to the king's spiritual needs. Its staff comprised officiating clergy, almoners and the king's confessor. The chamber under the Great chamberlain (*Grand chambellan*) or First gentleman of the chamber (*premier gentilhomme de la chambre*) was concerned with all the daily activities in and around the royal bedroom: namely, the king's *lever* and *coucher*, his personal toilette, his clothes and furnishings. The *hôtel*, under the Grand Master (*Grand maître de l'hôtel*) and his staff, was mainly responsible for feeding the king and his entourage. It was sub-divided into departments: the *paneterie*, *échansonnerie* and *fruiterie* which respectively provided the bread, wine, and fruit. The *cuisine de bouche* fed the king, and the *cuisine du commun* fed all those officials, who could claim board and lodging at court (*domestiques et commensaux du roi*). The *fourrière* was responsible for moving the court from place to place. Its staff of *maréchaux des logis* and *fourriers* supervised the transportation of furniture, allocated lodgings and issued lodging permits. Other departments included the *argenterie*, which purchased clothes, furniture and other necessities, and the stables (*écurie*) under the Master of the Horse (*Grand écuyer*), which looked after the king's horses. It also had a large staff of royal messengers (*chevaucheurs*) and comprised a riding school for pages, who were sons of noblemen trained at the king's

[46] *Comptes de l'hôtel*, pp. ii–vii.
[47] Zeller, pp. 94–5; Y. Labande-Mailfert, *Charles VIII et son milieu* (1975), p. 139.
[48] B.N., ms, fr. 7853, ff. 255r–262r; A.N., KK 98, ff. 1r–25v.   [49] Zeller, p. 101.

27. This tomb of Charles de Maigny, captain of the gateway to the king's household, was carved by Pierre Bontemps in 1557. Maigny's attitude has perplexed scholars. He seems to be sleeping on duty.

expense for a military career. The *vénerie* and *fauconnerie* shared the task of organizing the king's hunts.[50]

Alongside the royal household in the strict sense there was a military establishment made up of units created in different reigns. The oldest was the Scottish guard (*garde écossaise*), founded by Charles VII, which provided the king's bodyguard. The archers (*archers de la garde*) consisted of three companies of one hundred men each, the last being a creation of Francis. The Hundred Swiss (*Cent-suisses*) were set up by Charles VIII. Lastly, there were the Two Hundred Gentlemen of the household (*Deux-cents gentilshommes de l'hôtel*), divided into two companies. All these troops were mounted, except the Swiss who escorted the king whenever he walked in public ceremonies. In 1539, when Francis was unable to ride after a serious illness, he was carried in a litter from Compiègne to Paris by his Swiss guard.[51]

Law and order at court was maintained by the *Prévôt de l'hôtel* and his staff of three lieutenants and thirty archers. He could punish crimes committed in a royal residence or within five miles of the king's person. When the court was on progress, it was the *Prévôt*'s duty to ensure adequate supplies, by requisition if necessary, and to prevent overcharging by unscrupulous victuallers. The finances of the household were administered by the *Chambre aux deniers* whose annual budget was subject to the approval of the *Chambre des Comptes*. But the king's privy purse (*menus plaisirs*) escaped this control. Many people, who were not actually part of the household staff, had to attend there frequently on state business: they included councillors, *maîtres des requêtes*, notaries and secretaries.

The queen's household, though smaller than the king's, was nevertheless sizeable. It comprised more or less the same departments, but the chamber staff was entirely female, comprising various *dames*, *femmes* and *filles de la reine*. The king's mother and children had their own households. In 1523 the latter had a staff of 240, including five chamberlains, nine stewards and some twenty pages.

The court also included permanent or semi-permanent guests, such as princes of the blood, foreign princes, prelates and ambassadors with their respective suites. Finally, there were numerous hangers-on, including merchants and artisans, who were exempted from tolls and guild regulations provided they served only the crown. Under Louis XII, they had numbered about 100; Francis raised the number to 160 in March 1544.[52] Among the hangers-on were the camp followers or *filles de joie suivant la cour*, who, in accordance with ancient custom, received a New Year's gift of 20 *écus* from the king; in May they gave him a bouquet of flowers for which he paid them another 20 *écus*.[53]

---

[50] *Ibid.*, pp. 106–7.   [51] *L.P.*, xiv (pt. ii), 492.   [52] Zeller, p. 96.
[53] *C.A.F.*, iv. 121; viii. 66.

Overall control of the court was vested in the Grand Master, who was one of the *grands officiers de la couronne*. He drew up each year a roll of the household staff, supervised appointments to it, controlled its expenditure, kept the keys of the king's residence and ensured the security of his person. An office of such importance could only be given to someone the king trusted completely. Francis first appointed his old governor, Boisy, then his uncle, René of Savoy, but the most famous holder of the office was Anne de Montmorency, who held it for more than thirty years. He was also Constable of France and virtually ran the government from 1528 till 1541. His household duties were necessarily performed by deputies, headed by the First steward (*Premier maître d'hôtel*), but Montmorency did introduce foreign ambassadors to the king whenever possible.[54]

Although it had been customary for the royal household to be dissolved on the death of a king, Francis at his accession reappointed many of Louis XII's officials, and those who were too old were pensioned off. Continuity was demonstrated in Francis's entry into Paris in 1515, when the procession included members of Louis XII's household wearing his emblem of a porcupine, while Francis's archers wore the salamander. By the end of Francis's reign the household had grown to such an extent that it would have been difficult to rebuild it from scratch. Henri II accordingly decreed that in future the household would outlive the king.[55]

The absence of any major household ordinance for the reign of Francis suggests that he was broadly satisfied with the structure of the household as he found it. He did, however, introduce an important change of nomenclature. Under Charles VIII the king's most intimate companions, who took it in turn to sleep in his chamber, were called *valets de chambre*.[56] By 1515, however, the title of 'valet' had become so debased as to be unacceptable to nobles. Francis accordingly gave his aristocratic companions a title better suited to their social status: they became known as gentlemen of the chamber (*gentilshommes de la chambre*). As a consequence of this change it became possible for commoners to become *valets de chambre*, but their duties were different from those of the *gentilshommes*.[57] The effective head of the chamber was the First gentleman of the chamber (*Premier gentilhomme de la chambre*), an office held for much of the reign by Jean de La Barre, comte d'Etampes and *Prévôt de Paris*. His duties included looking after the crown jewels, holding money for the king's private use and signing contracts for work on the royal châteaux. He coupled the office

---

[54] F. Decrue, *Anne de Montmorency*, ii (1885), p. 77; Brigitte Bedos Rezak, *Anne de Montmorency* (1990), p. 115.
[55] L. M. Bryant, *The King and the City in the Parisian Royal Entry Ceremony: Politics, Ritual and Art in the Renaissance* (Geneva, 1986), p. 110; A.N., KK98, f. 23r; C. Loyseau, *Cinq Livres du Droit des Offices* (1610), p. 442.
[56] Labande-Mailfert, p. 139–40.   [57] J. du Tillet, *Recueil des Roys de France* (1602), ii. 295–6.

with that of *Maître de la garderobe*. De la Barre was richly rewarded for his services with gifts of land, offices and royal revenues. The wages paid to household officials were modest enough – 1,200 *livres* per annum was the norm for a gentleman of the chamber – but the perks they could pick up 'on the side' were considerable.[58]

The gentlemen of the chamber were the king's constant companions and enjoyed free access to his presence. Not all of them, however, were present all the time: they had a duty roster, and were often employed as ambassadors, which could take them away from court for considerable periods of time. Thus the seigneur de Castillon, was paid in September 1533 for 120 days' service as ambassador in England.[59] Another gentleman of the chamber who served as diplomat, soldier and administrator was Guillaume du Bellay, seigneur de Langey. He was sent on embassies to England, Italy and Switzerland, but especially to Germany.[60] Some portraits of the gentlemen of the chamber are to be found among Jean Clouet's drawings at Chantilly, and it is likely that many an 'unknown gentleman' in that splendid series belongs to that category of royal servant.[61]

The activities of the *gentilshommes de la chambre* conferred upon the chamber a special cultural significance, for it was here that they brought back and exchanged impressions and ideas gathered abroad. One of the ways in which rulers could demonstrate their friendship and trust was by exchanging gentlemen of their respective chambers. This could compensate for the shortcomings of ambassadors who might lack the personal status necessary for courtly assimilation. Bishop Bonner, for example, was a disastrous ambassador, not only because of his tactlessness, but also because, as a churchman, he did not easily fit into Francis's aristocratic entourage. By contrast, Sir Thomas Cheyney, who became ambassador in April 1526, was invited by the king to join his most intimate circle. 'He commanded me', Cheyney informed Henry VIII, 'to use myself in his chamber at all hours, as your Grace has appointed me in yours.' When the ambassador with some hesitation availed himself of the privilege, the Grand Master made him present the king's towel at his *lever*, saying that Henry had 'used him so at his being in England'.[62] Englishmen, who were admitted to Francis's chamber, inevitably drew comparisons between the life styles of his court and of Henry's

By 1535 the number of household oficials at Francis's court had risen from 540 to 622 and the amount spent on wages from 65,915 *livres* in 1517 to 214,918 *livres*.[63] But the expansion of the court was neither uniform nor continuous; while some sections grew, others contracted or even vanished. The

[58] C.A.F., i. 2636, 3071; ii. 6529; iii. 7993; vi. 20613.   [59] C.A.F., ii. 6238.
[60] V.-L. Bourrilly, *Guillaume du Bellay* (1905). See below pp. 291–4, 323.
[61] See below, p. 435.   [62] L.P., iv. 2087, 2092.
[63] A.N., KK94, f. 60r; B.N., ms. fr. 2953, f. 20r.

number of almoners, for example, grew from fourteen in 1515 to fifty-six in 1546, that of *gentilshommes de la chambre* from twenty in 1515 to sixty-eight in 1545. But the *enfants d'honneur* went down from forty-seven in 1515 to seventeen in 1536 after which they vanished from the payroll. The explanation for this may be found in an ordinance of July 1534 which laid down that in future no *enfant d'honneur* would be admitted to the royal household unless he had served at least four years in the king's heavy cavalry or *compagnies d'ordonnances*.[64] It seems that certain departments of the household reached their maximum size under Francis about 1523 and that an effort was then made, presumably for economy reasons, to limit the size of some of them.

Although the papal nuncio, Capodiferro, thinking mainly of the court, stated in January 1542 that Francis was wasting a huge amount of money daily, a recent examination of the king's expenditure has suggested that his reign marked 'a phase of relative level-pegging between the substantial rises during the reigns of Charles VIII–Louis XII and of Henri II'. Between 1516 and 1546 expenditure on the court rose from 622, 899 *livres* to 811,236 *livres*, a percentage increase of only 30 per cent over thirty years. Certain departments of the household cost relatively more than others. Thus the king's passion for hunting was reflected in a 71 per cent rise in the cost of the *vénerie* and *fauconnerie* between 1516–20 (33,773 *livres* p.a.) and 1542–46 (57,988 *livres* p.a.) Expenditure on certain departments fell at times of crisis, notably in the 1520s.[65]

It is impossible to know precisely how large the population of the court in the widest sense was at any given time, for it was subject to fluctuations. It tended to be larger in peace than in war, when the king and his courtiers might absent themselves, leaving behind a rump of women, elderly men and clerics. Young noblemen were in the habit of rushing off to fight the moment a war seemed imminent. Even in peacetime, the court's population was variable. As it travelled across the kingdom, noblemen from a particular region would tag on for a few days or weeks and then go home; their place might then be filled by nobles from another region, also for a limited period. Such visitors seldom stayed for long, since life at court was expensive and not always rewarding. Few noblemen chose to remain permanently at court; even the greatest of them liked to go back to their own châteaux from time to time.[66] Yet, even allowing for a variable attendance, the court at its widest was the size of a small town. It may have contained as many as 10,000 people. About 1550 only twenty-five towns in France had larger populations.

Francis's court was not only larger than its predecessors; its manners were

---

[64] *Ordonnances*, vii. 136–7.

[65] P. Hamon, 'L'Argent du roi: finances et gens de finances en France au temps de François Ier' (unpublished doctoral thesis, University of Paris I, 1993), i. 40; B.N. ms. fr. 4523, ff. 11a–13a.

[66] J.-F. Solnon, *La cour de France* (1987), p. 20; J.-M. Constant, *De la noblesse française aux XVIe-XVIIe siècles* (1985), pp. 55, 72.

also more polished, at least on the surface, a change commonly ascribed to Italian influence. As the French monarch became a key political figure south of the Alps, Italians sought his aid or protection. They came in waves reflecting the political situation. Among the first were the Fregosi of Genoa, the San Severini and Caraccioli of Naples and the Trivulzi of Milan.[67] By 1515 Galeazzo di San Severino had become *Grand écuyer* and Gian-Giacomo Trivulzio a marshal of France. Their children and grandchildren continued to serve France in various capacities. Not all Italians, of course, came to France as political exiles; Lorenzo de' Medici and Ercole d'Este came in response to the king's matrimonial diplomacy. The marriage of Catherine de' Medici to Francis's second son, Henri duc d'Orléans, in October 1533, added substantially to the number of Florentines at the French court.

An early arrival at Francis's court was the young Federico Gonzaga, who became the fifth marquis of Mantua in 1519 and first duke in 1530. He first met the French king in Milan in October 1515 and followed him to France, where he remained till March 1517 as a hostage for the good behaviour of his father, Francesco, marquis of Mantua. Francis showed great sympathy, even affection, for Federico, who at sixteen, was only five years his junior. He admired him not only for his affability and polished manners, but also as the representative of a court noted for its cultural and artistic prestige. Francis and Federico talked mainly about horses, love, Italy and France, art and architecture. Federico, whose suite comprised fifty persons and forty-one horses, continued to enjoy the king's favour till the end of his stay. When finally he took his leave, he was almost embarrassed by the warmth of Francis's declaration of affection.[68]

There were many Italians on the staff of the royal household in 1523, including two doctors, a steward, a trumpeter and two cornet players, but the largest contingent was to be found among the *écuyers du roi*.[69] This was doubtless due to the high reputation for horsemanship enjoyed by Italians at this time. Two names stand out in the 1523 list; 'Francisque', that is Francesco di Noceto, who later became a gentleman of the chamber and was employed by the king on a number of diplomatic and military missions, and 'Merveilles', Giovan-Alberto Maraviglia, who had entered Louis XII's service as *écuyer* in 1508 and continued to serve Francis in the same capacity.[70] Another Italian, this time among the *valets de chambre* in 1523, was 'Viscontin', Filippo Visconti, who, in 1530,

[67] E. Picot, 'Les italiens en France au XVIe siècle' *Bulletin italien*, vol. 1 (Bordeaux, 1901), 92–137.

[68] R. Tamalio, 'Federico and Ferrante Gonzaga at the courts of Francis I and Charles V. The training of a prince and courtier: Aspects of the political and familial strategy in the time of Isabella'. Unpublished paper given at a seminar at the Institute of Historical Research, London, on 12 June 1992.

[69] A.N., KK 98, f.6.

[70] Picot in *Bulletin italien*, vol. 2 (Bordeaux, 1902), 19–20; V.-L. Bourrilly, 'Les diplomates de François Ier: Maraviglia à Milan' in *Bulletin italien*, vol. 6 (Bordeaux, 1906), 133–46.

was described as one of two 'plaisantins du roi'. In other words, he was the king's fool. Marot wrote an epigram about him (*De Viscontin et de la Calendre du roy*) and Ortesio Lando in his *Sette libri* (1552) states that 'Il Vescantino Milanese' was highly esteemed by Francis 'per le sue buffonerie'.[71]

Traffic between France and Italy was not one-way only; Frenchmen were given many opportunities, as soldiers, diplomats or administrators, of observing Italian life and manners at close quarters. Women in Italy were considered an essential adornment of court society and close attention was given to literature and the arts. In the light of this experience, the French court became more refined. Sophistication, however, entailed extravagance, particularly with regard to buildings, clothes, jewellery and entertainment. Francis was most anxious that the ladies of his court should keep abreast of current fashions south of the Alps. He asked Federico Gonzaga to obtain dolls from his mother, Isabella d'Este, dressed in the latest Mantuan fashions, with a view to having them copied by the ladies of his court. Isabella also received a request from her son for some of her famous cosmetics. 'Send me perfume in goodly quantities', he asked, 'to give these ladies, and in particular a large basket of your compositions and lots of gloves, as well as a "soap-tree" which will be big enough to give them to many ... and further, oils, powders and distilled waters, when you have the opportunity to send such things.'[72]

Frenchmen tried to emulate Italians, often at the risk of ruining themselves, and many looked to the king's favour and munificence to rescue them from the consequences of their prodigality. This was grist to the mill of contemporary satire. Criticism of court life was not new, but it became wider in scope and more barbed in the sixteenth century. Extravagance was criticized not simply as lack of thrift, but as a sign of physical and moral decay.[73] Contemporary criticism of the court, however, has created a distorted impression. Among foreigners who attached themselves to the court, Italians were preponderant, but never more than a minority. Although the court looked to Italy for its code of manners (Castiglione's *Cortegiano* had a great success there), it was subject to other foreign influences as well. The military establishment included many Scots and Swiss, and the household of Queen Eleanor was full of Spaniards. The painter, Jean Clouet, who was a *valet de chambre* in 1523, probably hailed from the Low Countries. If cornet-players were invariably Italians, fife-players were always Swiss.[74]

Not enough, alas, is known about the day-to-day life of Francis's court. In September 1563, Catherine de' Medici urged her son to restore the routine that

[71] Picot, in *Bulletin italien*, vol. 3 (Bordeaux, 1903), 21–2.   [72] Ex inf. R. Tamalio.
[73] P. M. Smith, *The Anti-Courtier Trend in Sixteenth-Century French Literature* (Geneva, 1966), pp. 57–97.
[74] F.-X. Michel, *Les écossais en France et les français en Ecosse*, 2 vols. (1862); P. Mellen, *Jean Clouet* (London, 1971), p. 11; A.N., KK 98, f. 13r.

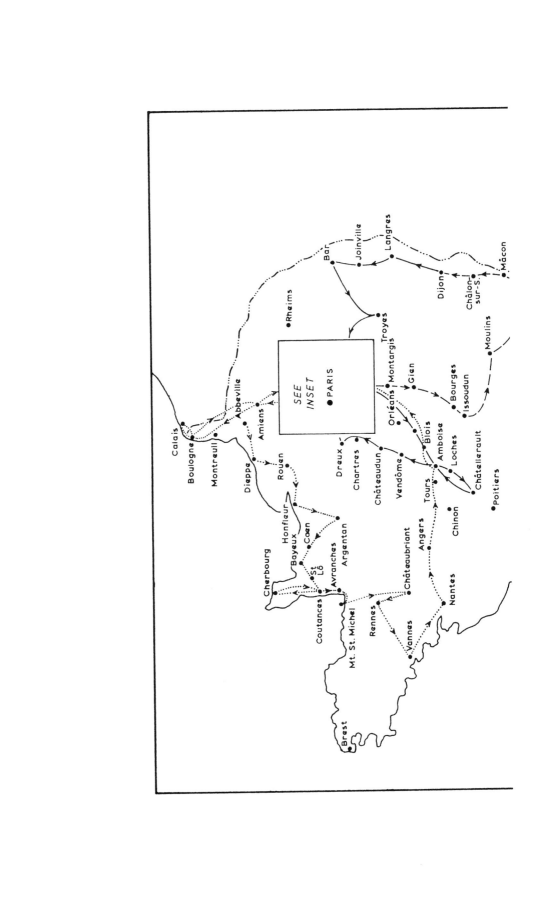

Calais
Boulogne
Montreuil
Abbeville
Dieppe
Amiens
Rouen
Rhaims
SEE INSET
• PARIS
Troyes
Bar
Joinville
Langres
Mâcon
Dijon
Châlon-sur-S.
Moulins
Orléans
Montargis
Gien
Bourges
Issoudun
Blois
Amboise
Loches
Châtellerault
Poitiers
Dreux
Chartres
Châteaudun
Vendôme
Tours
Chinon
Angers
Châteaubriant
Nantes
Vannes
Rennes
Mt. St. Michel
Coutances
Avranches
St. Lô
Argentan
Bayeux
Caen
Honfleur
Cherbourg
Brest

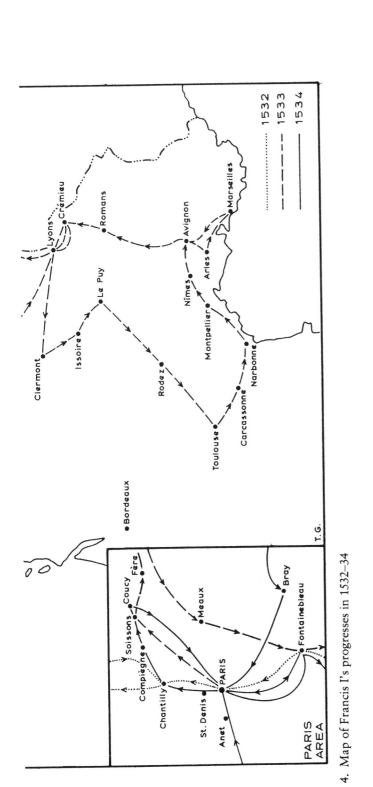

4. Map of Francis I's progresses in 1532–34

had existed under his father and grandfather.[75] The day began with the king's *lever* in the presence of his main courtiers and distinguished guests. He would be handed his shirt by the most honoured person present. Then he would retire to his *cabinet* with his secretaries and deal with state papers, or he would hold a council meeting in his chamber. At 10 am the king would go to Mass escorted by 'all the princes and lords'. Lunch followed at 11, when he ate alone, albeit normally in public, in his reception hall or *salle*. He was served by the *panetier*, *échanson* and *écuyer tranchant*. The greatest lords, the physicians and the almoner stood near him, while his meal was carried in procession from the kitchens by pages preceded by archers, the stewards and *écuyers servans*. While the king ate, he might be read to aloud. Twice a week lunch was followed by an audience in which people would approach him individually or deputations be admitted to his presence. Afterwards, he might spend an hour or so with the queen. He would then retire to his study for privacy before re-appearing about 3 pm to 'devote himself to some honest exercise': a walk or ride in the open air, a game of tennis or a hunt. In the evening he would sup with his family and perhaps offer an indoor entertainment, such as a ball or masque. Francis said that he needed to give a ball at least twice a week to live at peace with his subjects, who liked to be kept merry and engaged in some honest exercise. The day ended with his *coucher*, again in the presence of the great nobles.

Except when an outbreak of plague forced the king to shut himself up in his room, as in October 1520, he was very accessible. An ordinance of 1523 states that 'a greater conglutination, bond and conjunction of true love, pure devotion, cordial harmony and intimate affection have always existed between the kings of France and their subjects than in any other monarchy or Christian nation'.[76] Access to the court was certainly easy; anyone who was decently dressed or could claim acquaintance with a member of the royal entourage was admitted. The consequences were sometimes unfortunate: in November 1530 Francis complained that ornaments had been stolen from his chapel, as well as silver plate and clothes from his wardrobe. Such thefts were to be punished in future by death regardless of the value of the objects stolen.[77]

In an important respect the court in the early sixteenth century did not differ from its predecessors: it remained peripatetic. Indeed, as the kingdom grew larger and more peaceful, the court travelled more extensively than before. 'Never during the whole of my embassy', wrote a Venetian envoy, 'was the court in the same place for fifteen consecutive days.'[78] Yet Francis's movements were seasonal: in the winter and spring, when roads were little better than quagmires, he tended to stay put. Such nomadism was not a feudal survival. In

[75] *Lettres de Catherine de Médicis*, ed. H. de La Ferrière-Percy (1880–95), ii. 90ff.
[76] Zeller, p. 97.
[77] *Ordonnances*, vi. No. 547.
[78] *Relations des ambassadeurs vénitiens sur les affaires de France*, ed. N. Tommaseo (1838), i. 107–11.

an age of growing royal centralization, it was important for the king to know his realm at first hand and to make personal contact with the subjects. Francis's wanderings were far from haphazard. At the start of his reign he systematically visited several French provinces: Provence (1516), Picardy (1517), Anjou and Brittany (1518), Poitou and Angoumois (1519), Picardy again (1520) and Burgundy (1521). He then became involved in war with the Emperor, so that his movements became determined by military exigencies. When peace returned in 1526, he resumed his progresses, and even when his health declined seriously, he continued to tour his kingdom at regular intervals. The reign's most extensive progress lasted from November 1531 till February 1534. The court visited north-west France in 1532, the centre and south in 1533 and the east in 1534. In 1546, when Francis was fifty-two and ailing fast, he spent four months visiting his kingdom's borders from Bresse to Flanders.[79]

Though the king's movements were often related to the political or military situation, they were also inspired by more mundane considerations. Travel offered opportunities of hunting in various places. Nothing pleased Francis more, it seems, than to shed cares of state and vanish, sometimes for days on end, in some dense forest with a few friends. He did not enjoy city life: by comparison with the cramped and unhygienic conditions of any sixteenth-century town, the lure of the open country must have been irresistible. Yet Paris was too important, politically and economically, to be ignored by the king.[80] France had in effect two capitals: the court and Paris. While the *conseil étroit*, where major policy decisions were taken, continued to follow the monarch about France, some of the chief departments of state had 'gone out of court' and fixed themselves in Paris. Only by holding a *lit-de-justice* in the Parlement of Paris could the king finally overcome its opposition to a controversial piece of legislation. He also looked to the capital for financial assistance in an emergency, and since it was a *ville franche*, he could best do this by appealing in person to the generosity of its inhabitants. Various ceremonies, such as the queen's entry, a visit by a foreign prince, an aristocratic wedding or a religious procession, would draw the king to Paris. He also liked to shop there, his personal accounts being full of payments to Parisian goldsmiths and jewellers.[81] Francis visited Paris more often than any other town in France: he went there at least once in every year, except 1525 (when he was a prisoner in Spain), 1526, 1541 and 1547. He spent a total of more than a month in Paris in each of seventeen years and less than ten days in four.[82] Admittedly, he was seldom there in summer. In the course of his reign he spent a total of only thirty-one days in Paris during August. He resided there usually in the winter or spring.

---

[79] C.A.F., viii. 417–20.   [80] *Paris: fonctions d'une capitale*, ed. G. Michaud (1962), pp. 157–8.
[81] J.-P. Babelon, *Paris au XVIe siècle* (1986), pp. 45–50, 56–60, 148–9, 151.
[82] These figures are based on the king's itinerary in C.A.F., viii. 411–548.

Parisians probably viewed the occasional visits of the court with misgivings. An immature streak in Francis's character found an outlet (but only at the beginning of his reign) in senseless pranks at the expense of the citizens. In May 1517, he and his companions shocked them by riding disguised and masked through the streets almost daily, and frequenting houses of ill-repute.[83] Two years later some distinguished English visitors were invited by Francis to join him in similar sport. They 'rode daily disguised through Paris, throwing eggs, stones and other foolish trifles at the people, which light demeanour of a king was much discommended and jested at'.[84] Could any behaviour express more blatantly the contempt of the courtier for his social inferiors?

In the course of his progresses, Francis visited many churches and monasteries, and inspected fortifications, castles and harbour installations. At Marseilles, in 1516, he took a trip out to sea to look at a rhinoceros which was being taken in a galley as a gift from the king of Portugal to the pope.[85] Soon afterwards the king and his courtiers walked all the way from Lyons to Chambéry on a pilgrimage to see the 'Holy Shroud'.[86] Whenever Francis visited a major town for the first time he was given an *entrée joyeuse*. This was a most effective form of royal propaganda. Neither royal proclamations nor official tracts could move the hearts of the people as much as ceremonies in which the king appeared amidst a *décor* carefully designed to project his ideal personality and the nature of his rule. Impressive as it was, a coronation or royal funeral was seen by relatively few subjects; an entry could be repeated several times within the reign and in various places. As it was organized by the townspeople themselves, it identified them closely with the mystery of kingship. This, however, could be rudely dispelled. In 1518, for example, the captain of Brest had to pay 100 gold *écus* 'following artillery accidents during the king's entry ... as indemnity to the injured and to widows of the deceased'.[87]

From a relatively simple affair in which the townsfolk had offered victuals and sometimes fodder to the king, a royal entry had become, by the end of the Middle Ages, a magnificent spectacle with sacred and political overtones. The king was met outside the town by the citizens, wearing colourful liveries, and escorted into it to the accompaniment of trumpeters and other musicians. The presentation of gifts, either in the form of money or some precious *objet d'art*, was preceded by an exchange of oaths: the king promised to maintain the town's privileges, and the inhabitants swore to obey him. After receiving the town keys, the king rode through it in procession under a rich canopy or *dais* along a carefully prepared route. The road surface was usually covered with sand or rushes, and tapestries were hung over the façades of the houses. By the

[83] *J.B.P.*, p. 49.   [84] Hall, *Henry VIII*, i. 175.
[85] Barrillon, i. 193. This was the same animal that Dürer drew; it never reached its destination as the ship that was carrying it was wrecked off the Italian coast.
[86] Barrillon, i. 218.   [87] *C.A.F.*, v. 16800.

early sixteenth century roadside theatricals had become the rule. The procession culminated in a thanksgiving service at the town's main church, followed by a banquet and jollification lasting well into the night.[88]

One of Francis's most spectacular entries was at Lyons in July 1515. As he neared the city, he was greeted by a ship towed across the Saône by a white stag. This recalled the legend of Clovis to whom a stag had indicated a ford across which he might pursue his enemies. The city gateway was decorated with a Tree of Jesse and a salamander, flanked by figures representing *Lyons* and *Loyalty*. At intervals along the processional route, which had been decorated with the king's colours, young women stood on columns, each holding a letter of his name. Between the columns, *tableaux vivants* were enacted by members of Lyons's principal families: one of them showed Francis defending Peace against the duke of Milan and the Swiss bear; in another, he appeared as Hercules gathering fruit in the garden of the Hesperides. It was on this occasion, too, that a mechanical lion designed by Leonardo da Vinci performed for the king.[89]

The reign of Francis marks an important transition in the development of the royal entry in France. Whereas in 1515 the symbolism of the *tableaux vivants* was still essentially medieval, by 1547 this had incorporated many classical features. The transition was gradual, with medieval and classical existing side by side or even overlapping; but as from 1530 the classical began to dominate. Instead of being acclaimed as a second David or Solomon, Francis was now hailed as a new Caesar. Allegories inspired by the *Roman de la Rose* or *Songe du Vergier* were displaced by the Roman triumph. The chariot, the equestrian statue and the triumphal arch began to figure among the entry's ceremonial trappings, albeit in association with the Carolingian and Trojan legends.[90]

Moving the court was like moving an army. According to Cellini, 12,000 horses were used to transport it, and this was an exceptionally low figure. In peacetime, when the court was at full strength, 18,000 horses were used.[91] Dr Taylor, the English ambassador, who witnessed the court's arrival in Bordeaux in 1526, reported that stabling had been provided for 22,500 horses and mules.[92] Nor were these the only animals 'suivant la cour'. Many dogs and birds were attached to it, as well as a lion and a lynx. The latter, it seems,

---

[88] B. Guénée and F. Lehoux, *Les entrées royales françaises de 1328 à 1515* (1968), pp. 7–8; L. M. Bryant, *The King and the City*, pp. 99–124.
[89] Lecoq, pp. 144–8; J. Chartrou, *Les entrées solennelles et triomphales à la Renaissance (1484–1551)* (1928), pp. 26–7, 32–3, 37; C. Pedretti, *Leonardo da Vinci: The Royal Palace at Romorantin* (Cambridge, MA, 1972), p. 2.
[90] Chartrou, pp. 49, 62, 69.
[91] *The Life of Benvenuto Cellini Written by Himself*, tr. J. A. Symonds, ed. J. Pope-Hennessy (London, 1949), p. 264.
[92] *L.P.*, iv (pt. 1), 1938.

proved a handful, for, in August 1537, it was left behind at an inn in the Faubourg Saint-Honoré. The innkeeper's wife was paid 67 *livres* by the king for
feeding the animal and also to help her husband recover from a leg bite.[93]

The court, or at least its more important members, often travelled by water.
Thus in May 1534 the sum of 627 *livres* was paid to several men and horses
'who have taken the king's great boat and that of his kitchens from Paris to
Melun'.[94] The baggage was enormous: it included furniture, gold and silver
plate, and tapestries. Only royal châteaux that were frequently visited by the
court were kept furnished; the rest stayed empty from one visit to the next. In
the autumn of 1533, when Francis met the pope at Marseilles, the sum of 4,623
livres was spent on moving the court's furniture, plate and tapestries.[95]

Feeding the court could be a problem. In May 1533 the Venetian ambassador reported from Lyons: 'This town cannot accommodate so many men and
horses, and this has caused a great scarcity of all things and most especially of
lodgings, bread, corn, stabling; and the quantity of bread sold for one French
sou, equal to rather more than three *marchetti*, is so small, that I never remember to have got less for three *marchetti* in Venice, however great the scarcity
may have been there. The poor people eat very coarse and bad bread; corn has
trebled in price; and should the court remain here some days longer, the cost
will become unbearable.'[96] In August 1540, France suffered a terrible drought,
and the Imperial ambassador described the court's plight as it travelled to Le
Havre: there was no fodder for the horses, no wine or cider for the men. As all
the wells were dry, courtiers had to drink polluted water with predictable
results: Lautrec and the duc de Guise's son fell seriously ill and the duc d'Orléans had a 'bloody flux'.[97]

Finding accommodation was often difficult. Wherever possible, Francis
stayed in one of his own châteaux or accepted the hospitality of a courtier. Not
every member of the court could expect to share the king's roof. Accommodation within a royal residence was distributed according to strict rules of
precedence. These are known for 1547 at Saint-Germain-en-Laye. All the
ladies, princes accompanied by their wives and most cardinals were housed in
the château proper, while single noblemen were lodged in outbuildings along
with royal secretaries, household officials and the Dauphin's physicians. The
stable-grooms slept in the stables. Office-holders deemed 'necessary to the
service' (i.e. those whose titles were prefixed by the word *grand* or *premier*)
were given precedence over persons of higher social standing.[98]

[93] C.A.F., viii. 30314, 30843, 32168.   [94] *Ibid.*, ii. 7047.
[95] B.N. ms. fr. 10390, f.33r. See S. Schneebalg-Perelman, 'Richesses du garde-meuble parisien de
François 1er: inventaires inédits de 1542 et 1551', *G.B.A.* 6th ser., lxxviii (1971), 253–304.
[96] C.S.P., *Ven.*, iv (1527–33), no. 902.   [97] *Ibid.*, vi (pt. 1), 120.
[98] M. Chatenet, 'Une demeure royale au milieu du XVIe siècle: la distribution des espaces au château
de Saint-Germain-en-Laye' *Revue de l'Art* (1988), p. 28. See below, pp. 419–23.

In the absence of a suitable château, the king might put up at an abbey or inn, while his followers looked for lodgings round about. This often became a wild scramble. The bishop of Saluzzo complained that an isolated house would be found for the king and the ladies, while the rest of the court had to find lodgings up to six miles away.[99] Occasionally, they were reduced to pitching tents. As Cellini discovered, the hardships for the court's rank and file could be severe. 'Sometimes', he writes, 'there were scarcely two houses to be found and then we set up canvas tents like gipsies, and suffered at times very great discomfort.'[100] It was partly to ease this problem of accommodation that Francis embarked on his ambitious building programme.

The early châteaux: Amboise, Blois and Chambord

The early sixteenth century was marked by an outburst of architectural activity all over France, motivated by functional and aesthetic concerns. Until the mid fifteenth century the houses of the aristocracy had been built for defence rather than comfort with thick walls, few windows, massive angle towers, machicolations, portcullises and moats filled with water. With the return of domestic peace after the Hundred Years War, the need for such military features receded. They were not abandoned overnight, but were now treated mainly as decorations and status symbols. The nobility began to rebuild their homes with an eye to comfort: large mullioned windows appeared in the walls, the angle towers were reduced to graceful turrets and machicolations became a sort of frieze.

At the same time, the Italian Wars brought French nobles into contact with Renaissance architecture, and if they lacked the necessary education to grasp its basic principles, they nevertheless responded to its decoration and imported into France classical features, like columns, pilasters, triangular pediments and medallions, which they applied to façades of buildings that remained structurally Gothic.[101] A pioneer of this trend was King Charles VIII, who, on his return from Naples in 1495, set a team of Italian craftsmen to work at Amboise. Another was Georges d'Amboise who added Italianate features to his château at Gaillon.[102]

Under Francis I, the classical influence ceased to be merely decorative and began to determine structure. His earliest architectural activities were centred on the Loire valley: at Amboise, where he spent much of his childhood; at

---

[99] Terrasse, iii. 23–4.   [100] Cellini, p. 264.

[101] F. Gebelin, *Les châteaux de la Renaissance* (1927), pp. 5–16; A. Blunt, *Art and Architecture in France, 1500–1700* (Harmondsworth, Middlesex, 1957), pp. 3–13; J.-P. Babelon, *Châteaux de France au siècle de la Renaissance* (1989), pp. 17–22.

[102] R. Weiss, 'The Castle of Gaillon in 1509–10', *J.W.C.I.*, 1–12, 351; Babelon, pp. 86–93.

Blois, which was the property of his first queen, Claude; and at Chambord at the heart of a forest near Blois.

Amboise had been the scene of much building activity under Charles VIII. This was continued by Louis XII and Francis, but little survives of their work. Amboise was the principal royal residence during the first three years of Francis's reign and was the setting for some magnificent court festivities. During the king's first Italian campaign, building at Amboise was supervised by his mother. It consisted mainly of the addition of a storey to an existing wing and was characterized by its facing of white stone and exterior decoration of horizontal bands and nicely proportioned pilasters.[103]

A far more impressive survival is the wing built by Francis at the château of Blois. This narrowly escaped destruction in the seventeenth century, when Gaston d'Orléans, Louis XIII's turbulent brother, planned to rebuild the entire château in the classical style of his own day. Fortunately, he ran out of money and could not accomplish his purpose, so that Blois offers a fascinating juxtaposition of styles reaching back to the Middle Ages. The building accounts show that Francis began work there in June 1515 and continued till the death of Queen Claude in 1524.[104] His enthusiasm for the project is reflected in a letter written on 12 August 1516 by Stazio Gadio, the secretary of the young Federico Gonzaga, who spent two years at the French court. He describes how Francis led Federico by the hand. After showing him the beautiful gardens at Blois:

> His most gracious majesty, not content with such great proofs of affection as he had given him, although it was midnight, wished to show him some parts of the château, which has been very well arranged and embellished since he became king, on the side where the lodgings of King Louis once stood. After demolishing these, he has rebuilt them and made a very beautiful façade of freestone decorated in the most excellent manner, with very beautiful galleries. It is actually being worked on now both inside and out, while a beautiful façade all of stone is being erected on the courtyard side.[105]

Francis's wing at Blois was built, as Gadio's letter indicates, on the site of an earlier medieval building whose outer wall was retained and used as a dividing wall within the new structure. This involved a realignment of the roof and the removal of some dormer windows. On the garden side, Francis erected the *Façade des loggias*, widening the original building by fifteen feet. This must have been the work of French master masons whose technical skill was not matched by any deep understanding of the rules of classical architecture. There are two sets of loggias one above the other, and over them a third floor of

---

[103] *Ibid.*, pp. 108–10; Gebelin, pp. 37–9.
[104] *Ibid.*, pp. 55–62; Blunt, pp. 9–10; Babelon, pp. 110–18; F. and P. Lesueur, *Le château de Blois* (1914–21), pp. 76–105.
[105] M. H. Smith, 'François Ier, l'Italie et le château de Blois', *Bulletin monumental*, 147 (1989), 315–19.

28. Château of Blois: façade of the loggias. No precedent existed in France for outward-looking loggias on this scale. They were doubtless inspired by those of Bramante at the Vatican palace. At Blois, the loggias commanded a view of the château's gardens, of which Francis was especially proud.

flat-headed openings separated by free-standing columns. The idea of an arcaded loggia on the outside of the château was not altogether new in France, but the scheme at Blois was grander than anything of the kind yet seen north of the Alps. It was evidently intended to offer courtiers and visitors a view of the gardens below and was doubtless inspired by the loggias Bramante was building more or less at the same time at the Vatican palace. But the Blois loggias lack the regularity and lightness of Bramante's work. They are irregularly spaced and the arches are slightly flattened at the top in the traditional French manner. They are also deep recesses rather than genuine loggias.[106]

The most important feature of the Francis I wing on the courtyard side is the monumental staircase, which may be regarded as the last of a long line of spiral staircases erected all over France in the fifteenth century. Some of them are incorporated within the fabric of a building; others stand out from a façade in

[106] *Ibid.*; Blunt, pp. 9–10.

29. The Francis I staircase, standing within the courtyard of the château of Blois. Such staircases were a traditional feature of French civil architecture, but this one was more massive and combined classical with Gothic decoration.

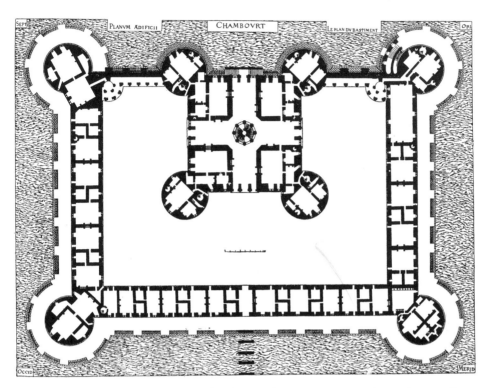

5. Plan of the château of Chambord, J. Androuet Du Cerceau, *Les plus excellents bastiments de France (1576–1607)*

a polygonal pavilion and are sometimes open. But the Blois staircase marks a new departure. As Blunt explains: 'For the first time one can speak of a feeling of monumentality in French Renaissance architecture. Compared with the light surface patterning of Azay or the façade itself at Blois, we have here the impression that the architect has thought in three dimensions. The ramp carves out a definable space, and both it and the piers create emphatically the impression of weight.'[107]

Chambord, unlike Amboise and Blois, was a château built from scratch. It was the first of a series which Francis was to build in the midst of forests where he liked to go hunting. They were intended to be glorified hunting lodges rather than long-term residences. Although Chambord was begun in 1519, it did not rise above the foundations till after 1526 and the decorations of the upper storeys were not completed till about 1540. Its plan is essentially that of a medieval fortress with a square keep flanked by four large round towers, from which run lower buildings with towers at the corners. The château was originally surrounded by a moat filled with water. The interior plan of the keep,

[107] *Ibid.*

30. The château of Chambord. The most important of several châteaux newly built by Francis in the midst of forests where he liked to go hunting.

however, marks a complete break with French tradition. It is divided into four parts by a Greek cross, the arms of which lead to a double-spiral staircase in the middle. This arrangement leaves a square space in each corner which is sub-divided into a lodging (*logis*) of three rooms. This ground-floor pattern is repeated on two storeys above so that altogether there are three cruciform vestibules and twelve lodgings, all of equal size. The origin of this plan, as in the case of the Blois loggias, is Italian. Except for the staircase, it recalls the internal arrangements of the villa built by Giuliano da Sangallo for Lorenzo de' Medici at Poggio a Caiano near Florence in the 1470s.[108]

Who designed Chambord? Two names have been suggested: Domenico da Cortona and Leonardo da Vinci. Domenico was a pupil of Sangallo who worked in France early in the reign of Francis and in 1531 was paid 900 *livres* by the king for making wooden models of various buildings, including Chambord, over the previous fifteen years. Such a model could still be seen at Blois in the seventeenth century when it was drawn by the architect and historian, André Félibien. It looks like a model of the keep at Chambord, though it differs in several respects from the keep that was actually built. In particular, it has a straight staircase instead of the double-spiral. Does this suggest that it was Domenico who designed Chambord? He was certainly more than a model-

---

[108] Babelon, pp. 162–3.

31. The double-spiral staircase at the centre of the keep of the château of Chambord. Its design may have been influenced posthumously by some of Leonardo da Vinci's sketches.

maker. He may have built a house for Francis in Ardres in 1520, and in 1532 he was commissioned by the king to design a new town hall for the city of Paris. This project, however, does not suggest a man of genius capable of designing a building as imaginative as Chambord.[109]

Leonardo came to France in 1516, when he was given the manor of Cloux outside Amboise by the king, and he died there three years later. He had been employed as an architect in Milan by Galeazzo da San Severino and Charles d'Amboise and his interest in architecture is reflected in the notebooks that he kept during the last years of his life. One of the sketches in the *Codex Atlanticus* is the ground plan of a château, flanked by a river on one side and a road on the other. The road, described as 'strada d'Ambosa' has been identified with the present rue des Capucins in Romorantin, and it has been suggested that Leonardo was commissioned by Francis to build a new palace for Louise of Savoy in that town. However, this project, if it was seriously mooted, was never carried out.[110]

Leonardo has also been acclaimed as 'the architect of Chambord', yet any direct participation by him in the actual building can be ruled out since he died about the time the first stone was laid.[111] Some of his ideas, however, may have been adopted by the king's master-masons. This cannot be proved, but Jean Guillaume has put forward a strong case in support of Leonardo's posthumous influence. It rests mainly on the evidence of the two staircases: the straight one of the wooden model and the double-spiral that was actually built. The only source for the former, Guillaume believes, is a design made by Leonardo in 1506 for Charles d'Amboise, and the only precedent for the latter is another drawing by him of a quadruple staircase within a square tower. Guillaume thinks it would be very surprising if Francis, having invited Leonardo to France, failed to make use of his architectural expertise.[112]

The example set by Francis as a patron of Renaissance architecture was enthusiastically followed by his courtiers. When Thomas Bohier, *général des finances* acquired the lordship of Chenonceaux in February 1513, he demolished the old castle, except a tower which he kept for his treasure and muniments, and built an elegant residence in the Renaissance style on the foundations of a water-mill. In 1518, more than 400 workmen were toiling, day and night, on the foundations of Azay-le-Rideau, the home of another fiscal

---

[109] L. de Laborde, *Les comptes des bâtiments du roi (1528–1571)* (1878–90), ii. 204; P. Lesueur, *Dominique de Cortone, dit Le Boccador* (1928).

[110] C. Pedretti, *Leonardo da Vinci; Leonard de Vinci ingenieur et architecte* (Montreal, 1987), pp. 278–82.

[111] L. H. Heydenreich, 'Leonardo da Vinci, Architect of Francis 1', *Burlington Magazine*, xciv (Oct. 1952), 277–85; M. Reymond and M.-R. Reymond, 'Léonard de Vinci, architecte du château de Chambord' *G.B.A.*, i (1913), 337; *Léonard de Vinci, ingénieur et architecte*, pp. 282–4.

[112] J. Guillaume, 'Léonard de Vinci, Dominique de Cortone et l'escalier du modèle en bois de Chambord', *G.B.A.*, i. (1968), pp. 101, 108 n.22; *Léonard de Vinci, ingénieur et architecte*, pp. 282–4.

official, Gilles Berthelot; Le Lude was rebuilt at the same time by Jacques de Daillon, the king's chamberlain, while Oiron was begun by Artus Gouffier, the Grand Master. Chancellor Duprat was building the château of Nantouillet in 1521, and three years later Anne de Montmorency set to work on the long gallery at Chantilly.[113]

[113] Gebelin, pp. 51, 65, 75, 81, 141–2, 153, 155; Babelon, *Châteaux de France*, pp. 119–27, 138–42, 188–91, 343–7.

Chapter seven

Humanism and heresy

France, like other parts of Christendom, was afflicted by a serious religious malaise at the end of the Middle Ages. Although far from moribund, the church contained some glaring abuses. Many prelates lived ostentatiously away from their flocks, and there was much poverty and ignorance among the lower clergy. The monastic ideal was often disregarded; instead of living in common according to the rules of their orders, monks frequently had their own rooms where they entertained relatives and friends. Many could be seen wandering about the streets of Paris in low company. Public opinion was shocked by the violence, insubordination and coarseness of the mendicant friars who competed fiercely with the parish clergy in administering the sacraments and officiating at funerals. The registers of the ecclesiastical courts for this period offer many instances of clerical violence, drunkenness and immorality.[1]

The situation, however, was not universally grim. Many voices including those of John Standonck, Jean Raulin and Olivier Maillard, spoke out in favour of church reform. All stressed the importance to salvation of pastoral care while Raulin criticized clerical ignorance. Such criticisms, of course, were a commonplace of sermons since the fourteenth century; what was new was a realization that reform to be effective needed to come from the bishops. As Raulin pointed out, they needed to lead their flocks and watch over them with vigilance. Another positive aspect was the survival of a genuine popular faith. New churches were being built and new forms of devotion invented, like the Stations of the Cross and the Rosary. Pilgrimages remained as popular as ever, and no one thought of making a will without including a number of pious bequests. Religious books formed the bulk of the printers' output, and art

---

[1] A. Renaudet, *Préréforme et humanisme à Paris pendant les premières guerres d'Italie* (1953), pp. 10–11.

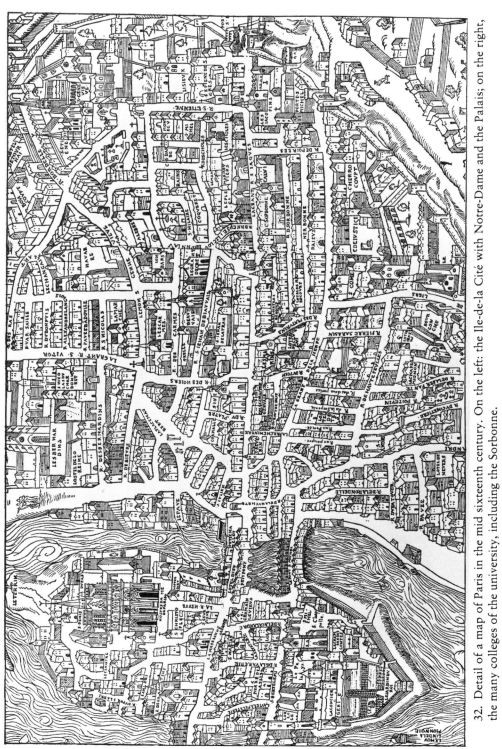

32. Detail of a map of Paris in the mid sixteenth century. On the left: the Île-de-la Cité with Notre-Dame and the Palais; on the right, the many colleges of the university, including the Sorbonne.

continued to dwell on sacred themes.[2] Anticlericalism, far from denoting a loss of faith, stemmed rather from a sharpened awareness of the discrepancy between the Christian ideal and the way of life of many of its professional exponents. However, on a more sophisticated level, that of the theologians in the universities, sharp differences arose regarding the philosophical foundations of Christian belief. Three currents of thought existed side by side: scholasticism, mysticism and humanism.

The most important centre of theological studies in Europe was the University of Paris. This comprised four faculties: Theology, Canon Law, Medicine and Arts. The first three were graduate faculties whose members had to be doctors. The five-year course in arts was the essential prerequisite for doctoral study in one of the other faculties. The doctorate in theology demanded a further fifteen years of study. Once a man had become a doctor of theology he was licensed to 'read, dispute, deliberate and teach' in the faculty. The doctors' main function was to preside over disputations and inaugural lectures by students. They were also expected to attend regular meetings of the faculty, which normally took place at the convent of Saint Mathurin. Sometimes such meetings were held at the Sorbonne which explains why historians have often confused this college – one of nearly forty – with the Faculty of Theology. They were, in fact, quite distinct. Only about 20 per cent of doctors of theology between 1500 and 1536 had any connection with the Sorbonne.[3] The main attraction of a doctorate in theology was the prestige attached to it: the holder was able to deliberate on the highest matters of faith and help decide matters of religious and political significance.

Meetings of the Faculty were presided over by the Dean or Pro-Dean. In addition the post of syndic was created in 1520 with responsibility for the good order of the faculty's deliberations, preparing the agenda for meetings, ensuring that the statutes were respected, that decisions were carried out and that minutes were kept. The post was intended as an annual appointment, but Noël Béda, the first syndic, was reappointed from 1520 till his exile in 1533.[4] There were fifteen universities in France in 1520, though not all had a faculty of theology. In theory each had authority in its own area, but in practice the authority of the Paris Faculty in defining doctrine and censoring books was overriding.[5]

The Faculty of Theology was, by virtue of its teaching, the preaching of its masters and the doctrinal judgments of its assembly, the sovereign interpreter of dogma. All of its learning was drawn from the Bible and the *Book of Sentences* of Peter Lombard. However, by the fifteenth century any notion of a

[2] L. Febvre, *Au coeur religieux du XVIe siècle* (1957), pp. 27–37.
[3] J. K. Farge, *Orthodoxy and Reform in Early Reformation France* (Leiden, 1985), pp. 3–4.
[4] J. K. Farge, *Biographical Register of Paris Doctors of Theology, 1500–1536* (Toronto, 1980), pp. 31–6.
[5] F. M. Higman, *Censorship and the Sorbonne* (Geneva, 1979), p. 15.

critical study of Scripture had been lost. A conciliar decision of 1311 that oriental languages should be taught in the principal European universities had been
ignored. Consequently, theologians were unable to read the Old Testament in
the original Hebrew or the New in the original Greek. They were content
instead with the quadruple method of exegesis: historical, allegorical, analogi-
cal and tropological. In applying this method they preferred the interpretations
of mediaeval scholars, like Nicholas of Lyra, to those of the early church
fathers. Above all they relied on the *Book of Sentences*.

Outstanding among thirteenth-century doctors at the university was St
Thomas Aquinas whose philosophy was largely shaped by Aristotle's meta-
physical writings. In his judgment, knowledge of God was attainable through
reason with the assistance of Scripture and the traditional teaching of the
church. However, the certainties inherent in his teaching were challenged, first
by Duns Scotus (*c.* 1265–1308), then by William of Ockham (*c.* 1285–1347).
The latter denied that spiritual concepts could be grasped merely through
reason. Divine truth, in his opinion, lay beyond the reach of the human intellect; it was held in trust by the church and could only be apprehended through
its teaching. The new doctrine, called Nominalism as distinct from the Realism
of Aquinas, seemed to demote knowledge into a mere study of ideas. For this
reason it was twice condemned by the University of Paris, but in the second
half of the fourteenth century it affirmed its dominance. The Nominalists,
instead of building on Ockham's ideas, merely repeated them; they even nar-
rowed their scope by retreating into a study of formal logic that was both
abstract and sterile. Their teaching became for sixteenth-century humanists the
epitome of intellectual backwardness and confusion. Nominalism effectively
paralysed the study of theology in Paris. It reduced Christianity to a collection
of affirmations that had to be accepted without thought of love, and the Christian life to the observance of formal practices and the performance of good
works.[6]

Nominalism, being too dry and formal to satisfy many Christians, was
bound sooner or later to provoke a reaction. This took the form of mysticism.
Although a strong mystical tradition existed in Paris reaching back to such
fourteenth-century teachers as Pierre d'Ailly and Jean Gerson, it was in the
Low Countries that mysticism flowered at the end of the Middle Ages. A major
ascetic movement was the *Devotio Moderna*. Its followers, the Brethren of the
Common Life, avoided formal vows while sharing a life in common dedicated
to poverty, chastity and obedience. Their founder, Gerard Groote, wanted
religion to be simple, devout and charitable. By the early fifteenth century the
Brethren had numerous houses in the Low Countries, Germany and the Rhine-
land. Their ideals were best expressed in the *Imitation of Christ* by Thomas à

6 A. Renaudet, pp. 53–67, 98.

Kempis. Rejecting the Nominalists' uncritical acceptance of the church's teaching, the Brethren found the truth of Christianity in the Bible and liked to read St Augustine and St Bernard, those great exponents of the inner life and divine love.[7] An important link between the mysticism of the Low Countries and France was John Standonck, a pupil of the Brethren who settled in Paris. Having completed the arts course, he entered the collège de Montaigu to study theology, becoming its principal in 1483. He imposed a harsh discipline on the students, hoping to develop among them an active, mystical piety. He was succeeded in 1504 by Noël Béda.[8]

The third component of Parisian thought at the close of the Middle Ages was humanism. Having originated in fourteenth-century Florence, it gradually reached the University of Paris. Around 1470 Guillaume Fichet, who visited Italy several times, was the central figure of a group professing a love of ancient Rome. It keenly felt the need for accurate texts of the Latin classics, especially Cicero, Virgil and Sallust. In 1470 the first Parisian press was set up in the cellars of the Sorbonne. Within three years it had printed several humanistic texts. Fichet's aim was to bring to Paris not merely the eloquence of Italian humanism but also its philosophy. He and his followers combined respect for the scholastic tradition with a love of Latin letters and an interest in Platonic ideas. Among Fichet's heirs in Paris the most important was Robert Gaguin, who gathered a small group of scholars sharing an interest in ancient letters. They discussed literary and ethical questions and tried to imitate Cicero's style. Yet they never allowed their classical enthusiasms to undermine their Christian faith. Many were churchmen who retained a strict, almost monastic, ideal. They were helped in their labours by a number of Italian humanists, notably, Filippo Beroaldo, Paolo Emilio, Girolamo Balbi and Fausto Andrelini, who came to Paris and did some teaching.

The early Parisian humanists soon developed an interest in ancient philosophy. As they did not know enough Greek to read the original works of Aristotle and Plato, they obtained good Latin translations from Italy. A few were also published in Paris. These were only first steps, however. Parisian teachers and students needed also to become acquainted with the philosophical speculations of the leading Italian humanists.[9] One of them, Pico della Mirandola, visited Paris in 1485. His major goal was to reconcile Platonism and Aristotelianism. He was well acquainted with mediaeval Aristotelianism and also with the sources of Jewish and Arabic thought.[10]

Parisian teachers needed to know Greek before they could become conversant with the Greek philosophers. In 1476 Greek studies received a boost when

[7] Ibid., p. 67–72; M. Aston, The Fifteenth Century (London, 1968), pp. 157–61.
[8] Renaudet, pp. 175–82, 359, 456–9; also his Humanisme et Renaissance (Geneva, 1958), pp. 114–61.
[9] Renaudet, Préréforme et humanisme, pp. 80–9, 114–30.
[10] P. O. Kristeller, Eight Philosophers of the Renaissance (London, 1965), pp. 54–71.

George Hermonymos, a Spartan, settled in Paris. For more than thirty years he lived by copying Greek manuscripts and teaching the language. His pupils included Erasmus, Beatus Rhenanus and Budé. In 1495 King Charles VIII brought back from Italy Janus Lascaris, an excellent Hellenist who taught Greek to a number of humanists, including Budé. He also began organizing the royal library at Blois. After about 1504 there were some excellent teachers of Greek in Paris. The first Greek printing there was in 1494 though until 1507 it consisted of only passages in a few works. Greek typography began in 1507 with François Tissard's edition of the *Liber Gnomagyricus*. He urged Frenchmen to study Greek in order to combat Italian charges of barbarism. In 1508 Girolamo Aleandro came to Paris. He began giving private lessons in Greek to people rich enough to buy the books being produced by the Aldine press. In 1509 he went public and published three small works by Plutarch. His intention, as he grandly announced, was to edit all the works of Greek authors.[11]

Despite the humanists, scholasticism remained firmly entrenched in the University of Paris in the early sixteenth century. Outstanding among the new generation of schoolmen was John Mair, who taught at the collège de Montaigu. He resented the charge of barbarousness levelled at the schoolmen by the humanists, yet his works exemplified some of the worst aspects of scholasticism, such as the endless chewing over of insignificant problems. Statutes drawn up for Montaigu by Béda in February 1509 did not forbid humanistic texts, but they provided for teaching only in Latin, not Greek.

The first Frenchman to break away significantly from the scholastic tradition was Jacques Lefèvre d'Etaples. Like many others of his generation, he was profoundly disturbed by the state of religion, and in 1472 thought of entering a reformed monastery; but he decided that he could serve Christianity more effectively by remaining in the world as a teacher. He began to devote himself to the restoration of Aristotelianism by replacing the pedestrian and often misleading translations of the schoolmen. He also wrote commentaries on the *Ethics*, *Politics* and *Economics* and prepared paraphrases of nearly all Aristotle's works.[12] But Lefèvre's enthusiasm for Aristotle was deeply permeated by mysticism. Along with Ficino and Pico della Mirandola, both of whom he had met in Italy, he believed that beyond Aristotelian logic lay another, more mysterious, world of forces and spirits accessible only to a privileged few capable of absorbing esoteric knowledge. After being attracted to Neoplatonism, he turned to the religious philosophy of Dionysius the Aeropagite. Above all, he succumbed to the spell of Nicolas of Cusa, who held that the supreme and unimaginable reality can only be intuitively received through extasy.[13] But

---

[11] Renaudet, *Préréforme et humanisme*, pp. 83–9, 114–26, 501–3, 509–13.   [12] *Ibid.*, pp. 130–55.
[13] *Ibid.*, pp. 207–8; E. F. Rice, 'Humanist Aristotelianism in France' in *Humanism in France at the end of the Middle Ages and in the Early Renaissance*, ed. A. H. T. Levi (Manchester, 1970), p. 143.

33. This medal of Erasmus of Rotterdam by Quentin Matsys (1519) bears an inscription to the effect that the portrait is taken from life and also a warning in Greek that Erasmus's real portrait is to be found in his writings.

Lefèvre wanted to reform not only the teaching of philosophy in Paris, but also that of theology. It was high time, he felt, to get away from the interminable and sterile discussions of the *Book of Sentences* and to study the neglected works of earlier writers. In 1509 he published an edition of the Psalter with a commentary in which theological questions were deliberately set aside and the inner life stressed. Three years later he published an edition of St Paul's Epistles. In short, Lefèvre became a Christian humanist.

The greatest exponent of Christian humanism was, of course, Erasmus of Rotterdam. He came to Paris in 1495 to study theology, and entered the collège de Montaigu, where Standonck's régime instilled in him a deep and lasting aversion to abstinence and austerity. He attended lectures on the Bible and *Book of Sentences* but derived no satisfaction, intellectual or spiritual, from the schoolmen's teaching' 'They exhaust the mind', he wrote, 'by a certain jejune and barren subtlety, without fertilizing or inspiring it. By their stammering and by the stains of their impure style they disfigure theology which had been enriched and adorned by the eloquence of the ancients.'[14] The schoolmen, however, were not wholly to blame for Erasmus's attitude: his mind, despite its breadth and acuteness, was not well suited to philosophical or dogmatic speculation. For the present he was interested in ancient letters, not in theology or philosophy. He joined Gaguin's circle of friends, and in 1499 published a small collection of ancient proverbs. This contained some of the earliest Greek printing by a French press and marked the beginning of a gigantic project for the rehabilitation of classical literature, which was to occupy Erasmus for the rest of his life. However, his enthusiasm for the classics did not lessen his appreciation of the Christian legacy, quite the contrary. After making the acquaintance of John Colet in England in 1499, he set out to place the wisdom of the ancients at the service of the interpretation of Christianity and, in his *Enchiridion militis Christiani* indicated the place of secular learning in the training of the Christian mind; the study of the classics, poetry and philosophy was to be simply the prelude to that of Scripture.[15] In April 1511 Erasmus was back in Paris, mainly to see his *Encomium Morae* (*Praise of Folly*) through the press. This famous work contains a satiric attack on current abuses, especially on worthless monks, vain schoolmen and warring popes. In June Erasmus left Paris never to return, but his influence lived on. His works continued to be published and read in the capital for many years.[16]

Francis I and humanism

In 1517 Francis I was anxious to show himself not only as a great soldier, but as a great patron of learning. The time was ripe for such a gesture, as Europe was for once at peace; Erasmus even hoped that this was the dawn of a new age. Francis was an avid collector of manuscripts and books.[17] He also shared an interest, common among princes of his day, in the occult sciences: astrology, alchemy and the Cabala. They were believed to hold the key to the hidden forces animating the universe. Thus the king was extremely interested in the 'theatre of memory' of Giulio Camillo, a system of universal mnemotechnique. When Camillo visited Paris, Francis paid him 500 gold

[14] J. Huizinga, *Erasmus of Rotterdam* (London, 1952), pp. 22–3.
[15] M. Mann, *Erasme et les débuts de la réforme française, 1517–1536* (1934), pp. 24–46.
[16] Renaudet, *Préréforme et humanisme*, pp. 606–11.
[17] Quentin-Bauchart, *La bibliothèque de Fontainebleau, 1515–89* (1891), pp. 8–9.

ducats for the completion of the theatre whose secret was to be revealed to him alone.[18]

The revival of interest in Jewish studies among Christians in the late fifteenth century entailed an interest in the Cabala, the esoteric tradition of Jewish mysticism. This rests on the belief that there is a hidden meaning in Scripture which opens the way to an understanding of the divine world. By using the methods of Hebraic cabalism, Christian scholars hoped to find in Holy Writ confirmation of the Christian mysteries and also to prove that, even before Christ's coming, the Jewish prophets and theologians were already Christian. Christian cabalism, like its Jewish counterpart, became closely associated with magic and astrology. Among its exponents was Agrippa of Nettesheim, who spent some time in Louise of Savoy's circle before becoming one of Charles V's intimates.

French interest in cabalism stemmed from the publication in 1517 of Reuchlin's *De arte cabalistica*. In 1518 Symphorien Champier devoted a chapter of his *Pronostics ou présage des prophètes, des astrologues et des médecins* to the Cabala. Whereupon Francis asked Jean Thenaud for a treatise on the subject. But Thenaud evidently disapproved of the king's interest, for his *Cabale métrifiée* (1519) treats with a truly Erasmian irony the combinations of words, permutations and anagrams that are basic to cabalism. 'It is far better', he writes, 'to be ignorant than to ask or look for what cannot be known without sinning.' Francis, however, was not deterred; he asked Thenaud for another work on the Cabala, this time in prose. Thenaud obliged by producing a more serious work, drawing upon the writings of Reuchlin and his Italian precursors. Yet even this warns the king of the danger of cabalism. It resorts to a device favoured by the *rhétoriqueurs*: the allegorical dream. Thenaud is rescued by Dame Simplicité from the synagogue into which he has been led by Dame Curiosité. She reminds him that God's book is sealed till the end of the world, and that it is a sin to seek to know its contents beforehand. Dame Simplicité leads Thenaud into the library of the church of the Holy Sepulchre and shows him a book, the *De laudibus sanctae crucis* of Raban Maur, the ninth-century Benedictine, which he uses to show the king that as much mystery is contained in Latin works as in those of Jews and Greeks.[19]

Francis enjoyed the company of intelligent, well-educated men. His entourage included several humanists, notably his secretary Guillaume Budé, his doctor Guillaume Cop, his old tutor François Demoulins, and his confessor Guillaume Petit. The most important of these men was Budé, who at the age of twenty-three gave up a life of hard drinking and hunting for scholarship. He learnt Greek, became something of a recluse and impaired his health by over-

---

[18] Frances A. Yates, *The Art of Memory* (London, 1966), pp. 129–32.
[19] A.-M. Lecoq, *François Ier imaginaire* (1987), pp. 301–8.

34. Portrait of Guillaume Budé, the great French humanist who encouraged Francis to set up the *lecteurs royaux*, by Jean Clouet (tempera and oil on wood). The Greek inscription reads: 'It may seem a great thing to realize one's desires, but truly the greatest thing is not to desire what one shouldn't.'

work. His two major works were the *Annotationes ad Pandectas* (1508) and *De Asse* (1515), but his scholarship, though profound, was long-winded and untidy. *De Asse*, a treatise on ancient coinage, contains innumerable digressions in which Budé reveals his ardent patriotism by rebutting claims to intellectual hegemony.[20] Like other northern humanists, he was a committed Christian and applied his philological expertise to the study of Scripture. But he was also aware of the fundamentally secular assumptions of classical thought, and unlike Lefèvre d'Etaples, saw no possibility of compromise between Hellenism and Christianity. In his last book, *De transitu Hellenismi ad Christianismum*, he went so far as to deny the value of ancient philosophy.[21]

At the beginning of Francis's reign the greatest need felt by humanists in France was for an institution devoted to the teaching of Greek and Hebrew which were excluded from the traditional university curriculum. The king's first response to this need was to appoint a Genoese scholar, Agostino Giustiniani, to teach Hebrew in Paris, but he was an incorrigible nomad and left after five years. In February 1517 Francis announced his intention of founding a college devoted to the study of classical languages.[22] This was not a new idea: in the fourteenth century there had been a move to set up in France an institution where the so-called oriental languages (i.e. Greek, Hebrew and Arabic) might be taught, but nothing happened till 1457 when Gregorio da Città di Castello began to teach Greek in Paris. He left after only eighteen months.[23] By the time Francis took up the idea of a classical college, two had been or were being, set up elsewhere: a college of young Greeks was founded in Rome by Leo X in 1515, and a trilingual one at Louvain by Busleiden two years later.

At the instance of Petit and Demoulins, the king decided to invite Erasmus to take charge of his new college, offering him a rich prebend as a bait. Why did he not choose Budé? This question was posed at the time. In January 1519 Christophe de Longueil expressed surprise that Francis should have preferred 'a German to a Frenchman, a foreigner to a compatriot and an unknown person to an intimate acquaintance'.[24] Yet the king's choice is understandable. Budé was as good a Greek scholar as Erasmus, possibly even a more profound one, but Erasmus was the only notable scholar who combined satisfactorily the classical and Christian elements of the Renaissance and whose international standing was commensurate with the prestige Francis hoped to gain from his foundation. He had already published his *Enchiridion*, *Adages*, New Testament and *St Jerome*, as well as many other editions of the classics and early church fathers. He was, as Lefèvre said, 'the splendour of letters'.[25]

---

[20] L. Delaruelle, *Guillaume Budé* (1907), pp. 58ff. 161–2; D. O. McNeil, *Guillaume Budé and Humanism in the reign of Francis I* (Geneva, 1975), pp. 3–36.

[21] R. R. Bolgar, 'Humanism as a Value System' in *Humanism in France*, ed. A. H. T. Levi (Manchester, 1970), p. 204.

[22] A. Lefranc, *Histoire du Collège de France* (1893), p. 45.

[23] G. Di Stefano, 'L'Hellénisme en France à l'orée de la Renaissance', in *Humanism in France*, ed. A. H. T. Levi, pp. 31–42.

[24] D. Erasmus, *Opus epistolarum*, ed. P. S. Allen and H. M. Allen (Oxford, 1906–34), iii. 473.

[25] M. Mann, *Erasme et les débuts de la réforme française*, pp. 7–8.

Far from being offended by the king's choice, Budé urged Erasmus to accept Francis's invitation. 'This monarch', he wrote, 'is not only a Frank (which is in itself a glorious title); he is also Francis, a name borne by a king for the first time and, one can prophesy, predestined for great things. He is educated in letters, which is usual with our kings, and also possesses a natural eloquence, wit, tact and an easy, pleasant manner; nature, in short, has endowed him with the rarest gifts of body and mind. He likes to admire and to praise princes of old who have distinguished themselves by their lofty intellects and brilliant deeds, and he is fortunate in having as much wealth as any king in the world, which he gives more liberally than anyone.'[26]

Erasmus, though flattered by the king's invitation and tempted by the rich prebend, valued his freedom too much to tie himself to any prince, however generous and enlightened. He was also afraid of offending Charles of Habsburg from whom he was drawing a pension. On 14 February, therefore, he wrote to Etienne Poncher, who had brought him the king's invitation, explaining that he could not leave the Netherlands because of his age, health and indebtedness to Charles. He suggested in his place Heinrich Loriti *alias* Glareanus, a young Swiss humanist.[27] In a letter thanking Francis, Erasmus expressed his admiration for what seemed to him the dawn of a new age, but this merely irritated the king. 'What, then, are Erasmus's intentions?', he asked. 'For he does not explain himself clearly.' In April, Budé and the queen's secretary, Germain de Brie, tried to persuade Erasmus to change his mind, but he would not yield. 'France', he replied, 'has always smiled on me, but so far I have been detained by any number of obstacles.'[28]

Seeing that no good would come out of the negotiations with Erasmus, Francis approached Janus Lascaris, the principal of Leo X's college in Rome, whom he had already invited to France in 1515. Lascaris had then refused for fear of offending the pope; this time he accepted. The scheme for the classical college, however, was not implemented at once. Francis's enthusiasm had waned during the protracted talks with Erasmus, and the French humanists were divided as to precisely what kind of college they wanted. Some favoured a trilingual college on the Louvain model, others preferred a college of young Greeks on the Roman model. In the end, Francis decided to set up a college in Milan, probably as the first step towards creating a more ambitious one in France. He allocated 10,000 *livres* to it in addition to an annual payment of 2,000 *livres* for the maintenance of twelve Greek students and two teachers,

[26] Lefranc, pp. 48–9.   [27] Erasmus, *Opus epistolarum*, ii. 454–8.
[28] Lefranc, pp. 53–6; M. Mann, p. 7. Late in 1521 or early in 1522 Erasmus met François de Tournon, the young archbishop of Embrun, at Basle and expressed the wish to visit France. This was for health reasons, not as a result of any new invitation by the king of France. The archbishop got him a safe-conduct, but Erasmus did not use it. See M. François, *Le cardinal François de Tournon* (1951), pp. 29–31.

one of Greek, the other of Latin. Lascaris returned to Italy in 1520 and, after finding suitable premises in Milan, moved to Venice, whence he sent agents to Greece to recruit suitable pupils. Pending their arrival, he worked in the library of St Mark's and collected manuscripts for the king of France.[29] It was largely thanks to him that Francis acquired one of the finest collections of Greek manuscripts in western Europe.[30]

Francis's interest in scholarship, though genuine, was easily supplanted by more urgent considerations, such as war, and needed to be kept alive by tactful reminders. This was where Budé made an important contribution. Much as he detested court life, he put up with it, if only to remind the king from time to time of his promises and obligations to scholarship. One day he followed Francis to his chamber and produced a letter from Lascaris. Francis asked to see it and, when Budé failed to respond, snatched it from him only to find that it was in Greek. This gave Budé the chance to show off 'like a monkey among a crowd of asses'. He so impressed the king by translating the letter aloud that he was able to say 'all that seemed opportune and useful'. In January 1521 Budé took advantage of the king's escape from a nearly fatal accident to remind him of his promise to found a college.

The upshot was a formal declaration on 22 January in which Francis announced his intention to set up a college for the study of Greek at the Hôtel de Nesle, in Paris. It was to comprise a chapel with a staff of four canons and four chaplains, and be maintained with the revenues of the chapels of old royal palaces. This represented a watering-down of his original scheme, and Budé was disappointed. 'I would not say', he wrote, 'that this zeal [the king's] is completely extinguished; I even believe that it will be revived without difficulty, but it is no longer active. I do what I can to rekindle the fire, which is only smouldering at present, but I lack the ability to influence the courtiers, who sometimes deride my plans and try unfairly to discredit me.' Lascaris, too, could feel despondent, for no money reached him from France after he had spent 2,000 *livres* recruiting young Greeks. He dug into his own pocket to pay for the college in Milan, but in August 1523 informed Montmorency that he would not be able to keep it going beyond the end of the month. He received no reply; the college was therefore dissolved.[31]

The rise of heresy

French humanism was not a purely intellectual movement: as exemplified by the writings of Lefèvre it aimed at reviving religion through a mystical approach to Scripture. To achieve this, however, it required practical assistance from influential churchmen. As Nicole Lemaitre has shown in her study of

[29] Lefranc, pp. 63–74.   [30] Di Stefano, p. 29.   [31] Lefranc, pp. 75–82.

the Rouergue, a keen desire for church reform existed among French bishops in the late fifteenth century. Among them was Claude de Seyssel, bishop of Marseilles (1511–17), then of Turin (1517–20) whose *Tractatus de triplici statu viatoris* laid down some of the guidelines for pastoral reform, including the need for bishops to reside in their dioceses. Between 1518 and 1520, at the same time as the Lutheran reformation was taking shape, several French bishops began to take their pastoral duties seriously. They included Guillaume Briçonnet at Meaux, François d'Estaing at Rodez, Louis Guillart at Courtrai, Pierre Filhol at Aix, Lodovico di Canossa at Bayeux and Philippe de Montmorency at Limoges. In 1518 bishops, who had too many other duties, appointed suffragans. Under the influence of Briçonnet and Etienne Poncher, Francis I ordered the holding of provincial synods 'to reform the church, to remove many abuses and to ensure that vacant benefices no longer leave the kingdom of France'. Between 1520 and 1529 many small manuals were published to assist parish priests in their cure of souls.

Although Francis I, in nominating bishops favoured the nobility of sword and turned a blind eye to the educational requirements laid down in the Concordat, there were more graduates among his bishops than previously. In the 1520s 27 per cent were graduates as compared with 8.5 per cent over the period 1490–1550. It was between 1523 and 1529 that the largest number of theologians were to be found, whereas lawyers had predominated before. This phenomenon may reflect the educational revival in the University of Paris between 1480 and 1510. Attendance at such colleges as Navarre or Montaigu and to a lesser extent Boncourt and Cardinal Lemoine brought future bishops into contact with advocates of church reform like Jean Raulin, Louis Pinelle, John Standonck and John Mair and later Jacques Lefèvre d'Etaples, Charles de Bovelles and Josse Clichtove. Having acquired their sees the bishops liked to surround themselves with some of the brilliant minds they had known in their student days. In this way a number of humanists became attached to episcopal courts. For example, François d'Estaing invited the poet and philosopher, Alain de Varènes, to join him at Rodez; Louis Guillart invited Josse Clichtove to Chartres; and Guillaume Briçonnet asked Lefèvre d'Etaples to promote reform at Meaux in 1521. Bishops who were unable to reside on a regular basis, and this was true of the majority, had to rely on suffragans to carry out their pastoral duties. The intellectual qualifications of these men were far from negligible. Unlike the bishops, they had risen on account of their degrees, not their birth. Out of thirty-eight suffragans between 1523 and 1529 not less than sixteen (42 per cent) were graduates, most of them products of Parisian colleges or prestigious Italian universities. They had nearly all been influenced by the *Devotio moderna*, and, more or less, by humanism. This was the generation of bishops and suffragans who were confronted with the enormously difficult task of fighting heresy and promoting reform at the same time.[32]

The problem showed itself most acutely in the diocese of Meaux. Briçonnet, on visiting his diocese in 1518 was shocked to find his flock 'starved of divine food' and poisoned by the superstitious claptrap of the local Franciscans.[33] To help him remedy this state of affairs, he invited Lefèvre to join him and gathered a group of evangelical preachers, who became known as the *Cercle de Meaux*. They included Gérard Roussel, Guillaume Farel, Martial Mazurier and Pierre Caroli. After dividing his diocese into twenty-six zones, Briçonnet assigned preachers to each of them for Lent and Advent while he himself preached every Sunday in his cathedral. Inevitably, this upset the local Franciscans (Cordeliers) whose livelihood depended on retaining the loyalty of the people. They accused the bishop and his friends of heresy and looked to the Faculty of Theology and Parlement of Paris for assistance.[34]

Heresy was not unknown in France at the end of the Middle Ages, but except in Dauphiné and Provence where there was an infiltration of Waldensianism from the Alpine valleys of Piedmont, it was not an organized movement.[35] In 1517 Erasmus described France as 'the purest and most prosperous part of Christendom' and the only country not infected with heresy.[36] This happy state of affairs did not last long. In 1519 Lutheranism first made its appearance in Paris. On 14 February, the Basle printer, John Froben, informed Luther that he had sent 600 copies of his works to France and Spain. 'They are sold in Paris', he wrote,' and are being read even at the Sorbonne; they meet with everyone's approval.' In May, Pierre Tschudi, a Swiss student informed Beatus Rhenanus that Luther's writings were being received in Paris 'with open arms'.[37] Even the Faculty of Theology, it seems, seemed to sympathize with Luther's views, notably his attack on indulgences.

The Faculty was consulted at least seventy times on matters of doctrine and morals between 1500 and 1542. A few examples will serve to demonstrate its attitudes to some major issues of the time. In 1512, for example, the doctors were asked by the Council of Pisa to pass judgment on a book by Cajetan which defended papal superiority over councils. The Faculty, being tradi-

---

[32] I am indebted for this information to Nicole Lemaitre whose paper on 'Les évêques réformateurs français et leur personnel dans le choc de la réformation luthérienne (1523–29)' was given on 10 May 1991 at the Institut français, London. On Bishop François d'Estaing see her *Le Rouergue flamboyant* (1988), pp. 217–45.

[33] Febvre, *Au coeur religieux*, pp. 145–61; Imbart de la Tour, iii. 110–15; M. Veissière, *L'évêque Guillaume Briçonnet (1470–1534)* (Provins, 1986), p. 131.

[34] Farge, *Orthodoxy and Reform*, pp. 124, 171, 237–40; Veissière, *Guillaume Briçonnet*, pp. 197–220, 233–7.

[35] E. G. Léonard, *Histoire générale du Protestantisme* (1961), i. 240–2; E. Cameron, *The Reformation of the Heretics: The Waldenses of the Alps, 1480–1580* (Oxford, 1984), pp. 15–24. See below, pp. 323–25.

[36] M. Mann, p. 23.

[37] W. G. Moore, *La réforme allemande et la littérature française* (Strasbourg, 1930), pp. 46–9.

tionally Gallican, opposed the book on principle, but it was also doubtful about the legitimacy of the Pisa assembly. In the end, it gave no opinion, as Francis, who was negotiating the Concordat, asked it to drop the matter. Two years later, the Faculty was drawn into the conflict over Reuchlin's promotion of Jewish studies. He believed that biblical studies should be reviewed in the light of recent exegetical advances and expertise in Hebrew and Greek. Such a programme threatened to upset the existing curriculum of theological faculties. On 2 August 1514 the Paris Faculty condemned Reuchlin's views only to be reprimanded by the Holy See which had recently cleared him of all charges. Historians have usually taken this affair as marking the decisive breach in Paris between scholasticism and the 'New Learning'.[38]

Within weeks of Luther's famous attack on indulgences in October 1517 the Paris Faculty prosecuted a similar case in France. It was much concerned by the crusade appeal launched by Leo X and Francis I. It decided to bring to the king's notice 'scandals and abuses which are taking place both in preaching and in crafty exactions of money for the said crusade ...'. Several people were accused of 'preaching things false, ridiculous, scandalous and perilous to faith and morals in order to extort money from the poor and the inhabitants of this kingdom'. The Faculty decided to examine certain passages in the papal bull, but it was forbidden to do so by the king. His instructions to preachers of the crusade were patently simoniacal, yet he would brook no opposition. Like Luther, the Faculty rejected the superstitious preaching of indulgences, but unlike him it did not reject the doctrine of indulgences as such.[39]

In July 1519 Luther and Eck held their famous debate in Leipzig. Soon afterwards they agreed to submit their positions to the Universities of Erfurt and Paris. Many observers believed that Paris would decline to rule on the matter, since a judgment in favour of Eck would buttress papal authority. Yet the Parisian doctors did not evade the issue. If Luther was not mentioned in their proceedings till 17 July 1520, this was because they wished for secrecy. A plenary discussion by the Faculty on 14 August may have focused on papal primacy, the main issue at Leipzig, and this would explain the doctors' failure to agree. But Luther offered them an escape from the question of papal authority by publishing three radical books in 1520. On 15 April 1521 the Faculty published its *Determinatio*, a unanimous condemnation of 104 Lutheran propositions. Not all were condemned with equal force: some were described as 'heretical', others as 'schismatic', 'false' or 'temerarious'. It may be significant that the *Determinatio* failed to deal with indulgences and papal authority, but the Faculty had only recently given its opinion on these matters.[40]

---

[38] Farge, *Orthodoxy and Reform*, pp. 115–18, 223–5.   [39] *Ibid.*, pp. 164–5.
[40] *Ibid.*, pp. 165–9; D. Hempsall, 'Martin Luther and the Sorbonne, 1519–21' *B.I.H.R.*, xlvi (1973), 29–36.

35. This woodcut by Geoffroy Tory (1480–1533) from *Praxis criminis persequendi* by Jean Milles de Souvigny shows the proclamation 'to the sound of trumpets' of an edict against heretics.

It is commonly said that Francis instructed the Parlement to ensure that no work was published without the university's *imprimatur* before the Faculty of Theology had issued its *Determinatio*. This has now been disproved. It was the Faculty which took the initiative in convincing both the king and the Parlement of the need to suppress Lutheranism.[41] On 6 May it called on the *gens du roi* to give special consideration to this matter of faith 'of which the most Christian king ought to be and is the guardian and protector'. On 13 June the Faculty, after consulting the Parlement, produced a decree establishing joint control of the book trade in and around Paris. It now became an offence to print or sell any religious book without the Faculty's prior approval. But this was not easily enforced. In July the Faculty complained about the persistent appearance in Paris of printed works, translated from Latin into French, which were offensive to the Catholic faith. More consultations took place, and a new decree was drawn up. On 3 August a proclamation was made 'to the sound of trumpets' in the streets of the capital. All booksellers, printers and other persons owning Lutheran works were to hand them over to the Parlement within a week on pain of a fine of 100 *livres* and imprisonment. This was an eloquent testimony of Luther's success in Paris to date: within four months it had become necessary to turn an academic condemnation into a police measure. Yet even this failed to check the circulation of Lutheran books. In the autumn Melanchthon's reply to the *Determinatio* appeared in Paris, only two months after its publication in Germany. It was an immediate success and the Faculty of Arts allowed it to circulate among its members, causing consternation and anger among the theologians. At attempt by the latter to muzzle the students of the junior faculty failed, whereupon they sought help from the king. On 4 November he made any breach of the decree of 3 August punishable by banishment.[42]

So far the Faculty of Theology had largely ignored the squabbles between the schoolmen and the humanists. In 1515 Lefèvre d'Etaples had been summoned to be 'amicably interrogated' about his support for Reuchlin and between 1518 and 1520 two doctors, Grandval and Béda, had defended traditional doctrine against the teachings of Lefèvre and Clichtove, but they had acted for themselves, not for the Faculty. Béda was not yet the syndic, yet he already held views which would eventually lead him to prosecute humanists as heretics. He believed that they were trying to change the text of the Bible that had been used for 1100 years and to substitute 'human' words for divinely inspired ones. 'God wills', he wrote, 'that the faculties and prelates make provision without delay that this foyer of scandals does not spread any further'.[43]

[41] Farge, *Orthodoxy and Reform*, pp. 253–4.
[42] *Ibid.*, pp. 168–9; D. Hempsall, 'Measures to suppress "La Peste Luthérienne" in France, 1521–2', *B.I.H.R.*, xlix (1976), 296–9; F. Higman, p. 23.
[43] Farge, *Orthodoxy and Reform*, p. 170.

36. Miniature from the *Orationes devotissime* (B.N., ms. n. acq. lat. 83, f. 2) written for Marguerite d'Angoulême *c.* 1527. The artist has emphasized the physical likeness, especially the long nose, between the king, his mother and sister. The manuscript stresses the analogy between the royal trio and the Holy Trinity.

The religious conscience of Francis I is not easily probed. All that is known for certain is that he attended Mass daily. He also repeatedly expressed his opposition to heresy, sharing the view, almost universally held in his day, that religious toleration was incompatible with national unity. The oath sworn at his coronation bound him not only to defend the faith, but also to root out heresy. This, however, was not easily recognized, especially in a period so aptly described by Lucien Febvre as one of 'magnificent religious anarchy'. Where, for example, did the boundary lie between Christian humanism and Lutheranism? The king was not obliged to accept any definition of heresy, even that of the Faculty of Theology, particularly if it conflicted with other principles he held dear or with the opinions of relatives, friends and advisers. Francis, as we have seen, had shown a lively interest in humanism.[44] Thus he must have found it difficult to accept Béda's view that 'Luther's errors have entered this [kingdom] more through the works of Erasmus and Lefèvre than any others'.[45]

A powerful influence on the king was undoubtedly his sister, Marguerite d'Angoulême, for whom he had a strong affection. A deeply devout person, she corresponded with Bishop Briçonnet from June 1521 until October 1524 and through his spiritual teaching imbibed the ideas of Lefèvre d' Etaples.[46] This did not make her a Lutheran. Yet the ideas of Lefèvre and Luther, sharing an interest in the writings of St Paul, did overlap a fair amount. Lefèvre in his *Commentarii* stated his belief in justification by faith, and denied the effectiveness of the sacraments *ex opere operato*. He did not, however, accept all Luther's ideas (e.g. his reduction of the number of sacraments) and continued to hope that the church would reform itself. Marguerite, for all her interest in Lefèvre and Luther, never broke with the Roman church. Her faith has been described as neither Catholic nor Lutheran, but as a strange personal mixture derived from a variety of sources, including Lutheranism.[47]

Sooner or later trouble was certain to break out between the king and the Faculty of Theology. While Francis was ready to act against Lutheranism, at least in respect of the censorship of books, the Faculty was anxious to silence the voice of Christian humanism. The first sign of trouble occurred in November 1522 when the king's confessor, Guillaume Petit, complained to the Faculty about sermons being preached at court by Michel d'Arande, an Augustinian hermit who had become Marguerite d'Angoulême's almoner on Briçonnet's

[44] See above, pp. 149–54.   [45] Imbart de la Tour, iii. 258 n. 2.

[46] G. Briçonnet and Marguerite d'Angoulême *Correspondance (1521–1524)*, ed. C. Martineau and M. Veissière (Geneva, 1975–79). In return for his spiritual guidance the bishop expected Marguerite to gain her brother's support for the cause of reform, but he advised her against being too impetuous. 'Cover up the fire for a time', he wrote, 'for the wood you wish to burn is too green.' P. Jourda, *Répertoire analytique et chronologique de la correspondance de Marguerite d'Angoulême* (1930), p. 85; Veissière, *Guillaume Briçonnet*, pp. 189–94.

[47] L. Febvre, *Autour de L'Heptaméron* (1944), pp. 106–22.

recommendation. His admirers said that he preached 'only the pure Gospel'. The Faculty decided to look into his activities, but on learning that it had incurred the king's displeasure, it proceeded no further. D'Arande continued to preach as he followed Marguerite on her travels about the kingdom.[48]

By 1523 the Faculty of Theology and the Parlement of Paris had become seriously concerned about the progress of heresy in France. Lutheran books were reported from many parts of the kingdom and evangelical preachers were increasingly active. In June 1523 Pierre Lizet, *avocat du roi* in the Parlement, asked for the Faculty's help in fighting heresy at Meaux. The Faculty was told of 'various doctrines and several scandals' raised by Lefèvre's *Commentarii initiatorii in IV Evangelia*. On 18 June, however, members of the Faculty were warned by Duprat in front of Briçonnet and two other bishops of the king's displeasure. After rebuking them, Duprat ordered them to submit by 25 June to him and the three bishops any allegedly heretical passages in Lefèvre's work. Rather than submit to this humiliating procedure, the Faculty decided against pursuing its examination. On 11 July Francis evoked the whole matter to the *Grand Conseil*. Next day Lizet announced that he had been ordered by the king to investigate the Faculty.[49]

On 29 July 1523 Béda submitted to the Faculty twenty-two allegedly heretical propositions taken from sermons by Mazurier and Caroli. They denied that the propositions (*articles de Meaux*) truly reflected their teaching and requested a public debate. Ignoring this request, the Faculty condemned the propositions in September and called the two preachers to account. Briçonnet was asked to put pressure on them to obey. This marked a change of policy by the Faculty: whereas in the past it had been content simply to judge doctrine, it was now encroaching on episcopal jurisdiction. Mazurier and Caroli appealed unsuccessfully to the Parlement: on 16 January 1524 Caroli recanted and was followed, on 12 February, by Mazurier.[50]

The Faculty's persecution of the two preachers was in effect an attack on the entire *Cercle de Meaux*. In August 1523 the Faculty debated the pros and cons of translating Scripture. Some of the doctors saw nothing wrong with this, but Béda forced through a resolution condemning as useless and pernicious all editions of Scripture in Greek, Hebrew and French. This move, which was evidently prompted by the recent publication of Lefèvre's New Testament caused Francis to intervene again. In April 1524 he forbade any discussion of Lefèvre's works on the ground that he was a scholar highly esteemed in and outside France. In October 1523 he nipped in the bud an attempt by the Faculty to

[48] Imbart de la Tour, iii. 226–7; Farge, *Orthodoxy and Reform*, pp. 169, 237, 255; Veissière, *Guillaume Briçonnet*, pp. 225–6.
[49] Farge, *Orthodoxy and Reform*, pp. 171–2.
[50] *Ibid.*, pp. 171–3, 175; Imbart de la Tour, iii. 230–2; Doucet, i. 343; Veissière, *Guillaume Briçonnet*, pp. 254–8.

condemn Erasmus. The bishop of Senlis, acting on the king's behalf, asked the Faculty to submit a signed statement of the errors allegedly contained in Erasmus's works. In the face of this new threat to their jurisdiction, the theologians dropped their examination of Erasmus, while defiantly refusing to sanction publication of his *Paraphrases*.[51]

By 1523 the progress of heresy had become so rapid that the Faculty and Parlement saw the need for strong counter-measures: censoring books was not enough; an example had to be made of some of the heretics themselves. But the king was determined to protect humanists from what he regarded as unfair persecution. On 13 May the home of Louis de Berquin, a young aristocratic scholar, was searched by the Parlement. On his shelves were found books by Luther, Melanchthon, Karlstadt and von Hutten. There were also books written by Berquin himself which the Faculty asked to examine. Francis at first authorized the examination, disclaiming any wish to protect a heretic, but the Faculty's attempt to widen the scope of its enquiry so as to include works by Lefèvre and Erasmus angered him. On 24 June he forbade the Faculty to examine Berquin's works and handed over the task to a special commission headed by the Chancellor. His letter, however, arrived too late. The Faculty had already completed its examination. Berquin's works were condemned on 26 June and about a fortnight later he was invited by the Parlement to retract his views. This he must have refused to do, for he was committed to prison on 1 August. Four days later he was sent to the bishop of Paris for trial on a heresy charge, but Francis immediately evoked the case to the *Grand Conseil*. Berquin was released by royal command from the bishop's prison. He was allowed to return home and resume his literary activities. His books, however, were burnt outside Notre-Dame.[52]

In October 1523 Bishop Briçonnet issued two decrees at Meaux. The first, addressed to all the faithful, was directed against Luther; the other, addressed to the clergy, was directed against those who denied Purgatory and the invocation of saints. Like Erasmus, he was trying to dissociate the Lutheran reformation from the movement of church reform. On 13 December he revoked all preachers showing Lutheran sympathies, thereby precipitating the departure from Meaux of Guillaume Farel, Calvin's precursor at Geneva. Throughout 1524 Lefèvre and Roussel, while damping down radical preaching, sought to understand the German and Swiss reformers. From this time on, the *Cercle de Meaux* comprised moderates and radicals, but this was not a distinction that commended itself to the Faculty of Theology and the Parlement.[53] The king's

[51] Imbart de la Tour, iii. 232–5; Farge, *Orthodoxy and Reform*, p. 177; Higman, pp. 24–5.
[52] Doucet, i. 336–40; Moore, pp. 102–4; Imbart de la Tour, ii. 228; *J.B.P.*, p. 142; Farge, *Orthodoxy and Reform*, pp. 173–4, 255–6.
[53] Veissière, *Guillaume Briçonnet*, pp. 247–51, 258–9, 277–90; H. Heller (*The Conquest of Poverty*, Leiden, 1986, pp. 32–3) argues that the upheavals at Meaux were not simply religious; they were

departure for Italy in the autumn of 1524 followed by his defeat and captivity offered them a chance of dealing with heresy in their own way.

The religious policy of Francis I has often been described as inconsistent. While he professed to be opposed to heresy and issued decrees banning the publication and sale of Lutheran books, he impeded the efforts of the Faculty of Theology and Parlement to silence various scholars and preachers whose views seemed to them dangerously at variance with traditional dogma. He protected Lefèvre, Berquin and some other scholars and preachers from persecution. Rightly or wrongly, he did not regard them as heretics. In the 1520s the borderline between evangelical humanism and heresy was far from clear. Only by endorsing the extremist standpoint of a Noël Béda, who thought they were one and the same, could the king have been both orthodox and consistent. It was only later in his reign that heresy was more easily recognized. For the present Francis was content, as his sister explained, to show that 'the truth of God is not heresy'.[54]

'enmeshed in the social and political conflicts that shook the town' in the early 1520s. Mazurier urged his parishioners to help the poor rather than spend money on masses and other religious works.

[54] Herminjard, i. 78.

Chapter eight

Valois versus *Habsburg (1519–23)*

On 12 January 1519 the Emperor Maximilian died, throwing open the contest for the succession to the Holy Roman Empire. This was an elective not an hereditary, dignity. The Emperor was chosen by seven electors: the archbishops of Mainz, Cologne and Trier, the king of Bohemia, the Elector-Palatine, the duke of Saxony and the Margrave of Brandenburg. They were not bound to choose a member of the house of Habsburg or even a German. Thus it was possible for the king of France to stand for election. The Empire attracted Francis for two reasons: though based in Germany, it was a supranational dignity, the secular counterpart of the papacy, and therefore had enormous international prestige.[1] Secondly, Francis knew that Maximilian wanted to be succeeded by his grandson, Charles, who already ruled the Netherlands, Franche-Comté, Spain and Naples. 'You understand', he wrote, 'the reason which moves me to gain the empire, which is to prevent the said Catholic king from doing so. If he were to succeed, seeing the extent of his kingdoms and lordships, this could do me immeasurable harm: he would always be mistrustful and suspicious, and would doubtless throw me out of Italy.'[2]

Towards the end of 1516 two of the electors, the archbishops of Trier and Mainz offered to vote for Francis when the moment arrived. In June 1517 the Margrave of Brandenburg gave a similar undertaking, as did the Elector-Palatine, so that a majority of electors seemed prepared to support Francis I's imperial candidature.[3] However, they were less interested in his success than in

---

[1] Earlier French kings had also toyed with the idea of becoming Holy Roman Emperor. See M. François, 'L'idée en France à l'époque de Charles-Quint', *Charles-Quint et son temps* (1959), p. 25; G. Zeller, 'Les rois de France candidats à l'Empire', *R.H.*, clxxiii (1934), 273–311, 497–534.

[2] L. Schick, *Une grand homme d'affaires au début du XVIe siècle, Jacob Fugger* (1957), p. 163.

[3] *Ordonnances*, ii. no. 123. Another German who promised the king his support was Franz von Sickingen, the redoubtable knight, who could raise an army of 20,000 men at the drop of a hat. Barrillon, i. 251–2. He received a pension and a chain worth 3,000 *écus*. Sickingen went over to the imperial side after Francis had cut off his pension following an offence against Milanese merchants. In exchange for an annuity from Charles he took up a command in the army of the Swabian League. Florange, i. 233–4, 238–43; Le Glay, ii. 207.

promoting a contested election. Although an imperial election was supposed to be conducted with the highest integrity, it offered marvellous opportunities for bribery and corruption. The electors could hope to acquire large fortunes by selling their votes to the highest bidder. Maximilian, who was well acquainted with the seamier side of German political life, advised his grandson accordingly. 'If you wish to gain mankind', he wrote, 'you must play at a high stake. Either follow my counsel and adopt my suggestions or abandon any chance of bringing this affair to a termination satisfactory to our wishes and creditable to our fame. It would be lamentable if, after so much pain and labour to aggrandize and exalt our house and our posterity, we should lose all through some pitiful omission or penurious neglect.'[4] Taking this advice to heart, Charles sent money to Germany, and in August 1518 Maximilian managed to bribe five electors into promising to vote for his grandson. Only the archbishop of Trier and the duke of Saxony refused to be bought.

Francis, meanwhile, pursued his imperial ambitions with vigour. He sent envoys to the electors and to the king of Poland, who was expected to vote in place of the young king of Bohemia. To co-ordinate their efforts he also sent Admiral Bonnivet, the seigneur d'Orval and Charles Guillart, president of the Parlement, to Lorraine. They were empowered to promise money to the electors and carried 407,000 crowns in cash to Coblenz.[5] Francis seemed ready to go to any lengths to satisfy the electors. He brushed aside Guillart's suggestion that persuasion might be preferable to bribery. 'If I had only to deal with the virtuous', the king explained, 'or with those who even pretend to a shadow of virtue, your advice would be expedient and honest; but in times like the present, whatever a man sets his heart upon, be it the papacy, be it the empire or anything else, he has no means of obtaining his object except by force or corruption.'[6]

Francis's agents in Germany created the impression that their master had inexhaustible funds at his disposal. 'In this affair of the empire', one Habsburg agent remarked, 'we must not haggle at any fixed sums. Fresh disbursements will be constantly required, as these devils of Frenchmen scatter gold in all directions.'[7] In fact, Francis had difficulty raising the necessary cash. He was forced to alienate parts of his domain and to sell offices, and confiscated Boisy's inheritance. He is also said to have raised a loan of 360,000 crowns from Italian bankers in London.[8] But raising money was not his only problem:

---

[4] *L.P.* iii, p. iv.

[5] Barrillon, ii. 120–1. In his memoirs Florange does not mention Guillart and exaggerates his own role in the campaign. Florange, i. 244–5.

[6] *L.P.* iii, p. x. See also F. Mignet, *La rivalité de François Ier et de Charles-Quint* (1875), i. 197 where Francis is quoted as saying: 'Je veux qu'on soulle de toutes choses le marquis Joachim'.

[7] *L.P.* iii. p. xiii.

[8] Schick, p. 169; A. Spont, *Semblançay (?–1527): la bourgeoisie financière au début du XVIe siècle* (1895), p. 166; *L.P.* iii. 161, 385. P. Hamon ('L'argent du roi: Finances et gens des finances en France

it had to be sent to Germany. The safest way of transferring large sums of money from one country to another was by bill of exchange, but Francis was denied this facility by the German bankers whose own interests were best served by supporting the Habsburg cause. Thus Jacob Fugger, the Augsburg banker, refused to accept a bill of exchange for 300,000 gold crowns from the king, while he agreed to place more than half a million florins at Charles's disposal. In February 1519 the town council of Augsburg forbade any merchant to transfer money from France to Germany under pain of death, and other German towns followed suit.[9] Francis was thus obliged to send ready cash and to risk its seizure by the many robbers at large on German roads. In May Richard Pace reported that Francis was sending 'money comptable without bills of exchange' through the diocese of Trier.[10] Various subterfuges had to be used to ensure its security. Thus sacks of French gold were allegedly attached to boats and dragged along the bottom of the Rhine. The archbishop of Trier certainly carried French money intended for two of the electors as he travelled up the Rhine to Frankfurt.[11]

The actual amount spent by Francis on his electoral campaign is by no means certain. It is possible that part of the 407,000 *écus* paid to French agents in Germany in the spring of 1519 were intended for military purposes, for the expenditure of the *extraordinaire des guerres* doubled between October 1517 and September 1519. Too much has perhaps been made of Francis I's naïvety in distributing bribes to the electors. He was as liberal in handing out promises as was his rival. Thus he promised not only gifts, but also pensions for life which would only come into effect if and when the electors honoured their own pledges. In September 1518 the king authorized his agents to promise 30,000 *écus* to the archbishop of Mainz, and 2,000 *écus* and a pension of 800 *écus* to three other electors '*le cas advenant et le service fait*'; in other words, on condition they satisfied his wishes. At the beginning of 1519 Francis likewise stressed promise. It was only on the eve of the election itself that Barrillon began to write of gifts 'among the high costs incurred to gain the empire'.[12]

Money, however, was not the only decisive factor in the election: German public opinion was also crucial. Habsburg agents used various forms of publicity, such as sermons and broadsheets, to stir up hatred of everything French. They were instructed to inform the Germans 'through preaching or otherwise

---

au temps de François Ier'. Unpublished doctoral thesis, University of Paris I, 1993, vol. 1, p. 196) has found no archival confirmation of Spont's allegation. He points to a possible confusion with the 360,000 *livres* owed by Francis to the London bankers at the time of the Field of Cloth of Gold. Alternatively the sum of 360,000 *écus* may have been part of the 600,000 *écus* he had to pay Henry VIII for the return of Tournai.

[9] Schick, p. 170; Le Glay, ii. 244, 249; R. Ehrenberg, *Capital and Finance in the Age of Renaissance*, (New York, 1928), pp. 76–7.
[10] *L.P.* iii. 274.   [11] Schick, p. 170.   [12] P. Hamon, 'L'argent du roi', i. 86–8.

of the condition of the French people, especially of the great demands made upon them, of the innovations and expedients by which they are daily fleeced, how in a single year three clerical tenths have been levied and other things which may help to bring them [Francis's agents] into disrepute and contempt'.[13] Francis countered this propaganda by claiming that he would be better able to defend Christendom against the Turks than his rival. Writing to the bishop of Brandenburg, Duprat stressed Charles's youth and the distance between Spain and Germany which would prevent him giving attention to either. 'Furthermore', he explained, 'the customs and way of life of the Spanish people are not only different from, but clean contrary to, those of the German people. The French nation, on the other hand, is like the German in almost every respect, since it has sprung from it, namely from the Sicambri, as is described by the ancient historians.'[14] Such arguments, however, failed to convince the Germans. As Pace reported, it was dangerous to speak one good word of a Frenchman in Germany.[15]

On 8 June the electors gathered in Frankfurt. Under the Golden Bull, which regulated electoral procedure, no foreigner could remain in the city. Bonnivet, wearing disguise and under the assumed name of 'Captain Jacob', had to watch the proceedings from Rüdesheim.[16] The atmosphere was anything but placid; the summer heat was intense and plague was rife. Outside the city, the army of the Swabian League stood waiting. The electors were told that it was there for their protection, but they were also made to understand that their safety depended on their choosing the right man. No Frenchman, Henry count of Nassau declared, would enter Germany except on the points of spears and swords.[17] Francis's cause seemed hopeless, and, at the eleventh hour, the pope who had so far favoured him rather than Charles, performed a characteristic *volte-face* by agreeing conditionally to the union of the imperial and Neapolitan crowns. On 26 June Francis withdrew from the election and instructed his agents to support the Margrave of Brandenburg or the duke of Saxony.[18] Two days later Charles was elected unanimously. As wild rejoicing greeted the news throughout Germany, Francis's agents fled home with help from the archbishop of Trier.[19] On receiving news of the result, Francis retired to Fontainebleau to hunt. He told Sir Thomas Boleyn that he thanked God for sparing him the trouble he would have incurred by becoming Emperor. Although Francis had been defeated, he could take some comfort from the fact that by contesting

---

[13] *Ibid.*, p. 169.   [14] Barrillon, ii. 126–40.   [15] *L.P.* iii. 297.   [16] Barrillon, ii. 143.
[17] *L.P.* iii. 326.   [18] Pastor, vii. 285–6.
[19] Bonnivet retired to Plombières for a cure. He was apparently suffering from syphilis and stayed away from court for three months. He was reported to be 'sore sick and not like to recover', but, on 14 October, Thomas Boleyn saw him at Orléans 'leap up and down of his mule as well as he was wont to do'. On 22 October he was appointed governor of Dauphiné in place of Boisy. Florange, i. 261; Barrillon, ii. 145, 150; *L.P.* iii. 468.

37. An anonymous portrait of the Emperor Charles V in his middle years. Although
he has been idealized by some historians, the contemporary view could be less
flattering.

the election he had obliged Charles to spend more than he might otherwise have done, thereby worsening his financial position.[20]

The Field of Cloth of Gold

An almost inevitable consequence of the rivalry between Francis I and Charles of Habsburg was a marked improvement in Anglo-French relations. Bonnivet led an embassy to England in July 1518 which was accompanied by more than eighty 'young fresh galants of the court of France'.[21] The English, having been left high and dry by the treaty of Cambrai, welcomed the opportunity of forging a new diplomatic link. On 2 October England and France signed a treaty bringing all the great powers and several lesser ones to perpetual peace. Any party to the treaty who came under attack was to be defended by the rest acting together. On 4 October, a number of subsidiary treaties were signed. Tournai was to be handed back to France for an indemnity of 600,000 gold *écus* payable in annual instalments of 50,000 *livres*. Eight French noblemen were to be sent to England as hostages, pending final settlement. Wolsey was to receive 12,000 *livres* as compensation for the loss of his see of Tournai. The Dauphin was to marry Henry's daughter, Mary. Other treaties provided for the suppression of piracy by subjects of both countries and envisaged a meeting between Henry VIII and Francis I before 31 July.[22] In December an English embassy, led by the earl of Worcester, visited Paris, and was magnificently entertained for a month; on 9 February 1519 Tournai was formally returned to France.[23]

England's international significance had been enhanced by the result of the imperial election. Whereas in the past there had been four major powers in Europe – France, Spain, England and the Empire – now there were only three, Spain and the Empire having become united in the person of Charles. Of these, France and the new Habsburg state seemed of roughly equal weight, so that England found herself in a peculiarly influential position: 'her alliance would bestow dominance, while her neutrality could, in theory, guarantee peace'. It was in 'pursuit of this policy of imbalance', as it has been called, that Wolsey revived the idea mooted in the treaty of 1518 of a meeting between his master

[20] Louise of Savoy claimed that Francis had spent only 100,000 crowns on the election; in fact, he may have spent far more. *L.P.* iii. 352, 416; Barrillon, ii. 146–7; Ehrenberg, pp. 78–9; Michaud et Poujoulat, v. 91. But see Hamon, 'L'argent du roi', i. 86–8.

[21] E. Hall, *Henry VIII*, ed. C. Whibley (London, 1904), i. 168.   [22] *Ordonnances*, ii. 165–9.

[23] A tournament on 22 December was followed by a memorable banquet in the courtyard of the Bastille (see A.-M. Lecoq, 'Une fête italienne à la Bastille en 1518' in *'Il se rendit en Italie'. Etudes offertes à André Chastel* (Rome and Paris, 1988), pp. 149–68). One of the eight hostages was Anne de Montmorency, the future Constable. *L.P.* ii. 4652; Hall, i. 173–4; Florange, i. 227–30; Barrillon, ii. 114–15; *J.B.P.*, pp. 64–7; du Bellay, i. 97–8.

and Francis.[24] In January 1520 Francis took the unusual step of commissioning Wolsey to arrange the meeting, and, on 12 March, the cardinal produced a draft treaty which both monarchs ratified. This laid down that they would meet near Guînes early in June and take part in 'a feat of arms'.[25]

The Anglo-French rapprochement was viewed with anxiety by Charles, who was about to leave Spain for Germany. He decided to stop in England on the way, doubtless in the hope of preventing the Anglo-French meeting or of damaging its prospects. However, he was held up by adverse winds in Corunna, and asked Henry to postpone his meeting with Francis, but the latter would not agree to this. His wife, he explained, was pregnant; any delay would preclude her attendance. In fact, the delay proved unnecessary, as a sudden change of wind wafted Charles to England in record time. He and Henry celebrated Whitsun together at Canterbury and agreed to meet again soon.[26]

Although the Emperor's visit to England caused unease in France, it did not disrupt preparations for the Anglo-French meeting. The two commissioners in charge picked the Val Doré as the site of the meeting. This was a shallow valley on English soil half way between Guînes and Ardres. It was reshaped to give it symmetry and a sumptuous tent set up nearby. The commissioners also fixed on the site for the 'feat of arms', which comprised stands for the spectators, small wooden houses in which the kings were to put on their armour, and a 'tree of honour' on which the shields of the jousters were to be hung. Accommodation was a major headache for the organizers of the Field of Cloth of Gold, for Ardres had been sacked in the war of 1513–14 and Guînes castle was partly in ruins. Efforts were made to repair both, but it was realized from the start that many people would have to sleep in tents. The French pitched three or four hundred in a meadow outside Ardres: they were covered with velvet and cloth of gold, emblazoned with the arms of their owners and surmounted by pennants or golden apples. Taller than the rest, Francis's tent was supported by two ship's masts lashed together, covered with cloth of gold and topped by a life-sized statue of St Michael. An eye-witness described the French tents as more magnificent than 'the miracles of the Egyptian pyramids and the Roman amphitheatres'. However, many people were more impressed by the temporary palace erected by Henry VIII near Guînes. This had walls of timber painted to look like brick and many large windows. Even Leonardo, an Italian commented, could not have done better.[27]

---

[24] J. J. Scarisbrick, *Henry VIII* (London, 1968), p. 81. During the election campaign for the Empire, Henry VIII had secretly opposed Francis's candidature while tentatively putting himself forward as a third candidate. Francis was aware of this yet pretended to be grateful for Henry's support and even called his second son after him. See *L.P.* iii. 289, 306; Scarisbrick, pp. 99–103.

[25] Hall, i. 182–7.   [26] *L.P.* iii. 637, 672, 681, 725–8, 733, 788–9; *C.S.P. Ven.*, iii. 50, 53.

[27] J. G. Russell, *The Field of Cloth of Gold* (London, 1969), pp. 23–46. Work on the French tents began at Tours in February and continued till June. The operation, which involved a large labour

38. Bas-relief from the Hôtel Bourgtheroulde in Rouen showing the meeting of Henry VIII and Francis I at the Field of Cloth of Gold on 7 June 1520.

39. Detail of an anonymous painting of the Field of Cloth of Gold showing the English temporary palace in the foreground and the French tents and the tournament field beyond.

The English court crossed the Channel on 31 May and arrived at Guînes on 5 June, slightly later than the treaty had stipulated. Meanwhile Wolsey called on Francis at Ardres. Under a treaty signed on 6 June, France reaffirmed her obligation to pay one million gold crowns to Henry in two annual instalments. The pension was to be prolonged indefinitely if the marriage between the Dauphin and Mary Tudor took place. Wolsey and Louise of Savoy were jointly to seek a settlement of Anglo-Scottish differences.[28]

Francis and Henry met for the first time on 7 June, the feast of Corpus Christi. They set off simultaneously with their escorts from their respective camps as a signal was fired by the guns of Guînes and Ardres. After the two processions had come to a standstill on opposite sides of the Val Doré, a fanfare sounded and the kings detached themselves from their companies. They rode towards a spot marked by a spear at the bottom of the valley, and, drawing closer to each other, spurred their mounts as if about to engage in combat, but instead they doffed their hats and embraced.[29] They then retired to the tent nearby where they were joined by Wolsey and Bonnivet. What exactly happened inside the tent is not known: Wolsey, it seems, read out certain diplomatic documents (presumably the treaty of 6 June) and a polite altercation followed over Henry's claim to the French throne. The two ministers then withdrew, leaving the kings alone. About an hour later they came into the open and presented their nobles to each other. Refreshments were consumed by all, and, as darkness fell, the kings retired to their respective lodgings.[30]

The 'feat of arms' began on 9 June, when the kings displayed their horsemanship in the lists.[31] The shields of the 'challengers' were hung up on the 'tree of honour', and those of the 'comers' on railings at its foot. The next day being Sunday, there was no jousting. Francis dined with Catherine of Aragon at Guînes and Henry with Queen Claude at Ardres. The joust began on 11 June when the queens arrived on the field in richly covered litters, their ladies on palfreys and their servants in waggons. The 'feat of arms' comprised three sorts of contest: jousting at the tilt, tournament in the open field and combat on foot at the barriers. In the tournament, which began on 20 June, the challengers faced their opponents in pairs, not singly as in the jousts; and in the foot combat the contestants fought in pairs with puncheon spears,

force, was supervised by Galiot de Genouillac, Grand Master of the Artillery. The accounts are in B.N., ms. fr. 10383.

[28] *L.P.* iii, 869–70; Hall, i. 194–5; *C.S.P. Ven.*, iii. 62, 73, 87; *Ordonnances*, ii. no. 257.

[29] The Field of Cloth of Gold derived its name from the expensive clothes worn by the nobles and their servants. 'Many', writes du Bellay, 'carried their mills, forests and meadows on their backs.' Du Bellay, i. 102.

[30] Hall, i. 195–200; *C.S.P. Ven.*, iii. 60, 67. For a recent discussion of some of the contemporary descriptions of the meeting, including a long poem in Latin by the contemporary humanist, Jacques Dubois, see *Renaissance Studies*, v (1991).

[31] For a full treatment of the meeting see Russell, pp. 81–181; S. Anglo, *Spectacle, Pageantry and Early Tudor Policy* (Oxford, 1969), pp. 124–69.

swords and two-handed swords. The kings won high praise for their martial qualities, but, contrary to common belief, they did not fight each other; as 'challengers' they fought against teams of noblemen. A royal wrestling match, however, may have taken place. According to Florange, the kings were drinking together one day, when Henry challenged Francis, who instantly threw him to the ground with a 'tour de Bretagne'.[32] The English records are silent about this incident.

The Field of Cloth of Gold was punctuated by banquets, dances and mummings, which need not be described here. One incident, however, deserves a mention. About 17 June Francis, casting aside etiquette, rode to Guînes early one morning and surprised Henry in his bedchamber. Calling himself Henry's prisoner, Francis handed him his shirt and accompanied him to Mass. A few days later Henry reciprocated by bursting into Francis's room at Ardres as he was getting out of bed.[33] On 23 June Wolsey celebrated Mass at an altar on the tournament field. He was assisted by a papal legate, three cardinals and twenty-one bishops, music being provided in alternation by the choirs and organists of the two royal chapels.[34] At the end of the service, Pace made a speech pointing to the great benefits both nations could expect from the meeting. Wolsey conferred the pope's blessing on the two monarchs and granted a plenary indulgence and absolution to everyone present. The congregation then sat down to an *al fresco* meal, which was followed by a display of foot combat with spears and swords. On 24 June each queen gave a ring as a tournament prize to the other's consort. Then came the sad farewells. Louise of Savoy told some foreign ambassadors that the kings had parted with tears in their eyes, intending to build, in the Val Doré, a chapel dedicated to Our Lady of Friendship and a palace where they might meet each year.[35] Francis left Ardres on 25 June. Henry, meanwhile, met Charles V at Gravelines. They agreed to hold a conference in Calais and, in the meantime, not to make a separate treaty with France.

War with the Emperor

On 23 October 1520 Charles of Habsburg was crowned King of the Romans at Aachen. Two days later, Pope Leo X allowed him to use the title 'Roman Emperor elect'; but in order to become a full-fledged Emperor, Charles needed to receive Charlemagne's crown from the hands of the pope in Rome. This was something deeply dreaded by Francis, who foresaw that if Charles was allowed to go to Italy with an army, he would be tempted to use it against

---

[32] Florange, i. 272. Michelet's claim that the incident had 'incalculable consequences' for Anglo-French relations is mere conjecture. J. Michelet, *Histoire de France* x. *La Réforme* (n.d.), 137–8.
[33] Hall, i. 208; Florange, i. 268–70; C.S.P. Ven., iii. 50, 77–8, 90. [34] See below pp. 458–61.
[35] C.S.P. Ven., iii. 50, 93, 95.

the French in Milan. For not only did he not relish the idea of losing the duchy, he also shared the widely held belief that control of Italy was the key to world domination. Powerful traditions, notably memories of the Roman empire, associated the peninsula with supremacy, and the papacy's residence in Rome reinforced its supra-national character. Nor did Francis trust Charles to show restraint. Historians have been largely brain-washed by Charles's propaganda: they have consistently portrayed him as upright and moral. Contemporaries saw him otherwise: as a restless, acquisitive and aggressive prince who ignored dynastic rights and morality if it suited him. So Francis's distrust may not have been misplaced. The events leading up to the outbreak of war between the two rulers are best understood as part of an attempt by Francis to prevent Charles from going to and controlling Italy. The traditional text-book explanation of the long Valois-Habsburg conflict that ensued (viz. that it represented an attempt by France to break through Habsburg encirclement) is a simplification which fails to take into account Francis I's immediate objectives. He merely wanted to keep Charles out of Italy and was not planning a major war at this stage.[36]

Francis had hoped to forestall the Emperor by going to Italy himself in the autumn of 1520, but he remained in France, possibly because his mother was prevented by an attack of gout from acting as regent. To add to his difficulties, early in 1521 he was nearly killed during a mock battle at court. Two months elapsed before he fully recovered.[37] Consequently, he had to look to others to draw the Emperor's attention away from Italy. He relied principally on Robert de La Marck, lord of Sedan, and Henri d'Albret, king of Navarre. In February, La Marck visited the convalescent king at Romorantin and agreed to serve him in return for a lump sum of 10,000 écus, an annuity and twenty-five men-at-arms. Soon afterwards, he declared war on Charles and invaded Luxemburg.[38] About the same time Henri d'Albret set off to reconquer that part of Navarre which Castile had annexed in 1512. On 1 April the imperial ambassador Naturelli, delivered a strong protest to Francis, accusing him of being the instigator of these moves and warning him of the dangerous consequences of his policy. Francis hotly denied the charge. Not only had he given no help to La Marck, he said; he had actually forbidden his subjects to serve him. As for d'Albret, he was only doing his duty and could not refuse him help if he asked for it.[39] However, such transparent excuses carried no weight with Charles. In

---

[36] M. J. Rodriguez-Salgado, *The Changing Face of Empire: Charles V, Philip II and Habsburg Authority, 1551–1559* (Cambridge, 1988), pp. 31–2.

[37] Barrillon, ii. 176; *L.P.* iii. 1100, 1183.

[38] *L.P.* iii. 1176; du Bellay, i. 107–12; *Fragments de la première Ogdoade de Guillaume du Bellay*, ed. V.-L. Bourrilly (1905), pp. 21–36. The English ambassador, Fitzwilliam, reported: 'Though it [the invasion of Luxemburg] is called Messer Robert's act, it is done by Frenchmen and at the King's charge.' *L.P.* iii. 1176.

[39] Barrillon, ii. 180–2; Le Glay, ii. 468–72.

April an imperial army led by Nassau threw La Marck out of Luxemburg, overran his lordship of Sedan and took up a threatening posture on France's northern border.[40] In the south, André de Foix, lord of Lesparre, after conquering Navarre, rashly invaded Castile just as the revolt of the *comuneros* was being crushed. He soon had to beat a hasty retreat and, on 30 June, was heavily defeated at Ezquiros. Within a few days Spanish Navarre had reverted to Castilian rule.[41]

In Italy, too Francis faced trouble. On 29 May Leo X, having gained nothing from his alliance with France, signed a treaty with the Emperor. He promised to crown Charles Emperor in Rome and signified his willingness to invest him with Naples. The treaty was kept secret until the pope was given a suitable pretext for overthrowing his alliance with France. He did not have to wait long. In June, the seigneur de Lescun, who had been left in charge of Milan by his brother Lautrec, entered the States of the Church with troops in pursuit of some Milanese rebels. Denouncing this violation of papal territory, Leo announced his intention of allying with the Emperor.[42] On 28 June a disaster befell the French garrison in Milan. Lightning struck an ammunition dump in the castle, causing a huge explosion in which 300 French troops died.[43] The pope acclaimed the event as a divine punishment on the French, and next day made public his treaty with Charles. He accepted from him the white mare which was the traditional token of investiture to Naples. Soon afterwards pope and Emperor formed a league with the marquis of Mantua and the Florentines. On 13 July, after several unsuccessful attempts to win back the pope, Francis issued a manifesto complaining of his ingratitude. He banned the dispatch of all ecclesiastical revenues to Rome, boasting that 'he would ere long enter Rome and impose laws on the pope'.[44] He also levied a ransom from the Florentine bankers in France under threat of heavy penalties. The Lyons bankers alone paid 100,000 *livres*.[45]

The Calais conference (1521)

By the summer of 1521 northern France was under threat of invasion; Navarre was once more in Castilian hands; the pope had turned imperialist and the French hold on Milan was precarious. The English ambassador noted

---

[40] Du Bellay, i. 120–2.

[41] *Ibid.*, i. 104–6; Barrillon, ii. 186–7. The *comuneros* were defeated at Villalar on 23 April.

[42] L. von Pastor, *The History of the Popes*, tr. F. I. Antrobus and R. F. Kerr (London, 1891–1933), viii. 35–6, 42–3.

[43] Barrillon, ii. 189–90; *J.B.P.*, pp. 110–11.   [44] Pastor, viii. 46; *J.B.P.*, p. 95.

[45] A. Spont, *Semblançay* (1895), p. 174; *J.B.P.*, pp. 88–9. Hamon ('L'argent du roi', i. 199–200) suggests that the Florentine merchants in France may have been arrested by way of retaliation for the decision taken by merchant-bankers in Florence to give a loan of 400,000 *écus* to the Emperor which they had previously promised to the king of France. Cf. *J.B.P.* p. 103.

a change of mood at the French court. 'For about half a year past', he wrote, 'they would by their words have overrun all the world, and cared for nothing save our master; and by as much as I can see, they would now have peace with all their hearts.'[46]

In June Francis accepted Henry VIII's offer of arbitration and, on 20 July, he sent a delegation, led by Duprat, to a conference at Calais under Wolsey's chairmanship. The king, it seems, wanted to draw back from the dangerous course on which he had embarked, but he wanted peace, not simply a truce that would give Charles a breathing space in which to solve his own domestic problems. But Gattinara, who led the imperial delegation at Calais, argued cogently against peace. He showed that if there were good reasons for making it, there were even better ones for continuing the war.[47] He hoped to draw England on to the Emperor's side by proving that France had broken the peace.

Wolsey's role at the conference has perplexed historians. Was he genuinely looking for peace or secretly committed to England entering the war on the Emperor's side? The latest view is that he favoured an Anglo-imperial alliance but kept his options open, and was above all anxious that England should be given time to prepare a major campaign.[48] Wolsey's behaviour certainly aroused French distrust. He suddenly left for Bruges, where, on 23 August, he signed an alliance with Charles. Under this treaty, Henry was to declare war on France unless hostilities were ended by November. A joint campaign led by Henry and Charles would be mounted in May 1523. Henry's daughter, Mary, was substituted for Francis's daughter Charlotte as Charles's prospective bride.[49] The Bruges conference has been called 'a monument of perfidy worthy of Ferdinand the Catholic', yet it seems that the terms of the treaty had not been worked out in advance. Hard bargaining at Bruges kept Wolsey there longer than he had expected. He secured a respite for his master when Charles would have liked him to enter the war immediately. Charles was persuaded to empower his representatives at Calais to negotiate a truce with France, thereby opening up the possibility of ending the war by November.[50]

Meanwhile, on 20 August, the Emperor attacked the north-east border of France. His army, commanded by Nassau, after capturing Mouzon laid siege to Mézières. For three weeks its artillery battered the town walls, but the garrison commanded by Bayard put up a heroic resistance.[51] This allowed Francis time to assemble a relief force at Rheims.[52] Meanwhile, at Calais, the French

[46] L.P. iii. app. 29.   [47] Le Glay, ii. 473–82.
[48] P. Gwyn, 'Wolsey's Foreign Policy: The Conferences at Calais and Bruges reconsidered' H.J. 23 (1980), 755–72.
[49] Barrillon, ii. 205–16; L.P. iii. 1508.   [50] Gwyn, pp. 765–70.
[51] Du Bellay, i. 139–42; Barrillon, ii. 264n; J. Jacquart, Bayard (1987), pp. 269–71: S. Champier, Les gestes ensemble la vie du preulx Chevalier Bayard, ed. D. Crouzet (1992), pp. 196–201.
[52] On 26 August he informed his envoys at Calais that 9,500 Swiss troops had arrived in France and that 3,000 more were on the way. He had summoned the gendarmerie of Burgundy and the military

grew restive as the peace talks seemed to get nowhere. Their impatience turned to anger on 9 September when an imperial force sacked Ardres, which had been left undefended in response to English wishes. Francis ordered Duprat to leave Calais, yet even now he had not given up hope of a settlement. His sister, Marguerite, was less optimistic. 'See ye not', she asked Fitzwilliam, 'how the cardinal is ever treating for peace almost to the day of battle?'[53] Without mutual trust the Calais conference became little more than a farce. Even diplomatic civility was forgotten. When Duprat wagered his head if it could be proved that Francis had colluded with La Marck, Gattinara replied that a pig's head would be more palatable.[54]

On 23 September a small French force under de Lorges managed to bring supplies to Mézières, thereby dashing imperial hopes of reducing it by starvation. Three days later Nassau, knowing that Francis was approaching with a large army, lifted the siege. As he retreated into Hainault, he left behind a trail of destruction. The sack of Aubenton was, according to du Bellay, 'the origin of the great cruelties committed in wars for the next thirty years'.[55] Elsewhere too the French chalked up successes: in Italy, Lautrec relieved Parma and, on 19 October, Bonnivet captured Fuenterrabía, commonly regarded as 'the key to Spain'. These victories inevitably made an impact on the talks at Calais. Wolsey did not wish Henry VIII to be dragged into a war on the losing side: on 4 October he announced that the Emperor and the pope were prepared to sign a truce. However, Francis was even less interested in a truce now that success was smiling on his arms. He was also keen to use the army he had assembled. 'Ye see what charge I am at', he told the English ambassador, 'and also how my men eat up my subjects, wherefore I will march on straight, and live upon their countries as they have done on mine.'[56] On 4 October Francis reviewed his Swiss troops at Attigny and marched with them pike in hand.[57] His aim was to relieve Tournai, which was being besieged by the imperialists, but the weather suddenly changed. Torrential rains brought his advance into Hainault almost to a standstill. As most of the villages had been destroyed by the enemy during their retreat, his troops suffered terrible hardships. 'Their horses', wrote Fitzwilliam, 'waste sore about by stabling without, and men weary and sick very fast; and for my part, I had never worse journey in all the wars that ever I had been in.'[58]

On 22 October, as the deadline laid down at Bruges for ending the war drew closer, Wolsey made a last attempt to secure a truce. The earl of Worcester and

personnel of his household, in all some 700 men-at-arms. Vendôme had been ordered to gather 10,000 infantry and 200 cavalry near Saint-Quentin and Laon, and Bourbon to come to Rheims with 6,000 infantry and 200 cavalry. Barrillon, ii. 253 n. 2.

[53] *Ibid.*, ii. 262n; *L.P.* iii. 1544, 1552, 1581.   [54] Granvelle, *Papiers d'état*, i. 184; Barrillon, ii. 267.
[55] Du Bellay, i. 145–52; Barrillon, ii. 263–4.   [56] *L.P.* iii. 1631, 1651.
[57] B. de Chantérac, *Odet de Foix, vicomte de Lautrec* (1930), pp. 61–2; du Bellay, i. 154–8.
[58] *L.P.* iii. 1698.

the bishop of Ely called on Francis at his camp near Valenciennes but found him intractable. He was afraid that Charles would use a truce to strengthen his own position before resuming the war. On the following day, however, Francis narrowly missed an opportunity of defeating the enemy near Bouchain. 'That day', writes du Bellay, 'God placed the enemy in our hands and our refusal to accept him has since cost us dear; he who refuses what God offers through good fortune cannot get it back when he asks.'[59] By 27 October Francis had lost the chance of relieving Tournai before the winter. He, therefore, signified his readiness to accept a truce. Duprat thought this was a mistake. He advised the king to wear down the enemy by waging a 'guerre guerroyable' or 'dribbling war', which, he believed, would oblige Charles to sue for peace, whereas a truce would be merely 'the wetnurse of a bigger war'.[60]

As winter closed in and the talks in Calais dragged on, Francis inflicted as much damage as possible on Hainault. 'Here', it was reported, 'is the most piteous destruction of towns and spoiling of so fair a country as never have been seen among Christian men.' Charles accused Francis of burning everything and of cutting off the fingers of small children.[61] This, however, was the king's last throw before the winter: on 1 November he began to retreat towards Arras; nine days later, at Amiens, he disbanded his army. At the end of November Tournai capitulated.

Meanwhile, the imperialists launched an autumn offensive in north Italy. Having disbanded part of his army owing to a lack of funds, Lautrec shut himself up in Milan and prepared for a long siege, but his cruel administration exemplified by the execution of Cristoforo Pallavicini, an elderly and respected citizen, had alienated the inhabitants. The imperialists were thus assured of a friendly reception when they broke through the city's defences on 19 November. Leaving a garrison in the castle, Lautrec retreated first to Como, then to Cremona, where he planned to spend the rest of the winter. The fall of Milan was quickly followed by the expulsion of the French from other cities in the duchy.[62]

The Calais conference, meanwhile, came to an end. Francis's willingness to sign a truce, had been enough to deter the Emperor from so doing. The French delegation left Calais on 22 November; two days later, Wolsey signed the treaty of Bruges. England was now definitely committed to enter the war on the Emperor's side in 1522.[63] Francis used the winter to replenish his coffers in preparation for a new campaign. In December he asked the Swiss for 16,000 troops. All the cantons, except Zürich, complied and the troops were soon on their way to Italy.[64] In January 1522 Francis inspected Normandy's coastal

[59] Du Bellay, ii. 161–3.   [60] Barrillon, ii. 315–6.
[61] *L.P.* iii. 1715, 1727. The destructive impact of the Habsburg – Valois wars on the countryside of Picardy is examined in Potter, *War and Government*, pp. 200–32.
[62] Du Bellay, i. 191–202; Chantérac, pp. 63–70.   [63] *L.P.* iii. 1728, 1802.   [64] Decrue, i. 22.

40. Odet de Foix, seigneur de Lautrec and marshal of France. One of Francis I's principal commanders whose record was anything but glorious. He lost the battle of La Bicocca in 1522 and died in Naples in 1528. The drawing is by Jean Clouet.

defences and his new ship, *La Grande Françoise* at Le Havre.[65] Henry VIII's pension was stopped and John Stuart, duke of Albany, heir presumptive to the Scottish throne who had been living in France, was sent home to stir up trouble for the English. But, as Francis wanted to concentrate his efforts in Italy, he kept up an outward show of friendship towards England. Henry's pension, he explained, had only been delayed, and Albany had slipped away without permission. Louise of Savoy played her part in this comedy of deceit. She told Cheyney that she would rather never see her son again than see his friendship with England broken.[66]

La Bicocca (27 April 1522)

The death of Pope Leo X on 1 December 1521 put a new complexion on the situation in Italy. As the flow of money from the papal treasury to Colonna's army dried up, enemies of the Medici everywhere raised their heads. Francis viewed the conclave, which opened on 27 December, with apprehension. He threatened to sever his allegiance to the Holy See if Giulio de' Medici, leader of the imperial faction in the Sacred College, were elected.[67] In the event, the cardinals chose Adrian of Utrecht, Charles V's old tutor and regent in Spain. This caused consternation in France. Louise of Savoy said that the Emperor might as well call himself pope, and Francis began by refusing to recognize the new pope, calling him 'the Emperor's schoolmaster'.[68] But Adrian assumed his new duties in a truly Christian spirit. While denying that he owed his election to Charles, he refused to join the league against France. He set himself the aim of pacifying Christendom and uniting its rulers against the Turks, who were threatening Rhodes, the last Christian bastion in the eastern Mediterranean. But Adrian's concern was not shared by Francis. 'We are ready', he told the pope, 'to make a peace or truce and to come with great power against the Turk, provided Milan which is our patrimony is returned to us.'[69]

In March 1522 Lautrec, whose army had been reinforced by the Swiss, laid siege to Milan, but finding its defences too strong, he turned against Pavia instead. This enabled Sforza to reinforce Colonna's garrison in Milan, much to Francis's disgust. He denounced his captains in Italy as worthless and promised to go there himself to put things right, but he was overtaken by events.[70] Colonna came out of Milan and threatened Lautrec's rear by capturing the Certosa of Pavia, whereupon the marshal lifted the siege of Pavia and marched

---

[65] On 28 February 1521 Francis ordered payment of 2,875 *livres* for the completion of this ship (*Ordannances*, iii. no. 281). The mainmast was not yet up on 18 August 1552 (*L.P.* iii. 2446).
[66] *L.P.* iii. 1946, 1992, 1994, 2036, 2059.   [67] *Ibid.*, iii. 1947, 2203.
[68] Pastor, *History of the Popes*, ix, pp. 32–3.
[69] F. Mignet, *La rivalité de François Ier et de Charles-Quint*, i. 354.   [70] *L.P.* iii. 2176.

41. Pen and ink drawing by Hans Holbein the Younger depicting an infantry battle *c.* 1530.

north to Monza. Colonna followed him at a safe distance and pitched camp in the grounds of a country house, called La Bicocca, fortifying it with deep ditches, an earthen rampart and artillery platforms. Lautrec saw that it would be madness to attack, but his Swiss troops were tired of marching and counter-marching to no purpose. Their rations were fast dwindling and their pay was overdue. They demanded immediate action, otherwise they threatened to go home. After pleading in vain, Lautrec sent them into action. The result was a foregone conclusion. The Swiss encountered a fierce artillery barrage as they made a frontal assault on the imperial camp. Those who were not mown down by the guns were picked off by arquebusiers. About 3,000 were allegedly killed. The survivors fled to their homeland.[71] The Swiss never again tried the head-long assaults which in the past had swept away enemies of superior strength. In the words of Guicciardini, they 'returned to their mountains diminished in number, but much more in audacity; for it is certain that the loss they received at Bicocca humbled them to that degree that for several years afterwards they did not show their accustomed vigour'.[72] Without them Lautrec was unable to retain control of Lombardy. After a vain attempt to hold on to Lodi, he

[71] Chantérac, pp. 70–7; du Bellay, i. 224–31.
[72] F. Guicciardini, *The History of Italy*, tr. A. P. Goddard (London, 1763), vii. 352.

returned to France, bitterly disappointed and angry. Soon afterwards, Lescun surrendered Cremona; on 30 May the French defeat was completed when Genoa capitulated. Only the castles of Milan and Cremona remained in French hands.

Chapter nine

The sinews of war

Francis I incurred some very heavy expenses from the start of his reign. He inherited a deficit of 1.4 million *livres* from Louis XII and had to pay for his funeral and also for his own coronation. But his principal expenditure (estimated at 1.8 million *livres*) was on preparations for the first Italian campaign.[1] Some historians have suggested that the early Italian Wars paid for themselves, and it is certainly true that Francis exploited the financial resources of the duchy of Milan. It largely paid for its own administration and for the French army of occupation. Yet France still had to pay a substantial share of military expenses beyond the Alps. The overall cost of the Marignano campaign has been estimated at 7.5 million *livres*.[2]

In August 1516 Charles of Habsburg agreed to pay 100,000 gold *écus* per annum to Francis as a tribute for Naples, and this encouraged the king to be extravagant, as did the pope's permission to levy a clerical tenth. The Peace of Fribourg (29 November 1516) cost the French crown one million *écus*. It also inaugurated a system of pensions that were paid to certain Swiss cantons and individuals.[3] Also in 1516, Francis agreed to pay a large sum to the Emperor Maximilian. By June 1517 he had accumulated a debt roughly equal to his regular annual income, yet, in 1518, he paid Henry VIII 600,000 gold *écus* for the return of Tournai. He also repaid Mary Tudor's dowry and disbursed pensions to various Englishmen.[4] The imperial election in 1519 may have cost Francis 400,000 *écus* and the Field of Cloth of Gold, in 1520, at least 200,00 *livres*.[5]

[1] A. Spont, *Semblançay* (1895), pp. 120–64.

[2] P. Chaunu and R. Gascon, *Histoire économique et sociale de la France*, vol. 1: 1450–1660. *L'Etat et la ville* (1977), pp. 156–58; P. Hamon, 'L'Argent du roi: finances et gens de finances en France au temps de François Ier'. 2 vols. (unpublished doctoral thesis. University of Paris 1. 1993), i. 80, 170–2.

[3] *Ibid.*, i. 88–92; M. Körner, *Solidarités financières suisses au XVIe siècle* (Lausanne, 1980), pp. 411–13.

[4] Hamon, i. 92–3. See C. Giry-Deloison, 'Money and Early Tudor Diplomacy. The English Pensioners of the French Kings (1475–1547)' in *Medieval History* (forthcoming). I am grateful to the author for allowing me to read his article in advance of publication.

[5] A. Spont, *Semblançay*, pp. 160, 164; Hamon, i. 85–8.

In June 1517 the king's council decided to levy supplementary taxes worth 1,100,043 *livres* in an attempt to reduce the government's deficit of 3,996,506 *livres*.[6] Certain items of expenditure were also cut from the budget. In 1520 Francis set up commissions of enquiry aimed at discovering commoners and churchmen who had acquired fiefs without paying the proper dues. These were of three kinds: the *franc-fief*, a fine on commoners buying noble land; the *droit d'amortissement*, a lucrative fee on land falling into 'mortmain' (i.e. transferred to the 'dead hand' of an ecclesiastical community); and the *nouveaux acquêts*, a fine on land acquired by ecclesiastical bodies and other permanent associations which, for some reason, had been excused the *amortissement*. Francis also set about extending the salt tax to areas hitherto exempt. He applied it to Anjou in 1517, but when he tried, soon afterwards, to do likewise to Brittany, he encountered such strong local opposition that he gave up the attempt.[7]

On the evidence of the central records it seems that Francis did not substantially change either the burden or the structure of taxation in the course of his reign. Royal income from taxes rose by an annual average of 1.44 per cent, which is moderate by comparison with the average of 2.38 per cent per annum under Louis XII and 5.7 per cent under Henri II.[8] The *taille* rose most in absolute terms: from about 2.4 million in 1515 to some 4.6 million in 1544–45 with a fall to 3.6 million in 1547.[9] The rate of the *gabelle* in north and central France trebled, but over the whole kingdom its value was only about 700,000 *livres* in 1547 as compared with less than 400,000 in the early part of the reign. Although little dependable information exists on the *aides* and other indirect taxes, they allegedly rose from about 1.2 million to 2.15 million. Revenues from the demesne, on the other hand, did not rise at all. Many lordships escheated to or were seized by the crown, but they were given away almost at once. Tolls, chancery rights, feudal dues and the rest brought in about 400,000 *livres* at the end of the reign, almost exactly the same as in 1523. The only tax created by Francis was one on walled towns. In 1522 the most important ones were each asked to pay the *solde* of 1,000 infantry and the less important ones of 500.[10]

Taxation estimates based on the yield that actually reached the king's coffers, are misleading, for a high proportion of tax receipts were disbursed at the point of collection. Thus in Dauphiné the estates are known to have raised

[6] Spont, p. 141.   [7] C.A.F., i. 845–52, 1142, 1237–40, 1258, 1387.
[8] Hamon, i. 115; M. Wolfe, *The Fiscal System of Renaissance France* (New Haven, CT and London, 1972), p. 99, gives a higher annual percentage increase of 2.2 per cent for Francis I; Potter, *War and Government*, pp. 250–3.
[9] Hamon, i. 103; Wolfe (p. 99) gives the figure of 5.3 million in 1547.
[10] G. Zeller, *Les institutions de la France au XVIe siècle* (1948), p. 259; P. Benedict (ed.), *Cities and Social Change in Early Modern France* (London, 1989), pp. 9–10; Wolfe, pp. 99–100, 116.

662,000 *livres* for military purposes which never reached the king's treasury.[11] Similarly, in Languedoc, they contributed nearly 700,000 *livres* during the first half of the century towards the fortification of Narbonne, yet this considerable outlay is not reflected in the crown's accounts. Thus the actual weight of taxation was much heavier than is suggested by the central records.[12] Allowance should also be made for abuses by the collectors. The sums they imposed commonly exceeded legal limits. In the *pays d'états*, for example, additional sums were levied for the benefit of provincial governors, presidents of the sovereign courts, and other office-holders. The yield of taxation was also eroded by the collection costs. In 1523 the cost of collecting the *gabelles* was estimated at 10,700 *livres*; that is, 3 per cent of the total collected.[13]

The French church was by no means immune from fiscal exploitation. A regular feature was the clerical tenth or *décime*. In theory, this was a voluntary gift to assist the king in an emergency. Following the Concordat of Bologna, the pope allowed Francis to levy a tenth on the French clergy. He did so again in 1527 and 1533, but papal authorization was not deemed essential to levying a tenth; the initiative was often taken by the king alone. Sometimes the Holy See gave its approval retrospectively. Francis might receive one or more tenths simultaneously. Bishops often acted as his agents, though sometimes they tried to obtain reductions for their diocesan clergy. The king occasionally put pressure on the clergy to pay up: in 1523 he even threatened to billet troops on the clergy of Rieux when they demanded a reduced contribution. The sanction most frequently invoked by the crown was the seizure of clerical temporalities, but this had a serious disadvantage: they were expensive to administer. Generally, however, the king could count on the clergy's docility. 'His Majesty uses their money as though it were his own', wrote the Venetian ambassador Cavalli in 1546.[14] A major part of collecting the tenth was left to the clergy themselves; royal officials intervened only to constrain or to redress incompetence. A *décime* was certainly less than a tenth of the income of a benefice; Cavalli equated it with a twentieth. In fact, the tenth yielded about 379,000 *livres* in 1516, and 474,000 *livres* in 1518. Altogether 57 tenths were levied under Francis, which may have yielded a total of at least 18 million *livres*.[15]

It was outside his regular income that Francis innovated most. Taxation was slow to collect, and not all of it reached his treasury. The king was consequently starved of cash for emergencies and forced to resort to expedients: he borrowed from bankers and private individuals, imposed forced loans on

[11] L. S. Van Doren, 'War Taxation, Institutional Change and Social Conflict in Provincial France – the Royal *Taille* in Dauphiné, 1494–1559', *Proceedings of the American Philosophical Society*, cxxi (February 1977), pp. 93–4.
[12] P. Contamine, *Histoire militaire de la France* (1992), vol. 1, pp. 266–7.   [13] Hamon, i. 110–11.
[14] *Relations des ambassadeurs vénitiens sur les affaires de France au XVIe siècle*, ed. N. Tommasco (1838), vol. I, p. 301.
[15] Hamon, i. 133–6.

towns, alienated crown lands and sold offices and titles of nobility. Unlike other sixteenth-century rulers, however, he did not devalue the currency to any significant extent.[16]

It has been suggested that kings of France seldom borrowed from foreign bankers in the century that followed the Hundred Years War.[17] Yet Francis borrowed quite heavily from merchants and merchant-bankers. Hamon has identified 124 lenders in the course of the reign. Eighty-seven of them were Italians of whom the largest proportion had settled in Lyons while retaining contacts with their country of origin; some others were based in Antwerp or London. They lent to the crown sometimes under constraint or in exchange for commercial concessions, but usually out of free speculative choice. The Florentine *fuorusciti* also hoped to gain French support for their political designs. Sometimes go-betweens helped to secure loans for the king. One of the best-known was Jean Cléberger (Hans Kleberg), nicknamed '*le bon Allemand*'. Another was Pierre Spine or Spina, who was described in 1518 as *banquier suivant la cour*. Roberto Albizzi (Albisse), a Florentine merchant who had settled in Lyons, lent the king 31,500 *écus* in 1521, 25,000 in 1531, 10,000 and 6,700 in 1536 and 30,300 *livres* in 1538.[18]

Lenders to the crown normally expected reimbursement within a year; any defaulting by the crown was likely to damage its credit-rating. Francis tried to placate creditors by giving them concessions such as exemption from the *droit d'aubaine* or from letters of marque or reprisal. Usually, however, he offered them high rates of interest. Thus a loan of 100,000 *écus* raised for the Field of Cloth of Gold in 1520 carried an annual interest of 32,400 *livres*; that is to say, 16.2 per cent. The interest on a Genoese loan in October 1515 reached 28 per cent and possibly 42 per cent per annum.[19]

Francis raised many loans in the first decade of his reign. In October 1515 three royal officials promised to pay 60,454 *écus* to two Genoese bankers at the next Easter fair in Lyons in return for a loan of 50,000 *écus*. By 1516 the crown was already heavily indebted to the Lyons bankers. In 1518 they were asked to advance 100,000 *livres* promised by the king to Lorenzo de' Medici, duke of Urbino, at the time of his marriage. Smaller loans were raised in Lyons in 1516 and 1517 possibly to pay the Swiss, the Emperor and Massimiliano Sforza. A loan of 120,000 *écus* was also raised by the *trésoriers des guerres* for a possible military intervention in Germany. Early in 1519 two Italian merchants were holding 100,000 *livres* for the king, though it is not certain that the money was

---

[16] In June 1545 the imperial ambassador Saint-Mauris warned his government that 10,000 crowns had been melted down and mixed with copper etc. to produce 150,000 crowns. These had been paid to the troops taken by de Lorges to Scotland. *C.S.P. Span.*, viii, additions no. 82; *L.P.*, xx (pt. 1), 1069.

[17] Wolfe, p. 64.

[18] Hamon, i. 181–7; R. Ehrenberg, *Capital and Finance in the Age of the Renaissance* (New York, 1928), pp. 184–6, 210–11.

[19] Hamon, i. 189–90.

actually used. What is certain is that between 1518 and 1520 Francis resorted to credit 'for several and good causes and reasons touching the estate and preservation' of his kingdom.[20]

The arrest of Florentine merchants in Lyons in 1521 marked the beginning of a deterioration of relations between the king and the city's bankers. Although Francis did manage to obtain a loan in June 1522, the confidence of the Lyons bankers was undermined even more seriously by the government's onslaught on Semblançay and other *gens de finances* who had traditionally guaranteed loans and acted as go-betweens. The bankers could no longer count on reimbursement. In September 1525 the principal Florentine creditors initiated a suit in the *Grand Conseil* to recover their moneys. As from 1523 Francis was unable for some time to borrow on the Lyons money market. This, according to Guicciardini, crippled his war effort and led to the peace of Cambrai. But this is an overstatement. Francis did manage to borrow elsewhere, though not on the same scale. A number of Parisian merchants (viz. Thomas Turquam, Nicolas Le Coincte and Etienne Delange) lent him 140,000 *livres* in 1527. In the following year Duprat borrowed 80,000 *livres*.[21]

Francis borrowed heavily from his own tax officials, who were invariably recruited from men of substance, not only so that they should be less tempted to cheat the king and his subjects, but also because they were expected on occasion to lend him money. If for some reason the tax yield was lower than expected or expenses higher, a tax official would be asked to advance money out of his own pocket. In return, he would receive a warrant to reimburse himself out of the following year's tax receipts or would be granted a salary increase. This was how taxes were 'anticipated'.[22]

On a number of occasions the king helped himself to the inheritances of wealthy subjects. His first victim was Artus Gouffier, seigneur de Boisy, who died in Languedoc on 13 May 1519. As soon as Francis learnt of his death, he ordered an inventory to be made of the Grand Master's 'savings'. They comprised 154,247 *livres* in gold *écus*, gold plate worth 34,635 *livres* and silver plate worth 17,558 *livres*. In 1523 the king seized the inheritance of Ymbert de Batarnay, seigneur du Bouchage, which consisted only of specie worth 46,000 *livres*.[23]

Although many French towns were exempt from the *taille*, they were often asked for forced loans, which could be more burdensome still. Loans were sometimes levied on individual towns or on several towns at once. The king used different methods: he would send commissioners to large towns with instructions to negotiate a loan or to impose it. In the case of small towns, a royal letter was deemed sufficient, local officials being entrusted with the

[20] *Ibid.*, i. 193–6; *Ordonnances*, iii. p. 118.   [21] Hamon, i. 201–4.   [22] Wolfe, p. 65.
[23] C.A.F., i. 268, 327, 372, 461, 817, 1263, 1328 etc.; Hamon, i. 245–8.

levy.[24] In 1515 and 1516, for example, Francis asked for sums ranging from 1,500 *livres* to 6,000 *livres* each from Toulouse, Lyons, Troyes and Angers.[25] Paris was asked for a gift of 20,000 *livres* to help defend the kingdom against the Swiss.[26] Sometimes a town was reimbursed by being allowed to levy a local tax, or *octroi*. Thus in July 1516, Paris was allowed to levy a tax on wine until it had recovered 20,000 *livres* which it had advanced to the king.[27] This was, in effect, an extension of allowing towns to use local taxes for a worthwhile purpose, such as the repair of their walls. But Francis was not content to let towns administer such revenues (*deniers communs*) independently. In March 1515 he created officials called *contrôleurs des deniers communs*, and, in July, ordered each town to declare the true value of its revenues. These measures caused consternation, nowhere more so than in Paris, where the municipal authorities successfully resisted the appointment of the *contrôleur*. But this was at the price of granting the king another subsidy of 20,000 *livres*.[28]

Towns did not readily submit to royal demands. They frequently claimed that they were too poor, but such excuses cut little ice with Francis, so that in the end they had to negotiate. The results varied in accordance with circumstances. Thus in 1524 Paris managed to reduce a royal demand for 200,000 *écus* to only 10,000 *livres*. On the other hand, Nantes and other towns in Brittany failed in their efforts to avoid contributing to the 1523 levy on 'free towns'. Larger towns were generally more successful than smaller ones in gaining concessions. Even when a compromise was reached, the king could not be certain of receiving his due. Sometimes he tried to sweeten the pill by giving the town a large measure of autonomy in collecting a tax and accounting for it. Yet he could not afford to relax pressure. This could range from relatively mild measures against recalcitrants to the imprisonment of citizens.

The towns responded in various ways to the crown's fiscal demands. This was demonstrated in Paris during the 1520s. In 1522 a tax was imposed on the various trades (*métiers*). In November 1523 a levy of 20,000 *livres* was described by the Bourgeois of Paris as a *taille*. Towns were often obliged to borrow in order to satisfy royal demands. Lenders were repaid gradually from municipal revenues as they came in. Francis might insist on all the inhabitants of a town, whether privileged or not, having to contribute. This could cause tension among the urban élites responsible for allocating the tax; some would try to evade it altogether; others would seek to lighten their own load by spreading the burden as widely as possible.[29]

An expedient much used by Francis was the alienation of crown lands by gift or sale. This was repeatedly opposed by the Parlement as a breach of the

[24] Hamon, i. 139–44.   [25] *C.A.F.*, i. 233, 283, 247, 1218.
[26] *R.D.B.V.P.*, i (1499–1526), 222.
[27] *C.A.F.*, i. 496.   [28] *Ibid.*, i. 163, 310; *R.D.V.P.*, i. 223–36; *J.B.P.*, p. 7.
[29] Hamon, i. 139–44, 232–6.

'fundamental law' that proclaimed the inalienability of the royal demesne. It pointed to the adverse effects on the king's 'poor subjects' of any diminution of his 'ordinary' revenue. However, Francis would not give way; in the end, his alienations were always ratified, albeit under protest. In April 1517 he resumed all crown lands which he and his predecessors had alienated, but this was an empty gesture; soon afterwards he issued letters of exemption to past recipients of these lands.[30]

Two fiscal expedients became notorious under Francis: the sale of titles of nobility and of royal offices. The exact number of letters of ennoblement issued is not known because of a fire that destroyed the *Chambre des Comptes* and its archives in 1737. As far as we know, only 183 such letters were issued in the course of the reign, of which 153 were sold. They cost between 100 and 300 gold *écus* before 1543 and considerably more afterwards.[31]

Such restraint as Francis may have shown in selling titles of nobility was not reflected in respect of offices: he turned their sale or venality into a system. He sold them directly to bourgeois, who were anxious to acquire the social status they conferred or gave them away as rewards for services rendered or as reimbursement for loans, leaving the recipients free to sell them, if they wished. Francis also sold *résignations* and *survivances*, which enabled office-holders to nominate their successors. The price of a councillorship in the Parlement of Paris was fixed by 1522 at 3,000 *écus*. Other offices commanded variable amounts. Payment for an office was officially a loan, but it was sometimes difficult for an office-holder to recover the purchase price. The sale of offices in the long run created a serious situation in which offices tended to be monopolized by a limited number of families.[32] In addition to selling existing offices, Francis also created a large number which were put on the market. Here again he met with resistance. In 1515, for example, the Parlement amended a royal ordinance creating *enquêteurs* in all the *bailliages* so as to reduce the number. But the court was most obstructive when its own interests were under threat. In theory, the king was supposed to choose the Parlement's councillors from a list of candidates submitted by the court, but, in practice, he often imposed his own nominees.[33]

The *gens de finances*

The *trésoriers de France* and *généraux des finances* responsible for the administration of the crown's finances between 1515 and 1527 were closely related to each other and shared common interests. Alongside their duties to

[30] Doucet, i. 60–3; C.A.F., i. 102, 115, 379, 578, 648, 676, 742; Hamon, i. 150–4.
[31] J.-R. Bloch, *L'anoblissement en France au temps de François Ier* (1934), pp. 152–97.
[32] R. Mousnier, *La vénalité des offices sous Henri IV et Louis XIII* (second edn, 1971), pp. 35–92.
[33] Doucet, i. 65–8; E. Maugis, *Histoire de Parlement de Paris* (1913–16), i. 136–86.

the crown, they ran highly profitable businesses of their own. Inevitably their public and private functions overlapped, offering them speculative temptations. Given the generally chaotic state of the king's finances, it was easy enough for one of the privileged oligarchy to put his hand in the till without anyone noticing.

Typical of this group of royal servants was Pierre Le Gendre, who between 1500 and his death in 1524 was simultaneously *général des aides* and one of the four *trésoriers de France*. His colleagues were Florimond Robertet, Jean Cottereau and his own brother-in-law, Louis Poncher. Through the latter, Le Gendre was connected to such powerful families as those of Berthelot, Ruzé and Beaune. In 1511 he drew closer to the ruling élite by marrying Charlotte Briçonnet. Le Gendre acquired a considerable fortune, as revealed by his probate inventory. He owned an *hôtel* in Paris, a sort of miniature palace with chapel, gallery and two courtyards. He also drew a substantial income from country estates as seigneur de Villeroy, Magny-en-Vexin and Alincourt. Yet, rich as he was, his fortune was small by comparison with that of other financiers, like Gilles Berthelot or Thomas Bohier, who built the châteaux of Azay-le-Rideau and Chenonceaux respectively.[34]

An outstanding member of the financial oligarchy in the early years of the reign was Jacques de Beaune, baron de Semblançay. The son of a rich merchant of Tours, he had entered the royal administration through Anne of Brittany's household. In 1515 he was *général* of Languedoïl, and, as such, played a leading part in gathering funds for Francis's first Italian campaign. From September 1515 until January 1516 he collaborated closely with the regent, Louise of Savoy, being in frequent attendance at her council. In December 1515 she gave him the barony of Semblançay. After the king's return from Italy in January 1516, Semblançay continued to attend his council whenever financial matters came under discussion. In September he resigned his office in favour of his son Guillaume, yet continued to deal with the king's financial business. His position was regularized on 27 January 1518, when he was given powers of supervision covering all the king's revenues, both ordinary and extraordinary. Yet he was not given authority over the *généraux*, his task being simply to co-operate with them and guide their actions. At the same time he was put in charge of the accounts of the households of the king, queen and royal children, just as he was already responsible for Louise's privy purse.

It was, however, as an agent of credit that Semblançay was probably most useful to the crown, for, in addition to being a civil servant, he ran his own banking business and was closely related to many leading financiers of his day. His private fortune was such that he could borrow more easily than the king, whose credit inspired less confidence.[35]

[34] J. Jacquart, *François Ier* (1981), pp. 202–3.   [35] Spont, *Semblançay*; Hamon, i. 304–7.

Important as they were, the *gens de finances* did not have ultimate control of the crown's financial policy. This rested with the king's council whose records are, alas, too fragmentary to yield a consistent picture of how policies were made. Yet it is clear that one councillor, usually the *Grand maître*, was singled out to oversee financial business. First to do so under Francis was Boisy, who was succeeded by the Bastard of Savoy.[36] On 12 August 1521 Admiral Bonnivet sent the king a plan for a rational allocation of financial responsibilities among councillors. Gilles Berthelot was to answer for expedients, and the *généraux* Bohier, Hurault and de Beaune for all other funds to Semblançay and Meigret. All were to be under the authority of the Bastard of Savoy, and each morning Saint-Marsault and Villeroy were to inform the king at his *lever* of what had been done and still needed doing so that decisions might be taken promptly.[37] In December 1523 Guillaume de Montmorency informed his son, Anne, who was in Italy with the army, that the king's councillors were hard at work each day trying to bring order to the royal finances. A fortnight later, the Bastard of Savoy wrote to Anne that the whole administration, including the king, was working 'flat out' to the same end.[38]

Frequent references, particularly in diplomatic correspondence, to Francis's elusiveness and obsession with hunting have created the impression of a ruler who cared little for serious business. But this impression is belied by several archival references to his personal participation in financial discussions. Thus in April 1519 he spent three days with Semblançay, Babou and *gens de finance* looking for ways to raise money needed to levy troops. In 1523 he was said to be frequently at pains to advise and think about his finances. His influence on policy-making, therefore, cannot be ruled out. Francis evidently left much routine business to ministers, but he did show an interest, particularly in difficult times.[39]

The financial crisis of 1521–23

Although Francis resorted to fiscal expedients from the start of his reign, it was only in 1521, after going to war with the Emperor, that the gulf between his revenues and expenses became almost unbridgeable. For war had become very expensive, a particularly heavy burden being the hire of Swiss mercenaries. 'These people', wrote Montmorency, 'ask for so much money and are so unreasonable that it is almost impossible to satisfy them.'[40] Yet, as long as Francis lacked an efficient native infantry, he could not do without them. Military costs from the declaration of war in 1521 until the king's defeat at Pavia

---

[36] Hamon, i. 428–31.   [37] B.N., ms. fr. 2994, f.13 b.   [38] Hamon, i. 415–16.
[39] *Ibid.*, i. 425–7.
[40] Decrue, i. 22.

amounted to nearly 20 million *livres*. The fighting on three fronts in the second half of 1521 may have cost as much as 700,000 *livres* per month. Between October 1520 and February 1522 the average monthly expenditure of the *extraordinaire des guerres* was 294,663 *livres* as compared with an average of 47,652 in the period from October 1519 to September 1520.[41]

The year 1521 has been described as a 'terrible year' in respect of royal loans.[42] Within a few months the king's indebtedness to money-lenders increased at an alarming rate. He borrowed 75,000 *livres* from merchants of Lucca and nearly 30,000 *écus* from a consortium of Italian merchant-bankers. A forced loan of 100,000 *livres* was levied from Florentine merchants in Lyons. In 1521 Geoffroy Ferrier, *général des finances* for Milan paid 320,000 *livres* to the *extraordinaire des guerres* in Italy. Much of this sum, it seems, had been lent. By the spring of 1522 Francis owed one million *livres*; he would not repeat such a level of indebtedness till the mid 1540s. The debt represented only a small proportion of his current income (possibly 15 per cent in 1521), yet the king was unable to clear it while the war dragged on.[43]

At the beginning of 1521 Semblançay had in his keeping 300,000 *écus* which the king had received from Charles V as part of the Neapolitan pension; he also had 107,000 *livres* belonging to his mother. When, on 10 April, Louise implored the baron to do everything possible to help her son out of his difficulties, he naturally assumed that she meant him to use her savings as well as her son's. Between 25 April and 15 May he placed 200,000 *livres* at Francis's disposal, but this sum fell far short of the king's immediate needs. On 29 May, therefore, his council decided to raise 187,500 *livres* by alienating crown lands. But this too was inadequate. An *état de l'extraordinaire*, drawn up on 6 June, called for 480,000 *livres* immediately and 220,000 *livres* in each of the following three months.[44] On 13 September Semblançay informed the king that he had only enough money for one month and urged him to fight a 'good battle' in the meantime.[45]

The war, however, dragged on through the winter, and Francis had to resort to yet more expedients. He decided to raise 120,000 *livres* by creating twenty councillorships in the Parlement of Paris. His excuse was the need to speed up justice, but, as his mother frankly admitted, Francis was only interested in money. She told the Parlement that he would drop his proposal if the court could think of another way of raising the same sum. But the Parlement disliked meddling in financial matters; it resorted to procrastination before eventually giving way.[46] Among other offices created by the king in 1522 were sixteen *commissaires examinateurs* and forty *notaires* at the Châtelet of Paris, twenty

---

[41] Hamon, i. 79–81. The evidence on which these figures are based is contained in B.N., ms. fr. 4523, ff. 49–51. See also F. Lot, *Recherches sur les effectifs des armées françaises des Guerres d'Italie aux Guerres de Religion, 1494–1562* (1962), p. 250.
[42] Hamon, i. 197.,   [43] *Ibid.*, i. 197–9.   [44] Spont, *Semblançay*, pp. 170–3; C.A.F., i. 1353.
[45] Spont, *Semblançay*, p. 176.   [46] Barrillon, ii. 308–14; Doucet, i. 160–4.

councillors in the Parlement of Dijon, twenty *serjents* in the *sénéchaussée* of Guyenne and a *procureur de roi* in every *bailliage*.[47]

Crown lands worth 200,000 *livres* were alienated in February 1522 'to put the kingdom in a state of defence', and the *taille* of 1523 was anticipated to the tune of 1,191,184 *livres*. Unpaid expenses amounting to 2,638,855 *livres* were passed on to the budget for the following year.[48] The king also called on a number of towns to pay for a specified number of infantry. At a meeting at the Hôtel de Ville in Paris he asked for 500. While the Parisians debated the matter, Francis went to Rouen and persuaded its inhabitants to pay for 1,000. He then returned to the capital and shamed it into doubling its contribution.[49]

Following England's entry into the war, Francis made still heavier demands on his subjects. The clergy in particular were hard hit. In 1522 the king seized church treasures to the value of 240,000 *livres* which the clergy were allowed to recoup from the demesne, *aides* and *gabelle* in Languedoc and Outre-Seine. Even so, contemporaries were shocked by the violence of the king's officials, particularly those who tore down the silver grill surrounding the shrine of St Martin at Tours. This, once melted down, yielded 60,800 *livres*, which helped pay for Albany's expedition to Scotland. At Laon cathedral, Francis seized three or four statues of apostles in gold worth 4,000 *écus*; the others, which were of silver, were left alone.[50] Many *droits d'amortissement* were levied, and, in December, a subsidy of 1,200,000 *livres* was demanded from the clergy to pay for 30,000 infantry during six months.[51]

An important innovation dating from the same year was the system of public credit, known as the *rentes sur l'Hôtel de Ville de Paris*. On 22 September 1522 the government raised a loan of 200,000 *livres* from the Parisian public against the security of the municipal revenues. Each contributor to the loan was assured of a life annuity or *rente*, carrying a rate of interest of 8$\frac{1}{3}$ per cent, which was to be paid out of the revenue from various local taxes. As the interest payments were entrusted to municipal officials sharing the same social background as the lenders, the system rested on a fair measure of mutual trust. Even so, Parisians showed little enthusiasm for the scheme. In the words of the Bourgeois de Paris: 'the town was forced to give the king up to 100,000 gold *écus*'.[52] Versoris is more outspoken. The Parisians, he says, were hostile to the measure, yet they provided the amount required 'more out of fear and dread than out of love or generosity ... not without much grumbling directed against the king's council'.[53] The *rentes* of 1522 have been acclaimed as the start of a new era in financial history, yet Francis used them sparingly. The next issue, for

[47] C.A.F., i. 1479, 1528, 1644.   [48] C.A.F., i. 1472; R. Doucet, *L'état des finances de 1523*, p. 8.
[49] J.B.P., pp. 102–4; C.A.F., i. 1495.
[50] C.A.F., i. 1584–5; J.B.P., p. 135; Spont, *Semblançay*, p. 190; L.P., iii. 2522.
[51] C.A.F., i. 1627, 1647–8, 1681–2, 1685, 1713.   [52] J.B.P., p. 104.
[53] *Livre de Raison de Me. Nicolas Versoris*, ed. G. Fagniez (1885), p. 25.

only 100,000 *livres*, was not floated till 1536. More *rentes* were sold in 1537 and 1543, bringing the total mount for the reign to 725,000 *livres*, slightly more than one year's yield from the *gabelles*.[54]

Despite all these expedients, Francis was virtually bankrupt in 1523. The *état-général des finances* for that year estimated a total revenue of 5,155,176 *livres* and a total expenditure of 5,380,269 *livres*, leaving a deficit of only 226,069 *livres*. In fact, the situation was far worse, for the officials who had drawn up the *état* were extraordinarily careless: they quoted amounts wrongly, were inaccurate in their sums (sometimes by as much as 100,000 *livres*) and failed to allow for emergencies. They overestimated the king's normal income by 1,961,369 *livres*, yet also failed to take into account supplementary taxation such as *crues de taille* and clerical tenths, which, in 1523 brought in about 4,641,257 *livres*. Thus the total income, not allowing for the yield from expedients, was 7,835,064 *livres*. Unfortunately for Francis, his expenses were also much greater than anticipated by his officials. They amounted to 8,650,333 *livres*, so that the real deficit for 1523 was 815,269 *livres*. And this is only an approximation; the gap between the king's needs and his resources was almost certainly far wider.[55]

The enquiry commissions of 1523–24

Louise of Savoy's *Journal* contains the following entry: 'In 1515, 1516 1517, 1518, 1519, 1520, 1521, 1522, my son and I were continually robbed by the *gens de finances* without being able to do anything about it.'[56] By the beginning of 1523 there was no money left in the royal coffers, not even from expedients, to meet the costs of the war. The king therefore began to look for new revenues. He suspected that many officials responsible for the collection of the *deniers casuels* (i.e. revenues not anticipated in the *état-général*) had kept some of his money for themselves and decided to make them disgorge it. On 17 January he set up a commission to examine their accounts and to punish any dishonesty on their part. The commissioners were drawn from the Parlement and *Chambre des Comptes*. By the end of January they had examined a number of fiscal officials, notably Guillaume Preudomme, *receveur-général* of Normandy, whose accounts were approved, and Jean Prévost, *commis à l'extraordinaire des guerres*, who was sent to prison.[57]

Not even Semblançay, who had done so much to help the king out of his difficulties, was spared. Indeed, he was the principal object of royal suspicion

[54] P. Cauwès, 'Les commencements du crédit public en France: les rentes sur l'hôtel de ville au XVIe siècle'. *Revue d'économie politique*, ix (1895), 97–123; B. Schnapper, *Les rentes au XVIe siècle* (1957), pp. 151–4; Wolfe, pp. 91–3; Hamon, i. 236–40.

[55] Doucet, *L'état des finances de 1523*, pp. 9–26.   [56] Michaud et Poujoulat, v. 90.

[57] C.A.F., i. 1730; Doucet, i. 180–4.

and his accounts were examined by commissioners appointed on 11 March 1524; but the only fault detected by them was a failure to distinguish clearly between the king's purse and that of Louise of Savoy. This was true particularly of the Neapolitan pension, which had changed hands twice: the king had given it to his mother, who had given it back to help pay for the war. Semblançay had entered it among the king's receipts; the commissioners thought it should have appeared among Louise's receipts. After the baron had amended his accounts, they showed that he had lent the king 1,574,342 *livres* and been repaid 662,994 *livres*. Louise's receipts, on the other hand, were now put at 760,267 *livres* and her expenses at 53,000 *livres*. In other words, Semblançay now owed Louise 707,267 *livres* while the king owed him 911,348 *livres*. Since Louise's money had been used exclusively in her son's interest, Semblançay suggested, not unreasonably, that Francis should repay her directly; alternatively he asked for permission to defer settlement of Louise's debt until he had been reimbursed by the king. On 27 January 1525 the commission gave its verdict: Francis was to settle his debt to Semblançay, which by then amounted to 1,190,374 *livres*, while Semblançay was to pay back his debt to Louise. He was given permission, however, to delay this until Francis had supplied him with a *décharge* in respect of the Neapolitan pension.[58] In short, the commission had failed to uncover any serious malpractice on Semblançay's part. His only mistake had been to confuse the purses of Francis and his mother, but, as he repeatedly explained, they had always insisted on their purses being identical.

The *Trésor de l'Epargne*

The enquiry commissions of 1523–24 were part of a more ambitious effort to improve the effectiveness of the fiscal administration handed down by Charles VII. For it was necessary not only to discover and punish corruption, but also to reform or even abolish institutions which had given dishonesty scope. Among the king's revenues the most vulnerable to corruption were the irregular ones, which were collected and handled in an *ad hoc* way by many officials. Some sort of centralization was needed to ensure that they were properly collected, used and accounted for. Bitter experience had also taught Francis the need to build up a reserve of cash for use in wartime to meet sudden and unexpected demands and, in peacetime, to buy back parts of the royal demesne which he had been forced to alienate. In looking for a solution he may have been inspired by the central treasuries that already existed in the duchies of Burgundy and Brittany.

The first step taken towards achieving the king's objectives was the creation

[58] Doucet, i. 186–201; Spont, *Semblançay*, pp. 208–28; Hamon, i. 344.

on 18 March 1523 of a new official, called *Trésorier de l'Epargne* with powers
to collect and disburse all royal revenues save those from the demesne and
regular taxation. Alone among financial officials, he was exempt from supervision by the *trésoriers* and *généraux*. He took his oath of office only to the
king. The man appointed to the new post was Philibert Babou, *trésorier* of
Languedoïl.[59]

Babou could expect to receive seven kinds of revenue (*deniers casuels*) in
1523: namely, two and a half tenths from the clergy in place of the *droits
d'amortissement*, a contribution of 35,100 *livres* per quarter from the *villes
franches* for the upkeep of infantry, a loan of 50,000 *livres* and a supplement of
4 *sous* per *livre* from all office-holders, loans from private persons, the profits
from the sale and resignation of offices, and various irregular revenues, such as
fines imposed by the enquiry commissions of 1523–24. Unfortunately, it is
impossible to put an even approximate total on these revenues, as only a tat-
tered fragment of Babou's register for 1523 survives. This shows that he
received only 900,000 *livres* from the clergy instead of 1,185,221 *livres*, as
expected. Even so, the amount of cash he received during 1523 cannot have
been negligible.

The next major step in the reform of the fiscal system was taken by Francis
on 28 December, when he greatly increased the powers of the *Trésorier de
l'Epargne*.[60] He was now to receive all royal revenues after deduction of customary local expenses. He was also authorized to make payments sanctioned
by royal warrants without endorsement by the *trésoriers* and *généraux des
finances*. But this put too heavy a burden on Babou's shoulders. In June 1524,
therefore, he was given responsibility for revenues only from the demesne and
from taxation (henceforth called *finances ordinaires*), while another official,
the *receveur des parties casuelles*, was given charge of the rest (henceforth
called *finances extraordinaires*). Thus there were now two treasurers at the top
of the fiscal pyramid, while beneath them remained a host of officials competing for the funds they controlled. In other words, the reform of 1523 created
two new posts without reducing the number of fiscal officials, at least in the
short term.

How well did the new system work? According to the preamble of the edict
setting up the *Trésorier des parties casuelles* (9 July 1524), it had already
proved extremely successful. The king had allegedly been spared the need to
cut back on wages and pensions and had even managed to clear many debts.
But it seems that money did not reach the *Trésorier de l'Epargne* as fast or as
plentifully as had been hoped. This is indicated by the fact that the old system
of disbursement was not completely abandoned. In 1528 only about a quarter
of the payments effected by the *Epargne* were in cash; the rest were in *assigna-*

[59] C.A.F., i. 1780.   [60] *Ibid.*, i. 1953; *Ordonnances*, iii. 318–24.

tions on local treasurers. Yet, even this was an improvement and the fact that all payments were now authorized by a single official instead of a dozen meant that the king had more control over disbursements. He was also better placed to know how much cash he had in hand for emergencies, as the *Trésorier de l'Epargne* had to report to the king's council each week on the state of his holdings. Another important effect of the reforms was the destruction of the influence of the *trésoriers de France* and *généraux des finances*. Their offices were not abolished, for, as they were venal, the king would have had to redeem them. Their powers, however, were drastically reduced; they continued to carry out inspections of their respective districts, but ceased to share in policy-making, which was now firmly in the hands of the king and his council.[61]

Wolfe has suggested that the reforms of 1523 were the first stage of a master-plan to reform the fiscal administration, but Hamon can see no valid reason for such a graduated approach. 'It was under the spur of necessity', he writes, 'and above all by feeling its way that the new organization was established.'[62]

[61] G. Jacqueton, 'Le Trésor de l'Epargne sous François 1er, 1523–1547', *R.H.*, lv (1894), i–43; Wolfe, pp. 77–86. For the fiscal reforms of Francis I as they affected Picardy, see Potter, *War and Government*, pp. 234–40.
[62] Hamon, i. 311.

Chapter ten

Treason

The French defeat in Italy in April 1522 was followed almost at once by England's entry into the war on the imperial side. At the end of May Charles V visited England on his way back to Spain from the Netherlands. He and Henry VIII planned a joint invasion of France before May 1523, and Henry promised to send a preliminary expedition across the Channel by August 1522. On 29 May an English herald appeared before Francis in Lyons and declared war in Henry's name. According to Louise of Savoy, the herald quaked as he delivered his message, whereas her son delighted everyone present by his eloquent and scornful reply.[1] Hostilities began in July when the earl of Surrey raided Morlaix. In September he marched out of Calais at the head of an Anglo-imperial army and tried to provoke the French into giving battle by destroying the countryside. This merely earned him a rebuke for his 'foul warfare' from the duc de Vendôme. Within a month the English had exhausted their supplies, and, after an unsuccessful attempt to capture Hesdin, they retired to Calais.[2]

The English invasion of Picardy was the signal for a Scottish attack on northern England. In September the duke of Albany marched on Carlisle at the head of one of the largest armies ever assembled in Scotland, but the Scots, being tired of fighting France's wars, accepted a truce offered to them by Lord Dacre, Warden of the Marches, over their commander's head. Profoundly humiliated, Albany slipped back to France, hoping to raise a new army.[3] Many rumours circulated in the spring of 1523 to the effect that he and Richard de la Pole, Edward IV's nephew who had fled to the continent in 1501, were preparing some great enterprise against England. The earl of Desmond promised in June to start a rebellion in Ireland, and, in August, Francis ordered 200,000 *livres* to be paid to de la Pole, but his enterprise never materialized. Five

[1] *L.P.*, iii. 2290, 2292, 2309; Michaud et Poujoulat, v. 92.
[2] *L.P.*, iii. 2362, 2530, 2541, 2560, 2614. See Potter, *War and Government*, pp. 71–2.
[3] *Ibid.*, iii. 2524, 2532, 2536, 2645.

hundred French troops were sent to Scotland in June, but another three months elapsed before Albany followed them with a much larger force.[4]

Francis, in the meantime, prepared to invade Italy, where he faced a hostile coalition, including Venice and the Holy See. Pope Adrian VI had been deeply upset by the Turkish capture of Rhodes in December 1521. On 3 March 1522 he called on all Christian princes to prepare for a new crusade by sinking their differences. But Francis insisted on Milan being restored to him first. About the same time, compromising letters written by Cardinal Soderini, leader of the French faction in the Sacred College, fell into the hands of Cardinal Medici. Adrian ordered Soderini's arrest and Cardinal Medici, who had been living in Florence since the last conclave, returned triumphantly to Rome. Francis interpreted Soderini's arrest as a hostile act; he also objected to a papal bull ordering the princes of Christendom to sign a truce under threat of spiritual censures. The pope, he claimed, was breaking canon law. Francis threatened to set up an antipope, while reminding Adrian of the fate that had befallen Pope Boniface VIII when he had dared to oppose Philip the Fair.[5] Adrian could not afford to punish the king's insolence. 'I shall not declare myself against France', he said, 'because such a step would be immediately followed by the stoppage of all supplies of money from that kingdom, on which I chiefly depend for the maintenance of my Court, and because I know on good authority that the French king would become a protector of the Lutheran heresy and make a settlement of the ecclesiastical order in his dominions.'[6] Yet, on 18 June, Francis banned the dispatch of money from his kingdom to Rome; he also dismissed the papal nuncio from his court. Thus was Adrian finally driven into the imperial camp: on 3 August he joined a league for the defence of Italy.

Francis, meanwhile, completed his preparations for war. On 23 July he attended Mass at the abbey of Saint-Denis and placed the saint's relics on the high altar where they were to remain for the duration of the forthcoming campaign. Next day he formally took leave of the citizens of Paris at the Hôtel de Ville and recommended his queen and his mother to them. The court then travelled south to Gien, where Louise of Savoy was appointed regent on 12 August for the second time.[7] While she and Queen Claude travelled to Blois, Francis continued on his journey to Lyons. However, about 16 August at Saint-Pierre-le-Moûtier, he received a letter from Louis de Brézé, *sénéchal* of Normandy, warning him of a plot led by the duc de Bourbon.

Charles III, duc de Bourbon, belonged to the younger branch of a house founded in the fourteenth century by Robert de Clermont, sixth son of King

---

[4] *Ibid.*, iii. 2755, 2768, 2799, 2870, 3118; C.A.F., i. 1858.
[5] L. von Pastor, *The History of the Popes*, tr. F. I. Antrobus and R. F. Kerr (London, 1891–1933), ix. 174, 185–8, 195, 197–200. See also K. J. P. Lowe, *Church and Politics in Renaissance Italy: The Life and Career of Cardinal Francesco Soderini, 1453–1524* (Cambridge, 1993), pp. 132–5.
[6] Pastor, ix. 201.   [7] *J.B.P.*, pp. 116–17; Versoris, pp. 31–2; *Ordonnances*, iii. 282–9.

42. Charles duke of Bourbon and Constable of France. Drawing attributed to Jean Clouet.

Louis IX. In 1443 the territory owned by this house in central France had been divided between the two sons of duc Jean I, and for a time it looked as if the two branches would go their separate ways, but in 1488 the lands of the elder branch passed into the hands of Pierre de Beaujeu, who, having no son, bequeathed his property to his daughter, Suzanne. Her right to inherit, however, was challenged by her cousin Charles, head of the younger branch of Bourbon-Montpensier, the future Constable. The quarrel was submitted to the Parlement and an ingenious solution found: Suzanne and Charles were married, the lands of the two branches being thus reunited. In 1521 the Bourbon demesne formed an unusually compact territorial block in central France with its own distinctive administration, including a high court of justice. The duke was all-powerful within his demesne: he raised troops, levied taxes, dispensed justice and called the local estates. He owned several fortresses and his château at Moulins was among the largest in France.[8]

Until 1521 Bourbon's relations with the king were friendly rather than intimate. The duke was slightly older than Francis and seems never to have commanded the same influence as the king's childhood friends. It has been suggested that Francis was jealous of the military reputation Bourbon had acquired in Italy under Louis XII and that he marginalized him from the start of his reign. The duke was certainly starved of funds during the Marignano campaign but this had happened before, under Louis XII. He ceased to receive his wages and pensions from the crown after 1516. In January he was appointed lieutenant-general in Milan and it was largely thanks to his efficient administration that the Emperor Maximilian failed to recapture the city. Yet he was soon afterwards replaced by Marshal Lautrec, but this was not necessarily a snub. Having served his term, the duke returned to the court where he was warmly received by Francis and his mother. In 1517 the king was godfather to Bourbon's short-lived son; in 1518 the duke took part in celebrations for the Dauphin's birth; in 1519 he and the king spent Christmas together at Châtellerault and in 1520 Bourbon figured prominently at the Field of Cloth of Gold.[9]

The first clear sign of a rift between Francis and the Constable occurred in the autumn of 1521 during the campaign against Charles V in northern France. Having assembled a formidable army near Rheims, Francis gave command of the vanguard to the duc d'Alençon and that of the rearguard to the duc de Vendôme, while he himself took charge of the 'battle'. Normally, the vanguard would have been entrusted to the Constable, and Bourbon was apparently vexed. 'Some say', wrote Fitzwilliam, 'that Monsieur de Bourbon is not contented that he hath not the vaward.'[10] Yet he concealed his true feelings and

[8] Doucet, i. 203–14; A. Lebey, *Le connétable de Bourbon* (1904), pp. 10–24, 122.
[9] Lebey, pp. 90–1; Doucet, i. 218.
[10] *L.P.*, iii. 1651; du Bellay, i. 159.

later that year captured Hesdin for the king. But the death of Bourbon's wife, Suzanne, on 28 April 1521, precipitated the collapse of his relations with Francis. For the duchess's death raised two important issues: her inheritance and the Constable's remarriage.

Suzanne's inheritance, as we have seen, was juridically of three kinds. Some of her lands (viz. Auvergne, Clermont-en-Beauvaisis and Montpensier) were appanages, which normally would have escheated to the crown on the extinction of the elder branch of the royal house. This had been confirmed by a clause in the marriage contract of Pierre de Beaujeu and Anne de France (1474), but annulled by Charles VIII (1488) and Louis XII (1498). Other lands (e.g. Bourbonnais and Châtellerault) were meant to escheat to the crown in case of a failure of the direct or male line of descent. Thirdly, other lands, acquired by the Bourbons over the centuries (e.g. Forez, Beaujolais, Dombes), were patrimonial and could be handed down to direct or collateral heirs of either sex.[11] For a long time, as we have seen, the dukes of Bourbon had striven to preserve the unity of their demesne. But this was now challenged from two sides. While Louise of Savoy, who was Suzanne's first cousin and nearest blood relative, claimed her entire inheritance, the king requested the return to the royal demesne of all the fiefs transmissible only to male heirs. Both suits were submitted to the Parlement of Paris, the only court empowered to deal with matters affecting a peer of the realm. But Francis did not wait for the court's verdict to dispose of Bourbon lands. On 7 October Louise did homage to him for the Bourbonnais, Auvergne, Clermont, Forez, Beaujolais, Marche, Carlat and Murat. By receiving her oath Francis prejudged the suits being considered by the Parlement. Furthermore, following the death of Suzanne's mother, Anne de France, on 14 November, he gave Louise property which Anne had bequeathed to her son-in-law, the Constable.[12] This gift contradicted Louise's claim to the Bourbon inheritance since it implied that this had escheated to the crown; but Francis and his mother were more interested in grabbing Bourbon lands than in legal niceties.

Meanwhile, the lawsuit in the Parlement followed its course. The three counsels concerned – Poyet for Louise, Lizet for the king and Montholon for Bourbon – argued for and against the validity of various legal transactions reaching back to the fifteenth century. The historian, Roger Doucet, after carefully examining the arguments, concluded that 'all reasons of law and equity supported the duc de Bourbon' and that the next strongest claim was the king's. That of Louise, in his opinion, could only be sustained by an arbitrary and selective interpretation of the documents.[13] The Parlement, unfortunately,

[11] J. Jacquart, *François Ier* (1981), pp. 134–6.
[12] *C.A.F.*, i. 1649–5, 1721; vii. 23738; Doucet, i. 227–9.
[13] *Ibid.*, i. 251–2.

never gave its verdict. On 6 August 1523 the case was adjourned until 11 November, but, at the end of August, the court ordered the sequestration of the Constable's lands. The decree has not survived, but it is mentioned by well-informed contemporary sources. The Parlement may have acted under pressure from Louise, who had become regent on 12 August, and failed to register the decree by way of protest, or it may have entered the decree into a secret register, now lost.[14] But, even allowing for duress, was there any justification for the sequestration order? To answer this question we need to consider another aspect of the Bourbon case.

Suzanne's death had raised a second major problem: since she left no children, her husband needed to remarry in order to ensure the continuity of his line. Even in Suzanne's lifetime, imperial agents had hinted at a possible future remarriage between the duke and one of Charles V's sisters. After her death the hint became a firm offer, but Bourbon was careful not to rush into a course which would inevitably alienate the king. Yet he also resisted pressure to marry him off to a French princess of royal blood. Did he reject an offer of marriage from Louise of Savoy, as historians of a romantic disposition have often claimed? There is some evidence for this. In May 1523, the imperial ambassador in England reported that Bourbon had refused to marry the king's mother, who was 'much in love with him'.[15] Marillac says nothing about this in his contemporary life of Bourbon, but de Laval, who completed his work, does mention such a marriage project, though he presents it as an unsentimental affair whereby Louise hoped to acquire the Bourbon lands.[16] Such a match would certainly have suited the crown. At the age of forty-four, Louise was unlikely to bear children; thus, in the event of her outliving the duke, the Bourbon demesne would ultimately revert to the crown. There is evidence, too, that Louise tried to reach some amicable arrangement – possibly a marriage – with Bourbon before she laid claim to his lands. Legally she was supposed to act within a year and a day following Suzanne's death, yet she waited till the last moment before doing so. This lends substance to the story that she sued the Constable only after he had rejected her advances.[17]

During the winter of 1522–23 Francis and the Constable were rumoured to have patched up their quarrel. Bourbon, it was said, would marry Renée, the queen's younger sister, and take up a military command in Italy.[18] Early in 1523, however, Francis accused him of becoming engaged – presumably to the Emperor's sister – behind his back. The story, as reported by the English ambassador in Spain runs as follows. Bourbon was dining with Queen Claude one day, when Francis burst into the room. 'Senyor', he exclaimed, 'it is shown

[14] *Ibid.*, i. 229–44.
[15] Quoted by F. Mignet in *La rivalité de François Ier et de Charles-Quint* (1875), i. 380 n. 1, who merely gives 'archives of Vienna' as the source.
[16] Doucet, i. 215–17.   [17] *Ibid.*, i. 221–2.   [18] *L.P.*, iii. 2799.

to us that you be or shall be married; is it true?' Bourbon denied the report, but Francis insisted that it was true. 'Sir', retorted the duke, 'then you menace and threaten me; I have deserved no such cause.' Whereupon he returned to his lodging accompanied by 'all the noblemen of the court'.[19] In May Bourbon told the bishop of Le Puy that he no longer expected fair treatment from the king; he would, therefore, surrender his sword and collar of St Michael and retire to Germany, where he expected to be joined by more than a thousand French nobles.[20]

Bourbon only severed his allegiance to Francis on 7 September, after the Parlement had ordered the confiscation of his lands. He was a vassal of both the king and in respect of certain lands situated east of the Saône, the Emperor. Under feudal law, a vassal who felt unjustly treated by one suzerain could seek redress from another. But Bourbon had been plotting rebellion for some time. In August 1522, one year before the decree of sequestration, two of his friends, François d'Escars and Philibert de Saint-Romain, seigneur de Lurcy told the Emperor's chamberlain, Adrien de Croy, seigneur de Beaurain that their master was prepared to rebel with 500 men-at-arms and 10,000 infantry.[21] Henry VIII was keen to accept the offer, but Charles V preferred to wait. By May 1523, however, the Emperor was ready to conclude with Bourbon if Henry would do likewise. Beaurain travelled to England and, after securing Henry's co-operation, went to Franche-Comté with powers to negotiate with Bourbon on behalf of both allies. As the Constable refused to meet him outside France, Beaurain had to go secretly to Montbrison, where he met Bourbon and some of his associates on the night of 11 July. The talks ended in a treaty between Bourbon and Charles: the duke was promised the hand of one of the Emperor's sisters, either Eleanor or Catherine, with a dowry of 100,000 écus; the Emperor would invade Languedoc from Spain and place 10,000 landsknechts at Bourbon's disposal. Henry was not a party to the treaty, as his plenipotentiary Dr Knight, failed to reach Montbrison in time. The king's role in the forthcoming campaign was none the less set out: he was to invade Normandy and pay a subsidy of 100,000 crowns to Bourbon.[22]

The Constable now began preparing his rebellion in earnest. He planned to lie low until Francis had crossed the Alps with his army and Henry and Charles had invaded France from two directions, then to attack Francis from the rear with the help of the landsknechts promised by Charles. Aymar de Prie was to pave the way for this operation by occupying Dijon.[23] But Bourbon was a half-hearted traitor. Even now, he still hoped to come to terms with Francis. His advisers, too, were divided: some favoured a revolt, others a settlement

[19] *Ibid.*, ii. 2879.   [20] Doucet, i. 259.   [21] *Ibid.*, i. 257–8; *L.P.*, iii. 3030.
[22] Doucet, i. 260–4; *L.P.*, iii. 3055, 3123–4, 3154, 3194, 3203; Le Glay, ii. 589–92.
[23] Doucet, i. 264–5.

with the king. Nor did Bourbon get much aristocratic support, for d'Escars refused to co-operate, while two Norman nobles, Matignon and d'Argouges, revealed the plot to their confessor, the bishop of Lisieux. He informed Louis de Brézé, who warned the king on 10 August.[24] It was his letter that Francis received as he travelled south to join his army.

The king's reaction was remarkably cool. He rode strongly escorted to Moulins, the Constable's residence, and, finding him in bed seemingly unwell, told him of the warning he had received. Then, pretending not to believe it, he promised to ensure an amicable settlement of Bourbon's suit in the Parlement, to increase his pensions, to raise him in honour 'as far as it was possible for him to go' and to give him command of the army in his own absence. But Francis laid down one crucial condition: Bourbon had to accompany him to Italy. This put the Constable on the spot: if he refused, the king's worst suspicions would be confirmed; if he accepted, his own plan of campaign would fall through. In the end, he agreed to follow the king, but asked for a week's grace so that he might recover his health. This was conceded. Having been assured that Bourbon's illness was genuine, the king resumed his journey to Lyons. On 22 August he sent Perrot de Warty to Moulins to remind the Constable of his undertaking.[25]

Eventually, Bourbon did set out for Lyons, but he travelled very slowly and, at La Palisse, suddenly turned back, saying that he was too weak to continue. On 6 September, at Gayette, he met Sir John Russell, whom Henry VIII had sent out in place of Dr Knight, and formalized his relations with England. While refusing to recognize Henry's claim to the French throne, he agreed to have it referred to the Emperor's judgment.[26]

Bourbon's failure to turn up in Lyons convinced Francis of his treasonable intentions. On 5 September three of the Constable's associates, Jean de Poitiers seigneur de Saint-Vallier, Antoine de Chabannes, bishop of Le Puy, and Aymar de Prie were arrested in Lyons, while troops were sent to Moulins to round up Bourbon's servants. Yet no drastic action was taken against the Constable himself: Francis merely asked him to explain his conduct. Bourbon, in the meantime, retired to Chantelle, where he severed his allegiance. But, as he needed more time to prepare his rebellion, he sent Jacques Hurault, bishop of Autun, to the king with an offer of loyal service in return for his property. The bishop, however, was arrested before accomplishing his mission.

The Constable's plight was now desperate. Royal troops were closing in on him, yet no immediate help was forthcoming from his allies. The landsknechts were still far away, and neither Henry nor Charles had invaded France. The

[24] *Ibid.*, i. 266–7; B.N., ms. fr. 5770; *L.P.*, iii. 3254.
[25] Doucet, i. 267–8; B.N., ms. Dupuy 211, fols. 4, 6–7.
[26] Doucet, i. 269; *L.P.*, iii. 3217, 3307.

only course left to Bourbon was flight. During the night of 8 September he left Chantelle with a few companions intending to reach Carlat, a fortress in the mountains of Cantal. He may have intended to reach Spain. Before leaving, he wrote six letters, including one to Louise of Savoy, asking for her intercession with her son. A few days later, after wandering through the Auvergne, Bourbon crossed the Rhône near Vienne. On 23 September he reached Chambéry and a few days later turned up at Sainte-Claude within imperial territory. On 9 October he informed the Swiss cantons that henceforth he would be serving the Emperor. A few days later, his sister, the duchess of Lorraine, who had tried to reconcile him with the king, wrote to Francis telling him of her failure. Bourbon had told her of his resolve to press on with his enterprise; he intended to drive the king like a wild boar into the woods.[27]

Although Bourbon's plot had misfired, its discovery prevented Francis from leading his army to Italy, as planned. On 17 September he informed Bonnivet, who had already crossed the Alps, of his decision to remain in France for the time being.[28] He needed to take stock of the situation and, remaining in Lyons, he devoted his energies to finding out the full extent of the plot and bringing Bourbon's accomplices to justice. Altogether about thirty were arrested ranging in status from the chancellor of the duchy of Bourbon to humble servants and messengers. It soon became clear that the plot was less widespread than had been feared. There were no provincial revolts, not even within Bourbon's demesne. Even so, Francis was determined to make an example of the conspirators. On 11 September, while the Constable's whereabouts were still unknown, the king ordered his arrest, offering a reward of 10,000 *écus* for his capture.[29] He also appointed a commission of four *parlementaires* to interrogate and try suspects. They were empowered to use torture, if necessary, to obtain the names of Bourbon's accomplices, and to inflict swift and exemplary punishment on all, save the Constable whose sentencing was reserved to the king alone. The commissioners felt uneasy about their task; they believed that it was really a matter for the Parlement, but Francis threatened to dismiss them unless they showed more zeal.[30]

Meanwhile, the French army under Bonnivet invaded the duchy of Milan. After crossing the Ticino on 14 September, the Admiral forced Prospero Colonna, the imperial commander, to fall back on Milan, but he then stopped for a few days. Colonna was consequently able to repair the city's defences. By the time the French resumed their advance, Milan was so strong that they could only blockade it.[31]

On 19 September the duke of Suffolk invaded Picardy with a huge army. His

[27] B.N., ms. fr. 5109, fols. 87–90; Doucet, i. 273; Jacquart, p. 140.
[28] B.N., ms. fr. 3897, fol. 244.
[29] *Ordonnances*, iii. 297–8.   [30] Doucet, i. 277–84.
[31] Du Bellay, i. 280–2, 285–90, 300–2; B.N., ms. fr. 3897, fol. 244a.

aim had originally been to capture Boulogne, but he was persuaded to march on Paris instead. This he did with remarkable speed. Within three weeks he had crossed the Somme; by late October he was only fifty miles from the capital.[32] The inhabitants, panic-stricken, appealed to Francis for help. His response was to send Philippe Chabot, who assured them of the king's willingness to sacrifice his life in their defence. If Francis could not come in person, Chabot declared, he would send them his wife, children, mother and all his possessions, for the king knew that if he lost his kingdom, he would be able to regain it as long as he kept control of Paris. Meanwhile the duc de Vendôme took steps to defend the capital. A special tax was levied, the *francs-archers* were called up, trenches dug, chains stretched across the streets and ramparts erected.[33] But all this proved unnecessary, as the English retired of their own accord after they had been let down by their allies.

Bourbon, instead of leading a rebellion, had left France. Many of the landsknechts he had been promised by Charles V had deserted, while the rest had invaded Champagne only to be routed by the comte de Guise. Bourbon was thus denied any chance of invading eastern France from his new headquarters in Franche-Comté. So he went to Italy, hoping eventually to join the Emperor in Spain.[34] As for Charles V, he had abandoned his plan to invade Languedoc for lack of money. The prince of Orange recaptured Fuenterrabía instead, but his attack on Bayonne in September was repulsed.[35] Thus Suffolk found himself fighting the war alone. His predicament was compounded by the desertion of his Burgundian troops and by a sudden cold spell which decimated his men and horses. By mid December he and the remnants of his demoralized army were back in Calais.

Paris had been saved, but not by Francis. The Parisians felt that while he had spent their money in pursuit of his Italian ambitions, he had left them largely defenceless. Their resentment took the form of sympathy for Bourbon, whom they regarded as a man of 'wisdom, virtue and valour', driven into treason by Duprat's insatiable greed. Such sentiments were expressed in popular songs.[36] Sympathy for the Constable was not confined to the populace; it seems also to have existed among the *parlementaires*, which may help to explain their leniency to his accomplices. On 20 December Francis reluctantly agreed to have them tried by the Parlement instead of the special commission he had appointed. The prisoners were accordingly moved to Paris and their trial began soon afterwards. On 16 January 1524 Saint-Vallier was sentenced to death and

[32] J. J. Scarisbrick, *Henry VIII* (London, 1968), pp. 128–30; du Bellay, i. 293–400; S. J. Gunn, 'The Duke of Suffolk's march on Paris in 1523', *E.H.R.*, 101 (1986), 596–634.

[33] *J.B.P.*, pp. 146, 148–50; Versoris, pp. 37–9.

[34] Du Bellay, i. 290–3; *L.P.*, iii. 3399, 3440, 3455, 3490, 3498.

[35] Du Bellay, i. 282–5.

[36] E. Picot, *Chants historiques français du XVIe siècle* (1903); B.N., ms. fr. 2200; Champollion-Figeac, p. 375.

to the loss of all his property and titles. It was also decided that he should be put to the question. On 17 February he was stripped of his knighthood, but his interrogators found him too ill to undergo torture. He was taken to the Place de Grève for execution. He mounted the scaffold, made his confession and placed his head on the block, but the axe did not fall, for a messenger suddenly appeared, waving a royal reprieve. Instead of losing his head, Saint-Vallier was to be imprisoned in a cell with an aperture wide enough only to allow the passage of food. As the crowd cheered, Saint-Vallier kissed the scaffold, crossed himself several times and returned to prison 'looking happier than when he had left it'. On 1 April he was taken to Loches where he remained until his release in 1526. According to the Bourgeois de Paris, Saint-Vallier had threatened to kill the king for having raped his daughter, and would have been beheaded but for the intercession of his son-in-law, the *Grand sénéchal* of Normandy.[37] The sentences passed on the other accused by the Parlement were far more lenient, possibly because, unlike Saint-Vallier, they had informed on their fellow plotters who had fled abroad. Saint-Bonnet was pardoned, de Prie was placed under house arrest, and d'Esguières and Brion were each sent to prison for three years.

Was Bourbon a second Coriolanus driven into treason by a jealous and ungrateful prince or just a selfish and ambitious plotter? The question has long been debated by historians. Bias and romantic fantasy have often intruded upon the discussion. The duke certainly acted under strong provocation, but not simply for personal reasons. He has been fairly described as France's last great feudatory. His power and wealth were such that he was less dependent on royal favour than other French nobles. This capacity for independence was in itself an anomaly which the crown had cause to resent at a time when it was seeking to strengthen its authority. Bourbon's divided feudal allegiance was also a potential danger. Clearly, he attracted a good deal of sympathy among his countrymen, who had no great love for the king or his mother and heartily detested the Chancellor. This was particularly true of the Parisians. The Parlement was lukewarm, if not sympathetic, in prosecuting the duke and his accomplices. Why then did Bourbon's rebellion fail? Several answers may be suggested: first, his plot was badly planned and executed; secondly, he was a malcontent, not a reformer: the wrongs he wished to avenge were his own; thirdly, he lacked the support of the nobility without which few sixteenth-century rebellions were likely to succeed. The nobility had less cause for dis-

---

[37] Doucet, i. 299–303; *J.B.P.*, pp. 157–60; Versoris, p. 41. This presumably is the origin of the story that Saint-Vallier's daughter, Diane de Poitiers, obtained his reprieve by becoming the king's mistress, which provided Victor Hugo with part of the plot of *Le roi s'amuse*, later used by Verdi in his opera *Rigoletto*. More probably Saint-Vallier owed his reprieve to the fact that it was his son-in-law, Diane's husband, who had warned Francis of the Bourbon conspiracy. Gaillard, *Histoire de François Ier* (1766), 247–8; Jacquart, pp. 150–1.

content than other social groups in France, for it was less heavily taxed than other social groups and benefited more from royal largesse. Rebellion was, in any case, a serious gamble few were prepared to risk.

In Italy, the winter of 1523–24 was notable for the election of a new pope to succeed Adrian VI who had died in September. Francis tried to bring pressure to bear on the conclave, but none of his candidates stood any chance of success. The favourites, Giulio de' Medici and Pompeo Colonna, were imperialists, and, when after five weeks and several scrutinies, Colonna stood down, Medici's success was assured. He was elected on 19 November and took the name of Clement VII. The result was acclaimed by the Emperor's ambassador in Rome. 'The Pope', he wrote to his master, 'is entirely your Majesty's creature. So great is your Majesty's power, that you can change stones into obedient children.'[38] He assumed that the new pope would adhere to the policies he had promoted as cardinal, but from the start of his pontificate Clement aimed to be neutral. He refused to be drawn into an offensive alliance with Charles V or to subsidize his army in Lombardy. In March 1524 he sent a nuncio to the principal courts on a peacemaking mission, but, as Francis would not accept a truce that included Bourbon, and Charles insisted on exchanging Milan for Burgundy, the mission proved abortive.[39]

Early in March Charles de Lannoy, Viceroy of Naples, who had replaced Colonna as commander of the imperial army in north Italy, launched an offensive which threatened to encircle Bonnivet's camp at Abbiategrasso.[40] The Admiral managed to extricate himself, but his army had been hard hit by the severe winter. He had no ammunition left and his supplies were running out. So many horses had died that the men-at-arms were reduced to riding ponies. An additional hazard was plague: Montmorency, who commanded the vanguard, became so ill that he had to be carried in a litter. Soon afterwards the French suffered heavy casualties as they crossed the river Sesia. Bonnivet, his arm shattered by shot from an arquebus, handed over his command to the comte de Saint-Pol. On 30 April Bayard, the *chevalier sans peur et sans reproche* was fatally wounded, also by an arquebus. Legend has it that, as he lay dying at the foot of a tree, Bourbon came to commiserate with him. 'Monsieur', replied Bayard, 'you need not pity me, for I die a worthy man; it is I who pity you, for you have betrayed your prince, your fatherland and your oath.'[41]

On reaching the Alps, the French went one way and the Swiss, who had joined Bonnivet during his retreat, went another. 'The Swiss', wrote Beaurain, 'swear a great oath never again to serve the French, and the French never to

[38] Pastor, ix. 253.   [39] *Ibid.*, ix. 257–8.   [40] *J.B.P.*, p. 153.
[41] Du Bellay, i. 314; J. Jacquart, *Bayard* (1987), p. 310. For a perceptive interpretation of the contemporary legend of Bayard as God's warrior fighting the forces of evil see Denis Crouzet's introduction to S. Champier, *Les gestes ensemble la vie du preulx Chevalier Bayard* (1992), pp. 7–76.

trust the Swiss.'[42] Money was the cause of their quarrel: the Swiss had not yet been paid, but a report that they kidnapped Bonnivet as a security for their wages was unfounded. The Admiral accompanied them because his wound prevented him from keeping up with his cavalry. He eventually returned to France, where he recovered slowly. His defeat had been truly crushing. The Emperor estimated that only 350 French men-at-arms returned home out of a total of 1,500. Twenty-four guns left by the French in Savoy were added to seventeen already taken by the enemy.[43] Within a few weeks the garrisons at Lodi and Alessandria surrendered, completing the French debâcle.

When Francis returned to Paris on 4 March after an absence of seven months, the mood of the citizens was distinctly hostile. Not only had they been left to face the English invasion alone, they had also endured an exceptionally harsh winter. Six days of frost in November had wiped out the next harvest, and many fruit trees and vines had been blighted. Vegetables were almost unobtainable and, in spite of legislation to curb profiteering, the price of bread had rocketed.[44] On 6 March the king addressed a meeting of leading citizens at the Hôtel de Ville. For once he did not ask them for money. Instead, he tried to justify his policy by presenting himself as the innocent victim of his neighbours' envy and of Bourbon's treachery. He praised them for their steadfastness in the recent crisis, thanked them for their support and promised to reward them. 'The king's speech', wrote Versoris, 'was most acceptable to the bourgeois of Paris, and the people were partly satisfied.'[45]

Two days later Francis went to the Parlement for the opening of the trial *in absentia* of the duc de Bourbon. The *advocat du roi* Lizet, after reading out the indictment, asked that the duke be immediately sentenced to death and all his property confiscated. Alternatively, he asked that he should be arrested or summonsed and prosecuted for default so that his sentence might be prefaced by a proper trial. After debating the matter, the Parlement ordered Bourbon's arrest and detention in the Conciergerie, failing which he was to be summonsed. In the meantime, his property and titles were to be seized for the king.

At a *lit de justice*, on 9 March, the whole Bourbon affair, not just the duke's trial, came under examination along with other business. After reminding the court of Saint-Vallier's fate, Francis asked for information about Bourbon's other accomplices, who, in his view, deserved exemplary punishment. President de Selve, outlined what had been done in each case, but was interrupted by Duprat. 'And what of their property?', he asked, 'have you not confiscated it?' To which the answer was 'no', for the case was a *relégation*, which did not allow confiscation. At this point Francis intervened. It was wrong, he declared, for a matter touching his person and the kingdom so closely to be treated like an ordinary civil suit. He intended to appoint several worthy persons to re-

---

[42] *L.P.*, iv. 305.   [43] *Ibid.*, iv. 351, 358.   [44] *J.B.P.*, pp. 155, 160–1.   [45] Versoris, p. 42.

examine the case of Bourbon's accomplices alongside the existing judges. Meanwhile, he forbade the prisoners to be moved.[46]

The king's rebuke, however, did not hasten the outcome of the trial; on the contrary. The judges, knowing that their sentences would be reviewed, were even less zealous than before. Much time was lost as summonses were pronounced against Bourbon and his accomplices. Francis, for his part, waited until 16 May to add nineteen judges, mostly drawn from the parlements of Toulouse, Bordeaux and Rouen, to those already conducting the trial. At the same time, he ordered this to be reviewed and forbade the court to pass new sentences without his knowledge. The Parlement responded by flatly refusing to review its earlier judgments and by appointing thirty of its own members to sit alongside the nineteen royal commissioners.[47]

Despite repeated admonitions from the king, the Parlement allowed several weeks to pass after the deadline set for Bourbon's appearance in court before pronouncing the first default against him. As for his accomplices they were not sentenced until 2 and 7 July. De Prie and Popillon were released on condition they remained in a town of the king's choice; their property was returned to them. A similar sentence was passed on d'Escars, though he was confined to a town for two years, because he had attempted to escape from the Conciergerie.[48] By contrast, savage and unenforceable punishments were inflicted on the duke's men who had fled abroad and had failed to answer the court's summonses. The only sentence outstanding was Bourbon's own, which had to await the king's pleasure.

Francis was understandably furious. Not only had the Parlement not reviewed its past judgments; it had virtually acquitted Bourbon's accomplices who had been in its custody. On 10 July he forbade the court to publish its sentences or to release its prisoners. He warned that it would hear from him again after his return from Italy. However, the Parlement was not easily browbeaten: while agreeing not to release its prisoners, it decided to publish its sentences in order 'to obviate the murmuring of the people and so that it should not be said that the court denies or conceals justice'.[49] The king accused it of putting its own wishes before his honour and service and the general good of the kingdom. He repeated his earlier commands.[50] A few days later he left Paris to take charge of his army in Italy. De Prie and d'Escars remained in prison for the present; Popillon died in the Bastille on 15 August.

Meanwhile, on 25 May, Henry VIII and Charles V had concluded a new treaty. Bourbon was to invade France with all possible speed, each prince contributing 100,000 crowns towards the cost of his army. He was to swear allegiance to Henry as king of France, otherwise the latter's contribution would

[46] Doucet, i. 306–9.   [47] *Ibid.*, i. 310; *C.A.F.*, v. 17782; *J.B.P.*, p. 161.   [48] *J.B.P.*, pp. 165–6.
[49] B.N., ms. fr. 5109, fols. 400–1.   [50] B.N., ms. fr. 5109, fols. 401–2.

lapse.[51] On 28 May Wolsey informed Richard Pace, who was with Bourbon near Turin, that Russell was bringing the duke 20,000 *livres*.[52] At first, Bourbon refused to swear allegiance to Henry, saying that this might alienate his supporters with France and drive the pope into the French camp. On 25 June, however, he changed his mind. 'I promise unto you upon my faith', he assured Pace, 'that I will by the help of my friends, put the crown of France upon the king our common master's head, or else my days shall be cut off.'[53] But he declined to do homage for his duchy to Henry.

On 1 July, Bourbon, acting as the Emperor's lieutenant-general, led his army across the Var, marking the frontier between Italy and France. As he waited for his artillery to arrive by sea from Genoa, his galleys were intercepted by the French fleet. Most of them managed to shelter in Monaco harbour, but three ran aground and their precious cargo was saved only after a fierce engagement on the beach in which Bourbon almost lost his life.[54] Inland, however, his army encountered little resistance as it advanced towards Aix. The French, under Marshal Lapalisse, were too weak numerically to put up a fight. As they retreated, town after town capitulated. On 7 August the consuls of Aix, led by the seigneur de Pras, surrendered its keys. Two days later Bourbon entered the town and assumed the title of comte de Provence. He had hoped to find money there, but was disappointed, as nearly all the wealthy citizens had fled.

So far the duke had received little help from his allies. Left to himself, Henry VIII would perhaps have invaded northern France, but Wolsey was sceptical about Bourbon's chances. He could see no sign of an impending revolt in France and thought the season too far advanced for an English expedition to be worth while. On 16 August Charles V complained that Henry's lethargy was endangering Bourbon's campaign, yet he himself was no more helpful: his army was still in Catalonia. Thus Bourbon was left to fight alone. Even the financial help sent by his allies was inadequate. Russell reached the duke's camp nearly two months after the start of his campaign, and the Emperor's subsidy arrived only in dribs and drabs. Bourbon had to borrow from his captains in order to pay his troops.[55]

About mid August Bourbon had to decide whether or not to besiege Marseilles. The town was protected by the sea to the south and west, and by fortifications, recently strengthened by Francis, to the north and east. The garrison consisted of 4,000 troops under Renzo da Ceri and Chabot de Brion; there was also a citizen militia of 8,000 men. The town was well provided with artillery and could, if necessary, invoke the additional fire-power of the French navy anchored in the harbour. Bourbon may have been tempted to by-pass such

[51] *L.P.*, iv. 365.   [52] *Ibid.*, iv. 374.   [53] *Ibid.*, iv. 442.
[54] *Ibid.*, iv. 483; Lebey, pp. 237–9.
[55] *L.P.*, iv. 552.

a formidable obstacle, but he must have seen the danger of penetrating deeper into France without removing it first. For Marseilles might threaten his rear and cut off his supplies. By capturing the port, the French fleet would be deprived of its chief base in the Mediterranean, Bourbon's communications with Spain and Italy would be improved, and other French towns might be induced to capitulate as well. On 19 August, therefore, he laid siege to Marseilles. Four days later his guns tore open a breach in the northern wall, but this was swiftly filled by the defenders using stones, logs and barrels of earth. Bourbon's sappers then tried to mine the wall, but the citizens countered the threat by hastily digging deep longitudinal trenches. On 2 September the imperialists captured Toulon along with nine guns, which they added to the batteries bombarding Marseilles. This alarming development prompted the defenders to appeal for help to Francis.[56]

The king was with his army near Avignon: it comprised 6,000 Swiss troops and most of the *gendarmerie* that had been defending Picardy. Praising Marseilles for its courage and loyalty, he promised to come to its aid soon. For the present, he ordered victuals and 1,500 troops to be sent there by sea.[57] On 14 September Bourbon launched a new assault on Marseilles; he opened a new breach in the wall and ordered his landsknechts to attack, but they refused to obey after seeing the obstacles that awaited them beyond the breach. Bourbon was reduced to black despair; having been let down by his allies, he now had to face mutiny. He thought of saving his honour by challenging the king of France to battle, but his captains dissuaded him from such recklessness. On 29 September he lifted the siege and began retreating along the coast. Two days later, as Montmorency's cavalry gave chase, Francis regained control of Aix.[58]

Francis could now think of carrying out his long-deferred plan of invading Italy. For several years he had longed to repeat his triumph at Marignano, but circumstances had forced him to delegate the task to lieutenants, who had proved incompetent or unfortunate. The tide had now turned in his favour: the enemy was on the run; Milan lay almost defenceless. Louise of Savoy tried to dissuade her son and some of his councillors advised him to wait till the spring. However, Bonnivet, who by now had recovered, was keen to avenge his recent defeat. The weather was unusually clement for the time of year and the opportunity of striking a blow at the enemy seemed too good to miss. Francis, therefore, decided to act before the imperialists could regroup. He left Aix on 5 October, narrowly missing his mother who made a last-minute dash to Avignon in a vain effort to restrain him. On 17 October he confirmed her as regent and immediately afterwards crossed the Alps for the second time.[59]

---

[56] Mignet, *La rivalité*, i. 522–30; Lebey, p. 246. On the long-term significance of the siege see E. Schalk 'Evolution and the Traumatic Event in the History of Marseille from the Fifteenth to the Eighteenth Century' in *Evénement, identité et histoire*, ed. C. Dolan (Quebec, 1991), pp. 25–38.

[57] Mignet, *La rivalité*, i. 539.   [58] *Ibid.*, i. 540–3, 549–51; Jacquart, pp. 156–7.

[59] *Ordonnances*, iv. no. 380.

Chapter eleven

Defeat and captivity

As the French entered the Milanese, the imperialists threw garrisons into Pavia and Alessandria, but abandoned Milan. They left the city by one gate, as the French entered by another. Francis could either prevent them digging in at Lodi or lay siege to Pavia. He chose to do the latter, thereby prompting the marquis of Pescara to exclaim: 'We were defeated; soon we shall be victorious.'[1] For Pavia was a tough nut to crack: it was enclosed by a wall except on the south side, where the river Ticino formed a natural line of defence, and the garrison, comprising 6,000 Germans and Spaniards, was commanded by Antonio de Leyva, one of the best captains of his day. The French began to bombard Pavia on 6 November, and within three days they had breached the wall, but their first assault was repulsed with heavy losses. They then tried to divert the course of the Ticino to facilitate an assault on the town from the south, but torrential rains swept away a dam they had built upstream. The siege gradually turned into a blockade punctuated by skirmishes and artillery duels.[2]

Francis's next move has been described as 'the maddest of all the strategical errors for which he and his two predecessors had been responsible'.[3] He detached 6,000 troops from his army and sent them under the duke of Albany to conquer the kingdom of Naples. But there may have been method in the king's madness. He possibly had two objectives in mind: first, to oblige Charles de Lannoy, the Viceroy of Naples, who shared command of the imperial army with the duc de Bourbon, to leave the Milanese in order to defend southern Italy; and secondly, to pressurize Pope Clement VII into taking the French side in the war.[4] The first objective was not achieved, for the Viceroy remained in Lombardy. If Albany had moved faster, he might have conquered Naples,

---

[1] F. Mignet, *La rivalité de François Ier et de Charles-Quint* (1875), i. 522–30; A. Lebey, *Le connétable de Bourbon* (1904), p. 246.
[2] *L.P.*, iv. 789, 826, 837, 839–40.
[3] C. Oman, *A History of the Art of War in the XVIth Century* (New York, 1937), p. 191.
[4] *L.P.*, iv. 872.

43. Portrait by Sebastiano del Piombo of Cardinal Giulio de' Medici (1478–1534), who became Pope Clement VII.

which was in a rebellious state, but he moved at a snail's pace, allowing himself to become embroiled in Sienese politics.[5] His expedition, however, did help to win the pope over to the French side.

Clement VII had so far abstained from open commitment to either side in the conflict. In November 1524 he had sent Gian Matteo Giberti to both camps with peace proposals, but neither had shown interest. 'I hope soon to occupy Pavia', Francis had declared. 'I have taken all the necessary measures; my supplies are ready and my troops are paid. I am expecting 1,400,000 francs next month and I have summoned fresh troops. I have not crossed the Alps in person or invaded Italy with 30,000 good infantry and the support of a fleet with 6,000 or 7,000 troops on board to stop now. I want nothing less than the entire state of Milan and the kingdom of Naples.'[6] Since neither side was prepared to talk, Clement signed a treaty with Francis, on 5 January 1525, binding himself and the Florentines not to support the king's enemies and granting Albany free passage through the States of the Church. Francis, for his part, promised to cede Parma and Piacenza to the Holy See and to maintain Medici rule in Florence.[7]

Historians have exaggerated the military significance of Albany's expedition. It did not seriously reduce the numerical strength of Francis's army outside Pavia, for the duke's troops were replaced by an equal number of Swiss reinforcements. The real blunder was the siege of Pavia itself which immobilized the king's forces for nearly four months. Some of Francis's captains urged him to retire to Milan for the winter, but he refused, saying that no king of France had ever besieged a town without taking it. He also underestimated the enemy's powers of endurance, believing that Pavia's garrison would soon capitulate. Thus he condemned his troops to a wretched winter in the open.[8]

The battle of Pavia (24 February 1525)

By mid January 1525 the imperial commanders were unable to pay their troops and feared a mutiny. They needed a swift end to the war, yet the French seemed unwilling to come into the open and fight; they remained stubbornly within their camp. This stood on the east side of Pavia behind earthworks and gun batteries. The French also occupied Mirabello, a country house standing in the north-west corner of an extensive walled park, situated on the north side of the city. This was used for grazing by the French cavalry, and openings had been made in the wall dividing it from the camp. Within the park the terrain

[5] *Ibid.*, iv. 1010, 1045–6, 1054, 1085, 1102; *C.S.P., Span., 1525–26*, pp. 28–9.
[6] *L.P.*, iv. 826, 837; *St.P*, vi. 359.
[7] L. Pastor, *The History of the Popes*, tr. F. I. Antrobus and R. F. Kerr (London, 1891–1933), ix. 267–8.
[8] *L.P.*, iv. 872, 912, 1053.

was open and rolling, with clumps of trees and shrubs and many brooks and streams. Other French troops occupied various positions around Pavia, including the so-called 'five abbeys'.

On 22 January the main imperial army, based at Lodi, tried to draw the French into the open by simulating an offensive against Milan. When this tactic failed, the army altered course, captured the village of Sant'Angelo, and stationed itself within a stone's throw of Francis's camp. For the next three weeks the two armies faced each other across the Vernavola, a small tributary of the Ticino. On 4 February the imperialists tried to storm one of the park gates, but were thrown back.[9]

Meanwhile, on the Ligurian coast, an attempt by an imperial army and fleet to capture the port of Varazzo was repulsed by the French. Elsewhere, however, they suffered setbacks. The most serious was the sudden departure from Pavia of some 5,000 troops from the Grisons, who had been recalled to defend their homeland. Early in February, 1,000 Italian infantry, marching to assist the French outside Pavia, were routed near Alessandria. On 9 February, a small imperial force managed to reach Pavia with a large quantity of gunpowder for the garrison, and on the 17th Giovanni de' Medici, the famous *condottiere*, who had recently entered French service, was wounded in a skirmish at Pavia and retired to Piacenza taking his famous 'black bands' with him.[10]

By 23 February the imperial commanders had failed to lure the French into the open, so they tried a new ploy. About 10 pm they moved out of their camp, leaving only a token force behind, and marched northwards along the outside of the east wall of the park. At midnight they halted at a spot that has not been identified precisely (it may have been at the northern end of the east wall or near the middle of the north wall), and their sappers, using only picks and rams to avoid making a noise, demolished the wall in three places.[11] This task took longer than expected; it was dawn by the time the imperial troops began filing into the park in three columns, one through each gap in the wall. Their objectives are not altogether clear: were they trying to bring relief to Pavia itself or planning a surprise attack on the French camp? We cannot be sure, but some troops, led by the marquis del Vasto, charged across the park with a view to capturing the country house. As they did so, the French guns opened fire.

[9] *Ibid.*, iv. 1064, 1072, 1075.

[10] Du Bellay, i. 332–4, 348–52; *L.P.*, iv. 1064; *Correspondenz des Kaisers Karl V*, ed. K. Lanz (Leipzig, 1844–45), i. 684.

[11] Oman, p. 198; P. Pieri, *Il Rinascimento e la crisi militare italiana* (Turin, 1952), p. 558. For a bibliography on the battle, see p. 562n. The standard work remains R. Thom, *Die Schlacht bei Pavia* (Berlin, 1907). J. Giono, *Le désastre de Pavie* (1963) is often closer to fiction than history. See also F. L. Taylor, *The Art of War in Italy, 1494–1529* (Cambridge, 1921), pp. 49, 54, 65–6, 68, 79, 101, 126–8 and G. Treccani degli Alfieri, *Storia di Milano*, viii (Milan, 1957), 254–7; also J. Jacquart, *François Ier* (1981), pp. 163–5.

44. The battle of Pavia (24 February 1525). The labels attached to the participants stress the role played by members of the house of Savoy. Francis is alleged to have killed a standard-bearer by mistake and to have been captured by a Burgundian nobleman.

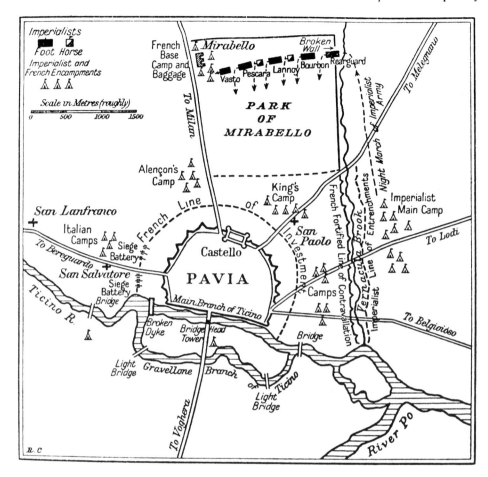

6. The battle of Pavia (Sir Charles Oman, *A History of the Art of War in the XVIth century*. New York, 1937, p. 197).

Meanwhile the bulk of the imperial army, after forming up, moved southward across the park, clambering over the many ditches. As they approached the French camp, Galiot de Genouillac's guns raked them with fire, opening up gaps in their ranks. According to du Bellay, 'you would have seen only arms and heads flying'.[12]

The imperial attack, it has been said, took the French by surprise. Yet, according to John Russell, Francis had been warned before midnight of the impending attack. He had accordingly drawn up his army within the park, so that the imperialists encountered the French marching towards them in good order.[13] This account tallies with another by Frundsberg, who commanded the imperial landsknechts. He tells us that the imperialists, on entering the park,

[12] Du Bellay, i. 353.   [13] *L.P.*, iv. 1175.

were spotted by French horsemen who promptly fell back. Francis then advanced with his cavalry and infantry. Meanwhile, his artillery 'shot terribly but did not do much damage'.[14] A third contemporary account states that Francis had been told during the night that the imperialists were about to retreat. He was about to pursue them, when, to his astonishment, he saw them enter the park.[15]

The sequel is difficult to unravel. Contemporary reports offer little more than glimpses of the battle, while the attempts of military historians to reconstruct it rely heavily on guesswork. The broad outlines are nevertheless clear. As the Emperor's troops were regrouping within the park, Francis charged at the head of his cavalry. But his action got in the way of his own guns, obliging them to hold fire. At first, the French men-at-arms carried all before them. The marquis of Sant'Angelo, who commanded the imperial horse, was killed and his men were thrown into confusion. 'Now is the time to call me duke of Milan!' shouted the king to Lescun.[16] But his joy was premature. Having broken through the enemy's cavalry, the French men-at-arms, came within range of a thousand Spanish arquebusiers, whom Pescara had concealed in copses near the park's northern perimeter. The shining suits of armour of the *gendarmerie*, their plumed helmets and distinctive horse trappings, offered easy targets. As the men-at-arms were picked off one by one by the Spanish marksmen, they crashed heavily to the ground. The wounded, who could not lift themselves up on account of the weight of their armour, were easily butchered by enemy foot-soldiers, using daggers. Francis, however, continued to fight on foot, striking out in all directions with his sword, after his horse had been killed beneath him. Meanwhile great blocks of infantry on both sides moved into action. The French landsknechts, under François de Lorraine and Richard de la Pole, fought heroically, but, being heavily outnumbered, were almost wiped out. The Swiss, by contrast, put up a poor showing. They arrived late on the field and, finding themselves caught between the imperial infantry and the garrison of Pavia, which chose this moment to come out into the park, they took to their heels. Many were drowned as they tried to swim across the Ticino whose bridges had been destroyed. By noon on 24 February, which happened to be Charles V's birthday, the battle was over. His troops had won and Francis was their prisoner.

Many accounts exist of the king's capture, some of them highly coloured.[17] He was apparently engulfed by a crowd of soldiers, who competed among themselves to snatch his gauntlets and other pieces of his armour; for each man wanted to claim the king's ransom. Eventually, the Viceroy of Naples arrived

[14] *Ibid.*, iv. 1123. The fact that the French guns were pointing the right way at the start of the action suggests that the imperial attack did not take them completely by surprise.
[15] *Ibid.*, iv. 1189.　[16] M. Sanudo, *Diarii* (Venice, 1879–1903), xxxviii. 53.
[17] Florange, ii. 231–3; du Bellay, i. 356–7; *L.P.*, iv. 1124, 1131.

45. Francis I charging at the head of his *gendarmerie*. One of a set of tapestries, designed by B. van Orley, showing various moments during the battle of Pavia. In the background Pescara's arquebusiers prepare to open fire.

on the scene and Francis gave up his sword to him. The answers to two questions remain uncertain: when was the king taken prisoner and by whom? A suggestion that he was captured early in the battle is disproved by contemporary evidence that he was still fighting after his main army had been crushed.[18] His captor, it seems, was not the viceroy but a steward of the duc de Bourbon, called La Mothe. When Lannoy later claimed the honour of capturing the king, La Mothe went to Spain to acquaint the Emperor with the truth and to challenge the Viceroy to a duel. Another nobleman of unknown identity, who claimed to have saved the king's life, reported that Francis had been captured half an hour before the Viceroy appeared on the scene.[19] According to Florange, the king refused to surrender to anyone other than the Viceroy.[20]

Francis was lucky to survive the battle, which was the biggest slaughter of French noblemen since Agincourt. The dead included many of his closest friends and advisers, notably Bonnivet, San Severino and Lapalisse. Lescun and René of Savoy soon died of their wounds. The comte de Saint-Pol, who had been badly injured, unexpectedly recovered; he was imprisoned in Pavia castle, but escaped on 15 May after bribing his guards. The bodies of François de Lorraine and Richard de la Pole were found among the landsknechts. Prisoners taken included Henri d'Albret, king of Navarre, Louis, comte de Nevers, Anne de Montmorency, and the seigneurs de Florange, Chabot de Brion, Lorges, La Rochepot, Annebault and Langey.[21] The only important French nobleman to escape death or capture was the king's brother-in-law Charles d'Alençon, but he died on 15 April, soon after returning to France, some said of shame, others of sorrow over the loss of his king.[22] About 4,000 prisoners whose status did not command worthwhile ransoms were released on parole; among them Blaise de Monluc, the future marshal and author of the *Commentaires*.[23]

Imperial losses were comparatively small. According to Frundsberg, about 10,000 Frenchmen were killed and only 400 or 500 imperialists. Ferdinand of Habsburg reported that 14,000 Frenchmen had been killed. Figures, quoted by Russell on 11 March, inspire more confidence: he estimated that not more than 400 out of 1,400 French men-at-arms escaped, that 1,200 men were killed in addition to a large number who drowned in the Ticino, and that 10,000 prisoners were taken. He put imperial losses at not more than 1,500.[24]

Why was Francis defeated at Pavia? Numerically, there was little to choose between the two sides. In mid January the imperial army comprised 22,000 infantry, 800 men-at-arms and 1,500 light cavalry, while the French had

[18] Pieri, p. 562n.
[19] *L.P.*, iv. 1127, 1425. Du Bellay (i. 356) states that Pompérant shielded the king until the Viceroy arrived.
[20] Florange, ii. 232–3. [21] *Ibid.*, ii. 235–41; du Bellay, i. 357–8; Champollion-Figeac, pp. 85–8.
[22] *J.B.P.*, p. 198. [23] P. Courteault, *Blaise de Monluc historien* (1908), p. 101.
[24] *L.P.*, iv. 1123, 1127, 1175.

between 24,000 and 26,000 infantry, 1,200 men-at-arms and more light cavalry. In the following five weeks, they lost some troops through desertion, but Francis estimated that, in the battle, he disposed of 26,000 infantry in addition to the men-at-arms and light cavalry.[25] Military historians differ by as much as 10,000 in their estimates; they agree, however, that the French were marginally superior in numbers.[26] They certainly had more cavalry and many more guns: fifty-three as against seventeen, but the imperialists had more arquebusiers. Strategically, French mobility was restricted by the need to encircle Pavia. This probably explains why the Swiss arrived late on the field, while other French troops never arrived at all. The imperialists had much more freedom of movement; they could also operate from inside Pavia and outside.

How far was Francis personally to blame for his defeat? Florange criticized him for silencing his own guns at the start of the battle, while modern historians have argued that he made other mistakes as well.[27] He has been criticized for relying too much on the protection of the park wall and for advancing towards the enemy instead of remaining within his strongly fortified camp from which it might have proved difficult to dislodge him. It is easy to be wise after the event. The imperialists risked being bottled up when they penetrated the walled enclosure, and it was a credible option for the king to attack them immediately before they could effectively regroup. His chief mistake was to lead his cavalry into a trap. Although Spanish arquebusiers had inflicted grievous losses on Frenchmen in recent campaigns, Francis still did not appreciate their potential. He may have shared the contempt for portable firearms felt by many noblemen at the time: the arquebus was viewed as an unchivalrous weapon.[28] Francis himself blamed his defeat on the Swiss, but even if they had shown their customary valour, they could not have won the battle, which was as good as lost by the time they came on the field.[29]

The king's captivity

Immediately after the battle, Francis was taken to the Certosa of Pavia, a monastery on the road to Milan, where he was given a meal, served by Lannoy

[25] F. Lot, *Recherches sur les effectifs des armées françaises des guerres d'Italie aux guerres de religion, 1494–1562* (1962), pp. 54–5.

[26] The French had 20,000 troops of all arms, according to Oman (p. 197); 31,000, according to Pieri (p. 558).

[27] Florange, ii. 227. 'The king, seeing them repulsed, caused the gendarmerie of the van to advance in front of the artillery, so that it could not fire any more, which was the main cause of the loss of the battle.'

[28] Monluc writes (*Commentaires*, i. 66): 'the battle was badly led in several places on our side, which caused those who did their duty to lose'. F. L. Taylor (p. 101) writes: 'The imperialists ... owed their victory on both occasions [i.e. Pavia and La Bicocca] chiefly to their bold use of the improved infantry firearms.' See also S. Champier, *Les gestes ensemble la vie du preulx Chevalier Bayard*, ed. D. Crouzet (1992), p. 41.

[29] *L.P.*, iv. 1175.

and Bourbon. Reports that he had been wounded were dispelled by a medical examination, which revealed only a bruise on one leg and a scratch on one hand.[30] Francis attributed his escape from serious injury to his finely crafted suit of armour. He now wrote two letters, one to his mother, the other to the Emperor. 'All that is left to me', he wrote to Louise, 'is my honour and my life which is safe.'[31] He appealed to her customary prudence and recommended his children. Writing to Charles V, he appealed to his magnanimity: 'You may be sure, should it please you mercifully to offer the ransom which the imprisonment of a king of France warrants, that, instead of acquiring a useless prisoner, you will turn a king into your slave for ever.'[32]

Charles V received news of his victory in Madrid on 10 March. Characteristically, he forbade noisy celebrations, arranged services of thanksgiving and retired to his private oratory. At the same time, he instructed Lannoy to take care of Francis's health and ensure that the king's mother received news of him frequently. The king was, in fact, well treated. From Pavia he was taken to the castle of Pizzighettone situated on the river Adda, near Cremona, where he remained for nearly three months in the custody of Fernando de Alarçon, a Spanish captain. Sharing his prison were Montmorency, Chabot de Brion, Jean de La Barre and the treasurer, Babou de la Bourdaisière. The king was allowed to write to his mother, and his companions were given safe-conducts enabling them to travel back and forth between Italy and the regent's court in Lyons. On 4 March Babou informed Louise that the king was sending Chabot to Spain and that Montmorency was leaving for France to collect money for his own ransom. On the same day, La Barre wrote, assuring Louise that her son was well and hoping for an early release; but he added: 'He will not eat eggs or anything but fish, which does not suit him, and he wishes to fast a few days each week.'[33] Montmorency assured the king's sister, Marguerite, on 22 March, that Francis was in good health and being well treated. He asked her to send frequent news of herself and of her mother, for this alone gave the king the utmost pleasure.[34]

News of Francis's defeat reached Louise at Saint-Just, near Lyons, on 1 March. Replying at once to her son, she thanked God for sparing his life and honour, and also for allowing him to fall into the hands of a man of honour. She urged him to accept whatever God had in store and promised to take care of his children and kingdom.[35] Marguerite, for her part, urged Francis to stop fasting and sent him the Epistles of St Paul to read. But he had time for other pursuits as well: he played billiards with Florange, the count of Egmont and even Bourbon.[36]

On 27 March a papal nuncio saw Francis in his prison. The king was on his

---

[30] *Ibid.*, iv. 1164; *C.S.P. Span., 1525–26*, p. 57.   [31] Champollion-Figeac, p. 129.
[32] *Ibid.*, pp. 130–1.
[33] *Ibid.*, p. 133.   [34] *Ibid.*, p. 141.   [35] *Ibid.*, p. 134.   [36] Florange, ii. 256.

way to church, surrounded by many Spaniards; he was wearing an ash-coloured garment trimmed with inexpensive fur, which he had not changed since his capture. The nuncio saw no sign of anxiety in the king's behaviour during Mass. Afterwards, he was allowed to speak to him in private. Francis eagerly asked for news of Albany and was astonished to learn that he had left Italy; he also asked about Giovanni de' Medici and was told that he would soon ride again. As the nuncio remarked that all was lost, Francis seemed deeply moved and replied that nothing else could be expected. At breakfast, Alarçon held his napkin and toasted his health. Francis was asked if he had any message for the pope. He replied that he had none and wished simply to be recommended to Fortune. He then left the room without looking at his visitor. 'It was a pitiable sight', wrote the nuncio, 'for he does not seem a prisoner of the emperor and his captains, so much as of his guards, who all claim a right in him. He behaves courteously and liberally and jokes with them, thinking it no less virtue to accommodate himself to fortune than to command a kingdom. Montmorency is his only comfort.'[37]

The defence of the kingdom

Francis's captivity lasted just over a year. During this time France was governed by his mother, Louise of Savoy, who resided throughout at the monastery of Saint-Just, near Lyons. She was assisted by her council and the team of ministers, headed by Chancellor Duprat. Though Louise was fully capable of shouldering her new responsibilities, the idea of a female regent did not command universal acceptance among Frenchmen. Some adhered to the tradition that the regent should be the king's nearest male kinsman. This was, Charles de Bourbon, duc de Vendôme and governor of Picardy, and it seems that, early in the captivity, a group of *parlementaires* and members of the *Bureau de la Ville* of Paris urged him, as he passed through the capital, to take over the government, but he refused, saying that he did not wish to divide the kingdom in an emergency. Far from supplanting Louise, he joined her council, sometimes acting as its spokesman.[38] In March 1525 the Parlement assured the regent of its devotion; it urged Frenchmen to regard their present misfortunes as a divine punishment for their own sins and not to blame their rulers.[39] Louise responded by enlisting the Parlement's co-operation in running the kingdom. The First President, Jean de Selve, was admitted to her council and

---

[37] *St.P.*, vi. 409–11; *L.P.*, iv. 1219.
[38] Du Bellay, ii. 2. Cf. Doucet, ii. 30 n.4. Vendôme had been called to Lyons by the regent, not by the Parlement, as stated in *J.B.P.*, p. 195. He was in Paris on 10 March. Even so, Vendôme was dissatisfied with his position at Lyons. See Potter, *War and Government*, pp. 71–2.
[39] Doucet, ii. 30–2.

46. The *échevins* of Amiens present a manuscript to Louise of Savoy. Miniature from B.N., ms. fr. 145 f. 1b). The king's mother sits in the place occupied in the rest of the manuscript by the Virgin Mary.

became the link between it and the Parlement. Later she sent him as ambassador to Spain.

Three important tasks awaited Louise: she had to defend the kingdom against foreign aggression, uphold her son's authority in his absence and secure his release on the best possible terms. The Emperor's victory did not end the war. For several months afterwards, France was threatened with invasion, particularly from across the Channel. Henry VIII had rejoiced over Francis's defeat. 'Now is the time', he declared, 'for the Emperor and myself to devise means of getting full satisfaction from France. Not an hour is to be lost.'[40] He began to assemble an army, looked for military help in the Netherlands and asked his subjects for an 'Amicable Grant'. He also sent an embassy to Spain in the hope of winning Charles V's approval for a joint attack on France. His proposals envisaged nothing less than the total dismemberment of the French kingdom. It would be folly, he thought, to restore Francis even to a diminished kingdom; his line and succession ought to be extinguished completely. Henry wanted the French crown for himself. At the very least he hoped to gain Normandy or Picardy in addition to Boulogne and other towns.[41] But Charles had not forgiven Henry for his failure to invade France, when he had wanted him to do so. He was also aware of secret negotiations between Wolsey and Louise on the eve of the battle of Pavia, and remembered the cardinal's rough treatment of his ambassador in England.[42] Furthermore, Charles had more pressing problems to deal with: an unpaid army threatening mutiny in Italy, the Peasants' War in Germany and the Turkish threat to eastern Europe. So he cold-shouldered Henry's plan, leaving him to invade France alone, if he so wished.

Had the allies been able to agree, France would have been at their mercy, for she had been largely denuded of troops, armaments and supplies in the interest of Francis's Italian campaign. A shortage of cash had obliged the commanders of garrison towns in the north to disband many troops. These were now living off the countryside, which had little enough to offer after a series of bad harvests. They were terrorizing villages near Paris and even penetrating its suburbs. In the south, the situation was less critical, as remnants of the king's army trickled back over the Alps. In April, Albany's expeditionary force returned almost intact from central Italy.[43] By May Louise disposed of 4,000 *lances* and a sizeable infantry. To pay for them she anticipated the *taille*, demanded a *crue* of 1,200,000 *livres* and cut expenditure on the royal house-

[40] C.S.P., Span. 1525–26, p. 82. 'My friend', he said to the messenger who brought him the news of Francis's defeat, 'you are like St Gabriel who announced the coming of Christ.' J. J. Scarisbrick, *Henry VIII* (London, 1968), p. 136.
[41] St.P., vi. 412–36 (L.P., iv. 1212).
[42] L.P., iv. 1093. G. Jacqueton, *La politique extérieure de Louise de Savoie* (1892), pp. 64–83.
[43] Doucet, ii. 73–7. For the situation in Picardy, see Potter, *War and Government*, p. 203.

47. Etienne Le Blanc begs to be 'cured' (i.e. asks to be given an office) by Louise of Savoy. Miniature from B.N., ms. 5715 f.Av°. Louise is shown wearing large wings and holding a rudder signifying 'governance'.

hold.[44] Even so, she could not afford to pay all the troops returning from Italy, so many drifted northwards to join the countless vagabonds swarming around the capital.

In providing for the kingdom's defence, Louise paid particular attention to Burgundy, for she distrusted its inhabitants, many of whom regarded Charles V as their lawful ruler. To ward off the threat of invasion from Franche-Comté, she posted spies to watch the enemy beyond the Saône and sent the comte de Guise to inspect the province's fortifications and ensure that they were sufficiently provided with artillery, gunpowder and money. At the same time, she avoided upsetting local feelings. Thus she refrained from imposing a garrison on Dijon out of respect for the right of self-defence claimed by the citizens.[45] In July she persuaded her cousin Margaret of Austria, governor of the Netherlands, to renew a truce which neutralized the border between Franche-Comté and Dijon.[46]

In the north, Louise depended almost entirely on the Parlement for preparations against a possible English invasion. Being unaccustomed to such a role, the court was at first reluctant to act alone: it formed a special assembly, called *Chambre de la Salle Verte*, comprising various Parisian bodies, but its powers were ill-defined and its membership was quarrelsome. So the assembly was soon dissolved, leaving the Parlement to act alone.[47] The disbanded and unpaid troops threatening the capital were a problem requiring urgent attention. The situation called for firm military leadership, but the comte de Saint-Pol, governor of Paris and the Ile-de-France, had been taken prisoner at Pavia. His deputy was Pierre Filhol, archbishop of Aix, but Jean Morin, the *prévôt des marchands* argued that the emergency required the services of a soldier, not a churchman. The regent sent the comte de Braisne to deal with the vagabond soldiery. But this led to rivalry between Filhol and Braisne which was only resolved in July, when Saint-Pol reappeared in the capital after escaping from prison.[48] Another problem was that of supplying the garrison towns of northern France. Theoretically, this was the responsibility of the victualler, Favier, but he was in Lyons and seemed only interested in his own private affairs. So the Parlement had to intervene: it obtained funds directly from the *receveur-général* Ruzé, purchased grain and sent it to Picardy, and persuaded the *Bureau de la Ville* to send arms and gunpowder from its arsenal to the province.[49]

---

[44] *Ibid.*, ii. 24–5.
[45] H. Hauser, 'Le traité de Madrid et la cession de la Bourgogne à Charles-Quint', *Revue bourguignonne*, xxii (1912).
[46] *C.A.F.*, i. No. 2183.
[47] Doucet, ii. 36–45; M. Félibien, *Histoire de la ville de Paris* (1725), ii. 953.
[48] *Ibid.*, ii. 946, 961, 964, 967–70.   [49] Doucet, ii. 93; Potter, *War and Government*, p. 190–1.

The regent versus the Parlement of Paris

On 10 April 1525 the Parlement submitted remonstrances to the regent. Normally, remonstrances were concerned with a particular legislative proposal, but this time they criticized a whole range of policies pursued since the start of the reign. They complained, in particular, of leniency shown to heretics, of the Gallican liberties being undermined, of abuse of fiscal expedients and of interference with the normal processes of justice.[50] Though not mentioned by name, Francis was clearly implicated, for who else had appointed unworthy prelates and shielded heretics? Louise accepted the remonstrances with good grace, calling them 'to the honour of God, exaltation of the faith, and very useful and necessary for the king and commonwealth'. But she never mentioned them again, and ruled as if they had never existed.[51] The Parlement took advantage of the king's captivity to challenge the regent over the application of the Concordat of Bologna. In February 1525 she appointed Chancellor Duprat as archbishop of Sens and abbot of Saint-Benoît-sur-Loire. Louise doubtless believed that she was applying the Concordat, but under this agreement the chapter of Sens retained the right to elect the archbishop, while, at Saint-Benoît, no abbot could be appointed who was not a Benedictine. Duprat, as a secular priest, did not qualify.[52] The two chapters were consequently within their rights in electing candidates of their own.[53]

On 7 April, Louise vetoed the election at Sens, whereupon the chapter appealed to the Parlement. She then evoked the suit to the *Grand Conseil*. Since Duprat, as Chancellor, was the president of this court, Louise's action effectively made him the judge of a suit to which he was a party. This caused outrage in the Parlement, which proceeded to examine the appeal. Jean Bochart, counsel for the chapter, used the opportunity to denounce the Concordat as contrary to divine law. Louise summoned him to her presence, but he excused himself and sought the Parlement's protection. Meanwhile, the court ordered the release of the chapter's temporalities which the regent had seized.[54]

At Saint-Benoît, events took a more dramatic turn still. The election led to another appeal to the Parlement which the regent evoked on 29 March. Duprat, meanwhile, sent agents to occupy the abbey. Among them were Jacques Groslot and P. Berruyer. The monks asked the Parlement to expel

---

[50] A.N., X[1a] 1527, f. 321; E. Maugis, *Histoire du Parlement de Paris* (1913–16), i. 559–66; Doucet, ii. 103–10; C. W. Stocker, 'The Politics of the Parlement of Paris in 1525' in *French Historical Studies*, viii (1973), 191–212.

[51] A.N., X[1a] 1528, f. 411.   [52] Doucet, ii. 120.

[53] The vacancies were created by the death of Etienne Poncher (23 Feb. 1525). *J.B.P.*, pp. 190–1). The rival candidates were Jean de Salazar (Sens) and François Poncher, Etienne's nephew and successor as bishop of Paris (Saint-Benoît). For a fuller discussion of this affair see my 'Francis I and the *Lit de Justice*: a "Legend" defended', in *French History* vii (1993).

[54] Doucet, ii. 119–25.

48. Terra-cotta bust of Antoine Duprat (1464–1535) cardinal-archbishop of Sens and Chancellor of France, who was Louise of Savoy's chief minister during the captivity of Francis I.

Duprat's men, so that their election might proceed freely. While ordering the abbey's evacuation, the Parlement refused to obey the regent's letters of evocation and imprisoned the usher of the *Grand Conseil*, who had delivered them. When its own usher turned up at Saint-Benoît to enforce the Parlement's *arrêt*, he was refused admission. Another *parlementaire*, Nicole Hennequin, was equally unsuccessful. He was told that, if the monks continued to resist, they would be banished from the kingdom and their revenues seized to help pay the king's ransom. On 6 May the Parlement ordered the arrest of Groslot and Berruyer and summonsed the men occupying Saint-Benoît. A third *parlementaire*, François Disque, was sent there, but was powerless in face of the occupants who by now had been reinforced by fifty men-at-arms.[55]

On 11 May Louise wrote to the Parlement: she reaffirmed her intention to uphold the Concordat, accused the court of undermining the king's authority and of playing into the hands of his foreign enemies. She denied its right to judge beneficial disputes and announced her intention to examine the affairs of Sens and Saint-Benoît herself with the advice of competent persons. Finally, she summoned Hennequin to explain his actions.[56] The Parlement, in reply, put forward a moderate proposal: namely, that any discussion of the Concordat's future should be deferred till the king's return provided capitular elections were restored at once. At the same time, it complained of the Chancellor, who was allegedly seeking to 'abolish and confound, remove and pervert all the ordinary justices and jurisdictions of this kingdom'.[57] On 3 June, the *Grand Conseil*, cancelled all the Parlement's decrees issued since 11 April; it also forbade anyone who had been prosecuted by the court to appear before it and ordered an enquiry into the Saint-Benoît affair. Meanwhile, it issued summonses against Hennequin and the *procureur-général*, François Roger.

Having tried moderation and failed, the Parlement adopted a more militant posture: it forbade Hennequin and Roger to obey the *Grand Conseil*'s summons and received appeals from both men. It also ordered its decrees regarding Saint-Benoît to be given effect. On 30 June, it affirmed its resolve to administer justice to everyone in respect of both secular and ecclesiastical cases. The Parlement ordered Groslot, Berruyer and the occupiers of Saint-Benoît to be brought to the Conciergerie and summonsed two judges of the *Grand Conseil* along with some monks of Saint-Benoît who had appealed to that court. The regent's response was to order the Parlement and *Grand Conseil* to hand over the Sens and Saint-Benoît affairs to the special commission. She also sent several companies of men-at-arms to Paris, presumably to intimidate the Parlement.[58]

And there was worse to come. The Parlement had never forgiven Duprat for having negotiated the Concordat. On 27 July he was summoned to Paris by the court to discuss 'certain matters regarding the good of the king and his children, the regent's authority and the administration of justice'.[59] He was given the deadline of 12 November to appear; if he broke it, he was to be summonsed personally. Meanwhile five *parlementaires* were appointed to examine his alleged misdemeanours while the *gens du roi* were instructed to draw up his indictment. Sens and Saint-Benoît were almost forgotten as the Parlement

---

[55] *Ibid.*, ii. 125–8; C.A.F., i. 401 (No. 2135). [56] A.N., X[1a] 1528, f. 453.
[57] A.N., X[1a] 1528, ff. 478a–482b.
[58] Doucet, ii. 136–8.
[59] A.N., X[1a] 1528, f. 654b. The text has been crossed out in the Parlement's register.

fastened on the regent's interference with the administration of justice and esp-cially on the role of Duprat.

On 5 September the Parlement again declared the decrees of the *Grand Conseil* to be null and void. Three *parlementaires* (La Barde, Tavel and Ruzé) were instructed to go to Lyons and show Louise the error of her ways. At the same time, the Parlement wrote to Vendôme and other members of the regent's council, reputed to be hostile to Duprat, in the hope of enlisting their support. It also decided to call a meeting of peers to consider matters 'for the relief of the subjects of the said kingdom'.[60] Its real purpose was to judge Duprat. However, before taking this step, the Parlement decided to await the council-ors' reply. On 12 November it wrote to Louise, urging her to respect the law and tradition. She was reminded that the kingdom's prosperity was linked to the Parlement's independence. This was now being threatened by certain indi-viduals acting under cover of the *Grand Conseil*. She was urged to put an end to their activities.

But the Parlement's hopes were soon dashed. Although some members of the regent's council disliked Duprat's arrogance, they chose to ignore the court's letter. Meanwhile, Louise and her Chancellor grew more confident after the treaty of the More had removed the threat of invasion from the kingdom (see below p. 244). The three *parlementaires* who had come to see Louise were kept waiting for six weeks before she would grant them an audience. She then trounced them. The Parlement, she said, had sown division in the kingdom, as France's neighbours had been quick to notice. It had even thought of calling the Estates General, which would have undermined her authority. While the Parlement accused others of judicial abuses, it was itself devoid of integrity; it would need to reform itself if it was ever to regain its reputation for fairness.[61] Louise invited the spokesmen to share in a debate with representatives of the *Grand Conseil* in front of her own council. But they declined, invoking their instructions as an excuse. When asked by the regent why Duprat had been called to Paris, they explained that it was only to discuss *évocations*. After rebutting her accusations, the representatives denied that the Parlement had ever thought of calling the Estates General. As for the current disputes, Louise had only herself to blame, for she had continued to use *évocations* after promising to renounce them. Finally, they denied that the Condordat was under attack, saying that the Parlement had not yet declared for or against it; it simply claimed the right to hear beneficial lawsuits.

The Chancellor decided to send La Barde to Paris to get the necessary instruc-tions, while detaining his two colleagues in Lyons. On 14 November La Barde informed the Parlement that the government was about to arrest some of its members. By now, the court had lost hope of finding support among the

[60] A.N., X[1a] 1528, f. 742. [61] Doucet, ii. 148–50.

regent's councillors. It therefore agreed to suspend its action regarding Sens and Saint-Benoît, if the *Grand Conseil* would do the same. It excused itself for abstaining from the debate before the regent's council on the ground that this would involve lengthy preliminary research in the archives. As for Duprat, the Parlement said that it had only wanted a 'brotherly and good discussion' with him in order to guarantee unified justice and 'a good union and concord'. Louise accepted these terms, knowing that her son would soon call the Parlement to order.[62]

The fight against heresy

Another area of friction between crown and Parlement had been the protection given by Francis to scholars and preachers whose evangelical opinions had been condemned as heretical by the Faculty of Theology of the University of Paris. His captivity and the regent's absence in Lyons left the Parlement and Faculty free to regain ground seemingly lost to orthodoxy. Their hand was strengthened by a wave of hysteria sweeping the country. Rumours of imminent catastrophe were reaching the Parlement almost daily. On 17 June it was reported that 80,000 Lutherans were marching on Rome after capturing Trent; on the 21st that Hungary, Poland and Bohemia had broken with Rome and on the 24th that the duke of Lorraine had burnt 16,000 Lutherans after seeing a fiery cross in the sky.[63] The threat of heresy was also perceived as home-based. A masquerade, held in the cloister of Notre-Dame, included a woman on horseback drawn by devils with placards on their chests and backs bearing Luther's name.[64] This reflected the belief, widely held in Paris, that Lutheranism flourished at the French court, for the woman was almost certainly meant to portray Marguerite, the king's evangelically minded sister.

The Parlement and the Faculty of Theology had reason to expect more support for their religious policy from Louise than they had previously got from her son, for she was 'the most consistently traditional member of the royal family, the most uneasy about the spread of Lutheranism in France'.[65] On 20 March 1525 the bishop of Paris was instructed by the Parlement to set up a commission, comprising two *parlementaires* and two theologians, to try cases of heresy. Though limited at first to his diocese, the competence of the new tribunal was soon extended to all other dioceses within the Parlement's area of jurisdiction. Among them was Meaux where recently there had been serious public disturbances. The setting up of the commission effectively deprived bishops of their traditional right of judging heresy cases. What is

[62] A.N., X¹ᵃ 1529, ff. 16b–18b, 99.
[63] J. K. Farge, *Orthodoxy and Reform in Early Reformation France* (Leiden, 1985), p. 181.
[64] A.N., X¹ᵃ 1530, ff. 33b–34a.   [65] Farge, p. 132.

more, its members were expected to prosecute bishops suspected of holding heretical views. Such authority, of course, could only come from the pope. So Louise asked Clement VII for a rescript which he duly conceded on 17 May. This delegated apostolic powers to the four commissioners, who consequently became known as *juges délégués*. They were authorized to judge heresy cases independently of the church courts and to act, if necessary, against bishops. An appeals procedure was established from them to the Parlement, which thus acquired an overriding control of heresy jurisdiction.[66]

The creation of the *juges délégués* enabled the Parlement to give more effective support to the Faculty of Theology in its fight against the *Cercle de Meaux*. On 23 June the Faculty ordered Mazurier to yield his pulpit to Jean Corion, head of the local Franciscan monastery. Mazurier complied; but such was the popular unrest provoked by Corion's sermons that Bishop Briçonnet had to intervene. Taking to the pulpit himself, he denounced Corion and cited him before the Parlement. Bochart, the counsel for the Franciscans, accused the bishop of inciting popular violence by his patronage of heretics. Indirectly, he implicated the king who had repeatedly protected Lefèvre d'Etaples, whom Bochart viewed as the most dangerous heretic among the bishop's acolytes. He urged the Parlement to 'draw its sword and show its fury against the malice of such men'. Poyet, who defended Briçonnet, blamed both Lutherans and Franciscans for the troubles at Meaux. The useless and hypocritical arguments of the Franciscans, he claimed, had created spiritual inertia among the people and provoked an evangelical backlash, which, if pushed to extremes, could lead to heresy. Briçonnet, he argued, had tried to steer a middle course and had shown his orthodoxy by endorsing the cult of the Virgin and saints. Poyet asked the Parlement to proceed against Corion and to forbid the Franciscans to preach.

The *procureur général* Lizet found Briçonnet suspect of heresy because of the errors preached by his protégés. He accused him of exceeding his episcopal authority by suing Corion. He also condemned on principle all translations of Scripture, proposed that all books in the vernacular should be kept provisionally under lock and key and demanded that the action against Lefèvre, which the king had suspended, be resumed. The Faculty, he declared, should examine his writings and pass a sentence that would end the scandals they had caused.[67]

The troubles at Meaux and pressure from the Faculty of Theology stiffened the Parlement's resolve to defend orthodoxy. On 27 August owners of religious books in French were ordered to hand them over within a week. The court was particularly intent on seizing copies of Lefèvre's *Epître et évangiles des cinquante et deux dimanches*, which had just been published anonymously. This

[66] *Ibid.*, p. 258; Doucet, ii. 160–4, 168–9; *Ordonnances*, iv. No. 387.
[67] Farge, pp. 124, 237–40; Doucet, ii. 162, 178–86; M. Veissière, *L'évêque Guillaume Briçonnet* (Provins, 1986), pp. 329–66.

was condemned by the Faculty of Theology on 6 November, and Briçonnet, who was suspected of being the author, was ordered to appear before the Parlement. On 5 January 1526 the Parlement defined heresy so broadly as to include the slightest deviation from orthodoxy. Censorship was now carried to greater lengths than ever before, printers and booksellers being forbidden to publish or even to stock translations into French of religious works. Bishops throughout the kingdom were instructed to preach against heresy and to prosecute suspects.[68]

Books were not the only victims of the persecution. In October 1525 eight artisans of Meaux were sent to Paris on a heresy charge, but the Parlement was chiefly interested in silencing the leaders of the *Cercle de Meaux*. The *juges-délégués* were ordered to prosecute Lefèvre, Caroli, Mazurier, Roussel and Mangin. This move prompted Francis to make one of his rare interventions from his Spanish prison in the domestic affairs of the kingdom. On 12 November he ordered the Parlement to suspend all proceedings against Lefèvre, Caroli and Roussel. They were being unfairly persecuted by the Faculty of Theology, he said, and Lefèvre had already been cleared of heresy; any new complaints about the three men should be referred to his mother.[69] The king's letter greatly irritated the Parlement. It particularly resented his insinuation that the Parlement was the Faculty's poodle. In its reply, the court said the king was being unfair: why, it asked, was he protecting only three of the accused and the most guilty at that? When Louise endorsed her son's demand, it asked her why she was impeding the work of the *juges-délégués* after she had set them up herself? 'The character of the times in which we live', the court said, 'makes it imperative that all offences and scandals committed directly against God and His Catholic church should be promptly ... punished and extirpated.'[70]

On 29 November, the *juges-délégués* were instructed by the Parlement to press on with their work regardless of royal interference. Consequently, the *Cercle de Meaux* continued to be harassed, its leaders being forced to recant or flee abroad. Lefèvre and Roussel were given sanctuary by Capito in Strassburg, where they were soon joined by Michel d'Arande. They found there the kind of revitalized Christian community they had been trying to establish in Meaux. As Roussel reported, the people were receiving from diligent preachers 'wholesome food, unmixed with pharisaic chaff and leaven'. Teachers were drawing on their knowledge of the original biblical languages, the poor were

---

[68] *Ibid.*, ii. 188–90; *J.B.P.*, 232–3; Farge, p. 184; F. M. Higman, *Censorship and the Sorbonne* (Geneva, 1979), pp. 26–7, 80–1.
[69] Herminjard, i. 401–3; Veissière, *Guillaume Briçonnet*, pp. 351–2. The king had probably been informed of the situation in France by his sister during her visit to Spain. See below, p. 245.
[70] Doucet, ii. 192–3.

being cared for; images were being removed from the churches and Christ alone was being worshipped.[71]

Caroli did not go to Strassburg. In September 1525 he asked the Faculty of Theology to readmit him as a member, but it refused on the ground that he was still being tried by the Parlement and *juges-délégués*. However, Marguerite d'Angoulême protected him from imprisonment. Using her patronage she gave him the parish of Alençon.[72] Mazurier was thrown into the Conciergerie as a relapsed heretic. To obtain his release he had to go through a second recantation: he promised always to obey the Faculty, asked for Béda's pardon, agreed to pay the costs of his own prosecution and to allow Corion to preach in his parish at Meaux.[73] As for Briçonnet, he earned the contempt of reformers, by becoming strictly orthodox. Pierre Toussain denounced him as a 'false prophet' who was 'more anxious to please men than God'.[74]

Another victim of persecution was Louis de Berquin, who was arrested for the second time in January 1526, his books being seized and condemned by the Faculty of Theology. Having previously recanted, he now faced the possibility of being sentenced to death as a relapsed heretic. The *juges-délégués* found him guilty and sent him to the Parlement for sentencing, but the court held back when it heard that the king was on his way home.[75]

The Spanish captivity

Francis had hoped that the Emperor would release him for a cash ransom, but Charles V's terms were far more sweeping. They were listed in a set of instructions sent to the imperial representatives in Italy, Bourbon, Lannoy and Beaurain.[76] Francis was to be reminded of claims to the crown of France, Dauphiné and Languedoc, which the Emperor could legitimately make, but was prepared to set aside along with the demand for a ransom. However, Charles wanted the duchy of Burgundy and all the territories, which had belonged to Charles the Bold at the time of his death in 1477; also Thérouanne, Hesdin and all that Francis was holding in Artois, along with Tournai and sovereignty over Flanders. He also wanted Francis to give back to Henry VIII all that belonged to him by right and to pay Charles's debts to the English monarch. Provence was to be separated from France and turned into a kingdom for the duc de

---

[71] Herminjard, i. 404–8. Roussel used the pseudonym Jean Tolninus. He was still at Meaux on 25 September 1525 and Michel d'Arande at Lyons on 8 October. Lefèvre reached Strassburg in October. *Ibid.*, i. 408 n.1; Veissière, *Guillaume Briçonnet*, pp. 369–71.

[72] J. K. Farge, *Biographical Register of Paris Doctors of Theology, 1500–1536* (Toronto, 1980), p. 68.

[73] *Ibid.*, p. 320.

[74] Herminjard, i. 446; P. E. Hughes, *Lefèvre: Pioneer of Ecclesiastical Revival in France* (Grand Rapids, MI, 1984), pp. 173–4.

[75] Doucet, ii. 199–202; *J.B.P.*, p. 234. Cf. Berquin's letter to Erasmus (17 April 1526) in Herminjard, i. 422–7.

[76] Champollion-Figeac, pp. 149–59, 170–3.

Bourbon, who would soon become the Emperor's brother-in-law. The duke's accomplices were to be pardoned. Francis was to surrender his claims to Milan, Genoa and Asti. Finally, to complete his humiliation, he was to accompany Charles to Italy for his imperial coronation and lend him troops, if these proved necessary, at his own expense. The settlement would be sealed by a marriage between the Dauphin and the Emperor's niece, Mary of Portugal; also by a crusade.

These conditions were presented to Francis at Pizzighettone by Beaurain in the presence of Lannoy and Bourbon. Replying point by point, the king emphatically refused to give up Burgundy, showed willingness to cede Hesdin, refused to give up Arras and thought the cession of Tournai might prove difficult. He was prepared to assist Charles with troops provided they were paid on a monthly basis. He envisaged no difficulty in suspending the lawsuit between his mother and Bourbon. The duke could have his property back as well as his offices, but Francis added 'let him never be seen'. He was ready to give up his Italian claims. As for the Dauphin's marriage, he liked the idea, but thought that a more significant token of reconciliation would be his own marriage to Charles's sister, Eleanor, the king of Portugal's widow. Lastly, he added proposals of his own. Without prejudice to his own right to Burgundy, he suggested its ownership might be submitted to arbitrators. If they decided against him, then the duchy might be given to Francis's future son by Eleanor. Finally, he offered the Emperor a ransom worthy of a king of France. But Francis refused to negotiate as long as he remained a prisoner: he, therefore, handed over full responsibility for making peace to his mother.[77] However, when Beaurain conveyed the Emperor's terms to Louise, she rejected them outright, saying that only the king in his own kingdom could persuade his subjects to accept them. On 28 April she appointed François de Tournon, archbishop of Embrun, as her ambassador in Spain. He was forbidden to cede any part of France to the Emperor, but allowed to compromise regarding other territories.[78]

After Francis had been in Pizzighettone for some weeks, his captors decided to transfer him to the greater security of the *Castel Nuovo* in Naples. He was alarmed by the decision, for Naples was much further from his kingdom than Pizzighettone; it was also notoriously unhealthy. On the other hand, a sea journey offered him the prospect of being rescued by the French Mediterranean fleet, a possibility he secretly broached to his mother in a letter, dated 12 May.[79] But the king soon changed his mind. He saw that his best chance of freedom lay in a tête-à-tête with the Emperor, which would by-pass tiresome negotiations by third parties. Two princes, sharing the same knightly code, would, he believed, soon settle their differences honourably. So he begged

[77] *Ibid.*, pp. 166–9.   [78] *Ibid.*, pp. 174–7.   [79] *Ibid.*, pp. 180–1.

49. Letter written by Francis I to his mother from his prison at Pizzighettone on 12 May 1525. He suggests that he might be rescued at sea whilst in transit to Naples.

Lannoy, who had become a friend, to take him to Spain. The Viceroy agreed, provided six French galleys were placed at his disposal. This was duly arranged by Montmorency with the regent and her council.[80] The galleys were presumably intended as hostages for the good behaviour of the French fleet based

[80] Decrue, i. 55.

in Marseilles. On 31 May Francis was taken to Genoa harbour where fifteen Spanish galleys lay at anchor. He embarked on the *Capitana of Castile*, which had been lavishly decorated in his honour. The fleet sailed first to Portofino, where it was joined on 8 June by the French galleys, now manned by Spanish crews, and thence to Spain. As the flotilla passed close to the Iles d'Hyères, local people came out in small boats to greet their king and offer him gifts. On 15 June it was sighted off Collioure; two days later, it reached Palamos.[81]

The decision to take Francis to Spain had been taken by the Viceroy alone. Bourbon was not told about it until the eve of the king's departure and was not well pleased; on 10 June he wrote protesting to the Emperor.[82] Not even Charles V knew of Lannoy's decision until Francis had landed in Spain.[83] Yet, he accepted the move, urged the Viceroy to show his prisoner every hospitality, and, in a letter welcoming Francis to Spain, expressed the hope that his coming would lead to a general peace.[84]

The king was given a truly royal welcome in Barcelona on 19 June. After attending Mass in the cathedral amidst a pomp normally reserved for Spanish monarchs, he touched a large number of sick people, who had come to benefit from the almost unique powers of healing traditionally enjoyed by the French monarch.[85]

A few days later, he was taken by sea to the castle of Tarragona, where he was nearly killed by a stray bullet from an arquebus, as he looked out of a window at some mutinous troops rampaging in the streets below.[86] Towards the end of June he was moved to Valencia, but was so hard-pressed by more sightseers and sick people seeking his healing touch, that he was taken to a country house, built in the Moorish style at Benisanó, a few miles away.[87] Montmorency, meanwhile travelled to Toledo with requests from Francis: he asked the Emperor first for a safe-conduct to be given to his sister, Marguerite, so that she might come to Spain to negotiate a peace; secondly, for himself to be allowed to come nearer the conference table in order to be more easily consulted; and thirdly, for a truce while the talks were in progress. All three

---

[81] *C.S.P., Span. 1525–26*, pp. 179–80; *L.P.*, iv. 1419; *C.S.P., Ven.*, iii. Nos. 1041, 1048.

[82] Champollion-Figeac, pp. 216–18; *L.P.*, iv. 1405.

[83] This is made clear by a letter written on 15 June by Charles to Lannoy. He had not yet received the Viceroy's message sent from Villefranche on 11 June, announcing the change of plan. L. E. Halkin and G. Dansaert, *Charles de Lannoy* (Brussels, 1934), pp. 284–7; *L.P.*, iv. 1407.

[84] *L.P.*, iv. 1442; Champollion-Figeac, p. 233.

[85] *Ibid.*, pp. 253–4; M. Bloch, *Les rois thaumaturges* (1961), p. 313; C. Terrasse, *François Ier* (1945–70), i. 331.

[86] *C.S.P., Ven.*, iii. No. 1057.

[87] Champollion-Figeac, p. 236. I am indebted to Dr J. Casey of the University of East Anglia for the identification of 'Venyssolo' (the name given in some contemporary letters) with Benisanó. Pandolfo, writing to Isabella d'Este from Toledo on 26 June reported that Francis would probably be held at the castle of Jativá, near Valencia. See R. Tamalio, *Ferrante Gonzaga alla corte spagnola di Carlo V* (Mantua, 1991), p. 250.

requests were conceded by Charles, whereupon Montmorency travelled to France to report to the regent and obtain the powers needed to conclude a truce.[88]

When the French ambassadors, Tournon and de Selve, met the Emperor in Toledo on 17 July he told them plainly that he would not release Francis for a ransom. As both sides began to examine the obstacles standing in the way of a peace settlement, it became clear that the main one was Burgundy. While de Selve argued that the duchy had escheated to the French crown on the death of Charles the Bold, Gattinara claimed that it had been annexed unlawfully by Louis XI. There would be no lasting peace, he said, as long as the duchy remained in French hands.[89] Soon afterwards, Tournon and de Selve were joined by Philippe Chabot whom the regent had sent to arrange a truce. This was signed on 11 August, but it was merely an 'abstinence of war' designed to facilitate the movements of diplomats and messengers; normal trading relations between France and Spain were not restored.[90]

Meanwhile, at the end of July, Francis was taken to Madrid. His journey, which lasted three weeks, was like a royal progress. At Guadalajara, he was lavishly entertained by the duke of Infantando, one of the principal Spanish grandees. Banquets, bullfights and other entertainments were laid on for him, and among the gifts he received was a horse with trappings worth more than 5,000 ducats. Francis also visited the famous university of Alcalá de Henares, founded less than twenty years before, by Cardinal Jiménez de Cisneros. Wherever he went he made an excellent impression. 'He bears his prison admirably', wrote a Venetian, 'and in all places through which he passes is so well greeted by reason of the extreme affability and courtesy evinced by him towards everybody, that he is well nigh adored in this country.'[91] Francis arrived in Madrid on 11 August and was given a room in the Alcázar, which occupied the site of the present royal palace.[92] Five days afterwards, he made a secret declaration, in the presence of the French ambassadors, to the effect that he would never surrender Burgundy of his own free will, and that, if forced to do so, his action would be null and void. When the talks in Toledo were resumed on 24 August, Alarçon announced that Francis was willing to give up Burgundy forthwith, pending arbitration on its lawful ownership. But Tournon corrected him: the king, he explained, had offered to send Burgundian representatives to the French court of peers (i.e. the Parlement of Paris)

[88] Le Glay, ii. 610–11.   [89] Champollion-Figeac, pp. 255–62.

[90] *Ibid.*, pp. 244–9, 294; *L.P.*, iv. 1557–8.

[91] *C.S.P., Ven.*, iii. No. 1093; Tamalio, p. 267.

[92] A theory that Francis stayed for a time in the tower of Los Lujanes has been disproved by A. Lopez de Meneses in *Anales del Instituto des Estudios madrileños*, vii (1971), 121–47. The Alcázar was destroyed by fire in 1734. Among the last persons to see the room traditionally occupied by Francis was the duc de Saint-Simon.

which was to judge the question. Such an arrangement was, of course, wholly unacceptable to the imperial negotiators.[93]

Louise of Savoy, meanwhile, sought to drive a wedge between Charles V and his ally, Henry VIII. The English government was afraid that Charles would soon make a separate peace with France. In an effort to counter this threat, it invited the regent to resume the secret negotiations which the battle of Pavia had interrupted.[94] The result was the treaty of the More (30 August 1525) which restored peace between England and France. By removing the threat of an English invasion, the treaty greatly strengthened the regent's authority within France as well as her negotiating position *vis-à-vis* the Emperor. Henry promised to use his influence to secure her son's release on favourable trms, and Louise promised in Francis's name to pay Henry 2 million gold *écus* in annual instalments of 100,000 *écus*. Steps were also taken to settle maritime disputes between the two countries. The Scots, who were conditionally admitted to the peace, were to stop armed incursions across England's northern border; Albany was barred from Scotland during James V's minority. Finally, France promised to compensate Louis XII's widow, Mary, now duchess of Suffolk, for losses incurred during the war.[95]

Because Francis was for the time being unable to ratify the treaty, the English government demanded special guarantees: namely, registration by the parlements and provincial estates of France, and financial securities from eight leading nobles and nine major towns. The nobles complied, particularly as Louise promised to indemnify them for any losses, but the Parlement, the estates of Normandy and some towns were less amenable. The Parlement did not register the treaty till 20 October, and the Norman estates never did so. Among the towns, Paris, Rouen, Bordeaux, Tours and Orléans were the most obstreperous. The regent was fortunately able to obtain concessions from the English government which facilitated Parisian compliance with her wishes on 24 January 1526. The other towns soon followed suit.[96]

In Italy, Louise stirred up opposition to the Emperor as discreetly as possible, so as not to prejudice a future settlement with him. In June 1525 she proposed to the pope and to Venice an alliance aimed at driving the imperial troops out of Italy and at pressurizing Charles into releasing her son, but she offered them only a few troops and a monthly subsidy. The Venetians eventually accepted her terms, while the pope drew back.[97] Louise did not limit her

[93] Champollion-Figeac, pp. 300–3; M. François, *Le cardinal François de Tournon* (1951), pp. 39–40.
[94] Scarisbrick, *Henry VIII*, p. 141.
[95] *Ordonnances*, iv. Nos. 394–5, 398–400; Jacqueton, *La politique extérieure*, p. 119. The treaty of the More, named after a manor owned by Wolsey in Hertfordshire, comprised five separate agreements; hence it is sometimes referred to as the 'treaties of the More'. C. A. Mayer and D. Bentley-Cranch in their *Florimond Robertet, homme d'état Français* (Geneva, 1994), pp. 71–2, 86–7, suggest that Robertet rather than Duprat inspired the policy leading to the treaty.
[96] Jacqueton, *La politique extérieure*, pp. 155–98.   [97] *Ibid.*, pp. 204–11, 229–39.

diplomatic activity to western Europe. Shortly after the battle of Pavia, she sent an envoy to Constantinople with a request for aid to the Ottoman sultan, Suleiman the Magnificent. He was warned that unless the aid materialized, Charles V would become 'master of the world'. Suleiman promised to send an expedition against him, but a letter he addressed to Francis contained nothing more than florid words of encouragement.[98]

Charles V, in the meantime, continued to make the surrender of Burgundy the *sine qua non* of peace with France. On 11 September, however, he nearly lost the only diplomatic card he had to play, when Francis almost died. For three weeks he ran a high fever and seemed lost to the world. He was suffering, it would appear, from a combination of acute depression, anorexia and a nasal abscess. His condition became so critical that his doctors gave up hope. The Emperor, who so far had avoided meeting his prisoner, now rushed to his bedside. On 18 September the two rulers embraced each other, protesting their friendship. Francis described himself as the Emperor's slave. Next day, they were joined by the king's sister, Marguerite, who had come post-haste from Barcelona. On 22 September Francis lapsed into a semi-coma. The end seemed near, when suddenly the abscess burst and he regained consciousness.[99] On 1 October de Selve wrote to the Parlement an account of how the king was cured as he was receiving the Blessed Sacrament. 'From this time onwards', he wrote, 'he has improved steadily and, thanks be to God, he is now rid of the fever that had gripped him for twenty-three days without respite. Nature has performed all its functions, as much by evacuation above and below as by sleeping, drinking and eating, so that he is now out of danger.'[100]

News of the king's recovery produced a mixed response in Paris. A few days after it had reached the capital, four men disguised as royal messengers rode through the streets shouting that 'the king was dead and that madam the regent was in great pain; that as wise men were concealing the truth, madmen had to proclaim it ...'.[101] There followed a wave of popular recrimination against the king, his mother and the government generally. Some people exclaimed that if Francis were not dead, he was unfit to rule and should be deposed. They called for the execution of more than fifty *grands officiers* and rich bourgeois. Much of this seditious talk doubtless emanated from the university, and in December the Parlement banned the farces and *morisques* traditionally staged by students to celebrate Epiphany. The ban, it explained, was necessary 'to prevent

[98] E. Charrière (ed.) *Négociations de la France dans le Levant* (1548–60), i. 112–18.
[99] *C.S.P., Ven.*, iii. Nos. 1112, 1115, 1119; P. Jourda, *Marguerite d'Angoulême* (1930), i. 116–17.
[100] Champollion-Figeac, pp. 331–3. Writing to Henry VIII, Louise described her son's recovery as a near miracle. *L.P.*, iv. 1692.
[101] Félibien, ii. 973; Champollion-Figeac, pp. 379–80.

wickedness taking advantage of such games to spread words which would carry serious consequences'.[102]

The peace of Madrid

The king's recovery was followed by the resumption of peace talks in Toledo, but the terms offered by Marguerite were unacceptable to Charles. On 11 October, therefore, the talks were suspended, and she returned to Madrid.[103] Meanwhile, an Italian captain, called Emilio Cavriana, formed a daring plan for Francis's escape from prison, but it was betrayed by Clément Champion, one of the king's servants.[104] Despite this incident, the talks in Toledo began again on 14 November. The French negotiators offered Charles a ransom of 3 million gold *écus* and proposed a marriage between Francis and the Emperor's sister, Eleanor of Portugal. When these terms were flatly refused, Marguerite decided that she might as well go home. She left Madrid on 27 November and on her journey back to France wrote several times to her brother, urging him not to despair.[105]

Deceit seemed the only course left to Francis if he was ever to regain his freedom. During November he drew up a deed of abdication in favour of the Dauphin, who was still only a child, but it was never registered by the Parlement and was almost certainly a move designed to frighten Charles into being more flexible.[106] But he stood firm on his original demands. Since nothing seemed likely to move him short of surrender, Louise of Savoy decided to abandon Burgundy. In a memorandum addressed to Chabot, she described the duchy as a price worth paying for her son's freedom. France, she explained, would suffer irreparable damage if he remained a prisoner, for the Dauphin was too young to rule and she could not carry the burden of regency for much longer. Far more, she said, had been given away following King John's capture at Poitiers in 1356. It seemed senseless to risk destroying the kingdom for the sake of a duchy.[107] Rallying to this view, Francis now decided to accept Charles's terms. Under the treaty of Madrid (14 January 1526) he abandoned Burgundy and also his claims to Italy and Artois. Henri d'Albret renounced his claim to Navarre, while Bourbon and his accomplices were reinstated. The

---

[102] Félibien, ii. 973–4. See also my 'Francis I and Paris' in *History*, lxvi (1981), 18–33.

[103] Champollion-Figeac, pp. 359–69. Francis seemed to have suffered a relapse in the interval. It was reported on 2 December that he had had a second sickness, more serious than the first, which had left him 'very weak and melancholy'. *L.P.*, iv. 1799.

[104] G. Salles, 'Un traître au XVIe siècle: Clément Champion, valet de chambre de François Ier', *R.Q.H.*, n.s. xxiv (1900), 41–73.

[105] Jourda, *Marguerite d'Angoulême*, i. 130–3.   [106] Champollion-Figeac, pp. 416–25.

[107] *Ibid.*, pp. 408–15.

king also agreed to hand over the Dauphin and his second son as hostages pending fulfilment of the treaty.[108]

Francis thus threw away every principle his ambassadors had been strenuously defending for months, yet his surrender was not unconditional, for he made two vital demands. First, he asked to be set free before the treaty was given effect so that he might persuade his subjects to endorse the cession of Burgundy; secondly, he requested the hand of Charles's sister, Eleanor, whom the Emperor had already promised to the duc de Bourbon. Both demands carried obvious risks. If the king was freed before the treaty was implemented, there was a possibility that this might never take place. Secondly, Bourbon would be alienated. The imperial chancellor Gattinara saw these dangers clearly: he advised Charles either to release Francis unconditionally and thereby gain his lasting gratitude and friendship, or to keep him locked up. History has proved Gattinara right, but Charles preferred to listen to Lannoy, who thought Francis could be trusted.[109] However, two days before the treaty was signed, Francis made another secret declaration nullifying in advance the surrender of Burgundy.

Francis was not released immediately after the peace had been signed. He remained at the Alcázar in Madrid until mid February, possibly for health reasons. He was still unwell on 20 January, when he was betrothed by proxy to Eleanor, and Bishop Tunstal found him weak and pale on the 28th.[110] On the following day, however, he was taken by litter to the church of Nuestra Señora de Atocha, where he attended vespers. As he rode back on a mule, he declared himself fit enough to hunt a stag. On the 30th he was given lunch by a Spanish countess and visited a convent, where he touched thirty scrofulous nuns.[111] Charles V came to Madrid on 13 February and spent a few days with Francis. They travelled together to Illescas, where Charles introduced him to Eleanor. She tried to kiss the king's hand, but he insisted on embracing her as a husband. Next day she performed a Spanish dance for him. The two monarchs parted company at Torrejon on 19 February: while Charles set off for Seville to marry Isabella of Portugal, Francis began his long journey back to France.[112] Travelling by way of Madrid, Burgos, Vittoria and San Sebastian, he remained under guard but was allowed to go hunting. At Aranda, on 26 February, he and Lannoy worked out the details of the exchange between himself and his sons. They agreed that this would be on 17 March at a specified place on the river Bidassoa, near Fuenterrabía. All troops were banned from the area as well as ships and boats, gatherings of local people were forbidden, and no member

---

[108] *Ordonnances*, iv. No. 412.   [109] Halkin and Dansaert, p. 91.
[110] Francis complained later that he was forbidden to leave the Alcázar, even during a fire, and that guards continued to peer into his bed at night. These allegations may have been fabricated to excuse his failure to honour the treaty of Madrid. Champollion-Figeac, pp. 506–7.
[111] *Ibid.*, p. 488.   [112] *Ibid.*, pp. 503–4, 508–9.

of the king's household was allowed further south than Bayonne. Before leaving Spain, Francis distributed gifts to his gaolers, including Alarçon who had followed him everywhere since Pizzighettone. He also wrote to Charles, asking him to send Eleanor to France before Holy Week.[113]

Montmorency had, in the meantime, carried news of the peace to France. Arriving at Lyons on 29 January, he was able to reassure Louise who had had no news out of Spain for over a month. She promptly informed the Parlement of the king's impending return and ordered prayers and processions for his safe deliverance.[114] On 1 February, she left Saint-Just. Despite a bad attack of gout, high winds and floods in the Loire valley, she travelled to Amboise where she picked up the Dauphin and his brother, and thence southward to Bayonne.[115]

On 17 March, two rowing boats were moored on opposite banks of the Bidassoa: one carried the king of France, and the other his sons. At an agreed signal, the boats crossed to a pontoon mid-stream, where they exchanged passengers. With tears in his eyes, Francis blessed the Dauphin and his brother Henri, promising to send for them soon. The boats then returned to their original moorings, and Francis found himself once more on French soil. Escorted by Lautrec and a few servants, he rode at full gallop to Saint-Jean-de-Luz and Bayonne, where his mother, sister and friends were waiting for him. An artillery salvo greeted his arrival about 3 pm; otherwise there was no public rejoicing on account of Lent. On 20 March, Francis and Louise attended a service of thanksgiving in Bayonne cathedral.[116] His long ordeal was over; only the future would tell whether he had learnt anything from it.

---

[113] *Ibid.*, pp. 504, 510–12, 516–18.   [114] *Ibid.*, p. 484.   [115] *L.P.*, iv. 1999, 2009, 2032.
[116] *Ibid.*, iv. 1938; Champollion-Figeac, pp. 522–3.

Chapter twelve

The king's return (1526–28)

Following his return from Spain, Francis was briefed by his mother and her ministers about events that had taken place in France during his absence. They doubtless told him of the attempts made by the Parlement to backtrack on the Concordat of Bologna and even to bring the Chancellor to justice. They will have told him of the obstructionism encountered by the regent in securing the obligations required by the treaty of the More; also of the efforts of the Paris Faculty of Theology to hound scholars and preachers of an evangelical persuasion. All these acts of defiance required punishment, but for the time being Francis allowed matters to stand while he went on a leisurely progress through south-west and central France. Among the more important places he visited were Bordeaux (9–23 April), Cognac (27 April–28 May), Angoulême (30 May–4 July) and Amboise (30 July–13 September). At Chartres, the king fulfilled a vow he had taken in Spain by performing a novena in the cathedral. Much of his time, of course, was devoted to hunting. On 9 June he broke his arm while chasing a stag and wore a sling for more than a fortnight.[1]

Tradition has it that it was at Mont-de-Marsan in March 1526 that Francis first met Anne, the daughter of Guillaume d'Heilly, seigneur de Pisseleu, who was to become his mistress. Anne was eighteen at the time and attached to the household of Madame de Vendôme.[2] By 1527 she had joined the 'fair band' of ladies which accompanied the king on hunting expeditions. The aftermath of a royal hunt near Amiens in August 1527 was described by Sir Anthony Browne in a letter to Henry VIII as follows:

> Furthermore, the king's bed is always carried with him, when he hunts; and anon, after that the deer is killed, he repairs to some house near at hand, where the same is set up, and there reposes himself three or four hours, and against his

---

[1] C.A.F., viii. 450–1; L.P., iv (pt. 1), 2243; J.B.P., pp. 241–2.
[2] P. Paris, *Etudes sur François premier* (1885), ii. 208–9, 231–4. According to Brantôme, Varillas and other early historians, Anne was a maid of honour of Louise of Savoy. The Picard family of Pisseleu, sieurs d'Heilly, is discussed by Potter in *War and Government*, pp. 134–6.

> return there is provided for him a supper by some nobleman, as by Monsr. de
> Vendôme, Monsr. de Guise or other; whereunto a great number of ladies and
> gentlewomen, used to be in his company be sent for, and there he passes his time
> until ten or eleven o'clock, among whom above others, as the report is, he
> favours a maiden of Madame de Vendôme, called Hely, whose beauty, after my
> mind, is not highly to be praised.[3]

Browne was probably prejudiced, for Anne was renowned for her beauty, intelligence and vivacity.

At the end of October the bodies of Queen Claude and of her six-year-old daughter Louise, whose funerals had been postponed because of the war, were carried in procession from Blois to Paris. Among the mourners were the king's mother and sister, the duc and duchesse de Vendôme, the comte de Saint-Pol and marshal Lautrec. On 5 November a funeral service was held at Notre-Dame and next day the bodies were taken to their final resting place in the abbey of Saint-Denis. The interment took place in front of a huge congregation including prelates, nobles and noblewomen, members of the Parlement, Chât-elet and municipal government of Paris. The king was not present. He stayed at Vincennes during the funeral and only came to Saint-Denis on 8 November when he removed the sacred relics from the high altar where he had placed them on the eve of his last Italian campaign. Francis then spent a few days at Ecouen, the home of Anne de Montmorency, before joining his mother, sister, sister-in-law and the rest of the court at Saint-Germain-en-Laye.[4]

On 26 December the king's recently widowed sister, Marguerite, was betro-thed to Henri d'Albret, king of Navarre, who had become something of a hero after escaping from the castle at Pavia. The marriage, which followed on 30 January 1527, prompting eight days of continual festivities and tournaments, had important political implications since Henri's claim to Spanish Navarre had yet to be satisfied. Though Marguerite visited her small kingdom, she soon returned to the French court and was present, in June 1528, at the marriage of her sister-in-law, Princess Renée with Ercole d'Este, son of the duke of Ferrara. On 16 November Marguerite gave birth to a daughter, Jeanne, the future mother of King Henry IV of France.[5]

The 'second accession'

Francis I's homecoming has been fairly described as a 'second accession', for it was accompanied by a distribution of honours comparable to that in 1515.[6] The treason of the duc de Bourbon and the slaughter of so many French noblemen at Pavia had created vacancies in the royal administration which

---

[3] *St. P.*, vi. 58. I have modernized the spelling.   [4] *J.B.P.*, pp. 248–51.
[5] *Ibid.*, pp. 253, 304–5; P. Jourda, *Marguerite d'Angoulême* (1930), i. 145–53.
[6] C. Terrasse, *François Ier* (1945–70), ii. 21.

Mons.^{re} le Grand Mais.^{tre} de Mohmorency

50. Anne de Montmorency (1493–1567), Grand Master of France and future Constable, who shared Francis I's captivity for a time and helped to negotiate his release. Drawing by Jean Clouet.

needed filling. The king's household around which the court was organized was of crucial importance to a personal monarchy. Offices in the household were used to reward men who had proved loyal, to maintain great lords in their duty and to give noblemen resources essential to the maintenance of their social status. Foremost among the new appointments were Anne de Montmorency and Philippe Chabot, both of whom had been captured with the king at Pavia and had since helped to secure his release.

Montmorency was thirty-three years old and a member of one of the oldest and richest aristocratic houses in France. He had been brought up with the king and, since 1515, had participated in several military campaigns. In August 1522 he had become a marshal of France, a knight of the Order of St Michael and a king's councillor. On 23 March 1526 he was appointed Grand Master in place of the king's uncle, René of Savoy, who had died of his wounds at Pavia, and governor of Languedoc in place of Bourbon. Montmorency soon became one of Francis's chief ministers, although the influence on policy-making of the king's mother, of Chancellor Duprat and of councillors, like Robertet, was not immediately eclipsed. But these men were ageing fast and there was a need for new blood. Montmorency rose to some extent at the expense of Duprat, who was over sixty and becoming increasingly preoccupied by ecclesiastical ambitions. The lawyer–churchman was giving way to the soldier–courtier. As Jacquart has written, 'the administration of the *Roi-Chevalier* was more than ever that of the nobility'. Montmorency was a strict, even brutal, disciplinarian who stood for a strong royal authority and religious conservatism. On 10 January 1527 he entered the royal family by marrying Madeleine of Savoy, daughter of René, and was henceforth addressed as 'my nephew' by the king's mother and sister. Madeleine brought her husband a sizeable dowry which helped to swell his already considerable fortune.[7]

The career of Philippe Chabot, seigneur de Brion, who replaced Bonnivet, the king's deceased favourite, as Admiral of France on 23 March was remarkably similar to Montmorency's. Roughly of the same age, he had also been brought up with the king. Soon after Francis's accession he had become a gentleman of the king's chamber, captain of a company of forty *lances*, a knight of St Michael and mayor of Bordeaux. Among his military exploits was the successful defence of Marseilles against Bourbon in 1524. For his many

---

[7] Decrue, i. 28, 67, 70–1, 75–8; C.A.F., i. 2307–8; J. Jacquart, *François Ier* (1981), p. 196. Montmorency's landed revenues amounted to 11,548 *livres* per annum in 1522. Thereafter he added considerably to his estates. By 1560–64 their annual revenue had risen to around 125,000 *livres*. He also drew substantial revenues from his royal offices: about 32,450 *livres* per annum in 1532; and in 1538, following his appointment as Constable, 56,450 *livres*. He also received large *ex gratia* payments as governor of Languedoc from the local estates in return for his protection and advancement of their interests at court. See M. Greengrass, 'Property and Politics in Sixteenth-Century France: The Landed Fortune of Constable Anne de Montmorency', *F.H.*, ii (1988), 371–98.

services, including his part in securing the king's release, Chabot was well rewarded: in addition to the admiralship, he was appointed captain of Honfleur and of Dijon and governor of Burgundy and of Valois. He also received many gifts of land and money, though he never became as wealthy as Montmorency. In January 1527 he too entered the royal family by marrying Françoise de Longwy, daughter of Francis's bastard sister.[8]

Other notable appointments made by Francis in 1516 were the following: Galiot de Genouillac became Master of the Horse (*Grand écuyer*) in place of San Severino. Robert de La Marck, seigneur de Florange, who had served his imprisonment in Flanders, was appointed a marshal of France. Jean de La Barre became comte d'Etampes and *prévôt de Paris*, while François de Tournon was promoted archbishop of Bourges.[9]

The League of Cognac (22 May 1526)

The main concern of the king and his council early in 1526 was to find ways of evading the terms laid down in the peace of Madrid and of securing more acceptable ones from the Emperor. They began by playing for time.

On 17 March, while Francis was still in south-west France, the imperial ambassador, de Praet, came to fetch the king's ratification of the treaty of Madrid. He was told that his powers were insufficient and sent home empty-handed. Charles sent new powers on 27 March. But Francis found other reasons for delay. He explained that a new Great Seal had to be engraved, the original having been lost at Pavia. On 2 April he complained that the treaty had been published in Antwerp, Rome and Florence, before he had been able to consult his subjects regarding the surrender of Burgundy. They were angry and were asking to be heard before the treaty was ratified.[10] Was the king's complaint genuine, or was he looking for an excuse to break his promise to the Emperor? Historians once believed that Francis called a meeting of the Estates General at Cognac in May 1526 and that the Burgundian representatives proudly refused to be separated from the French kingdom. This, however, is a myth created in 1548.[11] No meeting of the Estates General was ever held during Francis's reign. Burgundian delegates did call on him in April 1526, but they refused to act on their own; they advised the king to call a meeting of the

[8] *D.B.F.*, viii. 134–5; *C.A.F.*, i. 2305, 2086, 2408, 2861; v. 18592, 18661; viii. 32430.

[9] *C.A.F.*, i. 2313; ii. 6169; v. 18548; vii. 23873; Versoris, pp. 91–2; M. François, *Le cardinal François de Tournon* (1951), p. 47.

[10] H. Hauser, 'Le traité de Madrid et la cession de la Bourgogne à Charles-Quint', *Revue bourguignonne*, xxii (1912), 150–3; Le Glay, ii. 656–8.

[11] The story of the Estates General of Cognac was invented by G. Paradin (*Memoriae nostrae libri quatuor* (Lyons, 1548), iv. 47) and repeated by all eighteenth-century historians. See Hauser, 'Traité de Madrid', pp. 1–4.

Burgundian estates, which he did, but only after his council had decided on 10 May to break the treaty.[12]

Francis invoked popular consultation simply to give himself more time in which to cement his relations with England, Venice and the Holy See. Henry VIII feared an enormous expansion of the Emperor's power that would accrue from his acquisition of Burgundy and his sister's marriage to the French king.[13] Francis, for his part, professed gratitude to Henry for not invading France during his captivity and for aiding his release. As a mark of special favour, he invited the English ambassador, Sir Thomas Cheyney, one of Henry's gentlemen of the chamber, to enter his own chamber as freely as he would that of his master.[14] On 15 April Francis ratified the treaty of the More, declaring his willingness to meet Henry at any time. On 8 August England and France signed another treaty binding themselves not to negotiate separately with the Emperor.[15]

At the end of March envoys from Venice and the Holy See tried to persuade Francis to join a league against the Emperor. He seemed interested and even prepared to leave his sons in Spain for two or three years. They would be well looked after, he said, and would learn Spanish and make useful friends. On 20 April he told the Venetian envoy that he would join a league, not so much in his own interest, as in the cause of Italian liberty.[16]

Charles V, meanwhile, pressed Francis to ratify the peace. Early in May, Lannoy arrived at Cognac with an escort of 200 noblemen. He had saved Francis's life at Pavia and had been instrumental in securing his freedom. On both counts he deserved, and was given, a warm welcome, but Francis did not allow personal gratitude to deflect him from the only course he had set for himself.[17] On 10 May the Viceroy was informed by the king's council that Francis could not hand over Burgundy because his subjects would not permit such a diminution of his patrimony. The king further explained that promises extorted from him while he was a prisoner had no binding force. However, he added that he wished to remain the Emperor's friend and was ready to observe those clauses

[12] Hauser doubted whether any Burgundian deputies had come to Cognac (*ibid.*, p. 83). But see M. François, *Le cardinal François de Tournon*, p. 52 n.2. On 21 April English ambassadors reported the presence in Cognac of 'a gentleman from Burgundy, who had remonstrated with the king against delivering Burgundy into the Emperor's hands without their own consent, and rather than they would be so delivered they will refuse obedience either to the King or the Emperor'. *L.P.*, iv. 2115.

[13] G. Jacqueton, *La politique extérieure de Louise de Savoie* (1892), pp. 256–8; *L.P.*, iv. 1963.

[14] *L.P.*, iv. 2087, 2092. Cheyney's embassy was intended as a mark of special esteem for Francis, who reciprocated by sending the seigneur de Morette, a gentleman of his own chamber, to Henry VIII. *L.P.*, iv. 2104.

[15] *Ibid.*, iv. 2135; *Ordonnances*, iv. No. 428.

[16] Jacqueton, *La politique extérieure*, pp. 262–3, 269; *C.S.P. Ven.*, iii. 1236, 1253.

[17] Hauser, 'Le traité de Madrid', pp. 158–9; L.-E. Halkin and G. Dansaert, *Charles de Lannoy* (Brussels, 1934), p. 101; *C.S.P. Ven.*, iii. 1270, 1272–3, 1285.

of the treaty which were acceptable. In place of Burgundy, he again suggested a cash ransom.[18]

On 4 June the estates of Burgundy met at Dijon in the presence of the king's representative, Philippe Chabot. They endorsed the decision already taken by the king's council to repudiate the treaty of Madrid. Denouncing it as 'contrary to all reason and equity', the deputies affirmed their desire always to remain under the French crown. Using an identical phraseology (doubtless prompted by Chabot), the neighbouring estates of Auxonne made a similar declaration a few days later.[19]

In July a royal apologia intended for international consumption was published. It emphasized the 'fundamental law' which forbade the king to alienate any part of his demesne and laid down the principle that no province or town could change ownership without the consent of its inhabitants. Replying for the Emperor, Valdés denied that popular consent was needed to restore a territory to its lawful owner. He thought it strange that Francis, who had always boasted of his 'absolute authority' should now be the champion of 'popular consultation'.[20]

Francis, meanwhile, acted to prevent the Emperor from taking over Burgundy by force. Chabot was instructed to inspect the province's fortresses, receive an oath of loyalty from the inhabitants, draw up an inventory of available victuals and munitions, punish looters and set up a kind of espionage centre in Dijon. In carrying out these tasks, he took care not to ruffle local feelings: Burgundian officials were paid on the nail and parts of the province that had been heavily taxed were given relief. These precautions, however, were unnecessary, for Charles V was not in a position to attempt an invasion of Burgundy: his army in Franche-Comté was unpaid, and no help was forthcoming from his aunt, Margaret of Austria, or his brother Ferdinand. An unsuccessful attempt by imperial troops to capture Auxonne merely exposed Franche-Comté, which had been declared neutral, to a possible reprisal attack. Soon afterwards, the Emperor disbanded his army; his dream of reuniting 'the two Burgundies' had vanished for ever.[21]

Francis was doubtless keen to avenge the humiliation he had suffered at Pavia and since; but he wanted to recover his sons before embarking on another conflict with the Emperor. His negotiations with other powers in 1526 were aimed at putting pressure on Charles, nothing more. The so-called Holy League of Cognac was signed by France, the Holy See, Venice, Florence and Sforza on 22 May.[22] Though Henry VIII was called its 'protector', he was not yet included in it. The Emperor, ironically, was invited to join on four con-

---

[18] Halkin and Dansaert, pp. 102–3; Le Glay, ii. 660–1.
[19] Hauser, 'Traité de Madrid', pp. 78–81.
[20] *Ibid.*, pp. 90–6.   [21] *Ibid.*, pp. 74, 85–9.   [22] *Ordonnances*, iv. No. 418.

ditions: he was to release Francis's sons for a reasonable cash ransom, restore Sforza to the duchy of Milan, limit the size of the retinue he intended taking to Italy and pay his debts to Henry within three months. If Charles refused, the treaty provided for a future war against him, the contribution of each confederate being specified. Francis promised to send 500 *lances* across the Alps and pay a monthly subsidy of 40,000 *écus* to the pope and the Venetians for the hire of Swiss troops. He also undertook to send an army across the Pyrenees. A powerful fleet was to be assembled with a view of capturing Genoa; later it was to join a combined land and sea attack on the kingdom of Naples, which, once captured, was to be disposed of by the pope with the consent of his allies. Francis gave up his claims to Milan and Naples, but was promised handsome compensation: namely, an annuity of 50,000 ducats and the county of Asti from Sforza along with Genoa, and another annuity of 75,000 ducats from the eventual recipient of Naples.

The treaty of Cognac shattered the Emperor's plans. Having made peace with France and married Isabella of Portugal, he had planned to go first to Italy to receive the imperial crown from the pope, then to Germany, where his authority was under threat from the Reformation. Luther was as active as ever, and his supporters among the princes had formed a defensive league. In March Charles had informed the Catholic princes of his intention to come to their aid. He hoped to leave Spain on 24 June, but long before that date he learned of Francis's breach of faith. 'He is full of dumps', reported an English envoy, 'and solitary, musing sometimes alone three or four hours together. There is no mirth or comfort with him.'[23] Charles should have listened to Gattinara rather than Lannoy; he should not have released Francis before gaining Burgundy. Now he had to pay for that mistake: instead of going triumphantly to Italy, he had to remain in Spain and prepare for a new struggle. Pavia might as well not have happened.

The Italian members of the League of Cognac were the first to go to war. They confidently believed that the hour of their independence had struck, for the imperial army in north Italy was penniless and disorganized. The League's army, under the duke of Urbino, captured Lodi on 24 June and prepared to attack Milan, but it was forced to retire after Bourbon had introduced money and troops into the city.[24] As the tide of war began to turn against the League, Francis was criticized by his allies for not helping them. As yet, he had sent no troops to Italy, his fleet was still at Marseilles, and there was no sign of the subsidies he had promised.[25] He did not object to the Italians fighting the Emperor, but did not wish to become involved at this stage; yet he was anxious

[23] *L.P.*, iv. 2094.   [24] J. Hook, *The Sack of Rome* (London, 1972), pp. 77ff.

[25] Clement VII suspected he was being blackmailed by Francis, who wanted a red hat for Duprat and the see of Riez for François de Dinteville. V.-L. Bourrilly, *Guillaume du Bellay, seigneur de Langey* (1905), p. 20.

not to lose them as allies. On 18 July Francis sent Guillaume du Bellay to reassure them.[26]

Soon afterwards, however, the League suffered two more blows: Sforza, who had been defending Milan castle, surrendered on 25 July, and an attempt by the papal army to capture Siena was repulsed. Clement VII blamed the French for these misfortunes. They became exceedingly unpopular at the Curia. 'You have no idea', wrote the secretary of the French embassy, 'what things are said about us by persons of high standing in the Curia on account of our delays and our behaviour hitherto. The language is so frightful that I dare not write it!'[27] By mid August Clement had become disenchanted with the League: he told du Bellay that he could no longer carry the main burden of paying for the war. On 21 September he signed a four months' truce with the Emperor.[28]

Charles, meanwhile, rejected the terms of membership offered him by the League. Replying to the French ambassador, Calvimont, who had asked him to release Francis's sons for a cash ransom, Charles said:

> I will not deliver them for money. I refused money for the father: I will much less take money for the sons. I am content to render them upon reasonable treaty, but not for money, nor will I trust any more the king's promise, for he has deceived me, and that like no noble prince. And where he excuses that he cannot fulfil some things without grudge of his subjects, let him fulfil that that is in his power, which he promised by the honour of a prince to fulfil; that is to say, that if he could not bring all his promise to pass he would return again hither into prison.

Charles added that he would resist to the bitter end any attempt by Francis to recover his sons by force. 'Would to God', he declared, 'that he were content, in the avoiding of Christian blood, to try the right with me, hand for hand, I would, upon confidence of my right take it on me, which I trust in the right-eousness of God should defend me.'[29] Yet even now Charles did not rule out a peaceful settlement. He soon regretted his intemperate outburst and offered to discuss the release of the king's sons.

By the autumn of 1526 Francis had come to see the need to bring more pressure to bear on the Emperor by giving more effective support to his Italian allies and by turning his friendship with England into an alliance. He promised to send a subsidy to Rome, to assemble an army in Lyons and to go there himself before Christmas. This encouraged the pope, who anathemized the Colonna and sent an army to destroy their towns, fortresses and villages. By late November, however, no help from France had reached Clement, who was being threatened from several quarters: while in the south, the Colonna

---

[26] *Ibid.*, pp. 20–2.
[27] L. von Pastor, *The History of the Popes*, tr. F. I. Antrobus and R. F. Kerr (London, 1891–1933), ix. 323–4.
[28] Bourrilly, *Guillaume du Bellay*, pp. 26–30.
[29] *L.P.*, iv. 2470. Cf. F. Mignet, *La rivalité de François Ier et de Charles-Quint* (1875), ii. 228–31.

51. Medal of Pope Clement VII by Benvenuto Cellini, 1534.

invaded the States of the Church; in the north, Frundsberg's landsknechts reached Mantuan territory. The crisis was aggravated by the decision of the duke of Ferrara to throw in his lot with the Emperor. The last straw was the arrival in a Tuscan port of an imperial fleet carrying Lannoy and 9,000 troops. On 28 November it was reported that Clement looked 'like a sick man whom the doctors have given up'.[30]

Francis looked to friendship with England as a more economical way of bringing the Emperor to heel than military involvement in Italy. But it had to be bought, and Wolsey could drive a hard bargain. Although he had helped to create the League of Cognac, he had so far refused to join it on the ground that

[30] Pastor, ix. 345.

England could mediate between France and the Empire more effectively by remaining neutral. The cardinal also never missed a chance of playing one off against the other. Thus in October 1526 he embarrassed Francis by proposing that he should marry Henry's daughter, Mary. Francis explained that he was engaged to the Emperor's sister. 'I must do things', he said, 'as near as I can without displeasure of God and reproach of the world.'[31] The English government, however, continued to press for a marriage alliance: if Francis agreed to take Mary, it said, Henry would join the League and Charles would be forced to release Francis's sons.[32]

In Italy, meanwhile, the pope continued to vacillate. At the start of 1527 he seemed ready to carry on the war, but when the subsidy promised by Francis failed to arrive, Clement made a truce. This infuriated Francis who gave the papal nuncio a piece of his mind: 'I hope to act in such a way', he declared, 'that the Emperor will not succeed in his aim of subordinating everything to his tyranny, but I will leave those who have fallen into servitude through their own baseness and fear.'[33] He had no sooner uttered these words than news reached him that the pope had broken the truce and attacked Naples. This time Francis rejoiced. He told the nuncio that an Anglo-French alliance was imminent and gave him details of help Clement would soon receive.[34] By mid March, however, the pope was once more in deep trouble: Lannoy had invaded the States of the Church and another imperial army, led by Bourbon and Frundsberg, was about to march into central Italy from the north. On 15 March Clement signed a truce with Lannoy.

The League's failure in Italy brought France and England closer together in opposition to the Emperor who seemed no longer willing to compromise. On 30 April the treaty of Westminster was signed: Francis and Henry agreed to send a joint embassy to Charles to demand the release of Francis's sons and the payment of Charles's debts to Henry.[35] If the Emperor refused, they would declare war on him and Princess Mary would marry either Francis or his second son, the duc d'Orléans. The treaty also envisaged another meeting between the kings of England and France, albeit a less costly one than the Field of Cloth of Gold.

From the pope's standpoint the Anglo-French alliance came too late. Nothing could now stop the southward march of Bourbon's cold and hungry troops. By-passing Florence, they marched on Rome with incredible speed, intent on getting the loot they had been promised. Clement, realizing that he had been duped, rejoined the League on 25 April, but his allies could not save

---

[31] *L.P.*, iv. 2606.   [32] *Ibid.*, iv. 2728.   [33] Mignet, ii. 289–90; Desjardins, ii. 900ff.
[34] Bourrilly, *Guillaume du Bellay*, p. 38. Francis had sent Rabodanges with 50,000 *écus* to the pope in February.
[35] *Ordonnances*, v. No. 452; *L.P.*, iv. 3080.

him. On 6 May the sack of Rome began.[36] Bourbon was killed as he scaled the city's wall, but his troops poured into it like a torrent in flood, destroying all in their path. Clement along with fourteen cardinals took shelter in Castel Sant'-Angelo and, on 5 June, signed a humiliating peace which made him virtually the Emperor's prisoner. The first result of the news was a revolution in Florence and the overthrow of the Medici.

The persecution reversed

During the king's captivity a vigorous attempt had been made by the Parlement of Paris, aided and abetted by the Faculty of Theology, to check the progress of heresy in France. With the help of new powers obtained by the regent from the pope, a campaign had been mounted against the *Cercle de Meaux*, forcing its members either to recant or go into exile. Berquin had been arrested for the second time and tried as a relapsed heretic; but he still awaited sentence when the king returned.

Francis, who had been kept informed of these events by his sister during her visit to Spain, expressed disapproval of the persecution. On 1 April 1526 he rebuked the Parlement for its disobedience regarding Berquin, forbade it to pass sentence on him and threatened to call his judges to account. The Parlement duly obeyed, while offering excuses for its actions. In July, Francis ordered Berquin's release within Paris or, at least, that he be allowed unrestricted access to the Conciergerie's courtyard. But the Parlement would only allow him to use it for two hours each day and in silence. Soon afterwards, Berquin fell ill, and Francis ordered his transfer to the Louvre, but the Parlement again refused, saying that construction work at the Louvre made it unsafe. It did, however, allow Jean de La Barre, *bailli* of Paris to visit the prisoner, who seemed well treated and in good health. In October, the Parlement sent representatives to the king to explain why Berquin could not be released, but, after following Francis around for a fortnight, they were denied an audience. On 19 November he again requested Berquin's release only to meet with another refusal. Whereupon La Barre removed the prisoner from the Conciergerie by force and took him to the Louvre.[37]

Francis also gave his protection to members of the *Cercle de Meaux*. Lefèvre d'Etaples and Gérard Roussel, who had gone into foreign exile during the captivity, were now able to come home. Lefèvre took charge of the royal library at Blois and became the tutor of the king's youngest son, while Roussel was

---

[36] *L.P.*, iv. 3114–16, 3136; See also Hook, pp. 156ff. and A. Chastel, *The Sack of Rome, 1527* (Princeton, 1983), pp. 25–33.

[37] J. K. Farge, *Orthodoxy and Reform in Early Reformation France* (Leiden, 1985), pp. 259–60; Doucet, ii. 210–13. The king's letters to the Parlement are in A.N., X[1a] 1529, fols. 198–9, 316, 442–3.

appointed Marguerite de Navarre's almoner. As for Caroli, whom she had sheltered at Alençon, he resumed preaching in Paris with the bishop's permission.[38] But the Faculty of Theology did not readily submit to this state of affairs. On 16 May it condemned Erasmus's *Colloquies* and, soon afterwards, Noël Béda published his *Annotationes*, in which Erasmus and Lefèvre were accused of every kind of heresy. Erasmus wrote to Francis, blaming Béda for disturbing the peace and obstructing the progress of learning in France. If Béda's books were in French instead of Latin, Erasmus declared, everyone, even gardeners and shoemakers, would see that he was mad; the University of Paris had become a den of thieves. Its doctors, while claiming to defend the faith, were merely lusting for power: they threatened even the king's authority for they were capable of claiming the right to depose a monarch on a trumped-up heresy charge.[39]

While the Parlement indicated that it could not restrain the Faculty, Francis rose to the defence of Erasmus and Lefèvre. He banned the sale of Béda's book and forbade the Faculty to publish any work without the Parlement's *imprimatur*. On being invited by the Parlement to expound his views, Béda said that Francis was being badly advised: Erasmus and Lefèvre were bringing Lutheranism into France and the king would be acting differently if only he understood what was happening. The Parlement, however, was not prepared to defend the syndic. It accordingly obeyed the king, but only in 'order to avoid scandal', not out of conviction.[40] The Faculty, meanwhile, drew up a list of the alleged errors of Erasmus, Lefèvre and others for submission to the king and the Chancellor. In March 1527 Francis expressed concern at the Faculty's continued harrassment of Lefèvre, Roussel and Caroli, and asked the dean and syndic to see him. In September, he denounced Béda's book, which, he said, had scandalized many people and was allegedly full of errors and heresies. Yet the Faculty was unmoved: on 16 December it formally condemned Erasmus's works.[41]

Early in 1527 Francis deprived the Parlement of all involvement in the prosecution of heresy. After consulting the pope, he changed the composition of the *juges délégués*. In place of the two *parlementaires*, he appointed three bishops and two other churchmen; he also increased the number of theologians on the panel from two to three. In 1528 he removed Berquin's case from their jurisdiction.[42] The king's actions created the impression abroad that he sympathized with the Reformation. 'The king favours the Word', Capito wrote to Zwingli on 1 January 1527.[43] This, however, was an illusion. Francis was reasserting

[38] J. K. Farge, *Biographical Register of Paris Doctors of Theology, 1500–1536* (Toronto, 1980), p. 68.
[39] Farge, *Othodoxy and Reform*, p. 192.   [40] *Ibid.*, pp. 260–1; Doucet, ii. 217.
[41] Farge, *Orthodoxy and Reform*, p. 193.
[42] *Ibid.*, pp. 262–3; Fraikin, *Nonciatures de Clément VII* (1906), i. 428–33; Doucet, ii. 219.
[43] Herminjard, ii. 4.

52. Bas-relief from the tomb of Cardinal Duprat in the cathedral of Sens showing his entry into the city.

his authority after a concerted bid by the Parlement and Faculty of Theology to deal with heresy as they saw fit. He may have 'favoured the Word' in the sense of not understanding how a more evangelical faith could be construed as heretical, but he continued to oppose any religious dissent that offended orthodoxy as he understood it, particularly if it disturbed the public peace. Thus in December 1527, after the clergy had called for the extirpation of 'the damned and insufferable Lutheran sect', he promised to show that he was 'the Most Christian King' in deed as well as name.

Duprat's triumph

One of the most important tasks facing the king on his return from captivity was to endorse the actions taken by his mother as regent during his captivity. As we have seen, her authority had been seriously challenged by the Parlement, notably in respect of her appointment of Duprat to the see of Sens and the abbey of Saint-Benoît-sur-Loire. It had tried to set aside the Concordat of Bologna in favour of the electoral system enshrined in the Pragmatic Sanction of Bourges. An attempt had even been made by the Parlement to indict the Chancellor. Such actions could not be allowed to go unpunished by the king.

On 9 April 1526 he authorized Duprat to take possession of Saint-Benoît and a few weeks later gave effect to the decree of the *Grand Conseil* conferring Sens on him. But Francis also wanted to humiliate the *parlementaires* who had dared to challenge royal authority. He began by arranging a debate between representatives of the Parlement and *Grand Conseil* in front of his council. This took place on 4 December. After three representatives of the *Grand Conseil* had presented their case, the Chancellor explained why the government had become involved in the dispute over Saint-Benoît: the Parlement, he said, had defied the regent's authority and issued decrees harmful to the king. The four *parlementaires* tried to justify their conduct but to no avail: on 10 December the king's council ruled that the Parlement had acted unlawfully in a manner likely to encourage the enemies of the kingdom. It nullified the Parlement's decrees, including those directed against members of the *Grand Conseil*, and forbade the four *parlementaires* to resume their normal duties till further notice.[44] On 10 January 1527 Francis ordered the clerk of the Parlement to bring him the record of its debates during his captivity. At first the Parlement would send only transcripts, but he insisted on seeing the original minutes. The court eventually complied after certain passages concerning Duprat had been deleted. As for François Poncher, bishop of Paris, who had been elected abbot of Saint-Benoît in opposition to the Chancellor, he was accused of sedition and the *Grand Conseil* was ordered to look into his activi-

[44] Doucet, ii. 220–3; *C.A.F.*, i. 2504; v. 18563.

ties. He was eventually imprisoned at Vincennes where he died in September 1532.[45]

The King returns to Paris (14 April 1527)

Francis also needed to teach the Parisians a lesson, for, as we have seen, they had imperilled the success of Louise of Savoy's foreign policy by refusing the obligation demanded under the treaty of the More.

According to the Bourgeois de Paris, the king spent much of the winter of 1526–27 at Saint-Germain-en-Laye and stayed away from Paris 'except at night'.[46] He did not reappear officially in the capital until 14 April 1527. The authorities were given so little advance notice that the customary ceremonial – even the canopy under which the king traditionally made his entry – could not be prepared.[47] His entry, moreover, was immediately preceded by the arrest of eight citizens who had led the opposition to the guarantees required under the treaty of the More. They comprised a canon of Notre-Dame, Jacques Merlin, three *parlementaires*, Jean Bouchard, Jean Dugué and François Boileau, a notary of the Châtelet and three merchants. The notary and merchants were released almost at once, but the rest were allowed to languish in prison for two years. They would probably have remained there but for the intervention of the *Bureau de la Ville* when the king asked for a subsidy. The sentences they eventually received were not severe: Merlin was banished to Nantes for a year, while Bouchard was fined 400 *livres*, suspended from his practice for a year and banned for life from holding municipal office. The rest had only to pay costs.[48]

The *Lit de Justice* of 24 July 1527

The king's authority, as we have seen, had been challenged by the Parlement during his captivity. This challenge had focused on the application of the Concordat and had taken the form of an attempted indictment of the Chancellor. Such an undermining of royal authority could not be allowed to go unanswered. Francis had already taken steps to bring the Parlement to heel. After returning to the capital, he needed to reaffirm his authority in the most solemn manner. This he did in the *Lit de Justice* of 24 July 1527.

The setting in the *Grand' Chambre* was magnificent. The king sat on an elevated throne under a canopy of blue velvet embroidered with gold fleurs-de-lis. Running at angles on either side of the throne were two tiers of seats. An upper tier was occupied, on one side, by two lay peers and five other nobles, on

[45] Doucet, ii. 223–4; *J.B.P.*, p. 370.   [46] *Ibid.*, p. 252.
[47] *Ibid.*, pp. 266–7; L. M. Bryant, *The King and the City in the Parisian Royal Entry Ceremony* (Geneva, 1986), p. 226, wrongly dates this entry 1526.
[48] Jacqueton, *La politique extérieure*, pp. 188–9; *J.B.P.*, pp. 266–7; Versoris, p. 102.

53. A *lit de justice*. Contemporary woodcut showing Francis I presiding over a meeting of the Parlement.

the other, by three ecclesiastical peers and one archbishop. A lower tier was filled by nine *maîtres des requêtes* and by three presidents of the Parlement. Seven steps carpeted with the same fabric as the canopy led from the throne to the floor of the *Grand' Chambre*. Reclining on them were the Great chamberlain, the First chamberlain and the *prévôt de Paris*. Kneeling at the foot of the steps were two ushers of the king's chamber and, below the throne, on a chair upholstered like the royal throne was the Chancellor. The seventy-five councillors of the Parlement occupied benches on the main floor of the chamber and behind them sat many courtiers. The chief clerk of the court sat at a desk along with two other clerks and two notaries. Various members of the king's bodyguard were stationed near the door. Altogether there were about 120 people in the *Grand' Chambre*.[49]

As the meeting began, Duprat exchanged a few words privately with the king. He then turned towards the *parlementaires* and haughtily invited any one wishing to speak to do so, whereupon they all fell upon their knees. Francis asked them to rise and the Fourth President, Charles Guillart, began a lengthy address, in which he tried to justify the Parlement's past actions. While admitting that the king ruled by the grace of God, he said that his authority also rested on his subjects' obedience, which in turn depended on his use of good ministers and laws. The king, Guillart continued, should observe the laws of his predecessors who had ruled well; but he went even further. The Parlement, he claimed (without any historical justification), held its power not from the king, but from the people, for it had originally been a popular assembly, a sort of 'convention of estates'. Finally, he denounced royal policies which had produced friction between the Parlement and the crown, such as the protection of heretics and the use of *évocations*. He expressed indignation at the way in which the *Grand Conseil* had been absolved, even praised, for its illegal acts concerning the benefices of Sens and Saint-Benoît, while the Parlement's representatives had been 'condemned ignominiously'.[50]

Guillart's speech was not calculated to please the king. That afternoon he held a council meeting at which an edict was drawn up defining the Parlement's authority. In accordance with royal policy before the captivity, the Parlement was forbidden to meddle in affairs of state and confined to its judicial role. Even this was narrowly defined to exclude lawsuits concerning ecclesiastical benefices. While the Parlement was allowed to submit remonstrances, it was forbidden to amend any piece of royal legislation at the time of

[49] Sarah Hanley, *The 'Lit de Justice' of the Kings of France* (Princeton, 1983), pp. 52–3. This work offers an interpretation of the events of July 1527 which I find completely unacceptable. It turns a hypothesis – viz. that the meeting on 24 July was the first *Lit de justice* – into a proven fact, and dismisses the quarrel between the king and the Parlement that preceded it as 'peripheral'. For a critical view of Professor Hanley's ingenious but, in my opinion, unconvincing theory see my article: 'Francis I and the *Lit de Justice*: a "Legend" Defended' in *F.H.*, vol. 7 (1993), pp. 53–83.

[50] Doucet, ii. 252–4; E. Maugis, *Histoire du Parlement de Paris* (1913), i. 580–1.

registration. It was also required to obtain each year formal confirmation from the king of its delegated powers; any action taken by the Parlement in excess of these powers was annulled retrospectively and in the future. While the court was forbidden to restrict Louise of Savoy's powers as regent, all her past decisions were now confirmed and all the Parlement's contradictory ones revoked. The edict also confirmed the Chancellor's independence of the Parlement. Finally, it announced the setting up of a royal commission to reform the administration of justice, which, it claimed, was suffering because of the domination exercised by a few families of venal office-holders.[51]

The edict's presentation was as painful to the Parlement as were its contents. Once the king's council had completed its business, representatives of the Parlement were called before the king in the *Salle Verte* and Robertet read the edict to them. Normally they would have been given a chance to reply, but on this occasion, before they could utter a word, the king and his councillors swept out of the room. Francis then added insult to injury by insisting that the edict be registered not only by the Parlement but also by his own council and by the *Grand Conseil*. By insisting on the edict being registered after he had left the *Grand' Chambre*, the king deprived the Parlement of its customary excuse that the registration was under duress; it underlined its humiliation.[52] Though deeply wounded, the Parlement offered no resistance: it merely demonstrated its contempt for the edict by registering it without the customary formalities. Having made his point, Francis could afford to be magnanimous: on 26 July he pardoned the four *parlementaires* who had been suspended for their parts in the Sens and Saint-Benoît affairs.[53]

The next matter requiring the king's attention was the punishment of the late duc de Bourbon. In 1525, as we have seen, Francis had been angered by the lenient sentences passed on some of Bourbon's accomplices by the Parlement; he had forbidden their release. During his captivity he seems to have relented somewhat, perhaps in line with his mother's concern to achieve a *modus vivendi* with the Parlement. De Prie and d'Escars had been released. By March 1526 only three of Bourbon's main accomplices – the seigneur de Saint-Vallier and the bishops of Autun and Le Puy – remained in prison. Saint-Vallier was released in July, the bishop of Autun was pardoned in 1527 and the fate of the bishop of Le Puy is unknown. But the king had no intention of reinstating Bourbon despite the promise contained in the treaty of Madrid. The fact that the traitor was now dead did not preclude the need for a judgment.

In July 1527 the *procureur général* submitted two indictments to a special

---

[51] *Ordonnances*, v. No. 463, pp. 81–3.

[52] Hanley (p. 71) argues that the king's action shows that he 'took pains to dissociate a willful act of royal legislation from the other event, the *Lit de Justice* assembly'. This misses the point that his very absence served to underline the Parlement's humiliation.

[53] Doucet, ii. 256–7.

commission appointed to try the duke: the first, repeated some wild accusations dating back to 1523 and subsequently disproved, while the second focused on Bourbon's more recent crimes, notably his invasion of Provence and the sack of Rome. Only four days were needed to prepare the case against him. On 26 July Bourbon's trial by the court of peers began in the king's presence. It took place in the *Grand' Chambre* of the Parlement and the attendance comprised *baillis* and *sénéchaux* who had been specially chosen because some of Bourbon's alleged crimes had been committed in their jurisdictional areas. The trial began with an usher summoning the dead duke to appear; when no one responded the court got down to business. The *procureur-général* demanded that Bourbon's memory be condemned, his coat-of-arms effaced and his property sequestered. A purely formal debate ensued, after which the court drew up its verdict, which was announced the following day. This second session was even more solemn than the first: a large gathering of distinguished spectators, including foreign ambassadors, marshals of France, gentlemen of the household and officers of the king's guard listened to the Chancellor as he read out the sentence. This declared Bourbon guilty of '*lèse-majesté*, rebellion and felony' and conceded all the chief prosecutor's demands: the duke lost his coat of arms and title; his fiefs were formally annexed to the royal demesne; and all his personal property was confiscated. Some of this was restored to Bourbon's heirs under the peace of Cambrai, but only after protracted litigation. Thus, in August 1538 the Constable's aunt, Louise, princesse de La Roche-sur-Yon, received the county of Montpensier, the *dauphiné* of Auvergne and three lordships. Final settlement was not achieved till the reign of Charles IX.[54]

The fall of Semblançay (January–August 1527)

Finally, as part of the king's campaign to remove anything likely to cast a shadow on his restored authority, he came down heavily on the financial officials whom he held largely responsible for his recent misfortunes. The Parlement, in its remonstrances to the Regent of 10 April 1525, had already drawn attention to corruption among the king's servants and had proposed the establishment of a commission to investigate cases of embezzlement. On 26 November 1526, Francis set up a six-man commission with powers of detention and punishment equal to those exercised by the Parlement. This was the effective beginning of the *Commission de la Tour Carrée* which was officially set up on 17 November 1527, the day after Francis had wound up the auditing activities of the commission of January 1523. These were now

---

[54] Doucet, ii. 246–50; C.A.F., iii. 10231.

entrusted to the *Chambre des Comptes* which regained its full powers, while the *Tour Carrée* acted as a quite distinct criminal court.[55]

The principal victim of the new commission was the elderly Jacques de Beaune, baron de Semblançay, who had been such a powerful member of the royal administration until 1523, when his accounts had been originally scrutinized. Although he had been cleared by the commissioners in 1525, he had not regained royal favour and had retired to Tours during the regency of Louise of Savoy. Here, it seems, he spent much of his time pursuing creditors.[56] However, on 13 January 1527, after Semblançay had returned to Paris on business, he was arrested and thrown into the Bastille.[57] The decision to arrest him was taken by the king and his council. Among the members present were three men (Jean de Selve, Antoine du Bourg and Jean Ravier) who were close associates of Duprat. On 10 January they had been looking for ways of raising within five days 370,000 *livres* needed for the payment of troops.[58] Semblançay was known to be a very rich man and the prospect of confiscating his property must have been tempting. What is more, the king still owed him 1,190,374 *livres*. Other financiers arrested at the same time were Roberto Albizzi, the Lyons banker, and Jean Prévost, *trésorier des finances*. Albizzi was one of Semblançay's business associates, but Prévost was a protégé of Louise and his arrest was widely interpreted as a move by the government to create an illusion of fairness.[59]

Semblançay's trial in 1527 was not a retrial, for no criminal charges had previously been levelled against him. Now, however, he had to face a formidable indictment amounting to a charge of *lèse-majesté*. He was accused *inter alia* of misappropriating royal funds, obliging the king to borrow while he himself owed Francis money, taking bribes, fiddling taxes and fraudulently concealing the extent of his private wealth.[60] By modern standards, his bookkeeping was not impeccable, but discrepancies in his accounts were due less to dishonesty than to the complexities of sixteenth-century fiscal practice. Semblançay's situation was also complicated by his combining the roles of private banker and public servant. He tried to keep them separate by the use of intermediaries in London and Lyons, but his devious operations created misunderstandings and exposed him to the charge of misappropriating royal funds. Yet the number of people who testified against him was surprisingly small.

Semblançay's trial was a travesty, his judges being government creatures or

---

[55] P. Hamon, 'L'Argent du roi: finances et gens de finances en France au temps de François Ier', 2 vols. (unpublished doctoral thesis. University of Paris 1. 1993), i. 348–51; Doucet, ii. 106–7.

[56] A. Spont, *Semblançay* (1895), pp. 239–42; Doucet, ii. 225–6; Hamon, i. 399–400.

[57] *J.B.P.*, pp. 253–4.   [58] Hamon, i. 417.   [59] Doucet, ii. 225–6.

[60] Doucet, ii. 228–30

personal enemies. Although the baron produced documentary refutation of the charges against him, the verdict was never in doubt: he was found guilty on 9 August and sentenced to death.[61] The sentence was unusually terse: it failed to discuss the charges in detail and offered no reason for setting aside the decision of the enquiry commission in 1523. An appeal lodged by Semblançay with the Parlement was dismissed on the ground that his judges had been *parlementaires* whose verdict was final. The accused wrote to Francis reminding him of his past services to the crown; but the king was unmoved. He ordered the baron's immediate execution.[62]

On 11 August Semblançay was taken from the Bastille to the gibbet at Montfaucon. The old man (he was about eighty) was escorted through Paris by troops under Gilles Maillart, *lieutenant-criminel* of the Châtelet. He appeared calm and acknowledged friends in the crowd of spectators. It was not hostile. The *gens de finances* were not popular, yet Semblançay attracted sympathy on account of his age and dignified bearing. 'He was much pitied and mourned by the people' wrote a chronicler, 'who would have been pleased if the king had seen fit to spare him.'[63] Their sympathy may have stemmed from the unpopularity of Duprat, who was known to be Semblançay's enemy. An *Epigramme* by Clément Marot expressed their feelings:

> *Lorsque Maillart, juge d'enfer, menoit*
> *A Montfaulcon Semblançay l'âme rendre*
> *A vostre advis, lequel des deux tenoit*
> *Meilleur maintien? Pour le vous faire entendre,*
> *Maillart sembloit homme que mort va prendre,*
> *Et Semblançay fut si ferme viellart*
> *Quo l'on cuidoit, pour vray qu'il menast pendre*
> *A Montfaulcon le lieutenant Maillart.*[64]

Twice on the way to the gibbet and once at its foot Semblançay had to listen to a public recital of his crimes. Outside the convent of the Filles-Dieu his bonnet was removed and he was handed a wooden cross after receiving the customary gifts of bread and wine. At Montfaucon, he had to wait six hours before he was hanged. Thus ended the career of the man once described as 'quasi king in France'.[65] A few days later, his body vanished mysteriously. Duprat, who never missed an opportunity for vindictiveness, ordered a search so that the corpse might be strung up again. It was eventually found dismembered in a graveyard

---

[61] *J.B.P.*, p. 255.   [62] Spont, p. 262.   [63] Versoris, p. 106.

[64] C. Marot, *Les épigrammes*, ed. C. A. Mayer (London, 1970), p. 129. 'When Maillart, judge of hell, led Semblançay to Montfaucon to render up his soul, which of the two, in your opinion, had the better bearing? You should know that Maillart looked like a man whom death was about to carry off, whereas Semblançay was such a strong old man that he seemed to be leading the lieutenant Maillart to Montfaucon to be hanged.'

[65] Versoris, p. 106.

near Pantin by one of Semblançay's servants and decently buried in the church of Sainte-Catherine-des-Ecoliers.[66]

As an act of cruelty untypical of Francis, Semblançay's execution calls for an explanation. It may be taken as another aspect of the king's campaign to regain mastery of his kingdom after the crisis of 1525–26. It may also have been intended as a warning to all royal servants, and not merely those responsible for the royal finances.[67]

This was not the end of the Semblançay affair. For his widow, Jeanne Ruzé, and his son, Guillaume, appealed against the sentence. They did so probably to focus public attention on a miscarriage of justice for which they blamed the Chancellor. They said they would press their appeal until justice had been restored in France. The challenge could not be ignored by the crown. A commission made up of two presidents from every Parlement was appointed to examine the appeal. On 11 February 1529 Semblançay's sentence was confirmed and the appellants condemned. Jeanne's property was confiscated and her son, who had fled to Germany, sentenced to death. Two lawyers, who had advised them, were suspended. Eventually, however, the sentences were commuted. Jeanne recovered part of her property, Guillaume was pardoned and the two lawyers were reinstated.[68]

Yet the hunting-down of allegedly corrupt financiers continued till 1536. Among the victims were many of Semblançay's relatives, notably his nephew, Gilles Berthelot, who had to repay 29,399 *livres* in addition to paying a fine of 20,000 *livres*, his daughter, Marie de Beaune, widow of Raoul Hurault, who was fined 100,000 *livres*, and his grandnephew, Antoine Bohier, who was fined 190,000 *livres*. Nor was Semblançay the only financier to die for his alleged malpractices: Jean Poncher, *trésorier-général* of Languedoc was executed in September 1535.[69]

---

[66] Spont, pp. 263–4. According to Brantôme, many people thought Francis should have pardoned Semblançay because of his venerable age, his services to four kings and because Francis was in the habit of calling him 'father'. Brantôme, *Œuvres complètes*, ed. L. Lalanne (1864–82), iii. 90.

[67] Hamon, i. 406.   [68] Doucet, ii. 238–9; *J.B.P.*, pp. 262, 422–3; *C.A.F.*, i. 3316, 3646.

[69] Spont, pp. 274–7; *J.B.P.*, pp. 393–4; Guiffrey, p. 139. See below, pp. 347–9.

Chapter thirteen

The 'Peace of the Ladies' (3 August 1529)

In 1527 Francis I was anxious to recover his two sons who were being held in Spain by Charles V as hostages pending fulfilment of the treaty of Madrid, but he also wanted to renegotiate that treaty. He had broken it by his refusal to hand over Burgundy, yet the Emperor would not accept a cash ransom instead. Francis was as yet unprepared for war. He hoped still to persuade Charles to release his sons on reasonable terms by simply putting pressure on him diplomatically. He had joined the League of Cognac and stirred up trouble for Charles in Italy but had failed to help his allies. Pope Clement VII blamed Francis for his misfortunes which had culminated in the sack of Rome.

The treaty of Amiens (18 August 1527)

An immediate consequence of the sack of Rome was a closer understanding between France and England, for Henry VIII was afraid that the pope, who had become virtually the Emperor's prisoner, would not be free to grant him his divorce from the Emperor's aunt, Catherine of Aragon. A new sense of urgency animated Wolsey's foreign policy: peace remained his objective, but now he wanted it not only for reasons of national or personal prestige, but also to free the pope.[1] It was primarily with this end in view that early in August he met Francis at Amiens.[2] On the 16th the cardinal informed Henry VIII that he had finished his business with the king of France, save for one thing: he had not told him of Henry's intended divorce. This he proposed to do in 'so cloudy and dark a sort' that Francis would not realize Henry's 'utter determination'.[3]

---

[1] S. J. Gunn. 'Wolsey's Foreign Policy and the Domestic Crisis of 1527–8' in *Cardinal Wolsey: Church, State and Art*, ed. S. J. Gunn and P. G. Lindley (Cambridge, 1991), pp. 149–77.

[2] On 23 June Francis explained that he could not leave Saint-Denis because of a tertian fever. But on 2 July he was said to be out of danger. His health, however, remained troublesome. When Wolsey saw him on 5 August, he was 'lying on a couch with a white sheet made for the easement of his leg, which was so swelled he could not stand'. *L.P.*, iv. 3193, 3225, 3309, 3337.

[3] *Ibid.*, iv. 3350.

54. The golden *bulla* used to seal the treaty of Amiens, 1527. Francis I is seated under a rich cloth of estate of which the curtains are being drawn back by angels. On the reverse, the arms of France encircled by the collar of the order of St Michael.

On 18 August the treaty of Amiens was signed: Mary Tudor was promised to the duc d'Orléans, and Henry waived his objection to the marriage of Francis and Eleanor of Portugal (which was less dangerous to England now that Charles had a son). In the event of war with the Emperor, English merchants would have the same privileges in France as they had previously enjoyed in the Netherlands. Neither party would attend a General Council as long as the pope remained a prisoner.[4] The meeting at Amiens was followed by a conference at Compiègne, which considered measures for the government of the church during Clement's captivity. The Anglo-French talks were rounded off by an exchange of honours: Montmorency went to England to confer the order of St Michael on Henry VIII who reciprocated by sending the Garter to Francis. Louise of Savoy was delighted: now that the two kings were 'under one clothing', she hoped they would continue 'in one mind and heart'.[5]

Francis, in the meantime, committed himself to armed intervention in Italy. In August 1527 an army under Marshal Lautrec crossed the Alps and overran Lombardy, except Milan, while Andrea Doria, who had entered the service of France, captured Genoa. In the autumn Lautrec was ordered to march on Naples instead of completing the conquest of Milan. He moved to Parma,

[4] *Ibid.*, iv. 3356; *Ordonnances*, v. No. 466.
[5] *L.P.*, iv. 3574; Decrue, i. 97–9. See *Henry VIII: A European Court in England*, ed. D. Starkey (London, 1991), pp. 96–7. The book containing the statutes of the Order of St Michael was presented to Henry VIII by Montmorency during a brilliant ceremony at Greenwich on 10 November 1527.

remaining there from 7 November till 14 December. Meanwhile, Alfonso d'Este, duke of Ferrara, joined the league. He was given the towns of Modena and Reggio by some cardinals acting for the pope and promised the hand of Princess Renée, daughter of Louis XII, for his son Ercole, along with the county of Chartres. Alfonso, for his part, promised to pay 6,000 ducats a month to Lautrec for half a year.[6] This must have pleased the marshal who had complained repeatedly of not receiving enough money from France to pay his troops.[7]

The Assembly of Notables (16 and 20 December 1527)

On 16 December Francis held a meeting in Paris which has traditionally been called an Assembly of Notables.[8] It took place in the *Grand' Chambre* of the Parlement but was representative of various estates and corporations. The 200 delegates were drawn from the nobility, clergy, parlements and Paris. The assembly's purpose was twofold: first, to give legitimacy to the decision already taken by the king and his council to break the treaty of Madrid; secondly, to raise money with which to pay either the ransom for the king's sons or to make war on the Emperor should he persist in demanding Burgundy as the price of their release.

In an opening speech the king tried to justify his policy since the start of his reign.[9] His aim had always been peace, he explained, but his enemies, including the duc de Bourbon, had driven him to war. It was as a defensive measure that he had again invaded Italy. As for the treaty of Madrid, it had been negotiated by his mother and his ambassadors; he did not feel bound to honour it or his oath, as both had been extorted under duress. Turning to recent events, Francis explained that he had simply used the League of Cognac to force the Emperor to waive his demand for Burgundy, while he himself concluded an alliance with England. He and Henry VIII, he said, had submitted reasonable terms to the Emperor and were awaiting his reply. But, whatever this might be, 2 million *écus* would be needed either for his sons' ransom or to make war on

---

[6] *L.P.*, iv. 3578; *C.A.F.*, i. 2822. The marriage between Ercole and Renée was concluded on 10 February 1528, when the county of Chartres was turned into a duchy. See *Ordonnances*, v. p. 36n.

[7] Decrue, i. 101–3; B. de Chantérac, *Odet de Foix, vicomte de Lautrec* (1930), p. 100.

[8] S. H. Hanley, *The 'Lit de Justice' of the Kings of France* (Princeton, 1983), pp. 72–87. The author regards this meeting as another *Lit de Justice* and describes it as 'a constitutional assembly designed to reaffirm precepts of French Public law through ritual and discourse'. Its essential purpose, in my view, was to raise money for the ransom. This explains the assembly's representative nature and procedures. In a letter of 26 February 1528 to the *Bureau de la Ville* of Paris Francis refers to '*la grosse Assemblée par nous derrenièrement faicte en nostre Court de Parlement à Paris*' *R.D.B.V.P.*, ii. 10. See my 'Francis I and the *Lit de Justice*: A "Legend" Defended', *F.H.*, 7 (1993), pp. 53–83; see also below p. 533.

[9] T. Godefroy, *Le cérémonial françois* (1649), ii. 478; Doucet, ii. 288–96; *R.D.B.V.P.*, ii. 1–3.

the Emperor. In conclusion, the king asked the delegates for their views on the validity of the peace of Madrid: on whether or not, having broken his oath, he was bound to return to prison; and on his demand for money. He made it abundantly plain, however, that he was consulting them simply to 'honour' them, not because he was constitutionally bound to do so.

The king's speech was, it seems, well received. Each group of delegates met separately to consider its response. On 20 December they unanimously gave Francis all he wanted: the treaty of Madrid was declared null and void, as was his oath. He was therefore released from the obligation to return to prison. All four groups, moreover, agreed to contribute the sum demanded by Francis. Speaking for the clergy, cardinal de Bourbon offered 1.3 million *livres* to be divided among the clergy in their provincial assemblies. In return, Francis was asked to rescue the pope, to stamp out Lutheranism and to uphold the Gallican liberties. The duc de Vendôme offered him the goods and lives of the nobles present at the meeting and expressed the hope that the others would do likewise. President de Selve gave an assurance that members of the parlements, would offer their lives and goods. Lastly, the *prévôt des marchands*, speaking for Paris, offered to pay part of the royal ransom.[10]

Promises were one thing; raising the money was another. At provincial synods held in Paris and Bourges the clergy agreed to raise four tenths (i.e. 40 per cent) of one year's revenues from benefices, but several prelates asked that payment should be made in two annual instalments. Tournon complained that he had not encountered so much opposition since he was in Spain. In the end, however, the clergy paid up, though we cannot be certain that the full amount promised by them was collected.[11]

The nobles proved less open-handed. At a gathering in Paris of nobles from the Ile-de-France, on 28 September 1529, Francis admitted that in the past they had served him with only their persons; he had always tried to spare them the *arrière-ban*. His present request for aid, he said, would help preserve their liberty. He repudiated a rumour that he intended subjecting them to the *taille*. 'I am a *gentilhomme*', he said, 'it is the principal title I bear and the one I esteem most ... I pray you ... to offer me such gifts and presents as will enable me to know the love and affection you bear me.' They agreed to contribute 10 per cent of the annual revenues of their fiefs and sub-fiefs. Francis then looked to the rest of the provincial nobility. On 5 October the *baillis* were ordered to summon all nobles and other royal fief-holders. In October 1529, Francis asked the nobles of Anjou to be at least as

[10] Russell Major, *Representative Institutions*, pp. 136–7.
[11] M. François, *Le cardinal François de Tournon* (1951), pp. 61–2; A. Buisson, *Antoine Duprat* (1935), p. 295; P. Hamon, 'Un après-guerre financier: la rançon de François premier' in *Etudes Champenoises*, vol. 7 (1990), p. 13.

generous as those of the Ile-de-France. In the Boulonnais, they began by offering only a fifth. Montmorency was so upset by their meanness that he refused to transmit their offer to the king. He instructed the *sénéchal* not to accept anything from them until they were 'prepared to do as all the others have done'. In the end, they complied. In Touraine, Normandy and Langue-doc, the nobles were more forthcoming, and in Lyons they even showed enthusiasm.[12]

In Paris the ransom demand caused a great stir. On 26 February 1528 royal commissioners came to the Town Hall with a request for 100,000 gold *écus*. The *Bureau de la Ville* was so appalled by the size of the demand that it promptly sent a delegation to the king at Saint-Germain. He agreed to take only 150,000 *livres*, provided this concession was kept secret from other towns. The *Bureau* decided to levy contributions based on a valuation of house rentals. On 28 August, after the various *quartiers* had submitted assessments, it was decided to levy 114,000 *livres* from a third of all rentals. The balance of 36,000 *livres* was to be raised by a surcharge on the wealthiest house-owners and tenants. By 27 November Francis had become impatient. He wrote to the *prévôt de Paris*:

> I have seen the reply given to you by the Parisians. I find this business very slow; when one difficulty has been overcome, they find another; meanwhile, time is passing to my prejudice and damage. All the other towns of my kingdom, which are willing to help me, are waiting to know what arrangements Paris will make, which is delaying my affairs everywhere ... To conclude, bring this matter to an end to-morrow or I will consider what action to take ...[13]

The following day the levy was authorized, but the money came in only slowly and incompletely. On 25 September 1529 Francis created a duty on wine to make up for the shortfall. The *Bureau de la Ville* was also afraid that the assessment by the *quarteniers* might be used for a future levy. To avert this danger it obtained permission to return its accounts, not to the *Chambre des Comptes*, but to its own *Chambre du Conseil*, and thereafter to destroy them. This meant that, if the king ever asked for a similar contribution, the whole laborious exercise would have to be repeated from scratch.[14] The actual collection of the levy was by no means straightforward. Such was the resistance encountered by the *quarteniers* that they were instructed not to visit recalci-trant houses more than twice or three times, but to send in the troops. But even these were not always reliable: they were threatened with the loss of their

---

[12] Russell Major, *Representative Institutions*, pp. 138–9; P. Hamon, 'Un après-guerre financier', pp. 13–14; Decrue, i. 136–7.
[13] *R.D.B.V.P.*, ii. 44.   [14] *Ibid.*, ii. 42–3.

uniform (*hocqueton*) if they refused to enter houses 'to collect the moneys given to the king'. A captain of arquebusiers resigned rather than accompany his men on their round. Yet, Francis apparently got his due.[15]

The response of the provincial towns to the king's demand for ransom money was generally unenthusiastic. The reduction conceded to Paris was evidently not kept secret for long. When Lyons was asked for 35,000 *livres*, it asked the king for a reduction 'such as he had granted the town of Paris'. On 2 May his commissioners asked Rouen for 75,000 *livres*. The town sent a deputation to plead for a reduction. It cornered the king on his return from Mass and was referred to his council. Duprat told the deputies the tax was just, that Francis could force the Rouennais to pay though that was not his wish, and that everyone, including himself, was contributing. The deputies, however, stood their ground, as did the king. Finally, in January 1529 Rouen offered 30,000 *livres*. When this was refused, it raised its offer to 40,000. Finally, after further haggling, the king agreed to take 50,000. Similar deals were made with other towns: Orléans won a reduction from 30,000 to 20,000 *livres*, Bourges from 15,000 to 7,500 *livres*, and Beauvais from 12,000 to 4,000 *livres*.[16] Rheims still owed 4,000 *livres* out of 10,000 as late as 4 May 1531, when its revenues were temporarily seized by the crown. The dispute was only resolved after the local *grenetier* had agreed to lend the money owed by the town. The provincial estates, like the towns, had to contribute to the ransom. The heaviest burden – 400,000 *livres* – was imposed on Burgundy as the price of remaining French. Contributions from the other estates were negotiated in the same traditional way as were taxes.[17]

Finally, various methods were used to raise money from royal office-holders. As the Italian bankers, to whom the crown was still heavily in debt, were unwilling to make new advances, Francis had to borrow from his entourage, including great nobles and bishops. Montmorency's mother-in-law lent 7,000 *écus*, his sister the *maréchale* de Châtillon 6,000 and Guillaume du Bellay 10,000. The Grand Master himself acted as guarantor for part of the royal loans. Money was also saved by cutting the wages of public servants. Thus on 6 April 1527 financial officers of the *prévôté* of Paris were taxed one-eighth of the value of their offices under pain of suspension. In certain cases wages were stopped altogether: for example, the king stopped the wages of the *compagnies d'ordonnances* for the last quarter of 1528.[18]

---

[15] *Ibid.*, ii. 53. On 2 July 1530 Francis informed the Parisians that his sons had been set free. He wanted them to be among the first to know 'as those who, we believe, will be more pleased than any of our other subjects'.

[16] Russell Major, *Representative Institutions*, p. 139.

[17] P. Hamon, 'Un après-guerre financier', p. 15.

[18] *Ibid.*, pp. 15–16.

Catastrophe in Italy

Charles V refused to release Francis's sons at any price unless Lautrec's army was first recalled from Italy and its conquests restored. As this condition was unacceptable to France and England, war became inevitable. On 22 January 1528 a herald from each country bade the Emperor defiance. They justified their action by reciting Charles's alleged misdeeds, including the pope's imprisonment. Replying to the French herald, the Emperor expressed surprise that Francis should feel the need to declare war, considering that he had been fighting him for six or seven years without such a formality. As for the pope, the royal champions could set their minds at rest: Clement was a free man.[19] The pope had indeed escaped to Orvieto on 6 December with the Emperor's connivance.

Among the first to feel the effects of the declaration of war were the two French hostages in Spain. So far they had been well treated, but in February the Emperor ordered their removal to a castle near Segovia and dismissed nearly all their French attendants. Eleanor of Portugal was apparently so upset that she retired to a monastery for a time. Louise of Savoy complained to Wolsey of the Emperor's inhumane treatment of her grandsons: not only had they been deprived of their servants, Charles intended to send these to the galleys. Perhaps she was exaggerating in order to prick the cardinal's conscience; for England was not yet showing much enthusiasm for the war.[20]

Even after the declaration of war, Francis and Charles engaged in a strangely archaic ritual. On 18 March Charles repeated the challenge to a duel he had already made in 1526. This time, however, he put it in writing. Ten days later Francis accepted the challenge. Charles proposed that the duel should be fought on the river Bidassoa, but his herald was kept waiting by Francis for more than a month at the Franco-Spanish border for a safe-conduct. When he eventually reached the French court, Francis would not let him carry out his instructions. He had to return to Spain, his mission unfulfilled. The Council of Castile declared that Francis had once again shown that he was no gentleman.[21]

In the end, it was in Italy, not on the Bidassoa, that the king and the Emperor fought out their quarrel. On 9 February Lautrec invaded the kingdom of Naples after overrunning the Romagna. He was greeted as a liberator by the towns of the Abruzzi and soon gained control of Apulia as well. At the end of April he reached the outskirts of Naples which was being blockaded by a fleet

---

[19] *L.P.*, iv. 3453, 3455, 3597, 3826; K. Brandi, *The Emperor Charles V*, tr. C. V. Wedgwood (London, 1939), p. 265.

[20] *L.P.*, iv. 3982, 4266.

[21] Mignet, *La rivalité de François Ier et de Charles-Quint*, ii. 394–408; Granvelle, *Papiers d'état*, i. 360–424.

under Filippino Doria, Andrea's nephew. An imperial attempt to break the blockade ended in disaster on 28 April and no one expected Naples to hold out much longer. Francis wrote of his joy to Montmorency.[22] But the situation was not quite as he imagined it. Andrea Doria was dissatisfied with his French employer. As a Genoese, he backed his compatriots' claim to the Ligurian port of Savona, which Francis refused to give up. Doria also complained that he had not been rewarded for capturing the prince of Orange in July 1527; nor had he been paid his expenses for the reconquest of Genoa and an expedition to Sardinia. The last straw was the appointment of a Frenchman to lead the fleet that was about to leave for Naples. In June 1528 Andrea retired to La Spezia and ordered his nephew to join him. Only then did Francis take the Genoese seriously: he ordered Savona to be restored to them but Andrea had already decided to switch his services to the Emperor.[23]

On 4 July Filippino Doria withdrew his fleet from the bay of Naples, so that supplies were again able to reach the city. Soon afterwards there was an outbreak of plague or cholera in Lautrec's camp outside Naples. His captains urged him to retire to neighbouring hills, where the air was purer, but he preferred to stay in his sun-baked camp amidst a fast growing heap of rotting corpses. On 17 August he himself was carried off.[24] By then his army was only a third of its original size. Lautrec's successor, the marquis of Saluzzo, ordered a retreat, but surrendered soon afterwards. On 9 September the prince of Orange informed Charles V that the war in southern Italy was almost over: only a few pockets of resistance remained in Apulia and Calabria. Other disasters awaited the French in north Italy. On 12 September Genoa regained its independence with Andrea Doria's help, and on 21 October the French garrison in Savona surrendered. The whole Ligurian coast fell into enemy hands. And there was worse to come. In 1529 the comte de Saint-Pol attempted to retake Genoa only to be defeated and captured on 21 June at Landriano.

The French collapse in Italy convinced the pope that he had nothing to gain by being neutral. Only the Emperor could provide him with the military support needed to restore his Medici kinsmen to power in Florence; only he could halt the progress of Lutheranism in Germany and the westward expansion of the Turks. So for once Clement acted decisively. 'I have quite made up mind', he announced, 'to become an Imperialist, and to live and die as such.'[25] On 29 June he signed the treaty of Barcelona with Charles V. This provided for the restoration of Medici rule in Florence and the return of Ravenna, Cervia, Modena and Reggio to the pope. Clement, for his part, promised to crown Charles Emperor and to absolve all those responsible for the sack of

[22] Chantérac, pp. 99–107; Mignet, ii. 430.
[23] V.-L. Bourrilly, *Jacques Colin, abbé de Saint-Ambroise* (1905), pp. 14–35; *Ordonnances*, v. No. 489.
[24] Chantérac, pp. 111–14; *L.P.*, iv. 4663.   [25] *C.S.P. Span.*, iv. 73.

A res ſcilicet maxima laude
digna : quæ paucis annis
tranſactis Pariſiẛa te Chriſtianiſſimo
rege Franciſco celebrata eſt / nam cum
in vrbem hanc Lutherani quidam

55. Francis I making reparation for the mutilation by heretics of a statue in
Paris of the Virgin and Child, 1528. Miniature from Chantilly Ms. 892/1485.
The king, holding a lighted candle, kneels to receive from the bishop of Paris a
new statue to replace the old one in the empty niche. Pieces of the broken statue
can be seen next to the king.

56. Francis I and his suite receive communion. Detail from one of the 'puys d'Amiens', a series of altarpieces commissioned by the town's principal confraternity. The king holds out a hand to receive a gold coin symbolizing the Eucharist. Behind him a fool apes his gesture, a grotesque touch typical of the anonymous artist. Two pages hold the royal sword and a falcon.

Rome. A marriage was arranged between his nephew Alessandro and Charles's illegitimate daughter Margaret.[26] A direct consequence of the treaty was Clement's decision, on 16 July, to revoke Henry VIII's divorce suit to Rome which precipitated Wolsey's fall and led ultimately to England's breach with Rome.

The fight against heresy

In December 1527, after the French clergy had called for the extirpation of 'the damned and insufferable Lutheran sect', Francis promised to demonstrate that he was 'The Most Christian King' in deed as well as in name. His profession of orthodoxy may have been, at least in part, a *quid pro quo* for the clergy's generous offer of 1.3 million *livres* towards his sons' ransom.

In June 1528 the king was offered a chance to fulfil his pledge after the mutilation of a statue of the Virgin and Child in Paris. This, one of the earliest acts of iconoclasm of the French Reformation, may be taken as evidence of a more radical form of religious dissent than had previously been seen in France. For the smashing of religious images was less typical of Lutheranism than of the movement commonly known as the 'Radical Reformation'. It was Karlstadt, not Luther, who called for the removal of images in 1522; Luther described them as 'useful and commendable as a remembrance and a sign'. The fiercest opponents of images were the Zürich radicals, Ludwig Haetzer and Leo Jud. Francis showed his revulsion from the mutilation of the statue in Paris by offering a substantial reward for information about the culprits and by commissioning a new statue of wood covered with silver to replace the damaged one. He also took part in a solemn procession to the scene of the sacrilege and devoutly placed the new statue in its niche.[27]

From 3 February till 9 October 1528 a synod of the province of Sens met at the Grands Augustins, in Paris under the chairmanship of Archbishop Duprat. Some of the prelates evidently questioned the king's orthodoxy, for Duprat wrote as follows to Francis: 'A cunning spirit has tried to divert them from their good purpose. To achieve this end, it has been said that you have been displeased by their attack on Luther. I have denied this. If you please, Sire, to write them words of encouragement, this would be a most worthy deed.' We can assume that Francis followed his Chancellor's advice, for the synod pronounced its unanimous support for orthodoxy. 'Felicity and glory', it declared, 'have only belonged to princes, who, while attaching themselves unshakeably to the Catholic faith, have hunted down and exterminated heretics as the

[26] Pastor, *History of the Popes*, x. 56–7.
[27] Imbart de la Tour, iii. 262; *J.B.P.*, pp. 290–3; *R.D.B.V.P.*, ii. 24–26.

principal enemies of their crown.' Stringent measures were accordingly laid down for the suppression of heresy.[28]

Yet the reformers had not given up hope of converting the French king. They could derive some comfort from the fact that he was still protecting certain scholars and preachers from persecution. In March 1528 Berquin's trial was resumed before a commission of twelve laymen specially appointed by the pope at the king's request. The Faculty of Theology, however, accused them of being 'Lutherans' and the pope was persuaded to revoke their powers. This infuriated Francis who protested to Salviati, the papal nuncio: 'If I thought that the theologian-judges had obtained this brief', he declared, 'I would send them all to the galleys.' He added that he knew how to deal with heresy and would see to it that it did not take root in his kingdom. The news of Lautrec's crushing defeat in Italy, however, deprived Francis of leverage in his dealings with the pope. He had no choice but to accept Clement's decision.

On 15 April 1528 Berquin was found guilty of heresy and sentenced to life imprisonment. He should have accepted the verdict, as he was advised to do by his friends. But he preferred to appeal to the Parlement. Two days later, while the king was absent from Paris, the appeal was rejected and the sentence changed to one of death. Before the king could intervene a third time to save Berquin's life, he was hurriedly taken to the Place de Grève and burnt.[29]

The 'Peace of the Ladies' (3 August 1529)

By December 1528 Francis was anxiously seeking an opportunity to reopen peace negotiations with the Emperor. This was provided by a truce England and France had recently signed with Margaret of Austria, regent of the Netherlands. She was not only the Emperor's aunt, but also the sister-in-law of Louise of Savoy, who put out peace feelers when Margaret's secretary visited Paris about ratifying the truce. Margaret reacted cautiously at first, but when it became clear that Charles V would also welcome a respite from war, she sent ambassadors to Paris and eventually agreed to meet Louise at Cambrai.[30] As news of the negotiations leaked out, France's Italian allies became anxious lest Francis should desert them; but he reassured them: 'I protest', he said, 'that I would rather sacrifice my life and the lives of my children than abandon the confederates.'[31] Louise gave similar assurances. By negotiating through his

[28] Imbart de la Tour, iii. 262–7; A. Buisson, *Le chancelier Antoine Duprat* (1935), pp. 393–5; M. Veissière, *L'évêque Guillaume Briçonnet (1470–1534)* (Provins, 1986), pp. 399–409.

[29] R. Rolland, 'Le dernier procès de Louis de Berquin' in Ecole française de Rome: *Mélanges d'archéologie et d'histoire*, 12 (1892), 314–25; J. K. Farge, *Orthodoxy and Reform in Early Reformation France* (Leiden, 1985), p. 264; M. Mann, *Erasme et les débuts de la réforme française* (1934), pp. 144–8; *J.B.P.*, pp. 317–22, 423–7.

[30] Mignet, ii. 457–9.   [31] C. Terrasse, *François Ier* (1948), ii. 116.

mother, rather than directly, Francis avoided the embarrassment of bringing his Italian and English allies into the talks; he also remained free to reject any settlement that did not satisfy him. The talks at Cambrai, which began on 5 July, lasted nearly a month. Louise was accompanied by members of the king's council. Francis did not take part. He went hunting with Chabot at La Fère and Coucy, but a regular traffic of messengers kept him in touch with the progress of the negotiations. They proved far more gruelling and protracted than he had expected. Only the intervention of the papal nuncio averted a breakdown after Margaret had asked for certain border towns as securities.[32] Thereafter progress was rapid; on 3 August the treaty, which became known as 'the Peace of the Ladies', was signed. Two days later, it was celebrated in Cambrai cathedral in Francis's presence.

In all essentials, the treaty was a revision of the peace of Madrid. In place of Burgundy, the Emperor accepted a ransom of 2 million gold *écus*. Francis gave up all his Italian claims, as well as the towns of Hesdin, Arras, Lille and Tournai; also his suzerainty over Flanders and Artois. He agreed to lend Charles twelve galleys for six months and guaranteed the rights of Bourbon's heirs. Finally, he deserted his Italian allies by allowing them to be left out of the treaty; England was only accommodated at the eleventh hour. The Emperor, for his part, promised, on fulfilment of Francis's obligations, to send his sister Eleanor to France and to return the Dauphin and the duc d'Orléans.[33]

The peace of Cambrai has been described as 'wholly favourable to Charles'.[34] This is an exaggeration. It certainly contained terms humiliating to the king of France, but in two respects it was a triumph for his diplomacy: he retained Burgundy and recovered his sons for a cash ransom.[35] The peace was enormously valuable to Charles in that it enabled him to settle Italian affairs peacefully before tackling the German situation. Having been deserted by France, the Italians were unlikely to offer much resistance. Early in November Charles met the pope in Bologna where they spent four months negotiating against a background of civic revelry. The Emperor was afraid Francis would break the peace as soon as he had recovered his sons. To avert this danger a league of Italian states was formed on 23 December.[36] The Venetians agreed to restore Ravenna and Cervia to the pope, and Sforza was restored to Milan. A clause provided for the eventual admission of the duke of Ferrara. Only Florence was omitted because of its refusal to restore the Medici. Charles placed his army at the pope's disposal. On 12 August 1530 Florence surrendered after an eight months' siege. Eighteen months later, Clement's nephew Alessandro became its hereditary duke. In the meantime, Charles attained his highest

---

[32] V.-L. Bourrilly, *Guillaume du Bellay, seigneur de Langey* (1905), pp. 72–4.
[33] *Ordonnances*, v. No. 507. Potter (*War and Government*, pp. 272–5) examines closely the impact of the peace of Cambrai on the complexities of France's northern border.
[34] Brandi, *Charles V*, p. 279.   [35] J. Jacquart, *François Ier* (1981), p. 219.   [36] *L.P.*, iv. 6101.

ambition: on 24 February, the anniversary of his birth and of his victory at Pavia, he was crowned Holy Roman Emperor in San Petronio at Bologna. A month later he left for Germany to preside at the diet of Augsburg.

The princes' ransom

There was as much scepticism in Europe about the peace of Cambrai as there had been about that of Madrid. It was widely believed that Francis would again break his word once his sons had been returned to him. This time, however, he could not say that he had acted under duress. He duly ratified the treaty on 20 October 1529 and instructed the parlements and local estates to follow suit.[37] On 21 February he appointed Montmorency and Tournon to supervise arrangements for the return of his sons.[38] The two commissioners arrived in Bayonne on 22 March and for the next three months they worked closely together, helped by a large team of financial experts. While the Grand Master dealt mainly with diplomatic business, Tournon (who had become a cardinal on 10 March) supervised the collection of the ransom for the king's sons.[39]

The treaty of Cambrai stipulated three ways in which the ransom of 2 million gold *écus au soleil* were to be paid: first, a single lump sum of 1.2 million *écus*; secondly, reimbursement of Charles V's debts to Henry VIII, estimated at 290,000 *écus*; and thirdly, payment of an annuity of 25,500 *écus* to be raised from the lands held by the duchesse de Vendôme in the Netherlands. Francis managed to get some relief from Henry VIII. On 6 August he promised to pay Henry 185,000 *écus* in half-yearly instalments of 50,000 *écus*. The agreement, however, did not allow redemption of the *Fleur-de-lis*, a rich jewel the Emperor Maximilian had pawned in England in 1508 for 50,000 crowns; nor did it cover the so-called 'Windsor indemnity', which Charles had promised Henry in 1522 as compensation for the loss of his French pension. On 16 August, therefore, Francis sent Guillaume du Bellay to England to seek further alleviation of his financial obligations.[40] Henry would not consider this until he had been shown a complete text of the treaty, but on 31 August he agreed not only to remit the redemption money for the *Fleur-de-lis*, but also to return the jewel. As an additional concession, he remitted an instalment of his French pension for 1529, provided this was spent on the French princes' ransom.[41] In exchange for such generosity, Henry looked to Francis to help him get his divorce from Catherine of Aragon.

In spite of the English concessions, Francis still found it difficult to raise the

---

[37] C.A.F., i. 3514. [38] *Ibid.*, i. 3624. [39] François, *François de Tournon*, p. 77.
[40] Bourrilly, *Guillaume du Bellay*, pp. 75–80; L.P., iv. 5871, 5911.
[41] L.P., iv. 6227; Bourrilly, *Guillaume du Bellay*, pp. 88–9; *Ordonnances*, vi. Nos. 524–5; Potter, *War and Government*, p. 275.

huge ransom for his sons. France had been bled white by his earlier demands, and although his subjects had made generous promises at the assembly in December 1527 they did not pay up with any great alacrity, as we have seen. The collection of the moneys was also hampered by corruption and inefficiency within the royal administration. The weight and alloy of the gold crowns arriving in Bayonne were found to be below the standards laid down in the treaty. Following an enquiry, the mints of Dauphiné and Provence were temporarily shut down. Additional gold crowns had to be found to make up the deficiency in the amount collected. By 9 April no more *écus au soleil* could be found, so foreign coins circulating in France were rounded up. These, however, were of inferior alloy and the imperial commissioners insisted on their being melted down and re-minted as *écus au soleil* at Francis's expense. The collectors of the *taille* were also very slow in sending their revenues to Bayonne. As late as 2 April one of them had still not sent money due from the October quarter. Nor did the imperial commissioners help: they quibbled over every transaction and asked concessions not mentioned in the treaty. In each case Francis instructed his agents to give way.[42]

Because of all these complications and others too numerous and petty to mention here, the date of 1 March, originally fixed for the release of the king's sons, had to be repeatedly postponed. It was not until 10 June that Don Alvares de Lugo formally acknowledged receipt of the ransom on the Emperor's behalf, and 1 July that it was actually exchanged for the two princes and their future step-mother, Eleanor of Portugal, on the Bidassoa. On 3 July Francis met his new wife at Roquefort-de-Marsan. Although they had already been married by proxy, a second ceremony in the presence of both partners was evidently felt to be desirable, if only to underline Francis's sincerity. This took place on 7 July in a chapel adjoining the monastery of Beyries.[43] Thus was the peace of Cambrai sealed; Francis was now the brother-in-law of his chief rival and enemy.

Queen Eleanor and the duchesse d'Etampes

The successful outcome of the Bayonne talks greatly enhanced Montmorency's standing at court. Congratulations reached him from all parts. As the court travelled back to Paris, the Grand Master retired to Chantilly. Already a very rich man, he became even more so following the death of his old and much respected father, Guillaume, in May 1531. Anne acquired two-thirds of the paternal inheritance, leaving the rest to his brother François.[44]

---

[42] François, *François de Tournon*, pp. 76–82; Decrue, i. 141–53; *Correspondance du cardinal François de Tournon*, ed. M. François (1946), p. 62.

[43] François, *François de Tournon*, pp. 85–7; Decrue, i. 159–62.   [44] Decrue, i. 166–7, 170–1.

57. A satirical portrait of Francis I and his second queen Eleanor of Portugal.

Early in 1531 Montmorency supervised arrangements for the coronation of Queen Eleanor. This took place at Saint-Denis on 5 March and was followed two days later by the queen's entry into Paris. The Grand Master's feelings for Eleanor were nothing short of a cult. Frenchmen, he thought, should thank

58. Francis I. Oil painting attributed to Jean and François Clouet. This splendid portrait is one of only two large-scale portraits of the king. It probably dates from soon after his release from captivity in Spain. He wears the collar of the order of St Michael. The knotwork embroidered in the clear vertical bands of his doublet recall the girdle that was his mother's emblem.

God for giving them 'so beautiful and virtuous a lady'.[45] But Francis was less enthusiastic. As Sir Francis Bryan told Henry VIII, all was not well with the royal couple. His reasons were as follows:

> For the first, being both in one house they lie not together once in four nights; another he speaks very seldom unto her openly; another, he is never out of my lady's chamber, and all for Hely's sake, his old lover; another is, there has been no feast or banquet yet, since the beginning of the triumph, but, the table furnished, he has come and sat in the midst of the board, where Hely has sat, and the Cardinal of Lorraine and the Admiral likewise with their lovers. He has also divers times ridden six or seven miles from the Queen and lain out four or five days together, as it is said, at the houses of his old lovers.

The king's behaviour during the queen's entry into Paris must have raised many eyebrows:

> and the same day she should make her entry into Paris, he, having knowledge where Hely and divers other ladies and gentlewomen stood, took with him the Admiral and Cardinal of Lorraine; and they, finding these gentlewomen in the said house, the French king took Hely and set her before him in an open window and there stood devising with her two long hours in the sight and face of all the people, which was not a little marvelled at of the beholders.[46]

Two years later Marguerite de Navarre told the duke of Norfolk that no man could be less satisfied with his wife than her brother; for the past seven months 'he neither lay with her, nor yet meddled with her'. Norfolk asked why. '*Purce quil ne le trouve plesaunt a son apetyde*', she replied, 'nor when he doth lie with her, he cannot sleep; and when he lieth from her no man sleepeth better.' Again Norfolk pressed for an explanation. 'She is very hot in bed', replied Marguerite, 'and desireth to be too much embraced', whereupon she 'fell upon a great laughter, saying "I would not for all the good in Paris that the king of Navarre were no better pleased to be in my bed than my brother is to be in hers".'[47]

Eleanor, it seems, also failed to get on with her mother-in-law, but she did not have to put up with her for long. Louise, who had been riddled with gout for many years, died at Grez-sur-Loing on 22 September 1531. Her 'Caesar' was not at her bedside, being with Montmorency at Chantilly. But he gave her a splendid funeral. Her body was taken first to the abbey at Saint-Maur-des-Fossés, where her wax effigy was displayed, then to Paris for the funeral service at Notre-Dame, and finally to the abbey of Saint-Denis for burial on 19 October. Louise's inheritance was even larger than her avarice had led people to expect: her moveables were valued at 150,000 *écus*, while her lands included Angoumois, Anjou and Maine (given to her by Francis) and Bourbonnais, Beaujolais, Auvergne, Châtellerault, Forez, Marche, Montpensier and Cler-

---

[45] *Ibid.*, i. 164.   [46] *St.P.*, vii. 891. I have modernized the spelling.   [47] *L.P.*, vi. 682.

mont (taken from the Constable of Bourbon). All were now absorbed into the royal domain.[48]

As for the king's official mistress, Anne d'Heilly, her position at court grew from strength to strength. Following the death of the king's mother, she became the governess of his daughters, Madeleine and Marguerite. About 1534 Francis married her off to Jean de Brosse, seigneur de Penthièvre, and on 23 June he gave them both the county of Etampes, raising it later to ducal status. Thus did Anne become the duchesse d'Etampes, the title by which she is best remembered. In spite of her marriage she remained at court and exercised a powerful influence on the king till the end of the reign.[49]

[48] Terrasse, *François Ier*, ii. 150–2.
[49] P. Paris, *Etudes sur François Ier* (1895), ii. 204–323; E. Desgardins, *Anne de Pisseleu duchesse d'Etampes et François Ier* (1904); C.A.F., ii. 7189, 7256; ix. 8768. See also below, pp. 497–9.

Chapter fourteen

Protestants and Turks (1529–34)

The peace of Cambrai did not bring about a fundamental change in Francis I's foreign policy whose principal objective continued to be the recovery of Milan. The peace merely provided a breathing space in which to replenish the king's coffers, rebuild his armed forces and consolidate his alliances. Between 1530 and 1534 Francis stirred up trouble for the Emperor in Germany and in the Mediterranean without, however, openly contravening the peace treaty. At the same time, he built up a coalition of anti-Habsburg powers, comprising the German princes, the king of England, the pope and the Turks. But the Protestant Reformation, which divided the Holy Roman Empire into two rival religious camps, and Henry VIII's divorce, which incurred the pope's condemnation, were serious obstacles in the path of a unified opposition to the Habsburgs. They obliged Francis to assume the role of religious peacemaker at a time when the Reformation in France was challenging his authority. His reputation as a Christian monarch was also imperilled by his secret intrigues with the Infidel Turk.

Henry VIII's 'Great Matter'

In 1528 Henry VIII tried to put pressure on the pope to concede his divorce by consulting theologians in various universities, including Paris. The theologians were asked not merely to judge the validity of the dispensation issued by Pope Julius II in December 1502 which had enabled Henry to marry his deceased brother's widow, but also whether any pope had the right to issue such a dispensation. The task of canvassing support for Henry's cause among the theologians in Paris fell to Guillaume du Bellay, seigneur de Langey. In assuming the responsibility, he was less interested in the theological aspects of the case than in the political advantages he might derive for Francis; for the Emperor was Catherine of Aragon's nephew and a decision

59. Guillaume du Bellay, seigneur de Langey (1491–1543), one of the gentlemen of Francis I's chamber, who served him well, as a diplomat and administrator. He and his brother, Jean, bishop of Paris, had evangelical sympathies. Guillaume was Rabelais's patron.

favourable to Henry was likely to drive a deep wedge between the two monarchs.

The English government attached too much importance to the consultation to entrust it simply to diplomats. An extraordinary embassy led by George Boleyn, Anne's brother, asked Francis to use his influence in support of Henry's cause. But the king of France could not do so openly as long as the Emperor continued to hold his sons hostage in Spain. He was not prepared to allow his friendship for Henry to compromise the peace of Cambrai, yet he was aware that support for Henry's cause might gain him useful financial concessions. His way out of the dilemma was to give Langey secret encouragement and assistance until such time as he could do so openly.

Langey persuaded many Paris theologians to subscribe to a statement supporting Henry's divorce. The matter was then aired in the Faculty and a vote taken which proved favourable to Henry. This result, however, was challenged by two Spanish doctors, Garay and Moscoso, and by the syndic, Noël Béda. In late December Montmorency rebuked Béda, but the syndic pressed on regardless. He and Garay gathered signatures in support of an alternative statement condemning the divorce. However, on 4 February 1530 the collecting of signatures for or against the divorce was formally banned by the Faculty after a doctor had shown that it might incur discredit from the exercise. The signatures so far collected were handed over to Gervase Wain, an agent of the du Bellays, while the statement opposing the divorce was deposited by order of Pierre Lizet, First President of the Parlement, with the clerk of the episcopal tribunal (*officialité*) of Paris. Garay moved heaven and earth to retrieve it, but in vain. On 9 April he wrote to Charles V, complaining bitterly of Langey's activities. He was allegedly holding dinner parties for twelve or more theologians during which he would show them a decision already prepared supporting Henry's case, intimidate them by disclosing Francis's wishes and even bribe them with cash.

On 7 June Henry's 'Great Matter' was debated by the Faculty of Theology, which had been deliberately 'packed' for the occasion. Langey presented Henry's case most persuasively. The king, he said, was asking only for advice, not a judgment. But Béda argued that true doctrine was being sacrificed to the Anglo-French alliance. A discussion followed which produced three different opinions: first, that the affair should be examined forthwith; secondly, that the pope or at least the king should be consulted before any action was taken; and thirdly, that the king's opinion should be sought and the examination of the case begun pending his reply. But, as the Faculty's bedel listed the speakers to find out where the majority lay, one of the doctors snatched the list from him and tore it up. Out of the ensuing chaos, Garay and his friends emerged claiming victory for their side. The English ambassadors, who had witnessed the scene, protested energetically to Langey, who complained to Francis in writing about Béda and his friends. He asked the king to order their submission and to bring discussion of the divorce to a speedy conclusion.

Francis, who was in Bordeaux at the time, was infuriated by Langey's report. On 17 June he ordered Lizet to threaten Béda with his wrath. Any consultation of the pope, he said, would constitute a breach of the kingdom's rights and privileges. The king's letter left the Faculty in no doubt as to where its duty lay. Hitherto its discussions had been merely provisional; it now had to reach a definite conclusion without delay. On 2 July it decided by fifty-three votes against forty-seven that neither divine nor natural law permitted the pope to issue a dispensation allowing a man to marry his deceased brother's widow. Henry's marriage to Catherine was, therefore, null and void. Four days later a copy of the decision was dispatched to England. Yet even now the opposition refused to accept defeat. Garay and Béda tried to prevent the decision from being sealed. Then they attempted to appeal against it on procedural grounds but were unable to find a lawyer prepared to draw it up in proper form. They also tried to get hold of the register containing the minutes of the Faculty's debates, which Guillaume Petit had removed from the archives by royal command. They also tried to dissuade doctors, who had been absent on 2 July, from adding their signatures to the Faculty's pronouncement.[1]

After their defeat the Bédaists tried to get their own back by spreading a report that Jean du Bellay, bishop of Bayonne, Langey's brother, had been charged with heresy in the Parlement. The bishop complained to the king, who demanded an explanation. The Parlement denied that any such charge had been made, but the bishop requested an opportunity to clear his name. Francis accordingly referred the matter to the *Grand Conseil*, which presumably found du Bellay innocent, since he was sent to England as ambassador in October 1531 and appointed bishop of Paris in September 1532.[2]

Francis and the German princes

The election of Charles V's brother, Ferdinand, as King of the Romans in January 1531 widened the rift between the Emperor and many German princes. No constitutional warrant existed for such a choice during the Emperor's lifetime, and Protestant princes were naturally alarmed by the election of a Catholic ruler dedicated to the defence of his faith. On 16 February they appealed to the king of France for help and eleven days later six Protestant

[1] V.-L. Bourrilly, *Guillaume du Bellay, seigneur de Langey* (1905), pp. 92–107; J. K. Farge, *Orthodoxy and Reform in Early Reformation France* (Leiden, 1985), pp. 135–43.
[2] V.-L. Bourrilly and N. Weiss, 'Jean du Bellay, les Protestants et la Sorbonne', *B.S.H.P.F.*, lii (1903), 114–20.

princes and ten cities formed the Schmalkaldic League to defend their interests.[3]

Although Francis had undertaken at Cambrai not to meddle in German affairs, he found the appeal of the Protestant princes irresistible. In May 1531 he sent Gervase Wain to Germany to assess the situation.[4] This was far from clear-cut. The Elector of Saxony, for example, though opposed to Ferdinand's election, was loyal to the Habsburgs, whereas the Landgrave of Hesse and the two dukes of Bavaria were prepared to fight them. Another controversial issue was the duchy of Württemberg, which the Habsburgs had seized in 1519. Philip of Hesse wanted to restore Duke Ulrich, but the dukes of Bavaria opposed this. They hated Ulrich, who was their brother-in-law, and, as Catholics, were afraid that the Landgrave would use his restoration to introduce Lutheranism into Württemberg.

As a first step towards creating an effective opposition to the Habsburgs, Wain mediated between the Bavarian dukes and the Schmalkaldic League. Such was his success that they signed an alliance at Saalfeld on 26 October.[5] This was the foundation-stone of Francis's future policy in Germany: a coalition of Catholic and Protestant princes had been formed ostensibly to defend German interests against the Habsburgs. Francis refused to join it, but promised the confederates financial aid for defensive purposes only.[6] However, he soon changed his mind and agreed to an armed reconquest of Württemberg. On 26 May 1532 an alliance was signed at Scheyern between France, Saxony, Hesse and Bavaria, Francis promising to contribute 100,000 *écus* towards the cost of the forthcoming war. Before this could be declared, however, the Turks invaded central Europe.

Francis and the Turks

Francis had been intriguing with the Turks for some time. The disputed succession to the Hungarian throne, which had followed the death of King Louis II at the battle of Mohács, had allowed him to undermine Habsburg interests in central Europe. In February 1527 he sent Antonio Rincon, a Spanish renegade, to offer French aid to John Zápolyai, Voivode of Transylvania, who had been elected king in opposition to Ferdinand of Habsburg. Rincon also attempted to win the support of King Sigismund of Poland for Zápolyai's cause. By the end of 1527, however, Zápolyai lost his throne to

---

[3] *Corpus Reformatorum*, ed. C. G. Bretschneider (18 vols., Halle, 1834), ii. cols. 472–7, 478–80.

[4] C.A.F., ii. 4042.   [5] Bourrilly, *Guillaume du Bellay*, p. 126.

[6] Francis helped to bring about the peace of Bremgarten (20 November) between the Catholic and Protestant cantons in Switzerland. E. Rott, *Histoire de la représentation diplomatique de la France auprès des cantons suisses*, i (1900–35), 281, 383–5; A. Hyrvoix, 'François Ier et la première guerre de religion en Suisse, 1529–1531' *R.Q.H.*, lxxi (1902), 465.

Ferdinand. He did not, however, give up the struggle. In the autumn of 1528 a Hungarian bishop called John Stafileo came to Paris and signed an alliance with Francis. In return for a promise of financial aid, Zápolyai agreed to bequeath his kingdom, in the event of his dying childless, to the duc d'Orléans. This alliance had far-reaching consequences, for Zápolyai was allied to the Turkish sultan, who, in 1529, confirmed him as king, as he overran Hungary on his way to besiege Vienna.[7]

While Francis celebrated the withdrawal of the Turks from Vienna in October 1529 along with the rest of Christendom, he continued to have dealings with them. In July 1530 Rincon went to Constantinople with the purpose, so the imperialists claimed, of persuading the Sultan to attack Charles V in Italy. In March 1531 Giorgio Gritti, a Venetian employed by the Turks, came to Paris, ostensibly on business but probably for more sinister reasons.[8] As Thomas Cromwell remarked, no Christian scruple would deter Francis from bringing the Turk and the devil into the heart of Christendom if they could help him regain Milan.[9] The king almost admitted as much: 'I cannot deny', he told the Venetian envoy, Giustinian, 'that I keenly desire the Turk powerful and ready for war, not for himself, because he is an infidel and we are Christians, but to undermine the Emperor's power, to force heavy expenses upon him and to reassure all other governments against so powerful an enemy.'[10]

Yet Francis could not determine Turkish strategy. Nothing, for example, was more damaging to his interests in Germany than a Turkish attack on central Europe. This always had the effect of rallying support for the Habsburgs. From the French standpoint a Turkish attack on Charles V in Italy was far preferable since it offered Francis a pretext for invading the peninsula himself as the champion of Christendom. Thus in March 1532 Francis sent Rincon to the Sultan, who was preparing a new offensive in the west, to persuade him to attack Italy rather than Hungary. Rincon, however, reached the Sultan's camp too late to influence his strategy.[11] The Turks, after sweeping through the Balkans, pushed towards the valley of the Danube. Rincon's presence among them served merely to confirm imperial allegations of collusion between Francis and the Infidel. In the end, the Turkish offensive failed. The Sultan, after being held up for three weeks by the heroic defenders of Güns, retreated, and on 23 September Charles V entered Vienna in triumph.

---

[7] V.-L. Bourrilly, 'Antonio Rincon et la politique orientale de François Ier', *R.H.*, cxiii (1913), 76–83.

[8] J. Ursu, *La politique orientale de François Ier* (1908), pp. 58, 60–1.

[9] *C.S.P. Span.*, v. No. 157, p. 455.

[10] *Relations des ambassadeurs vénitiens sur les affaires de France*, ed. N. Tommaseo (1838), i. 67.

[11] Ursu, pp. 66–72; *C.S.P. Span.*, iv. 456–7; Bourrilly, 'Antonio Rincon et la politique orientale de François Ier', pp. 276–7.

Clement VII and Henry VIII

The widening rift between England and the papacy caused by Henry VIII's repudiation of Catherine of Aragon was a matter of serious concern to Francis who wanted them both as friends. In April 1531 he sent Cardinal Gramont to Rome to help solve the problem of Henry's divorce and to propose a marriage between the duc d'Orléans and the pope's niece, Catherine de' Medici. Following the cardinal's return in July, Francis appointed Cardinal Tournon as ambassador extraordinary to the Holy See.[12] Meanwhile, Francis and Henry met for the second time.

Although ostensibly directed against the Turks, the meeting of the two kings was really aimed at co-ordinating their efforts in Germany and Rome. Francis wanted Henry to share the burden of subsidizing the League of Scheyern, while Henry, having recently got rid of Wolsey, depended on French cardinals to advance his cause at the Curia.[13] The meeting was far less elaborate than the Field of Cloth of Gold: it lasted only eight days (21–29 October 1532); took place half in Calais, half in Boulogne; and the expenses were shared by the two kings.[14] Henry was accompanied by Anne Boleyn, at Francis's suggestion, and Queen Eleanor stayed away. The entertainments provided included bear-baiting, a wrestling match between Cornishmen and French priests, and dancing in which Francis partnered Anne.[15] Gifts and honours were also exchanged: Anne received a diamond worth 15,000 *écus* from Francis, while Henry remitted 300,000 *écus* owed him by the king of France. As another gesture of friendship, Henry sent his natural son, the duke of Richmond, to be brought up at the French court with Francis's sons. Finally, the dukes of Norfolk and Suffolk were admitted to the order of St Michael, while Montmorency and Chabot became knights of the Garter.[16]

On 28 October the two kings formed an alliance against the Turks, but this was a smoke-screen: their real concern was the Emperor's avowed intention of soon returning to Italy.[17] Francis was afraid that the peninsula would be closed to him once Clement VII had fallen under Charles's domination, while Henry dreaded a formal condemnation of his divorce, which would force him to choose between surrender and schism. Both monarchs consequently agreed to send Cardinals Gramont and Tournon to the pope.[18] They were given a

---

[12] M. François, *Le cardinal François de Tournon* (1951), pp. 94–7.
[13] J. J. Scarisbrick, *Henry VIII* (London, 1968), p. 305.
[14] Le P. Hamy, *Entrevue de François Ier avec Henri VIII à Boulogne-sur-Mer en 1532* (1898).
[15] E. W. Ives, *Anne Boleyn* (Oxford, 1986), pp. 198–200.
[16] *L.P.*, v. 1484–5. The Order of St Michael was founded by Louis XI on 1 August 1469. See P. Durrieu, 'Les manuscrits des Statuts de l'Ordre de Saint-Michel', *Bulletin de la Société française de reproductions de manuscrits à peintures*, 1 (1911), 17–47.
[17] *Ordonnances*, vi. No. 605; *C.S.P. Ven.*, iv. Nos. 820–5.
[18] François, *François de Tournon*, pp. 99–100.

60. Henry VIII's departure for Calais. Detail of an anonymous painting at Hampton Court Palace. Though traditionally associated with the Field of Cloth of Gold, this painting should probably be linked to Henry's second meeting with Francis at Boulogne in 1532.

message combining promises with threats and instructed to arrange a meeting between Francis and the pope. The cardinals arrived in Bologna on 3 January 1533, several weeks after the Emperor. Yet they soon made progress: Clement secretly agreed to meet Francis and also to the latter's marriage proposal.[19]

Some headway was even made regarding Henry's divorce; although Clement was being pressed by the Emperor to condemn the English king, he issued the bulls Cranmer needed to become archbishop of Canterbury. However, Francis's efforts on Henry's behalf were frustrated by the latter's impatience. About 25 January he married Anne Boleyn secretly, and, in March, sent her brother Rochford to put Francis in the picture. The marriage was not officially announced till May, but it had become common knowledge long before, if only because Anne's pregnancy could not be concealed. Henry subsequently claimed that he had married her with Francis's encouragement. This may have been true, for Francis stood to gain from a match that was bound to drive a

[19] *Ibid.*, pp. 101–5; *L.P.*, vi. 38, 64, 92.

deep wedge between Henry and Charles V.[20] Yet he was not prepared to sacrifice his good relations with the pope for Henry's sake. Thus he flatly refused Rochford's suggestion that he should put pressure on the pope to grant Henry's divorce by threatening to break off the proposed marriage between his own son and Clement's niece. Such a move, he said, would only drive the pope into the Emperor's arms.[21] All that he was prepared to do at this stage was to try to dissuade Clement from excommunicating Henry immediately.

The fate of the English monarch depended to some extent on Francis's meeting with the pope. This had to be postponed for a variety of reasons: the refusal of the duke of Savoy to allow Nice to be used for the meeting, the activities of Turkish pirates off the Italian coast, bad weather in August and the intrigues of France's enemies. The delay was a serious embarrassment to Henry, who wanted his second marriage to be legalized before the birth of Anne's child, which was due in September. On 23 May Cranmer, usurping the pope's jurisdiction, declared the king's second marriage lawful, and on 1 June, he crowned Anne queen. Clement retaliated on 11 July by condemning Henry's remarriage and giving him till September to take back Catherine under threat of excommunication. Meanwhile, Henry sent the duke of Norfolk to France. He tried to persuade Francis to call off his interview with the pope, but the king refused, saying that he did not think such a step was warranted by Clement's sentence on Henry. He believed that a solution might still be found, if Henry would send to the meeting a representative empowered to negotiate. In September, Tournon persuaded the pope to extend the deadline for Henry's excommunication.[22]

Francis meets Pope Clement VII (October 1533)

In July, an envoy from Khair ad-Din Barbarossa, the famous Algerian corsair, met Francis at Le Puy, as he was travelling south to meet the pope. The envoy brought with him a number of Frenchmen who had been captured by the Turks and whom the Sultan now released as a gesture of goodwill. The purpose of his mission, it seems, was to pave the way for an ambassador from the Sultan, who arrived soon afterwards, bearing words of encouragement for Francis in his struggle with the Emperor and also offers of military help.[23] But Suleiman was too busy fighting the Persians in 1534 to attack the Habsburgs. He relied instead on Barbarossa, who, in August, captured Tunis, expelling its ruler, Muley Hassan, who was the Emperor's ally. In November the corsair sent another envoy to the king of France ostensibly to sign a commercial truce,

---

[20] *L.P.*, vi 230; E. W. Ives, *Anne Boleyn*, pp. 202, 204.   [21] *L.P.*, vi. 254.
[22] *Ibid.*, vi. 954, 1038, 1070, 1155.
[23] Ursu, pp. 77–8.

but more probably to agree on joint military action in the future. French observers were mystified by these intrigues. The Bourgeois de Paris reported that the envoy had come to seek a marriage alliance and baptism for the Sultan and his son![24]

On 1 September Catherine de' Medici sailed from La Spezia to Villefranche where she was joined a month later by her uncle, the pope. On 11 October the papal fleet – some sixty ships in all – arrived at Marseilles, prompting a huge welcoming salvo from the shore batteries. Next day, Clement and fourteen cardinals, riding mules, entered the town. Francis arrived on the 13th when he prostrated himself at the feet of the Holy Father. On 27 October the contract for the marriage of Henri duc d'Orléans and Catherine was signed, and next day they were married amidst great pomp. That night the newly weds, both aged fourteen, were led by Queen Eleanor and her ladies to a sumptuously decorated nuptial chamber where allegedly they consummated their union in the presence of Francis who declared that 'each had shown valour in the joust'. Next morning Clement found the young couple still in bed and noted with pleasure their satisfied looks. There followed an exchange of gifts. Clement gave Francis a beautiful casket with panels of engraved crystal by Valerio Belli depicting twenty-one scenes from the life of Christ, and also a unicorn's horn (actually a narwhal's tusk) said to be useful for detecting the presence of poison in food. Francis gave the pope a Flemish tapestry depicting the Last Supper. He also distributed pensions to the cardinals in the pope's entourage. Ippolito de' Medici was given a tame lion that Barbarossa had recently presented to the king. On 7 November Clement created four French cardinals: Jean Le Veneur, Philippe de La Chambre, Odet de Coligny and Claude de Longwy. Among other concessions obtained by Francis was permission to levy another clerical tenth. The meeting, which did not produce any formal treaty between France and the Holy See, ended on 12 November, when Francis and his court left for Avignon. The pope's departure from Marseilles for Italy was delayed until the 20th.[25]

No one knows what the king and the pope decided at Marseilles, though a draft agreement written in the king's hand may offer a clue. It anticipates an offensive alliance for the conquest of Milan as well as the cession of Parma and Piacenza to the pope.[26] Clement was subsequently accused by his enemies of acquiescing in Francis's alliance with the German Protestants and the Turks, but this cannot be proved. What is certain is that he later betrayed some of Francis's confidences to the Emperor. 'Not only will I not oppose the invasion

---

[24] *J.B.P.*, p. 357.

[25] Du Bellay, ii. 225–31; le P. Hamy, *Entrevue de François Ier avec Clement VII à Marseille, 1533* (1900); J. Heritier, *Catherine de Médicis* (1940), pp. 49–57; I. Cloulas, *Catherine de Médicis* (1979), pp. 53–8.

[26] R. Reumont and A. Baschet, *La jeunesse de Catherine de Médicis* (1866), pp. 325ff.

61. Back view of a casket with crystal panels engraved by Valerio Belli, showing scenes from the life of Christ, which was given to Francis I by Pope Clement VII in October 1533 on the occasion of the marriage between the king's son, Henri, and the pope's niece, Catherine de' Medici.

of Christendom by the Turk', the king allegedly declared, 'but I will favour him as much as I can, in order the more easily to recover that which plainly belongs to me and my children, and has been usurped by the Emperor.'[27]

Three topics were certainly discussed at Marseilles: the spread of heresy in France, the calling of a General Council and Henry VIII's divorce. Francis is said to have promised to eradicate heresy from his kingdom, while refusing to act against the German Protestants. Be that as it may, Clement issued a bull against French Lutherans on 10 November.[28] As regards a General Council, Francis argued that it could serve no useful purpose as long as he was on bad terms with the Emperor and Clement was only too glad of this excuse to postpone it indefinitely. This decision caused great bitterness among German Catholics. Duke George of Saxony complained that the pope had allowed himself to be duped by Francis. If the Roman church lost 10,000 ducats, he said, bulls of excommunication would be hurled, swords drawn and all

[27] *C.S.P. Span.*, v. No. 131, p. 396.
[28] Decrue, i. 212; L. von Pastor, *The History of the Popes*, tr. F. L. Antrobus and R. Kerr (London, 1891–1933), x. 304. See also below, p. 312.

Christendom asked for help; but if 100,000 souls were lost, the pope listened only to a man who was bent on injuring and enslaving Christendom.[29]

Henry VIII's divorce proved more troublesome. Francis asked for a further delay of six months before Henry's excommunication was given effect, but the pope would concede only one. Meanwhile Stephen Gardiner, bishop of Winchester, acting on Henry's behalf, asked Clement to lift the sentence and give his approval to the king's divorce. Both demands were politely refused, but, at Francis's behest, Clement offered to submit Henry's suit to a Franco-papal commission at Avignon. On 7 November Edmund Bonner delivered Henry's reply. Forcing his way into the pope's chamber, he 'intimated' the king's appeal to a future General Council. This angered Francis almost as much as the pope, for, without consulting him, Henry had insulted his guest. 'As fast as I study to win the pope', he told Gardiner, 'ye study to lose him.'[30] In late November he sent Jean du Bellay to England to complain that Henry's envoys had undone a week's work in an hour and to warn him to behave less strangely if he valued the friendship of 'the most powerful king and best friend in Christendom'. But Henry no longer trusted Francis: he kept du Bellay waiting four days, then complained that Francis had been treating with his worst enemy.[31] On 23 March 1534 Clement fulminated his anathema against the king of England, whereupon Henry completed England's breach with Rome.

The question of Württemberg

By the autumn of 1533 the German signatories of the treaty of Scheyern had decided to wrest Württemberg from the Habsburgs. Before doing so, however, they wanted to be sure of receiving the subsidy promised by Francis, and also to bring about the dissolution of the Swabian league, which was due for renewal. On 16 November Francis received an appeal for help from Christopher of Württemberg, who had been invited to submit his case to the next diet of the Swabian League at Augsburg. Francis needed no prompting to fish in the troubled waters of the Empire. He instructed Langey to attend the diet and lend Christopher his support. In a speech to the diet on 10 December Langey claimed that his master only wanted fair play. He asked the delegates to restore two towns to Christopher and to temper justice with clemency in respect of the rest of Württemberg. He then withdrew from the diet as a demonstration of disinterestedness. Yet behind the scenes he did his utmost to stir up trouble for the Habsburgs. 'The Frenchman', it was reported, 'is up to his neck in this affair; he acts as if he would like to see war break out, and if he

[29] C.S.P. Span., iv. No. 1136, p. 825; Pastor, x. 321–2.
[30] L.P., vi. 1403, 1425–6; Scarisbrick, Henry VIII, pp. 319–20.
[31] L.P., vi. 1558, 1572; Correspondance du cardinal Jean du Bellay, ed. R. Scheurer (1969–73), i. 322–32.

is not offering help openly, he is distributing cash by the fistful so as to create discord in our midst.'[32] On 28 January 1534 Langey signed a secret treaty committing Francis to pay a third of the cost of a war in defence of German liberties. Three days later he again addressed the diet. This time, he warned the delegates against refusing to grant redress to Ulrich of Württemberg and his son. He also urged them not to renew the Swabian League or at least to exclude Württemberg from it so that Christopher might recover his property more easily. On 1 February the diet adjourned indefinitely without renewing the League.[33]

Meanwhile, Francis and Philip Landgrave of Hesse signed a treaty at Bar-le-Duc on 20 January. While Philip promised to declare war on the King of the Romans within three months, Francis undertook to pay Ulrich of Württemberg a subsidy of 125,000 *écus*. This, however, was disguised so as to protect Francis from the charge of breaking the treaty of Cambrai; Ulrich sold him the county of Montbéliard for the amount of the subsidy with the option of buying it back.[34] Soon afterwards, Philip overran Württemberg and restored Ulrich to power. On 29 June he made peace with Ferdinand, and the dukes of Bavaria soon did the same.

The attempt to reunify the churches

A major obstacle to the formation of a large anti-Habsburg coalition in Germany was the religious schism dividing its princes; hence Francis's decision in 1534 to become a religious peacemaker. His agent was once again Langey, who returned to Germany by way of Switzerland in May.

The main purpose of this mission was to persuade the reformers that Francis's recent meeting with Clement VII had produced a climate favourable to a reunion of the churches. Langey told the diet of Baden that the pope had shown a desire not only to modify anachronistic institutions, but also to accept 'some of the views of those in Germany who call themselves evangelicals'. He invited the reformers to submit statements indicating how far they believed compromise with the Catholics over doctrinal differences was possible.[35] Though the reformers suspected Francis's motives, they were sufficiently impressed by Langey's eloquence to respond to his invitation. Among the first to do so was Philip Melanchthon, Luther's lieutenant. His submission, which arrived in Paris in the summer of 1534, was most conciliatory. He denied that he and his fellow reformers had ever wanted to overthrow the Roman church and acknowledged the need for episcopal authority, even for papal supremacy.

---

[32] Du Bellay, ii. 236; Bourrilly, *Guillaume du Bellay*, pp. 160–1. [33] *Ibid.*, pp. 150–62.
[34] *Ordonnances*, vii. No. 651.
[35] Bourrilly, *Guillaume du Bellay*, pp. 173–7.

Melanchthon felt sure that a mutually acceptable definition of justification was possible provided the preponderant role of faith was recognized. The Mass, he admitted, was a more difficult problem, but he thought a synod would be able to solve it. Although he himself wished to see the cult of saints abolished, he thought it might be reprieved if God's prerogative were safeguarded. Monasteries might be turned into colleges or schools. This matter, like clerical celibacy, could be left to the pope's decision. On 17 August two other reformers, Bucer and Hedio, replied to Langey's questionnaire in more or less the same spirit.[36] All this was most encouraging to Francis. He could reasonably imagine that the religious schism preventing a united opposition to the Habsburgs was about to be healed.

Two important embassies

In October 1534 Charles V sent Henry of Nassau to France with two proposals: first, that Sforza should give a pension to the duc d'Orléans in exchange for French recognition of his own dukedom; secondly, for a marriage between Henry VIII's daughter, Mary, and Francis's third son, the duc d'Angoulême. The first proposal was immediately rejected by Montmorency, who, on 20 October, gave Nassau a written statement renewing Francis's claims to Milan and Genoa. As for the second proposal, which may have been intended to damage Anglo-French relations, Montmorency's response was sufficiently encouraging for the Emperor to take it further.[37]

By the autumn of 1534 Anglo-French relations had become ambiguous. Henry VIII, following his breach with Rome, was more than ever dependent on French support, yet did not know if he could trust Francis now that he had become the pope's kinsman and ally. Francis, for his part, played on Henry's sense of insecurity to extract from him more financial concessions. He sent Philippe Chabot to England with the Emperor's proposal. The Admiral was magnificently entertained, but when he requested Mary's hand for the duc d'Angoulême, Henry told him that he must be joking. Chabot proved that he was not by showing his instructions, whereupon Henry put forward a counter-proposal: he would give Mary to Angoulême if both renounced all claim to the English throne; alternatively, he would give Elizabeth, his daughter by Anne Boleyn, to the duke and would renounce his own claim to the French throne if Francis would persuade the pope to lift his excommunication. Chabot, however, was unenthusiastic about both proposals, and soon returned to France apparently much disgruntled.[38]

By the end of the summer Francis could feel reasonably satisfied with the

---

[36] *Ibid.*, pp. 179–83.   [37] Decrue, i. 230–1; Granvelle, *Papiers d'état*, ii. 224.
[38] *C.S.P. Span.*, v. Nos. 111–12, 114, 118.

results of his diplomacy. Without openly contravening the peace of Cambrai, he had undermined the Emperor's power in several quarters. He had won over the pope and tied him down with a family compact. In Germany, the Emperor and his brother were being harassed by a coalition of Protestant and Catholic princes; they had lost Württemberg. Furthermore the religious schism which had hampered the formation of a large-scale coalition against the Habsburgs seemed about to be healed. In the Mediterranean, the foundations had been laid of a useful partnership between Francis and the Turks. Only in respect of England could Francis feel less than satisfied. He had worked hard to avert a breach between Henry VIII and the pope, but his efforts had been frustrated by Henry's lack of self-control. Even so, the Anglo-French alliance had survived.

Before the year was out, however, two events radically altered the international situation: the death of Clement VII on 25 September destroyed the basis of the new Franco-papal alliance. All would have been well if Clement had been succeeded by another member of the Medici family, but on 12 October Alessandro Farnese was chosen to occupy St Peter's throne. This turned the marriage of Henri duc d'Orléans with Catherine de' Medici into a *mésalliance*. The new pope, who took the name of Paul III, announced that his pontificate would be dedicated mainly to three tasks: the pacification of Christendom, the calling of a General Council and a crusade against the Turks. Francis paid lip-service to all three objectives, but did not really favour any of them. Paul's accession consequently necessitated a revision of French policy towards the Holy See. The second event, which profoundly affected the king's foreign policy was the Affair of the Placards of 18 October 1534 which provoked a savage campaign of religious persecution in France. This shocked Protestant opinion throughout Europe and called into question Francis's sincerity as a religious peacemaker.

Chapter fifteen

The threat of heresy

The '*lecteurs royaux*'

Following the peace of Cambrai in 1529, Budé and his friends reminded Francis I of his undertaking to found a college for the study of classical languages, and in March 1530 he set up four regius lectureships. Pierre Danès and Jacques Toussaint were appointed to teach Greek, François Vatable and Agazio Guidacerio to teach Hebrew. Humanists everywhere acclaimed the king's action. 'The river which the king is about to let flow', wrote a Flemish scholar, 'will water many lands and make them fertile.' Erasmus urged the teachers of Louvain to redouble their efforts in face of the new challenge from France. She was more fortunate, he thought, to have the *lecteurs royaux* than if she had conquered the whole of Italy. Rabelais also acclaimed the event in *Pantagruel*:

> still, as you may well understand, the times were not as fit and favourable for learning as they are to-day, and I had no supply of tutors such as you have. Indeed the times were still dark, and mankind was perpetually reminded of the miseries and disasters wrought by those Goths who had destroyed all sound scholarship. But, thanks be to God, learning has been restored in my age to its former dignity and enlightenment ... Now every method of teaching has been restored, and the study of languages has been revived: of Greek, without which it is disgraceful for a man to call himself a scholar, and of Hebrew, Chaldean, and Latin. The elegant and accurate art of printing, which is now in use, was invented in my time, by divine inspiration; as, by contrast, artillery was inspired by diabolical suggestion. The whole world is full of learned men, of very erudite tutors, and most extensive libraries, and it is my opinion that neither in the time of Plato, of Cicero, nor of Papinian were there such facilities for study as one finds today. No one, in future, will risk appearing in public or in any company, who is not well polished in Minerva's workshop. I find robbers, hangmen, freebooters, and grooms nowadays more learned than the doctors and preachers were in my time. Why, the very women and girls aspire to the glory and reach out

for the celestial manna of sound learning. So much so that at my present age I have been compelled to learn Greek ...[1]

The foundation of the *lecteurs royaux* marked a major step in the advancement of French education. Students from far and wide were drawn to Paris by the free and independent courses provided by them. Such was their success and renown that additional lectureships were soon created. Oronce Finé was appointed to teach mathematics, a subject recently neglected in France, and in 1531 a third lecturer in Hebrew was appointed in the person of Paul Canossa, *alias* Paradis, a converted Venetian Jew. At first, no provision was made for the teaching of Latin which was regarded as the university's responsibility. Many people, however, believed that this needed to be brought up to date, and it was doubtless with this end in view that in 1534 Barthélemy Le Masson *alias* Latomus, a dedicated Ciceronian was appointed by the king.

Important as they were, the *lecteurs royaux* represented a modest achievement by comparison with the college originally envisaged by Francis, for they were given no building of their own. They were consequently obliged to lecture either in existing colleges or in the open, and sometimes had to interrupt their teaching on account of obtrusive street smells and noises. Their salaries, which the *Trésorier de l'Épargne* was supposed to pay, seldom materialized, forcing them to give up valuable teaching time to press their claims at court. Eventually, they were put on the payroll of the royal household, but their remuneration continued to cause trouble till the end of the reign.[2]

The Roussel affair

On 10 May 1529 Farel wrote to Capito: 'I cannot see what progress can be made among the French under so insane a sovereign who has allowed the New Testament to be forbidden to the people, so that there remains no way of making the truth known.'[3] Similar pessimism was expressed by Oecolampadius in a letter to Zwingli of 4 May 1530: 'It is getting too late for France to turn to Christ, for persons who arrived here [Basle] at Easter brought news that the bishops and theologians are extremely hostile to those who profess Christ, and that the king is not merely silent about this but actually threatens the most learned Gérard Roussel and Jacques Lefèvre and others with burning if they do not dissuade his sister from the beliefs they have induced her to embrace.'[4]

---

[1] F. Rabelais, *The Histories of Gargantua and Pantagruel*, tr. J. M. Cohen (Harmondsworth, Middlesex, 1955), p. 194. For the original French text see F. Rabelais, *Pantagruel*, ed. V. L. Saulnier (Geneva, 1965), pp. 43–5.

[2] A. Lefranc, *Histoire du Collège de France* (1893), pp. 101–23.

[3] Herminjard, ii. 179. The ban dated back to 5 February 1526 (*J.B.P.*, p. 276). It was for this reason that Lefèvre's edition of the New Testament was not reprinted in France as from 1526 and that his translation of the New Testament was published in Antwerp in 1528.

[4] *Ibid*, ii. 249.

Oecolampadius, however, had been misinformed. True, Francis had failed to countermand the Parlement's ban on French translations of Scripture, but there is no evidence of his threatening either Roussel or Lefèvre with execution. At the end of May, Marguerite asked Montmorency as Grand Master to allow Lefèvre to leave Blois whose climate was harmful to his health. 'He has put the royal library in order', she explained, 'classified the books, and drawn up a complete inventory which he will give to whomsoever the king pleases.' Permission was readily given and Lefèvre moved to Nérac where he spent his last years peacefully under Marguerite's protection.[5]

The absence of any hostility on the part of Francis towards Lefèvre is indicated by a letter from Bucer to Luther of 25 August. The Gospel, he declared, was making good progress in France, but disagreement over the Eucharist between Lutherans and Zwinglians was a serious hindrance. If it could be removed, there was hope that Christ would soon be received by the people 'for the king is not opposed to the truth, and now that he has received back his children he will cease to be so dependent on the pope and the Emperor'. Bucer wrote of the unfailing support of 'that most Christian heroine', the king's sister, adding that 'in a certain region of Normandy so many have now professed the Gospel that the enemy has begun to call it "little Germany"'.[6] Bucer's mention of the king's sons helps to explain Francis's seemingly inconsistent attitude towards the Reformation: as long as they were held captive, he could not do anything publicly that might prejudice their return.

In Lent 1531 Gérard Roussel, a former member of the *Cercle de Meaux* and now Marguerite de Navarre's almoner, was accused by the Paris Faculty of Theology of preaching heresy in her presence at the Louvre. The king ordered him to give advance notice in future of whatever he intended to say in his sermons. This pacified the Faculty for the time being, but in 1533 Roussel was again accused of preaching heresy to large crowds at the Louvre. Six bachelors of theology were accordingly instructed to preach in Paris against the errors and perverse doctrines of the Lutherans. They were cautioned to preach against errors, not persons; but they exceeded this brief. On 16 April the Chancellor said that Francis was worried about the Faculty's preachers, who 'indiscreetly sought to stir up the people against Roussel'. The Faculty promptly called a meeting of all its members who had heard Roussel preach. Two reported meeting the king: he had received them promptly and courteously, and had listened carefully to their explanation of the Faculty's actions. He had spoken with great admiration about the need to extirpate heresy from the kingdom.

[5] *Ibid.*, ii. 250–1; P. E. Hughes, *Lefèvre: Pioneer of Ecclesiastical Renewal in France* (Grand Rapids, MI, 1984), pp. 178–9.
[6] Herminjard, ii. 271–2.

On 9 May a committee of sixteen doctors was appointed to draw up articles of heresy preached by Roussel for submission to the king. But his attitude hardened following a report that a bachelor of theology, François Le Picart, had publicly accused Marguerite's husband, the king of Navarre, of heresy. Writing from Moulins on 13 May, Francis banished from Paris Béda and the bachelors who had attacked Roussel. He declared that 'persons worthy of credence' had charged Béda with 'plots and monopolies' causing scandals in the Faculty. Several days of demonstrations for and against the syndic followed, and enemies of the Faculty rejoiced. Le Masson wrote, in June, that the theologians had suffered such a defeat that their only hope was for Marguerite, who was pregnant, to die soon, or for a sudden and violent change of circumstances. Be this as it may, the Faculty elected a new syndic and appointed a delegation of sixteen theologians to argue its case against Roussel. This was presented to the Parlement six months after Béda's exile.[7]

Much of the university's resentment was directed at the king's sister. In October 1533, during the king's absence from the capital, students of the Collège de Navarre staged a satirical play. This showed Marguerite preaching heresy at the instigation of a fury, called Mégère (a pun on Roussel's name) and tormenting anyone who would not listen. The play came to Marguerite's attention and the college was soon afterwards raided by the *prévôt de Paris*. The author was not discovered, though two senior members of the college were detained. It is not known how the affair ended.[8]

Later that month, Marguerite again came under fire when the *Miroir de l'âme pécheresse* ('Mirror of the Sinful Soul'), a poem she had published anonymously appeared on a black list drawn up by the University of Paris. The king demanded an explanation, whereupon the rector, Nicolas Cop, called a meeting of all the faculties. He blamed a few theologians for what had happened and called on other members of the university to dissociate themselves from their action. The theologian, who had blacklisted the poem, denied that any offence to Marguerite had been intended. It had figured on the list, he explained, because it had been published without the Faculty of Theology's *imprimatur*, an essential requirement for all religious works. Cop then moved that the poem be removed from the list and an apology sent to the king. The Faculty, finding itself isolated, had to back down: on 8 October fifty-eight theologians signed a statement to the effect that they had never read the poem

[7] V.-L. Bourrilly and N. Weiss, 'Jean du Bellay, les Protestants et la Sorbonne', *B.S.H.P.F.*, lii (1903), 120–2, 193–213; C. Schmidt, *Gérard Roussel prédicateur de la reine Marguerite de Navarre* (Strasbourg, 1845), pp. 85–99; J. K. Farge, *Orthodoxy and Reform in Early Reformation France* (Leiden, 1985), pp. 201–3.
[8] *Ibid.*, pp. 203–4; Herminjard, iii. 93–5, 107; P Jourda, *Marguerite d'Angoulême* (1930), i. 178–80.

62. Marguerite d'Angoulême (1498–1549), duchesse d'Alençon and later queen of Navarre. She was Francis I's sister, the author of the *Heptaméron* and a patron of evangelical scholars and preachers. This anonymous portrait was painted about 1544 and derives from a drawing attributed to François Clouet.

and had, therefore, neither condemned it nor given it their approval. This apparently satisfied the king.[9]

Cop's sermon (November 1533)

In the autumn of 1533, while Francis was in the south of France, a new crisis blew up in Paris. It was customary for a newly elected rector of the university to preach on the feast of All Saints in the church of the Mathurins. But the sermon delivered by Nicolas Cop on 1 November 1533 was more controversial than usual. He was a close friend of Jean Calvin, who may have had a hand in writing the sermon. At this stage in his career Calvin was a humanist, not the Protestant reformer he would soon become. His first published work, a commentary on Seneca, praised Budé as 'the first ornament and pillar of literature' and Erasmus as its 'second ornament'.[10] Cop's sermon opened on an Erasmian note of appreciation for 'the philosophy divinely given to man by Christ to show forth the true and surest felicity'. It pardoned sin by the grace of God alone and Cop urged his audience to pray that Christ, the 'intercessor with the Father' should flow into their souls and shower them with 'the dew of his spiritual grace'. He went on to compare the Gospel and the Law in a way characteristic of evangelical humanism. He also attacked salvation by good works. 'Who could be so obtuse', he asked, 'as to think and assert that eternal life is a repayment for our good deeds, or that our good deeds are worthy of eternal life?' All Christians, Cop declared, were bound to proclaim these truths publicly. 'Why then do we conceal the truth rather than speak it out boldly?', he asked.

> Is it right to please men rather than God, to fear those who can destroy the body but not the soul? Oh the ingratitude of mankind, which will not bear the slightest affliction in the name of Him who died for the sins of all, Him whose blood has freed us from eternal death and the shackles of Satan! The world and the wicked are wont to label as heretics, imposters, seducers and evil-speakers those who strive purely and sincerely to penetrate the minds of believers with the Gospel ... But happy and blessed are they who endure all this with composure, giving thanks to God in the midst of affliction and bravely bearing calamities ... Onward, then, Oh Christian men. With our every muscle let us strive to attain this great bliss.[11]

Cop's sermon owed much to Erasmus's *Paraclesis* and to Luther's *Kirchenpostille* yet as a modern commentator has said 'a Roman Catholic of our own day would find little in the address to make him uneasy'.[12] It nevertheless

[9] Farge, *Orthodoxy and Reform.*, p. 204; Herminjard, iii. 108–9.
[10] W. J. Bouwsma, *John Calvin* (Oxford, 1988), p. 13.
[11] *Ibid.*, pp. 15–16. For a discussion of Calvin's responsibility for Cop's sermon see F. Wendel, *Calvin* (London, 1965), pp. 40–1.
[12] T. H. L. Parker, *John Calvin* (London, 1975), p. 30.

offended members of his audience who complained to the Parlement. Even before the court could act, however, Cop called a meeting of the whole university. He had been misrepresented, he claimed, and the university's privileges impugned. He asked for his critics to be called to account. But, failing to get the support of all the faculties and anticipating danger, he vanished, taking with him the university's seal. Three months later he turned up in Basle. The king ordered the arrest of the *parlementaire* who had let Cop escape.[13] Calvin too was obliged to flee. He retired probably to Noyon, then returned and was granted a friendly audience by Marguerite de Navarre. He decided none the less that he would be safer away from the capital and withdrew for several months to the home of his friend Louis du Tillet, a canon of Angoulême, where he may have begun work on his *Institutes*.[14]

At the end of November the Parlement made a number of arrests. Precisely how many is not known: some authorities say fifty, other 300. The Faculty of Theology was also active: it set up a commission to collaborate with the Parlement while investigating its own members. Both bodies warned the king about the growth of heresy in the capital. 'We are angry and displeased', he replied from Lyons, 'to learn that ... this damned heretical Lutheran sect is flourishing in our good town of Paris.'[15] He ordered three counter-measures: the appointment of two *parlementaires* to judge heresy cases on appeal, the publication of two recent papal bulls against heresy and the appointment by the bishop of Paris of two commissioners, to be chosen by the Parlement, to try heretics in the diocese. This last measure was strongly resisted by the bishop's vicar-general, René du Bellay, who thought it an unnecessary infringement of the bishop's authority. The threat of heresy in the capital had been much exaggerated in his opinion; he also rejected the implication that the bishop had been negligent in pursuing heretics. If heresy had grown, René argued, the Parlement and Faculty of Theology had only themselves to blame, for they had prevented the registration of royal letters patent aimed at strengthening episcopal control of preaching in the diocese. The Faculty's own preachers had much to answer for: instead of preaching the Word of God, they had given Luther widespread publicity by denouncing his errors. Finally, René rejected the allegation that heresy suspects had been released from the bishop's prison without trial after only a few days.[16]

Béda's banishment

In January 1534 Béda was recalled from exile to answer charges of heresy arising from a book called *Confession et raison de foy de maistre Noel Beda*. In

---

[13] M. Mann, *Erasme et les débuts de la réforme française, 1517–1536* (1934), p. 165; Farge, *Orthodoxy and Reform*, p. 204.
[14] Parker, pp. 30–1.   [15] Herminjard, iii. 114–18.   [16] Bourrilly and Weiss, pp. 219–24.

a dedication to Francis the author likened himself to St Paul; having persecuted the Gospel, he was now helping to reform the church along Lutheran lines. The book was obviously a spoof aimed at incriminating Béda, and the king was deceived to the extent of ordering the poor theologian publicly to denounce the errors in the book. This move, however, did not turn Béda into a docile instrument. He soon added to the king's irritation by mounting an attack on the *lecteurs royaux*. He accused them of undermining the authority of the Vulgate Bible by comparing it unfavourably to Greek and Hebrew versions. He asked the Faculty to ban their brand of biblical criticism and warn them that they needed a licence from the Faculty of Theology. Marilhac, who defended the lecturers, argued that the licence they had received from the king to teach the 'humane letters' took precedence over the Faculty's licence. He also pointed out that ordinary churchmen were teaching Scripture without a licence. Another lawyer recalled that the Clementine decretals had enjoined universities to teach Hebrew. The Parlement, however upheld Béda's position and forbade the *lecteurs* to criticize the Latin Vulgate. Béda's triumph, however, was short-lived. He was soon rearrested and, after an imprisonment lasting several months, was publicly degraded on 31 January 1535. It is often said that he was banished to the Mont Saint-Michel for the rest of his life, but evidence has come to light that he was in Paris after January 1535, two years before his death.[17]

The Affair of the Placards (18 October 1534)

For nearly two decades the Protestant Reformation in France offered no clear-cut confessions of faith; its adherents felt free to switch doctrines in their search for the truth. Guillaume Farel, for example, after belonging to the *Cercle de Meaux*, turned to Lutheranism. Then, in the mid twenties, he adopted the more radical ideas of Karlstadt and Zwingli. Yet he would still have been called a 'Lutheran' by the French authorities, for this was the label they attached to all religious dissenters, whatever their beliefs.[18] In 1534, however, an event took place which indicated how radical certain French reformers had become since 1519, when Lutheranism had first penetrated their country.

On the morning of 18 October Parisians going to church were startled to find that Protestant placards or broadsheets had been put up in several public

---

[17] Farge, *Orthodoxy and Reform*, pp. 205–6; G. Berthoud, 'La "Confession" de maître Noël Béda et le problème de son auteur', *B.H.R.*, 29 (1967), 373–97; A. Hyrvoix, 'Noël Bédier d'après des documents inédits, 1533–1534', *R.W.H.*, 72 (1913), 578–91; J. K. Farge, *Biographical Register of Paris Doctors of Theology, 1500–1536* (Toronto, 1980), pp. 31–6.

[18] 'Men of the sects of Zwingli and Oecolampadius, whom the populace call Lutherans' (A. Fabrice, 23 January 1535) Herminjard, iii. 252 n. 8. Saint-Mauris, the imperial ambassador, reported (27 July 1545) that there were many Lutherans in France, chiefly in Guyenne and Normandy, and that most of them were sacramentarians. B.L. Add. ms. 28594, fol. 144.

¶ Articles veritables sur les horribles/grandz z importables abuz de la Messe papalle: inuentez directement contre la saincte Cene de Jesus Christ.

Je inuocque le ciel z la terre/ en tesmoignage de Verite...

Premierement/ ...

Secondement/ ...

Tiercement/ ...

Quartement/ ...

63. The Placard against the Mass which was displayed in Paris and elsewhere on the night of 18 October 1534. It was written by Antoine Marcourt and printed in Neuchâtel by Pierre de Vingle.

places during the previous night. Each placard consisted of a single sheet of paper, 37 by 25 centimetres, printed in Gothic type. It was entitled *Articles véritables sur les horribles, grandz & importables abuz de la Messe papalle* (*True articles on the horrible, great and insufferable abuses of the papal Mass*), and the text was made up of a preamble and four paragraphs. The Mass was attacked on four grounds: first, there has been only one sacrifice, that of Christ on the Cross, which being perfect, cannot be repeated; secondly, the Mass implies the Real Presence of Christ in the host, yet Scripture tells us that He is with God the Father till the Day of Judgment; thirdly, transubstantiation is a human invention contrary to Scripture; and lastly, communion is a memorial service, not a miracle.[19] Here, in short, was a brief, clear statement of the Zwinglian or sacramentarian position on the Mass, not the Lutheran one. Neither Luther nor Zwingli saw the Mass as a sacrifice, but Luther continued to believe in the Real Presence.

The authorship of the *Articles véritables* was for a long time in doubt. Farel was suspected by many, but we now know that the author was Antoine Marcourt, a Frenchman exiled in Switzerland, who in 1530 had become the first pastor of Neuchâtel. In November 1534 he also published a pamphlet, entitled *Petit traicté ... de la Sainte Eucharistie* (*Small treatise ... on the Holy Eucharist*) in the preface of which he states that he alone had written the *Articles véritables* in order to expose publicly the 'seducers' who were holding the people in ignorance. But Marcourt alone could not have distributed copies of the placard. They were, it seems, smuggled into France by Guillaume Feret, a servant of the king's apothecary, and displayed in Paris by a group of radical dissenters who may have wanted to show their implacable hostility towards any Protestant compromise with Rome at a time when Francis was seeking to heal the religious schism in Germany.[20]

The effect of the placards on Parisian public opinion was traumatic. A wave of hysteria swept across the capital as it was rumoured that the reformers were about to sack the Louvre, burn down the churches and massacre the faithful at Mass.[21] Foreigners came under suspicion. Thus a Flemish merchant was lynched by a mob which shouted: 'He is a German! His death will gain us indulgences!'[22] Soon Parisian fears were heightened by reports that similar placards had been found in about five provincial towns (Orléans, Amboise, Blois, Tours and Rouen) and even at the château of Amboise where Francis was residing. The immediate sequel was a campaign of persecution more

---

[19] R. Hari, 'Les placards de 1534', in *Aspects de la propagande religieuse*, ed. G. Berthoud *et al.* (Geneva, 1957), pp. 114, 119–20.

[20] G. Berthoud, *Antoine Marcourt* (Geneva, 1973), pp. 174–6.

[21] *J.B.P.*, pp. 379–80; Berthoud, pp. 181–7.

[22] Herminjard, iii. 236 n. 5. See also Andrew Baynton's letter to Cromwell (Paris, 1 February 1535): 'the common people imagine that we and the Germans are all one, that is Lutherans'. *L.P.*, viii. 165 (Public Record Office, London: SP1/89/f. 137a).

savage than any yet experienced by the French reformers. Within twenty-four hours of the discovery of the placards, the Parlement ordered a general procession in Paris; it also began the search for culprits. Soon the prisons began to fill up. On 10 November the first sentences were passed and three days later a shoemaker's son, nicknamed 'the Paralytic', was burned at the stake; on the 14th it was the turn of Jean du Bourg, a rich draper. By the end of the month four more dissenters – a printer, a weaver, a bookseller and a stone-mason – had been executed.

Francis, in the meantime, left Amboise and travelled slowly back to Paris. On 9 December he wrote to Duprat from Bonneval: 'Monsieur the legate, I have received your letters of the 7th of this month from which I have learnt of the diligence with which the matter of the Lutherans has been and is being dealt with each day. This has given me much pleasure and nothing would satisfy me more than that it should continue so that the damned and abominable sect may neither set foot nor take root in my kingdom.'[23] On 16 December the Chancellor sent Francis a list of persons who were not to be allowed to escape. Five days later the king set up a special commission of twelve *parlementaires* to try suspects. His zeal earned him a vote of thanks from the Paris Faculty of Theology on 29 December.[24] But the Protestants soon struck again.

On 13 January, shortly after Francis's return to the capital, some copies of Marcourt's *Petit traité* – an elaboration of the doctrine of the placards – were found in the streets of Paris. This second 'affair', though less dramatic than the first, was more provocative since it cocked a snook at the authorities, just as they were congratulating themselves on having stamped out the October 'plot'.[25] It was presumably this second affair which prompted Francis to ban all printing till further notice and to order a procession for 21 January.[26] Such processions, as Philip Benedict has shown, 'served as a rite of purification for a city soiled by heresy, thereby conveying very clearly to the onlooking crowds the message that the Protestants formed a force within society whose polluting actions required community atonement'.[27]

The procession on 21 January was one of the most spectacular ever seen in the French capital. It brought together the royal court and all the main corpo-

---

[23] Bourrilly and Weiss, liii (1904), 117.   [24] *Ibid.*, and Hari, p. 107.

[25] The evidence for this second 'affair' is an unsigned letter written from Paris to John Longland, bishop of Lincoln. It was transcribed into his register, and E. Peacock published it in *Athenaeum*, no. 2761 (25 September 1880), 401. It contains the following passage: 'Ther was within thise fewe dayes by the stretes of parrys scatoryd books which was Intitled Parantiphrasyn scilicet a right prouffitable Intreatise concernynge the Sacrament of the aulter, wherin as they say were scarsely soo many sentences as blasphemyes contrary to the said sacrament wherewith the Kynge was highly offended.'

[26] Bourrilly and Weiss, p. 118. The ban on printing was not registered by the Parlement (C.A.F., iii. No. 7461; A.N. X^{1a} 1538 f. 113) but an edict reiterating the ban on 23 February 1535 (C.A.F., iii. No. 7559) was registered. F. J. Higman *Censorship and the Sorbonne* (Geneva, 1979), p. 34.

[27] P. Benedict, *Rouen during the Wars of Religion* (Cambridge, 1981), p. 64.

rate bodies in Paris: the sovereign courts, university, religious orders, municipal government and trade guilds. A notable feature was the large number of shrines and relics that were brought out from the churches for the occasion. The most precious came from the Sainte-Chapelle and included the Crown of Thorns, at the sight of which, we are told, the 'people's hair stood on end'. At the centre of the procession was the Blessed Sacrament, which the placards had outraged; it was carried by the bishop of Paris under a canopy borne aloft by the king's three sons and the duc de Vendôme. Immediately behind, walked Francis, bareheaded, dressed in black and holding a lighted candle. To the accompaniment of church bells, hymn-singing and instrumental music, the huge cortège wound its way from Saint-Germain l'Auxerrois to Notre-Dame. Every now and then it came to a halt and the host was placed on a temporary altar. An anthem was sung and the king lost himself in prayer, a sight which allegedly drew tears from the spectators. Occasionally someone in the crowd shouted: 'Sire, do good justice!' and he replied with a sign indicating that he could be trusted to do so.[28]

After high mass at Notre-Dame, Francis and his queen were given lunch at the bishop's palace. Then, in the presence of a large and distinguished gathering, Francis urged his subjects to denounce all heretics, even if they were close relatives or friends. The day ended with six more burnings, but the king did not light the faggots himself. He did not even watch the burnings, but left Paris as soon as the victims had done public penance. This, alas, was not the end of the persecution. Many more burnings took place before it ended in May. Meanwhile, other repressive measures were taken: on 24 January a royal proclamation called on seventy-three 'Lutherans', who had gone into hiding, to give themselves up. They included some famous names, notably Pierre Caroli, Clément Marot, Marthurin Cordier and Simon du Bois.[29] On the 29th an edict made harbourers of heretics liable to the same penalties as the heretics themselves and offered informers a quarter share of the victims' property.[30]

Why did Francis react so savagely to the placards? The traditional explanation is that he was enraged by a placard that was discovered on his bedchamber door. The story rests on more or less contemporary evidence, though

---

[28] There are several contemporary accounts of this procession. One of the fullest is in *Cronique du roy Françoys premier*, ed. G. Guiffrey (1860). See also *Athenaeum*, no. 2761 (25 September 1880), 401. The best modern account is in Berthoud, *Antoine Marcourt*, pp. 190–5. For a discussion of comparable processions in Rouen see P. Benedict, *Rouen during the Wars of Religion*, pp. 62–4.

[29] For a full list see Hari, pp. 104–6.

[30] Bourrilly and Weiss, liii, 129. A letter written by Andrew Baynton to Thomas Cromwell from Paris on 1 February 1535 contains an interesting account of these momentous events. Paris, he states, is full of heretics of both sexes: twenty have already been burned, thousands are in hiding and about a hundred have fled. He alleges that Francis in his speech asked God to forgive his slackness in persecuting heretics over the previous two years and swore henceforth to burn all who fell into his hands. To do this, Baynton suggests, the king would need to shut the gates of Paris and set fire to the city. Public Record Office, London: SP1/89/136–7.

there is much confusion over details. Crespin states that the placard was found at the Louvre, de Bèze gives the location as Blois; both mention the bedchamber door, but Fontaine states that the placard was found 'in the king's cup (*tasse*) wherein he placed his handkerchief'. Florimond de Raemond describes how Guillaume Feret threw Protestant articles of faith into the king's *cabinet* and planted 'small bills in the *nef* from which he is served at table'. Nearly everyone mentions the king's anger. According to Crespin, he 'vomited rage through his eyes and mouth', and de Bèze writes that the king decided there and then to 'exterminate everyone'. Fontaine says that Francis 'entered into an incredible zeal' after the placard had been read out to him.[31] A distillation of all these stories has found its way into most modern text-books. 'It seems characteristic of the superficiality of Francis', writes A. G. Dickens, 'that a personal affront should have decided his policy.'[32]

Superficial Francis may have been, but it is difficult to believe that a personal affront alone was responsible for the persecution that followed. One placard was almost certainly planted in the royal apartment at Amboise, for the martyrs of 1535 included a chorister of the king's chapel who had allegedly introduced placards into the château when Francis was residing there.[33] But was this an offence of sufficient gravity to provoke a violent and protracted persecution far from the scene of the crime? Intrusions on the king's privacy were not unknown. Such was his accessibility that he once complained of thefts from his wardrobe and chapel.[34] In January 1533 three armed strangers were found in his bedchamber at the Louvre, yet his only response was to ask the Parlement to show more vigilance in policing the streets of Paris at night.[35] What is more, nothing in the king's behaviour immediately after the Affair of the Placards suggests a great explosion of anger. Nearly two months elapsed before he wrote to Duprat giving his approval to the persecution.[36] It is also unlikely that a royal command could have reached Paris so soon after the discovery of the placard at Amboise. The journey between the two towns normally took three days, though a royal messenger could have accomplished it in twenty-four hours.

Did Francis unleash the persecution or did he merely signal his approval of measures taken by others in his name? No archival evidence links the start of

---

[31] J. Crespin, *Histoire des martyrs* (1554); T. de Bèze, *Histoire Ecclésiastique* (1580), S. Fontaine, *Histoire catholique de nostre temps* (1558) and F. de Raemond, *Histoire de la naissance, progrez et décadence de l'hérésie de ce siècle* (1647). The relevant passages are quoted in Hari, pp. 84–8. Also Berthoud, p. 181.

[32] A. G. Dickens, *Reformation and Society in sixteenth-century Europe* (London, 1966), p. 98.

[33] *J.B.P.*, p. 384. He was allegedly sent to Paris by the king and burned at the 'carrefour du Gros Tournois' on 13 March 1535.

[34] *Ordonnances*, vi. 122–3.   [35] A.N., X^{1a} 1536, f. 68v.

[36] Francis left Amboise on 20 October. He stayed at Châtellerault from *c.* 7 until 22 November and at Saint-Germain-en-Laye from 20 December till 3 January. C.A.F., viii. 487.

the persecution to any incident in Amboise.[37] When the *Bureau de la Ville* met on 19 October it was in response to a call from the Parlement; the municipal register does not mention the king. It was also the Parlement which ordered the search for culprits and the general procession on 22 October.[38] Francis did not, it seems, react officially till 9 December. Thus it seems that it was the affair in Paris rather than the bedchamber incident in Amboise which prompted the persecution and that this was instigated by the Parlement, exactly as it had done in October 1533 following Cop's sermon. On that occasion Francis had called a halt to the persecution after his return to Paris from the south of France. Why did he not do the same in January 1535? The answer surely lies in the nature of the challenge. Cop's sermon had been a moderate statement of evangelical belief directed at an academic audience; the placards were an extremely violent attack on the fundamental tenet of Catholic belief aimed at the general public. Their clandestine distribution and display were calculated to provoke a public disturbance. Fixing a placard on the king's bedchamber door was an impertinence; displaying others in five towns on the same night pointed to the existence of a well-organized underground movement of radical dissent. But it was the message of the placards rather than the method of their dissemination which shocked the authorities: their language revealed how extreme some reformers had become. It was exceptionally abusive, even by sixteenth-century standards: thus transubstantiation was denounced as a 'horrible and execrable blasphemy', an act of 'public idolatry' and the 'doctrine of devils'. Priests were condemned as 'miserable sacrificers', 'false antichrists' 'ravishing wolves', 'brigands', 'lewd fellows' [*paillards*] and 'enemies of God'.[39]

Ironically, the placards were a gift to the Parlement and Faculty of Theology which had been trying for years to silence the voices of evangelicalism only to be repeatedly obstructed by the king. Now they had him in their power. He could not dispute the gravity of the offence committed by the perpetrators of the placards; nor could he stem the tide of popular hysteria they had provoked. Embarrassing as the persecution was for his diplomacy with the German Protestants, it was unavoidable. Had Francis tried to unwind it, his credibility as 'The Most Christian King' would have been irreparably damaged. The author and distributors of the placards had taken dissent far beyond the kind of evangelicalism which the king had so far tolerated. Finding himself without room for manoeuvre, he chose the only possible course of action, which was to fall in with the persecution and assume its leadership in defence of the faith.

The Affair of the Placards was a watershed in the history of the French Reformation. It did not produce a change of royal policy from toleration to

---

[37] A letter written by the king to the *Bureau de la Ville* from Pontlevoy near Blois on 19 October and delivered on 26 October makes no mention of the affair. *R.D.B.V.P.*, ii. 194.
[38] *Ibid.*, ii. 192–3.
[39] Opinions differ on this point. Compare Hari, pp. 120–1 with Berthoud, p. 218.

persecution. Religious toleration before October 1534 had been strictly selective: only scholars and preachers with influence at court had enjoyed Francis's protection; no toleration had been accorded to the general run of heretics. N. M. Sutherland has suggested that as early as April 1526 Francis was determined 'to permit no interference with the Sacrament of the Eucharist'.[40] This may be so, though the evidence is hardly conclusive. What is certain is that the king's attitude hardened after the Affair of the Placards. This may have been for political as well as religious reasons. D. R. Kelley has pointed to the treasonable implications of sacramentarianism. 'To reject immanence', he writes, 'and thereby traditional authority, on grounds of private conscience was merely heretical; but to proclaim these views publicly was treasonable.'[41] Yet, as Mark Greengrass has argued, the significance of the placards should not be exaggerated. In many French provinces there was no perceptible change in repression in the years 1534–35. Orthodoxy was not defined in France until 1543 when a confession of faith, drawn up by the Paris Faculty of Theology was accepted by the parlements and promulgated as a royal law. Censorship was not co-ordinated or given a national basis until the Faculty produced an index of prohibited books in 1545. The competence of the various courts, lay and ecclesiastical, responsible for suppressing heresy was not properly defined till 1539–42.[42]

The placards revealed the existence within France of a group of sacramentarians, not necessarily a large one, whose opinions offended both liberals and reactionaries. They did not mark the end of Lucien Febvre's 'long period of magnificent religious anarchy', when, in the absence of any clear confessions of faith, the boundary between orthodoxy and dissent was easily crossed, but they brought it into sharper focus. Some Frenchmen, who in the past had crossed it carelessly, became more circumspect. The advent of sacramentarianism helped to polarize opinion in certain quarters, but, as David Nicholls has shown, the formative period of French Protestantism remained 'largely formless' until the late 1550s.[43] The term 'Lutheran' continued to be applied indiscriminately to all sorts of dissenters, yet, as far as the authorities were concerned, the battle lines were now clearer and likely targets of repression reacted accordingly. While many people were still prepared to risk death or imprisonment for their religious beliefs, others drew back and looked for personal safety in conformity. Some authors who had used distinctively Protestant names, like 'Christ'

[40] N. M. Sutherland, *The Huguenot Struggle for Recognition* (New Haven and London, 1980), pp. 14–18.
[41] D. R. Kelley, *The Beginning of Ideology: Consciousness and Society in the French Reformation* (Cambridge, 1981), pp. 13–19.
[42] M. Greengrass, *The French Reformation* (Oxford, 1987), p. 26.
[43] D. Nicholls, 'The nature of popular heresy in France, 1520–1542', *H.J.*, 26 (1983), 261–75. See also his chapter on France in A. Pettegree ed. *The Early Reformation in Europe* (Cambridge, 1992), pp. 120–41.

without 'Jesus', carefully deleted them from their works. Although Marguerite de Navarre continued to protect reformers at her court in Nérac, she assured her brother that none was a 'sacramentarian'.[44]

The edict of Coucy (16 July 1535)

The persecution of French dissenters which followed the Affair of the Placards seriously damaged Francis's reputation in Germany just as he was trying to heal its religious division. Imperial agents pointed to the shameful contrast between the king's harsh treatment of his own Protestant subjects and his friendly reception of Turkish ambassadors. They claimed that he was the main obstacle to the calling of a General Council, and accused him of throwing Germans into Parisian prisons.[45] Francis defended himself in a manifesto addressed to the imperial estates on 1 February 1535. The persecution, he explained, was political, not religious; its aim was the suppression of sedition. The imperial estates, he continued, would have acted as he had done if they had found themselves in his situation. He denied that he was at fault in negotiating with the Turks: Christendom needed peace and the Emperor's brother had done the same. It was also untrue, he said, that Germans were being persecuted in France: 'My court, my towns and my lands are open to all of your nation ... they are as free in France as are my own subjects and even my children.' It was easy to see why he was being slandered, the king concluded: it was to sow discord between the French and the Germans because their friendship barred the way to Habsburg ambitions: its destruction would allow the Emperor to build a universal monarchy on the ruins of the German liberties.[46] On 25 February Francis denied that he was opposed to a General Council. A papal nuncio, he said, had just arrived at his court and he intended keeping him there till the date, venue and agenda of a council had been arranged.[47]

Imperial propaganda, however, needed to be countered by deeds as well as words, and this was doubtless why in June 1535 Francis asked the Parlement to treat heretics less harshly, and on 16 July he issued the edict of Coucy which stopped the persecution on the ground that heresy in France had been wiped out.[48] The edict ordered the release of all religious prisoners and allowed religious exiles to return home, both categories being offered a pardon. Yet the edict was not an edict of toleration, for sacramentarians were excluded from the amnesty. The pardon was also made conditional on dissenters abjuring within

[44] Berthoud, *Antoine Marcourt*, pp. 216–20; P. Jourda, *Marguerite d'Angoulême* (1930), ii. 1069–70. In a letter to her brother of December 1542 Marguerite wrote: 'Thank God, my lord, none of ours has been found to be a sacramentarian'. Herminjard, vii. 392; P. Jourda, *Répertoire analytique et chronologique de la correspondance de Marguerite d'Angoulême* (1930), no. 903.

[45] V.-L. Bourrilly, *Guillaume du Bellay* (1905), pp. 188–9; Granvelle, *Papiers d'état*, ii. 283.

[46] Herminjard, iii. No. 492, pp. 249–54.

[47] A.N., K. 1483, no. 61.   [48] He did so allegedly at the request of Pope Paul III. *J.B.P.*, p. 458.

six months; if they failed to do so, they were to be hanged. As N. M. Sutherland has rightly pointed out, the edict was 'the first regulation to introduce the death penalty for the propagation of heresy by any spoken or written means'.[49]

The edict of Coucy coincided with a resumption of negotiations between Francis and the German Protestants. On 16 July, the very day it was issued, Barnabé de Voré set off for Germany bearing an invitation from Francis to Philip Melanchthon to take part in a theological debate with doctors of the Paris Faculty. He was assured of a warm welcome whether he came on his own account or as the representative of German Protestants as a whole.[50] At the same time, Francis informed the Faculty that Melanchthon and other Germans had asked 'to be received in the church'. He invited the Faculty to send ten or twelve doctors to the debate, but it was not so easily duped. 'One must not listen to heretics', the doctors replied, 'or have any dealings with them.' The king thanked them for their 'good' advice, while reserving his decision. Meanwhile, Langey gave the Faculty twelve articles based on the replies he had received from Melanchthon, Bucer and Hedio, to the questionnaire circulated in 1534. He promised not to return to Germany until the doctors had given their opinion. On 30 August the Faculty rejected the articles as a trap and refused to take part in any debate with their authors. Francis was reminded that in Germany such debates had produced only division and the loss of numberless souls. If the Lutherans wanted a settlement, the Faculty concluded, they had only to submit to the church's teaching.[51]

In Germany, too, Francis's hopes of a religious compromise were dashed. Johannes Sturm urged Melanchthon to accept the king's invitation for the sake of the French Protestants. His coming to France, Sturm said, would be like a patch of blue sky in a storm; he might even convert the king. 'He is quick-witted, sensible, and not stubborn', he explained, 'he submits readily to reasoned arguments.' Melanchthon was left in a quandary: if he went to France, he might be trapped into making important doctrinal concessions in return for trivial ones; if he did not go, his French co-religionists would feel abandoned. In the end, his mind was made up for him. On 17 August, his lord, the Elector of Saxony, forbade him to go to France.[52]

Yet Francis persisted in his efforts to reach an understanding with the German Protestants. Bucer advised him to make a new approach to the German princes and to the city of Strassburg, while stressing the need to keep

---

[49] *Ordonnances*, vii. No. 701, pp. 248–51. For its effects see N. Weiss, 'Documents inédits pour servir à l'histoire de la réforme sous François Ier, 1536–1537', *B.S.H.P.F.*, xxxiv (1885), 164–77, also C.A.F., vi. 20990. For a discussion of Francis's edicts against heresy see N. M. Sutherland, *The Huguenot Struggle for Recognition*, pp. 1–39, 333–40.

[50] Herminjard, iii. No. 498, pp. 266–70; no. 512, pp. 300–1.

[51] Imbart de La Tour, iii. 575–8; Herminjard, iii. 341 n 2; *C.S.P. Span*, v (pt i), no. 225.

[52] Herminjard, iii. no. 515, pp. 306–12; Bourrilly, *Guillaume du Bellay*, pp. 193–4.

politics out of religion.[53] Langey was accordingly dispatched to the diet of
the Schmalkaldic League. On 19 December he urged it to send representatives
to a conference in France before accepting the pope's invitation to a General
Council in Mantua. He told Melanchthon, Bucer and Bruck, the Saxon Chancellor, that Francis shared most of their doctrinal opinions. The king, he
said, regarded the papal primacy as a human institution; he held their views on
the Eucharist, the intercession of saints, religious images and Free Will. He
favoured mutual concessions on the Mass. Only their attitude to Purgatory and
good works was likely to cause difficulty, yet Francis did not think this would
be insuperable. He wanted clerical celibacy to be maintained, but was in
favour of exempting priests who were already married. Lastly, he hoped to
gain concessions from the pope regarding communion in both kinds.

Was Francis really prepared to travel so far towards Protestantism? This is
unlikely. He was always ready to listen to new ideas, but never showed any
special interest in Protestantism. Langey had probably been instructed to exag-
gerate his master's willingness to compromise over religion in order to gain the
political support of the Schmalkaldic League. In December 1535 Francis was
preparing to invade Savoy. Sooner or later he was bound to come into conflict
with Charles V. He, therefore, needed the support of the German Protestants,
but fell into the trap which Bucer had warned him against: by intimating that
he was prepared to join the League, he mixed politics with religion, thereby
arousing the distrust of the delegates. They turned down the pope's invitation
to attend the General Council in Mantua, but at the same time evaded the theological debate in France. Nor would they admit Francis to their League.
Instead, they undertook not to help his enemies in any quarrel that did not
involve the Emperor or his dominions.[54]

The Vaudois of Provence

Distrust of the French monarch among German Protestants was sustained
by reports that their French co-religionists were still being persecuted in spite
of the edict of Coucy. In July 1535, for example, they received an appeal for
help from the Vaudois or Waldenses of Provence.[55] These were a religious sect
whose origins went back to the twelfth-century Poor Men of Lyons. They had
since spread to various parts of central and southern Europe, notably Piedmont
and Provence. The Vaudois of Provence in the early sixteenth century were
mostly peasants who lived in villages and small towns spread out along the
valley of the Durance between the Upper Alps and Aix-en-Provence. Their

---

[53] J. V. Pollet, *Martin Bucer* (1962), ii. 505; *L.P.*, ix. no. 544.
[54] Bourrilly, *Guillaume du Bellay*, pp. 206–11.
[55] Herminjard, iii. no. 521, pp. 327–32; no. 523, pp. 335–9.

main centres were Mérindol in Provence and Cabrières in the papal enclave of Comtat-Venaissin. Substituting their own apostolic forms for the authority and practice of the Roman church, the Vaudois believed spiritual probity to be essential to the administration of the sacraments. They rejected the doctrine of purgatory, the swearing of oaths, the cult of the Virgin and saints, religious images and many prayers. Believing that all of nature was sacred, they did not think that worship had to be centred on a church. Outwardly, however, the Vaudois were not easily distinguished from their Catholic neighbours, for they tended to keep their beliefs to themselves while continuing to attend the local parish church, to pay tithes, to confess to the local priest and take communion from him. In short, they practised outward conformity. It was only at night and in the privacy of their own homes that the Vaudois assumed a distinctive religious identity with the help of itinerant preachers, called *barbes*.

Of peasant stock, like their flocks, the *barbes* had learnt to read and write and earned their living by plying some peripatetic trade. Their pastoral role was not to seek converts, but to confirm existing Vaudois in their faith by preaching to them on biblical texts and taking their confessions. The *barbes* were celibate and tried to lead apostolic lives. Each year they would gather in some secluded Alpine valley to report on their mission, to examine the current state of the Vaudois community and to bring offerings they had received, part of which were given to the poor. They would then depart, always in pairs, on another round of preaching which might take them quite far afield.[56]

Intermittent persecution of the Vaudois had taken place since the fourteenth century. In 1487 Pope Innocent VIII had launched a crusade against them, but in France at least this had been stopped by Louis XII.[57] The persecution was resumed, unofficially at first, under Francis I. About 1528 Jean de Roma, the Dominican inquisitor of the faith, toured their villages extorting confessions under torture (his favourite method was to pour boiling fat into the boots of his victims). But his activities came to the king's notice. An enquiry commission was set up and a warrant issued for de Roma's arrest. He fled to Avignon where he died of plague in 1533.[58] But this did not end the persecution of the Vaudois who, among the Waldenses, were distinctly precocious in making contact with the early Protestants.[59]

In September 1532 an important meeting of *barbes* took place at Chanforan

[56] G. Audisio, *Les vaudois du Luberon: une minorité en Provence (1460–1560)* (Mérindol, 1984), pp. 149–78, 199–278; G. Audisio, *Les 'vaudois'. Naissance, vie et mort d'une dissidence (XIIe–XVIe siècles)* (Turin, 1989), pp. 133–51.
[57] J. Marx, *L'Inquisition en Dauphiné: étude sur le développement et la répression de l'hérésie et de la sorcellerie du XIVe siècle au début du règne de François Ier* (1914), pp. 158–67, 178–98.
[58] Audisio, pp. 71–87.
[59] E. Cameron, *The Reformation of the Heretics: The Waldenses of the Alps, 1480–1580* (Oxford, 1984), pp. 135–6, 148; Audisio, *Les 'vaudois'*, pp. 174–82.

in Piedmont.[60] Its main purpose was to consider relations between the Vaudois and the Protestant Reformation. Among those present was Guillaume Farel, Calvin's closest collaborator. As a Dauphinois with knowledge of *occitan*, the tongue spoken by the Vaudois, he was uniquely placed to bring them into the Protestant orbit, and it was almost certainly under his powerful influence that a majority of the *barbes* at Chanforan decided to adhere to the Reformation. Their decision dealt a fatal blow to the Vaudois movement, as it had existed since the Middle Ages, for they renounced all of its distinctive tenets. The Vaudois were ill-equipped theologically to hold their own in the great doctrinal debates of sixteenth-century Europe. Geneva offered them not only a possible refuge but the example of a New Jerusalem in which the reformed faith was realized within a social context. In Calvin's *Institutes* they were given a coherent doctrine such as they had never possessed. But the adoption of Calvinism by the Vaudois rank and file did not happen overnight: some thirty years elapsed before their day-to-day lives were affected.[61]

Another important decision taken at Chanforan was to commission a new Bible in French based, not on the Latin Vulgate, but on Hebrew and Greek sources. It cost the Vaudois the large sum of 800 gold *écus*. The translation by Pierre Robert, alias Olivétan, was published at Neuchâtel by Pierre de Vingle on 4 June 1535. Why was the translation into French rather than *occitan*? It seems likely that the *barbes* had allowed themselves to be pressurized by Farel and other Francophone reformers to accept a Bible that would have an impact on the whole of France rather than just the Midi.[62]

On 17 July 1531 Francis I ordered an enquiry into the 'Lutherans' of the diocese of Aix. This lasted throughout 1532 and the archbishop's court began trying suspects in 1533. A teacher of Avignon reported that the Vaudois (whose number he estimated at 6,000) were being burned and their property seized.[63] In March 1534 the prior of Pertuis was ordered to spread the Word among the heretics of his area. Two years later several were interrogated and burnt. After July 1535 some Vaudois apparently benefited from the amnesty contained in the edict of Coucy and in September 1535 Farel wrote to Langey raising the possibility of his interceding with Francis on their behalf.[64]

---

[60] Cameron (pp. 131–44) dismisses the synod of Chanforan as a myth, but his view is not shared by G. Audisio, who offers conclusive evidence that the synod did take place at or near Chanforan. For criticisms of Cameron's thesis see G. Audisio in *Histoire des Religions*, cciii (1986), 395–405; G. G. Merlo in *Bollettino Storico-Bibliografico Subalpino*, lxxxiv (1986), 285–6; P. Biller in *English Historical Review* (1987), 664–9; and J. Fr. Gilmont in *Revue d'histoire ecclésiastique*, lxxxiii (1988), 69–89.

[61] Audisio, *Les vaudois du Luberon*, pp. 178–82; Audisio, *Les vaudois*, pp. 182–88, 192–202.

[62] *Ibid.*, pp. 183–7; G. Audisio, *Les vaudois des origines à leur fin (XIIe–XVIe siècles)* (Turin, 1988), pp. 90–3; Audisio, *Les 'vaudois'*, pp. 188–92.

[63] J. Bonnet, 'La tolérance du cardinal Sadolet', *B.S.H.P.F.*, xxxv (1886), 484.

[64] Cameron, p. 151; Herminjard, iii. 327–32, 356–62.

The growth of persecution

Limited as it was, the edict of Coucy encouraged reformers to hope that Francis was still open to persuasion. They believed he had been deliberately misled by evil counsellors about the activities of his evangelical subjects. He had been told that they were trouble-makers bent on overthrowing church and state, and some reformers hoped that the king might still be prepared to hear the truth. This hope was most eloquently expressed by Calvin in the preface to his *Christianae religionis institutio* (*Institutes of the Christian Religion*) which was addressed to Francis. The work was completed in August 1535 and published in Basle in March 1536. Calvin's original purpose, he states, had been to write a work of pious instruction for those who hunger after Christ, but after the terrible persecution they had suffered, he had decided to write a confession of faith for the king's information. The evangelicals, Calvin explained, had been falsely charged with sedition, and their cause, the very cause of Christ, had been torn apart and trampled upon. 'This has happened', he writes, 'as a result of the tyranny of certain Pharisees rather than by your will.' Not even those who sympathize with the evangelicals are prepared to rise in their defence; they talk merely of pardoning the error and imprudence of ignorant men. It is the king's duty to listen to what the evangelicals have to say in their own defence. A true king is one who rules as God's minister on earth; otherwise he is not a king but a robber. Replying to the objections commonly raised to evangelical teaching, Calvin argues that it is the fashionable theology of the late medieval church that is new; the evangelicals are the true heirs of the primitive church. In a final appeal to the king, he writes: 'although your heart is at present alienated from, even inflamed against us, I trust that we may regain its favour, if you will only read our confession once without indignation or wrath'.[65]

We do not know if Francis ever read Calvin's epistle, but reformers were encouraged on 31 May 1536, when the king, allegedly in response to an appeal from the council of Berne, extended the pardon contained in the edict of Coucy to all heretics, including sacramentarians. Yet a dissenter was still required to abjure his faith within six months.[66] In July the governments of Strassburg, Zürich, Basle and Berne appealed to Francis to waive this condition, but he did not reply. Doubtless, he had more urgent matters to attend to: the Emperor had just invaded Provence, and the Dauphin died on 10 August. In November the four cities decided to send him two envoys. They were instructed to tell him

[65] Herminjard, iv. no. 545, pp. 3–23. See also T. H. L. Parker, *John Calvin* (London, 1975), pp. 34–7.
[66] *Ordonnances*, viii. no. 741, pp. 93–6; Herminjard, iv. 71 n. 2. The poet Clément Marot, who had been in Italy in April 1535, returned to Lyons, where he abjured in December 1536. See C. A. Mayer, *La religion de Marot* (Geneva, 1960), pp. 35–9; M. François, *Le cardinal François de Tournon* (1951), p. 145 n. 1.

that it was unreasonable to expect Protestants to abjure their faith. They were also to praise the 'good conversation and honesty' of French exiles: far from criticizing and cursing the king, they had sung his praises and prayed for him. He had no cause, therefore, to fear any rebellion on their part; all they wanted was freedom of conscience.[67] The envoys, who saw Francis on 17 February 1537, were pleased by his verbal assurances; they were less satisfied by a letter he sent after they had left his court. They ought to be content, he said, with the extension of the edict of Coucy which had been conceded on their account alone: all religious exiles were now free to return to France without danger to their lives and property. He would order the release of heretics who were still in prison and pardon them, like the rest. But Francis failed to mention the abjuration clause which was of such concern to the Protestants.[68] On 15 March the council of Berne reported to the other cities on the mission of the two envoys. Apart from Langey and Count Wilhelm von Fürstenberg, the mercenary captain, they had met few friends of the Gospel at the French court and had, therefore, been less successful than they had hoped. Marguerite de Navarre had done all in her power to assist them, and they wanted to know from Fürstenberg if the king's letter truly reflected his intentions.[69]

Whether or not Fürstenberg was able to sort out the discrepancy between Francis's verbal and written statements to the Swiss envoys is uncertain. In September he secured a promise from him that evangelical prisoners held at Grenoble, Lyons and elsewhere would be set free, but in November the Genevan pastors were dismayed to learn that two Protestants had been burnt at Nîmes. Believing that Zürich had recently signed a treaty with Francis in which he had promised to treat heretics more leniently, they asked the canton to protest without delay. On 17 November Berne appealed to Francis to stop the persecution, but to no avail.[70] In brief, the king's promises to the Swiss reformers were empty: religious persecution in France continued in spite of the edicts of 1535 and 1536. As long as he needed the political support of the Swiss against the Emperor, Francis was content to string them along with 'fair words'.

By 1538 it had become clear to the royal administration that the advance of heresy in France would only be checked by giving the parlements more powers. On 16 December Francis urged the parlement of Toulouse to prosecute heretics vigorously and to punish them in an exemplary way.[71] On 24 June 1539 all judges, both secular and ecclesiastical, were instructed to co-operate in fighting

---

[67] Herminjard, iv. no. 566, pp. 70–3; no. 577, pp. 95–8; no. 604, pp. 169–72.
[68] *Ibid.*, iv. no. 612, pp. 191–3.
[69] *Ibid.*, iv. no. 618, pp. 202–3. On Fürstenberg see *ibid.*, vi. 123 n. 9 and J. V. Wagner, *Graf Wilhelm von Füstenberg, 1491–1549* (Stuggart, 1966).
[70] Herminjard, iv. no. 658, pp. 293–4; no. 668, pp. 315–19; no. 669, pp. 320–1.
[71] C.A.F., iii. 10534.

heresy, but the procedure laid down for them was too complicated to be effective.[72] On 1 June 1540, therefore, a new law – the famous edict of Fontainebleau – gave the parlements overall control of heresy jurisdiction. The preamble recalled the measures so far taken by the king to extirpate 'evil errors' from his realm. Having been purged, they had now reappeared and were being spread partly by religious exiles, who had come home, partly by heretics, who had lain low during the repression. Both sorts were being helped and sheltered by 'a number of important people'; hence the need for exceptional measures.

The ordinance entrusted to all royal judges 'indifferently and concurrently' the right of enquiry in respect of all persons, lay and ecclesiastical, except clergy in major orders. Suspects were to be sent directly to the sovereign courts for trial, notwithstanding any privilege or franchise. All feudal lords with powers of higher justice (*hauts justiciers*) were enjoined to carry out investigations within their respective areas of jurisdiction and to refer suspects to the king's judges. The ecclesiastical courts retained their jurisdiction over clerks in major orders but were to be assisted by the secular arm. Finally, all subjects were ordered, on pain of *lèse-majesté*, not to harbour or assist heretics but to denounce them and assist in their extirpation 'just as each is bound to run in order to put out a public fire'.[73]

---

[72] Isambert, xii. 566; C.A.F., iv. 11072.   [73] Isambert, xii. 676–81.

Chapter sixteen

Montmorency's triumph (1535–38)

Western Europe stood on the brink of war in the spring of 1535. Charles V was preparing an attack on the Barbary corsairs of North Africa who were threatening Spanish shipping, and Francis made this a pretext for re-arming. 'The engagements entered into with me', he declared, 'are not kept at all. If the emperor arms, I cannot but do the same.'[1] The papal nuncio was alarmed by the king's belligerency. His hatred, he wrote, was such that 'he seems to make it his business to provoke the emperor'.[2]

Two important embassies

While Francis was inspecting his legions, his diplomats were active throughout Europe. Two were particularly important: Jean de La Forêt and Cardinal Jean du Bellay. La Forêt was sent to the Ottoman court in February 1535 with a view to gaining the Sultan's help in a future war with the Emperor. He stopped in north Africa on the way and offered Khair-ad-Din Barbarossa fifty ships as well as victuals and munitions in return for help against Genoa.[3] In Constantinople, La Forêt allegedly signed a commercial treaty, called the *Capitulations*, in February 1536. Although this agreement has long been regarded as the foundation of French influence in the Levant till the nineteenth century, its existence has of late been called into question, as its only surviving version is a draft. Negotiations certainly did take place between La Forêt and Ibrahim, the Sultan's chief minister, and they may have agreed to co-operate in the military field. No formal agreement, however, seems to have been con-

---

[1] *C.S.P. Span.*, v (pt. 1), no. 130.
[2] H. Jedin, *A History of the Council of Trent*, tr. E. Graf (London, 1957–61), i. 300.
[3] E. Charrière (ed.) *Négociations de la France dans le Levant* (1848–60), i. 255–63; V.-L. Bourrilly, 'L'ambassade de La Forest et de Marillac à Constantinople (1535–38)', *R.H.*, lxxvi (1901), 297–328. For the legions, see below pp. 350–2.

cluded, and a commercial treaty, if discussed at all, seems to have been shelved.[4]

Jean du Bellay was sent to Italy in June 1535 primarily to win over the new pope, Paul III, to Francis's side and to dissuade him from calling a General Council, which, the king believed, would merely serve to increase the Emperor's power. On the way south, he tried to patch up a quarrel between the duke and duchess of Ferrara. He also made contact with a number of *condottieri*. In Rome, the cardinal collaborated with Filippo Strozzi, leader of the Florentine exiles, who were plotting to liberate their city from the rule of Alessandro de' Medici, the Emperor's son-in-law. As far as the main object of his mission was concerned, du Bellay was only moderately successful. Paul III listened to him with interest, but reserved his position. He distrusted Francis's professions of devotion to the Holy See.[5] While claiming to be shocked by Henry VIII's religious policy, the king was unwilling to help the pope's efforts to depose the schismatic monarch.[6]

The invasion of Savoy

On 10 June 1535 Charles V sailed out of Barcelona at the head of a large expeditionary force, and on 14 July he captured La Goletta, a fortress guarding the entrance to the bay of Tunis. Among the booty he captured were several French cannon. Tunis fell soon afterwards, but Barbarossa managed to escape to Algiers with part of his fleet. On 22 August the Emperor landed in Sicily at the start of a triumphal progress that was to take him up the entire length of the Italian peninsula.

Francis, in the meantime, did nothing, much to the chagrin of the war-party at his court, led by Admiral Chabot. Montmorency, who had given his word to the imperial ambassador that Francis would take no unfair advantage of Charles during his absence, came in for much bitter criticism. In July he left the court and retired to Chantilly. Chabot became effectively the king's chief minister. But Montmorency's withdrawal from the court did not amount to a disgrace: he ceased to attend the council for a time, but remained head of the royal household and retained all his titles, offices and pensions. In October he presided over the estates of Languedoc as governor of the province, mustered its legion and inspected Narbonne's fortifications.[7]

Montmorency may not have been responsible for the king's inertia in the summer of 1535. Other reasons may be suggested. Francis, as yet, had no *casus*

[4] *Ordonnances*, viii. pp. 503–74.
[5] V.-L. Bourrilly, 'Le cardinal Jean du Bellay en Italie', *Revue des études rabelaisiennes*, v (1907), 246–53, 262–74.
[6] *L.P.*, viii. 837; ix. 148.   [7] Decrue, i. 241–4; Jacquart, *François Ier*, p. 238.

belli. He would also have seriously damaged his international reputation had he stabbed the Emperor in the back while Charles was fighting the Infidel. On a more practical level, Francis was not ready for war: in July he was still mustering his legions. By the time they were ready, the fighting season was almost over. The king was also detained in Lyons during the autumn by 'a fever, flux of the belly and stomach pain'.[8]

On 1 November the question of the Milanese succession was revived when Francesco Sforza, who had ruled the duchy since 1525, died without leaving a male heir. Francis, who had reluctantly abandoned his claim to the duchy in the treaty of Cambrai, immediately proposed that Milan should be given to his second son, Henri duc d'Orléans. This, however, was unacceptable to the Emperor, who, as suzerain, had the duchy's investiture in his gift. Henri was too close to the French throne; he also had a claim to the duchy of Urbino through his wife, Catherine de' Medici. If he acquired Milan and Urbino, he would need only Naples to be master of Italy. But Charles V did not rule out the possibility of conferring Milan on Francis's third son, Charles duc d'Angoulême.

Matters stood thus in February 1536, when Francis suddenly invaded the duchy of Savoy. His relations with his uncle, Duke Charles III, had been strained for some time. Francis claimed that the duke was clinging to territory that had belonged to his own mother, Louise of Savoy. He also bore him a grudge for his refusal to allow Nice to serve as the venue for his meeting with Clement VII in 1533. In December 1535 Francis asserted his claims, while the duke was engaged in a conflict with the city of Geneva. In January he sent Poyet to Savoy with an ultimatum. At this juncture, the Bernese threw in their lot with the Genevans, and ironically Duke Charles appealed to Francis for help. The king ostensibly offered his mediation, while he informed the Bernese of his own designs on Savoy. They accordingly called off their campaign, leaving the way clear for Francis to invade. Charles III was too weak to resist. On 24 February he lost Bourg-en-Bresse and, five days later, Chambéry. The conquest of Savoy was completed in March, when Chabot pushed eastward into Piedmont, capturing its capital, Turin. He then laid siege to Vercelli, but was careful not to trespass on Milanese territory. If there was to be war with the Emperor, Francis wanted to be able to blame Charles V for starting it.[9]

Francis claimed that he had acted in self-defence. He only wanted, so he said, to regain territories which were his by right; but this was a poor excuse. His real purpose in invading Savoy was to acquire either a bargaining counter in his negotiations with the Emperor on Milan's future or a springboard from

---

[8] M. François, *Le cardinal François de Tournon* (1951), p. 126 n3; *C.S.P. Span.*, v (pt. 1), no. 226; *R.D.B.V.P.*, ii. 209.
[9] Du Bellay, ii. 302 ff.

64. Bronze medal bearing the profile of the Emperor Charles V by Hans Reinhardt the elder (1537).

which to invade that duchy should the negotiations collapse.[10] However, Charles III was the Emperor's brother-in-law and ally. By attacking him Francis gravely offended Charles V. At the time of the French invasion the Emperor was in southern Italy, too far away to come to the duke's assistance. He needed time to reorganize his army and to establish his authority in the kingdom of Naples. He therefore played for time by keeping the Milanese question open to discussion. He even offered to consider the candidature of the duc d'Orléans. Privately, however, he made it clear that he would never entertain it.[11]

On 17 April the Emperor denounced the French invasion of Savoy in a

[10] Decrue, i. 253.   [11] C.S.P. Span., v (pt. 2), no. 26, p. 48.

speech to the pope and college of cardinals. He offered Francis the choice either of accepting Milan conditionally for his youngest son or of meeting him, the Emperor, in single combat. If he chose the second option, the prize would be Burgundy on the one side and Milan on the other. But before any talks could take place, Charles warned, all French forces would need to be withdrawn from Piedmont. Paul III, for his part, refused to allow a duel between the Emperor and the king of France. He promised to make every effort to reconcile them and to declare against the one who would oppose a reasonable settlement.[12]

On 24 April the cardinal of Lorraine met the Emperor at Siena and tried to persuade him to give Francis the life reversion of Milan, which in the meantime would be held by Orléans. But Charles no longer needed to temporize now that he had almost reached the Lombard plain. He repeated his offer to cede the duchy to the king's third son, but emphatically refused to give Francis its life reversion.[13] On 11 May Francis replied to the Emperor's speech. 'I cannot understand', he said, 'how the Emperor can claim that in making war upon the duke [of Savoy] I contravene any treaty made with him, for nothing belonging to the Empire has been touched by my troops; on the contrary, both the generals and captains of my army have received instructions not to attempt anything against the Emperor's territory.' He offered to submit his claims to Savoy to papal arbitration. As for the Emperor's challenge to a duel, Francis accepted it while making it clear that, in his view, Charles had no injury to avenge.[14]

In north Italy, meanwhile, an undeclared state of war between France and the Empire already existed. In April Chabot was instructed to plant garrisons in Pinerolo, Turin, Fossano and Coni and to bring the rest of his army back to France. He was replaced as lieutenant-general in Piedmont by Francis, marquis of Saluzzo. Cabot's recall may have been connected with Montmorency's return to court: on 7 May the Grand Master was again playing his full part in government. Nor is this surprising, for he was generally regarded as France's best general.[15] A strong hand was needed to take charge of military operations. In May de Leyva entered Piedmont threatening the garrisons left behind by Chabot. Saluzzo wanted to evacuate the entire province, except Turin, but was resisted by his captains who feared that such a move would facilitate an imperial attack on Provence. Their anxiety proved justified, for the marquis, who coveted the county of Montferrat, was secretly in league with the enemy. On 17 May he surrendered Coni and returned his insignia of the order of St

---

[12] L. von Pastor, *The History of the Popes*, tr. F. I. Antrobus and R. F. Kerr (London, 1891–1933), xi. 247–52; du Bellay, ii. 354–70.

[13] Du Bellay, ii. 383–4, 393–8; iii. 12–26; *C.S.P. Span.*, v (pt. 2) nos. 45–6.

[14] Du Bellay, ii. 402–12; *C.S.P. Span.*, v (pt. 2), no. 52. The king's reply was written by Guillaume du Bellay and circulated widely. See Bourrilly, *Guillaume du Bellay*, pp. 215–16.

[15] Decrue, i. 257; *C.S.P. Span.*, v (pt. 2), no. 50, p. 111; du Bellay, ii. 399–401; iii. 64–6.

Michael to Francis. His defection nearly caused the collapse of the French position in Piedmont, but Fossano held out for a month, allowing Francis time to
prepare the defence of south-east France.[16] He gathered as many troops as possible in Lyons, while Jean de Humières, the new lieutenant-general in Dauphiné, Savoy and Piedmont, concentrated supplies at Grenoble and distributed
troops and munitions among castles guarding the Alpine passes. Work also
began on fortifying Marseilles.[17]

On 11 June Francis dismissed the imperial ambassador from his court. The
pope, meanwhile, called a General Council for the following May and
appointed Cardinals Caracciolo and Trivulzio to mediate between the king of
France and the Emperor. But the latter would not listen: he complained that
Francis had continued to provoke him since he had left Rome and said that he
could only defend himself. On 13 July he decided to invade Provence.[18]

Charles V's invasion of Provence (1536)

On 14 July Montmorency was appointed lieutenant-general 'on either
side of the mountains' with powers to mobilize troops, direct military
operations, appoint officers, and, if necessary, negotiate with the enemy.[19]
Francis himself took no part in the fighting. On his council's advice he kept
well behind the front line so as not to compromise the defensive strategy;
otherwise he would have been in honour bound to respond to a personal challenge by the Emperor. He nevertheless took an active part in the military
preparations and was kept continually informed of developments in the campaign. Jean du Bellay reported on 13 July that Francis had decided to 'act
rather as captain than as soldier'.[20] Once it became clear that the Emperor
would advance into Provence along the coast road through Nice, the king's
army was directed to Avignon, which the French had recently occupied. Some
30,000 men had gathered there by 25 July, when Montmorency took up his
command; by the end of August their number had roughly doubled.

The Emperor would have been wise to drive the French out of Piedmont
before attacking France itself, but he preferred to revive the plan Bourbon had
failed to carry out in 1524: namely, to invade Provence and, at the same time,
launch an attack on northern France, thereby obliging Francis to divide his
forces. Charles had several advantages over Bourbon: his army was larger and
more experienced, he had better naval support and, above all, he did not have
to count on the king of England creating the diversion in the north. Henry of

---

[16] Du Bellay, iii. 9–12, 66–86, 94–108.   [17] *Ibid.*, iii. 33–44.
[18] *Ibid.*, iii. 116–30; *C.S.P. Span.*, v (pt. 2), nos. 62, 73, 74, 75; Decrue, i. 259.
[19] *C.A.F.*, iii. 8563.
[20] *Correspondance du cardinal Jean du Bellay*, ed. R. Scheurer (1969–73), ii. 378.

Nassau could be relied upon to do so at the right moment. On 24 July Charles V crossed the Var into Provence, confident that he would defeat the French before winter set in.[21]

Montmorency had the choice of engaging the enemy or waiting in carefully selected and strongly fortified positions. Though some of his captains wanted to defend Aix, he preferred to remain at Avignon. This was in line with a strategy outlined by the king in June: namely, not to offer the Emperor battle, but to harass him with continual skirmishes and force him to waste time and money.[22] However, before committing himself, Montmorency inspected the defences of Aix and Marseilles. Finding that a month would be needed to repair Aix's fortifications and that the town had not enough supplies for a garrison of 6,000 men which was needed to defend it, he ordered its evacuation. The inhabitants were given six days in which to destroy or remove anything of potential value to the enemy.[23]

The evacuation of Aix was part of a comprehensive strategy aimed at creating a vacuum in front of the advancing enemy. Lower Provence was systematically laid waste by troops under the deputy governor, Bonneval. Mills were destroyed, wells blocked, stocks of wood and grain burnt, wine barrels smashed open, salt spoiled and farm animals let loose. Only fruit trees and vines were spared in the hope of encouraging the spread of dysentery among the enemy. Here and there peasants resisted the destruction, but in general they co-operated with the royal troops.[24] Of course, the destruction or *gast* was not applied to Marseilles, which had contributed so decisively to Bourbon's defeat in 1524. Since May its fortifications had been strengthened and its garrison reinforced. A large fleet under Saint-Blancard was stationed in the harbour.[25] Montmorency also aimed to prevent any link-up of Charles V's army from Italy with a potential invading force from Spain. Thus, while Lower Provence was evacuated, towns guarding the Rhône – Arles, Tarascon and Beaucaire – were heavily fortified. The hub of the French defensive system was Montmorency's camp south-east of Avignon. It was easily accessible to supplies and reinforcements coming down the Rhône and there were useful vantage points nearby. The camp, which may have been inspired by the ancient Roman model, was enclosed by a wide ditch and an earthen rampart with artillery platforms. A watercourse running through the middle and linked to a network of channels ensured a high standard of hygiene. Strict discipline was maintained by segregating the various nationalities in the army, each being allotted

---

[21] Du Bellay, iii. 140; C.S.P. Span., v (pt. 2), no. 74.
[22] Du Bellay, iii. 285; C.S.P. Span., v (pt. 2), no. 59.
[23] Du Bellay, iii. 181–2; Decrue, i. 270–1.
[24] Du Bellay, iii. 183, 188, 191; G. Procacci 'La Provence à la veille des Guerres de Religion: une periode décisive, 1535–45', Rev. d'hist. mod. et contemp., v (1958), 249–50.
[25] Du Bellay, iii. 178–80.

65. Francis I in armour by Louis Claude Vassé (1716–1772). Bronze bust made in 1757 for King Louis XV and modelled on a sixteenth-century stone bust found in 1756 at Fontainebleau and since lost.

a compartment formed by the grid of water channels. Montmorency's tent stood on a central mound from which the entire camp could be surveyed. 'No camp', he wrote, 'was ever seen in our time which was stronger, more beautiful, more free from disease or as well supplied with victuals.'[26]

The king, meanwhile, established his headquarters further north at Valence, which became an important assembly point for troops, artillery and supplies bound for Avignon. It was also a useful base from which to co-ordinate the defence of northern France with that of the south. Francis kept in constant touch with his council in Lyons, with Montmorency at Avignon and with the authorities in charge of defending the north.

Charles V had timed his invasion of Provence to coincide with an attack on

[26] *Ibid.*, iii. 193–4, 208–11; Decrue, i. 271–3, 275, 279.

northern France led by Henry count of Nassau. The latter captured Guise but failed to take Saint-Quentin. On 12 August, he laid siege to Péronne.[27] The defence of northern France was entrusted to three men: Charles duc de Vendôme and governor of Picardy, Claude duc de Guise and governor of Champagne and Cardinal Jean du Bellay, governor of Paris and Ile-de-France. Their task was made difficult by the absence of the *gendarmerie*, which was in the south, and by a lack of funds. Vendôme felt certain that the legionaries and *aventuriers* under his command would take advantage of the *gendarmerie*'s absence to mutiny if they were not paid punctually. He looked for assistance to du Bellay, who, as governor of Paris, was best able to tap the wealth of its inhabitants, but the cardinal had been instructed by the king to undertake a costly fortification programme for the capital. The clash of priorities caused much tension between the two men. In the end, du Bellay's ingenuity prevailed: without sacrificing his fortification programme, he raised a loan of 140,000 *livres* from the Parisians and persuaded them to pay for 6,000 additional infantry for service in Picardy.[28] Vendôme's troops also proved more dependable than expected, so that Nassau was eventually obliged to lift the siege of Péronne and retire into Flanders.

Meanwhile, in Provence, Montmorency's defensive strategy paid off handsomely. The Emperor, after capturing Aix on 13 August, pitched camp a few miles outside the town. He could advance either north or west, but either way his path was blocked by the French. In the south, he had to contend with Marseilles which had been such a thorn in Bourbon's side twelve years earlier. After carrying out reconnaissances in all three directions, Charles decided to stay put, but his troops began to succumb to hunger and sickness. Convoys travelling to the imperial camp from the coast were regularly plundered, while soldiers who searched the countryside for food were set upon and butchered. On 2 September Montmorency reported that the Emperor had already lost 7,000 or 8,000 men from famine or dysentery.[29] Five days later de Leyva, Charles's principal lieutenant, died.

Francis also suffered a great loss at this time. On 10 August his eldest son, the Dauphin François, died suddenly at Tournus, almost certainly of natural causes. Poison was suspected, however, and Sebastiano de Montecuculli, one of the Dauphin's servants, was accused of his murder. Incriminating documents, including a treatise on poisons and an imperial safe-conduct, were found among his possessions. Montecuculli admitted the charge under torture, but subsequently retracted. He was none the less executed with appalling cruelty in Lyons on 7 October. Meanwhile, the French government accused the

---

[27] Du Bellay, iii. 212–14; *C.S.P. Span.*, v (pt. 2), no. 96.
[28] *Correspondance du cardinal Jean du Bellay*, ii. nos. 387, 389, 395, 401, 402.
[29] Du Bellay, iii, 195–204, 241–8; Decrue, i. 276–9; *C.S.P. Span.*, v (pt. 2), no. 97.

Emperor and Ferrante Gonzaga, the imperial governor of Milan, of having
instigated the murder, a charge which they vigorously denied. Equally unfairly,
they accused the Dauphin's brother, Henri, and his wife, Catherine de' Medici.[30]
Such charges and counter-charges did nothing to mend Franco-imperial
relations; but the papal legate, Cardinal Trivulzio, pointed out that the Dauphin's death had removed the main obstacle to a peaceful settlement of the
Milanese succession. Henri, duc d'Orléans was now too near the French throne
to be a suitable candidate for the duchy. This left his younger brother, Charles
d'Angoulême, whom the Emperor had been prepared to accept. But the
Emperor was less inclined to accept Angoulême, now that he stood second,
instead of third, in line of succession to the French throne. He told the nuncio
that Francis would have to offer realistic peace terms or face the trial of
strength which he had so far avoided.[31]

On 11 September the Emperor began retreating towards Fréjus, having
already sent his heavy guns to the coast; yet Francis, who joined Montmorency at Avignon the next day, resisted the temptation to set off in pursuit.
News of Nassau's retreat from Péronne had not yet reached him, so that he
was not sure that his army would not be needed in the north. He was also
desperately hard up. The first year of fighting had virtually wiped out his
reserves. He had started out with only 1,500,000 *livres* and the war had so far
cost him more than 4,500,000 *livres*.[32] He had other resources, of course, but
needed every *sou* to prepare the next season's offensive. So, instead of trying
to cut off the Emperor's retreat by a quick dash across the Alps, Francis
merely sent his light cavalry to harass Charles's rear. Mocking the king's
timidity, the Emperor boasted that his retreat had been accomplished in
perfect order and without serious loss. It was, however, a sadly depleted army
that he brought back to Italy on 23 September. Soon afterwards he sailed from
Genoa to Spain.[33]

Stalemate

Francis, meanwhile, went on a tour of inspection of Provence. He visited
several towns, including Marseilles, but stayed away from Aix, whence plague
was reported. He saw how the province had been devastated, but refused to
compensate the inhabitants as long as the war lasted. A Marseillais chronicler
remarked that 'the donkey always carries the saddle'.[34] The task of disbanding

[30] François, *François de Tournon*, p. 132; Bourrilly, *Guillaume du Bellay*, pp. 229, 233; Guiffrey, pp. 188–9.
[31] *C.S.P. Span.*, v (pt. 2), no. 92.
[32] G. Jacqueton, 'Le Trésor de l'Epargne sous François Ier, 1523–1547', *R.H.*, lvi (1894), 20–1.
[33] Decrue, i. 286.   [34] Bourrilly, *Guillaume du Bellay*, pp. 230–1; Procacci, 'Provence', p. 251.

the army in the south was left to Cardinal Tournon, who was appointed lieutenant-general in south-east France. Using money borrowed from the bankers of Lyons, he paid off the foreign mercenaries, thereby saving Vienne from a sack, but he was unable to pay the garrisons in Piedmont. 'I could not send you a single *écu*', he wrote to Humières, 'even if the army were dying of hunger.'[35]

In mid October Francis left Lyons and travelled to Paris by way of the Loire valley. Meeting James V of Scotland on the way, he gave him the hand of his daughter, Madeleine. The marriage took place in Paris on 1 January 1537 and prompted the usual round of banquets, dances and tournaments.[36] Then, at a *lit de justice* on 15 January, Francis proclaimed the confiscation of Flanders, Artois and Charolais whose suzerainty he had surrendered in the peace of Cambrai. His purpose, however, was not to annex a large part of the Netherlands but to consolidate France's northern border by incorporating Thérouanne into his kingdom. The obvious man for this task was Montmorency whose prestige had been much enhanced by his recent triumph in Provence. On 10 March he was appointed lieutenant-general with the immediate object of recovering the counties of Artois and Saint-Pol.[37]

Early in March the king and Montmorency marched north from Amiens. After capturing Auxy-le-Château, the Grand Master laid siege to Hesdin, while Francis pitched camp at Pernes. On 6 May, however, after Saint-Pol had been reconquered, Francis suddenly called off the offensive in order to go to the rescue of his army in Piedmont. Humières was promised 10,000 landsknechts and told that the king would soon be going to Lyons. Francis knew that the Turks were planning a descent on the kingdom of Naples, but the prospect of a combined Franco-Turkish invasion of Italy faded when Charles V launched a counter-offensive in northern France. After capturing Saint-Pol and Montreuil, he laid siege to Thérouanne. Montmorency was immediately sent back to Artois and most of the troops intended for Piedmont were recalled. As the flow of money, which had started to trickle through to Piedmont, dried up, Pinerolo was sacked by Italian troops serving in the French army. Fortunately for Humières, the northern campaign came to an abrupt halt when the regent of the Netherlands called a truce. This was signed at Bomy on 30 July ending the siege of Thérouanne. Francis was allowed to fortify the towns he had captured in the spring; only Saint-Pol remained in enemy hands.[38]

---

[35] François, *François de Tournon*, pp. 133–7.
[36] G. Donaldson, *Scottish Kings* (London, 1967), pp. 155–9; du Bellay, iii. 338, 342. The long sea journey to Scotland proved too much for the princess, who died on 7 July.
[37] Decrue, i. 294, 297–302.
[38] *Ibid.*, i. 305, 307, 310; Bourrilly, *Guillaume du Bellay*, p. 244; J. Ursu, *La politique orientale de François 1er* (1908), p. 100.

The truce enabled Francis to go to the aid of his army in Piedmont, but it was now too late for his action to be co-ordinated with the Turks, who, after landing in Apulia, had turned their attention to Corfu.[39] Early in October Francis arrived in Lyons to prepare a new invasion of Italy, and on 8 October the bulk of the army set off for the Alps under Montmorency. After crossing the Mont Genèvre, the Grand Master forced his way along the Val di Susa and relieved the garrisons of Savigliano, Pinerolo and Turin. The king, who followed with the rest of the army, ordered prayers and processions of thanksgiving throughout France.[40] Within days the French had occupied Piedmont as far as Montferrat.

Both sides were now worn out. The campaign of 1537 had cost Francis 5,500,000 *livres*, even more than that of 1536 which had emptied his warchests.[41] The Emperor, too, was bankrupt. A three months' truce was, therefore, signed at Monzon, in Spain, on 16 November, and soon afterwards it was followed by peace talks at Leucate, near Narbonne. It was agreed that Milan should eventually be given to Charles d'Angoulême and that he should marry the daughter of the King of the Romans. But neither side could agree on the administration of Milan in the interim. Consequently, the talks collapsed after three weeks, leaving only the truce, which was extended till 1 June.[42]

On 10 February 1538 Montmorency was rewarded for his successes in Provence and elsewhere with the office of Constable of France, which had been vacant since Bourbon's treason. It was, symbolically, at Moulins, Bourbon's old capital, that he received the king's sword in the presence of all the court. Two new marshals of France, Claude d'Annebault and René de Montjehan, were created at the same time.[43]

The year 1536 has been acclaimed as the most glorious year in the reign of Francis I after 1515. Not only had he saved his kingdom from foreign invasion; he had also shown himself capable of pursuing an effective defensive strategy. While leaving much to chance in the north, he had shown foresight and prudence in the south. His Fabian tactics stood in sharp contrast to the foolhardiness that had marked the Pavia campaign.[44] Doubtless Montmorency deserves much of the credit for this change of policy. Yet the war had outlasted the king's capacity to fund it. Within a year he had spent all that had been set aside since 1532. If he had disposed of the means, he might have chased the Emperor back to Italy and defeated him decisively. As he could not fight a war on two fronts, he had been obliged to turn his attention to northern France, thereby

---

[39] *Ibid.*, pp. 103–4.   [40] Decrue, i. 326.   [41] Jacqueton, 'Le Trésor de l'Epargne', p. 21.
[42] Decrue, i. 332–5.
[43] *Ibid.*, i. 337–41. Annebault succeeded Robert de La Marck, better known as Florange, who died on 21 December 1536.
[44] H. Martin, *Histoire de France*, 4th edn (17 vols. 1858–60), viii. 244.

missing an opportunity of joint action with the Turks. Fortunately for Francis, the enemy was also bankrupt. Thus the war ended in stalemate. Francis still had a foothold in Italy, but in northern France he had lost ground. Provence lay impoverished and the succession to Milan remained unresolved.

Chapter seventeen

Domestic issues

Once Francis I had restored his authority following his Spanish captivity, he was able to attend to a number of important domestic issues, including further fiscal reform, the formal annexation of the duchy of Brittany, the creation of a national infantry, and judicial reform.

Rising expenditure

The financial records for the reign are incomplete and difficult to interpret. Global estimates of receipts and expenses are, at best, rough approximations, yet all the evidence points to the fact that in the 1530s and 1540s the government's expenditure continued to outstrip its resources.[1] The cost of the court was variable. The absence of a queen's household between the death of Claude in 1524 and the coming of Eleanor in 1530 helped to reduce costs, as did the death of Louise of Savoy in 1531 and the deaths of some royal children. Yet overall expenditure rose between 1531 and 1546 from 1,736,000 *livres* to 2,167,000 *livres*. The cost of the royal administration also went up, reflecting the inflationary effect of venality on the number of judicial offices. At the same time expenditure on foreign affairs exploded. As always, war was the biggest drain. Payment of the *compagnies d'ordonnances* (*Ordinaire des guerres*) rose from 143,000 *livres* in 1515 to 566,865 *livres* in 1529, and to 775,960 *livres* in 1532. The cost of hiring foreign mercenaries (*Extraordinaire des guerres*) rose from 113,937 *livres* in 1529 to 361,575 *livres* in 1536. The war of 1536–38 may have cost 15 million *livres*. The crown spent relatively more on the navy and fortifications in the 1530s than earlier. Until 1528 Francis relied largely on

---

[1] The most comprehensive and thorough survey of the financial history of the reign is P. Hamon, 'L'argent du roi: finances et gens de finances en France au temps de François Ier' (unpublished doctoral thesis. University of Paris I. 1993). Two contemporary manuscripts (B.N., ms. fr. 4523, ff. 1a–51b and ms. fr. 17329, ff. 82–92) provide valuable global figures for the king's receipts and expenses.

Doria's fleet, but after the Genoese admiral had defeated, the king had to build up his own navy. As from 1532 he spent an annual average of more than 200,000 *livres* on it.[2]

Even peace could be expensive. A contemporary account of expenses on 'journeys, embassies, *chevauchées* and *messageries*' indicates a dramatic rise in cost from 10,000 *livres* in 1515 to 34,500 *livres* in 1530 and 49,000 *livres* in 1531. Even more expensive relatively than diplomatic routine were the occasional summit meetings. The Boulogne interview of 1532 was much less expensive (86,469 *livres*) than the Field of Cloth of Gold, but the Emperor's visit to France in 1539–40 was another story. At a meeting of the king's council on 23 January 1540 the cost of 'rings, cloths of gold and silk bought by the king during the Emperor's visit and other associated expenses' was put at 200,000 *livres*.

Alliances too had to be paid for. Rather more than 4 million *livres* were paid by France to the Swiss cantons between 1516 and 1546, not counting secret bribes. Although the payment of Swiss pensions was disrupted between 1527 and 1532 owing to more urgent claims on the king's limited funds, they were not completely stopped and after 1532 some were doubled to cover arrears. Also burdensome were payments to Henry VIII under various treaties. In the course of his reign Francis paid a total of 1,784,643 *écus* to the English monarch and 232,234 *écus* to twenty-two influential Englishmen, including Wolsey. The marriage of James V of Scotland with Francis's daughter Madeleine in January 1537, was another notable expense: Francis had to pay for his daughter's dowry, for her husband's stay in France and for the fleet that carried Madeleine to Scotland. Under the League of Cognac (22 May 1526) he had to pay 40,000 *écus* to Venice and the papacy for the hire of Swiss troops. After 1529, Francis sent money to the Emperor's enemies in Italy, notably Florentine exiles, like Filippo Strozzi, who received 20,000 *écus* in 1537. The king also supported friends beyond the Rhine, albeit secretly in order not to break the peace of Cambrai. In 1534 he subsidized them to the tune of 100,000 *écus* by purchasing the county of Montbéliard from the duke of Württemberg and then selling it back to him at a heavy loss. On rare occasions Francis was the beneficiary of diplomatic payments: for example, in 1533 his daughter-in-law, Catherine de' Medici brought a dowry, given to her by the pope, of 292,500 *livres*. Henry VIII had to pay Francis 407,910 *écus* under treaties signed in 1527, but after deduction of pensions owed to him by France, he only paid out 168,438 *écus*.[3]

A financial burden of quite exceptional weight borne by Francis in the 1530s was the ransom of 2 million gold *écus* imposed by the peace of Cambrai. This,

[2] Hamon, 'L'argent du roi', pp. 38–83.
[3] *Ibid.*, pp. 83–95.

as we have seen, had to be paid initially as a single lump sum of 1.2 million *écus*, the equivalent of 4.2 tons of gold or almost as much as the totality of gold imports from the New World in the decade 1521–30. Almost certainly this was the largest single transfer of cash during the century; such a prodigious outflow of gold caused serious monetary problems within France. Even after the lump sum had been paid, Francis had to find the balance of 800,000 *écus*, a task which bedevilled his finances for another three years.[4]

Taxes, loans and expedients

As we have seen, the average rise of taxation in France under Francis I was relatively modest. Even so, the *taille* did rise. After reaching a peak in 1524 (5,761,000 *livres*), it declined slightly in 1525 and 1526, then picked up in 1527 and 1528 (5,061,000 *livres*). In 1529 it reached 5,661,000 *livres*. Between 1530 and 1531 it declined steadily from 4,100,000 *livres* to 3,600,000 *livres*. The annual average between 1524 and 1541 was 4,269,000 *livres*. Overall, direct taxation did not keep pace with the contemporary rise in prices; and the yield continued to suffer from corrupt practices at the local level. The *aides*, of course, reflected inflation, rising from 5,165,000 *livres* in 1523 to 5,625,000 *livres* in 1535, and 6,725,000 in 1537.[5]

To compensate for inadequate tax yields, Francis continued to use the full panoply of expedients we have already examined. By turning precious objects into cash he helped to accelerate the circulation of money. Not even his own *argenterie* escaped monetization. In September 1536 three out of twelve cups he had commissioned for his meeting with the pope in 1533 were sent to the Paris mint. The newly minted coins were destined for the king's war chests.[6]

Some of the pressures Francis had applied to his subjects before 1525 were tightened in the 1530s, notably, his demands on the clergy. In February 1535 he explained that he needed to seize their temporalities, as he could not impose a heavier burden on his other subjects. The threat, however, was not carried out; it prompted a compromise whereby the church agreed to pay three tenths. Between 1535 and 1537 Francis obtained the colossal sum of 3,173 million *livres* by way of clerical tenths.[7]

Towns too suffered from royal fiscality. Some were made to pay handsomely for confirmation of their privileges. On 31 March 1527 Francis levied half the municipal revenues (*deniers communs*) for one year only; but in 1533 he renewed this measure in respect of municipal taxes which towns had been allowed to levy. In 1535 and 1541 he asked for all the municipal revenues of a

---

[4] *Ibid.*, pp. 95–97; P. Hamon, 'Un après-guerre financier: la rançon de François Ier', *Etudes Champe-noises*, 1990–97. Special number on 'Les après-guerres (1525–1955)', pp. 9–20.
[5] Hamon, L'argent du roi', pp. 102–15.   [6] *Ibid.*, pp. 243–8.   [7] *Ibid.*, pp. 124–36, 229–32.

single year. But the returns were often late and disappointing. The year 1537 saw a wave of forced loans. Consequently, the king waited until 1538 before reviving the *solde des 20,000 hommes de pied* which had been levied on a few towns in 1520–21. This time, however, 227 towns were required to contribute. In 1539–41 the government claimed municipal revenues to pay for border forti- fications. As the towns of Outre-Seine remarked in 1538, it seemed intent on imposing some form of urban *taille*.[8]

Francis continued to be heavily dependent on loans after his return from captivity. As from the late 1520s he tried to mend his relations with the merchant-bankers of Lyons. Their confidence had been so shaken by events that they had refused to lend any more money to the crown after 1523. Sig- nificantly, they played no part in the elaborate transactions regarding Francis I's ransom. In 1530 he tried unsuccessfully to obtain loans in Flanders and England. However, an arrangement with Florentine merchants in Lyons did enable him to send financial help to the besieged city of Florence without openly breaking the peace of Cambrai. This signalled the beginning of a recon- ciliation with the Lyons money market. The king was, of course, obliged to accept interest rates determined by the lenders. In 1528 Duprat thought them too high but reflected that 'we need to consider the times we live in as well as our necessity'. The terms offered to Francis were no worse than those offered to other princes.

By the time war broke out again in 1536 Francis's finances were in better shape; he had even paid off some old debts. He could also count on the services of Cardinal Tournon, who was all the more effective as a negotiator with the bankers for being resident in Lyons. He took serious measures to regain their confidence: for example, in November 1536 he repaid to the Florentines a loan after only a month. 'You would not believe', he wrote to the Chancellor, 'how novel and good the merchants find this.' In September 1537 he refused to defer a repayment, saying 'the greatest displeasure you can give to the merchants is not to pay them on the day'. Tournon's strategy soon yielded dividends. He was able to raise new loans for the crown. By July 1537 he owed the Lyons bankers 102,500 *livres* in capital and 5,825 *livres* in interest. Early in 1538 he made repayments totalling 85,500 *livres*. Yet his credit-rating was not limitless and he was not able to supply all the needs of the French garrisons in Piedmont.[9]

Fiscal reform: (February 1532)

On 7 February 1532, Francis issued the ordinance of Rouen, regulating the duties and functions of the *Epargne*.[10] This laid down that the coffers in

---

[8] *Ibid.*, pp. 136–44, 232–40; Potter, *War and government*, p. 246.
[9] Hamon, 'L'argent du roi', pp. 204–19.   [10] *Ordonnances*, vi. 584.

which the *Trésorier de l'Epargne* kept his cash would no longer follow the court but be fixed at the Louvre, in Paris, and that all the king's revenues, except the *parties casuelles*, would be paid into them. The idea behind these arrangements was evidently to build a large reserve of ready cash. The same ordinance laid down regulations for the safekeeping of the coffers. In addition to the *Trésorier de l'Epargne* and two auditors, a committee was set up consisting of the First and Second Presidents of the *Chambre des Comptes*. Its powers, however, were purely supervisory: the commissioners had to be present whenever the coffers were opened or closed; but only the *Trésorier* controlled the *Epargne*'s receipts and expenses. He was not obliged, however, to reside at the Louvre; in fact, he continued to follow the king so as to provide for his day-to-day expenses and to assist him and his council in financial matters. He was also allowed to delegate the task of cashing and disbursing revenues, provided he always signed the warrants given to the receivers. In order to open the coffers at the Louvre or even to gain access to them, the collaboration of the three bodies which together constituted the *Epargne* was essential, for each coffer had three locks and as many keys. One of these was kept by the *présidents*, another by the *contrôleurs* and the last by the *Trésorier* himself and his assistants. The door of the tower containing the coffers was guarded by two archers of the king's guard.

The ordinance of Rouen did not affect the *trésoriers de France* and *généraux des finances*, but it was the first of a series of measures taken against the *Changeur du Trésor* and *receveurs-généraux*. These officials were accused of not handing over their revenues to the *Epargne*, as they had been instructed to do in 1523. Pending an investigation of their accounts, they were suspended and replaced by officials known as *commis à l'exercice*. In the following year three commissioners were assigned to each *recette-générale* to collect all the king's revenues, including those from the demesne. This meant, in effect, the suppression of the *change du Trésor*. In 1539 the three commissioners were replaced by a single *commis*, and this arrangement was apparently maintained until the creation of the *recettes-générales* in 1543.

More is known about the functioning of the *Epargne* after the reform of 1532 than before, thanks to the survival of six registers for the period 1532–35.[11] These show that the wages of the sovereign courts, *mortes-payes* and *gendarmerie* were paid out of the coffers at the Louvre in spite of the ordinance of 1532, which had exempted revenues destined for such uses from transfer to the *Epargne*. The registers also show that important sums of money in the hands of the *receveurs-généraux* never reached the Louvre. They were levied instead by the *Trésorier de l'Epargne* wherever he might be and used to pay the king's day-to-day expenses. From 1532 to 1535 the *Trésorier* received a total of

[11] B.N., mss. fr. 15628–33.

1,275,000 *livres* in this way. During the same period Preudomme also paid out 150,000 *livres* by means of warrants assigned on local tax collectors. Thus a total of 1,425,000 *livres* never reached the coffers at the Louvre.[12]

Commission de la Tour Carrée

One of the least attractive features of Francis I's government was its propensity to blame others for its own mistakes and failures. Its principal scapegoats were the *gens de finances*. Thus Gaillard Spifame was thrown into prison on a charge of 'having cheated the king of more than three or four hundred thousand francs when he had been in charge of the *extraordinaire des guerres* ... thereby causing the loss of the war and of the battle in which the king had been captured because the men-at-arms had not been paid'. The crown had good reasons perhaps for focusing blame on the financiers, since public opinion, as reflected in chronicles of the time, tended to hold the king's ministers responsible, especially Chancellor Duprat, for recent disasters. By picking on the financiers, the crown may have been deliberately deflecting the popular anger aroused by its exactions. For the king was able to claim that he, too, was being robbed.[13]

A high proportion of the *gens de finances* were prosecuted on criminal charges under Francis. The accused were the officials themselves or their heirs. Sometimes both were involved, as in the case of Jean Grolier who was made to account for his father's administration as well as his own. Altogether about forty out of a total of 118 *grands officiers des finances* were thus prosecuted by various commissions and courts, of which the most important was the *commission de la Tour Carrée*. This was set up officially on 17 November 1527 but it had already begun to act before that date. It was a new body with powers of criminal jurisdiction and not a revival of the commission established in 1523 to examine the accounts of royal officials. The commissioners of the *Tour Carrée* numbered seventeen in October 1528 and twenty-four later. Their task was not simply to try suspects but also to prepare their indictments. They thus had to gather, and sift through, a vast amount of evidence, verbal and written, much of it extremely difficult to interpret, for the relevant financial records were often scattered, incomplete or missing. Sometimes they had to travel far afield, even to Switzerland in the case of Morelet de Museau, although their activities were mainly centred in Paris.[14]

Over a ten-year period the commissioners of the *Tour Carrée* condemned at least eighteen officials or their heirs. They comprised three categories: the

---

[12] G. Jacqueton, 'Le Trésor de l'Epargne sous François Ier, 1523–1547', *R.H.*, lvi (1894), 1–13. See also M. Wolfe, *The Fiscal System of Renaissance France* (New Haven, CT and London, 1972), pp. 86–9; Hamon, 'L'argent du roi', pp. 307–25.
[13] Hamon, 'L'argent du roi', pp. 334–89, 590–5. [14] *Ibid.*, pp. 368–69.

trésoriers des guerres, généraux and *receveurs-généraux*. The *trésoriers de France* were largely spared, probably because they were *ordonnateurs* and not *comptables*: in other words, they did not actually handle money, and were, therefore, less susceptible to corruption. This functional distinction was of fundamental importance. The charges levelled at the accused were in the main financial, but sometimes there were political implications, as in the case of clients of Admiral Chabot at the time of his disgrace. Among the victims of the *Tour Carrée* were Philibert Tissart, Gilles Berthelot, Lambert Meigret, Jean Parajau, Menant, Daniray, Guillaume de Beaune, René Thizart, Henri Bohier, the heirs of Thomas Bohier, Jean Carré, Etienne Besnier, the heirs of Raoul Hurault, Gaillard Spifame, Jean Lallemant le jeune and the heirs of Morelet de Museau. Only one, Jean Poncher, suffered the same fate as Semblançay: he was sentenced to death by hanging on 18 September 1535. The court's last known victim was Jean Ruzé who was sentenced on 12 April 1536. Though the commission was never suppressed, it ceased to be active about 1537, some of its functions being taken over by other courts, notably the *Chambre des Comptes*. Its decline may have been due to the fact that some of the commissioners were themselves accused of self-enrichment at the crown's expense.[15]

Francis and his council had hoped for huge financial gains from the trials of the financiers. In the event, they were probably disappointed for the gains had to be set against the legal costs. The property of at least twenty-four officials was seized by the crown, usually at the start of their trial. Such sequestrations, however, were fraught with practical difficulties, some of them created by the victims themselves or their relatives. It was not easy for the crown to discover the precise extent of property. And once lands had been taken over, they had to be administered. The crown might sell off the movables by auction and farm out the administration of the estates, but none of this made for quick returns. Debts also needed to be ascertained and recovered, a process which might entail years of costly and diffuse litigation. Thus the commissioners responsible for Sapin's property became entangled in twenty-six lawsuits with his debtors. An *état* of 23 August 1533 estimated that 2 million *livres* arising out of the sentences passed by the *Tour Carrée* still needed to be collected. On 14 March 1535 the amount was still as high as 1.7 million *livres*.[16]

The revenues accruing to the crown from the prosecution of the financiers in the 1530s certainly fell short of the government's highest expectations; hence Duprat's comment in November 1531: 'I do not see that the king is being assisted by this *Tour Carrée*.' Yet the trials did yield substantial revenues. For example, the fines imposed on Tissart and Meigret yielded 13,584 *livres* and 15,000 *livres* respectively. In many cases the king accepted lump sums by way of commutation. They ranged from 150,000 *livres* from the heirs of Thomas

---

[15] *Ibid.*, pp. 355–7, 377–9.   [16] *Ibid.*, p. 521.

Bohier (May 1535) to 20,000 *livres* from those of Spifame. Altogether the com-
mutations totalled 707,082 *livres*. Sometimes they were partly in kind. Thus the
Ponchers ceded Limours to the king and the heirs of Thomas Bohier surrendered Chenonceaux (valued at 90,000 *livres* or 60 per cent of their commutation). The needs of war may explain the king's willingness to accept commu-
tations, for he needed funds quickly. He also recovered offices as a result of the
trials which he was able to resell. Unfortunately, no reliable global estimate
can be given of the profit made by Francis out of the trials of the financiers, for
it was not channelled into a centralized fund. However, it is likely to have run
into several hundreds of thousands of *livres*.[17]

The annexation of Brittany (August 1532)

It is often assumed that the duchy of Brittany became part of France in
1491 as a result of the marriage between King Charles VIII and the Duchess
Anne. Actually, it was in 1532 that the duchy was formally annexed to the
kingdom of France.

In April 1515 Francis had persuaded his first queen, Claude, who had inherited the duchy from Anne, her mother, to give him its administration during
her lifetime, and in June her grant had been turned into a perpetual gift. Thus
ever since 1515 Brittany had been administered by the king of France in the
right of his wife. Then, in 1524, shortly before her death, Claude had made a
will bequeathing the duchy to her eldest son, François, but, as he was a minor,
the king had continued to administer it. When François came of age in 1532 it
became necessary to regularize the duchy's status, for Claude's will had been
endorsed only by the Breton parlement (called *Grands Jours* till 1554) and a
case could be made out for his younger brother, Henri, under an arrangement
of 1499 which the Breton estates had ratified. If Brittany's permanent union to
France was to be guaranteed, it was necessary to establish the Dauphin's right
to it beyond dispute.

As a first step towards achieving this, Chancellor Duprat, who had also been
Chancellor of Brittany since 1518, invited a number of influential Bretons to
Paris. They included Louis des Désers, President of the *Grands Jours* of
Rennes, who suggested that the demand for permanent union with France
should come from the Breton estates themselves, and that it was only necessary
to bribe three or four nobles and a few members of the clergy and third estate
to secure this. The advice was well heeded, and in 1532 many bribes and
favours were distributed by the king of France to influential Bretons. Then, in
August, Francis took up residence at the castle of Suscinio, near Vannes, where
the Breton estates met to discuss the proposed union with France.

[17] *Ibid.*, p. 540.

Ardent patriots among the deputies argued that union with France would drag the duchy into foreign wars and subject it to heavy taxation, but their opponents pointed to all the hardships that had befallen Brittany in the late fifteenth century when it had been independent. Even the partisans of union, however, wanted certain conditions laid down. On 4 August, therefore, the estates sent four demands to the king: the Dauphin was to be sent to Rennes as duke and owner of the duchy; its administration and usufruct were to be reserved to the king; its rights and privileges were to be respected after the union; and the Dauphin was to take an oath to this effect.

Francis immediately agreed to these demands and issued an edict whereby Brittany was irrevocably annexed to France. On 12 August the Dauphin made his entry into Rennes; two days later, he was crowned as Duke Francis III. He was the last to hold the ducal title; when he died in 1536 Brittany became an ordinary French province. By completing the process initiated by Charles VIII forty-five years earlier, Francis made a notable contribution to French unification. A small, independent, yet vassal, state, which in the past had often called in the foreigner to defend its independence, was no more. From Calais to the Pyrenees the Atlantic seaboard now belonged to France.[18]

Military reform: the provincial legions (July 1534)

A most difficult problem facing the king of France in the early sixteenth century was how to find a large force of infantry that was efficient and reliable, yet cheap. The Swiss were efficient but not always reliable and anything but cheap. Francis could not dispense with them lest the Emperor should use them, but he wanted to lessen his dependence on them: hence, his decision to set up seven legions of foot-soldiers recruited within his own kingdom.

Under an ordinance of 24 July 1534 Normandy, Brittany, Picardy, Languedoc and Guyenne were each to raise one legion.[19] The sixth was to be provided by Burgundy, Champagne and Nivernais and the seventh by Dauphiné, Provence, the Lyonnais and Auvergne. Everyone serving in a legion was to be a native of the province that raised it, perhaps to stimulate competition among the legions. The ordinance is silent about the method of recruitment, but this was almost certainly voluntary enlistment. Noblemen who enlisted were promised exemption from the *ban et arrière-ban*, and commoners exemption from the *taille*.

Each legion was divided into six *bandes* of a thousand men each under a captain, who was to be a nobleman chosen by the king. One of the six captains

---

[18] J. de La Martinière, 'Les Etats de 1532 et l'Union de la Bretagne à la France', *Bulletin de la Société polymathique du Morbihan* (Vannes, 1911), pp. 177–93.

[19] *Ordonnances*, vii. no. 666.

was also the colonel commanding the whole legion. Each captain was free to appoint his own subordinates, who comprised two lieutenants, two ensigns, ten *centeniers*, forty corporals, four quartermasters, six sergeants, four drummers and four fifers. A captain was to be paid 50 *livres* per month in peacetime and 100 *livres* in wartime, proportional amounts being laid down for his subordinates. The rank and file were to be paid only in wartime. Those who were wounded or fell sick on service were to be paid as usual; those permanently disabled were exempted from the *taille* and given the chance to serve in garrisons as *mortes-payes*.

Legionaries were armed with pikes, halberds and arquebuses, the distribution of weapons varying with each legion. There were relatively more arquebusiers in the southern legions than in those from the north. Altogether there were meant to be 12,000 arquebusiers as against 42,000 pikemen and halberdiers. The defensive armour of the legionaries consisted of a gorget of mail and a light helmet. Musters were to be held twice a year and were intended partly as training exercises; false musters were subject to severe penalties.

The ordinance of 1534 laid down a strict code of discipline. No legionary below the rank of officer was to talk loudly or shout on pain of having his tongue pierced. Each was to swear an oath to protect sick and pregnant women. A legionary who stole from a church in peacetime was to be hanged and strangled; one who blasphemed was to wear a heavy iron collar (*carcan*) for six hours. If he repeated the offence a third time, his tongue was to be pierced and he was to be banished from the legion. Mutiny, desertion, arson, pillage and theft all carried the death penalty. No legionary could switch legions or be accompanied by a woman. But the ordinance also offered rewards. In imitation of the ancient Romans, a gold ring was to be awarded for outstanding valour, and a legionary who had achieved this distinction was to be allowed to rise through the ranks. On becoming a lieutenant, he was to be ennobled. This, at least, was the theory.

The ordinance of 1534 was swiftly put into practice. The Normandy legion was inspected by the king at Rouen in April 1535 and the Picardy legion at Amiens in June. On 6 August Francis reviewed the Champagne legion near Rheims and soon afterwards used it to bring to heel the seigneur de Lumes, who had been disloyal. Other legions were, in the meantime, being raised in the south.[20] But the ordinance was not carried out in every particular. For some unknown reason the Breton legion was never formed, and the rule governing the provenance of legionaries was interpreted flexibly. Monluc tells us that many of the troops serving in the Languedoc legion had actually been raised in Guyenne.[21]

[20] Du Bellay, ii. 288–92; C.A.F., iii. 7802–3, 7814, 1941.
[21] B. de Monluc, *Commentaires*, ed. P. Courteault (1911–25), i. 102.

Despite all the contemporary publicity given to the legions, they proved a disappointment. Their discipline left much to be desired, and they showed up badly in action. The main weakness was their lack of regular training. 'Sixteenth-century wars', Sir John Hale has written, 'were not to be won by clapping civilians into uniform and giving them a Roman name.'[22] The legions were soon relegated to the secondary role of garrisoning border towns and fortresses, and the king had to fall back on foreign mercenaries whenever he required a first-class infantry force.

Ordinance of Villers-Cotterêts (30 August 1539)

Probably the most important ordinance of Francis's reign was that of Villers-Cotterêts for which Chancellor Poyet was mainly responsible. It is chiefly remembered for four of its 192 clauses:

(1) that French instead of Latin be used in legal documents,
(2) that registers of births and deaths be kept by all parish priests,
(3) that the accused in a criminal case be denied counsel and
(4) that all confraternities be abolished.

The main purpose of the act, as stated in the preamble, was reform of the judicial system. The use of French in legal documents was intended to avoid retrials by eliminating from judgments all 'ambiguity, uncertainty and reason to demand an interpretation'. Likewise, the registration of births and deaths was to facilitate verification of the rights of parties to a lawsuit. The denial of counsel and retention of torture – measures much criticized at the time – were 'to shorten proceedings' rather than merely to harass the accused.[23] But how effective was the new law? To answer this question one would need to examine in detail the administration of justice after 1539. All that can be suggested here are certain doubts regarding three of its main provisions: the registration of births and burials, the use of French in legal documents and the abolition of confraternities.

Clause 50 of the ordinance demanded that registers be kept of all benefice-holders, and to establish the age of their majority, clause 51 prescribed the registration of all baptisms with an indication of the date and time of birth. Accuracy was to be guaranteed (clause 53) by the signatures of a notary and parish priest or his deputy. Each year the registers were to be submitted to the clerk of the court of the nearest *bailliage*. In the Nantes region such registers

---

[22] J. R. Hale, in *The New Cambridge Modern History*, II, *The Reformation*, ed. G. R. Elton (Cambridge, 1958), p. 491.

[23] J. H. Langbein, *Prosecuting Crime in the Renaissance* (Cambridge, MA, 1974), pp. 246–7. Cf. A. Esmein, *A History of Continental Criminal Procedure*, tr. J. Simpson (London, 1914), pp. 148–74.

had been kept since the early fifteenth century at the instance of the local ecclesiastical authorities. But it seems that the ordinance was not fully applied: there is no evidence that the registers were submitted to the *greffe* of the *bailliage*. Only in Nantes itself were they signed by a notary, and this was mainly in the second half of the century. As for the date and time of birth, they went unrecorded. In short, the ordinance, at least in the Nantes region, was applied only as far as it endorsed existing routine.[24]

As for the use of French in legal documents (clause 111), the evidence of parish registers in the Nantes area suggests a less than immediate or comprehensive local response to royal legislation. In both urban and rural parishes the use of Latin actually increased in the first half of the century, perhaps reflecting an improvement in clerical education. After 1550 French took precedence in urban parishes, but Latin survived in rural ones till the early seventeenth century. It cannot be assumed, therefore, that the ordinance of Villers-Cotterêts led to the immediate adoption of French for legal records throughout the kingdom.[25]

The ordinance may have been even less effective regarding confraternities (clause 185). These were associations of masters, apprentices and journeymen formed principally for religious and charitable purposes: they arranged masses and memorial services, provided aid for their poorer members, and threw banquets which sometimes upset the church authorities by turning into orgies. Confraternities, especially those limited to journeymen, were also frowned upon by the state because they provided a focus for political and religious agitation. Indeed, the decision to ban them was probably prompted by a strike of journeymen–printers in Lyons in April 1539, which had caused the local *sénéchal* to ban all gatherings of more than five journeymen. This decision was endorsed by the king ten days before the ordinance of Villers-Cotterêts was issued. Neither move succeeded in restoring good industrial relations in Lyons. As for confraternities generally, they too survived. Although in Paris their property was seized by the *prévôt*, some reappeared soon afterwards. The cloth-workers' confraternity, for example, was reprieved in April 1541, and other trades subsequently got similar concessions. In 1561 confraternities were reminded by the government that their funds should be used only for charitable and religious purposes, a clear enough indication of their survival.[26]

---

[24] A. Croix, *Nantes et la pays nantais au XVIe siècle* (1974), p. 24.   [25] *Ibid.*, pp. 30–1.
[26] H. Hauser, *Ouvriers du temps passé* (1927), pp. 161–7, 177–234; N. Z. Davis, 'A Trade Union in Sixteenth-Century France', *Econ. H.R.*, xix (1966), 48–69.

Chapter eighteen

Poverty and wealth

How prosperous was France under Francis I? De Beatis, writing in 1517, found much to praise, but described the peasants as 'in complete subjection, more ill-treated and oppressed than dogs or slaves'.[1] The earl of Surrey reported in September 1522 that poverty in France was universal.[2] Yet Marino Cavalli, writing in 1546, commented on the richness of the kingdom. 'This country', he wrote, 'thanks to its size, has a great variety of soil and products. These are of such high quality and so abundant that there are enough for France and even for foreign countries.'[3] Where does the truth lie?

The end of a golden age

Large-scale peasant unrest, which became so notable a feature of French history in the late sixteenth and early seventeenth centuries, was absent during Francis's reign. This is all the more surprising if one considers that the main direct tax, the *taille* rose to its highest level since the reign of Louis XI and that the peasantry had to bear the heaviest burden. But two mitigating factors need to be taken into account: first, the relative prosperity of the peasantry after 1450 and secondly, the fall in the real value of money during the same period.

As we have seen, the reign of Francis overlapped with the completion in many parts of France of the rural recovery that had begun in the fifteenth century. Plague was less frequent, extensive or virulent, and war no longer affected the French countryside, except in Provence, Picardy and some other border regions. The disappearance of those scourges enabled the population of the kingdom to double in size betweend 1450 and 1560. The need to feed more mouths stimulated agricultural production. Land which had gone to waste was

---

[1] *The Travel Journal of Antonio De Beatis*, ed. J. R. Hale (London, 1979), p. 165.
[2] *L.P.*, iii. 2549.
[3] *Relations des ambassadeurs vénitiens sur les affaires de France*, ed. N. Tommaseo (1838), i. 253.

reclaimed in many areas, a process that was followed by a spectacular increase in grain production, albeit an uneven one. In general, there was a return to the levels of the early fourteenth century, but almost everywhere the movement ran out of steam in the early sixteenth century. In the Ile-de-France, for example, a slowing down of production after 1500 lasted till 1540, when a new rise took place. In the Midi grain production reached a peak in the 1540s, then declined. Some areas witnessed an expansion of crops other than grain: for example, the chestnut in the Massif Central and the olive in Languedoc. Another feature of the agricultural renaissance was the development in certain regions of specialized crops in response to market demands at home and abroad. Such products were woad from Toulouse, hemp from Le Mans and wine from Burgundy, the Ile-de-France, the Atlantic seaboard and Languedoc.

All in all, French agriculture was prosperous in the first decade of Francis's reign; but about 1520 it began to show signs of strain. Most serious was the imbalance between the rise in population and agricultural productivity. While the population continued to grow, agricultural production suddenly slowed down and levelled off. In Languedoc there was even a recession after 1545. This was due to technical backwardness: agricultural tools remained primitive, and fallow was usually left bare. Agricultural expansion consequently ceased once the land had been reclaimed. As a result, supplies of grain began to run short and the price of grain to rise. Some shortages were so severe as to cause famine and deaths from starvation similar in kind to those we are, alas, witnessing in the Third World to-day. In the Nantes region, for example, grain famines occurred in 1528–32, 1538 and 1543–45. The two longest were accompanied by *mortalités* (1531–32, 1544–46). Such crises, however, were localized, nor were they sufficiently severe to halt the overall rise in population. A number of mitigating factors also helped the peasantry to overcome the difficulties of the mid century. Speculative crops, for example, were less susceptible than grain to the fall in production after 1520. The vineyards continued to produce more in response to the stimulus of international trade. Another asset was the spread of buckwheat, a crop of high, albeit variable, yield, undemanding in terms of soil and climate.

Another problem that developed under Francis was the fragmentation of peasant holdings. As the ratio of births to deaths increased, the limited arable pertaining to the village community was progressively sub-divided through the normal process of inheritance. Thus at Bessan, in Languedoc, where this was particularly marked, the number of peasant proprietors sharing the arable fields doubled and, in some cases, trebled between 1502 and 1559. A consequence was the growth of distrust among the villagers towards outsiders. Under Francis immigration, which had played a vital role in the agricultural revival, ceased to be significant. The village community had enough people of its own to accommodate; it did not need to attract more from outside. The reduction in the size of holdings inevitably undermined the self-sufficiency of the peasantry. By 1547 most peasants had not enough land to serve the needs of their families, the essential minimum of five hectares being seldom achieved. In Hurepoix, 94 per cent of holdings in seven parishes fell below this figure. But the peasant could often supplement his income in various ways. In many parts of France, there was an active cottage industry, producing various kinds of cloth. The peasants were generally paid piece-rates by a merchant, who provided the raw material and sometimes the tools, and collected the finished article for distribution. Peasants might also add to their income by taking up seasonal employment on large estates.

We have already noted that the reign of Francis saw the culmination of two important trends in the countryside: a reduction in the wealth and authority of the *seigneur* and the rise of a village aristocracy. But there was also a third: namely, the proletarianization of the lower orders of the peasantry. Until about 1450 agricultural workers had been well paid on account of their scarcity; thereafter, the real value of their wages had declined steadily. In the Paris region, for example, wages remained more or less static till 1530, while grain prices rose sharply. The price of the best wheat on the Paris market rose from 1.04 *livres* in 1440–60 to 1.56 *livres* in 1510–20, yet the abbeys of Saint-Denis and Saint-Germain-des-Prés paid their vineyard workers no more in 1510 than they had done in 1440. It has been estimated that the purchasing power of rural workers in the Paris region fell by as much as 50 per cent between 1450 and 1550. In Languedoc, where wages were normally in kind, the peasantry suffered less from inflation. Where the real value of wages fell dramatically, small peasant proprietors were driven to borrow money in order to buy food. Those who could not repay the interest on these loans might have to sell their holdings. The next step might be to lapse into vagabondage.[4]

The failure of grain production to keep pace with the rising population affected the towns as well as the countryside. As supplies ran short, speculators came into their own. Seeing that the price of grain rose at the mere prospect of a shortage, merchants were tempted to hoard it until the price reached a maximum. Such malpractices caused distress and, sometimes, social unrest. Local authorities, therefore, tried to limit speculation by controlling the grain trade in various ways: weekly checks were kept of the prices charged on the local market, and attempts made to fix a fair ratio between grain and bread prices. Sometimes municipal authorities tried to provide for emergencies by purchasing large quantities of grain in times of plenty and storing it in munici-

---

[4] G. Duby and A. Wallon (eds.), *Histoire de la France rurale*, ii (1975), 108–65; J. Jacquart, *La crise rurale en Ile-de-France 1550–1670* (1974), pp. 41–50. For a good recent summary see F. Bayard and P. Guignet, 'L'économie française aux XVIe, XVIIe et XVIIIe siècles' (1991), pp. 89–98.

pal granaries. Interprovincial problems, however, necessitated royal intervention. The Parisian authorities, for example, complained of having to allow the
transportation of grain down the Seine to Rouen, whence it might be exported
regardless of the capital's needs. Royal legislation tried as far as possible to
meet Parisian requirements by alternately allowing and forbidding grain
exports. The crown also intervened occasionally to persuade a province to
release grain for the benefit of a town. In 1520 and 1528 Lyons only managed
to get grain from Burgundy after such an intervention.[5]

Henry Heller has stressed the negative aspects of the French economy in the
early sixteenth century. In his judgment, it was far removed from Braudel's
vision of a 'beautiful century'. It was beautiful for some, he writes, but not so
for the commons and, focusing on their plight, he stresses the exploitation of
the countryside by the towns. 'From at least the sixteenth century the urban
oligarchies dominated not only the urban population but also the smaller
towns and villages in the surrounding area. Such control took the form of
economic as well as political and administrative subordination.' Thus the
oligarchy ruling Bordeaux, and acting through the local parlement, used its
control of the Garonne estuary to force Agen and its region to serve its own
economic needs. The Agenais was made to serve Bordeaux as a granary, and
by way of compensation the oligarchy of Agen was given extensive control
over the neighbouring countryside.[6]

The reign of Francis also saw the beginning of a sharp decline in the living
standards of the urban proletariat. The first five years marked the end of a
'golden age' of cheap bread. As from 1520, nominal wages began to lag behind
grain prices. By the end of the century the purchasing power of the working
man was 40 per cent less than at the beginning. Rents and the cost of fuel and
candles rose steeply during the same period; only prices of manufactured
goods, such as shoes and cloth, went up more slowly. As a result many of the
menu peuple joined the ranks of the poor.[7]

The growth of poverty

The activities of large gangs of vagabonds, who damaged and terrorized
the countryside, loom large in contemporary chronicles. Not all were disposs-
essed peasants; many were troops disbanded after a campaign. Their activi-

[5] P. Chaunu and R. Gascon, *Histoire économique et sociale de la France*, i. (1450–1660), pt. i, *L'état
et la ville* (1977), pp. 256–60. 'Picardy suffered more systematic military operations than any other
region of France in this period.' In the years between 1520 and 1560 'the impact of war on the
peasantry and townsmen made normal life at times virtually impossible'. Potter, *War and Government*, pp. 200–32.
[6] H. Heller, *Iron and Blood: Civil Wars in Sixteenth-Century France* (Montreal and Kingston, 1991),
pp. 5, 32–3.
[7] Chaunu and Gascon, pp. 410–20.

ties brought the poor generally into disrepute; they were commonly regarded as carriers of disease and as criminals. A public disaster invariably implicated them. In 1524, for example, after a large part of Troyes had been destroyed by fire, many vagabonds were accused of arson and punished.[8]

The most serious outbreak of popular disorder under Francis was the *Grande Rebeyne* of Lyons. In April 1529 placards were put up in the city calling on the people to rise against the speculators, who were blamed for the high price of bread. A mob, mainly of poor people, ransacked the Franciscan monastery and the homes of notables. The municipal granaries were broken into as well as that of the abbey of l'Ile Barbe. The municipal government, or Consulate, promised concessions so as to restore order, but a few weeks later it was busier hanging and whipping the leaders of the revolt than reducing the price of bread.[9]

The *Grande Rebeyne* was more than a grain riot. It was also a protest against new taxes on imports of wine and grain and marked another stage in the age-old conflict between the artisans and the consuls of Lyons; hence the inertia of the local militia (which was mainly composed of artisans) at the start of the riot. Religious factors may also have intruded, though this has been disputed. Lyons's population of artisans included many Germans, who doubtless brought news of Lutheran activities in their own country and of the recent Peasants' War. Symphorien Champier, whose house was ransacked by the mob, believed that heretics were largely responsible. He blamed the city's immigrant population for much of its troubles. What is certain is that the *Grande Rebeyne* coincided with a sharp decline in the standard of living of the common people. The index, which had stood at 126 in the previous decade, had now fallen to 85. The riot also expressed the feeling of alienation from their urban environment felt by the *menu peuple*. It pointed to the self-interested fiscal policies of the wealthy oligarchy ruling the city.

The impact of the *Grande Rebeyne* was widely felt. It was mentioned by chroniclers in Paris and Le Puy, and within Lyons it generated a deep-seated fear of the *menu peuple* among the Consulate and the rich, which was henceforth expressed in all their policies regarding the poor. Thus it partly inspired the creation of the *Aumône-générale* in 1531 and 1534 and it contributed to the establishment in 1536 of the silk industry which was expected to offer opportunities of employment to humble folk, women and children. Finally, the *Grande Rebeyne* strengthened the alliance between the urban patriciate and the crown. It has been described as 'a stage in the history of the eclipse of urban liberties in the face of the rise of royal authority'.[10]

[8] J. P. Gutton, *La société et les pauvres en Europe (XVIe-XVIIIe siècles)* (1974), p. 98.
[9] J. P. Gutton, *La société et les pauvres: l'exemple de la généralité de Lyon, 1534–1789* (1971), pp. 229–30; R. Gascon, *Grand commerce et vie urbaine au XVI siècle: Lyon et ses marchands* (1971), ii. 768–74.
[10] Chaunu and Gascon, pp. 449–52.

Lyons may have been exceptionally volatile, but many other towns in France experienced some kind of social unrest in the 1520s. For example, unrest at Meaux in those years was not simply religious, but also stemmed from economic and political conditions. In 1521–22 and again in 1524–25 Brie and the Ile-de-France suffered plague and famine. These afflictions, coupled with war and brigandage, drove many peasants to seek shelter within the walls. At the same time, artisans in the cloth industry were thrown out of work by war and famine. This crisis ignited a revolt in October 1522 against the ruling oligarchy. The municipal government was democratized for a time, while more serious unrest was dampened by the organization of poor relief. But this had the effect of widening the rift between reforming and conservative clergy. Thus Mazurier urged his parishioners to help the poor instead of spending money on masses and other religious works.[11]

Royal concern with vagabondage was reflected in a large number of edicts and ordinances. Several forbade soldiers to take on vagabonds as their 'servants', while others ordered vagabonds to move only in small groups on pain of being 'cut to pieces'. Such measures, however, proved ineffective. Vagabondage in the wake of armies remained a serious problem throughout the century. Royal legislation tried to improve policing methods. In January 1536 responsibility for arresting and punishing vagabonds was transferred from the *baillis* who were accused of lethargy to the *prévôts des maréchaux*. In May 1537 the king empowered anyone to kill vagabonds as rebels.

Coercion, however, was not the only method used to deal with poverty in the sixteenth century. In the Middle Ages poor relief other than private almsgiving had been of two kinds: public handouts and hospitalization. No attempt had been made to discriminate between the impotent poor and sturdy beggars. All hospitals had been either ecclesiastical or private foundations; neither the state nor the municipal authorities had been responsible for them. In the early sixteenth century, however, poor relief underwent a radical change. This began in Flanders and was marked by state intervention. The theory behind the reform was propounded by Juan Luis Vives in *De subventione pauperum* (Bruges, 1526), a work which was to prove successful in France.

Two notable developments regarding poor relief took place under Francis I; the reform and laicization of hospitals and the creation of municipal relief organizations, called *Bureaux des pauvres* or *Aumônes-générales*. As from 1519, the king set about reforming the hospitals and leper houses. His Grand Almoner was instructed to see that they carried out their duties and to inspect their accounts. A zealous reformer of hospitals was Pierre du Chastel.[12] The

---

[11] H. Heller, *The Conquest of Poverty: The Calvinist Revolt in Sixteenth Century France* (Leiden, 1986), p. 32.
[12] R. Doucet, 'Pierre du Chastel, grand aumônier de France', *R.H.*, cxxxiv (1920), 38–45.

laicization of hospitals was also encouraged: in December 1543 the financial administration of leper houses was entrusted to 'bourgeois'. But such measures were not applied universally owing to strong clerical resistance.

Sixteenth-century legislation insisted on the need for each town or village to care for its own poor. The existing hospitals, however, were for the most part inadequate. So the municipal authorities set up organizations designed to bring relief to the poor in their own homes and funded out of taxes on the well-to-do (*aisés*). In Paris, poor relief was traditionally administered by the Parlement, but in November 1544 Francis transferred this responsibility to the *Bureau de la Ville*. A *Bureau des pauvres* of sixteen notables and sixteen commissioners was set up, the latter's task being to receive donations and collect the poor tax. The impotent poor were allowed to share in public handouts and to receive medical treatment in their own homes. At the same time the *Bureau* employed sergeants to hunt down sturdy beggars and assign them to public works.

The most perfect example of the institutional response to the new ideas on welfare was the *Aumône-générale*, founded in Lyons after a grave famine in 1531. It was a temporary measure at first, but, in 1534 a permanent *Aumône* was established. It consisted of eight commissioners (later called 'rectors') and a treasurer with wide discretionary powers to deal with the poor. Unlike mediaeval hospitals, the *Aumône* had no endowment: its income was made up of police fines, legacies, collections in churches and inns, and especially a tax, voluntary in theory but compulsory in practice, on a wide cross-section of Lyonnais society. The two main aspects of the *Aumône*'s work were the care of orphans and foundlings, and the public distribution of bread.[13]

Royal control of trade

In the early sixteenth century it was generally believed that a nation's power lay in its stock of bullion and, therefore, that every effort should be made to conserve and enlarge it. Francis shared this view and, in March 1517, put forward a far-reaching programme of economic reform. Realizing, however, that 'many things profitable to one area may be harmful to others', he decided to consult the 'good towns' of his kingdom before finally drawing up an ordinance. Fifty-two delegates representing nineteen towns met in Paris on 25 March, when, in the king's presence, Chancellor Duprat delivered a long speech. France, he declared, was so rich in life's necessities as to be virtually self-sufficient, whereas her less fortunate neighbours could not do without her. It was necessary to stop money leaving the kingdom in exchange for goods 'tending to voluptuousness rather than necessity' and to attract foreign money into the kingdom; hence the programme suggested by the king. This consisted

---

[13] Gutton, *La société et les pauvres: Lyon*, pp. 256–7, 266–79.

of nine main proposals: a ban on imports of spices and drugs, except through the kingdom's seaports; a ban on imports of woollen cloth from England, Italy and Spain; the obligation on French merchants to pay for two-thirds of foreign purchases with French goods and on foreign merchants to accept such goods in exchange for two-thirds of their imports; a revaluation of the coinage; the unification of weights and measures; a ban on imports of luxury fabrics and furs; the regulation of inns and inn-keepers; and a ban on gold and silver exports to the Holy See.[14]

The government's economic thinking, however, was too national for the towns. Their representatives felt unable to comment on the king's proposals without consulting their constituents. They were accordingly sent home after three days and ordered to send their replies in writing. Nine of these are known, and they show the parochialism of each town. Thus Bordeaux rejected any move designed to give Frenchmen control of the spice trade; it opposed a ban on imports of English cloth for fear of retaliation against its own wine exports. Rouen pointed to its profits from trade with Flanders and Portugal and to the impossibility of trading direct with Calicut without permission of the Portuguese crown. As a cloth-producer, it opposed silk imports, but, fearing reprisals, was against banning foreign cloth. Limoges pressed for a ban on all foreign wool and woollen cloth. Yet Bourges, which needed foreign wool for its own cloth industry, wanted its importation to be free. On the other hand, it advocated a ban on imports of foreign cloth likely to compete with its own. Only in respect of one government proposal did the towns rise above local particularism: namely, the unification of weights and measures.[15]

The government, it seems, chose to ignore the replies from the towns. According to Barrillon, they were dropped unopened into a large leather bag and quietly forgotten. But if the reform programme of March 1517 was never embodied in a single ordinance, its principles were not abandoned. Many ordinances regulating imports and exports were issued during the reign, and various attempts were made by the crown to lessen dependence on foreign imports by encouraging home industries. In April 1540 Francis instituted a single unit of measurement for textiles (*l'aune du roi*) but this attempt to bring some degree of standardization to the existing chaotic system of weights and measures was unsuccessful. So too was the long series of edicts aimed at clearing France's rivers of seigneurial obstacles, such as tolls and mills.[16] As many as 120 illicit tolls still punctuated the course of the Loire in 1567. Other

---

[14] E. Coornaert, 'La politique économique de la France au début du régne de François Ier', *Annales de l'Université de Paris*, viii (1933), 414–27.
[15] Chaunu and Gascon, i. 320–1.
[16] C.A.F., iv. 11483, 11687; E. Levasseur, *Histoire du commerce de la France* (1911), i. 185.

royal measures for the encouragement of trade were more successful, notably the creation and restoration of a large number of fairs.[17]

Many royal ordinances attempted to regulate trade for various reasons. Fear of famine, coupled with the desire occasionally to dispose of harvest surpluses, prompted a long series of regulations authorizing, restricting or banning grain exports. In the winter of 1520–21, for example, Francis allowed grain to be exported to England, where it was scarce. Conversely, in October 1535, he banned its export from Dauphiné.[18] Another series of regulations sought to prevent gold and silver leaving the kingdom.[19]

Francis's reign marked an important stage in the development of customs duties. These had been originally levied on exports only, but Louis XI had introduced a 5 per cent duty on silk imports, obliging them to enter the kingdom through Lyons only. In 1517 Francis extended this duty to imports of cloth of gold and silver and, later, goldsmiths' work and jewellery. In 1543 he revived a duty on alum, which Louis XII had created and abandoned. A year later, he extended it to all spices and drugs. Meanwhile, Francis undertook an ambitious reform of export duties. In 1540, following abuses by tax farmers, he decided that the *imposition foraine*, a duty of one *sou* per *livre* of the declared value of goods, would henceforth be collected by royal agents. In 1541 merchants who were not leaving the kingdom, were spared the declaration; the complicated system of *acquit-à-caution* (whereby a merchant was reimbursed the duty paid at the point of dispatch on goods sold in provinces where the *aides* were in force) was also relaxed and in certain cases even abolished. In 1542 a tariff for goods subject to the *foraine* was published: it comprised no fewer than 450 items, but the values were exceedingly moderate. In 1544 the first *douane* in France was set up. This was a duty of six *deniers* per *livre* on all goods entering Lyons. It was discontinued in 1545 but revived ten years later. Also in 1544 Francis appointed a *contrôleur-général des traites* to supervise the customs systems.[20]

Among state activities with a direct bearing on the economy the most important was control of the coinage. In France the right to mint coins had been regalian for a long time; jurists saw this as a sign of absolute sovereignty. But the coinage was not yet national: foreign coins circulated freely within the realm and were accepted as legal tender unless the crown ruled otherwise. Further complication was caused by the fact that prices were usually given in money of account (*livre tournois* subdivided into *sous* and *deniers*), whereas payments were made in real money. The principal coins under Francis were of three kinds: gold (*écu au soleil*), silver (*teston*) and billon (a mixture of copper

[17] *Ibid.*, i. 187, 189–92.   [18] *L.P.*, iii. 1092, 1157; *C.A.F.*, iii. 8153.
[19] E. Coornaert, *Les Français et le commerce international à Anvers* (1961), i. 73.
[20] *Ibid.*, i. 76; G. Zeller, 'Aux origines de notre système douanier: les premières taxes à l'importation (XVIe siècle)', *Mélanges 1945*, Faculté des lettres de Strasbourg, Etudes historiques, vol. iii (1947).

and silver) *douzains, dizains, sizains*). The value of coins was determined in relation to a fixed weight – the mark of gold or silver – and to the *livre tournois*, but this dual relationship was subject to frequent fluctuations.

The large number of monetary ordinances issued by Francis were concerned mainly with regulating the mints themselves and upholding the value of the *livre tournois*. Minting was farmed out to rich merchants whose workshops were subject to occasional visits by royal commissioners. Samples of their coins were sent in boxes to the *Chambre des monnaies* in Paris for testing. In June 1515 Francis closed all French mints except four: Paris, Lyons, Rouen and Bayonne. But the number soon increased, and measures had to be taken to eradicate and discourage malpractices by their masters. In July 1536 coin-clippers were made liable to the same harsh penalties as counterfeiters. In 1540 several measures were aimed at safeguarding the quality of the coinage, and in March 1541 an important step was taken towards a more unified system of minting, when Burgundy, Dauphiné and Provence were forbidden to encroach on the jurisdiction of the *Chambre des monnaies*. The government tried to prevent depreciation of the *livre tournois* by fixing the relative values of gold and silver. As far as possible, it tried to adhere to the traditional ratio of one to twelve, but inflationary pressures at home and abroad forced periodic adjustments of the official rates.[21]

In addition to controlling the coinage, the crown regulated bills of exchange. Italian merchants had used them for a long time, but it was only under Francis that the French monarchy regulated them in a series of ordinances between 1537 and 1541. This legislation bore witness to the growth of credit and the problems this posed for the government, notably the question of interest on loans. Public opinion viewed this as normal, even if unjustified, but governments took a different view. While the imperial government fixed a rate of 8.333 per cent as lawful, the French crown continued to condemn all interest as usury.[22]

Can Francis's economic policy be described as 'mercantilist'? Many historians have argued that the doctrine of national self-sufficiency, as enunciated by Duprat in March 1517, anticipated Colbert's views. Indeed, the phrase 'Colbertism before Colbert' has become a cliché among French economic historians. But mercantilism, in the seventeenth-century sense, was a more sophisticated doctrine than that which inspired Francis's policy. He and his ministers may have vaguely understood that the yield from indirect taxes would rise and fall in response to national prosperity and depression, but the farming of such taxes inevitably restricted such fluctuations. Consequently, an essential aspect

---

[21] F. C. Spooner, *L'économie mondiale et les frappes monétaires en France, 1493–1680* (1956), pp. 108–36.

[22] Coornaert, *Les Français et le commerce*, i. 65–6.

of mercantilism – namely, the encouragement of trade and industry as a means of boosting the kings' revenues – was missing from Francis's policy, which is more correctly described as 'bullionist'.[23]

Three areas of growth

Three aspects of economic growth under Francis deserve special mention: the rise of Lyons, the expansion of trade in the Mediterranean and the opening up of the Atlantic ports. In each, the king made a contribution.

Lyons's prosperity rested on textiles, which accounted for more than 75 per cent of its imports in 1522–23. They comprised a wide variety of fabrics, ranging from the finest Italian silks to coarse cloth from central France. Among the city's other chief imports were spices, which Italians brought from the Levant, either by sea through Marseilles or overland across the Alps. In the twenties and thirties, Portuguese spices began to arrive in Lyons, mainly from Antwerp, but in January 1540 Francis ensured the triumph of the Mediterranean spice trade by banning the import of spices except through Lyons, Marseilles and Rouen. Like silk, most spices sold at Lyons were for the home market, Paris being the largest single consumer.

In addition to being one of Europe's most important money markets, Lyons was noted for its printing and silk industries. The fact that it was a city of 'free work' – that is, one in which no fee or masterpiece or guild membership was required by artisan or entrepreneur – encouraged industrial enterprise. All that was needed to open a printing shop was capital. Lyons's first press was set up in 1473; forty years later it had more than a hundred. Most books sold in Lyons were also printed there, and each year large consignments were sent to the Frankfurt fair.

The introduction of the silk industry to Lyons was closely related to the policy of conserving the kingdom's bullion stock; if silk could be produced at home, there would be no need to use cash for its purchase abroad. In 1466 Louis XI had ordered the Consulate to set up a silk industry in the city; he had authorized it to levy a tax in order to cover its costs and had conferred privileges on the new industry so as to attract foreign workers. But the merchants of Lyons had not wanted to give up their profitable trade in Italian silk for the sake of an experiment of uncertain future. After only three years, therefore, Lyons had sent its silk-workers and looms to Tours, where a similar experiment had borne fruit.

Under Francis the attitude of the Lyonnais changed. The home demand for luxury cloth had grown to such an extent that it was now possible to envisage a native industry coexisting with foreign imports. Italian silk was, in any case, far superior to anything France could yet produce. Italian merchants, moreover, saw profits to be gained from a venture which would make demands on their capital, technical expertise and business contacts. At the same time, the *Grande Rebeyne* of 1529 alerted the Consulate to the danger of harbouring a large number of unemployed poor in the city. Charity alone could not solve the problem; additional employment was needed. The silk industry could be the answer. By 1536, therefore, Lyons was prepared to accept a new royal initiative.

Francis's decision to revive Louis XI's experiment was a direct response to Genoa's so-called treason in 1528, when Andrea Doria sealed the fate of the French army in Naples by transferring his services to the Emperor. Francis retaliated in 1530 by banning imports of Genoese velvet. This, however, caused resentment in Lyons, where the Consulate feared a boycott of the city's fairs. Cardinal Tournon, who was trying to raise a loan for the king from the city's Italian bankers, secured a compromise: the ban on Genoese velvet was lifted in January 1537 in exchange for a duty of two *écus* per piece. But Francis did not yet forgive the Genoese: in October 1536 he exempted all Lyons's silk-workers from municipal taxes in the hope of bringing 'total ruin' to the Genoese 'rebels'. In March 1538, two months before the king's letters were published in Lyons, a merchant, called Etienne Turquet, asked the Consulate for a subsidy to set up looms for the manufacture of velvet. He was granted 500 *écus* over five years. Other local merchants contributed funds to the venture, and a company was formed, soon to be followed by others. By 1554 Lyons's silk industry was employing 12,000 workers. Four years later Italian merchants were importing less than a third or a quarter of the silks they had previously imported from Italy; instead, they were buying Lyons silk at far less cost.[24]

For much of the Middle Ages, France's window on the Mediterranean had been restricted to the coast of Languedoc. But in 1481 she had acquired Provence and some excellent ports, notably Marseilles. The rise of Lyons as an international market offered them a useful outlet for their imports and a precious source of capital.

The development of Marseilles can be traced in notarial acts and port books. For example, the yield from harbour dues rose from about 400 *livres* around 1500 to 1,300 in 1519–20 and to more than 3,000 in 1542. In the forties the annual average was 8,000 *livres*. The population of Marseilles shows a parallel rise: from 15,000 inhabitants in 1520 to 30,000 in 1554. These figures reflect an expansion of Marseilles's trade along existing routes (to Languedoc, Catalonia, Corsica, Liguria, Tuscany, the States of the Church and Sicily) and the opening

[24] Gascon, *Grand commerce et vie urbaine*, i. 308–12.

up of new ones. From the start of Francis's reign there were Marseillais at Alexandria. In 1528 the Sultan confirmed privileges formerly given to French merchants in Egypt by the Mameluk sultans. He also gave them permission to go to Cairo. Francis's friendship with the Ottoman empire favoured the establishment of French trading posts at Beirut and Tripoli. Closer ties were also established with the Barbary coast. But penetration of the eastern market by the Marseillais did not seriously challenge the Italian spice monopoly. The Italians were superior in navigation, wealth and business experience; their spices were cheaper and of better quality than the French imports. A large colony of Italian merchants in Marseilles reflected their dominance of Mediterranean trade. But if the Marseillais as yet played only a subordinate role, they could learn from their masters and might eventually displace them.[25]

The early sixteenth century witnessed a remarkable expansion of trade in the Atlantic as a consequence of Europe's overseas discoveries. The Portuguese and the Spaniards, who pioneered that movement, were, naturally enough, the first to benefit from it. But their principal ports, Lisbon and Seville, were not ideally suited to distribute goods to the rest of Europe. Antwerp offered better prospects, as the Portuguese recognized when they established their spice staple there in 1502. This marked the beginning of Antwerp's rapid rise to international pre-eminence as a market.

France, too, benefited from the growth of Atlantic trade, albeit in a more limited way. By now she had recovered all the coastline that had once been under English occupation. Since 1491 Brittany, too, had virtually passed under her control. Among the most important Atlantic ports were Rouen, Nantes, La Rochelle and Bordeaux. Rouen was the principal market for north-west France. In addition to distributing local produce, it served as a market for goods from all over France and overseas. Its imports far exceeded in quantity and variety its own needs or even those of its province. A significant proportion of the trade between Antwerp and Lyons passed through Rouen. Though not comparable to Antwerp as an international market, Rouen was none the less important: its sailors and merchants travelled widely in Europe and beyond; many foreign merchants were to be found among its inhabitants. 'Rouen', said Francis, 'is the first town of France, for Paris is more than a town, it is a province.' Nantes served not only as a port of call for ships plying between Bilbao and the Netherlands, but also as an outlet for produce from the Loire region. Among foreign merchants established in the town, the most important was the Spanish family of Ruiz. Further south, economic life was dominated by two local products: salt and wine. The principal port south of Nantes was La

[25] R. Collier and J. Billioud, *Histoire du commerce de Marseille*, iii (1480–1599), (1951), 179–85; Chaunu and Gascon, pp. 240–4.

Rochelle, which exported wine, paper, linen cloth and cheese, and imported a wide variety of goods, ranging from spices and herrings to varnish and mercury. Bordeaux's prosperity in the sixteenth century was due to the revival of the local vineyards, the rapid development of woad cultivation in the Toulouse region and the extraordinary upsurge of inland water traffic. In an average year it exported between 20,000 and 30,000 barrels of wine.[26]

Francis's main contribution to the development of France's Atlantic seaboard was the foundation of Le Havre. This was in response to pressure from the community bordering the Seine estuary. The ports of Honfleur and Leure were so silted up that a new harbour was urgently required. A deep-water inlet at Grasse was already being used by ships, but it was undefended, and there was a real danger that it might be seized by the English in wartime. By 1517 the transformation of the inlet into a properly fortified harbour had become a defensive necessity. Francis also needed a good base from which to send a fleet to his ally, James V of Scotland. Thus the creation of Le Havre can be explained on other than purely commercial grounds.[27]

The task of building the new harbour at Grasse was given to Admiral Bonnivet on 7 February 1517, but he was too busy at court to attend to it personally, so he commissioned Guyon Le Roy, seigneur du Chillou, to act in his stead. He was empowered to force the inhabitants of a number of places near Grasse to contribute one day's work each month on the new harbour. The king was kept regularly informed of progress by Jacques d'Estimauville, who visited the court seven times between May 1517 and May 1518. In October 1517 Francis granted exemption from the *taille* and *droit de franc-salé* to anyone who came to build and live at Grasse. This privilege was confirmed by the king when he visited the new town in August 1520. By then work was so far advanced that ships were able to use the harbour 'without danger or inconvenience'.[28] Three years later it had fortifications and a shipbuilding yard, where a large vessel of 1,200 tons, called *Grande Françoise* was under construction for the king. She was completed in 1524 but never sailed; her draught was so deep that she could not leave the harbour and had to be dismantled.[29]

Six years after visiting Le Havre for the second time in 1535, Francis commissioned Girolamo Bellarmato, a Sienese military engineer, to add a new district, called Quartier Saint-François, to the town. Unlike the town built by Le Guyon, which had been a purely speculative venture without aesthetic pretensions, this one conformed with the new ideas of Renaissance town planning: it

[26] Coornaert, *Les Français et le commerce*, i. 217–25, 311–12, 318–21, 324–7; P. Benedict, *Rouen during the Wars of Religion* (Cambridge, 1981), pp. 1–45.

[27] A. E. Borély, 'Origines de la ville du Havre', *R.H.*, xiv (1880), 286–311.

[28] S. de Merval (ed.), *Documents relatifs à la fondation du Havre* (Rouen, 1875), pp. 9–13, 24, 28, 59, 115–20, 257–61, 266.

[29] *J.B.P.*, p. 125; C. de La Roncière, *Histoire de la marine française* (1899–1932), ii. 473; iii. 176.

was to comprise four blocks divided by two wide and straight streets crossing at right angles. All future houses were to conform to certain rules of alignment and decoration. Indeed, Bellarmato's commission (18 June 1541) has been called 'the first great document in the history of urban architecture in France'.[30]

The French economy, then, under Francis was in general healthy: agriculture had recovered from the fourteenth-century crisis, urbanization was growing apace, new industries were being set up, and trade, both domestic and international, was thriving. All this doubtless helps to explain the relative absence of popular unrest during the reign, in spite of an increasingly burdensome royal fiscality. Yet all was not well. The failure of agricultural production to keep pace with the needs of a fast-growing population was forcing a large number of people on to the breadline. Likewise, inflation was reducing the real wages and living standards of the lower orders of society. Unemployment and vagabondage were serious problems, and the state had been forced to intervene to solve or at best contain them. The seemingly contradictory comments of contemporary observers are not, therefore, irreconcilable: from about 1520 France's prosperity was under attack; it did not collapse, however, until the second half of the century.

[30] C.A.F., iv. 11768, 12279; vi. 22160, 22184, 22293; P. Lavedan, *Histoire de l'urbanisme* (1941), pp. 93–100. P. Manneville, 'La fondation du port du Havre (1517) et son développement' in P. Masson and M. Vergé-Franceschi (eds.), *La France et la Mer au siècle des grandes découvertes* (1993), pp. 322–38. Another example of town planning by Francis I is Vitry-le-François; see below, p. 491, n. 58.

Chapter nineteen

France overseas

France took no official part in the great movement of European expansion overseas until the reign of Francis I, yet she had as many advantages as Portugal and Spain, who had pioneered that movement: she had an extensive Atlantic coastline, many ports, good sailors and a generally sound economy. She also had as much interest as other Atlantic powers in breaking the Venetian monopoly of spices from the Far East. What she lacked until the early sixteenth century was a royal interest in overseas expansion.

The three immediate predecessors of Francis were interested mainly in reviving and developing trade along traditional routes, particularly with the Levant, which the Hundred Years War had disrupted. Louis XI reopened Bordeaux to English ships, gave the spice monopoly to the ports of the Languedoc and developed the port of Marseilles. Charles VIII was too preoccupied in Italy to be interested in the discovery of America or to object to Pope Alexander VI's bull *Inter caetera*, which had allowed the Catholic Kings to claim all territories beyond a line drawn 100 leagues west of the Azores and Cape Verde islands. In November 1511 the Mameluk sultan offered Louis XII freedom to trade in Syria and Egypt along with pilgrimage facilities. He expected that, in return, Louis would put pressure on the Grand Master of Rhodes to release captured Egyptian ships, but the king failed to achieve this. Consequently, the Venetians had their privileges confirmed, while France had to be content with a treaty guaranteeing freedom of trade.[1]

Under Francis, spices continued to reach France via the Levant in spite of the alternative route to the East Indies recently opened up by the Portuguese. The French government was aware of this competition. In March 1517 Chancellor Duprat, speaking to representatives of the 'good towns', alluded to the Portuguese spice trade. If it were true, he said, that the Portuguese were now getting cheaper spices, then he hoped that Frenchmen would soon emulate them. His

[1] C.-A. Julien, *Les voyages de découverte et les premiers établissements* (1948), pp. 1, 47–52.

chief concern, however, was not to facilitate this so much as to restrict the import of spices, which drained the kingdom of gold and silver.[2] Meanwhile, French merchants established depots at Constantinople, Beirut, Damascus and Nicosia of Smyrna. In 1528 the concessions previously accorded to them in Egypt were confirmed by the Ottoman sultan, and early in 1534 Francis concluded with him a commercial truce of three years. Whether further concessions were obtained from the Sultan in February 1536 is a matter of controversy. There is no evidence that the French ambassador, La Forêt, was instructed to negotiate a new trade agreement at this time.[3] Be that as it may, French merchants certainly occupied a privileged position in the Levant, which undermined any incentive to look for alternative markets.

However, if the French monarchy was for long content to look no further than the Mediterranean in promoting overseas trade, its subjects were more enterprising. From the mid fifteenth century onwards, seamen from France's Atlantic and Channel ports showed a considerable interest in the profits to be made in West Africa and Central and South America. As early as 1457 the king of Portugal was so concerned about French interlopers along the coast of Guinea that he planned to send a fleet to drive them off. The first Frenchman known to have reached Brazil was Paulmier de Gonneville, a captain of Honfleur. He went there in 1504 and, after a six months' stay, returned to France with Essomericq, the son of an Indian ruler. Gonneville said that other Frenchmen had preceded him to Brazil in search of dyewood, raw cotton, monkeys, parrots and other local products. The French got on well with the natives, and some stayed behind to learn their language and to organize resistance to the Portuguese.[4]

French pirates were also active from an early date. They attacked Portuguese ships carrying spices from the Indies and wood from Brazil, and Spanish treasure-ships from America. The outbreak of war between Francis and the Emperor in 1521 turned them into corsairs, among whom Jean Fleury of Honfleur was outstanding. In 1522 he caused a great stir by intercepting the ships sent by Cortés to Charles V with the treasures he had found in Mexico and sinking two of them near Cape St Vincent.[5]

Knowledge of French activities in the North Atlantic in the early sixteenth century is vague. Two Frenchmen, Jean Denys of Honfleur and Thomas Aubert of Dieppe, are said to have explored the coast of Newfoundland in 1506 and 1508 respectively. It was probably Aubert who, in 1509, brought back to Rouen seven Indians with their clothes, weapons and canoe. Bretons went to Newfoundland to fish as early as 1504. When the queen of Castile commis-

---

[2] E. Coornaert, 'La politique économique de la France au début du règne de François Ier', *Annales de l'Université de Paris*, viii (1933), 418–19.
[3] *Ordonnances*, viii. 560–7.   [4] Julien, pp. 18–21, 70.
[5] *Ibid.*, p. 72; C. de La Roncière, *Histoire de la marine française* (1899–1932), iii. 249–51.

sioned Juan de Agramonte to discover the 'secret of Newfoundland' in 1511, she allowed him to take two Breton pilots.[6]

A major figure in all this private maritime activity was Jean Ango of Dieppe (1480–1551), a shipowner, banker and entrepreneur, who fitted out a fleet of twenty to thirty ships. He entrusted them to captains well trained in navigation and sent them to Newfoundland, Guinea, Brazil and Indonesia. Despite his manifold activities, Ango also found time to lead a cultivated life. He built a handsome house overlooking the harbour at Dieppe and a summer residence at Varengeville, of which some traces remain. In 1535 he entertained the king, who ennobled him and made him governor of Dieppe. Ango was often asked to lend Francis money and ships, and it was he who victualled the forces sent to invade England in 1544. Such demands outstretched his means; his last years were spent fighting off creditors.[7]

Giovanni da Verrazzano

Francis I was already interested in overseas exploration in 1522, when John III of Portugal was warned of a French project likely to damage his interests. He promptly sent João da Silveira to the French court with a request that Francis should forbid his subjects to attack Portuguese subjects and their property. The ambassador was well received, but Francis answered him evasively.[8] The project which so alarmed the Portuguese monarch was almost certainly the first voyage of Giovanni da Verrazzano, which was apparently initiated by a syndicate of Florentine merchants in Lyons. Yet a royal commission must have been issued, since Verrazzano reported to the king on 8 July 1524 following his return: 'I have not written to tell Your Majesty', he wrote, 'of what happened to the four ships which you sent out over the Ocean to explore new lands ... [or how] we continued the original voyage with only the *Dauphine*; now on our return from this voyage, I will tell Your Majesty of what we found.' Later in the report he states that the voyage had been made by the king's command, and this was confirmed by his brother Gerolamo on a map of 1529. Nor was the king's role limited to granting a commission: the *Dauphine* was a royal ship and her captain was paid by the king during the expedition.[9]

It is tempting to connect Verrazzano's first voyage with the first circumnavigation of the world by Sebastiano Elcano. Not only was this achievement

[6] Julien, pp. 21–8; H. P. Biggar, *The Precursors of Jacques Cartier 1487–1534* (Ottawa, 1911), p. 107.
[7] E. Guénin, *Ango et ses pilotes* (1901)
[8] L. C. Wroth, *The Voyages of Giovanni da Verrazzano, 1524–1528* (New Haven, CT, 1970), p. 67.
[9] *Ibid.*, p. 65. Three versions exist of Verrazzano's letter to Francis. The most authoritative is the *Cèllere Codex* in the Pierpont Morgan Library, New York. For a facsimile reproduction, transcription, English translation and editorial commentary, see Wroth, pp. 96–152.

widely publicized by Maximilian of Transylvania's *De Moluccis insulis* (January 1523), but Antonio Pigafetta, a Venetian who had accompanied Elcano, visited the French court soon afterwards and made 'a gift of certain things from the other hemisphere' to Louise of Savoy.[10] It is likely that Verrazzano's aim was to find a more direct route to Cathay across the American continent than the Strait of Magellan used by Elcano. He set off about 1 January 1524 in four ships, but two were lost in a storm. Eventually, he took only one, the *Dauphine*, and, after crossing the Atlantic, made landfall near Cape Fear. Instead of landing, however, he sailed southward along the coast for about 160 miles in an unsuccessful search for a port. Then, turning back, he returned to his original landfall and set foot for the first time on American soil. A few days later he set out on a long north-easterly coastal voyage. On 25 March he sighted an 'isthmus' and, beyond it, water which he identified with the Pacific. In fact, the 'isthmus' was the barrier-island chain of the Carolina Outer Banks, and the 'Pacific' consisted of the three sounds of Pamlico, Roanoke and Albemarle. Verrazzano's error was to vex geographers, cartographers and explorers for more than a century.

Verrazzano gave the name of Arcadia to the coast of Virginia and Maryland 'on account of the beauty of the trees'. Landing there, he and his men spent three days exploring the interior, during which they kidnapped an Indian boy. From Arcadia, Verrazzano sailed north-eastwards along a coast 'very green and forested but without harbours', calling it Lorraine after the cardinal of that name. Other topographical features were named after the duc d'Alençon, the seigneur de Bonnivet, the duc de Vendôme and the comte de Saint-Pol. Eventually, he came to the bay of New York, which he called Santa Margarita after Francis's sister, 'who surpasses all other matrons in modesty and intellect'. As for the land around the bay, Verrazzano called it Angoulême. He described Manhattan island as 'a very agreeable place between two small but prominent hills; between them a very wide river, deep at its mouth, flowed into the sea'. This was, of course, the Hudson, which was not to be rediscovered till 1609. Taking a small boat for a short distance upstream, Verrazzano found himself in a densely populated area. 'The people', he wrote, 'were dressed in birds' feathers of various colours, and they came towards us joyfully uttering loud cries of wonderment'.

After this brief glimpse of New York Bay, Verrazzano continued to sail north-eastward. After noting Block Island, which he called Aloysia in honour of Francis's mother, he proceeded to Newport, Rhode Island, where he spent a fortnight recuperating. Here he was visited by many Indians, who proved most friendly. 'These people', he wrote, 'are the the most beautiful and have the most civil customs that we have found on this voyage. They are taller than we

[10] Wroth, p. 220.

are; they are a bronze colour, some tending towards whiteness, others to a tawny colour; the face is clear-cut, the hair is long and black.' After rounding Cape Cod, Verrazzano followed the coasts of Massachusetts and Maine. He then sailed northwards until, on reaching the latitude of Cape Breton, he turned east and sighted Newfoundland. Finally, his stores almost gone, he recrossed the Atlantic and, on 8 July 1524, arrived at Dieppe.[11]

Although Verrazzano had failed to discover a northern passage to Cathay, his achievement was none the less remarkable. By exploring, describing and mapping out the east coast of North America from Florida to Cape Breton, he had closed an important gap in contemporary geographical knowledge. The report he sent to Francis on his return is 'the most accurate and the most valuable of all the early coastal voyages that has come down to us'.[12] About a third of it is devoted to the physical appearance, manner of life, customs and character of the American Indians. Verrazzano also showed an appreciation of the American landscape, praising its beauty, its vegetation and, in places, its climate. He knew that it was not Asia, describing it as a 'new land which had never been seen before by any man, either ancient or modern', and called it Francesca in honour of his royal patron. Francis thus acquired a claim, albeit one without papal support, to territorial dominion in the New World.

Unfortunately for Verrazzano, his return coincided with Bourbon's invasion of Provence. Francis had already left Blois to take charge of his army in the south. He may not have found time to read Verrazzano's report or to meet him in Lyons in August, yet the explorer was commissioned by him about this time to undertake another voyage to the Indies. He was given four ships, but just as they were about to sail, they were requisitioned to help defend the French Channel coast.[13] Verrazzano's next moves are obscure: he may have looked for a new patron in England and Portugal. But in April 1526 he obtained the backing of Admiral Chabot and Jean Ango, who formed a joint-stock company with a view to fitting out three ships to do 'the voyage to the Spice islands in the Indies'. This time the expedition managed to get away, but where did it go? There is evidence that Verrazzano tried to round the Cape of Good Hope but was forced by bad weather to go to Brazil. By 18 September 1527 he had returned to France.[14] Three months later the Portuguese ambassador reported that Verrazzano had been ordered by Chabot to go with five ships to 'a great river on the coast of Brazil'. 'I think', he added, 'that they are going to establish a base there and thereafter, that they will push still further their

---

[11] *Ibid.*, pp. 71–90; D. B. Quinn, *North America from Earliest Discovery to First Settlements* (New York, 1978), pp. 154–9.
[12] B. Penrose, *Travel and Discovery in the Renaissance, 1420–1620* (Cambridge, MA, 1952), p. 146.
[13] Wroth, pp. 160–2; C.A.F., viii. 31508.
[14] One of the three ships did apparently manage to round the Cape and reach Sumatra, where part of her crew was massacred. The survivors recrossed the Indian Ocean westward and were shipwrecked off Mozambique. Wroth, pp. 219–35.

exploration.' In April 1528 Verrazzano made an agreement with the crew of the *Flamengue* of Fécamp for a voyage of trade and exploration to the Indies sponsored by a group of merchants. There is evidence that he looked for a strait leading to the Pacific somewhere in Central America, but he did not survive to tell the tale. The *Flamengue* returned to France before 26 March 1529 with a small cargo of Brazil-wood, but without Verrazzano. It was reported that he had been killed and eaten by cannibals on a Caribbean island.[15]

Franco-Portuguese rivalry

The last two voyages of Verrazzano, whatever their exploratory purpose may have been, were part of the long and bitter commercial rivalry between France and Portugal, which was fought out mainly in Brazil and along the West African coast. Although John III professed to be concerned only with the suppression of French piracy, he was, in fact, hostile to all French shipping in Brazilian waters and ordered its destruction. At the same time, he sought restitution of all Portuguese ships and cargoes that had been seized by the French, as well as guarantees for the future. Francis wanted to conciliate John, whose support he needed against the Emperor; but his attitude ran counter to the interests of French shipowners, like Ango, and also of the French admiralty, which claimed a share of all prizes. Thus Francis's assurances to John were seldom implemented. In September 1522 Bonnivet even granted letters of marque to one of Ango's associates, allowing him to intercept Portuguese ships.

Five years later the situation became dangerous when Christovão Jaques, acting on John III's orders, captured and executed some Breton merchants as they were loading wood at Bahia in Brazil. The governor of Brittany complained to Francis, but he was more concerned at this time to raise the ransom money for his sons than to champion the interests of French seamen. So he requested a loan of 400,000 *cruzados* from the Portuguese king, while demanding compensation for the relatives of the seamen massacred at Bahia. John III offered only a quarter of the sum requested by Francis; the rest, he said, might be levied by the French courts as compensation for 300 Portuguese ships captured by the French over thirty years. Once Francis had paid his sons' ransom, he was more inclined to listen to Admiral Chabot, who consistently championed the cause of French shipowners. In July 1530, after Portuguese coastguards had seized the *Marie* of Dieppe, Francis issued letters of marque to Ango, allowing him to recoup his loss at the expense of Portuguese shipping. In April 1531 John was dismayed to learn that Ango had placed an embargo on

[15] *Ibid.*, pp. 236–62

all Portuguese vessels entering French ports on their way to Flanders. He decided to get Ango's letters of marque revoked. When diplomacy failed, he resorted to corruption: Chabot, who was always susceptible to bribery, agreed to mediate and to ban all French ships from going to Brazil or Guinea. In July, after negotiators from both sides had reached an agreement, Ango surrendered his letter of marque. But, even with the co-operation of the French admiralty, Portugal failed totally to exclude French interlopers from her dependencies. Thus about 1531 Bertrand d'Ornesan, baron de Saint-Blancard, attempted to establish a French trading post at Pernambuco. That autumn more than ten ships at Harfleur and six at Rouen were preparing to set off for Guinea and Brazil. Ango, too, continued to trade with both places, and Chabot secretly encouraged such ventures in return for a share of the profits.

John III was uncompromising about the rights of discoverers. 'The seas', he declared, 'where everyone must and can navigate, are those which have always been known to all and common to all, but the others, which were not known and did not seem navigable and which were discovered at the cost of much effort on our part, are excluded from them.' Francis disagreed, believing that the seas were open to all. His doctrine, however, conflicted with Alexander VI's bull of 1493, which had divided the world between Castile and Portugal without taking effective occupation into account. This impeded French overseas enterprise, but in October 1533 Pope Clement VII was persuaded, apparently by the king's Grand Almoner, Jean Le Veneur, to reinterpret the bull: it applied, he said, only to 'known continents, not to territories subsequently discovered by other powers'. Francis could thus challenge the monopoly claimed by the Iberian powers without fear of incurring spiritual sanctions.[16]

The French in Canada: Cartier and Roberval

Le Veneur was also bishop of Lisieux and abbot of Mont-Saint-Michel. In May 1532 he entertained Francis at his abbey and, being keenly interested in maritime affairs, suggested sending an expedition of discovery beyond Newfoundland. He offered to contribute to its cost and to supply chaplains, if the king would accept as its leader, Jacques Cartier, a sea captain related to the abbey's treasurer.[17] Francis agreed, and in March 1534, after the pope had given his new ruling on the rights of discoverers, he commissioned Cartier 'to voyage and go to the New Lands and to pass the Strait of the Bay of the Castles [i.e. Strait of Belle Isle]'. Here, he was to discover 'certain islands and lands, where it is said he should find rich quantities of gold and other rich things'.[18]

[16] Julien, *Les voyages de découverte*, pp. 92–9, 109–17.
[17] Baron de La Chapelle, 'Jean Le Veneur et le Canada', *Nova Francia*, vi (1931), 341–3.
[18] *A Collection of Documents Relating to Jacques Cartier and the Sieur de Roberval*, ed. H. P. Biggar (Ottawa, 1930), pp. 42–3.

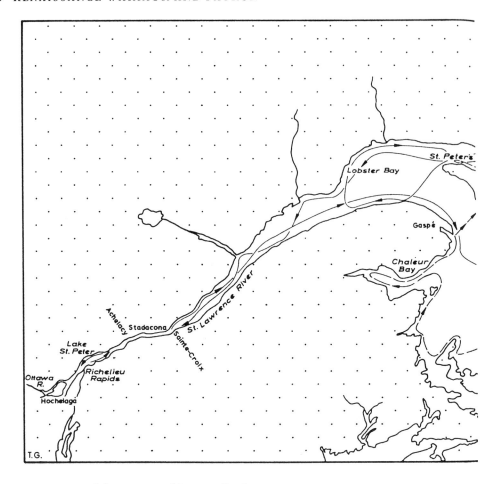

7. Map of the voyages of Jacques Cartier

Cartier was born in Saint-Malo in 1491. He became an experienced seaman with first-hand knowledge of the Newfoundland fisheries and was well-informed about Brazil. His main objective in 1534 was probably to find a passage to Asia which Verrazzano had failed to discover. He sailed from Saint-Malo with two sixty-ton ships in April and, after crossing the Atlantic in twenty days, made landfall at Bonavista in eastern Newfoundland. On 27 May he tried to enter the Strait of Belle Isle, but icebergs prevented him doing so till June. He then explored its northern shore and came across a fishing vessel from La Rochelle, proof that he was not the first Frenchman to reach this area. On 15 June Cartier began the first known exploration of the west coast of New-foundland. He then made for Prince Edward Island, sighting it on 1 July, and two days later began to inspect Chaleur Bay, only to find that it did not lead to the interior. The bay was full of Indians, who had come to fish. They invited

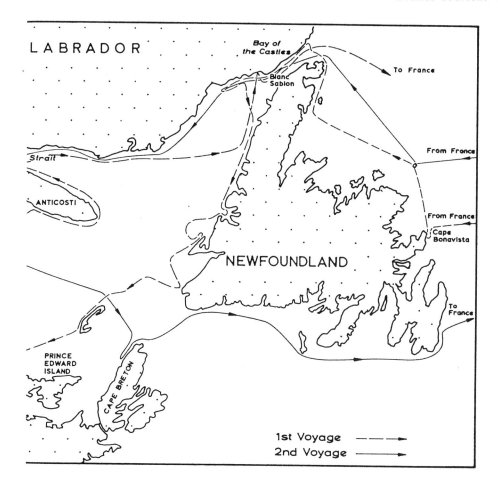

Cartier to come ashore, 'holding up to us some furs on sticks'. At first Cartier tried to frighten them off by firing several shots, but eventually mutual confidence was established, and the French bartered trinkets and weapons for furs. On 12 July, Cartier began to explore the coast of the Gaspé peninsula. He set up a cross at the entrance to Gaspé harbour and came across more Indians who had come from afar to fish. These, however, had no furs to trade and wore little clothing. With the consent of their chief, Donnaconna, Cartier decided to take two young Indians back to France. He planned to teach them French and to learn more about their country from them. Their names were Dom Agaya and Taignoagny. From Gaspé, Cartier sailed north-eastward to Anticosti, thereby missing the entrance to the St Lawrence river. He followed the island to its eastern extremity, then its north shore until it became clear that a strait separated it from the mainland. This he called St Peter's Strait, but, the season being late, he decided to postpone its exploration till the following year. He then returned to Blanc Sablon in the Strait of Belle Isle and, on 15 August, set sail for France. He returned to Saint-Malo on 5 September.[19] Although he had found no gold, Cartier had collected much valuable information about climate, anchorages, good and bad terrain and the local flora and fauna. He now knew that there was a passage north and south of Anticosti leading to the west, which might be a passage to Asia. Evidence supplied by the two captured Indians pointed to the existence of a great kingdom, called Saguenay, far inland from their own Canada.

Francis was sufficiently impressed by these results to order a new expedition without delay. On 30 October Cartier was empowered to take three ships, each victualled for fifteen months, 'beyond the New Lands' which he had discovered.[20] The *Grande Hermine*, *Petite Hermine* and *Emerillon* were fitted out at once, but an outbreak of plague delayed their departure from Saint-Malo till 19 May 1535. Cartier's company included the two Indians, who by now had learnt enough French to serve as interpreters and guides. After being dispersed in the Atlantic, Cartier's three ships met up at Blanc Sablon on 26 July. They then followed the coast of Labrador westward and passed through St Peter's Strait into the mouth of the St Lawrence river. Early in September, as Cartier made his way upstream, Donnaconna met him bearing gifts. He welcomed back Dom Agaya and Taignoagny, who were allowed to rejoin their tribe. Their village, Stadacona, was pleasantly situated (near modern Quebec), but Cartier was not yet prepared to settle down for the winter. He wanted to explore the kingdom of Hochelaga, further up the St Lawrence. However, the two Indians, who had promised to lead him there, now refused. They even tried to deter him by sending a canoe downstream with three Indians disguised as devils, who warned him of hazards ahead. But on 19 September Cartier set off from Sainte-Croix with the *Emerillon* and two rowing boats. At Achelacy, he was warned of the dangers of the Richelieu rapids, but the rich woods, the loaded grapevines and the abundance of bird life beckoned him on. After crossing Lake St Peter, he left the *Emerillon* and her crew behind, and with a small party made his way to Hochelaga, where more than a thousand men, women and children came out to greet them. Neither Cartier nor the Indians showed any fear of each other; the women even had him touch their babies. In exchange for gifts of fish and corn, the French handed out knives and beads to the Indians.

On 3 October Cartier led twenty-three of his men to Hochelaga, a village,

---

[19] *Les Français en Amérique pendant la première moitié du XVIe siècle*, eds. C.-A. Julien, R. Herval and T. Beauchesne (1946), pp. 79–112; Quinn, *North America*, pp. 169–75.
[20] *Documents re. Cartier and Roberval*, pp. 44–5.

encircled by a triple palisade and containing about fifty longhouses. The Frenchmen noted what the Indians ate and how it was cooked, how they slept and dressed and how they specially prized their white wampum beads. From the top of a mountain he called Mont Réal, Cartier was shown the Ottawa river, which, the Indians believed, flowed past the kingdom of Saguenay. 'And without our putting any question or making any sign', the French reported, 'our Indian guides took the silver chain of the Captain's whistle and the handle of a dagger hanging at the side of one of our sailors, which was of brass as yellow as gold, and made signs that such things came from up the said river.' But Cartier was unable to find out how far Saguenay was. Rather than go further at this stage, he decided to return to Sainte-Croix, where the men he had left behind had built a fort 'enclosed on all sides with large wooden logs, planted upright, with artillery pointing every way'. This was now strengthened with deep, wide ditches, a gate and a drawbridge.

For five months, from mid November 1535 till 13 April 1536, Cartier and his men were frozen in and snowed up at Sainte-Croix. Their fuel and supplies ran short, and many died of scurvy. The death toll would probably have been higher if Dom Agaya had not shown Cartier how to extract a healing mixture from the branches of a local tree. As other Indians came to barter fresh meat and fish for goods, the Frenchmen recovered. Yet in April Cartier decided to return to France without attempting further exploration. But first, he kidnapped eight Indians, including Donnaconna, and with two Indian children given to him by another chief further up the St Lawrence, set sail for France in two vessels (the third had been broken up) on 6 May after setting up a cross and taking formal possession for France. He reached Saint-Malo on 16 July, having passed into the Atlantic by way of the Cabot Strait.[21]

What had Cartier achieved in his second voyage? He had established the insularity of Anticosti as well as that of Newfoundland. More important still, he had determined the course of the St Lawrence as far as the Lachine rapids and discovered a territory beyond which lay Saguenay, where, according to Donnaconna, 'immense quantities of gold, rubies and other rich things were to be found' and the men were white and wore clothes like those worn by Frenchmen. But, apart from a few quills containing gold dust, Cartier brought back none of the riches he had been sent to find, so that in the eyes of Francis and Chabot, his expedition must have seemed a failure. The time, in any case, was not ripe for a new expedition to North America, for war had broken out again between France and the Empire. Not until the truce of Nice (18 June 1538) did Francis's interest in North America revive. In September he ordered two payments to Cartier: one for his past voyages, the other for feeding and looking

---

[21] *Les Français en Amérique*, pp. 115–83.

after the Indians he had brought back.[22] During the same month Cartier submitted a long memorandum to the king, setting out his needs for a successful voyage to Saguenay. He asked for six vessels of at least 100 tons each and two barques of about 50 tons, all furnished with provisions for two years. In addition to 120 sailors, Cartier required about 154 artisans and soldiers, including two goldsmiths 'skilled in handling precious stones' and six priests.

According to the memorandum's preamble, Francis, in spite of the exhaustion of his finances, wanted to establish Christianity 'in a land of savages far removed from France, at the other end of the world, knowing full well that it offered neither mines of gold or silver nor any other hope of gain, save the conquest of an infinite number of souls for God'.[23] This statement, however, is not easily reconciled with the rest of the document or with Cartier's own ideas and behaviour. He never showed a strong missionary zeal. His first two voyages produced no baptisms, and the Indians he brought back to France had to wait a long time for theirs. Nor does the king's renunciation of mineral wealth accord well with Cartier's request for two goldsmiths. His manifesto was probably aimed at the new pope, Paul III, who had not declared himself on French activities overseas. By claiming exclusively religious intentions, Cartier may have hoped to secure for his patron papal privileges similar to those already given to the Portuguese and Spanish monarchs.[24]

An indication of the true motives underlying Cartier's third voyage is contained in a reported conversation between Francis and a Portuguese pilot, called João Lagarto. After the latter had shown the king two marine charts and an astrolabe, Francis spoke to him 'with understanding and intelligence' for over an hour. Next evening, he showed Lagarto two charts of his own 'well painted and illuminated, but not very accurate'. He pointed to 'a river in the land of Cod marked out and set down at his request'. 'He has sent there twice', writes Lagarto, 'and he has in this matter a great desire and longing, as was clearly shown, and what he says and wishes to do in the matter would make men marvel. And he spoke of this to me many times until I seemed to see it with his eyes.' Francis spoke of Cartier's two voyages and their results. He said that the river he had sent him to discover was allegedly 800 leagues long. Well up the river there were two falls, and he planned to send with the ships two brigantines which might be taken overland. 'Beyond the falls', Lagarto continues, 'the King of France says the Indian King told him there is a large city called Sagana, where there are many mines of gold and silver in great abundance, and men who dress and wear shoes like we do; and that there is abundance of clove, nutmeg and pepper. And thus I believe he will again decide to

---

[22] *Documents re. Cartier and Roberval*, pp. 69–70. The sums were 3,499 l. 4s. 6d. and 50 *écus soleil* respectively. Donnaconna and all his adult companions died before Cartier's third voyage.
[23] *Ibid.*, pp. 70–4.   [24] Julien, *Les voyages de découverte*, pp. 137–8, 147.

send there a third time seeing his great desire.' Francis told Lagarto that he wished a fort to be built well up the river whence the brigantines might be sent to pass the falls. Summer was brief in that country, he explained, and the winter long and extremely harsh, but there were plenty of fish in the river as well as oranges and pomegranates at its mouth. There were animals with hides worth ten cruzados each and men with 'wings on their arms like bats', who flew 'but little, from the ground to a tree, and from tree to tree to the ground'. Cartier had brought him some goose quills containing fine gold from Sague-nay. He used to believe that the river would lead to a passage into the southern sea, but now knew that none existed. Lagarto expressed scepticism about the precious metals and spices, insinuating that Donnaconna had mentioned them so as to return to his own country, but Francis brushed aside this suggestion with a laugh. The Indian king, he said, was an honest man who would honour his promises.[25] Never in the course of this conversation was the religious con-version of the Indians so much as mentioned. Clearly, the king's intention was to emulate the Iberian rulers by having Indies of his own; the religious motive was mere propaganda.

A report that Francis had commissioned Cartier and others to go to the Indies and settle the New Lands reached the Emperor in the Netherlands in August 1540. Treating the French challenge as a serious breach of the truce of Nice, Charles V sent a spy to keep watch on shipping along the French Atlantic coast. Despite an assurance from him that Cartier would not be going to imperial territories, Charles took no chances: fearing that the French might establish a base from which to invade the Indies and control the Bahamas channel, he ordered all French ships bound for the Indies to be intercepted and their crews thrown into the sea 'as a warning against similar expeditions'.[26]

Charles also tried to enlist the support of the king of Portugal and the pope in opposing Francis's overseas ventures. But John III would only defend his own interests. He refused to close Portuguese ports to French ships and sent an agent to Fontainebleau, who apparently won the favour of the duchesse d'Etampes and an assurance that neither Brazil nor Guinea would be encroa-ched upon. As for Paul III, he received the Emperor's entreaties with sympathy, but times having changed, he was unwilling to alienate France for the sake of *Inter caetera*. Francis did not accept the doctrine enshrined in that bull, as he made clear to the imperial envoy in December 1540. Popes, he said, had spirit-ual jurisdiction, but could not distribute lands among kings. Neither the king of France nor other Christian rulers had been consulted when the partition had been made. He therefore rejected any Portuguese or Spanish privileges which failed to take account of his own interests. 'He said that he did not send these ships to make war or to contravene the peace and friendship [with the

---

[25] *Documents re. Cartier and Roberval*, pp. 75–81.   [26] *Ibid.*, pp. 104–27, 140–3, 259–66.

Emperor] . . . but that the sun gave warmth to him as well as to others, and he much desired to see Adam's will to learn how he had partitioned the world.'[27] Yet, while defending his rights, Francis was prepared to respect the Emperor's wherever he effectively occupied a territory. His subjects, he said, would not go to the Emperor's 'lands and ports' or to 'the parts not discovered by his predecessors, and belonging to his crown more than thirty years before the ships of Spain and Portugal sailed to the new Indies'. The imperial ambassador understood Francis's meaning: 'In truth', he explained, 'I think he has in mind the populated and defended places, because he said that passing by and discovering with the eye was not taking possession.'[28]

No amount of foreign pressure could persuade Francis to give up or modify his plans. On 17 October 1540 he commissioned Cartier to go to Canada or Hochelaga 'forming an extremity of Asia on the western side' and, if possible, Saguenay in order to convert the natives.[29] Soon afterwards, however, he radically altered his plan. Instead of an ostensibly proselytizing expedition, he now envisaged the establishment of a French province overseas. This necessitated a leader capable of assuming the full responsibilities of a royal lieutenant-general. Cartier, though talented enough, was a commoner. The king wanted a nobleman rich enough to shoulder some of the cost of the enterprise. His choice fell on Jean-François de La Roque, seigneur de Roberval, a Protestant nobleman from Languedoc, a soldier and allegedly an expert in fortification. Having lost money by living at court, he hoped to rebuild his fortune by investing what was left in the Canadian enterprise.

In the king's letters patent of 15 January 1541 Roberval was instructed to go to the 'lands of Canada, Hochelaga and others circumjacent' and to organize them in the king's name provided none was occupied by the Emperor, the king of Portugal or any other Christian prince. Although the religious aims of the expedition were restated, no particulars were given of any ecclesiastical personnel or institutions, a significant omission from a document otherwise rich in constitutional provisions. What the king had in mind was an occupation by peaceful means, if possible, or by force, if necessary. Once the country had been taken over, it was to be settled and organized, and towns and forts built, as well as temples and churches. As lieutenant-general, Roberval was to exercise legislative and judicial powers, to appoint to all offices and to distribute lands as fiefs or lordships to noblemen ready to defend their country or as leasehold to persons of lower social status in return for annual rents. The expedition's profits were to be divided into three parts: the first for the settlers, the second for Roberval and the third for the crown. It was intended that

---

[27] *Ibid.*, pp. 189–92.   [28] *Ibid.*, pp. 169–71.   [29] *Ibid.*, pp. 128–31.

Roberval should be accompanied by noblemen, merchants and 'subjects of goodwill and of all qualities, arts and industry'.[30]

Cartier, in his commission had been allowed to take fifty prisoners, except those convicted of heresy, *lèse-majesté* and false coining, in addition to other 'subjects of goodwill'. But his efforts to recruit crews at Saint-Malo and other Breton ports were strongly resisted, perhaps because word had got around of the appalling hardships suffered by his men in the winter of 1536. In February 1541, however, after the king had intervened, preparations reached an advanced stage. Roberval, too, was allowed to take prisoners under sentence of death, who were required to pay for their own transportation to Canada and for their upkeep over two years.[31]

Cartier, who served under Roberval, left Saint-Malo first, on 23 May 1541, with five ships carrying several hundred men and enough supplies for two years. After a difficult Atlantic crossing, he rallied his fleet at Newfoundland and, on 23 August, returned to his old anchorage at Sainte-Croix. This, however, was unsuitable for Cartier's new fleet and numerous company. He moved, therefore, to a better site nine miles further up the St Lawrence, where he established a settlement, called Charles-Bourg-Royal (after the king's third son) and two forts. Meanwhile, two ships were sent back to France with reports for the king. The new settlement seemed to answer all of the colonists' wishes: as they set to work, they discovered iron and, as they thought, gold and diamonds. Fruit trees abounded and vegetables prospered. But Cartier longed to reach Saguenay. On 5 September he made his way upriver in two boats to the island of Montreal. He managed to bypass two rapids, but before he could reach the third, he was informed by Indians that the Ottawa was unnavigable. He returned to Charles-Bourg, only to find strained relations between his men and the Indians. Blame for this lay squarely with the French, who, instead of returning the Indians' friendship, had exploited them and treated them cruelly. Consequently, the small French garrison found itself under attack almost daily. In May 1542 Cartier and his men left for France.[32]

Roberval, meanwhile, completed his preparations, but he was seriously delayed by lack of money. On 16 April he sailed from La Rochelle with three ships carrying about 200 men and women. At Newfoundland, on 8 June, they were surprised to see Cartier's ships heading for France. Roberval ordered him to turn back, but Cartier slipped away in the night, taking with him his valuable experience and help. Roberval pressed on none the less and, at the end of July, arrived at Charles-Bourg, which he rechristened France-Roy. He built two forts (the others having been presumably destroyed by the Indians) and, on 14 September, sent two ships home. As winter approached, Roberval tried to

[30] *Ibid.*, pp. 178–85.   [31] *Ibid.*, pp. 131–2, 153–4, 193, 199–202, 212–14, 228–30, 289–92.
[32] *Les Français en Amérique*, pp. 187–97.

eke out his dwindling supplies by rationing; he also imposed a harsh discipline on his followers. For a time the Indians brought the colonists quantities of shad, but, in the end, they were overcome by scurvy; at least fifty died before April 1543. By 5 June Roberval had only about a hundred men left. Taking seventy with him, he went upriver in eight boats. His objective, like Cartier's, was Saguenay. The journey proved hazardous. One boat overturned, drowning eight men, and the others failed to get past the Lachine rapids. Otherwise, nothing is known about the expedition. It probably got no further than the Ottawa river. By the end of June Roberval had returned to base.[33]

Meanwhile, Cartier's return to France had produced bitter disappointment. The diamonds and gold he had brought back were tested and found worthless. Francis, who was again at war with the Emperor, lost interest in the Canadian enterprise. He cut his losses by sending two ships to repatriate Roberval and the remnants of his colony in the autumn of 1543. Neither Cartier nor Roberval made any profit out of their expeditions. Cartier let it be known that, in addition to the king's subsidy, he had spent 8,638 *livres* out of his own pocket; Roberval lost whatever fortune he had left.[34] But, if contemporaries viewed the Cartier-Roberval expeditions as a failure, modern opinion is more charitable. They were genuine pioneering attempts to settle Europeans well inside North America, and they yielded much experience and knowledge.[35] A tradition had also been created that not only the coastline sketched out by Verrazzano but also the interior explored by Cartier constituted a New France, which could still be occupied by France whenever she wished. As such, the Cartier-Roberval expeditions represented 'a standing challenge to the Spanish claim to a monopoly of rights to North America as a whole'.[36] If Cartier had failed to achieve any of the fundamental objectives he had set himself, he had nevertheless taken possession in France's name of a new territory and shown the way, which was to be followed successfully by Champlain in the seventeenth century.

---

[33] *Ibid.*, pp. 201–7.   [34] *Documents re. Cartier and Roberval*, pp. 480–4.

[35] Ramusio published accounts in Italian of the first two Cartier voyages (1556). A published map associated with Sebastian Cabot (1544) was the first to record something of the St Lawrence discoveries

[36] Quinn, *North America*, p. 190.

Chapter twenty

Fruitless entente (1538–42)

Francis I's foreign policy underwent a remarkable change in 1538: after years of bitter hostility towards the Emperor, he suddenly chose to become his friend. The two monarchs met in July at Aigues-Mortes and astonished the world by exchanging tokens of friendship and agreeing to sink their differences. In the following year Charles passed through France on his way to the Netherlands and contemporaries marvelled that he should thus put himself at the mercy of his former prisoner. But the alteration in Francis's policy was one of method, not purpose: this continued to be the recovery of Milan. The only difference from the past was that, instead of using force, Francis was now prepared to try conciliation.

The minister responsible for this change was the Constable, Anne de Montmorency, who largely controlled the king's foreign policy between 1538 and 1540. No French ambassador wrote to the king without also writing to the Constable; conversely, a letter from the king to an ambassador was invariably accompanied by another from Montmorency. 'The Constable', wrote a Venetian, 'has a great influence over the king's mind. He does all that he wishes in France, and sees that only peace can preserve for him this great authority.'[1] The Constable wanted a peaceful solution of the Milanese question, but he appreciated the need to negotiate from strength. He therefore used the current truce to consolidate the French occupation of Savoy and Piedmont. Each region was given a parlement and a *Chambre des Comptes*, and Turin was fortified.[2] At the same time Montmorency urged his brother, La Rochepot, to complete the fortification of towns in Picardy and Champagne and to retaliate against any infringement of the truce by imperial forces based in the Netherlands.[3]

No one wanted peace more fervently than Pope Paul III, for without it there

---

[1] *Relations des ambassadeurs vénitiens sur les affaires de France*, ed. N. Tommaseo (1838), i. 181.
[2] Decrue, i. 343; Bourrilly, *Guillaume du Bellay*, p. 264.   [3] Decrue, i. 344.

could be neither general council nor crusade. In December 1537 he appointed two legates, one for France, the other for Spain, with the object of turning the truce into a lasting peace. Rodolfo Pio, cardinal of Carpi, who was sent to France, managed to persuade Francis to meet the Emperor and the pope in the summer.[4] However, the king soon changed his mind. On 8 February a Holy League, ostensibly directed against the Turks, was formed by the Emperor, the pope, the King of the Romans and the Venetians. Believing that it was really directed against himself, Francis protested to the legate. He was also angered to learn that Paul was trying to marry his grandson to the daughter of the King of the Romans.[5] By mid February he had decided against papal mediation and suggested a further extension of the truce.[6] He had no objection, however, to resuming peace talks directly with the Emperor, and early in March sent an envoy to Spain to bring this about. But Charles, having already decided to meet the pope in Nice, refused to be side-tracked. This forced the king's hand: rather than be left in the cold, he reluctantly agreed to attend the meeting.[7]

The meeting in Nice lasted from 15 May until 20 June. As the duke of Savoy would not place the castle at the pope's disposal, Paul put up at a monastery outside the town. Charles, for his part, stayed on board his galley at Ville-franche, and Francis resided at Villeneuve. The interview consisted mainly of four meetings between the pope and the Emperor, and two between the pope and the king. At his first meeting with Paul, on 2 June, Francis assured him of his total obedience, yet refused to meet Charles in the pope's presence or to promise aid against the Turks unless Milan were restored to him first.[8] On 9 June Paul put forward the following peace plan: the daughter of Ferdinand, King of the Romans, would marry the duc d'Orléans, and after three years they would receive Milan; in the meantime, the duchy would be held in trust by Ferdinand. Francis, however, rejected this proposal.[9] So Paul had to accept a truce, but even this proved contentious. Francis wanted it to last fifteen or twenty years, whereas Charles favoured a period of five years or less. Eventually, the truce was fixed for ten years on the basis of the *status quo*. The pope claimed to be happier than at the time of his election.[10]

The meeting at Aigues-Mortes (July 1538)

Although Francis and Charles did not meet in Nice, there were frequent contacts between their courts. On 1 June Montmorency persuaded the

---

[4] Pastor, *History of the Popes*, xi. 274–5; François, *Le cardinal F. de Tournon*, p. 163.
[5] Pastor, xi. 276–7; *C.S.P.Span.*, v (pt. 2), nos. 187, 192.
[6] *Ibid.*, p. 456 and no. 184.   [7] *Ibid.*, nos. 190, 191, 193.   [8] Pastor, xi. 287–8.
[9] *Ibid.*, pp. 289–90.
[10] *Ibid.*, pp. 290–1. The truce was signed on 18 June. A.N., X^{1a} 1541, fols. 484 a–b, 485a.

Emperor to meet his master after the pope's departure.[11] Ten days later, Queen
Eleanor and her ladies travelled by sea to meet her brother. As they dis-
embarked, a wooden pier collapsed, pitching them all into the sea, but no one
suffered anything worse than a soaking. On 19 June Eleanor paid a second visit
to Charles and begged him to meet her husband soon.[12] Pope Paul left Nice on
20 June and travelled to Genoa, where he had further talks with the Emperor
before returning to Rome. Charles then sailed to Aigues-Mortes, in Languedoc,
where, on 14 July, he was greeted on board his galley by Francis. Next day
Charles returned the compliment by stepping ashore. The two arch-enemies
exchanged warm greetings and tokens of brotherly love. Observers could
hardly believe their eyes. 'It seems', one of them wrote, 'that what we are seeing
is but a dream, considering all that we have seen in the past. God is letting us
know that he governs the hearts of men as he pleases.'[13] King and Emperor
agreed to co-operate in defending Christendom and bringing heretics back into
the church. Montmorency viewed their meeting as a triumph: they could
henceforth regard each other's affairs as the same, he wrote.[14]

In October there was a further demonstration of Valois-Habsburg reconciliation, when Francis met his sister-in-law, Mary of Hungary, regent of the
Netherlands, in northern France. They spent most of the time hunting, feasting
and dancing. On 23 October they signed a treaty at Compiègne: Francis
promised not to assist the Emperor's rebels in the Netherlands, and Mary
undertook to satisfy certain French nobles whose lands in the Netherlands had
been confiscated during the war. On the eve of her departure she was given a
superb diamond by Francis.[15]

The meetings at Aigues-Mortes and Compiègne were only the prelude to
new peace talks. In December two French ambassadors submitted the following proposals to the Emperor in Spain: the duc d'Orléans would marry
Charles's daughter or niece, and his son, Philip, would marry Francis's daughter, Marguerite. Francis, for his part, would sever relations with England and
join a crusade against the Turks; he would also collaborate with the Emperor
in matters of general concern to Christendom. To the great satisfaction of the
French, Charles accepted these proposals on 22 December. His action was seen
in France as almost equivalent to an alliance.[16]

Not everyone, however, believed that the entente would last. Pope Paul
thought it was worthless and prophesied that Francis would try to sabotage the
crusade. The Emperor also doubted the king's sincerity, but was reassured by
his ambassador in France. 'I can certify to Your Majesty', the latter wrote,
'under pain of being reproached as the lowest wretch in the world, that any

[11] Decrue, i. 352. [12] *C.S.P.Span.*, v (pt. 2), nos. 206, 226, 227.
[13] C. Terrasse, *François Ier: le roi et le règne* (1945–70), ii. 293.
[14] Decrue, i. 356. [15] *L.P.*, xiii (pt. 1), 690, 749; Decrue, i. 362–3; *C.A.F.*, iii. no. 10386.
[16] Decrue, i. 364–5; *L.P.*, xiv (pt. 1), 198; *C.S.P.Span.*, vi (pt. 1), no. 252.

promise made here will be completely fulfilled.'[17] At the French court, too, there was distrust of the Emperor, but Montmorency maintained that the truce had become a peace that would last for the lives of Francis and Charles, even if Milan's cession were delayed.[18]

In fact, the French government under Montmorency's direction did honour the Aigues-Mortes entente in the expectation that Charles V would eventually hand over Milan. Francis scrupulously abstained from any new involvement in Germany's domestic affairs. An embassy from the Schmalkaldic League which came to France in August 1538, hoping to form an alliance, left empty-handed, save for a letter from Francis assuring the German Protestant princes of his friendship. Montmorency was more honest: when the ambassadors reminded him of promises given to them by Langey, he told them bluntly that 'times had changed'. Yet Francis was keeping his options open. In December he replied evasively when the pope asked him to intervene against the German Protestants. However, he did eventually inform the League that it could no longer count on his support, thereby facilitating the truce of Frankfurt (April 1539) between it and the Emperor. The German princes were so convinced of the change in the king's attitude towards them that they now looked to England for assistance; hence the marriage alliance between the duke of Cleves and Henry VIII.[19]

Francis was also cautious in his attitude towards England. Henry VIII feared that the Franco-imperial entente was the opening shot in a Catholic offensive aimed at deposing him and bringing England back into the papal fold. There were signs pointing that way. In December 1538, for example, Paul III, angered by Henry's desecration of Becket's shrine, confirmed his excommunication, which had been suspended for three years; he also sent Cardinal Pole to Spain and France to gain secular backing for the bull.[20] Early in 1539 rumours of a Franco-imperial offensive against England caused Henry to make frantic defensive preparations. His anxiety turned to panic in February, when the French and imperial ambassadors in England were recalled simultaneously.[21] Yet Henry had nothing to fear. Charles was preoccupied with the Turks, and Francis did not intend breaking with England simply to please the pope. The simultaneous recall of their ambassadors was a pure coincidence. Although in his private dealings with the papacy Francis seemed to favour some kind of action against Henry, he still insisted on the Emperor making the first move. When Pole sought Francis's support, he met with a cool response.[22] Francis, meanwhile demonstrated his peaceful intentions towards Henry by

[17] *Ibid.*, no. 35 (p. 101).   [18] *Ibid.*, no. 77.

[19] J.-Y. Mariotte, 'François Ier et la Ligue de Smalkalde', *Revue suisse d'histoire*, xvi (1966), pp. 216–21; Herminjard, vi. 236 n.14.

[20] *L.P.*, xiii (pt. 2), 1087, 1110; xiv (pt. 1), 13.   [21] *Ibid.*, xiv (pt. 1), 337, 398, 418.

[22] *Ibid.*, xiv (pt. 1), 536, 602–3, 723, 1110, 1277; W. Schenk, *Reginald Pole* (London, 1950), p. 80.

appointing a new resident ambassador in England in the person of Charles de Marillac.[23]

Francis found it more difficult to reconcile his endorsement of the Emperor's crusade with the preservation of French interests in the Levant. He offered to mediate between Charles and the Sultan when a serious revolt in Ghent forced the Emperor to shelve his crusade. With the latter's consent, Francis instructed Rincon, his resident in Turkey, to seek a truce between Christendom and the Infidel. The Sultan, however, would only consider a settlement with the Venetians. Francis trimmed his mediation accordingly, but this did not suit Charles; failing a general truce, he wanted the Venetians to continue fighting the Turks until he was free to launch his crusade. Suspecting Francis of duplicity, he suggested a joint Franco-imperial embassy aimed at dissuading Venice from making a separate peace. Francis had to agree, and, in December, del Vasto and Annebault arrived in Venice. The doge and senate, however, refused to alter their policy, and eventually came to terms with the Turks. It has been suggested that they were secretly encouraged by Annebault, but this is only conjecture. What is certain is that Francis managed, in spite of his entente with Charles, to retain the Sultan's friendship. In September 1539 Suleiman even invited him to attend the celebrations for his son's circumcision.[24]

The Emperor visits France (November 1539–January 1540)

The climax of the entente forged at Aigues-Mortes was the Emperor's visit to France in the winter of 1539–40. It was suggested originally by Charles V. He needed to reach the Netherlands from Spain as quickly as possible. The sea route across the Bay of Biscay and up the English Channel was dangerous in winter, and the alternative route across the Mediterranean and overland through Italy, Switzerland and Germany was far too long. By crossing France as the guest of her king, Charles would also save money. But he needed to convince his council that he would be safe in France and that no attempt would be made by Francis to extort concessions from him. It was not even enough for the king to guarantee Charles's safety; Francis's health seemed so fragile that it was felt necessary to obtain an invitation from the Dauphin and chief ministers just in case he died during the Emperor's stay in France.[25]

All this was done. Montmorency avidly took up the idea of the Emperor's visit in the hope of persuading him to give up Milan, but he ruled out any idea of pressing for this during Charles's stay in France in case he should subsequently repudiate any concession on the ground that it had been extorted

[23] *L.P.*, xiv (pt. 1), 669, 670, 907–8.
[24] Ursu, *La politique orientale de Francois Ier* (1908), pp. 110–15; *L.P.*, xiv (pt. 1), 849, 884, 1229.
[25] L.-P. Gachard, *Relations des troubles de Gand sous Charles-Quint, par un anonyme* (Brussels, 1846), pp. 249–53.

66. Francis I and Charles V. A fresco painted by Taddeo Zuccari (1529–1566) for the Villa Farnese at Caprarola, commemorating the meeting and short-lived reconciliation of the two great rivals.

under duress, exactly as Francis had done after the peace of Madrid. The Emperor had to be treated fairly and honourably in the hope that he would respond in kind.

When Francis sent out the official invitation on 5 August, Charles accepted in principle but explained that he could not fix the date of his coming until he had ascertained Turkish intentions in the Mediterranean.[26] By the autumn, however, he had decided to leave, and, on 7 October, Francis wrote to him in the friendliest terms: he was anxious, he said, to spare him the hazards of sea travel and to help him solve his problems in the Netherlands; Charles could rest assured of a most honourable reception in France; he had only to say the word and Francis and his children would come to meet him in Spain. Charles also received letters urging him to accept the king's invitation from the Dauphin, duc d'Orléans, Montmorency and other leading figures at the French court.[27]

On 22 October Charles accepted Francis's invitation and prepared to leave Spain. His decision caused much satisfaction in France, particularly as he asked for no hostages or other guarantees; he even asked Francis to lend him his own cooks. As the French Chancellor pointed out, such a demonstration of trust called for a truly munificent welcome.[28] Francis only regretted that his health prevented him from meeting his guest sooner. He was recovering from a serious illness and still could not ride. He did, however, manage to get as far as Loches in a litter, while his sons and Montmorency travelled to the south of France, issuing instructions on the way to towns and provincial noblemen as to how they should welcome the Emperor.[29]

From his arrival near Bayonne on 27 November, Charles and his small retinue were magnificently entertained. The Emperor was given an entry at Bordeaux, Poitiers, Orléans and Paris, and the privilege of setting prisoners free. Each entry offered scope for appropriate symbolism, 'Peace' and 'Concord' being the dominant themes of the street decorations for Charles's entry into Paris on 1 January. In each town he was given costly presents. At Poitiers, for example, he was given a silver eagle and lily on a rock, while the Parisians offered him a life-size statue of Hercules holding two pillars, also in silver. This had been designed by Rosso, and Francis later disclosed to Cellini that it was 'the ugliest work of art that he had ever seen'. The trouble apparently lay with the Parisian silversmiths who had made it. 'Not even the best masters', wrote Cellini, 'were able to give to that statue either grace, beauty or style; and for the simple reason that they did not know how to solder properly,

[26] *L.P.*, xiv (pt. 1), 451, 550, 767, 810; (pt. 2), 16.
[27] Granvelle, *Papiers d'état*, ii. 540–2; Decrue, i. 372.
[28] *R.D.B.V.P.*, iii. 1–7.
[29] *C.S.P.Span.*, vi (pt. 1), 92. On the king's illness, see *L.P.*, xiv (pt.2), 353, 492; Kaulek, pp. 136–7; Decrue, i. 374.

and so had to stick on the legs and the head and the arms by means of fastening them with silver wire.'[30]

The Emperor's itinerary from Loches northwards had evidently been devised to show him the principal artistic achievements of the reign. He visited Chenonceaux (which Francis had recently acquired from the heirs of Thomas Bohier), Chambord, Fontainebleau, Madrid, the Louvre, Villers-Cotterêts and Chantilly. At Fontainebleau, where Christmas was celebrated, Charles was given accommodation in the *Pavillon des Poêles*, which Rosso and Primaticcio had decorated specially for him. From the windows he could look into the *Cour de la Fontaine*, where a tall pillar had been erected. This had a flame at the top burning night and day, and wine and water flowing from its sides.[31] In Paris, too, he had much to admire. The hall of the Palais, where a banquet and a ball were held on the evening of his entry, had been adorned with beautiful tapestries depicting scenes from the *Iliad* and Acts of the Apostles, while the courtyard of the Louvre, where Charles resided, was dominated by a colossal statue of Vulcan.[32] In short, no expense had been spared to make his stay memorable.

The Emperor's visit to France naturally aroused the interest of Europe's other rulers. The most anxious may have been Henry VIII, who sent Sir Thomas Wyatt to find out what lay behind it. He was soon able to reassure his master: he saw no sign of an impending Franco-imperial treaty. Charles and his suite seemed to be biding their time until they had 'wound themselves honestly out of France'. The Emperor, he believed, had been forced to go there by the urgency of the crisis in the Netherlands: he and Francis did not seem to be plotting to divide the world between them despite 'all those entries, joining of arms, knitting of crowns and such like ceremonies'.[33]

The fall of Admiral Chabot (1538–41)

Montmorency now reigned supreme under the king. He was not only rich and powerful, but also popular on account of his military and diplomatic successes. While adding to his considerable wealth, he advanced his relatives and friends at the expense of his rivals and enemies. Montmorency always courted the Parlement of Paris and in 1538 he secured the appointment of its First president, Guillaume Poyet, as Chancellor of France. The Constable could also count on the support of many friends at court. Apart from the king, they included the Dauphin Henri and his mistress, Diane de Poitiers. He was also on

---

[30] J. Pope-Hennessy, *Cellini* (London, 1985), p. 103; *Fêtes et cérémonies au temps de Charles Quint*, ed. J. Jacquot (1969), pp. 433–9. For a list of the Emperor's suite and of the people who shared his table in Paris, see Musee Condé, Chantilly Ms. 899 ff. 64a–66b.
[31] F. Herbet, *Le château de Fontainebleau* (1937), pp. 109, 132.   [32] *Fêtes et cérémonies*, p. 438.
[33] *L.P.*, xiv (pt. 2), 628, 741.

excellent terms with the cardinal of Lorraine and his brother and nephews. 'You may dispose of my person', wrote François de Guise, comte d'Aumale, 'my being as much at your command as any of your own children.' Although Montmorency was devoted to Queen Eleanor, he had not yet fallen foul of Madame d'Etampes, the king's mistress. But Marguerite d'Angoulême, after patching up her differences with him in 1536, would no longer associate with him, for he had failed to support her husband's claims to Spanish Navarre and had backed the persecution of her evangelical friends. Another of the Constable's enemies was Admiral Chabot, who had risen to power with him. Having been excluded from the meetings at Nice and Aigues-Mortes, he had retired to his own province of Burgundy.[34]

In 1538 stories began to circulate to the effect that the Admiral had confused his own interests with those of the king. A discreet enquiry held with the king's approval into the activities of Chabot's subordinates revealed various malpractices. As yet, Francis was unwilling to proceed against Chabot himself, who had been his close friend since childhood. But in February 1540 the Admiral's own conduct came under scrutiny. It was found that he had taken bribes from merchants in return for letters of marque and had exacted a high percentage of the profits they hoped to make by trading in Africa and elsewhere. Ango had given him a diamond worth 3,000 *écus* in return for a permit to harass Portuguese shipping. When the king of Portugal tried to buy off Ango, Chabot intervened, exacting a substantial commission. The enquiry also revealed certain abuses committed by him as governor of Burgundy. He was tried, not by the Parlement, but by a special commission under Poyet's chairmanship. On 8 February 1541 the Admiral was stripped of all his dignities and offices, heavily fined, deprived of all the gifts he had received from the king and declared unworthy of holding any public office. He was imprisoned at Vincennes.[35]

The entente collapses

Before Charles left France for the Netherlands, he and Francis discussed the Turks and matters touching the faith, but they did not talk about their own differences; the Emperor merely promised to attend to them after meeting his brother, Ferdinand, in Brussels.[36] He took leave of Francis at Saint-Quentin on 20 January, and was escorted as far as Valenciennes by the king's sons and Montmorency. They returned four days later, carrying gifts from Charles. It was generally assumed at the French court that the Constable and the cardinal of Lorraine would soon be called to Brussels to conclude a peace settlement.

---

[34] Decrue, i. 358–61.
[35] J. Jacquart, *François Ier* (1981), pp. 384–85; *C.A.F.*, iv. 11827, 12336, 12397, 12399, 12428.
[36] *C.S.P.Span.*, vi (pt. 1), 102.

For two months, however, Montmorency waited in vain, while the Emperor put down the Ghent revolt. In the meantime, rumours began to circulate to the effect that the Franco-imperial entente had broken down and that a new war between Francis and Charles was imminent. Such talk, Montmorency declared, stemmed from malice and jealousy; the entente was as firm as ever, but important matters could not be settled overnight.[37]

The Constable's valiant efforts to keep up appearances were soon frustrated. In March the Emperor recalled his ambassador from France, and a few days later, sent him back with peace proposals. Charles's daughter, Mary, would marry the duc d'Orléans, and both would eventually inherit the Netherlands, Burgundy and Charolais. They would administer these territories in the Emperor's lifetime, albeit under his supervision. If Mary died without issue, her lands would revert to Charles's heirs in the male line. Two other marriages were proposed: one between Francis's daughter Marguerite and the eldest son of the King of the Romans; the other between Charles's son, Philip, and Jeanne d'Albret, heiress to Navarre. Francis, for his part, would surrender his claim to Milan as well as Hesdin and the lands he had taken from the duke of Savoy. He would also ratify the treaties of Madrid and Cambrai, and join a league in defence of Christendom.[38]

When they received these proposals, Francis, the Dauphin and Montmorency shut themselves up in a room for an hour and a half; the Constable then took to his bed for two or three days. On 4 April Francis delivered his reply. The Netherlands, he explained, were not an adequate substitute for Milan, which was his by right of inheritance and by virtue of Maximilian's investiture of Louis XII. Their future enjoyment was a poor exchange for the immediate possession of Milan, which had been promised to the duc d'Orléans on condition he married the Infanta. As for Marguerite, Francis preferred to delay her marriage; he was ready, however, to accept the match proposed for his niece, Jeanne d'Albret. He was willing to exchange Hesdin for Tournai, Mortagne and Saint-Omer, but refused to ratify the treaties of Madrid and Cambrai. If it could be proved that he held parts of Savoy unlawfully, he would hand them back in exchange for his own lands held by the duke without valid title. As for the league, this was no problem.[39]

On 24 April Francis modified his terms in response to new proposals from Charles. He agreed to suspend his claim to Milan if Charles would hand over the Netherlands immediately to the duc d'Orléans. He also accepted their reversion to Charles in the event of Mary dying childless, but only if his own claim to Milan were recognized. He still refused to ratify the treaties of Madrid

[37] Decrue, i. 380, 388–9.
[38] *L.P.*, xv. 373; K. Brandi, *The Emperor Charles V*, tr. C. V. Wedgwood (London, 1939), pp. 430–1.
[39] *L.P.*, xv. 457.

and Cambrai, but offered to sign a new agreement covering such concessions as he could legitimately make.[40]

The two rulers continued to exchange proposals for several weeks, but their fundamental positions remained unchanged, Milan, as usual, being the stumbling-block; Francis wanted nothing else, while Charles was as determined as ever to prevent it passing into French hands. On 15 May he complained that the tone of Francis's last message was not what he had come to expect after the interviews of Aigues-Mortes and Paris.[41] Yet the last thing he wanted at this stage was a new conflict with France, for he still needed to restore order to the Netherlands, heal the religious schism in Germany and prepare his crusade. He instructed his ambassadors, if all else failed, to arrange another interview with Francis. But they were not given a chance to show their instructions. The cardinal of Lorraine told them bluntly that Francis felt he should be given Milan without fuss.[42] By June the talks had finally collapsed.

Montmorency's fall (1541)

The breakdown of the Franco-imperial entente played into the hands of Montmorency's enemies at court who had longed for such an opportunity to topple him. 'He is a great scoundrel', said the duchesse d'Etampes, 'for he has deceived the king by saying that the Emperor would give him Milan at once when he knew that the opposite was true.'[43] Yet Francis was still not prepared to discard the Constable. 'I can see only one fault in you', he told him, 'and that is that you do not love those whom I love.'[44] Although Montmorency continued to attend the king's council, he ceased in April 1540 to influence foreign policy. The king began to consult Cardinals Tournon, du Bellay and of Mâcon, as well as the bishop of Soissons.[45] In August it was noted that Francis attended council meetings more regularly; he was also having long consultations with Poyet and Tournon, who, together with Madame d'Etampes, were continually in his company. The imperial envoy described her as 'the real president of the king's most private and intimate council'. This did not bode well for Franco-imperial relations. 'I hear from a good quarter', wrote the same ambassador to Charles, 'that the reason for her angry feelings is that when Your Majesty passed through the kingdom you did not make so much of her as she expected which has hardened her heart in such a way that it will be very difficult, nay, almost impossible to appease her.'[46]

On 11 October the Emperor invested his own son, Philip, with the duchy of Milan, thereby precipitating Montmorency's fall.[47] Within a month the king's

[40] *Ibid.*, xv. 573; Ribier, i. 509.   [41] *C.S.P.Span.*, vi (pt. 1), 108.   [42] *Ibid.*,117.
[43] François, *François de Tournon*, p. 179 n.1.
[44] Decrue, i. 401.   [45] *L.P.*, xv. 574.   [46] *C.S.P.Span.*, vi (pt. 1), 117.   [47] Decrue, i. 400.

secretaries were forbidden to use the diplomatic cyphers he had given them; princes and ambassadors ceased to write to him, and Poyet took charge of the department Montmorency had previously run. Believing that he was already in disgrace, the Constable asked for permission to leave the court, but Francis said that he still needed his services. In February 1541 Montmorency staged something of a comeback. 'The Constable', wrote the imperial ambassador, 'is beginning to recover his breath and to take part in affairs of state'; but not for long.[48] In April Mary of Hungary received the following report from the French court: 'As for the government of the court, Madame d'Etampes has more credit than ever. The constable . . . is paying court to her; his credit is diminishing each day. He has had angry words with the chancellor.'[49] Soon Montmorency was no longer free to correspond even with his friends. He advised Langey, the king's lieutenant in Piedmont, to send his reports in future to Marshal d'Annebault. On 14 June he attended the marriage between the duke of Cleves and Jeanne d'Albret at Châtellerault.

Henri d'Albret had long been dissatisfied with Francis's policy which had failed to secure imperial recognition of his claim to Spanish Navarre. In 1537 he had entered into secret talks with Charles V and in March 1538, after an interruption, they were revived. How far Marguerite d'Angoulême connived at these negotiations is uncertain: she was allegedly disenchanted with her brother's policy towards Navarre.[50] Be this as it may, her position became difficult early in 1540, when Francis accepted a request from William, duke of Cleves, for the hand of her daughter, Jeanne. The king's alliance with Cleves, though ostensibly defensive, marked a reorientation of his foreign policy, for the duke was currently engaged in a dispute with the Emperor over the succession to Guelders. He was also the brother-in-law of the Elector of Saxony, one of the leaders of the anti-Habsburg opposition in Germany. Marguerite was appalled by the prospect of her twelve-year-old daughter marrying a man twice her age: she begged William not to hasten the match, describing it as premature 'in the eyes of God and nature'. But the duke came to France soon afterwards at the invitation of Francis. Jeanne d'Albret, after agreeing to be married, now changed her mind and had to be bullied into submission by Tournon.[51] On 14 June the little princess was carried to the altar by Montmorency acting by royal command. This seemed to him the final indignity; next day he left the court never to return during Francis's reign.[52]

Montmorency retained his offies despite his fall from grace, but in May 1542

[48] *Ibid.*, i. 402.   [49] *Ibid.*
[50] P. Jourda, *Marguerite d'Angoulême* (1930), i. 215–17, 222–4, 228–30; *C.S.P.Span.*, v (pt. 2), 196–7.
[51] A. de Ruble, *Le mariage de Jeanne d'Albret* (1877). Also Jourda, i. 251–67; N. L. Roelker, *Queen of Navarre, Jeanne d'Albret* (Cambridge, MA, 1968), pp. 46–59.
[52] P. de Bourdeille, abbé de Brantôme, *Oeuvres complètes*, ed. L. Lalanne (1864–81), viii. 117; Decrue, i. 403.

Francis annulled the powers of provincial governors and lieutenant-generals on the ground that they had become excessive. His ordinance, however, was nothing more than a polite means of depriving Montmorency of his governorship of Languedoc, for, two days after its publication, letters of confirmation were sent out to all the other governors. Francis, it seems, was unwilling to inflict a public humiliation on his former chief minister: having excluded him from court and council, he still needed to strip him of his provincial powers. By suspending all the governors and then restoring them, save Montmorency, he achieved his object with a minimum of offence to the Constable's pride.[53]

[53] Isambert, xii. 779–80; G. Zeller, 'Gouverneurs de provinces au XVIe siècle', *R.H.*, clxxxv (1939), pp. 243–5.

Chapter twenty-one

Madrid and Fontainebleau

In March 1528, two years after his return from captivity, Francis informed the municipal authorities in Paris of his intention 'henceforth to reside most of the time in our good town and city of Paris and its neighbourhood rather than elsewhere in the kingdom'.[1] In fact, he continued to travel about France as much and as widely as before, nor did he abandon the Loire valley. However, he did shift the centre of his building activities to Paris and the Ile de France. He began rebuilding the Louvre, erected the château of Madrid in the Bois de Boulogne, remodelled Saint-Germain-en-Laye to the west of Paris, built Villers-Cotterêts to the north of it, and embarked on the transformation of Fontainebleau into one of the most magnificent royal palaces in Europe.

What prompted this shift? It is possible that the disloyalty of certain Parisians during the king's captivity had persuaded him of the need to overawe them. Strategic considerations may also have influenced him: the highly vulnerable frontiers of northern and eastern France were more easily reached from the Paris area than from the Loire valley. Another reason may have been the political ascendancy of Anne de Montmorency (1528–41) whose principal estates – Chantilly, Ecouen, Fère-en-Tardenois – lay near the capital. Anne must have welcomed an arrangement which allowed him to keep an eye on his own châteaux while attending the court. Francis was often his guest during this period.

The Louvre

The only potential accommodation available to the king within the capital was the Louvre, but it was a decrepit medieval fortress without a courtyard suitable for the kind of entertainment favoured by Renaissance princes. The need had been underlined early in the reign when the courtyard of the

[1] *R.D.B.V.P.*, ii. 17.

398

Bastille had been used for a banquet in honour of an English embassy.[2] In 1528 Francis created an open space within the Louvre by demolishing the mediaeval keep. The moat was also filled and the approaches to the castle improved. The king ordered a street on the east side to be made 'beautiful, wide and straight' as well as the building of an embankment 'giving passage to the horses pulling merchandise along the river'. A letter of 13 August 1530 from Nicolas de Neufville to Montmorency describes work recently undertaken at the Louvre on the king's orders. It includes the building of various offices and the refurbishment of a council chamber. The king's lodging was situated beneath that of the queen above which were three rooms for her ladies. The royal lodgings were at the eastern end of the south wing of the Louvre. Their dimensions were far more modest than those of the suite once occupied by King Charles V, but they were richly decorated internally. The distribution of rooms was also carefully done, the king being provided with some curious emergency exits. The reduced size of the royal *logis* may have resulted from the multiplication of court officials and ladies, the king's acceptance of discomfort as part and parcel of a nomadic existence and also from his wish to cultivate an image of informality with his subjects.[3] Yet the rebuilding of the Louvre took a very long time. For twenty years Francis was content to make it simply more convenient while giving it an occasional facelift. Sauval tells us that in 1540, on the occasion of the Emperor's visit,

> many repairs were carried out. All the weathercocks were regilded. The arms of France were in several places repainted and displayed . . . Most of the casements were enlarged and the windows painted. The number of apartments was increased . . . This château thus became so liveable that Charles V, the king, the queen, the Dauphin, the Dauphine, the king and queen of Navarre, the Children of France, Cardinal Tournon, the Constable and even the duchesse d'Etampes, Francis I's mistress, each had apartments proportionate to their status. Such was the expenditure at that time that an entire register of the royal works is full of it and contains nothing else.[4]

It was only at the very end of his reign that Francis ordered Pierre Lescot to demolish the west wing of the Old Louvre and replace it by the south-west wing of the present *Cour Carrée*. The work was continued after the king's death in 1547 by his son, Henri II. Lescot has been described as 'a talented draughtsman, with perhaps a sound theoretical grasp of principles of architectural style, but with no practical or technical expertise'.[5]

The New Louvre was part of a plan for the embellishment of Paris envisaged

[2] A.-M. Lecoq, 'Une fête italienne à la Bastille en 1518' in *'Il se rendit en Italie'. Etudes offertes à André Chastel* (1988), pp. 149–68.
[3] M. Fleury and V. Kruta, *Le Château du Louvre*, (1990), p. 71; M. Chatenet, 'Le logis de Francois Ier au Louvre', *Revue de l'Art*, vol. 97 (1992), pp. 72–4.
[4] *Ibid.*, pp. 71, 74.   [5] D. Thomson, *Renaissance Paris* (London, 1984), p. 83.

by Francis. Another was the building of a new town hall. The *Maison des Piliers*, which had been the headquarters of the municipal authorities since the fourteenth century, had outlived its usefulness. In December 1529 the *Bureau de la Ville* informed the governor of Paris of its intention to erect a new Hôtel de Ville. On being asked for help to fund the project, Francis put forward a design by Domenico da Cortona, which the *Bureau* duly adopted. This consisted of a trapezoidal building facing the Place de Grève. At each end was a square pavilion pierced by a large archway and the intervening block had an arcade with Corinthian columns and recessed pedimented windows. Statues in niches filled the spaces between the first-floor windows. The pavilions and intervening block had their separate high pitched roofs. The whole was 'an intriguing mixture of imported decorative features applied to a building wholly French in form'.[6] Work on the Hôtel de Ville began in 1534 and continued with interruptions till the end of the reign. It was not completed till 1606, and the entire building was destroyed in 1871, the one now standing on the site being a crude and much enlarged modern version.

Madrid

Nothing remains of the château of Madrid which Francis I built in the Bois de Boulogne just outside Paris, though its plan and elevation are recorded in drawings, engravings and eye-witness accounts.[7] Work on the château began in the spring of 1528 and lasted for more than twenty years. By 7 January 1540, when Francis visited the château with Charles V, it was probably finished up to the second floor. In June 1544 the king imposed a temporary ban on decorating Madrid, presumably to save money at a time of national emergency. Two-thirds of the roof had been completed by 1547.

Why did Francis find it necessary to build a new residence only six kilometres from the Louvre? He gave the answer in letters patent of 1 August 1528 in which he expressed the wish 'to find his pleasure and relaxation in hunting'.[8] Although much smaller than the vast forests associated with other royal châteaux, the Bois de Boulogne had the advantage of being near Paris. In 1540 the king had it enclosed by a wall, and between 1544 and 1546 he enlarged it by many land purchases. Earlier French kings had had hunting parks, but none had ever built a palace inside one. Francis was the first to associate a traditional royal residence (the Louvre) with a house dedicated to 'recreation and pleasure'. When he appointed Duprat as captain of the château of Madrid in May 1530 it was described as a *maison de plaisance* where the cardinal might

---

[6] *Ibid.*, p. 76. See also P. Champion, *Paganisme et réforme* (1936), pp. 41–8; J.-P. Babelon, *Paris au XVIe siecle* (1986), pp. 119–22.
[7] M. Chatenet, *Le château de Madrid au bois de Boulogne* (1987), pp. 49–63.   [8] Laborde, i. 7.

find relaxation from the cares of state. The site chosen was close to the port de Neuilly, where the king used to cross the Seine on the way from Paris to Saint-Germain-en-Laye.[9]

The château of Madrid had neither courtyard nor moat. In plan, it was a rectangular mass comprising five blocks. The centre block was occupied by a large hall (*salle*) flanked by two open loggias. On either side, was another block containing a small hall (*sallette*) on an entresol flanked by two *cabinets*. The *sallette* had a fireplace 'in the manner of Castile' with a tall over-mantel and a hearth open on three sides. At either end of the château there were large square pavilions, each containing four apartments. An apartment comprised two living rooms. This arrangement was repeated on three floors. Thus the château had four large *salles*, each measuring 168 square metres. The *sallette* on the first floor opened on to a balustraded tribune overlooking the central hall. The pavilions contained a fourth floor with four large rooms lit by dormers. There was also an attic containing four small, badly lit, rooms. The apartments were reached by spiral staircases, four in square towers at the angles of the great hall, and two in circular turrets at each end of the building. Altogether there were thirty-two apartments, each with a fireplace and an alcove, an idea allegedly imported from Spain by the king. The basement was occupied by kitchens and offices. The elevation comprised on the ground and first floors two horizontal tiers of open loggias running round the entire building between the towers and linked by a corridor. The second floor had a terrace. High pitched roofs covered the various blocks and towers. Tall mullioned windows were regularly spaced. At the upper levels they were flanked by columns and pilasters. The dormer windows, instead of bearing complicated open-work designs, as at Blois and Chambord, were mostly covered by straight pediments.[10]

The most unusual feature at Madrid was the decoration, both interior and exterior, of brightly coloured glazed terracotta. The columns and capitals of the loggias were covered with a grey or dark brown glaze imitating marble, bronze or *pietra serena*. Medallions, containing busts of Roman emperors, occupied the spandrels above the columns. Their white frames were set against a bright blue background. The entablatures of the loggias were also adorned with majolica, while the pilasters flanking the ground floor windows had candelabra patterns comprising dolphins, putti and satyrs. Two friezes on the second and third floors had white circles against a blue background. The dormers too had majolica adornments as had the tall chimney stacks.[11]

The interior decoration at Madrid seems also to have been lavish. John Evelyn informs us in his *Diary* that 'earth painted like porcelain' was used 'for whole statues and relievos . . . chimney pieces and columns both within and

9 Chatenet, pp. 43–8.   10 *Ibid.*, pp. 65–71.   11 *Ibid.*, pp. 76–86.

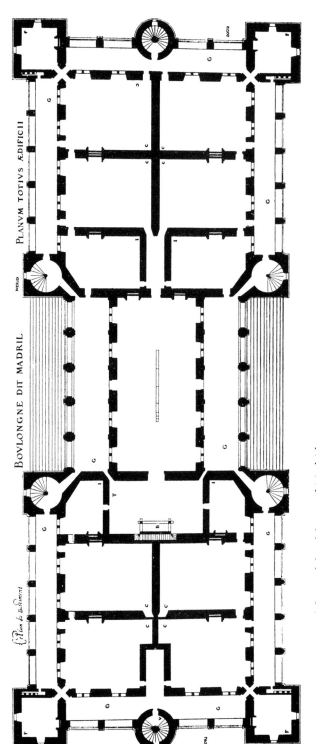

8. Plan of the ground floor of the château of Madrid

9. Elevation of the château of Madrid (J. Androuet Du Cerceau, *Les plus excellents bastiments de France*)

without'.[12] Few other visitors, however, point to the interior decoration as being of majolica, which suggests that this was mainly used on the outside of the building. The iconography of Madrid's interior decoration is for the most part unknown. As Chatenet writes: 'It is difficult to grasp the precise meaning of the fireplace adornments, and we do not understand, in particular, why the salamanders are winged like the phoenix, queen Eleanor's emblem.'[13]

According to a document of February 1530, two men were responsible for the building of Madrid: Pierre Gadier and Girolamo della Robbia.[14] Gadier was a master mason from Touraine who had worked at Amboise and Tours. When he died in 1531, he was replaced by Gatien François, a master mason of similar background. Girolamo was a Florentine sculptor. Born in 1488, he was the youngest son of Andrea della Robbia and grandnephew of the famous Luca. He first came to France early in the reign of Francis, who paid him a small pension as *imagier et paintre du roi*. After a spell in Florence, he returned to France in 1527 and settled at Puteaux, where the king provided him with a workshop. He became quite prosperous, built a house in Paris and about 1536 was appointed *valet de chambre ordinaire du roi*. The king ordered from him a large *chapeau de triomphe* for Fontainebleau (*c*.1536) and two triumphal arches for Charles V's entry into Paris (2 December 1539). In addition to such works, he was employed as master mason at Madrid from 1531 and continued

[12] *The Diary of John Evelyn* ed. E.S. De Beer (London, 1959), p. 284.   [13] Chatenet, p. 86.
[14] *Ibid.*, p. 17.

to work there till 1552. In 1564, at the age of seventy-seven, he carved the *gisant* of Catherine de' Medici for the tomb of Henri II. This together with a few fragments of ceramic in Sèvres museum are his only surviving works.[15]

Who was the architect of Madrid? We cannot assume that he was one of the three original master masons. Such a person was responsible for carrying out an architectural project; he did not have to be its creator. The term 'architect' in early sixteenth-century France was applied to three Italians – Leonardo, Pierre Paul and Domenico da Cortona – who were not workmen but scholars with a knowledge of Italian architectural theory. Although Girolamo della Robbia was described as 'the king's architect' in 1566, he was never described as such in any of the twenty-four relevant documents for the reign of Francis I. Chatenet, while conceding that he played a major part in the construction of Madrid and designed the arches for the loggias, does not believe that he designed the whole building. Its plan, in her view, is French in conception, as is much of the workmanship. Instead of Girolamo, she plumps for an unidentified designer: a man familiar with certain Italian theoretical principles, but without any real knowledge of the art of building as practised south of the Alps.[16]

How did the château get its name? The problem has caused much speculation over the centuries. The Bourgeois de Paris informs us that the king called it 'Madrid' because it was like the building in Spain where he had been held prisoner.[17] Yet the Alcázar was quite different. All the official documents of the reign refer to the château of 'Boulogne'. Would they have done so if the king had used a different name? According to John Evelyn, the king called the château 'Madrid' 'to absolve him of his oath that he would not go from Madrid (where he was a prisoner) in Spain, but from whence he made his escape'.[18] Another explanation is given by Sauval in his *Antiquités de la ville de Paris*. Francis, he writes, never wanted to be troubled with affairs of state when he vanished into the Bois de Boulogne, so much so that his courtiers complained that they saw as little of him as when he had been in Madrid. They called the new château 'his Madrid' and the name stuck.[19]

All this speculation, however, can now be laid aside, for a link has been firmly established between the château of Madrid and the Casa de Campo, a country house built to the west of Madrid not far from the Alcázar between 1515 and 1519 by Francisco de Varga, a royal treasurer and businessman. Though the Casa was destroyed in the Spanish Civil War, its elevation and plan are known from documents. It was a rectangular building with two storeys and an attic under sloping roofs. Two square pavilions, one at each

[15] *Ibid.*, pp. 17–21.
[16] *Ibid.*, pp. 21–4, 129–30. For Pierre Paul, known as *'l'Italien'*, see C.A.F., ii. 4270; vii. 28392, 28531
[17] J.B.P., p. 274.   [18] *Diary of John Evelyn*, p. 64.
[19] H. Sauval, *Histoire et recherches des antiquités de la ville de Paris* (1724), ii. 309.

end, were linked by a narrower central block. Each façade had arcaded galleries, open and superimposed. The arches rested on marble Corinthian columns imported from Italy with capitals adorned with escutcheons. The building was constructed of brick and faced with glazed tiles (*azulejos*). The square pavilions were subdivided internally by walls, while the central block consisted of a large vestibule. The Casa, however, was smaller than the château of Madrid. A connexion between the two buildings was noted as early as 1540 when a Spanish traveller published an anonymous account of Charles V's visit. He tells us that on 7 January the Emperor left Paris 'and dined in a house called Boulogne modelled on that of the *licenciado* Vargas of Madrid although it is a little better'. Thus it seems that the château was after all inspired by a Spanish prototype, though some of its features probably owed more to French and Italian sources. Francis presumably saw the Casa del Campo during his captivity and liked it so much that he decided to create a larger version outside Paris for his own lasting enjoyment.[20]

Saint-Germain-en-Laye

According to Du Cerceau, Francis was so knowledgeable (*ententif*) about architecture that one could almost say that he alone was the architect of Saint-Germain-en-Laye.[21] This suggests at least a close collaboration between the king and the Parisian master mason Pierre Chambiges, who began rebuilding the château in September 1539. Keeping as much as he could of the mediaeval château, Chambiges added two storeys and completely renovated the inner façades. His chief innovation, which the king may have suggested, was the terraced roof, constructed of large, superimposed stone slabs. Such was its weight that the supporting edifice had to be reinforced with large buttresses and held together by long iron tie-bars.[22]

Architecturally, Saint-Germain is not Francis I's most exciting château, yet, along with the Louvre and Fontainebleau, it was one that he used most frequently. The château proper was only the chief component of a vast complex of buildings. On the west side, there was an outer courtyard (*basse-cour*) adorned with a well and a fountain and surrounded by outbuildings (*communs*). On the north side lay the garden and, on the south and east sides, the park and forest. Three bridges linked the château to the park. Within the dry moat were a tennis court, the lists and a small building (*armerie*) 'in which

[20] F. Marias, 'De Madrid à Paris: François Ier et la Casa de Campo' *Revue de l'Art*, vol. 91 (1991), 26–35; M. Chatenet, 'Une nouvelle "cheminée de Castille" à Madrid en France'; *ibid.*, pp. 36–8; Chatenet, pp. 119–26;
[21] J. A. Du Cerceau, *Les plus excellents bastiments de France (1576–1607)* (facsimile repr., Farnborough, 1972), i. 5b.
[22] F. Gebelin, *Les châteaux de la Renaissance* (1927), pp. 161–6; J.-P. Babelon, *Châteaux de France au siècle de la Renaissance* (1989), pp. 318–23.

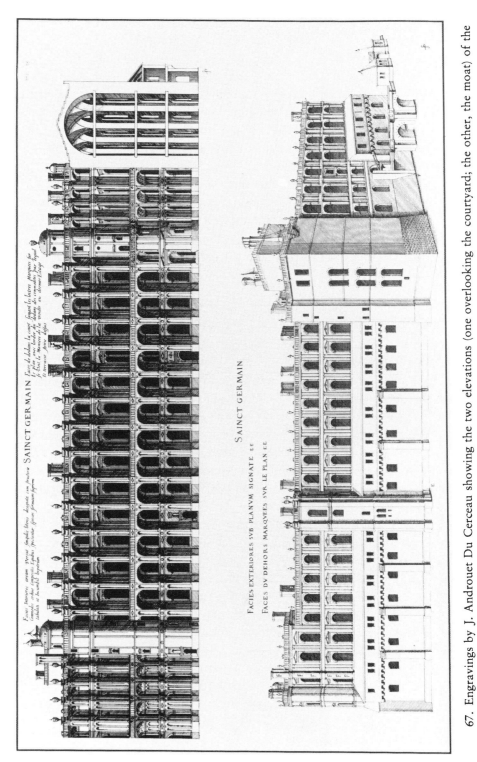

67. Engravings by J. Androuet Du Cerceau showing the two elevations (one overlooking the courtyard; the other, the moat) of the royal logis at the château of Saint-Germain-en-Laye.

the king armed himself'. Near the future Château-Neuf stood the royal menagerie. Elsewhere in the park there was a quintain (*jeu de bague*) and a piece of equestrian equipment called *chevalet de la jument*.[23] Finally, in the depths of the forest stood an ancillary residence, the château of La Muette, built as from 1542, at a spot where the king liked to watch the deer retire 'exhausted from the labours of the chase'. Though this château, too, had a terraced roof and stone walls decorated with brick, it differed from Saint Germain in plan and was also much smaller. It consisted of a square central block with four square pavilions, one at each corner. The chapel and an ingenious staircase were contained in two projecting wings, one on either side. There were superimposed galleries on two façades. Within ten years of its completion in 1549 the roof at La Muette had to be rebuilt. Nothing remains of this château to-day.[24]

Another small château built by Francis in the Ile-de-France was Challuau. It was demolished in 1803, but the plan and elevations are recorded in Du Cerceau's engravings. It was again a clever design with a cubic central block and four square angle pavilions. The lateral façades were adorned with superimposed galleries providing independent access to the apartments. From the main entrance a single-flight straight staircase led to the first floor. The walls were built of mortar and brick and the flat roof was balustrated. It was built, probably by Pierre Chambiges, between 1539 and 1545 and was given by the king to the duchesse d'Etampes.[25]

From 1532 onwards Francis was a frequent visitor to Villers-Cotterêts, situated 85 kilometres north-east of Paris. Work on the château began about 1533 and was largely completed in Francis's lifetime. It was carried out by two Parisian master masons, Guillaume and Jacques Le Breton. The château was built around two rectangular courtyards, one of which served as a tennis court. In its present state the main feature at Villers-Cotterêts is the wing that divides the courtyards. This contains a chapel (now the *Salle des Etats*) and two straight staircases of which the larger has a coffered vault decorated with scenes from Colonna's *Il sogno di Polifilo*.[26]

Fontainebleau

By far the most important château built by Francis in the last twenty years of his life was Fontainebleau. In December 1529 he announced his intention to spend more time there on account of the pleasure he derived from hunting deer

---

[23] M. Chatenet, 'Une demeure royale au milieu du XVIe siècle: La distribution des espaces au château de Saint-Germain-en-Laye', *Revue de l'Art*, 81 (1983), p. 22.
[24] Babelon, *Châteaux de France*, pp. 323–5. [25] *Ibid.*, pp. 325–7.
[26] Laborde, *Les comptes des bâtiments du roi (1528–1571)* (1878–80), i. 222–4.

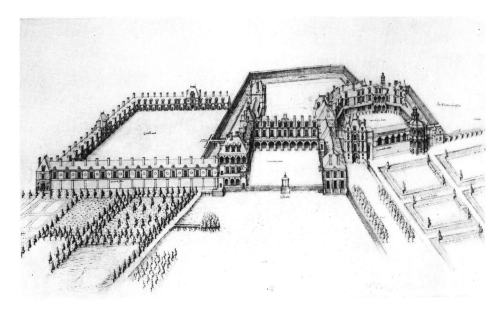

10. The château of Fontainebleau

and wild boar in the neighbouring forest.[27] Fontainebleau did, in fact, become
his favourite residence. He 'liked it so much', writes Du Cerceau, 'that he spent
most of his time there . . . all that he could find of excellence was for his
Fontainebleau of which he was so fond that whenever he went there he would
say that he was going home'.[28] This is confirmed by the king's itinerary: he
spent more time at Fontainebleau after 1528 than anywhere else save Paris.[29]

A castle, roughly oval in shape with a gatehouse, a square keep and flanking
towers, had existed at Fontainebleau since the twelfth century. By the sixteenth
century, however, it could no longer serve the needs of a large, sophisticated
court. To enlarge it, however, a Trinitarian monastery standing a short distance away to the west needed to be removed. This was progressively demolished, Francis acquiring the site in 1529. Meanwhile, in 1528, he accepted an
estimate for the reconstruction of the castle. A Parisian master mason, called
Gilles Le Breton undertook three tasks: first, to restore the original castle;
secondly, to build a new château with a vast courtyard on the monastic site;
and thirdly, to build a gallery projecting westward from the keep of the old
château.[30] Work on the original château included the construction of *corps
d'hôtel* between the towers and of turrets containing spiral staircases. The
mediaeval gatehouse was transformed into the *Porte Dorée*, a monumental

[27] Gebelin, pp. 181–4; Babelon, *Châteaux de France*, pp. 213–18.
[28] P. Guilbert (Abbé), *Description historique des château, bourg et forest de Fontainebleau* (2 vols.,
1731), ii. 262.
[29] Du Cerceau, ii. 3.   [30] C.A.F., viii. pp. 455–533, 541–8.

68. A contemporary cartouche showing the pond, the *Porte Dorée* and the wing of the château of Fontainebleau containing the baths, the *Galerie François Ier* and the king's library in their original state.

gateway with two superimposed loggias recalling those built by Laurana for palaces at Urbino and Naples. Instead of the beautiful white stone used in the Loire valley, Le Breton used *grès*, a hard local stone not easily carved. In the *Cour du Cheval Blanc*, he used brick for the pilasters and mouldings.

In 1531, following the king's remarriage and the death of his mother, important modifications were carried out in the *Cour Ovale*. Vertical access to the apartments by means of spiral staircases was abandoned in favour of a horizontal scheme. The staircase turrets were removed and a continuous open terrace was provided at the first-floor level. This had a simple iron railing and was carried by a row of pillars around much of the courtyard.[31] As the king's

[31] Babelon, pp. 198–206.

staircase near the *Porte Dorée* offered access only to his apartment, another staircase was built within the courtyard. This was an extraordinary structure consisting of two straight flights leading to a platform from which a third flight served as a bridge to the first floor. The staircase was attached to an arcaded portico on two storeys adorned with classical columns and reminiscent of a Roman triumphal arch. The apse of the chapel of St Saturnin on the opposite side of the courtyard was designed to match the staircase. It is unlikely that Le Breton, who was in many respects a clumsy architect, designed this original staircase. It was once attributed to the Italian architect, Sebastiano Serlio, but the staircase was built about ten years before he came to Fontainebleau in 1541. André Chastel has suggested that the designer was the Florentine artist, Rosso, who came to Fontainebleau in 1531.[32] He is remembered primarily as a painter, who initiated the château's interior decoration, but, according to Vasari, he was also an 'excellent architect' whose 'arches, colossi and such-like things were . . . the most stupendous ever made'.[33]

At the same time, work continued on the east wing of the *Cour du Cheval Blanc*. This included a central pavilion terminating the *Galerie François Ier* and another at each end. To the south was the *Pavillon des Poêles*, where Charles V probably stayed in 1539. As its name indicates, the ground floor housed stoves, which heated the floors above. At the northern end was the *Pavillon des Armes* which had open loggias and was topped by a belvedere. Two unusual atlantes, copied from Egyptian art and possibly designed by Rosso, flanked its entrance. It was here that Francis stored his ancient statues. The first floor contained the Constable's apartment and the second, the king's armoury.

Fontainebleau was built in a piecemeal fashion over a long period. Francis did not live to see it finished. For much of his reign it must have been a noisy, dirty place, full of scaffolding and workmen. A great deal of what he built has also been destroyed. Only the north wing of the *Cour du Cheval Blanc* is more or less in its original state, though it was shortened in 1565 to make way for a moat. The west wing was destroyed by Napoleon I, and the south wing was rebuilt by Louis XV. This involved the destruction of the *Galerie d'Ulysse*. This was the longest gallery in France (115 metres) and its vaulted ceiling and walls were adorned with paintings by Primaticcio. Recent research has shown that the gallery was an afterthought. As late as 1535 the south wing of the *Cour du Cheval Blanc* had no upper storey and was of the same length as the north wing. About 1536, however, it was decided to increase its length and add a first floor containing the gallery. These changes, marking a radical departure from Francis's original plan for an autonomous 'château neuf' to the west of the old

[32] A. Chastel, 'L'escalier de la Cour Ovale à Fontainebleau' in *Essays . . . to Rudolf Wittkower*, ed. D. Fraser, H. Hibbard and M.J. Lewine (London, 1967), pp. 74–80.

[33] G. Vasari, *The Lives of the Painters, Sculptors and Architects*, ed. W. Gaunt (London, 1963), ii. 355, 362.

one, can be directly related to the building of the *Pavillon des Poêles*. This was put up very rapidly and sumptuously decorated in time for Charles V's visit in 1539. It was given far more attention than the *Pavillon des Armes*. From 1534 onwards Francis became increasingly interested in the pond and gardens at Fontainebleau which lay close to the *Pavillon des Poêles*. Guillaume has suggested that initially the *Galerie d'Ulysse* was intended as a corridor providing easy access from the royal apartments in the *Cour Ovale* to the *Jardin des Pins*. But its potential as a great hall for receptions and festivities soon came to be appreciated. In other words, the king's new interest in the gardens at Fontainebleau led to a reorientation of the *château neuf*, necessitating a radical transformation of the south wing of the *Cour du Cheval Blanc*. The *Galerie d'Ulysse* may have been inspired by a gallery at the Belvedere in Rome which the pope used to reach his gardens. It was known to Rosso, who may have drawn Francis's attention to it.[34] The only part of the original south wing that survives is the *Grotte des Pins* with its giants emerging from a rocky background. This was for a long time one of Fontainebleau's most controversial features. In fact, it was built about 1543 as a summer-house. The notion that it was used as a bathroom and that James V of Scotland saw his future bride, Madeleine de France, bathing there naked is a figment of eighteenth-century imagination.[35]

In the early seventeenth century the *Cour du Cheval Blanc* (named after a plaster copy of the Capitoline statue of Marcus Aurelius, which Catherine de' Medici set up in the middle) was used for equestrian purposes, and it may have been used for this purpose by Francis whose stables occupied the ground floor of the south wing till 1537. The horses were then moved to Monceau and the ground floor placed at the disposal of merchants and artisans attached to the court. The courtyard was entered through the centre pavilion of the west wing which was traditionally occupied by the *Cent-Suisses*. What the other pavilions were used for is uncertain. One may have housed the foundry used to make bronzes of ancient statues from casts brought back from Rome by Primaticcio in 1541; it later became a tapestry workshop.

Today the most important survival of Renaissance Fontainebleau is the *Galerie François Ier*, which occupies the first floor of the wing that was added to the keep. In the early sixteenth century it served as a passage from the royal apartments to the church of the Trinitarians. The present building is twice the width of the original, so that instead of having windows on both sides, it is now lit from the south side only. Other differences should also be noted. At first there was no terrace on the south side: this was added in 1535 to accommodate six kitchens and larders. A passage beneath the gallery, which local

---

[34] *La galerie d'Ulysse à Fontainebleau*, ed. S. Beguin, J. Guillaume and A. Roy (1985), pp. 9–42.

[35] L. Golson, 'Serlio, Primaticcio and the Architectural Grotto', *G.B.A.*, 6th ser., lxxvii (1971), 95–108; K. Woodbridge, *Princely Gardens: The Origins and Development of the French Formal Style* (London, 1986), pp. 56–61.

people used to reach a pond and the *Porte Dorée*, was blocked, and Francis was thus able to turn the ground floor into an *appartement des bains*, comprising a bathroom and sweating rooms (*étuves*). According to an Italian visitor of the early seventeenth century, the bath was square and about five feet deep. It was reached by a flight of wooden steps, and two spouts provided hot and cold water. The bath was surrounded by a wooden balustrade, painted to look like bronze, around which people could walk two abreast. The vault and lunettes were decorated with paintings and stucco.[36]

Rosso and Primaticcio

It was at Fontainebleau, in the *Galerie François Ier*, the earliest example of a long gallery north of the Alps, that the Florentine artist Giovanni Battista Rosso evolved a distinctive style of interior decoration.[37] He arrived at Fontainebleau in 1531, where he was given a suite of rooms. He was followed in March 1532 by Francesco Primaticcio, a pupil of Giulio Romano, who came recommended by the duke of Mantua.[38] He was, it seems, particularly skilled in the art of stucco. Indeed, Vasari gives him credit for introducing it to Fontainebleau, yet the style of the *Galerie François Ier*, which contains the earliest stucco work in the château, is unmistakably Rosso's.[39] Between them Rosso and Primaticcio decorated many parts of Fontainebleau. Sometimes they collaborated, but more often they worked separately, each with his own team of assistants. Unfortunately, much of their work has been destroyed. It is known thanks to preliminary drawings which have survived, and a large number of contemporary etchings and engravings copied from or inspired by their designs.[40]

All that remains of Rosso's work at Fontainebleau is contained in the *Galerie François Ier*, which remains impressive in spite of drastic alterations and clumsy restoration over the centuries.[41] The walls are divided into two roughly equal parts, the lower containing carved wood panelling by Scibec de Carpi, and the upper a combination of stucco and painting. Each space between the windows has a painted panel in the middle, flanked by varied decorations in stucco, including nudes, herms, putti, garlands of fruit and

---

[36] F. Herbet, *Le château de Fontainebleau* (1937), pp. 153–6.
[37] J. Adhémar, 'Aretino: Artistic Adviser to Francis I', *J.W.C.I.*, xvii (1954), 311–18. Caroline Elam has indicated that Francis's awareness of Rosso's talent may have antedated the receipt of *Mars and Venus*. It seems that he had already received Rosso's *Moses and the daughters of Jethro*. See below p. 443. For Rosso generally, see E. A. Carroll, *Rosso Fiorentino, Drawings, Prints and Decorative Arts*, exh. catal. Washington, 1981, and articles in *Burlington Mag.*, cxxxi (1989).
[38] L. Dimier, *Le Primatice* (1900).
[39] G. Vasari, *Lives*, iv. 193; A. Blunt, *Art and Architecture in France, 1500–1700* (Harmondsworth, Middlesex, 1957), p. 31.
[40] H. Zerner, *The School of Fontainebleau* (London, 1969).
[41] The best account of the gallery is in the *Revue de l'Art*, special no. 16–17 (1972).

69. The *Galerie François Ier* at the château of Fontainebleau. Though much altered over the centuries, it remains the most impressive vestige of Francis I's rebuilding after 1528.

strap-work (i.e. stucco made to look like rolls of leather cut into fantastic shapes). All of this represents a rejection of High Renaissance classicism in favour of Mannerism.

The meaning of the decoration of the *Galerie François Ier* has exercised generations of art historians. The Panofskys have argued that it forms 'a coherent and, on its own complex premises, consistent system' aiming at the glorification of the monarch through mythological references to various moments of his life.[42] This view, however, has been seriously undermined by a fairly recent restoration of the gallery. Much more is now known about the chronology of Rosso's decorations. The frescoes were executed by four men of varying skill between 1534 and 1538 *after* the stucco had been completed. Thus some of the ingenious references to moments in the king's life, which the Panofskys read into the frescoes on the assumption of a piecemeal execution over a longer period, are no longer acceptable. Much haste was apparently applied to finishing the gallery for the Emperor's visit in 1539.[43]

[42] D. and E. Panofsky, 'The iconography of the Galerie François Ier at Fontainebleau', *G.B.A.*, 6th ser. lii (1958), 113–90.
[43] *Revue de l'Art*, special no. 16–17, p. 40.

70. Detail of the *Royal Elephant*, one of a series of frescoes designed by Rosso Fiorentino for the *Galerie François Ier* at Fontainebleau. The elephant (note the fleur-de-lis, the royal 'F' and the salamander on its trappings) symbolizes power and eternity. It dominates the elements embodied by the gods: fire by Zeus, water by Neptune and earth by Pluto.

71. *Venus and Cupid*. Another of Rosso's frescoes for the *Galerie François Ier* at
Fontainebleau. Venus, standing in a pool, appears to be addressing Cupid, who lies
prostrate on a ledge. Other putti fly around carrying various martial attributes: a
shield, a lance and a helmet. Bottom right: part of a twisted column and a half-open
book. In the centre, a draped woman clasping her hands. On the left: a fountain with
Tritons and two doorways. The meaning of this picture has yet to be convincingly
explained.

Yet, if the attempts of art historians to unravel the iconographical mysteries
of Rosso's frescoes have at times strained credibility, it cannot be doubted that
some of them at least were seeking to glorify the reign. The *Royal Elephant*
with its shabrack adorned with the fleur-de-lis and the crowned 'F' evidently
symbolizes the king. *The Unity of the State* in which a bearded ruler, wearing a
laurel wreath, receives a pomegranate (symbol of unity) may also be seen as a
commentary on Francis's achievement. Finally, the bearded figure holding a
book and a sword, who is shown striding through the door of a temple
towards a bright light within, is suggestive of Francis's dual role as victorious
soldier and enlightened patron. Throughout the frescoes there are features that
recall the triumphal art of ancient Rome. Seen from this perspective, the gallery
was more than a covered passageway; it was 'an official setting for the
deployment of an imperial programme'.[44]

[44] F. Joukovsky, 'L'Empire et les barbares dans la Galerie François Ier', *B.H.R.*, 1 (1988), 7–28. See
also E.A. Carroll, *Rosso Fiorentino*, pp. 222–91.

72. *Diana and Callisto*. This pen and ink drawing by Francesco Primaticcio was a design for one of the mural decorations in the baths at Fontainebleau. Diana discovers Callisto's pregnancy for which Jupiter is responsible.

Francis's pride in Fontainebleau is well attested by Sir John Wallop, the English ambassador to France in 1540. The king told the ambassador that he had heard that Henry VIII used much gilding in his houses, whereas he himself used little or none. He preferred 'timber finely wrought with divers colours of wood natural, as ebony, brazil and certain others', which he reckoned were richer than gilding and also more durable. Soon afterwards, Wallop was able to see all this for himself at Fontainebleau. He found the royal bedchamber 'very singular, as well with antique borders, as costly ceiling and a chimney right well made'. After helping the ambassador to stand on a bench so that he might touch the 'said matter and stuff', Francis led him to his gallery, the key of which he kept on his person. The king then took Wallop to see his baths. 'These', the ambassador reported, 'being warm and reeked so much, like it had been a mist, that the king went before to guide me.'[45] Yet it was here, in the hot and humid atmosphere of the *appartement des bains* that Francis chose to display his unique collection of paintings. The modern mind boggles, but a cultivated Renaissance man would have seen nothing incongruous in the dedication of a building simultaneously to the care of the body and pleasures of the mind.

[45] *St. P.*, viii (pt. v), 482–4. I have modernized the spelling.

The art of Primaticcio is even less well represented at Fontainebleau than Rosso's. All that survives of his work before 1540 is the upper part of a fireplace in the *Chambre de la Reine*, but his drawings for decorations in the *Chambre du Roi* and elsewhere show that until then he was still much under the influence of his master, Giulio Romano, who at that time was employed by Federico II Gonzaga, duke of Mantua. Francis had invited Giulio to come to France, but the artist was unable or unwilling to do so. In his place, he recommended Primaticcio, one of his team of assistants who had helped to decorate the Palazzo Te in Mantua. By comparison with Rosso, Primaticcio was virtually unknown. It seems unlikely that Francis would have given him a free hand to decorate the royal apartments at Fontainebleau until he had proven himself. Thus Primaticcio's early work at Fontainebleau must have been directly inspired by Giulio Romano. Among those who helped him decorate the king's chamber was Niccolò Bellin of Modena, who subsequently worked for Henry VIII at Nonsuch.

Primaticcio's originality may have been first manifested in the stuccos, a technique which he had already practised with skill in Mantua. This may explain Vasari's comment about him introducing the art of stucco at Fontainebleau ahead of Rosso.[46] It was later in the reign that Primaticcio asserted his own distinctive style on the decoration. In 1540 he was sent to Rome on an art-collecting spree for the king and came into contact with ancient sculpture and the art of Parmigianino. Following his return to Fontainebleau, he developed a style of figure-drawing exemplified by the caryatids of the *Chambre de la Duchesse d'Etampes* with their long, tapering limbs, thin necks and small heads with exaggeratedly classical profiles.[47]

Primaticcio's main work after 1540 was done in the *Salle de Bal* and *Galerie d'Ulysse*, but most of it dates from after Francis's reign. The gallery was destroyed in 1739 and none of its splendid murals was preserved. However, scholars have been able to reconstruct Primaticcio's iconographical programme from various sorts of documentary evidence.[48] His choice of the story of Ulysses for the paintings of the vault and side walls is not surprising, for Homer was much in fashion at Francis's court about 1540. But whereas the *Iliad* had been exploited for some time as a source of illustrations, the *Odyssey* had not. By choosing it as his inspiration, Primaticcio broke new ground. He

---

[46] Sylvie Béguin, 'Remarques sur la Chambre du Roi', in *Actes du Colloque international sur l'art de Fontainebleau*, ed. A. Chastel (1975), p. 200. Giulio Romano worked at Mantua for Federico II Gonzaga between 1524 and 1546. See C. Hope, 'Federico II Gonzaga as a Patron of Painting' in *Splendours of the Gonzaga*, ed. D. Chambers and J. Martineau (exh. catal. Victoria and Albert Museum, London, 1981–82), pp. 73–5.

[47] Blunt, p. 58. See also *L'Ecole de Fontainebleau* (exh. catal. Grand Palais, Paris, 1972–73), pp. 130–72.

[48] Sylvie Béguin, J. Guillaume and A. Roy, *La Galerie d'Ulysse à Fontainebleau* (1985). Work began on the gallery about 1537 and ended after 1560. Most of the decoration dates from after 1546.

73. *Alexander taming Bucephalus* by Francesco Primaticcio. A fresco flanked by stucco caryatids in the *Chambre de la Duchesse d'Etampes* (now the *Escalier du roi*) at the château of Fontainebleau. The elongated female nudes are characteristic of the style of the first School of Fontainebleau.

also gave himself more scope for illustrating the twenty-nine panels on either side of the gallery. Yet he travelled so much that he probably did only the sketches for the gallery, leaving the actual painting to Niccolò dell'Abbate and some assistants.[49] Primaticcio was also responsible for the decoration of the king's baths, which were, alas, destroyed by Louis XIV.

Cost of the royal châteaux

The building of royal châteaux in the Paris region was supervised by an office of works set up in 1527. It comprised three commissioners (Nicolas de Neufville, seigneur de Villeroy, *trésorier de France*, Pierre de Balzac, seigneur d'Entragues and Jean de La Barre, comte d'Etampes and *prévôt de Paris*), a controller and a treasurer. In addition to fixing the terms of contracts, the commissioners ordered and authorized expenses. When La Barre died in 1536, he

[49] *Ibid.*, pp. 45–64, 98–101.

was replaced by Philibert Babou, *Trésorier de l'Epargne*, who also controlled Chambord. Francis evidently trusted Villeroy's taste, for in 1535 he asked him to judge in his absence various designs for a grand staircase at the Hôtel de Ville. The controller's task was to see that work at Madrid and Fontainebleau was carried out in accordance with the king's instructions. The treasurer paid the workmen in accordance with the orders of the commissioners and kept the accounts.[50]

In a famous letter of 1535 Marino Giustiniani wrote: '[the king spends] on his private buildings 25,000 *écus* [56,250 *livres*]; as much on public buildings; scarcely less is required. When the king orders the construction of a private or public building, officers are appointed to supervise it who are paid a pension and are chosen among the families of office-holding noblemen. These offices still exist and that is why so many buildings are started and never completed.'[51] Giustiniani estimated Francis's total revenues at 5,625,000 *livres* (2,500,000 *écus*). Thus the 'private buildings' – presumably the châteaux – accounted for 1 per cent of the royal budget. The official building accounts (*Comptes des bâtiments*) yield a slightly higher estimate. In 1532–37 the king spent 43,233 *livres* annually on his Parisian residences alone. The cost rose from 53,600 *livres* in 1528 to 85,800 *livres* in 1546, that is about 1 per cent of the royal revenue which rose from 5 million *livres* in 1523 to rather more than 9 million in 1546. Taking into account Chambord, where the average annual cost of 22,000 *livres* rose to 60,000 *livres* in 1531, the percentage was 1.5 per cent of the annual revenue.

There were three categories of royal works: large (costing more than 20,000 *livres per annum*), middling (between 10,000 *livres* and 15,000 *livres per annum*) and small (not more than 5,500 *livres per annum*). Chambord and Fontainebleau belonged to the first category; Saint-Germain-en-Laye, Villers-Cotterêts and Madrid to the second and La Muette to the third. Annual expenditure at Madrid between 1528 and 1540 was 11,300 *livres*, yet it was expensive for its size. At 8,000 *livres per annum* the masonry was 70 per cent as expensive as at Fontainebleau.[52]

Internal arrangements of the royal châteaux

Until recently historians of French architecture have not paid much attention to the way living space was used within the royal châteaux. Much useful

[50] Chatenet, *Le château de Madrid*, pp. 14–15.
[51] *Relations des ambassadeurs vénitiens sur les affaires de France au XVIe siècle* ed. N. M. Tommaseo (1838), i. 101.
[52] Chatenet, *Le château de Madrid*, pp. 16–17; and her 'Le coût des travaux dans les résidences royales d'Ile-de-France entre 1528 et 1550' in *Les Chantiers de la Renaissance*, eds. A. Chastel and J. Guillaume (1991), pp. 115–29.

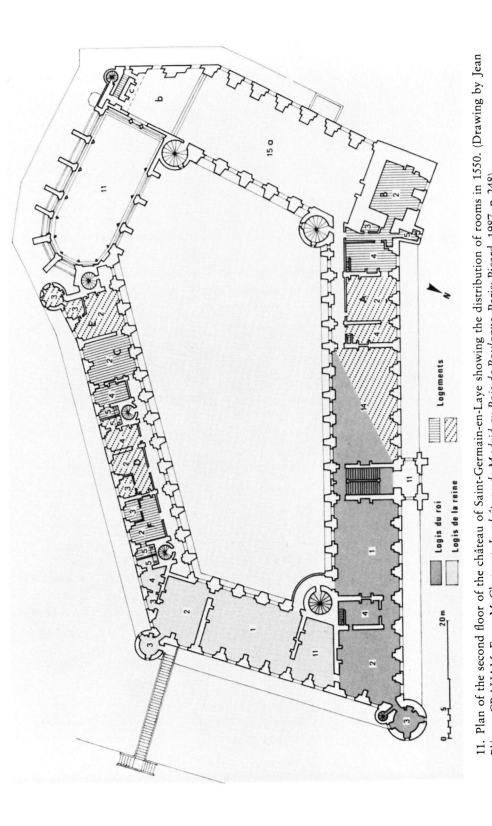

11. Plan of the second floor of the château of Saint-Germain-en-Laye showing the distribution of rooms in 1550. (Drawing by Jean Blécon, CRAHAM. From M. Chatenet, *Le château de Madrid au Bois de Boulogne*. Paris: Picard, 1987, p. 248).

information, however, is contained in building accounts for Saint-Germain-en-Laye covering the period from 1 January 1547 to 30 September 1550.[53] They list the names of the occupants of the various rooms at the start of Henri II's reign. The château comprised fifty-five apartments (*logis*): sixteen on the ground and first floors, eight on the second, eleven on the third and four on a mezzanine. There were another twenty-five in the outbuildings. In addition to these eighty apartments, the château had a ballroom, seven chapels, a kitchen, eight service rooms and a prison. The ground floor of the outbuildings contained about thirty kitchens and various offices.[54]

The royal apartments were on the second floor. That of the king was reached from the inner courtyard by a staircase leading to a reception room or *salle* followed by a chamber, *garderobe* and *cabinet*. The queen's apartment, which was reached by a separate spiral staircase, was similar to the king's, though it had a chapel and a second *cabinet*. The location of the royal apartments was deliberate: traditionally, no one, save a member of the royal family, was allowed to live above the king. The staircase played an important part in court ceremonial. When an important guest visited the king, it was customary for a guard of honour to be lined up in the courtyard, up the staircase and in the *salle*, while the king waited in his chamber to welcome him. The distance separating the king's chamber from the chapel was also intentional: it was so that his subjects might have a better chance of seeing him as he went to Mass each morning. As for the *salle*, the king had to cross it *diagonally* to reach the staircase from his chamber. This made it easier for courtiers to attract his attention as they stood in two long lines on either side of his path.[55]

The royal chambers were somewhat larger than the rest. The king's had 120 square metres and the queen's 80 square metres. The *cabinets* too were distinctive. A *cabinet*, according to Philibert de l'Orme, was intended to allow the king to 'retire into privacy and quiet, either to write or to discuss affairs in secret or otherwise'.[56] No one was supposed to enter the *cabinet* without being invited. At Saint-Germain, it was quite small with a diameter of only 4.20 metres. Elsewhere Francis disposed of more private space: in the Old Louvre he had several *cabinets* and, at Fontainebleau, his chamber opened out on to the *Galerie François Ier*. At Saint-Germain, a small spiral staircase led from his *cabinet* to an exterior gallery on the first floor, thence to a bridge leading to the park. Such secret exits, offering the king a chance of escape, existed in many royal châteaux.

Another resident of the second floor at Saint-Germain was Montmorency who, following the death of Francis, acquired the apartment that had belonged to the duchesse d'Etampes. Other occupants of the second floor were Henri II's

[53] B.N., ms. fr. 4480.   [54] Chatenet, 'Une demeure royale', p. 22.   [55] *Ibid.*, p. 29.
[56] *Ibid.*, pp. 22–8.

sister and daughter; marshal Saint-André, and two of the queen's ladies. The west wing was occupied by the ballroom. The next floor in order of import-ance was the third, which was occupied by the king's children. Henri II's mis-tress, Diane de Poitiers, lived on the first floor immediately beneath the queen. Other apartments on this floor were occupied by important courtiers and their wives. The ground floor was occupied by persons of slightly lower rank. It also comprised a dormitory for the *filles de la reine* and several service rooms. The kitchen of the *bouche* was situated behind the chapel, as were the latrines. In the west wing were three refectories, the guardroom and a prison. The 'great chapel' was reached across the courtyard and there were three other chapels.

The five blocks surrounding the *basse-cour* contained, on the ground floor, many kitchens and service rooms. There were also several refectories for the queen's ladies and for the royal stewards and chamberlains. The apartments on the first floor were smaller than those in the château, each comprising a chamber and a *garderobe*. The occupants were a mixed bag socially, including cardinals, great nobles, royal favourites, fiscal officials, the king's apothecary, the Dauphin's tutor, the captain of the château, the concierge and the gardener. There were also dormitories for the female attendants of some important ladies, the stewards and the Dauphin's doctors.[57]

Rooms at Saint-Germain were allocated according to strict rules. All the ladies, princes accompanied by their wives and most cardinals were housed in the château proper, while single noblemen were accommodated in the out-buildings along with the king's secretaries, officers of the household and the Dauphin's doctors. The grooms (*écuyers d'écurie*) slept in the stables which were situated near the park wall. Office-holders deemed 'necessary to the service' (i.e. those whose office was qualified by the title of *Grand* or *Premier*) were given precedence over persons of higher social standing.

All the apartments at Saint-Germain were independent of each other. Move-ment and access within the château were by means of staircases rather than corridors. Apartments were of two kinds according to whether or not they had a *salle*. Those with a *salle* were reserved exclusively for the royal family, the king's mistress and the Constable. The arrangement of rooms within each apartment was identical. All had fireplaces, while rush matting covered the floors, walls and sometimes the ceilings. A chamber was roughly square in shape, measuring between 45 and 120 square metres. The *garderobes*, measur-ing on average 7.50 metres by 2.50 metres, were used not only to keep clothes, but also to sleep servants and children in bunks. The *cabinets* were small, compact, yet variable in shape; they were situated either above the *garderobe* or were created within a chamber by means of wooden partitions. Several apartments at Saint-Germain had closets (*retraits*), but they were soon blocked

[57] *Ibid.*, p. 28.

off. Close stools were doubtless less malodorous. Many courtiers preferred to relieve themselves on the staircases.[58]

Arrangements similar to those at Saint Germain existed at Blois, Fontaine-bleau and the Louvre. They had the same sequence of *pavillons* and *corps d'hôtels* and the same distinction was drawn between the royal apartment and ordinary ones. At Fontainebleau the distinction was emphasized by the *Galerie François Ier* which completed the royal suite. In the Old Louvre, the royal lodging contained a *salle du conseil* and a *salle de la reine*. At the New Louvre, the royal apartment contained a large number of rooms. At both the Louvre and Saint-Germain the luxurious suite of reception rooms distinguished the king's lodging from the rest.[59]

These arrangements were in sharp contrast with those in the three 'new' châteaux of Chambord, Madrid and La Muette. Though not identical, the apartments in these châteaux, had one thing in common: none was more important than the rest by virtue of its size, location or decoration. In all three châteaux the *salles* were situated centrally: on each floor the *salle* communi-cated with four apartments and was linked to the rest by galleries. This sug-gests that informality was the rule in the king's *maisons de plaisance*. The amount of living space in each one, however, was variable. The thirty-two apartments occupied 4,700 square metres at Chambord, 2,900 at Madrid and 1,650 at La Muette. Equally variable was the amount of space given to the reception rooms: the three at Chambord filled a space of 1,950 metres, the four at Madrid measured 1,020 square metres and the two at La Muette only 307 square metres.[60]

Aristocratic building under Francis I

By the 1530s correct usage of the classical orders was becoming more widely known in France, not only among humanists capable of reading Vitru-vius in Latin or Alberti and Serlio in Italian, but also among master masons. They were now able to use the first popular works of Geoffroy Tory and also an abridgment in French of Vitruvius by Diego de Sagredo, published in Paris by Simon de Colines between 1526 and 1537. Thus nobles were not dependent simply on the king's example in the pursuit of classical correctness. By 1538 Montmorency's new château at Chantilly was one of the finest houses in France both for its architecture and setting. An almost perfect example of the Italian style was the long arcaded portico built at Châteaubriant by Jean de Laval, governor of Brittany. Its sober and repetitive articulation was ahead of much contemporary French taste which tended to identify modernity with lavish decoration. At La Rochefoucauld, François and Anne de Polignac built a

[58] *Ibid.*, pp. 28–9. [59] Chatenet, *Le château de Madrid*, pp. 91–2. [60] *Ibid.*, pp. 90–2.

courtyard with three superimposed galleries reminiscent of an Italian *cortile*. At Assier, Galiot de Genouillac adorned his château with a carved frieze displaying military emblems. It also had terracotta medallions containing heads of Roman emperors doubtless from the Della Robbia workshop. Finally, at Pagny, Admiral Chabot erected one of the finest palaces of his day, which was, alas, pulled down in 1774. It contained a straight marble staircase flanked by niches containing the busts of kings of France. Rarely had the Italian grand manner been so magnificently transplanted to French soil. All over France the early sixteenth century was marked by a frenzy of building comparable with that which England was to experience later in the century when Elizabeth's courtiers erected country houses on a lavish scale.[61]

[61] Babelon, *Châteaux de France*, pp. 193–7, 210–12, 245–9, 256–61, 262–6, 283.

Chapter twenty-two

Patron of the arts

Francis I's interest in art can be traced back to his childhood. On 12 June 1504 Niccolò Alamanni wrote from Blois to Francesco Gonzaga, marquis of Mantua, as follows:

> As I am the servant and familiar of our little prince of Angoulême, he has expressed the wish that I should obtain for him some pictures by those excellent Italian masters, as they give him so much pleasure. Since I know that M. Andrea Mantegna is among the best and also that he is liked by Your Lordship, I take the liberty of writing to beg you to cause M. Mantegna to suspend everything in order to make him something exceptional, as such a great prince deserves; the size and execution will be left to the painter's judgment. I know that no greater pleasure can be given to His Excellency. I have sent orders to Florence and elsewhere for others to be made.[1]

Such artistic precocity on the part of the ten-year-old count of Angoulême calls for an explanation. He did not appear regularly at the French court till 1508 and did not become personally acquainted with Italy till 1515. So where had he picked up his taste for Italian art? The likeliest source has to be his mother, Louise of Savoy. In 1516, another Italian, Rozone, wrote to Isabella d'Este from Crémieu: 'An idea has occurred to me: it would not be a bad thing, indeed it would be a good one, if Your Ladyship were to offer her some perfect picture of a saint, male or female, for she takes great pleasure in such things and is also knowledgeable.'[2]

When Federico Gonzaga visited the French court in 1516, art was among the topics he discussed with the king. Francis listened with delight to his account of the Mantuan collections and especially of Mantegna's *Triumphs of Caesar* (now at Hampton Court).[3] As a child, Federico had spent several years in Rome at a time when Michelangelo was painting the ceiling of the Sistine

---

[1] M.H. Smith, 'François Ier, l'Italie et le château de Blois', *Bulletin monumental*, 147 (1989), 307–8, 320.
[2] *Ibid.*, pp. 309, 322.   [3] *Ibid.*; see above p. 124.

Rancoys en guerre est vn Mars furieux
En paix Minerue & diane a la chasse.
A bien parler Mercure copieux
A bien aymer. vray Amour. plein de grace
O france heureuse honore donc la face
De ton grand Roy qui surpasse Nature.
Car lhonorant tu fers en mesme place
Minerue Mars. Diane Amour. Mercure.

74. Francis I as a composite deity. Miniature by Niccolò Bellin. The king is shown combining the attributes of Mars, Minerva, Diana and Mercury.

Chapel and Raphael the *Stanza della Segnatura* and the *Galatea*. He may have communicated some of his enthusiasm for these artists to the king of France. When Federico became marquis of Mantua in 1519, he had to rely on Costa and Leonbruno, old-fashioned artists favoured by his mother, Isabella d'Este, but eventually he induced Giulio Romano, Raphael's best pupil, to work at Mantua. As we shall see, Giulio was to have a considerable influence on the art of Francis I's court at Fontainebleau.[4]

Francis was not the first French monarch to collect pictures, but the royal collection was heterogeneous and of variable quality until he took it over.[5] The art of painting in France was at a low ebb about 1500, the only French artists of any significance being Jean Bourdichon and Jean Pérréal; Italian painters seldom troubled to visit France. In 1515, however, an important change came about as a result of Francis's conquest of Milan. We do not know how or when he met Leonardo da Vinci, who had been attached to the household of Giuliano de' Medici since 1513. It is possible that he met him in Bologna when he saw the pope, Giuliano's brother, in December 1515. Be this as it may, the king invited Leonardo to France, and he accepted, probably after Giuliano's death on 17 March 1516. This, however, was not Leonardo's first contact with the French monarchy. He had already designed a mechanical lion for King Louis XII. The lion, which walked a few steps and opened its chest disclosing a bank of fleur-de-lis against a blue background, was apparently used more than once: it greeted Francis during his entry into Lyons on 12 July 1515.[6]

Leonardo was sixty-five years old, when he arrived at the French court. He was given the manor of Cloux, near Amboise, and an annuity of 500 *livres*. The king seems to have asked for nothing in return except the pleasure of his conversation which he is said to have enjoyed almost daily. Vasari tells us that Francis wanted Leonardo to do 'the cartoon of St Anne in colours', but that the artist 'as was his wont, gave him nothing but words for a long time'. As Leonardo's health gave way, he began to think of death and occupied himself with 'the truths of the Catholic faith'. When the king called on him, he would sit up in bed, talk about his illness and 'show how greatly he had offended God and man in not having worked in his art as he ought'.[7] As Kenneth Clark

---

[4] *Splendours of the Gonzaga*, eds. D. Chambers and Jane Martineau (Catalogue of exhibition at Victoria and Albert Museum, London, 1981), p. 73.

[5] J. Cox-Rearick, *La collection de François ler* (1972), p. 7; J. Adhémar, 'The Collection of Francis the First'. *G.B.A.*, 6th ser. xxx (1946), 5–16.

[6] K. Clark, *Leonardo da Vinci* (Harmondsworth, Middlesex, 1958), p. 157; C. Pedretti, *Leonardo* (London, 1973), pp. 172–3. The author states wrongly that Francis's entry into Lyons was 'after his Italian campaign'. It seems unlikely that Leonardo could have met the king before he had conquered Milan. Leonardo's lion has been a subject of long-standing controversy. A mechanical lion, possibly the same one, appeared in the celebrations at Argentan in Oct. 1517 when Francis visited his sister. See E. Solmi, 'Documenti inediti sulla dimora di Leonardo da Vinci in Francia nel 1517 e 1518' in *Archivio Storico Lombardo*, IV. Ser ii (1904), pp. 390–4.

[7] G. Vasari, *Lives*, ii. 167.

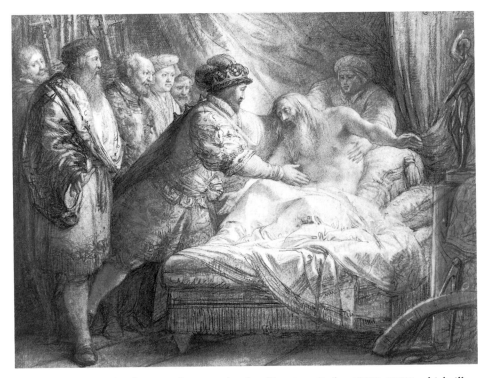

75. *The death of Leonardo.* Drawing by Giuseppe Cades (1750–1799) which illustrates the apocryphal story recounted by Vasari in his *Lives of the Artists*. Francis I was at Saint-Germain-en-Laye on 2 May 1519, when Leonardo died at Amboise.

states, Leonardo suffered from 'a disease of the will'. He was constitutionally incapable of following any task through from beginning to end without the intervention of a thousand experiments and afterthoughts. It seems that he produced almost nothing in France. Certainly, none of his paintings, not even the *St John* in the Louvre, can be dated to his time at Amboise. But some of his notes and drawings were done in France. They show that he was interested in canal-building, town-planning and architecture.[8] It has been suggested that Leonardo may have designed a palace for the king's mother at Romorantin, and also that some features of châteaux built by Francis, notably Chambord, owed their inspiration to these drawings. Nothing, however, is certain.[9]

On 10 October 1517 Leonardo was visited by Cardinal Luigi of Aragon, whose secretary, Antonio De Beatis, has left an intriguing account of him. The artist showed the cardinal three pictures: a certain Florentine lady done from life at the behest of Giuliano de' Medici, a youthful St John the Baptist and a

---

[8] Clark, *Leonardo da Vinci*, pp. 147, 153, 156; C. Pedretti, 'Leonardo da Vinci: Manuscripts and Drawings of the French Period, 1517–18', *G.B.A.*, 6th ser. lxxvi (1970), 285–318.

[9] See above, pp. 138, 140.

76. *The Virgin and Child with St Anne* by Leonardo da Vinci. This may have been the painting seen by Antonio De Beatis when he visited the artist at Amboise in 1517. A similar, possibly the same picture, was in Francis I's collection *c.* 1527.

77. *Charity*. The only picture certainly painted by Andrea del Sarto for Francis I during the artist's stay in France between June 1518 and March 1519. Of all the Italian paintings now in the Louvre it is the only one for which the king's patronage was directly responsible.

Virgin and child in the lap of St Anne. However, Leonardo could no longer produce such fine works, as he was paralysed in the right hand. But he had trained a Milanese disciple, who worked satisfactorily. Leonardo could also draw and instruct others. He had compiled an anatomical treatise and claimed to have dissected more than thirty bodies of men and women of all ages. He had also written about the nature of water and of divers machines.[10]

Leonardo died at Cloux on 2 May 1519, but not in the king's arms, as Vasari would have us believe; on the day in question Francis was at Saint-Germain-en-Laye.[11] His esteem for the artist was nevertheless high; twenty years later he told Cellini that Leonardo had been 'a great philosopher' who knew more than any other man about painting, sculpture and architecture.[12] By 1545 the royal collection at Fontainebleau included several major works by him. It has been generally assumed that *Mona Lisa* and other important paintings passed into Francis's collection immediately after the artist's death. Yet some of the works which found their way into the royal collection were apparently taken to Italy first by Leonardo's pupil, Salaì, for they are listed in the probate inventory drawn up after his death in January 1524. This suggests that the paintings were acquired subsequently by Francis's agents.[13]

Another Italian artist of the first rank who visited France early in Francis's reign was Andrea del Sarto. The king invited him to France after he had been sent his painting of *Christ being supported by angels* by a merchant, called Giovanni Battista Puccini, who served Francis as an artistic agent in Italy as early as 1516. Andrea was warmly received at court, and within a day of his arrival received rich vestments and money from the king. Without delay he did a portrait of the Dauphin, then only a few months old, and painted a *Charity* for the king which was much admired, and is now in the Louvre. According to Vasari, Francis gave Andrea a large pension and did everything to retain his services. He assured him that he would lack nothing, as he was pleased with his quickness and satisfied with his work. At the same time, Andrea worked for members of the court. But one day, as he was working on a *St Jerome* for Louise of Savoy, he received letters from his wife in Florence, urging him to return home. He asked Francis for permission to go, promising to return with his wife and also to bring valuable paintings and sculptures. The king trusted him and gave him money while Andrea swore on the Gospels that he would

[10] *The Travel Journal of Antonio De Beatis: Germany, Switzerland, the Low Countries, France and Italy, 1517–1518*, ed. J. R. Hale (London, 1979), pp. 132–3. Leonardo was left-handed.
[11] Pedretti, pp. 171–2. The legend apparently originated in Michelangelo's circle. It first appears in Francisco de Hollanda's *De Pintura antigua* (Lisbon, 1548). The evidence for Francis being at Saint-Germain in May 1519 is in C.A.F., viii. p. 428. For the painting by Ingres showing Leonardo dying in the king's arms see C. Scailliérez, *François Ier et ses artistes* (1992), pp. 76–7.
[12] Clark, *Leonardo da Vinci*, p. 156.
[13] Janice Shell and Grazioso Sironi, 'Salaì and Leonardo's legacy', *Burlington Mag.*, (1991), pp. 95–108; Scailliérez, pp. 76–7, 92–101.

return in a few months. However, once back in Florence, he allegedly squandered the king's money on his own account. His wife also persuaded him not to return to France. This breach of trust greatly angered Francis, who 'for a long time looked askance at Florentine painters, and he swore that if Andrea ever fell into his hands he would have more pain than pleasure, in spite of all his ability'.[14]

But it was after 1531, at Fontainebleau, that Italian artists were most consistently employed by Francis. Here, in the *Galerie François Ier*, Giovanni Battista Rosso evolved a distinctive style of interior decoration. He was a Florentine artist who had come under the influence of Michelangelo and Raphael while working in Rome. About 1529 he moved to Venice and did a drawing of *Mars and Venus* for Pietro Aretino. This drawing has been read as an allegory of the peace of Cambrai (for 'Mars' read 'Francis' and for 'Venus', 'Eleanor of Portugal'). It was presented to Francis and may have paved the way for Rosso's invitation to France. He arrived at Fontainebleau in 1531. Being not only a good painter but also a cultivated man, he made a good impression on the king, who appointed him as his First Painter. He was given a large salary and a house in Paris, but he lived most of the time at Fontainebleau where he had a suite of rooms. Antonio Mini wrote to Michelangelo late in 1531 or early in 1532 that Rosso was living like a nobleman with horses, servants and silk garments. In May 1532 he was given letters of naturalization and, in August, became a canon of the Sainte-Chapelle.[15] By this time he had been joined at Fontainebleau by Primaticcio, who had worked with Giulio Romano on the decoration of the Palazzo Te in Mantua. The two Italians, aided by their assistants, were the leaders of a group of artists, who are generally known as the first School of Fontainebleau.[16]

Rosso's art at Fontainebleau was widely diffused under different forms. A number of engravings were executed somewhat clumsily at Fontainebleau between 1542 and 1548 by artists, such as Antonio Fantuzzi, who had been directly associated with the gallery. Another studio based in Paris and dominated by Pierre Milan and René Boyvin produced engravings of higher quality between 1545 and 1580, the best-known being the *Nymph of Fontainebleau*.[17] Rosso's French period remains obscure, but new discoveries are continually being made. Sylvie Béguin has drawn attention to a newly restored painting of *Bacchus and Venus*, now in Luxemburg. This may be one of a pair of paintings

[14] Vasari, *Lives*, ii. 312–3; J. Shearman, *Andrea del Sarto* (Oxford, 1965), i. 3–4, 77, 314; S. J. Freedberg, *Andrea del Sarto* (Cambridge, MA, 1963), i. 47; Scailliérez, pp. 23, 116.

[15] J. Adhémar, 'Aretino: Artistic Adviser to Francis I', *J.W.C.I.*, xvii (1954), 311–18; C. Elam, 'Art and Diplomacy in Renaissance Florence', *RSA Journal*, 136 (1988), 813–25; E. A. Carroll, *Rosso Fiorentino, Drawings, Prints, and Decorative Arts*, (exh. catal. Washington, 1981) and articles by various scholars in *Burlington Magazine*, cxxxi (1989).

[16] L. Dimier, *Le Primatice* (1900).

[17] H. Zerner, *The School of Fontainebleau* (London, 1969); *Revue de l'Art*, special no. 16–17, p. 112.

78. *Mars disrobed by Cupid and Venus disrobed by the Graces*. Pen and ink drawing by Rosso Fiorentino. It was drawn in Venice by the artist for Pietro Aretino in April 1530 shortly before Rosso's arrival in France. The drawing may be an allegory of the Peace of the Ladies (1529) which produced not only peace between France and the Empire but also the marriage of Francis and Eleanor, the Emperor's sister.

79. *Bacchus, Venus and Cupid* by or after Rosso. This painting, now in Luxemburg, may have been originally in the *Galerie François Ier* at Fontainebleau.

(the other being a lost *Cupid and Psyche*) which Rosso is said to have executed in France before Primaticcio's arrival in March 1532. They were at opposite ends of the *Galerie François Ier*. The *Cupid and Psyche* disappeared when the west wall was transformed in 1639, but the *Bacchus and Venus* survived on the east wall till Louis XIV removed it out of prudery. The Luxemburg picture is a fascinating record of Rosso's inventiveness and of the new type of courtly painting he brought to Fontainebleau. It shares the refinement and erotic appeal of the *Mars and Venus*. In Béguin's own words: 'the composition is a skilful display of taste and culture, making reference to antique sculpture – then still very scarce at Fontainebleau'. Its rediscovery obliges us to reconsider the commonly held assumption that it was Primaticcio who formulated the eroticism of the School of Fontainebleau. Clearly, Rosso had sown the first seeds of the style before Primaticcio's arrival.[18]

From the beginning of his stay in France, Rosso undertook various tasks in addition to his work at Fontainebleau. He designed costumes for spectacles, tableware, horse trappings and a tomb. He may also have served as an architect. For the Emperor's visit in 1539 he designed costumes, festival decorations and the large silver statue of Hercules given to Charles V by the city of Paris. Sometimes he worked for other patrons than the king. Thus in 1534 he designed a tapestry for the cardinal of Lorraine and 1538 painted the *Pietà* (now in the Louvre) for the Constable of Montmorency. Rosso also did work for Notre-Dame after becoming a canon of the cathedral. By the end of his life, he was allegedly living like a prince with many horses and servants. On 14 November 1540, however, after he had falsely accused a friend of stealing a large sum of money, he committed suicide at Fontainebleau. 'When the news of [Rosso's death] was taken to the king', writes Vasari, 'it caused him indescribable regret, since it was his opinion that in losing Rosso he had been deprived of the most excellent artist of his time.'[19]

Francis's artistic interests were not exclusively Italian. For portraiture he turned mainly to Jean Clouet, an artist who hailed almost certainly from the Netherlands. Portraiture became very popular during the reign, and many chalk drawings have survived of the king, members of his family and entourage. Some are of high quality and are usually attributed to Clouet; others are contemporary copies of variable quality. These were put to different uses: they might be sent to friends and relatives of the sitter, as are photographs today, or gathered into albums containing fifty or sixty drawings each. Although Clouet was almost certainly French-trained, his use of parallel diagonal hatching strokes to obtain a three-dimensional effect was of Italian origin. For this

[18] Sylvie Béguin, 'New evidence for Rosso in France', *Burlington Magazine*, cxxxi (1989), 828–38.
[19] Cited by E. A. Carroll in 'Rosso in France' in *Actes du Colloque international sur l'art de Fontainebleau*, ed. A. Chastel (1975), p. 17.

reason he has been described as 'one of the first artists in France to comprehend the principles of the Italian High Renaissance'.[20] He died in 1540 and was succeeded as 'Painter to the King' by his son, François, who continued the series of court portraits.

Diplomatic gifts

Some of the most important works in Francis's art collection were gifts from various popes and Italian princes. In 1518 Pope Leo X sent four paintings to France through his nephew Lorenzo de' Medici and the cardinal-legate Bibbiena. They were a *St Michael* and a *Holy Family* by Raphael and a *St Margaret* and a portrait of *Joanna of Aragon* by Raphael and his pupil, Giulio Romano. All of them are now in the Louvre. They were given to Francis at Nantes by Bibbiena, following Lorenzo's departure from court. The *St Michael* was specifically painted for the king, who was grand master of the Order of St Michael. The gift coincided with an allegorical staging at Angers of the king being protected by the Archangel Michael.[21] The *Holy Family* was intended for Queen Claude, possibly as a celebration of the Dauphin's providential birth. At Bologna, the king had promised to take part in a crusade provided he was given a son, who would guarantee the succession to the throne. The *St Margaret* was probably intended for the king's sister. As for *Joanna of Aragon*, she was renowned for her beauty, and the gift of her portrait to Francis may have been suggested by her cousin, cardinal Luigi of Aragon, who was Bibbiena's friend.[22]

Other diplomatic additions to Francis's art collection, dating back to 1518 or soon after, were a *Venus* by Lorenzo Costa, given by Francesco Gonzaga, and a *Visitation* by Sebastiano del Piombo, given by the Venetian republic. We may perhaps ascribe to the same period the gift of a perfume-burner, designed allegedly by Raphael. However, it is not certain that this object, with its lid decorated with fleurs-de-lis and salamanders, was ever made. It is known only thanks to an engraving by Marcantonio Raimondi, but the Graces supporting the burner clearly influenced contemporary taste, as reflected, for example, in some of Primaticcio's stucco nudes at Fontainebleau.[23] Among some of the more curious items in Francis's collection was a seven-headed beast with the skin of a crocodile, which Antonio Rincon brought back from Constantinople

---

[20] P. Mellen, *Jean Clouet* (London, 1971), p. 29. See also R. de Broglie, 'Les Clouet de Chantilly: catalogue illustré', *G.B.A.*, 6th ser., lxxvii (1971), 257–336. Francis also looked to the Netherlands for tapestries. See S. Schneebalg-Perelman, 'Richesses du garde-meuble parisien de François Ier: inventaire inédits de 1542 et 1551', *G.B.A.*, 6th ser., lxxviii (1971), 253–304. See below p. 448.

[21] Scailliérez, pp. 21, 106; A.-M. Lecoq, *François Ier imaginaire* (1987), pp. 441–6.

[22] Scailliérez, pp. 21, 108–9, 111.

[23] *Ibid.*, pp. 21, 112–13; Lecoq, pp. 44–8.

80. *St Michael slaying the demon*, by Raphael. This painting, also known as *The Great St Michael*, was given to Francis I by Pope Leo X in 1518 in celebration of the new Franco-papal alliance. The king of France was deemed to be transformed by his coronation into the archangel's earthly equivalent.

81. *Joanna of Aragon*, by Raphael and Giulio Romano. This painting was given to Francis I by the papal legate, Cardinal Bibbiena, in 1518. The sitter, who became the wife of Ascanio Colonna, Viceroy of Naples, was renowned for her beauty.

in 1530 as a gift from the Ottoman Sultan.[24] Finally, in 1533, the marriage of the Dauphin Henri and Catherine de' Medici, produced more gifts. Pope Clement VII presented Francis with a unicorn's horn mounted in gold by the Milanese goldsmith, Tobia. Cellini had designed a mount for the same object, but the pope was apparently persuaded to choose Tobia's work because the French were said to be vulgar people incapable of appreciating Cellini's excellence. On the same occasion, Clement gave to Francis a casket with carved panels of crystal depicting scenes from the life of Christ by Valerio Belli. This eventually passed into the hands of Catherine who gave it to her grand-daughter on her marriage; it is now in the Palazzo Pitti in Florence.[25]

The king's artistic agents

By 1525 Francis's art collection comprised a significant number of paint-ings by Florentine and Roman artists of the High Renaissance.[26] Thereafter its scope was enlarged. Agents were employed by the king to find him paintings, statues, books and other rare and valuable items. Some were French diplomats, like Guillaume du Bellay, who was paid 2,050 *livres* in 1526 for sending certain 'articules' to the king from Rome; others were Italians, like Battista della Palla and Pietro Aretino.[27]

Della Palla's activities were closely connected with Florentine politics.[28] The republican régime, which had been set up following the overthrow of the Medici in 1527, faced the growing threat of attack by the Medici pope, Clement VII, possibly in alliance with the Emperor. Della Palla was one of many Floren-tines who looked to the king of France for help. He had lived in France as an exile between 1522 and 1527, and had established close contacts with the French court, more especially with Francis's sister, Marguerite. He had given her a portrait of Savonarola in addition to the friar's complete writings. In 1528 Battista returned to France as an envoy of the new Florentine republic, when he was commissioned by Francis to collect antiquities and works of art

[24] Scailliérez, p. 21. According to Père Dan (1642) it was embalmed in Venice and valued at 6,000 ducats.

[25] Scailliérez, pp. 21–2; J. Pope-Hennessy, *Cellini*, p. 51.

[26] Viz. Leonardo da Vinci's *Virgin of the Rocks*, *A Lady of the Court of Milan*, *Mona Lisa*, the *Bacchus-St John*, the *Virgin and St Anne* and *St John the Baptist*, Andrea del Sarto's *Charity* and Raphael's *Belle Jardinière* and *St Michael*.

[27] V.-L. Bourrilly, *Guillaume du Bellay* (1905), p. 36 n. 5.

[28] M.G. de La Coste-Messelière, 'Battista della Palla conspirateur, marchand ou homme de cour?', *L'Œil*, cxxix (1965), 19–24, 34. For a fuller account of della Palla's career and collecting activities see Caroline Elam, 'Art and Diplomacy in Renaissance Florence', *RSA Journal*, 136 (1988), 813–25. She cites evidence from the Carte Strozziane v. 1209 in the Archivio di Stato, Florence. See also Polizzotto, L. and C. Elam, 'La unione de' gigli con gigli', *Rinascimento*, 2nd Ser., xxxi (1991), 239–59; and 'Art in the Service of Liberty: Battista della Palla, art agent for Francis I' in *I Tatti Studies – Essays in the Renaissance*, V, 1993 (forthcoming). This article is the fullest treatment of the subject and contains twenty documents relating to della Palla's work for the French court. I am grateful to Miss Elam for allowing me to see these in advance of their publication.

82. This engraving by Marcantonio Raimondi may reflect a lost design by Raphael for a perfume-burner. The fleurs-de-lis and salamanders adorning the lid probably indicate that the perfume-burner was intended for Francis I, but we cannot be sure that it was ever made.

on his behalf. His task was to provide 'large numbers of antiquities of every sort, that is marbles and bronzes and paintings by masters worthy of his Majesty, in which things he had delighted greatly all his life, and is now more immersed than ever'.[29] After failing to persuade the Florentine government to make collecting for Francis public policy, Battista fell back on his own resources; he began investigating likely areas for purchase and to commission works from leading artists.

Della Palla's activities as an artistic agent are given a hostile treatment in Vasari's *Lives of the Artists*. As an employee of the Medici, Vasari disapproved of della Palla's spoliation of Florence's artistic heritage. He describes Battista's abortive attempt to strip the Borgherini nuptial chamber of famous panels painted by Pontormo, Andrea del Sarto and other artists. However, Battista was able to secure other works. He informed his friend and patron, Filippo Strozzi, in January 1529 that 'there are few painters and sculptors left here who are not working on a little something for me'.

Della Palla commissioned copies from Ridolfo Ghirlandaio of Pollaiuolo's *Labours of Hercules* (now lost). He also asked Andrea del Sarto to paint *Abraham and Isaac* (now in Dresden) and the *Charity* (now in Washington), but neither work reached France. Pontormo painted a lost *Raising of Lazarus* for della Palla. The only work commissioned by Battista for the king of France that survives at Fontainebleau is a statue of *Nature* by Niccolò Tribolo. Derived from ancient images of the multi-breasted Diana of Ephesus, it was intended to support an antique granite vase. In the Renaissance the image was taken to represent the abundance of nature; it gives suck not only to animals and human beings, but also to grotesque, unnatural monsters. Della Palla sent Francis at least two other statues by contemporary artists: one was Bandinelli's *Mercury Holding a Flute* and the other Michelangelo's *Hercules*. This early work by the artist was given to della Palla by its owner, Filippo Strozzi. 'Many people', wrote Filippo's brother, 'are displeased that we are parting with it, easpecially Michelangelo.'[30] At Fontainebleau, the statue formed part of a fountain. It stood originally in the *Cour de la Fontaine*, but was moved to the *Jardin de l'Etang*. When this garden was destroyed about 1714, the *Hercules* vanished. An idea of what it looked like is conveyed by an etching of 1649 by Israel Sylvestre. The statue has been identified with a drawing by Rubens and a wax model in the Casa Buonarroti, but this identification has been challenged. There is even some doubt as to whether the *Hercules* was presented to Francis or to his son, Henri II. When Francis wrote to Michelangelo in February 1546 he implied that he possessed none of the master's sculptures.[31] Francis twice

[29] Elam, p. 821.   [30] *Ibid.*, p. 822.
[31] De Tolnay, C. 'L'Hercule de Michel-Ange à Fontainebleau', *G.B.A.*, 6th ser. lxiv (1962), 125–40; P. Joannides, 'Michelangelo's Lost Hercules', *Burlington Magazine*, cxix (1977), 550–5 and 'A supplement to Michelangelo's lost Hercules', *Burlington Magazine*, cxxiii (1981), 20–3.

83. *Hercules*. This drawing by Peter Paul Rubens has been identified with the statue by Michelangelo which stood in the grounds of the château of Fontainebleau until its disappearance in the early eighteenth century.

invited Michelangelo to France, but the artist never made the journey. He promised, if he should live long enough, to execute for the king 'a work in marble, one in bronze, one in painting'; ironically, it was Francis who died first.[32] According to Vasari, Francis was the intended recipient of two famous statues by Michelangelo: the *Rebellious slave* and the *Dying slave*. He may have been offered them by Roberto Strozzi in 1546, but they did not reach France till 1550, three years after the king's death.[33]

Another notable work della Palla managed to obtain for the king was the *Moses and the daughters of Jethro* by Rosso Fiorentino, now in the Uffizi. This was originally painted by Rosso for Filippo Strozzi's licentious friend, Giovanni Bandini. Unlike Botticelli's treatment of the same Old Testament story in the Sistine Chapel, Rosso's painting is a ferocious battle of nude men. The motives of the shepherds pursuing Jethro's daughters seem far from pastoral, while the latter's bejewelled coiffures are reminiscent of courtesans.

We do not know what precise instructions, if any, della Palla received from the king. Did Francis ask for specific works which were known to him or for works by particular artists or with a predetermined iconography? If not, then della Palla 'seems to have had a remarkably good idea of Francis's preferences, both stylistic and iconographical'.[34] The contorted figures and the bizarre eroticism of some of the works he selected or commissioned would seem to have suited the king's character and stylistic preferences. Francis, we know, had early developed a taste for the erotic: in 1518 he wrote to Mantua asking for 'nude figures or a Venus' by Lorenzo Costa. In 1519 he received such a picture from Francesco Gonzaga. Federico de' Preti, who presented it to the king on 2 January, described his response, as follows: 'he liked it very much and could not take his eyes off it. He asked me to give a thousand thanks to Your Lordship [Francesco Gonzaga]. He took it at once to the queen and his mother and showed it to them, who praised it highly. His Majesty the king has asked me if it was the portrait *au naturel* of one of Madame's great ladies, but I said that I did not know. The king shows her to all these lords and gentlemen.'[35]

Like other collectors of his day, Francis was keen to collect antique sculpture. 'Our need', della Palla wrote to Strozzi, 'is not less for quantity – a great number of mediocre pieces, as long as they are antique – as for quality, for the most excellent.' Here he seems to have been only moderately successful: he acquired a number of minor pieces, but failed to capture any really important ancient sculpture. In a memorandum to Strozzi he expressed concern regarding

---

[32] Cox-Rearick, p. 44.   [33] Scailliérez, p. 25.   [34] Elam, p. 822.

[35] Francesco II Gonzaga sent the picture to Francis on 30 November 1518. See C. M. Brown, 'Lorenzo Costa in Mantua – Five Autograph Letters', *L'Arte*, xi–xii (1970), 120ff; M.H. Smith, 'François Ier, l'Italie et le château de Blois', *Bulletin monumental*, 147 (1989), pp. 309, 322. The painting has been identified with Costa's *Venus*, now in Budapest. See Scailliérez, p. 21.

84. *Francis I*, by Titian. This portrait was sent by Pietro Aretino to the king from Venice in 1538. It is likely that Titian painted the idealized profile from a medal, possibly Cellini's.

the condition of works he had sent to France. Forty crates of paintings, sculpture and antiquities – but mostly paintings – had been shipped to Marseilles, and Battista was worried lest they should be unpacked by uncaring hands, exposed to the elements or damaged in other ways. His concern was probably justified, for very few of the works he sent to France have survived.

Della Palla's activities as Francis's artistic agent were doubtless remunerated, but he was also motivated by zeal for the Florentine republic. He described them as 'most useful and necessary to the conservation of the city's liberty'.[36] His expectations, however, proved illusory. In August 1529 Francis abandoned his Italian claims in the peace of Cambrai and soon afterwards Florence was besieged by the imperial army. Della Palla was imprisoned by the Medici and died in 1530, possibly murdered. Yet Francis continued to add Florentine works to his collection, including Michelangelo's *Leda and the Swan* (now lost) and, possibly, Bronzino's *Venus and Cupid* (now in the National Gallery, London).[37]

Though most of the artists represented in the royal collection at Fontainebleau were Florentine, Venetians were not completely overlooked. In 1538 Pietro Aretino sent two pictures to Francis, 'one magnifying the honour of man, the other magnifying the glory of God'. The first was Titian's portrait of the king, now in the Louvre, which was painted from a medal, not from life; the other was obviously a religious work, possibly also by Titian. It may have been the *Penitent Magdalene*, now in Bordeaux. It was presumably on the evidence of these works that Titian was invited to France by the king, but the artist declined, allegedly because he 'never wanted to abandon Venice'.

Aretino's artistic services to the king began in 1529 when he attached himself to the circle of scholars and artists formed by Lazare de Baïf, the French ambassador in Venice. In the following year he was promised a gold chain by the king, but received it only three years later. It consisted of overlapping enamelled gold tongues, weighed eight pounds and was worth 500 crowns. Aretino wore it with pride, as may be seen in the engraved portrait serving as frontispiece to his works. But he failed to receive an annuity promised by Francis and warned him that 'the furnace of Murano', burning in his honour, would grow cold unless he kept his word. About 1539 Aretino sent two portraits, one of Plato, the other of Aristotle, to the cardinal of Lorraine, who gave them to the king. After looking at them for a long time and praising their colour, Francis said that he already had a bust of Aristotle and recognized him

---

[36] Elam, pp. 822–3.

[37] Vasari writes of Bronzino: 'he made a picture of singular beauty which was sent into France to King Francis. In it was a nude Venus and Cupid who kissed her . . .' For contrasting interpretations of this picture see E. Panofsky, *Studies in Iconology* (New York, 1962), pp. 86–91, and M. Levey, 'Sacred and Profane Significance in Two Paintings by Bronzino' in *Studies in Renaissance and Baroque Art presented to Anthony Blunt on his 60th Birthday* (London, 1967), pp. 30–3.

85. Pietro Aretino (1492–1557), the poet who acted as Francis I's artistic agent in Venice. In this portrait by Titian, Aretino wears the gold collar given to him by the king.

perfectly, but did not remember ever having seen a portrait of Plato. He ordered both pictures to be taken to the room at Fontainebleau where he kept his favourite possessions. Rossi, to whom we owe these details, adds that Francis commended Titian highly; his portrait of the cardinal, he said, was so perfect that it needed only movement and speech to be the real man.[38] In 1539–40 Aretino had his own portrait painted by the Florentine Francesco Salviati and sent it to Francis to whom he recommended the artist in 1542. He also backed the painter Girolamo da Treviso, who passed into the service of Henry VIII instead of staying in France. Competing for artists was an important aspect of the cultural rivalry that existed among European courts in the Renaissance. Finally, Aretino supported the efforts of Georges d'Armagnac, the French ambassador in Venice, to secure an invitation to France for the architect Sebastiano Serlio.[39]

Sculpture entered the royal collection later than painting. In 1520 Cardinal Bibbiena reported that it contained no statues, ancient or modern. This prompted Cardinal Medici to order for the king a copy by Bandinelli of the recently discovered *Laocoön*; but this was never sent. Pope Clement VII apparently liked it so much that he kept it at the Palazzo Medici in Florence (it is now in the Uffizi museum). Other ancient statues, so far unidentified, were sent to the king instead. During a visit to France in 1528 della Palla may have introduced to Francis the Florentine sculptor Giovanni Francesco Rustici. After he had shown the king some of his works, including perhaps a bronze relief of the *Virgin and child* (now in the Louvre), he was commissioned by Francis to make a 'bronze horse twice natural size', presumably an equestrian statue of the king, but it was never completed.[40] In 1540 Francis sent Primaticcio to Rome to buy and copy antiquities, and the artist returned in the following year with a number of plaster casts of ancient statues, mostly from the papal collection at the Belvedere. These included the *Ariadne, Laocoön, Apollo Belvedere, Cnidian Venus, Hercules Commodus, Tiber*, two sphinxes and two satyrs. They were turned into bronzes by Vignola, the future architect, who set up a foundry at Fontainebleau in 1541. The bronzes, however, were not exact replicas. For example, the attitude of the Fontainebleau *Ariadne* is different from that of her Roman counterpart. Such discrepancies were due in part to repairs necessitated by damage to the plaster casts while in transit from Rome or by faults in casting, partly to a conscious attempt to improve on the originals.[41] The bronzes, displayed initially in the *Galerie François Ier* were much admired

[38] Adhémar, 'Aretino', pp. 311–18. See also H. Tietze, 'Titian's Portrait of King Francis I', *Connoisseur*, cxxvi (October 1950), 83–5. It seems that the medal used by Titian was that made by Cellini in 1537 during his first visit to France. Scailliérez, pp. 27, 50.
[39] Scailliérez, p. 27.   [40] *Ibid.*, p. 25.
[41] S. Pressouyre, 'Les fontes de Primatice', *Bulletin monumental*, cxxvii, 3 (1969), 223–39. Five of the bronzes (the *Tiber*, sphinxes and satyrs) were melted down during the French Revolution; the rest were sent to the Louvre. They have since been returned to Fontainebleau.

by the king and his entourage. The sight of Venus inspired Francis to flatter the duchesse d'Etampes: her body, he said, was no less perfect than that of the goddess. Not all the bronzes in Francis's collection were acquired by Primaticcio in Rome. The *Boy Drawing Out a Thorn*, for instance, was given to the king in 1540 by the cardinal of Ferrara. Nor were bronzes made from all the casts brought back by Primaticcio: Michelangelo's *Pietà*, reliefs from Trajan's column, and a horse (presumably that of Marcus Aurelius on the Capitol) were reproduced in plaster only.

Among less important contributors to the royal collection was Renzo da Ceri, the king's lieutenant-general in Naples, who sent him a newly discovered ancient statue of Venus, which was installed at Amboise in 1530 and won the praises of Clément Marot and other poets. It may be the *Venus Genitrix*, ascribed to Callimachus, now in the Louvre. Another donor was the humanist Paolo Giovio, who sent a painting in *grisaille* by Aristotile da Sangallo after Michelangelo's lost *Battle of Cascina*. This is now at Holkham Hall.[42]

Francis I's art collection contained many works other than paintings and statues. Thanks to two inventories, we know that he owned 213 tapestries. A few of these may have been from Parisian workshops, but the bulk came from Brussels and Antwerp. In 1532 the Italian agent, Marchio Baldi, presented Francis with three tapestries depicting the *Story of Scipio Africanus*. The design was by Giulio Romano, and Primaticcio was sent to Brussels to supervise the weaving in 1532, soon after his arrival in France. The tapestry in twenty-two pieces was woven by several workshops simultaneously over a period of three years and cost a huge sum of money. It was among the king's tapestries in 1542 but was destroyed for its gold thread in 1797. Several preparatory drawings and two cartoons for the tapestry survive at the Louvre and in St Petersburg. Also in 1532 Pierre de Pannemaker, the famous Brussels weaver, executed for Francis a set of six hangings enriched with silk, silver and gold threads. The designs were supplied by Matteo del Nassaro, best known as an engraver of medals and gems, who also supervised their execution. In 1534 another Brussels merchant supplied the king with three sets: namely, a *Story of Romulus and Remus*, a set of *Espaliers* and a *Creation of the World* in five hangings. The *Stories of Actaeon and Orpheus* 'in gold and silk with verdure and little figures' followed in 1538. Once again the purchaser was Matteo del Nassaro.[43]

Perhaps with an eye to economy, Francis decided about 1540 to set up a tapestry workshop at Fontainebleau. It was apparently not intended to be permanent and its only known product is a set of six hangings, reproducing panels

---

[42] Scailliérez, pp. 27–8.

[43] *Ibid.*, p. 30. In 1539 Francis sent Jacques Ticquet, one of the tapestry-workers at Fontainebleau, to Flanders to choose 'certain tapestries of that country'; R. A. Weigert, *French Tapestry* (1962), pp. 90–1.

on the south side of the *Galerie François Ier* at Fontainebleau. They are now in Vienna and were already there in 1690. It has been suggested, without any archival evidence, that they were given by Charles IX, along with Cellini's salt-cellar, on the occasion of the king's wedding to Elizabeth of Austria. Francis, it seems, wanted to have a movable version of his famous gallery, and a minor artist, Claude Badouin was paid 20 *livres* per month to copy Rosso's work. His cartoons were then woven by a team of French tapestry-workers, including Jean Lebries, who was paid 12 *livres* 10 *sous* per month. Until the restoration of the *Galerie François Ier* in the 1960s, the tapestries were the most faithful reflection of Rosso's original conception.[44]

In 1546 on the occasion of the baptism of Catherine de' Medici's daughter, the *Cour Ovale* at Fontainebleau served for an exhibition of royal treasures assembled from all corners of the kingdom. An awning of blue silk was stretched across the courtyard and supported in the middle by a tall mast. At its foot was a pyramid with nine shelves on which the king's plate was displayed along with many vases and antique pieces. Specially appointed guides told visitors where all the precious objects had come from: some, they explained, had been brought to France by Charlemagne, others were the gifts of foreign potentates.[45] Fontainebleau became something of a great European cultural centre to which people flocked from different corners of Europe. Vasari described it as 'a kind of new Rome'.[46]

Benvenuto Cellini

Some of the most valuable objects in Francis's collection were made by Benvenuto Cellini, the Florentine goldsmith and sculptor. He has achieved immortality not only on account of his artistic achievement, but also of his autobiography which incidentally offers a unique picture of Francis I's patronage of the visual arts. Additional information is also contained in his treatises on goldsmith's work and on sculpture.[47]

Cellini visited France twice, in 1537 and 1540. The first visit was a disappointment to him: war between France and the Empire had just started again, and Francis had other preoccupations than art. Thus Cellini failed to secure any royal commission. But he did gain the patronage of Ippolito d'Este, the future cardinal of Ferrara, who paved the way for his return in 1540.[48]

[44] *Ibid.*; S. Pressouyre, 'Le témoignage des tapisseries' in *Revue de l'Art*, vol. 16–17 (1972), pp. 106–11; *Ecole de Fontainebleau*, Catalogue of exhibition at Grand Palais, Paris, 1972–73, p. 339.
[45] F. Herbet, *Le château de Fontainebleau*, (1937), pp. 240–1.
[46] 'Quasi una nuova Roma'. G. Vasari, *Le vite de piu eccellenti pittori, scultori ed architettori*, ed. G. Milanesi (Florence, 1878–85), vii. 408.
[47] J. Pope-Hennessy, *Cellini* (London, 1985).
[48] *The Life of Benvenuto Cellini Written by Himself*, tr. J. A. Symonds, ed. J. Pope-Hennessy (London, 1949), pp. 187–8.

86. Medal of Francis I in the guise of a Roman emperor by Benvenuto Cellini. It was apparently made during the artist's first visit to France in 1537.

Cellini's second visit lasted five years. He began to follow the court on its travels, but soon became restless, as he needed a fixed residence in which to carry on his work. The cardinal of Ferrara advised him to appear as often as possible at the king's table. 'This I did then', writes Cellini, 'and one morning at his dinner the King called me. He began to talk to me in Italian, saying that he had it in his mind to execute several great works, and that he would soon give orders where I was to labour, and provide me with all necessaries.'[49] However, Cellini was not satisfied by the salary of 300 *écus* offered him by the king. He left the court, but was ordered to return under threat of imprisonment. Cellini was then told that the king had decided to employ him on the

[49] *Ibid.*, p. 264.

87. *Juno* by Benvenuto Cellini. This drawing in black chalk is virtually all that remains of the commission given by Francis I to the artist for twelve life-size statues of gods and goddesses to serve as candlesticks around his dining table. Only the *Jupiter* was completed and it is now lost.

same terms as Leonardo da Vinci had enjoyed. He was also promised 500 *écus* for his travel expenses. For his accommodation, Cellini was given the Petit Nesle, a medieval building on the left bank of the Seine opposite the Louvre.

During his time in France Cellini occupied the post of Goldsmith to the King (*Orfèvre du Roi*). The exact sequence of his commissions for work in gold and silver is not precisely known. With the help of a cosmopolitan team of assistants, Cellini undertook several works for the king. The first was a statue of Jupiter in silver. Francis asked for twelve such statues to serve as candlesticks for his table; they were 'to represent six gods and six goddesses, and to have exactly the same height as his Majesty, which was a trifle under four cubits'. Cellini made small wax models of Jupiter, Juno, Apollo and Vulcan for the king's inspection. As he was working on his *Jupiter*, he received an unexpected visit from the king, accompanied by the cardinal of Lorraine, Madame d'Etampes, the king and queen of Navarre, and the Dauphin and Dauphine. Observing that Cellini was working on one of the silver plates, Francis said that he would prefer him to undertake less manual work himself and to employ as many apprentices as necessary for the rough work, but Cellini explained that if he left off work he would fall ill and the standard of his work would be impaired. The cardinal backed him up and advised Francis to let Cellini work in his own way.[50] Although Cellini spent five years working on the king's candlesticks, he completed only the *Jupiter*. All that survives of the project is a chalk drawing of Juno and a small model of the goddess in bronze.

The day after he had visited Cellini in his workshop, Francis called him and again expressed admiration for a ewer and vase the artist had made for Ippolito d'Este, which the cardinal had given to the king in March 1541. He explained that he now wanted a saltcellar to accompany them. Cellini had, in fact, a model for a saltcellar which he had brought from Rome. This he now submitted to the king. Francis asked Cellini how much gold he would need. 'A thousand *scudi*', replied the artist, and the money was handed over forthwith. When Francis saw the saltcellar for the first time in 1543, he 'uttered a loud cry of astonishment and could not satiate his eyes with gazing at it'. The saltcellar, now in the Kunsthistorisches Museum in Vienna, is the only major piece of precious metalwork by Cellini that survives. It has been described by John Pope-Hennessy as 'an allegory of consummate naturalness . . . a paragon of virtuosity . . . an evocative and memorable work of art'.[51]

Apart from the saltcellar the only major work to survive from Cellini's French period is a bronze relief, the *Nymph of Fontainebleau*, now in the Louvre. It is only part of a decorative scheme designed by Cellini for the *Porte Dorée* at Fontainebleau. In a model submitted to the king he corrected the proportions of Le Breton's doorway, and, instead of columns, he fashioned

[50] Pope-Hennessy, p. 106.   [51] *Ibid.*, pp. 106–15.

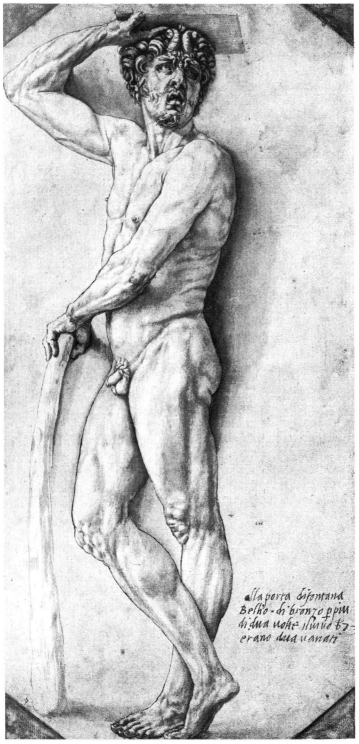

88. *Satyr*, drawing by Benvenuto Cellini. One of a pair designed by the artist as decorations for the *Porte Dorée* at Fontainebleau.

89. Francis I's saltcellar, by Benvenuto Cellini. The upper surface is divided between the Earth and the Ocean and this is reflected in the emblems on the base: Earth sits on the left and Neptune on the right. The triumphal arch is the pepper container balancing a nef for the salt on the opposite side.

two satyrs. Each supported the cornice with one hand whilst holding a club or lash in the other. The lunette above contained the reclining nymph, her left arm resting on a stag's neck. The imagery of the lunette echoes that of a fresco by Rosso in the *Galerie François Ier* (now known through an engraving by Pierre Milan). The subject is the legend from which Fontainebleau derives its name: a spring and its presiding goddess were discovered in the forest of Brie by a hunting dog named Bleu or Bliaud, and the site washed by the spring became known as 'Fontainebleau'. Out of this composition only the nymph was actually cast in bronze, nor did she ever adorn the *Porte Dorée*. She was eventually given by Henri II to his mistress, Diane de Poitiers, and placed over the entrance to her château at Anet.[52]

---

[52] Pope-Hennessy, pp. 133–41. The symbolism of the saltcellar and *Nymph of Fontainebleau* is described by Cellini himself in *The Life*, pp. 283, 305–6.

In February 1542 Cellini showed Francis, in addition to the model for the *Porte Dorée*, a model for a fountain for Fontainebleau which had not been commissioned. It was shaped 'in a perfect square, with handsome steps all round'. On a pedestal in the middle stood a nude male figure, holding up a broken lance in the right hand and resting the left on a scimitar. His right foot rested on a richly decorated helmet. At each angle of the fountain sat a figure 'accompanied by many beautiful and appropriate emblems'. Though pleased by the design, Francis was baffled by its symbolism until Cellini explained that the central figure, which he intended to stand 54 feet above the ground, was the king himself in the guise of Mars and the seated figures represented the arts and sciences which he so generously patronized.[53] Francis ordered his treasurers to disburse whatever money Cellini needed for the fountain. However, Madame d'Etampes persuaded the king to hand over the project to her favourite artist, Primaticcio. But Cellini pressed on regardless. When his great statue of Mars was seen by the king early in 1545, he admired it greatly. The account given by Cellini of the king's reaction in his *Treatise on Sculpture* is worth citing in full:

> I crossed the river [Seine] and waited upon his Majesty. He was quite gracious to me and asked me if I had anything lovely to show him. I replied that as for loveliness I was not so sure, but I had done some work with great study and with all the devotion that so noble an art demanded, and that if it was good it was due to him who allowed me to want for nothing, such freehandedness being the only way of getting the best work done. To this the King gave an affirmative reply, and the following day he came to my house. After I had shown him a variety of different work I made him enter the courtyard, placing him at the point at which my great statue told to the best advantage. He obeyed me with the greatest condescension and the most perfect breeding; and indeed never have I met any prince who had such a wonderful way with him. Now while I was conversing with his Majesty, I ordered Ascanio, my pupil, to let the curtain down. Instantly the King raised his hands and spoke in my praise the most complimentary words that human tongue ever uttered. After which, turning to Monsignor d'Aniballe [Claude d'Annebault], 'I command you' he said, most emphatically, 'to give the first good, fat Abbey that falls vacant to our Benvenuto, for I do not want my kingdom to be deprived of his like'. At this I bowed deeply and thanked the King, while he, well satisfied, went back to his castle.[54]

The story of Cellini's colossal statue is far from clear. The only fountain we know to have been commissioned for Fontainebleau was designed by Primaticcio for the *Cour de la Fontaine*. Cellini's must have been intended for another site. Alvarotti, the Ferrarese ambassador, writing on 29 January 1545, refers to 'a certain fountain which his Majesty intends to place in a court at Fontainebleau, which will, it is said, have a statue larger than any made by the Romans as far as is known'. The concentration with which Cellini approached his task annoyed the king who had not forgotten his earlier commissions. He declared:

[53] *The Life of Cellini*, pp. 284–5.   [54] Pope-Hennessy, p. 143.

> There is one most important matter, Benvenuto, which men of your sort, though full of talent, ought always to bear in mind; it is that you cannot bring your great gifts to light by your own strength alone; you show your greatness only through the opportunities we give you. Now you ought to be a little more submissive, less arrogant and headstrong. I remember that I gave you express orders to make me twelve silver statues, and this was all I wanted. You have chosen to execute a saltcellar, and vases and busts and doors, and a heap of other things, which quite confound me, when I consider how you have neglected my wishes and worked for the fulfilment of your own. If you mean to go on in this way, I shall presently let you understand what is my own method of procedure when I choose to have things done in my own way. I tell you, therefore, plainly: do your utmost to obey my commands; for if you stick to your own fancies you will run your head against a wall.

Bending one leg to the ground and kissing the king's coat, Cellini replied:

> Sacred Majesty, I admit that all you have said is true. Only, in reply, I protest that my heart has ever been, by day and night, with all my vital forces, bent on serving you and executing your commands. If it appears to your Majesty that my actions contradict these words, let your Majesty be sure that Benvenuto was not at fault, but rather possibly my evil fate or adverse fortune, which has made me unworthy to serve the most admirable prince who ever blessed this earth.

Finally, Cellini asked for permission to return to Italy. This was a mistake. Late in 1544 or early in 1545 the king cut his subsidy for casting in the foundry at the Petit Nesle and Cellini was obliged to dismiss his bronze casters. This was why neither the Satyrs nor the Colossus were cast. Economy may not have prompted the royal move so much as the wish that Cellini should apply himself to the work for which he had been originally engaged.[55]

Cellini's testimony shows that Francis delegated much of his patronage to subordinates, who were not always punctilious in carrying out his wishes. If Cellini is to be believed, he did not always get the rich rewards promised by Francis; yet his labours did not go unrewarded: in addition to cash payments, he received letters of naturalization free of charge and was given possession of the Petit Nesle. The grant of naturalization assumed that Cellini would spend the rest of his life in France, serving her king. When he left France in 1545 it was in breach of this agreement.[56]

Cellini's stay in France was anything but peaceful: attempts were made to dislodge him from the Petit Nesle, and he was attacked in the streets and in the courts. For many of his troubles, however, he had only himself to blame: his arrogance, bombast and violent temper earned him many enemies, the most important being the king's mistress, the duchesse d'Etampes. She allegedly did everything possible to poison the king's mind against him and even tried to sabotage the presentation of his *Jupiter*. Cellini was ordered to bring the statue

---

[55] *Ibid.*, pp. 142–4.   [56] *Ibid.*, pp. 269, 280–1; C.A.F., iv. 12681; vi. 22859.

to the *Galerie François Ier,* where Primaticcio's bronzes were already on display. The duchess hoped that their proximity would detract from Cellini's work; she also delayed the king's appearance till nightfall so as to darken the gallery for the presentation. But Cellini's ingenuity overcame her malice. He had mounted his statue on a movable plinth and introduced a wax torch among the flames of *Jupiter*'s thunderbolt. As the king entered the gallery, Cellini lit the torch and his apprentice pushed the statue forward. This made it seem alive, and Primaticcio's bronzes were eclipsed. But the duchess was not through yet; as Francis praised the *Jupiter,* she said that it would show to less advantage in daylight and pointed to a veil which, she claimed, was hiding its faults. This threw the artist in a rage. He pulled off the veil, which he had intended only for modesty. The duchess was outraged by his impertinence, and only Francis's timely intervention averted an ugly scene.[57]

Cellini last met Francis at Argentan. The king was allegedly indisposed, so that Cellini had to kick his heels for several days. When eventually he saw the king, he offered him two vases. Francis seemed well disposed, so Cellini again asked for permission to return to Italy. 'While I was uttering these words', he writes, 'the King kept gazing intently on the vases, and from time to time shot a terrible glance at me; nevertheless, I went on praying to the best of my ability that he would favour my petition. All of a sudden he rose angrily from his seat and said to me in Italian: "Benvenuto, you are a great fool. Take these vases back to Paris, for I want to have them gilt." Without making any other answer he then departed.' Ippolito d'Este agreed to intercede for Cellini. He instructed him to go to Paris and wait there for eight days; if no letter reached him in the meantime, he would be free to depart. No letter came, so Cellini left after appointing his assistants, Ascanio Napoletano and Paolo Romano, as guardians of the Petit Nesle and its contents. Three silver vases, which he took with him, had to be returned after he had been accused of stealing the king's silver. Once Cellini was back in Florence working on his *Perseus* for Cosimo I, Francis began to regret his loss. He told the cardinal of Ferrara that it had been a great mistake to let him go. To one of his treasurers he said: 'Send Benvenuto six thousand *scudi* and tell him to come back and finish his great colossus, and I will make it up with him.' Cellini was ready to return to France, but, while negotiations were still taking place, Francis died. 'Thus, was I deprived', writes Cellini, 'of the glory of my great work, the reward of all my labours, and of everything that I had left behind me.' Yet he remained grateful. In a poem, written in 1556, he described himself as 'in part immortal, since the French king set me on the path of sculpture'.[58]

---

[57] Pope-Hennessy, p. 104.   [58] *Ibid.,* pp. 144–6.

Music at the court of Francis I

Far less attention has been given to Francis I's patronage of music than to that of the visual arts or literature. Yet music was important in his reign: attached to the royal court were many musicians, both singers and instrumentalists, who performed regularly. No coronation or royal funeral, no princely birth or wedding, no *Te Deum* or religious procession, no royal entry or interview was complete without its accompaniment of voices or instruments or a combination of both. Music also accompanied the dances that were so popular at court. Composers wrote works to celebrate a person or event.

Francis did not compose music himself though some of his poems were set to music. He has also been depicted playing the pedal organ. His chapel had an excellent choir which he tried to build up, not always scrupulously. In 1517 two boys were kidnapped from the choir-school of Rouen for the king.[59] A list of singers who took part in Louis XII's funeral gives an idea of the composition of the famous *chapelle de musique*. It comprised twenty-three singers, most of them French. Francis's chapel played a prominent part in his meetings with the pope at Bologna in December 1515 and with Henry VIII at the Field of Cloth of Gold five years later. Florange tells us that at Bologna 'the singers of the pope and the king were together and sang beautifully'. At the Field of Cloth of Gold, the English and French chapels sang alternate sections of the Mass that was celebrated on the last day. The *Introitus* was sung by the English choir, the *Kyrie* by the French and so on till the *Agnus Dei* which was sung by the French. They followed it with several motets. Each choir was accompanied by its own organist, the French one being Pierre Mouton, a canon of Notre Dame. In the *Credo* the French enhanced the overall effect by using sackbuts and fifes.[60]

An expense account for 1532–33 distinguishes between two royal chapels, the *chapelle de musique* and a chapel of plainchant, newly created by the king. The former had Cardinal Tournon as its master and Claude de Sermisy as sub-master, while the master of the plainchant chapel was Guillaume Galiot. The personnel of the *chapelle de musique* numbered twenty-seven, including a clerk, a *sommelier*, a *noteur* and a *fourrier*; that of the plainchant chapel numbered fourteen, including a clerk and a muleteer. Total expenditure on the *chapelle de musique* was 9,580 *livres* and on the plainchant chapel, 2,140 *livres*. The lion's share of the wages bill went to Tournon, who was paid 1,200 *livres*. Sermisy received 400 *livres* for his wages, 180 *livres* for the food and upkeep of 'the children of the said chapel' and 250 *livres* 'for looking after the books of the said chapel and for recruiting singers' (*'pour envoyer quérir des chantres'*).[61]

---

59 Isabelle Cazeaux, *French Music in the Fifteenth and Sixteenth Centuries* (Oxford, 1975), p. 19.
60 P. Kast, 'Remarques sur la musique et les musiciens de la chapelle de François Ier au Camp du Drap d'Or' in *Fêtes et Cérémonies au temps de Charles-Quint*, ed. J. Jacquot (1960), 135–7.
61 B.N., ms. fr. 10389.

It was under Francis that musicians of the royal household, apart from the chapel, were classed as members of the chamber and of the *écurie*. Among the chamber musicians were lutenists, cornettists, fifers and drummers. In the 1530s the singer, Antoine le Riche (Antonius Divitis), appeared among the chamber musicians, but singers normally belonged to the chapel. The distinguished Italian lutenist, Alberto da Ripa (Albert de Rippe) worked at the French court, having been invited from Mantua by Francis. Like other artists attached to the royal household, he was a *valet de chambre*. In addition to his wages, which were roughly twice as much as lutenists had been paid before, he received several royal gifts, notably the captaincy of Montils-sous-Blois and the estate of Beauregard in Dombes.[62] His death in 1555 brought tributes from Baïf, Ronsard and others. Le Roy and Ballard dedicated a book of lute music to his memory, and his pupil, Guillaume Morlaye, collected six volumes of his works, which were published between 1553 and 1558. Francis I was evidently fond of lute music. In 1538 he was captivated by the playing of Francesco Canova da Milano, sometimes called *il divino*, whom Pope Paul III had brought to the meeting at Nice.[63] About 1535 Francis created a small vocal ensemble to sing chansons to which he added some instruments, such as flutes, hautbois and organs. Musicians of the *écurie* were not soloists, but formed a band which performed on various state occasions and in courtly entertainments. They comprised viols, hautbois and sackbuts. Socially, they were deemed inferior to the chamber musicians and were expected to travel on foot. A writer commented in 1533: 'if some of them now travel on foot, a time will come when they shall be raised on clouds and placed with the consort of angels, in whose glory they participate'.[64]

A distinguished composer employed by Francis before 1522 was Jean Mouton, a disciple of the great Josquin des Prez. After serving in churches at Nesle, Amiens and Grenoble, he was apparently introduced to the royal service by Anne of Brittany. Two letters of 1518 confirm his presence at Francis's court and show that he was held in high esteem. Glareanus who met him at the court of Francis, said that his music was 'in the hands of everyone'. He died as a canon of Saint-Quentin in 1522. Among several motets composed by him for certain occasions were *Domine salvum fac Regem* for Francis's coronation and *Exalta Regina Galliae*. Mouton's style is distinguished by a 'serene, smoothly flowing polyphony, with great technical finish and superb contrapuntal command'.[65] Apart from about one hundred motets, he wrote approximately fifteen masses and twenty chansons. The masses span the transition from

---

[62] C.A.F., ii. 5611; iii. 8594, 10393; vii. 28327, 26876, 27334.
[63] G. Reese, *Music in the Renaissance* (New York, 1959), pp. 527, 553.
[64] Cazeaux, p. 21.
[65] H. M. Brown, *Music in the Renaissance* (Englewood Cliffs, NJ, 1976), p. 176. On Mouton, see also Reese, pp. 280–5.

cantus firmus to paraphrase and parody. Like the motets, the chansons are in various styles: some are canonic, others are three-part popular arrangements and others still are wittily imitative pieces influenced by popular tunes. Three other composers, who worked at the French court early in Francis's reign, were Antoine de Longueval, Antoine le Riche and Pierre Moulu. The latter's motet, *Mater floreat florescat* was probably written for the entry of Queen Claude into Paris in 1517. It pays tribute to the most celebrated French musicians and names many of the court's composers.[66]

The first half of the sixteenth century witnessed notable developments in French music. While some composers developed techniques first explored by Josquin and his contemporaries, others developed new techniques and genres which transformed the sound of music. Old compositions were parodied and musicians looked for ways of expressing the meaning as well as the form of the words they set. An autonomous instrumental music grew up independent of literary associations or the dance. At the same time the distribution of music was transformed by developments in the art of printing. About 1537 Pierre Attaingnant acquired the title of the king's music printer. He was the sponsor, and probably the inventor, of an improved method of music printing, namely cutting the note and its own bit of stave in one punch, thereby eliminating the need to print the stave and the note in two processes, as was done by the Venetian music printers. Attaingnant published vast amounts of music mostly by composers living and working in and around Paris.[67]

The reign of Francis I corresponds closely with the first period of the sixteenth-century chanson. Then and later it drew on Italian and Netherlandish elements, spicing them with native French grace and wit. Its textual charm, of varying shades of respectability, was calculated to delight Francis and his courtiers. Despite the broad humour evinced, many chanson composers also wrote serious motets and masses. They even held positions in the church. The two earliest collections of polyphonic chansons were published by Attaingnant in 1528. Another, which appeared in the following year, included compositions by Claude de Sermisy and Clément Janequin. Sermisy, commonly called Claudin, served as *sous-maître* of Francis's chapel. In 1533 he became a canon of the Sainte-Chapelle, thus being assured of a substantial income. He accompanied Francis to Italy in 1515 and was among the musicians who performed at the Field of Cloth of Gold. About 160 of his chansons were printed in collections of the period. Some became so popular that they were arranged for lute and keyboard and were adapted to sacred texts. In contrast to typical Franco-Netherlandish music, the characteristic secular work of Claudin is predomin-

---

[66] Reese, pp. 273–8.

[67] D. Heartz, *Pierre Attaingnant, Royal Printer of Music* (Berkeley and Los Angeles, 1969), 45–60. Attaingnant's letters patent are not extant. See also R. Freedman, 'Paris and the French Court under Francis I' in *The Renaissance*, ed. I. Fenlon (London, 1989), pp. 184–9.

antly chordal in style, song-like, with syllabic treatment of the text. Without sacrificing melodic grace, there is a tendency to use rapidly repeated notes, producing a light declamatory effect. The whole is characterized by terseness, precision, simplicity, airiness and a generally dance-like quality. The simplicity made it suitable for performance by amateurs. A good example is *Tant que vivray* set to a poem by Clément Marot: although it reaches no great expressive heights, its charm and ability to delight listeners are immediately evident. Parisian composers in the second quarter of the sixteenth century no longer set their music to poems that followed the rigid conventions of the *rhétoriqueurs*; they preferred poems without any fixed rhyme scheme. Their subject matter reflects a new freedom, encompassing love fulfilled and unrequited, comic and serious. Many poems mix popular with courtly elements.[68]

The Renaissance liking for realistic tone-painting appears in a distinctive way in the programme chansons of Clément Janequin. A native of Châtellerault, he took holy orders early in his career. After serving in the choir-school at Angers, he enjoyed the patronage of the cardinal of Lorraine, Jean de Guise. He did not become a member of the royal chapel till 1555. Yet in 1530 he provided a song of welcome, *Chantons, sonnons, trompetes* for the return of Francis's sons from their captivity in Spain. His most famous chanson, *La Guerre*, may be cited to illustrate Janequin's descriptive style. It imitates vividly the confused noises of battle: drum-beats, fanfares, and rallying cries. Patter effects, common to chansons of the time, are also present. Janequin's large chanson production – 286 examples survive – was not limited to programme pieces or even to the chordal type. He has left many graceful works in a more conventional style, including *Qu'est ce d'amour*, one of several settings of poems by or ascribed to Francis I.[69]

[68] Reese, pp. 291–5; Brown, pp. 211–13.   [69] Reese, pp. 295–9; Brown, pp. 214–16.

Chapter twenty-three

'Father of letters'

The origins of humanism in France have been traced back to the fourteenth century, when the papacy created at Avignon a cultural centre under the aegis of Petrarch whose influence elsewhere in France was extensive and lasting.[1] Thus the claim advanced by Jacques Amyot in 1559 that it was Francis I who 'happily established and began the task in this noble realm of bringing good letters to a new birth and flower' cannot be endorsed.[2] As we have seen, the impact of Italian humanism was felt in Paris in the fifteenth century. All that Francis did was to provide the movement with a large-scale patronage it had previously lacked.

Poetry and prose: Marot, Saint-Gelais and Rabelais

Under Charles VIII and Louis XII court poetry was practised by a group of poets to whom posterity has applied the label of *rhétoriqueurs*. Studiously avoiding everyday speech, they aimed at harmonizing poetry and music. Much of their output was religious in inspiration and associated with the *puys*, yearly festivals in which prizes were awarded for compositions on the Immaculate Conception. But it was at court that the *rhétoriqueurs* were most prolific. However, they were rarely paid for their poetic services. They were usually secretaries or librarians, and as most of them were in holy orders, they might also hold benefices. Their love poems and pastime compositions were much appreciated, but they were also expected to write for and to help plan royal entries and ceremonies. By celebrating the king's military campaigns and victories, they were effectively his propagandists. The *rhétoriqueurs* were also historians, or rather chroniclers, a role which enabled them to propagate such

---

[1] F. Simone, *Il Rinascimento francese* (Turin, 1961), and N. Mann in *Humanism in France*, ed. A. Levi, pp. 6–28.
[2] *French Humanism, 1470–1600*, ed. W.L. Gundersheimer (London, 1969), p. 9.

90. The author of the *Panegyric of Francis I* (1531) offers his work to the king. Miniature from Chantilly Ms. 892/1485.

legends as the Trojan origin of the French monarchy. Of all historical writings of the time, the most immediately popular was the *Illustrations de Gaule* by Jean Lemaire de Belges (1473– ?1524). This traced the history of France back to ancient Troy and gave widespread currency to the theory of an *Hercule gaulois*. Lemaire's intense patriotism caused him to link Gaul with Greece, thereby transforming Roman culture into a product rather than a source of western civilization. He used the French language, decrying the Italian notion that it was barbaric, and praised Paris above Athens and Rome as 'the mother and mistress of all the world's studies'.

Under Francis I the form of poetry became much more varied than before. The *rhétoriqueurs*, though less firmly established, continued to be reprinted. Their forms were often used by Charles Fontaine and Marguerite de Navarre to express religious sentiments. Yet a growing awareness of the classical world, greater sophistication at court and various pedagogical developments combined to change the poetic climate. Classical authors, hitherto neglected, came into their own. While Virgil and Ovid remained dominant, Horace, Martial and Ausonius became popular. A latinization of genres got under way: the elegy came to stay, the epistle was renovated, the eclogue enjoyed some success and the epigram and epitaph took over from older genres. The *chanson*, with its popular origins, helped to make poetry more flexible and lively. In short, a shift took place from old forms to new, while contact with classical sources fostered a reappraisal of rhetorical techniques. The influence of the court in all of this was decisive. Poetry formed an essential component of royal propaganda, celebrating the king's martial prowess and reviling his enemies. Events at court, such as births, deaths and marriages, prompted a considerable output of encomiastic verse. The court had its accredited poets: Marot and Saint-Gelais for the vernacular, Salmon Macrin for Latin poetry. The presence of humanists, some of them foreign, led poets to widen their thematic range. Higher standards of elegance and urbanity became the order of the day. But, of course, the royal court was not the only centre of literary activity: Marguerite de Navarre had her own court and Lyons was for a time the pace-setter in poetic developments.[3]

Among the many poets, who frequented the court of Francis I, none was as gifted or significant as Clément Marot. His father, Jean, one of the last of the *rhétoriqueurs*, was one of Louis XII's *valets de garderobe* and continued to serve Francis till his death about 1526.[4] Meanwhile, Clément entered the household of Nicolas de Neufville, seigneur de Villeroy, as a page. In 1518 he offered a poem to the king (*Temple de Cupido*), who may have recommended

---

[3] I. A. McFarlane, *A Literary History of France: Renaissance France, 1470–1589* (London, 1974), pp. 31–50, 91–2.
[4] *Ibid.*, pp. 94–6.

91. The poet, Clément Marot. Portrait attributed to Corneille de Lyon.

him to his sister; for Marot soon became Marguerite's secretary. In 1521 he accompanied her husband, Alençon, on a military campaign in Flanders, describing the experience in his *Epistre du Camp d'Atigny*. Marot then disappears from the records for a few years. Scholars no longer believe that he was wounded and captured at Pavia. What is certain is that, in March 1526, he got into trouble with the authorities for breaking the Lenten fast. He was imprisoned, but soon released. In 1527, he was again detained, petitioned Francis and duly set free on 1 November. In 1526 Marot became a royal *valet de chambre*, but he had to petition the king in verse for his name to be put on the roll of the household. As court poet, he celebrated in verse the marriage of princess Renée to the duke of Ferrara (1528), the peace of Cambrai (1529), the return of the king's sons from captivity (1530) and the arrival in France of Queen Eleanor. In 1531 he fell victim to the plague, but was cured by royal physicians. He was also robbed and given 100 gold *écus* by Francis. In 1532 an attempt by the Parlement to rearrest Marot was foiled, it seems, by Marguerite. By this time, his fame was such that pirated editions of his work began to circulate. In August he authorized the publication of some of his poems under the title *Adolescence Clémentine*. It was followed in 1534 by a second volume, then by a translation of Ovid's *Metamorphoses*.[5]

In October 1534, the course of Marot's life was suddenly changed by the Affair of the Placards.[6] Though he had taken no part in it, his house was searched by the Parlement, his books and papers being confiscated. He fled to Marguerite's court in Navarre, but after his name had appeared, in January 1535, on a list of heresy suspects, he looked for safety further afield. He entered the service of Renée, duchess of Ferrara as her poet and secretary. At the same time, he wrote an epistle to Francis (*Au Roy, du temps de son exil à Ferrare*) in which he tried to justify his action. In November, he celebrated the king's recovery from illness in another poem. He hoped that Francis would recall him and pay his wages in the meantime. In June 1536 Marot was expelled from Ferrara by the duke, who had grown tired of his wife's French attendants. The poet fled to Venice with the connivance of Georges de Selve, the French ambassador. In another epistle to Francis, he insisted that being French had been his only crime. In Venice, he composed verses for the king and the Dauphin, requesting a safe-conduct for a six months' stay in France. He hinted that he might stay longer if Francis would retain his services. Eventually, the king granted him leave to return without, however, exempting him from the abjuration required by the edict of Coucy. On 14 December Tournon informed Montmorency that Marot was back in France, seemingly repentant and

[5] P. M. Smith, *Clément Marot, Poet of the Renaissance* (London, 1970), pp. 2–16; C. Marot, *Les épitres*, ed. C. A. Mayer (London, 1954), pp. 5–11.
[6] See above, p. 313.

anxious to be a good Christian in the future. After calling on friends in Lyons, the poet returned to Paris, where, in February 1537, he attended a dinner party held to celebrate Etienne Dolet's release from prison. Among others present were Budé and Rabelais.

On 8 March 1537, soon after returning to court, Marot composed *Dieu Gard à la Court de France*. Although he resumed his functions, his reinstatement on the roll of household servants required a campaign of epigrams to the king. Meanwhile, Marot continued to serve as Marguerite's secretary, accompanying her and her husband to south-west France. In 1538 he composed a *cantique* celebrating the talks at Aigues-Mortes between Francis and Charles V, and in the following year the poet was ordered by Francis to present a copy of his *Trente Psaumes de David* to the Emperor. Although unofficial editions of Marot's translations circulated abroad from this time onwards, it was only in 1541 that one was published with his consent; it was dedicated to the king. However, in 1542, Marot again fell foul of the religious authorities. His *Psaumes de David* were banned by the Faculty of Theology. Fearing arrest, he fled to Geneva where he translated another nineteen Psalms. These, added to the original thirty, were published in two separate editions: the first, by Calvin, was for use in Protestant churches, while the other was clearly intended for the French court. In spite of his religious beliefs, Marot did not find Geneva to his taste. Late in 1543 he moved to Savoy whence he sent an epigram to Francis, in which he compared Geneva to Hell. Early in 1544 he wrote an eclogue for the birth of the Dauphin's son. His last epistle celebrated the French victory at Ceresole. Marot then moved to Turin, where he died, probably in September.[7]

It was only after 1526 that Marot's poetry began to show signs of originality. Changes in the literary climate and the sharpening of religious issues doubtless influenced his development. Rejecting the genres of the *rhétoriqueur*, he showed a new sensitivity toward classical sources of inspiration. His gift for satire also appeared in his poem *L'Enfer*. We find it also in his epigrams, which became frequent from this time onwards. Though Marot was not a complete Latin scholar, he promoted classical influence on French poetry by the range of genres he exploited and by the themes he handled. Some of his earliest work involved translations from Virgil. Later he turned to Ovid and, most important, to the Psalms. However, it was in the *épitre* that he really found his form. This genre, by eliminating allegorical elements and reducing the number of metrical fireworks, helped to bring poetry closer to everyday life. Most of Marot's epistles are concerned with his personal circumstances and needs. But his success depended in the last resort on his use of language. He divested

[7] Smith, *Clément Marot*, pp. 16–36, 53–6.

himself of the monotonous tone and static rhythms of the *rhétoriqueurs* and turned to a more popular current.

Marot's poetry, it has been said, 'gives an impression of intelligence and alertness, but rarely of depth', yet some of it betrays strong feelings, particularly on religious matters. Even if it is conceded that Marot's poetry lacks a certain inward vitality, his historical importance as a transitional figure, particularly in respect of form, is undeniable. He took poetry beyond the limits within which the *rhétoriqueurs* had worked by exploring new genres, by experimenting with new metrical patterns, by widening the thematic range and by injecting life and movement into the poetic line. He anticipated the Pléiade's use of the ode and was one of the first Frenchmen to write a sonnet.[8]

A court poet did not need to be good by the highest standards of his art. Technical accomplishment combined with an inexhaustible capacity to flatter, please the ear and titillate were enough to win acceptance by Francis and his entourage. This was essentially the secret of Mellin de Saint-Gelais's success, though he had the additional advantage of being well-connected. The Saint-Gelais had long been closely associated with the house of Angoulême. The poet's grandfather, Pierre, had served Francis's father and mother. He had been chamberlain to Francis before his accession to the throne. Mellin was the illegitimate son of one of Pierre's six sons, possibly of Octovien, bishop of Angoulême, who was himself a poet. After studying at Poitiers, Bologna and Padua, he attached himself to the court of Francis I where he soon gained the reputation of being witty, amiable and gallant. He eulogized the king in verse at every opportunity, flattering his mistresses and entertaining the courtiers with erotic ditties. Incongruous as it may seem, Mellin was also a churchman. He was almoner, first to the Dauphin François, then to his younger brother, Henri. In 1531 he became abbot of La Fresnade, near Saintes, and, in 1532, abbot of Reclus.[9] In 1536 he was appointed keeper of the royal library at Blois with responsibility for controlling the export of printed books from France. In 1538, he was sent to Toulouse by the king in order to take an inventory of the library of the late Jean de Pins, bishop of Rieux. In addition to such income as Mellin drew from his office and benefices, he received occasional gifts from the king: 300 *écus* in July 1531 and 650 *livres* in December.[10]

Mellin refused to publish his poetry. Much of it has accordingly vanished or been wrongly ascribed. What survives is pretty worthless. 'One is tempted to think', Ian McFarlane has written, 'that today he would be lucky to obtain employment as a writer of mottoes for Christmas crackers.' Slight in length and

---

[8] McFarlane, *Literary History of France*, pp. 104–15.
[9] H.-J. Molinier, *Mellin de Saint-Gelays (1490?–1558): Etude sur sa vie et sur ses œuvres* (1910. Reprint 1968).
[10] C.A.F., ii. 5170, 6980; iii. 9476, 9599, 32656; v. 16728; vi. 20228; viii. 32302, 30461.

substance, many of Mellin's poems may have been written for accompaniment by the lute, which apparently he could play well. He also translated some Latin epigrams and helped to diffuse Horace. Being familiar with the Italian literary scene, he translated and adapted texts by Ariosto, Aretino and Petrarch. Finally, he helped to fashion court entertainments and experimented in new metrical forms, such as *terza rima* and the sonnet.[11]

The greatest French literary figure of the reign of Francis I was, of course, François Rabelais. The details of his career are too well known to need reciting here, but we should give attention to his contacts with the king and his entourage.[12] Unlike Marot and Saint-Gelais, Rabelais never held an office at court. There is not a single mention of him in the *Actes de François Ier*. However, when the *Tiers Livre de Pantagruel* appeared in 1546 it bore a fulsome privilege signed by Delaunay in the name of Francis, dated 19 September 1545. It describes the previous two volumes as 'no less useful than delectable' and suggests that in spite of daily badgering by the 'learned and studious people of our kingdom', Rabelais had been deterred from publishing the third by printers who had corrupted his texts. He was accordingly given a monopoly of his works for six years, Francis 'desiring that good literature should be encouraged throughout our kingdom, for the use and erudition of our subjects'.[13] The king, it seems, was personally acquainted with Rabelais's work. Evidence for this is a letter written by Rabelais to Cardinal Odet de Châtillon in 1552. The king had apparently wanted to find out if Rabelais's Chronicles were dangerously heretical. He had had them read out to him by his official reader, Pierre du Chastel, bishop of Mâcon, and had declared afterwards that he had not found them at all suspect.[14]

Even in 1523, when Rabelais was only a Franciscan friar at Fontenay-le-Comte, he attracted the notice of Guillaume Budé, the 'Prince of Hellenists'. Rabelais wrote to him on 5 March 1521 and was overjoyed to receive a long reply. Budé, who hated court life, expressed envy of the freedom enjoyed by Rabelais and his friend Pierre Amy to devote themselves to philosophy. But they were less free than Budé imagined. Following the confiscation of their books by their superior, they left Fontenay. Rabelais moved to the Benedictine house at Maillezais and secured the patronage of the local bishop, Geoffroy d'Estissac. For three years he accompanied him on various journeys in Poitou. Then, after visiting several universities, including Paris, Rabelais, who had trained in the law, was admitted to the medical faculty at Montpellier. Two years later he became a physician at the Hôtel Dieu in Lyons.

[11] McFarlane, *Literary History of France*, pp. 130–1.
[12] J. Plattard, *The Life of François Rabelais*, tr. L. P. Roche (London, 1968).
[13] M. A. Screech, *Rabelais* (London, 1979), p. 211.
[14] *Ibid.*, p. 29. The letter is the dedication to the *Quart Livre*. See F. Rabelais, *The Histories of Gargantua and Pantagruel*, p. 437.

In the summer of 1533 Francis I stopped in Lyons on his way south to meet Pope Clement VII. He brought with him many scholars and writers, including the physician, Hubert Sussanée and the poet, Salmon Macrin, both of whom were protégés of Jean du Bellay, bishop of Paris.[15] Some months later Rabelais accepted an invitation from the bishop to accompany him to Rome. From this time onwards, he became closely associated with the du Bellay brothers, Jean and Guillaume.

As M. A. Screech has demonstrated, Rabelais became wedded to the interests of his patrons and less directly to those of the king. His Chronicles are, in part, works of propaganda which, to be fully appreciated, need to be set against their historical context. Thus the satirical catalogue of the library of Saint Victor in *Pantagruel* reflects Rabelais's support for Jewish studies at a time when the Paris Faculty of Theology was seeking to prevent the *lecteurs royaux* from teaching the Hebrew Old Testament.[16] Likewise, the debate of Baisecul *versus* Humevesne shows Rabelais's awareness of the crown's difficulties in enforcing the Concordat even after its registration by the Parlement.[17] *Gargantua*, unlike *Pantagruel*, is a courtly book set against a sombre political background. Its aim is not only to win the ear of great courtiers and diplomats but also to amuse and influence the king. It is with reference to the rumpus caused by Roussel's preaching in 1533 that Rabelais has Janotus and his cronies process, debate and make their protests.[18] The Picrocholine War develops into a satire on the Emperor Charles V. There are allusions to the crippling ransom imposed by him on France and to the obligation laid on Francis to send his sons as hostages to the imperial court. 'Many parts of the Picrocholine War', writes Screech, 'show how the Holy Roman Emperor appeared to loyal monarchist Frenchmen in the 1530s, still smarting under the defeat of their king at Pavia, still resenting the loss of Milan, while they helplessly watched Charles's apparently unstoppable triumphs.'[19]

Rabelais's propaganda was also designed to buttress the religious policies of his du Bellay patrons. *Gargantua* mocks those aspects of Catholic worship which stood in the way of an ecumenical rapprochement with the Protestants. Rabelais's own religious beliefs, as reflected in his writings of the 1530s, may be summed up as 'royalist Gallican, truly Catholic within the wider tolerance of pre-Tridentine theology, yet close indeed on major issues, to the Philippists on whom the du Bellays pinned their hopes'.[20] In one respect at least Rabelais's mocking must have struck a chord with Francis. According to Brantôme, the king had a low opinion of monks: 'Cloistered monks are useless people [he would say], who were good for nothing except eating and drinking, visiting

---

[15] J. Plattard, pp. 138–43.   [16] Screech, p. 44; see also above p. 313.
[17] *Ibid.*, pp. 82–5; see above pp. 95–100.
[18] *Ibid.*, pp. 156–7.   [19] *Ibid.*, p. 169; see above p. 222.   [20] *Ibid.*, p. 179.

taverns, gambling, making cords for cross-bows and ferret nets, catching rabbits and whistling down linnets – those are their exercises, as well as the debauchery their idleness brings in its train.'[21]

The greatest influence on Rabelais's life was Guillaume du Bellay, whom he followed to Piedmont in the summer of 1540. It was during his stay in Turin (1540–42) that Rabelais finally recast *Gargantua* and *Pantagruel*, removing a number of satirical shafts. Thus he changed the word *théologien* to *sophiste* and deleted every reference to the Sorbonne. He also tried to avoid giving any offence to the royal dignity. Gargantua's novel way of wiping his bottom ceased to be 'le plus royal'. Consequently in 1542 the French public was able to read Rabelais in a new, less aggressive revision, but the Faculty of Theology condemned his two Chronicles just the same. In 1543 Guillaume Postel, the distinguished orientalist, denounced Rabelais as a disguised Moslem and 'atheist'.[22] Yet Rabelais' *Tiers Livre* appeared in 1536, bearing the king's privilege, and it was preceded by a *dixain* from Rabelais's own pen addressed to the ecstatic spirit of Marguerite de Navarre. The *Tiers Livre*, however, was condemned by the Faculty on 31 December 1546. By this time, Rabelais had gone to Metz, an imperial free city noted for its tolerant régime. On 28 March (1546?) Johannes Sturm wrote to Cardinal du Bellay: 'we are but men, even when we want to be wiser than others and more experienced. The times have driven Rabelais out of France; fie on such times.'[23] Rabelais's decision to leave France in 1546 tells us something about royal patronage at this juncture. As Screech says: 'the declining years of Francis's life were not ones in which the king was for long periods disposed towards the eirenic, tolerant policies of the du Bellays. On the whole it was a rival party which was in power, exerting fitful influence on the ailing monarch.' Yet if Rabelais felt unsafe, his *Tiers Livre* continued to circulate freely under the protection of the royal privilege. This entitles Francis to a share of the credit for a work that has been acclaimed as 'a watershed in literature'.[24]

The royal library

Among the marvels to be seen at Fontainebleau in the last years of Francis's reign, not the least remarkable was the library situated on the floor above the *Galerie François Ier*.

At the beginning of the reign the king's library was at the château of Blois, where it was seen in 1517 by Antonio De Beatis, who described it as follows:

> in the castle, or rather palace, we saw a library consisting of a sizeable room not only furnished with shelves from end to end but also lined with book-cases from

---

[21] *Ibid.*, p. 182. [22] *Ibid.*, pp. 208–9. [23] *Ibid.*, p. 213. [24] *Ibid.*, pp. 291, 294.

floor to ceiling, and literally packed with books – to say nothing of those put away in chests in an inner room. These books are all of parchment, handwritten in beautiful lettering and bound in silk of various colours, with elaborate locks and clasps of silver gilt.[25]

According to an inventory drawn up in 1518 the library contained 1,626 volumes, including forty-one in Greek, four in Hebrew and two in Arabic. Some of these books had been acquired by Francis's royal predecessors; others had come from his parents. In 1515 the Keeper of the Library at Blois was Adam Laisgre, almoner to Queen Claude. He was succeeded by Guillaume Petit, Jacques Lefèvre d'Etaples, Jean de La Barre and Mellin de Saint-Gelais, in that order.[26]

In 1522 the post of Master of the King's Library was created for Budé and it was probably under his influence that Francis began a search for manuscripts, especially Greek ones, in Italy and the Near East. This quest may have been related to the plan to set up a college for the study of classical languages in France.[27] Over 500 manuscripts were acquired in five years through the agency of envoys in Venice and Rome and by the purchase or gift of complete collections. On 1 January 1539 a Cretan scribe, Angelos Vergikios, who had been employed by Georges de Selve, the French ambassador to Venice, was engaged as Greek *scriptor* to the king's library. Later in 1539 the Dauphin's tutor, Girolamo Fondulo of Cremona, was sent to Italy on a book-buying expedition. Venice was the chief centre of trade in Greek manuscripts. Older codices could be obtained through the Republic's colonies on the Greek mainland and in the Archipelago, while modern copies were supplied by scribes from the Greek refugee colony in Venice itself. Fondulo returned with sixty manuscripts that had cost 1,200 *écus*. Among the most assiduous book-collectors for the king were his diplomats in Rome and Venice, who were instructed to buy all the Greek manuscripts they could find or to copy those that could not be bought. Georges d'Armagnac, bishop of Rodez, had fourteen Greek manuscripts copied during his four years in Rome, while Guillaume Pellicier employed twelve copyists continually during his Venetian embassy (1539–42). Other contributors to the royal collection of rare books were Antonios Eparchos, a refugee from Corfu who had settled in Venice, and Giovanni Francesco d'Asola, brother-in-law of Aldo Manuzio, the famous Venetian printer. Since Francis knew no Greek, Hugues Salet and other scholars translated the *Iliad*, some of Plutarch's

---

[25] *Travel Journal of Antonio De Beatis*, ed. J. R. Hale (London, 1979), p. 133.

[26] E. Quentin-Bauchart, pp. 6–7; A. Franklin, *Précis de l'histoire de la Bibliothèque du Roi* (2nd edn, 1875), pp. 63–70. The royal library at Blois was the subject of an exhibition at the Bibliothèque nationale, Paris, in October 1992 – January 1993. See *Des livres et des rois*, ed. U. Baurmeister and M.-P. Laffitte (1992).

[27] Franklin, pp. 65–6; Quentin-Bauchart, p. 42. See above pp. 152–4.

Lives and Heliodorus's romance of Theagenes and Charicleia into French for him.[28]

With the help of such men and under Budé's overall direction, Francis gradually built up a second library at Fontainebleau to which books from the duc de Bourbon's library were added after 1523. A third library followed the court on its travels; for Francis was not content simply to collect books; he liked to read them or have them read out to him at mealtimes. This was the role of the *lecteur du roi*, a post held in 1529 by Jacques Colin, translator of Castiglione's *Il Cortegiano* and in 1537 by Pierre du Chastel.[29] In 1536 the king's mobile library consisted of two chests, the contents of which tell us something about his taste in reading. Though no classical scholar, he was evidently interested in Roman history and the heroic deeds of antiquity. For the chests contained works by Justinus, Thucydides, Appian and Diodorus Siculus as well as the *Destruction de Troie la Grant*, the *Roman de la Rose* and other romances.[30] There is evidence, too, that Francis not only knew his library but could direct someone to a particular book on its shelves. Thus in 1531 Germain Brice (de Brie?) reported a conversation at the king's table. Francis asked Brice if he had read Vida's *Eclogues*. Brice replied that he had read some of his poems, but not the *Eclogues*, whereupon the king told Colin in which volume they were to be found and where in his library.[31]

The king's library, though rich in manuscripts, had relatively few printed books. It was ostensibly to remedy this deficiency, but also perhaps to hamper the diffusion of new religious doctrines, that the ordinance of Montpellier, generally regarded as the first law of legal deposit anywhere, was issued on 28 December 1537. All printers and booksellers were required to deliver a copy of every new book in any language by any author, ancient or modern, to the king's librarian at Blois. Books imported from abroad were to be deposited for examination and for purchase if they were found suitable. In this way, the ordinance explained, contemporary works would be assembled at Blois as a monument to the literary glory of the reign, the king's successors would acquire a taste for study and be more inclined to continue his patronage of letters, and posterity would find texts in their original purity which might otherwise become corrupt and disappear. The ordinance, however, seems to have been a dead letter, for an inventory of the library at Blois, drawn up in 1544, lists only 109 printed books. Had it been applied to Parisian book

---

[28] Quentin-Bauchart, pp. 13–17; A. Hobson, *Great Libraries* (London, 1970), p. 126. Odet de Selve tried during his English embassy (November 1546) to obtain a Plotinus from Oxford for Francis. *L.P.*, xxi (pt. 2), 346. A. Hobson, *Humanists and Bookbinders* (Cambridge, 1989), pp. 179–81.

[29] V.-L. Bourrilly, *Jacques Colin, abbé de Saint-Ambroise* (1905; repr. Geneva, 1970), pp. 36–41.

[30] Quentin-Bauchart, pp. 8–9.   [31] Bourrilly, *Jacques Colin*, pp. 40–1.

92. Francis and his courtiers listen to Antoine Macault reading from his translation of Diodorus Siculus. Anonymous miniature of *c.* 1530. Among the king's entourage are his three sons (on his right), Cardinal Duprat (on his left) and the king's pet monkey.

production alone, the royal library would have acquired some 400 new titles each year.[32]

By this time Francis thought it expedient to gather all his books in one place. On 22 May, therefore, he ordered the library at Blois to be moved to Fontainebleau, which thus acquired 1,894 volumes as well as a terrestrial globe and a crocodile's head in a leather case.[33] Unfortunately, no early description of the new library exists. It was probably equipped, as the library in Blois had been, with a combination of wall-shelves and double-sided desks at right angles to the windows. Portraits, busts and curiosities or small works of art probably completed the decoration. It was in a fit state to be shown to visitors by August 1546. Early that month an English embassy arrived at Fontainebleau to ratify the treaty of Ardres. One of the envoys was Cuthbert Tunstal, bishop of Durham, an excellent scholar in Greek and Latin. Francis addressed the ambassadors after dinner on the subject of Greek books he had had translated into French and conversed privately with Tunstal about his library.[34] In 1567 Pierre Ramus, one of the *lecteurs royaux* petitioned Catherine de' Medici for the king's library to be brought to Paris where it would be more accessible to scholars. Two years later the library – now consisting of 3,650 titles – was moved to an unidentified building in the capital.[35] It was to become the nucleus of the Bibliothèque Nationale.

About 1540 Francis ordered many of his books to be rebound, an undertaking which was continued on a more lavish scale by his successor. Gold-tooling, the most conspicuous feature of humanistic binding, had been imported into France from Italy in the early 1500s. By 1540 French binding had entered a great period of stylistic innovation. This has been ascribed to the availability of morocco leather from the Levant following the Franco-Turkish treaty supposedly signed in 1536, but this is unlikely: sixteenth-century French binders tended to use Italian goatskin. Some Greek manuscripts acquired by Francis were rebound in a style called *alla greca* which was new to France. Of the royal manuscripts listed in a catalogue of 1552, 170 bear the arms of Francis I. Some of his bindings, tooled in gold and silver, are striking, but the series as a whole is unimpressive. The goatskin employed, mostly green and red, is of indifferent quality and the decorative designs are stiff and awkward.[36]

Francis had wanted his collection of books to be made available to scholars; hence the great interest which he took in printing. Robert Estienne, who was

[32] Ordonnances, viii. no. 828, pp. 494–500; Quentin Bauchart, pp. 21–2; *Des livres et des rois*, p. 224.
[33] C.A.F., iv. 13866. The inventory drawn up on this occasion is now B.N., ms. fr. 5660; Hobson, *Great Libraries*, p. 128.
[34] A. Hobson, *Humanists and Bookbinders*, pp. 184–5; L.P., xxi. 1405.
[35] Quentin-Bauchart, pp. 36–7, 46–9; Franklin, *Bibliothèque du Roi*, pp. 77–9, 85–6.
[36] Hobson, *Humanists and Bookbinders*, pp. 172–89.

93. Two bindings in Francis I's library: a) a fairly crude one displaying the salamander and fleur-de-lis; b) another binding with gilded adornments marking a new stage in the art of bookbinding.

appointed in 1539 as the king's printer in Hebrew and Latin and in 1542 as his printer in Greek, explained Francis's intentions as follows: 'Far from grudging to anyone the records of ancient writers which he at great and truly royal cost has procured from Italy and Greece, he intends to put them at the disposal and service of all men.'[37] Thus three special founts of Greek type (the *grecs du roi*) cut by Claude Garamond and modelled on the writing of Vergikios, were financed by grants from the king. The first work to be published with the new type was Eusebius's *Ecclesiastical History* (1544), and the most influential was an edition of the New Testament (1550) based on nine manuscripts in the royal library. It is said that Francis himself chose the Roman history of Dionysius of Halicarnassus for publication in 1546–47 and suggested the small Greek type used for a pocket-size New Testament in 1546.[38]

[37] Hobson, *Great Libraries*, p. 126; E. Armstrong, *Robert Estienne, Royal Printer* (Cambridge, 1954), pp. 63, 117.
[38] Armstrong, p. 52; Hobson, *Great Libraries* p. 128.

Chapter twenty-four

The return to war (1542–44)

The Constable of Montmorency had worked for a peaceful settlement of the Milanese question and of other differences between Francis and the Emperor Charles V. The failure of his policy and his consequent fall from royal favour cleared the way for a return to an aggressive French foreign policy. Publicly, Francis continued to speak of his friendship with Charles; privately he boasted of his preparations for a new war and of the troubles he and the Turks could stir up for Charles.[1]

The change in French foreign policy was most clearly revealed in those two highly sensitive areas: Germany and the Levant. In May 1540 Francis sought an alliance with the Schmalkaldic League, but its leaders suspected his motives. 'French advances', the Chancellor of Hesse declared, 'are taking place because the king has not been able to agree with the Emperor; if they had been able to agree, these advances might not have taken place.'[2] The king was also distrusted on account of his persecution of French Protestants. Consequently, he failed to make any headway in Germany. In December 1540 the diet of Naumburg sent him a petition in support of his Protestant subjects instead of an embassy. The Emperor, on the other hand, signed a treaty with the Land-grave of Hesse in June 1541 in which the latter promised not to ally with Francis or to allow him to raise troops on his territory. In 1542 the Elector of Saxony, Francis's only potential ally in Germany, came to terms with the King of the Romans.[3]

Francis was more successful in the Levant. In February 1540 Rincon, the French ambassador, managed to restore the Sultan's confidence in his master which the Emperor's visit to France in 1539 had rudely shaken. Francis was also helped by the situation in Hungary, where the death of John Zápolyai in

[1] *C.S.P.Span* , vi (pt. 1), 120.
[2] J.-Y. Mariotte, 'François Ier et la Ligue de Smalkalde', *Revue suisse d'histoire*, xvi (1966), p. 226.
[3] *Ibid.*, pp. 227–32.

July was followed by a disputed succession between Zápolyai's infant son and the King of the Romans. The Sultan took the infant under his protection and, later in the summer, he invaded Hungary. In order to prevent the Emperor from aiding his brother, Suleiman encouraged Francis to stir up trouble for Charles in the west. On 5 March 1541 Rincon returned to the French court loaded with gifts from the Sultan.[4] Two months later he set off on the return journey to Constantinople, accompanied by Cesare Fregoso, a Genoese in French employment on a mission to Venice. On 4 July, as the two envoys were sailing down the Po near Pavia, they were murdered by imperial troops. Although the Emperor disclaimed all responsibility for the crime and ordered an enquiry, the French government accused him of breaking the truce and retaliated by arresting the archbishop of Valencia, the Emperor Maximilian's natural son, as he was passing through Lyons.[5]

Rincon's death was a mixed blessing for the Emperor: it rid him of a dangerous traitor and deprived Francis of a skilful diplomat with a rare expertise in Turkish affairs, but it could not have happened at a worse time. Charles was trying to disentangle himself in Europe in order to lead a new expedition against the Infidel in north Africa. But Francis thought that Charles's preparations were intended to oust the French from Piedmont. While preparing for war he was anxious not to incur blame for any collapse of the truce. At the king's request, the pope agreed to arbitrate in the Rincon affair, and Charles welcomed his intervention, if only to gain time for his African campaign.[6]

On 28 September Charles sailed to Majorca, where he was joined by an expeditionary force. Francis, now realizing the Emperor's true intentions, promised not to declare war on him while he was fighting the Infidel. This was not only good propaganda; it also gave the king more time to raise money and find allies. But the Emperor's campaign soon met with disaster. After his fleet had been battered in a storm, he called off the siege of Algiers. In November he returned to Spain, leaving behind his horses and guns. Francis was tempted to take advantage of Charles's discomfiture. On 8 March 1542 Baron de La Garde, Rincon's successor as French ambassador to the Porte, returned home from Constantinople with a promise of massive Turkish support on land and sea.[7] This was too good an opportunity to miss. On 12 July at Ligny-en-Barrois Francis declared war on Charles. In a proclamation, widely publicized in France, he listed the injuries he had received from Charles, including the murder of Rincon and Fregoso, 'an injury so great, so detestable and so strange

---

[4] J. Ursu, *La politique orientale de François ler* (1908), pp. 116–17, 123–30.
[5] The best account of this famous affair is in V.-L. Bourrilly, *Guillaume du Bellay*, pp. 327–41. See also C.S.P.Span., vi (pt. 1), 188.
[6] Bourrilly, pp. 339–40.   [7] *Ibid.*, p. 348; Ursu, p. 138.

to those who bear the title and quality of prince that it cannot be in any way forgiven, suffered or endured'.[8]

Having thrown down the gauntlet, Francis launched an offensive on two fronts: in the north, an army officially led by his son, Charles d'Orléans, captured Luxemburg, while, in the south, a much larger one, under the Dauphin and Marshal d'Annebault, laid siege to Perpignan. Francis himself abstained from the fighting. He went to Lyons early in August; then, leaving his council behind, he travelled to Avignon. On 22 August he reached Montpellier. Next day the Dauphin launched an assault on Perpignan, but it was beaten off and the king ordered his army to retreat. Meanwhile, in the north, Luxemburg was recaptured by the imperialists after Orléans had gone south to join his brother. Thus on both fronts the French offensive had failed.[9] As winter approached, Francis gathered up his forces in the south and sent them to reinforce the French garrisons in Piedmont, while he himself went to La Rochelle to put down a revolt.

The *gabelle* revolt (1542)

Instances of popular resistance to royal taxation during Francis's reign are remarkably few by comparison with the number later on. His subjects had the reputation abroad of being extraordinarily docile. In 1546, for example, the Venetian ambassador reported:

> the king has only to say I want such-and-such a sum, I order, I consent, and the thing is done as speedily as if it had been decided by the whole nation of its own volition. The situation has already gone so far that a few Frenchmen, who can see a little more clearly than the rest, say: our kings used to call themselves *Reges Francorum*, but at present they might as well be called *Reges servorum* [kings of the slaves]. The king receives all that he asks for and the remainder is at his mercy.'[10]

Royal taxation, however, was not always accepted without protest. In Dauphiné, as Le Roy Ladurie has shown: 'The tax squeeze of 1535–38 was so intense that it seemed to release all the repressed resentment in the kingdom.'[11]

In 1541 Francis attempted a radical reform of the *gabelle* or salt tax.[12] On 1 June he introduced a single tax of 44 *livres* per *muid* to be levied at the salt marsh.[13] Thereafter the salt was to circulate freely in the kingdom. This in

---

[8] Guiffrey, p. 392; C.A.F., iv. 12628; Granvelle, *Papiers d'état*, ii. 628.
[9] L.P., xvii. 755, 838; Du Bellay, iv. 63–6, 73, 75, 79–81.
[10] S.-C. Gigon, *La révolte de la gabelle en Guyenne, 1548–1549* (1906), p. 18.
[11] E. Le Roy Ladurie, *Carnival: A People's Uprising at Romans, 1579–1580* (London, 1980), pp. 49–51.
[12] See above, p. 58.   [13] Isambert, xii. 745–58; Gigon, pp. 22–3.

effect abolished the *greniers* in the *pays de grandes gabelles* and shifted the apparatus of state control to the area of production, depriving it of its privileged status. Henceforth, the *pays du quart de sel* would have to pay the same tax as the *pays de grandes gabelles*. The edict also severely penalized fraud and smuggling: a first offence was to be punished by a fine and confiscation of the salt concerned and the means by which it was being transported, a second by corporal punishment and a third by death. In April 1542 the amount of tax was reduced to 24 *livres* per *muid*, but extended to salt for export and fish curing, which had hitherto been tax-free.[14] The purpose of this legislation was clearly to simplify the *gabelle* and improve its yield. But it was bitterly opposed by the people of the salt marshes. According to an edict of 27 September 1542, the inhabitants of the 'isles' of Marennes, Oléron, Saint-Fort, Saint-Jean d'Angély, Saint-Just, Bourg, Libourne, Bordeaux, Saint-Macaire, Langart and elsewhere had taken up arms and, in large numbers, had resisted two waves of royal commissioners who had been sent to enforce the legislation. They had been prevented from accomplishing their mission and the king had had to summon the *ban et arrière-ban* of Poitou. But the rebels, knowing that he was engaged on several fronts at once and could not afford to put another army in the field, had rebelled again. Ten thousand or more, equipped with artillery, had barred the way to the commissioners, forcing them to retire. When Francis heard about these events, he summoned the salters to appear before him at Chizé. Without making excuses, they begged for pardon. Needing time to reflect, the king ordered the leading rebels to appear before him at La Rochelle on 31 December. Meanwhile he confiscated their salt marshes.[15]

La Rochelle, which stood in the midst of the salt marshes, had long been a centre of unrest. This, however, had been caused not by the *gabelle*, but by Francis's high-handed treatment of the local corporation. Traditionally this consisted of an elected mayor and 100 *échevins*, but in July 1535 Francis had decreed that the mayor would in future be a royal appointment; he had also reduced the number of *échevins* to twenty.[16] Thereafter, there had been nothing but trouble between the governor (who was also the mayor), Charles Chabot, seigneur de Jarnac, and the townspeople. Matters came to a head in August 1542 after Francis had been told of a conspiracy in the town. He ordered Jarnac to round up suspects and to raise infantry for the town's defence. But, as soon as the troops entered La Rochelle, a riot broke out between them and the townspeople, many being injured on both sides. The troops were withdrawn only to return soon afterwards with men-at-arms. Jarnac imposed a curfew on the town and disarmed the inhabitants. Mean-

---

[14] *Ibid.*, p. 23.   [15] Isambert, xii. 787–9.   [16] C.A.F., vi. 20929, 20931.

while, town representatives called on the king at Cognac, but instead of giving them redress, he ordered them to be detained at court.[17]

On 30 December Francis arrived at La Rochelle. At his own command, no townspeople came to meet him, no gun salutes were fired, no church bells rung. The town waited in silence for the king to appear. He was preceded by the captive rebels in chains who were taken to the castle by archers. The suspense was maintained on Sunday 31 December, as the king went to Mass and visited the harbour and town fortifications. Not until Monday did he pass judgment on the two groups of rebels. He sat on a dais four steps high, flanked on his right by the ducs de Vendôme and Orléans and other princes, and, on his left, by the cardinals of Tournon, Lorraine and Ferrara. Members of his council stood behind the throne, and Montholon, the Keeper of the Seals, sat at his feet. As for the prisoners, they stood in two groups on the floor below.

The formal proceedings began with a speech on behalf of the 'islanders' by a barrister from the parlement of Bordeaux. Offering no excuses for their actions, he expressed their remorse and begged the king to pardon them and return their marshes without which they could not live. At this juncture, the prisoners fell upon their knees, crying loudly 'Miséricorde!' Next to speak was the lieutenant of La Rochelle, who likewise asked for a royal pardon for his fellow citizens. The king then replied. He began by reminding the rebels of the seriousness of their crime at a time when he and his sons were busy defending the kingdom. They deserved, he said, to lose their lives and property, yet he could not refuse to pardon those who were truly repentant; nor did he wish to treat his subjects as harshly as Charles V had treated the people of Ghent. He therefore granted their request. As soon as he had spoken, sweet music was heard coming from the belfry of St Bartholomew's church. The bells rang out, as did those of all the other churches in La Rochelle. Bonfires were lit everywhere and the castle's guns thundered. That evening Francis was given supper by the townspepole. As proof of his trust, he allowed them to serve him, retaining only two of his own servants. Next morning he left La Rochelle amid the loud plaudits of its people. 'I believe that I have won your hearts', he told them, 'and I assure you, *foi de gentilhomme*, that you will have mine.'[18]

Three qualifications have to be applied to Francis's magnanimity. First, his pardon was not unconditional. The owners of the salt marshes of Guyenne and Saintonge were ordered to deliver 15,000 *muids* of salt to the *grenier* at Rouen.[19] This doubtless enabled the king, in September 1543, to repay some of

---

[17] Guiffrey, pp. 396–406.
[18] *Ibid*., pp. 413–25. Cf. *Le voyage du roy François Ier en sa ville de la Rochelle l'an 1542 etc.*, in L. Cimber and F. Danjou (eds.), *Archives curieuses de l'histoire de France depuis Louis XI jusqu'à Louis XVIII (1834–49)*, iii. 35.
[19] C.A.F., i. 12865.

his creditors with salt. Secondly, magnanimity was his only option. He was engaged in a foreign war, and having lost one campaign, was preparing another. If he had put down the rebellion by force, his military preparations would have been compromised; he would also have sown bitterness in an area of France vulnerable to English intervention at a time when Anglo-French relations were at a low ebb. Finally, he did not give up his plans for the *gabelle*. The 1542 ordinance was revoked in May 1543, but the idea of a unified salt tax was not abandoned. Two ordinances in 1544 extended the system of *greniers* to the whole kingdom, except Languedoc, Dauphiné, Brittany and Provence. But the new régime was not set up overnight, and this may be why Guyenne stayed fairly quiet for a time; the only disturbances in 1545 were in Périgord. In 1546, however, serious riots occurred in Saintonge. But salt smuggling on a large scale, in spite of the activities of a small force of archers, called *chevaucheurs du sel*, prevented the new system from yielding enough revenue. In March 1546, therefore, the government decided to farm out the *gabelle* for ten years. It became so oppressive that in July 1548 another revolt broke out in Angoumois and Saintonge, far more serious than that of 1542. This was savagely put down by Henri II.[20]

The growth of faction

In January 1543 William Paget, the English ambassador to France, explained to Henry VIII the difficulty of finding out Francis's designs in Scotland. 'This king', he wrote, 'never sojourns two nights in one place, disposing himself as the report of great harts is made to him, and continually removing at an hour's warning so that no man can tell where to find the Court.'[21] Similar complaints punctuate much of the diplomatic correspondence of the time.[22] Francis was continually dashing about the countryside, usually in the company of a few gentlemen and his 'privy band' of ladies. These included his mistress, the duchesse d'Etampes, and other favourites, like Madame de Canaples and Madame de Massy.[23] In May 1543 the papal nuncio, Dandino, wrote: 'The king is more than ever addicted to his lascivious pleasures, being totally in the power of Madame d'Etampes, who, in order to appear wise always contradicts others and lets the king believe that he is God on earth, that no one can harm him and that those who deny this are moved by selfish interest.'[24] Yet Francis's

---

[20] Gigon, *La révolte de la gabelle*, pp. 24–7; Y-M. Bercé, *Croquants et Nu-Pieds* (1974), pp. 19–43.
[21] *L.P.* xviii (pt. 1), 29.
[22] E.g. *Correspondance des nonces en France: Capodifero, Dandino et Guidiccione, 1541–1546*, ed. J. Lestocquoy (Rome, 1963), p. 65.
[23] Marie d'Acigné, wife of Jean de Créquy, seigneur de Canaples, and Marie de Montchenu, wife of Louis d'Harcourt, seigneur de Massy. See also Potter, *War and Government*, pp. 138–9.
[24] *Correspondance des nonces . . . Capodifero* etc., p. 220.

relentless pursuit of pleasure entailed no loss of authority. Decisions relating to peace or war were his alone. Each morning he would hear his councillors, and, in the evening, they would report on what had been done in his absence.[25] But Francis was growing old and his health was poor. Courtiers knew that his days were numbered and that his death would be followed by a palace revolution, for the court was far from united.

A powerful stimulus to faction was the rivalry between Francis's two sons, the Dauphin Henri and Charles, duc d'Orléans. This began in 1536 following the death of the Dauphin François, when Charles became the king's favourite son. The rift widened in 1541 as a result of Montmorency's fall. Henri remained loyal to him throughout his disgrace, whereas Charles became the darling of Madame d'Etampes, who had been the Constable's implacable foe. Each prince thus became the focus of a party at court: while Montmorency's friends rallied round Henri, his enemies including Admiral Chabot, Marguerite de Navarre and Madame d'Etampes gathered round Charles. After the outbreak of war in 1542 the brothers' rivalry was exacerbated by their military performance: whereas Charles enhanced his reputation as a soldier by conquering Luxemburg, Henri's was dented by having to retreat from Perpignan.[26] At the heart of much in-fighting at court was Madame d'Etampes whose political views were broadly in line with her personal sympathies: in foreign affairs, she leaned towards England rather than the Empire; in religion, she had Lutheran sympathies.[27] It has been suggested that she had no political influence, but a different impression is conveyed by contemporary observers.

In March 1541, following the fall of Montmorency, Philippe Chabot had been restored to his various offices. A year later he was cleared of *lèse-majesté* and, soon afterwards, of all other charges as well.[28] His rehabilitation led inevitably to the downfall of the Chancellor, Guillaume Poyet, who had helped to bring him to trial. On 2 August 1542 Poyet was arrested and sent to the Bastille. Various rumours circulated as to the reason for his detention, but he was evidently the victim of a court intrigue involving Madame d'Etampes.[29] With her help a certain La Renaudie had arranged for a lawsuit to be transferred from the Parlement of Paris to that of Toulouse, but Poyet had refused to seal the king's letters authorizing the transfer. When the duchess complained to the king, Poyet made rude remarks about women who meddle in affairs of state. He was arrested after his words had been reported to the king. Poyet

[25] *L.P.*, xix (pt. 1), 573.
[26] L. Romier, *Les origines politiques des Guerres de Religion* (1913), i. 1–11.
[27] E. Desgardins, *Anne de Pisseleu duchesse d'Etampes et François Ier* (1904). See also Potter, *War and Government* pp. 135–6.
[28] J. Jacquart, *François Ier* (1981), p. 386.
[29] G. Ribier, *Lettres et mémoires d'Estat des roys, princes, ambassadeurs et autres ministres sous les règnes de François Ier, Henri II et François II* (1666), i. 561.

begged Francis to let him know his offence and wrote grovelling letters to his enemies. 'Madame', he wrote to the duchesse d'Etampes, 'your kindness to me had been so constant that I only became aware of it after losing it, and my first realization was that I was unworthy of it.' His letters to Chabot and Tournon remained unanswered.[30]

In October 1542 Paget told Chabot that he was worried about the possible effects of the schism within the French court on Anglo-French relations. He identified two rival camps: on the one hand, the queen of Navarre, the duc d'Orléans, the duchesse d'Etampes and Chabot himself; and on the other, the queen, the Dauphin, the Constable and most of the cardinals. What would happen, he asked, if the papal legate were to win over the king with the help of Chabot's enemies? 'No man', replied the Admiral, 'can serve in my place without many and great enemies and yet man must serve and abide to adventure.'[31] On 10 October Chabot collapsed as he was talking to the king. He died on 1 June 1543; six days later, he was given a magnificent funeral by Francis.[32]

Poyet's fall and Chabot's death cleared the way for the ascendancy of two younger members of the king's council: Claude d'Annebault and Cardinal François de Tournon. They had been prominent in the administration since the thirties, but it was only after 1542 that they virtually ran it under the king. Annebault, who succeeded Chabot as Admiral in February 1544, was the senior of the two. This was made clear in September 1543, when Tournon was left in charge of affairs in the Admiral's absence.[33] In May 1544 an Englishman noted: 'the admiral is the king's factor to whom he commands all things', and in December a Florentine wrote: 'the admiral rules everything; without him one cannot speak to the king or obtain anything'.[34] Two years later Cavalli reported that Francis entrusted everything to Annebault and Tournon and did only as they wanted or advised. Francis, however, did insist on being consulted about all important matters of state and any war plans. Indeed, if Dandino is to be believed, the two ministers were only yes-men: 'Tournon and Annebault, who govern at present', he wrote in May 1543 '– Annebault being more dead than alive – grope their way along and dare not say a word which might upset the king.'[35]

[30] C. Porée, *Un parlementaire sous François Ier: Guillaume Poyet, 1473–1548* (Angers, 1898), pp. 104–7; *L.P.*, xvii. 567.

[31] *L.P.*, xvii. 935; *St. P.*, ix. 192.

[32] *C.A.F.*, iv. 11862, 11987; *St. P.*, ix. 200; A.N., U. 2035, fols. 20b–21b; A. Martineau, 'L'amiral Chabot, seigneur de Brion (1492?–1542) in *Positions de thèses de l'Ecole des Chartes* (1883), p. 83.

[33] Du Bellay, iv. 160.   [34] *L.P.*, xix (pt. 1), 573; Desjardins, iii. 140.

[35] *Correspondance des nonces ... Capodifero* etc., p. 220. In January 1577, during the Estates General of Blois, Catherine de' Medici recalled how Francis, after banishing the Constable of Montmorency, had wanted to open dispatches (*les paquets*) and do everything himself, but all had remained undone, whereupon he had become angry and had taken on Admiral d'Annebault and the cardinal of Lorraine. C. J. Mayer, *Des Etats Généraux et autres assemblées nationales* (The Hague and Paris, 1788–9), xiii. 106. I owe this reference to the kindness of Dr Mark Greengrass.

Although subordinate to the Admiral, Tournon's contribution was distinct-ive and significant. His particular expertise was financial, and one of his main tasks in 1542 on becoming lieutenant-general in the Lyonnais and south-east France, was to secure funds for the war. In February 1543 he was listed among people the king wished to admit to the financial committee of his council. An English agent noted in 1544 that this body met at Tournon's house, but the cardinal was concerned also with a whole range of public affairs. He was the king's chief adviser in the Admiral's absence and opened all letters addressed to Francis.[36]

The Anglo-imperial alliance (1543)

Relations between France and England had reached a low ebb by the spring of 1543. Henry VIII was annoyed by Francis's failure to keep up payments of his pension and other obligations under past treaties. Maritime disputes between the two countries also caused friction, as did Scotland, where the defeat of James V at Solway Moss and his death soon afterwards were followed by a bitter struggle for power between a pro-French and pro-English faction. For James's successor, Mary Stuart, was an infant, and the earl of Arran, who governed in her name, was weak. In July Henry persuaded the Scots to sign a treaty which provided for Mary's betrothal to his son, Prince Edward. However, the Scots soon repudiated the treaty and renewed their league with France.[37]

On 11 February Henry made a secret alliance with the Emperor, which pro-vided for a joint invasion of France within two years. He then recalled his ambassador, Paget, from the French court.[38] Francis was appalled. 'If my good brother will join with me', he told Paget, 'tell him I will stick upon no money matters; he shall rule me as he list.'[39] The last thing Francis wanted was war with England just as he was about to deal the Emperor another blow. But Henry's mind was made up: early in May he and the Emperor sent Francis an ultimatum threatening war unless impossible conditions were met within twenty days. On 22 June, as the deadline expired, the allies declared war. Soon afterwards an English army under Sir John Wallop entered the Boulonnais from Calais, destroying villages in its path.[40]

By now fighting had flared up along the borders of Artois and Hainault. The time seemed ripe for a French offensive, as many imperial troops had been withdrawn from the area to fight France's ally, William duke of Cleves, who had invaded Brabant. In April the duc de Vendôme revictualled Thérouanne

---

[36] M. François, *Le cardinal François de Tournon* (1951), pp. 189–93.
[37] *L.P.*, xvii. 185, 1144, 1159, 1220, 1236; *L.P.*, xviii (pt. 1), 804; (pt. 2), 481, 499; *C.A.F.*, iv. 13490.
[38] *L.P.*, xviii (pt. 1), 144, 182.   [39] *Ibid.*, 217.   [40] *Ibid.*, 622, 707, 754.

and captured Lillers, but Francis did not launch his main offensive till June, when Annebault captured Landrecies. But, instead of pressing forward to assist the duke of Cleves, Francis paused near Rheims.[41] In August Charles invaded the duchy of Jülich, capturing Düren. Francis decided to help his ally by recapturing Luxemburg, but his timing was at fault. Three days before Luxemburg fell to Orléans and Annebault (10 September), the duke surrendered to the Emperor.[42] By so doing he destroyed the *raison d'être* for his marriage to Francis's niece, Jeanne d'Albret, and Marguerite de Navarre promptly urged her brother to break it off. The marriage was, in fact, annulled by the pope in April 1545 and Duke William remarried the Emperor's niece.[43]

Francis was strongly advised to withdraw from Luxemburg which was inaccessible to supplies, but he refused, saying that it was part of his inheritance. He ordered Babou to mobilize supplies for the town, and on 28 September he celebrated Michaelmas there.[44] But Francis was soon obliged to march to the relief of Landrecies to which the Emperor had laid siege. As Charles withdrew, Saint-Pol and Annebault relieved the garrison, an event which caused much jubilation in France. The Emperor then tried to engage Francis in battle, but during the night of 4 November the king slipped away quietly and put his army into winter quarters at Saint-Quentin. Charles, for his part, retreated northwards, capturing Cambrai. Meanwhile, the English army under Wallop returned to Calais after taking part in the siege of Landrecies.[45]

The Franco-Turkish alliance

Unusual events had, in the meantime, been taking place in the Mediterranean area. In April, following two missions to the Porte by Baron de La Garde, the Sultan informed Francis that he was placing Barbarossa's fleet at his disposal for the coming season. The fleet, including 110 galleys, left the Dardanelles with the French ambassador on board, and after raiding the coasts of Sicily and Italy (but not the States of the Church, allegedly at Francis's request) it appeared off Marseilles in early July, to a warm welcome from François de Bourbon, comte d'Enghien, who commanded the French Mediterranean fleet. Having recently suffered a rebuff at Doria's hands during a surprise attack on Nice, he was delighted to add the Turkish fleet to his own. On 6 August the combined fleets appeared off Nice, and next day, the Turks landed troops and artillery at Villefranche. During the next two weeks Nice was bombarded from

---

[41] Du Bellay, iv. 124–32, 134–44. Twice during April Francis reported to the Parlement victories by the duke of Cleves. A.N., X^{1a} 1550, fols. 355b–356a, 397b–398a.

[42] *L.P.*, xviii (pt. 2), 143.   [43] P. Jourda, *Marguerite d'Angoulême* (1930), i. 281–2.

[44] Du Bellay, iv. 158–61.

[45] *L.P.*, xviii (pt. 2), 341, 346; Du Bellay, iv. 185–7.

94. The tomb of Philippe Chabot (1480–1543) seigneur de Brion and Admiral of France, by Pierre Bontemps. The Admiral was a life-long friend of the king and the main rival of the Constable of Montmorency. He was tried and condemned in 1541, then rehabilitated.

land and sea, and repulsed three assaults. On 22 August, however, the town surrendered, although the castle held out till 8 September, when the besieging army withdrew.[46]

The sight of Christian fighting Christian with the help of the Infidel was bad enough, but worse was in store. On 6 September Barbarossa threatened to leave unless Francis gave him the means of refitting and revictualling his fleet. Rather than lose his naval superiority, Francis placed the port of Toulon at his ally's disposal. The inhabitants, except for 'heads of households', were ordered to leave with their belongings on pain of death; as compensation they were exempted from the *taille* for ten years.[47] Toulon consequently became a Turkish colony for eight months, each of Barbarossa's captains being given a house, for himself, his servants and slaves. Turks, who could not be housed within the town (they numbered about 30,000), were allowed to pitch tents outside. Neighbouring villages provided them with food. The transformation of a Christian town into a Moslem one, complete with mosque and slave market, did not fail to amaze witnesses. They were also unanimous in praising the strict discipline of the Turks, which contrasted favourably with the manners commonly displayed by Christian armies.[48]

On the surface, Franco-Turkish relations were amicable enough. Barbarossa received the gift of silver plate and a clock from Francis, and his captains also benefited from the king's largesse. Yet Francis did not trust Barbarossa and instructed La Garde to watch him closely. He also began to find the Turkish presence on French soil embarrassing, as it earned him universal opprobrium and elicited many complaints from his Provençal subjects. He was, therefore, much relieved to recover Toulon in May 1544. Before departing, however, Barbarossa demanded the release of all Turkish and Barbary corsairs serving on French ships. He also revictualled his fleet by ransacking five French ships in Toulon harbour.[49]

Barbarossa left Toulon on 23 May accompanied by six French galleys under La Garde and Leone Strozzi, who had to witness harrowing scenes as the Turks ravaged the Neapolitan coast, carrying off the inhabitants into slavery. Eventually the French squadron broke free, but, instead of returning to Provence, it sailed eastwards, calling at Delos, Troy and other ancient sites in Greece and Asia Minor. On 10 August it reached the Bosphorus and was cordially received by the Sultan.[50]

---

[46] Du Bellay, iv. 132–4; C. de La Roncière, *Histoire de la marine française* (1899–1932), iii. 376–84.
[47] J. J. Champollion-Figeac, *Documents historiques inédits sur l'histoire de France tirés des collections manuscrites de la Bibliothèque Royale* (4 vols. 1841–48), iii. 559; C.A.F., iv. 13481.
[48] La Roncière, iii. 386–7.   [49] *Ibid.*, iii. 390; J. Ursu, *La politique orientale*, p. 150.
[50] La Roncière, iii. 390–5.

The Anglo-imperial invasion of France (1544)

On 31 December 1543 Henry VIII and Charles V signed a treaty in which they agreed to invade France in person before 20 June. Charles was to invade Champagne, and Henry, Picardy; and the two armies, each consisting of 35,000 foot and 7,000 horse, were then to converge on Paris.[51] However, before the treaty could be put into effect, Henry had to safeguard his rear from a possible Scottish attack and Charles needed to win the support, military and financial, of the German princes. Both conditions were soon met. On 15 May the earl of Hertford assured Henry that the Scots would never recover from the mischief he had done them.[52] Meanwhile, the Emperor won over the princes at the diet of Speyer. Francis had hoped to defend his policy at the diet, but his ambassadors were denied a safe-conduct. A French herald, who dared to go to Speyer without one, was sent home after being told that he deserved to be hanged.[53]

In the meantime, the French won a notable victory in Piedmont. Enghien, the lieutenant-general, had laid siege to Carignano in January. As del Vasto marched to its relief, Enghien asked Francis for permission to engage the enemy in battle. Blaise de Monluc tells us in his memoirs that he was the messenger and that it was thanks to his Gascon eloquence that, on 14 April, the battle of Ceresole (Cérisoles) was fought. Some of Francis's councillors had, it seems, grave misgivings about risking a battle in Italy at a time when northern France was under threat of invasion. But Monluc's bellicose ardour won over the king. 'Let them fight! Let them fight!' he cried, throwing his bonnet on the table. As news of the king's decision spread through the court, many young nobles left for Italy in search of glory. True or false, Monluc's account offers a unique glimpse of the council in session, with the Dauphin, standing behind the king's chair, laughing and egging on the messenger.[54] The battle of Ceresole, after starting badly for the French, turned into their victory; but Enghien failed to follow it up. It was also largely cancelled out by the defeat, at Serravalle on 4 June, of Piero Strozzi and the count of Pitigliano, who had been sent by Francis to raise troops in Italy.[55]

By now preparations for the Anglo-imperial invasion of northern France were complete. In May 1544 the Emperor had two armies ready: the first, under Ferrante Gonzaga, Viceroy of Sicily, lay north of Luxemburg; the other, under Charles himself, waited in the Palatinate. On 25 May Gonzaga recaptured Luxemburg easily. He then advanced rapidly southwards, taking Commercy and Ligny; on 1 July he issued a proclamation to the effect that the Emperor

---

[51] *L.P.*, xviii (pt. 2), 526.   [52] *L.P.*, xix (pt. 1), 314, 508, 510.   [53] *Ibid.*, 132, 137, 160, 167.
[54] B. de Monluc, *Commentaires*, ed. P. Courteault (1911–25), i. 239–50; P. Courteault, *Blaise de Monluc historien* (1908), pp. 152–5.
[55] *Ibid.*, pp. 155–71. Cf. du Bellay, iv. 196–235.

was fighting, not to dismember France, but to overthrow a tyrant allied to the Turks. On 8 July Gonzaga laid siege to Saint-Dizier, where the Emperor soon came with the rest of the imperial army.[56]

Henry VIII, meanwhile, sent a huge army to Calais under the dukes of Norfolk and Suffolk. After invading Picardy, it divided into parts: while Norfolk laid siege to Montreuil, Suffolk did likewise to Boulogne. On 14 July Henry himself crossed the Channel and took charge of operations outside Boulogne. The imperialists complained that the king, by allowing himself to get bogged down in Picardy, was breaking his agreement with Charles: they wanted him to march on Paris. Henry retorted that he needed to safeguard his supplies: he was really only interested in seizing a piece of French soil near Calais. He was not sorry to see his ally held up at Saint-Dizier, since this gave him an excuse for staying put.[57]

Saint-Dizier proved a tougher nut to crack than Charles had expected. It had been fortified by Girolamo Marini, one of the best military engineers of his day, and was bravely defended by the comte de Sancerre and Captain Lalande. On 24 July the imperialists captured Vitry, whence the French had been harassing the besiegers of Saint-Dizier, but this did not break the spirit of the defenders.[58] On 8 August, however, as their munitions began to run out, they sought honourable terms. The Emperor allowed them to leave with banners flying and two guns of their choice if they received no help within seven days. On 17 August the garrison capitulated.[59] Its heroic stand of forty-one days had broken the impetus of the imperial advance so that, on 21 August, the Emperor held a council of war to decide whether to march on Paris or retreat. Some of his captains advised retreat, as the fighting season was well advanced and the army was running short of provisions, but Charles did not wish to lose face. He, therefore, moved forward to the neighbourhood of Châlons, but was deterred from crossing the Marne by a French army stationed on the left bank

---

[56] C. Paillard, *L'invasion allemande en 1544* (1884), pp. 32–119.
[57] J. J. Scarisbrick, *Henry VIII* (London, 1968), pp. 446–8.
[58] Vitry-en-Perthois occupied an important strategic position near the junction of the rivers Saux and Marne. It was destroyed by Charles V's army on 27 July 1544. Francis decided to rebuild it on another site further south better suited to contemporary military conditions. Special privileges granted to the settlers included twenty years' exemption from the *taille*, three annual fairs and a market each week. C.A.F., iv. 14422, 14465. The plan of Vitry-le-François, as the new town was called, was the work of Girolamo Marini, the Bolognese engineer. It consisted of a square of 612 metres per side, divided into sixteen compartments by six main roads, three in each direction crossing at right angles. Each compartment was subdivided by a smaller street. A large square in the town centre offered scope for military displays. P. Lavedan, *Histoire de l'urbanisme* (1941), pp. 76–81. See also R. Crozet, 'Une ville neuve du XVIe siècle: Vitry-le François', *La vie urbaine*, 5 (1923), 291–309, and 'Naissance de Vitry-le-François', *Mémoires S.A.C.S.A. de la Marne* (1968). On G. Marini, see Potter, *War and Government*, pp. 181–2.
[59] Paillard, pp. 119–260; A. Rozet and J.-F. Lembey, *L'invasion de la France et le siège de Saint-Dizier par Charles-Quint en 1544* (1910), pp. 60–156. For the king's reports to the Parlement on the siege, see A.N., X^{1a} 1553, fols. 249b, 328a.

at Jalons. Without trying to capture Châlons, which might have resisted for as long as Saint-Dizier, Charles captured Epernay, where the French had built up provisions. As the imperialists marched on through Champagne, capturing Châtillon-sur-Marne, Château-Thierry and Soissons, observers were puzzled by Francis's inactivity. 'Who ever would have thought', exclaimed a Venetian, 'that the French would allow the invaders free passage and let them devastate their country?'[60]

It was in the course of the imperial advance on Paris that Lagny-sur-Marne was sacked by French troops under the command of Jacques de Montgommery, sieur de Lorges. We do not know exactly what happened. Du Bellay tells us that de Lorges was sent by the Dauphin with 7,000 or 8,000 infantry and 400 men-at-arms to help defend Paris, but that he chose Lagny as a more suitable place for his operations.[61] This, it seems, was the occasion for 'acts of disobedience and rebellion' by the local inhabitants which de Lorges put down savagely. Two months later, in November, Francis issued letters patent authorizing de Lorges to sack Lagny as if it were in enemy hands and endorsing such punitive actions as he had already taken. Any survivors were forbidden to prosecute de Lorges or his men for acts committed in pursuit of the king's order, and no court in the kingdom was allowed to receive their suit. Such harshness evidently upset the Parlement which registered the royal decree in March 1545 only after three *lettres de jussion*.[62] Francis's action on this occasion stands in sharp contrast to the magnanimity he had shown to the rebels at La Rochelle. Indeed it is difficult to imagine a more draconian step by a king against his own subjects. Lagny was wiped off the map for a time. It is not known if the sack left any survivors.

Panic gripped the French capital as the invaders drew closer to its walls. On 1 September all religious houses in and around Paris were ordered by the Parlement to hold processions and masses for the peace of Christendom. Nine days later the court's presidents called on Francis at the Louvre. He assured them that he had come to defend Paris and was resolved to live and die there. Parisians, he said, had nothing to fear. He ordered the Parlement to administer justice as usual, adding that within a few days he hoped to inflict shame and confusion on the enemy. The king also commanded that the city's gates and shops, which had been closed, should reopen. He then left the room before the presidents could reply. Turning to Tournon, they explained that justice could not be administered as usual, since many barristers and solicitors had fled the capital. Tournon replied that he did not think Francis expected the impossible: he would be satisfied if they did their utmost to prevent panic among the *petit peuple*.[63]

---

[60] Rozet and Lembey, p. 178.   [61] Du Bellay, iv. 268.   [62] A.N., X^{1a} 1556, fol. 84a–b.
[63] A.N., X^{1a} 1553, fols. 447b, 487a–b.

Francis, in fact, did almost nothing to hamper the imperial advance or even its retreat after Charles had decided, on 11 September, to abandon his march on Paris. But for a cavalry skirmish near Soissons in which more than a hundred Spaniards were captured, the French made no move against the imperialists after the fall of Saint-Dizier; they merely covered their movements from the left bank of the Meuse. The French strategy was sensible. Francis was fighting on two fronts. A defeat for his army in Champagne would have left Paris at the mercy of the English. That was a risk he could not afford to take.

The peace of Crépy (18 September 1544)

From the start of the invasion Francis put out peace feelers, but Henry VIII would not listen to overtures till he had captured Boulogne, an objective only achieved on 13 September. Charles, on the other hand, had shot his bolt. He was desperately short of money and mainly interested in settling the religious situation in Germany.[64] Thus it was he, not Henry, who first responded positively to Francis's peace moves. As Franco-imperial talks got under way, Charles sent a message to Henry asking him either to invade France at once or allow him to make peace. Before Henry could reply, Charles signed the treaty of Crépy (18 September).[65] This consisted of two agreements: one open, the other secret. The first laid down that Francis would help fight the Turks. It also restored the territorial *status quo* of 1538 and provided for a marriage between the duc d'Orléans and either Charles's daughter, Mary, or his niece, Anna. In the first case, he was to get the Netherlands and Franche-Comté as dowry; in the second, Milan. The choice of bride was to be made by Charles V within four months. Francis, for his part, was to give three duchies (Bourbon, Châtellerault and Angoulême) to his son. He also gave up his claims to Savoy and Piedmont, while the Emperor did likewise in respect of Burgundy. In the second, secret, agreement Francis promised to help Charles reform the church, to further the meeting of a General Council and to bring back the German Protestants into the Catholic fold. If they resisted, he was to give the Emperor as much help as against the Turks.

The peace was given a mixed reception in France. Queen Eleanor, who had tried to avert a conflict between her husband and her brother, was delighted. She left Paris on 22 September and travelled to the court of her sister, Mary of Hungary, in Brussels, where she was joined by the duc d'Orléans. Her entry into Brussels on 22 October was followed by several days of public rejoicing, culminating in a tournament on the Grand' Place.[66] Not everyone in France,

---

[64] K. Brandi, *The Emperor Charles V*, tr. C.V. Wedgwood (London, 1939), p. 522.
[65] Rozet and Lembey, pp. 164–9, 186–8; *L.P.*, xix (pt. 2), 198–9, 205, 213, 249, 291.
[66] C. Terrasse, *François Ier* (1945–70), iii. 132–3; *L.P.*, xix (pt. 2), 568, 570.

however, was pleased by the peace. The Dauphin Henri had every reason to resent it, for not only did it rob him of the chance to avenge his recent humiliation at Perpignan, it also advanced his brother's prospects. Ever since the early forties Francis had aimed to create an Italian patrimony for his younger son, while Henri had to be content for the time being with Brittany. Under the terms laid down at Crépy, Charles d'Orléans seemed set to become the duke of Milan. When he visited Antwerp in the autumn of 1544 he bore the arms of Milan quartered with those of France. Had the peace been implemented, Henri would have lost not only his rights in Italy but perhaps much of his kingdom, for Orléans was promised four French duchies as appanages. Thus it was with good reason that Henri protested formally about the treaty on 12 December 1543. His example was soon followed by the parlement of Toulouse, and that of Paris registered the treaty only at the second request from the king.[67] Abroad too the peace aroused mixed feelings. The pope seemed pleased, but Henry VIII felt that he had been betrayed by the Emperor. As for the Sultan, he nearly had the French ambassador impaled.[68]

The treaty of Crépy proved little more than a dead letter. Francis fulfilled some of the terms: he asked the pope to call a General Council and he returned Stenay, a fortified town in Lorraine, to the Emperor. But the core of the treaty – the alternative marriage proposed for the duc d'Orléans – never took effect. The Emperor, after hesitating for a long time, chose his niece, Anna, as Orléans's future bride, but on 9 September 1545 the duke died of a brief and mysterious illness. Francis was heartbroken. He had lost not only a much-loved son, but, as he himself put it, 'he by whom Christendom might have remained in perpetual repose and quietude; he would have nourished peace and tranquillity among the princes'.[69] Orléans's death effectively nullified the peace. It also removed the threat that had been hanging over the Dauphin's inheritance. Francis now drew closer to Henri, admitting him to his council. He also tried to give him a more significant role in government, but the old wounds were not so easily healed. Henri preferred to stay in the wings till the stage could be truly his.

[67] C.A.F., iv. 14267, 14306; L.P., xix (pt. 2), 597, 740.
[68] Rozet and Lembey, pp. 201–2; L.P., xix (pt. 2), 304; E. Charrière (ed.), *Négociations de la France dans le Levant* (1848–60), i. 593n.
[69] François, *Francois de Tournon*, p. 213; L.P., xix (pt. 2), 642.

Chapter twenty-five

Gathering clouds (1544–47)

For all his remarkable energy, Francis was desperately sick in the last five years of his life. Ever since his almost fatal illness in Spain he had suffered relapses. The most serious had occurred in 1539 on the eve of the Emperor's visit to France. In 1545 he succumbed at Fontainebleau to an intermittent fever, provoked by an excruciatingly painful 'apposthume' or abscess 'in his lower parts'. Physicians and surgeons cauterized the abscess and opened it up in three places, releasing a large quantity of pus. The king was then prescribed a course of 'Chinese wood'.[1] This was a sudorific root, imported from the Portuguese colony of Goa. First mentioned by Niccolò Massa in 1532, it was one of several woods and roots used for treating syphilis which reached epidemic proportions in sixteenth-century Europe. Francis is also said to have used Barberossa's notorious pills of which untreated mercury (quicksilver) was an ingredient.[2] While believing that he was a victim of the pox, his doctors also suspected an ulcerated bladder.

By about 7 February 1545 the king had recovered sufficiently to set off in a litter for the Loire valley. He declared himself fit again 'albeit dead in respect of the ladies'. In March, however, his abscess reopened. Some doctors thought his days were numbered, especially as he continued 'to indulge his appetite'; others were more hopeful. Yet they were unanimous about the king's 'inside' being 'rotten'.[3] In July he ruptured a vein on which, according to his physician, the life of a man depends, yet again recovered.[4] In January 1546 his abscess gave further trouble, prompting the imperial envoy to remark: 'if the game lasts much longer, he may cease to play altogether'. But it burst of its own accord, and early in February Francis was again hunting from a litter.[5] In July Sir

---

[1] *C.S.P.Span.*, viii. no. 115; B.L., Add. Ms. 28594, fol. 189a–b; *L.P.*, xx (pt. 1), 45.
[2] C. Quétel, *History of Syphilis* (Oxford, 1990), pp. 61, 63.
[3] B.L., Add. Ms. 28594, fol. 103b. [4] *Ibid.*, fol. 142; *C.S.P.Span.*, viii. no. 104.
[5] *Ibid.*, nos. 187, 194; B.L., Add. Ms. 28594, fols. 223–4.

95. Francis I. This drawing in black chalk probably dates from around 1540 when
François Clouet took over from his father, Jean, as the royal portraitist.

Thomas Cheyney found him in much better shape than when he had last seen him, and, later that month, Lord Lisle saw him leap on his mule and kill a stag.[6] In November the king rose early each morning and covered seven or eight leagues in a day, taxing the energies of those who followed him on foot.[7] In 1546 Cavalli described him as follows: 'The king is fifty-four years of age and of a regal presence, so that without knowing that he is the king or having seen his portrait, there is not a foreigner who, seeing him, does not say: "This is the king". He has an excellent complexion, a hale and hearty constitution . . . He eats and drinks very well, sleeps even better, and, what is more important, thinks of nothing but living joyfully without too many cares . . .'[8]

In spite of his health, Francis remained firmly in charge of state affairs. Foreign ambassadors, describing their audiences with him, offer no evidence of the mental disorders commonly associated with the tertiary stage of syphilis. Francis still showed a good grasp of international affairs, even if his judgment was sometimes at fault. His authoritarianism was also undimmed: he imposed a strict discipline on his courtiers. When Julien de Clermont murdered a fellow nobleman, no one save his sister dared to incur the king's displeasure by interceding on his behalf.[9] Yet everyone knew that Francis's days were numbered and that his death would signal a palace revolution. For there was no love lost between the king and the Dauphin or between their respective mistresses, the duchesse d'Etampes and Diane de Poitiers. There was consequently much jockeying for position in anticipation of the next reign. 'Thus', wrote Wotton in August 1546, '. . . the Court everywhere is the Court, that is to say, a place where is used good shouldering and lifting at each other.'[10]

A key figure in all these intrigues was Madame d'Etampes, who used her influence to advance her relatives and friends.[11] Being fickle, she was capable of abandoning one favourite for another. In 1545, for example, she tried to get her erstwhile protégé, Admiral Annebault, dismissed so that her new favourite, Nicolas de Bossut, seigneur de Longueval might take his place. Although previously she had opposed war with England, she now supported it, hoping that it would bring discredit on the Admiral.[12] But Madame d'Etampes did not always get her way. Thus Francis continued to employ Annebault even after the Admiral had bungled an expedition against England. In 1545 he led an embassy to the imperial court, and in 1546 was the chief French plenipotentiary at the peace talks at Ardres. In August Annebault was sent to England to obtain Henry VIII's ratification of the peace, and in January 1546 Francis gave

[6] *L.P.*, xxi (pt. 1), 1200, 1365, 1405.   [7] *C.S.P.Span.*, viii. no. 347.

[8] Cited by J. Jacquart, *François Ier* (1981), p. 389.

[9] Julien de Clermont, alias Tallard, was a friend of the Dauphin. He was executed despite an appeal for clemency from Henry VIII. *St. P.*, xi. 270, 272, 301; *C.A.F.*, v. 15322, vi. 22018; viii. 31004.

[10] *St. P.*, xi. 277.   [11] E. Desgardins, *Anne de Pisseleu, duchesse d'Etampes et François Ier* (1904).

[12] *C.S.P. Ven.*, v. no. 327.

96. Anne de Pisseleu, duchesse d'Etampes. Painting by Corneille de Lyon. She became Francis I's mistress after 1526 and came to exercise an important political and artistic influence. She used it to assist Primaticcio and to discredit Cellini.

him the lordship of the Compiègne as a reward for his services during the war and his management of the highest affairs of state.[13]

Madame d'Etampes also failed in her bid to oust Cardinal Tournon from the administration. She and the king's sister, Marguerite, disliked the cardinal for his religious conservatism, but they had other grievances as well. Marguerite blamed him for not insisting on the restoration of Navarre to her husband as one of the terms of the peace of Crépy. As for Madame d'Etampes, she fell out with the cardinal after he had ordered the arrest of her protégé, the count of Anguillara, and opposed her efforts to oust Annebault from the office of Admiral of France in favour of her favourite, de Bossut. She persuaded one of Tournon's servants to lodge an anonymous complaint about him with the king's council. The cardinal managed to defuse the situation by withdrawing temporarily from the court on medical grounds. When he returned, Francis treated him to a great show of friendship. 'Tournon', wrote the Florentine ambassador, 'has overcome everything, and is now greater than ever.'[14] But the duchess had another card up her sleeve: at her instigation the cardinal was accused of lining his own pockets during the war of 1536 by exploiting the special fund-raising powers given to him by the king. The charge was not groundless (Tournon had speculated over duties on Genoese goods passing through Lyons), but he extricated himself by offering Francis a loan of 25,000 *écus*. On 8 June he received new powers to raise loans from the Lyons bankers. By late July he was reconciled to the duchess: they often ate together and jointly pleaded with the king not to go to Picardy during a plague. The cardinal's position in the government remained unchallenged till the end of the reign.[15]

Madame d'Etampes doubtless knew that her fate was bound up with the king's. She could expect little sympathy from the Dauphin Henri or Diane de Poitiers. Henri did not care for his wife, Catherine de' Medici. She had given him no children and he was talking of divorce. Since the age of eighteen, he had been passionately in love with Diane, the widow of the *sénéchal* of Normandy, who had died in 1531. In spite of her age (she was now forty and twenty years older than Henri) she was universally praised for her beauty. Henri flaunted his passion in front of the court and already used the monogram, linking the 'H' of his name with the 'D' of hers arranged as three crescent moons. As for Catherine, she was well liked by Francis and, on 19 January 1544, secured her position as well as the dynasty by producing a son, the future Francis II.

Two women played virtually no part in court intrigues at the end of Fran-

---

[13] E. Dermenghem, 'Un ministre de François Ier: la grandeur et la disgrace de l'amiral Claude d'Annebault', *Rev. du XVIe siècle*, ix (1922), 34–50.
[14] Desjardins, iii. 160.   [15] M. François, *Le cardinal François de Tournon* (1951), pp. 205–11.

cis's reign. Queen Eleanor had long since given up any attempt to compete with Madame d'Etampes in the king's affections. As for his beloved sister, Marguerite, she now spent most of her time at Nérac or on her domains, making only fleeting appearances at court. It was in September 1546 at Cauterets that she composed the prologue of her *Heptaméron*. Four years had passed since she had thought of writing a collection of stories divided into ten days like the *Decameron* which her protégé, Antoine Le Maçon, was soon to publish in French translation. The task which, according to Brantôme, she accomplished while being transported in her litter, was to occupy the rest of her days.[16]

The trial of Guillaume Poyet (1544)

The trial of Guillaume Poyet did not begin till April 1544, two years after his arrest. As Chancellor, he was entitled to be tried by the whole Parlement, but Francis set aside this privilege on the ground that its implementation would disturb the normal course of justice. Instead, he appointed a special commission of thirty-four members, mainly drawn from the Parlement. Under a rule of Poyet's own devising, laid down in the ordinance of Villers-Cotterêts, he was denied any advance notice of the charges against him and allowed no time to prepare his defence. When he complained to his judges of this unfair procedure, he was curtly told: '*Patere legem quam ipse tulisti.*' Francis gave evidence against Poyet; he also suggested that the *gens du roi* should, contrary to normal usage, attend the final judicial review of the case, but strong opposition from the judges obliged him to back down. It was agreed that the *gens du roi* would only present the king's case.

Many charges were levelled against Poyet. He was accused of fraud in respect of a gift arising from Louise of Savoy's inheritance, of cheating the comtesse de Brienne over the purchase of an estate, of abusing his privilege of judging counterfeiters of the king's seal, of evoking lawsuits from the *Grand Conseil* and giving personal judgments in the name of the court as a whole, of misappropriating fines, of tampering with the decisions of the sovereign courts in return for bribes, of selling judicial offices for personal gain and usurping the king's exclusive right to create such offices. Poyet's role in Chabot's trial also came under attack: he was accused of intimidating the judges, withholding evidence from the court and of tampering with its verdict. We do not know how justified these charges were, for the prosecution failed to produce any conclusive evidence and witnesses frequently contradicted themselves.

Poyet, despite his physical debility, defended himself vigorously. He read out a long statement recalling his past services to the crown and his irreproachable

16 Jacquart, *François Ier*, p. 388.

parliamentary career. He tried to win over the judges by flattery and a display of humility in sharp contrast to his erstwhile arrogance. He also tried to get certain hostile judges removed or to discredit them by seeming to be in league with them. The judges admired Poyet's burning sincerity and remained mindful of his former eminence, but they were under pressure from his enemies to convict. None was more insistent than the king.[17] He complained of delays engineered by Poyet's relatives and ordered the trial to be suspended until his own return to Paris, presumably in the hope of securing a heavier sentence.

In the end, Poyet got off fairly lightly: he was fined 100,000 *livres*, deprived of the chancellorship, debarred from holding any royal office and sentenced to five years' imprisonment. Francis was told that two factors had mitigated the sentence: the prosecution's failure to produce evidence of guilt and the Chancellor's holy orders. But the king was not mollified: a chancellor who lost his office, he said, should also lose his life. He complained that lawyers in general were insufficiently punished for their misdemeanours and that Poyet's property should have been confiscated. He complained also that his own testimony had not been given sufficient weight and made no secret of his low opinion of the judiciary.

Poyet was sentenced in front of the whole Parlement on 23 April. He was then taken back to the Bastille. On 16 May he was required to pay his fine, but, as he did not have 100,000 *livres* in cash, he persuaded the king to take some of his lands. Francis then relented to the extent of cutting Poyet's term of imprisonment. The ex-Chancellor was released on 11 July 1545. In April 1548 he obtained the Parlement's leave to have a retrial but died before this could take place.[18]

The war with England (1544–46)

In the autumn of 1544 peace talks with England at Calais failed to make headway on account of Henry VIII's refusal to hand back Boulogne. He also insisted on France abandoning the Scots.[19] The French accordingly decided to force a settlement by launching an attack against the south coast of England to be coupled, if possible, with a Scottish invasion of the north. They probably did not intend a full-scale invasion of England, merely wanting to disrupt communications between England and her army in Picardy so as to facilitate a recapture of Boulogne by the Dauphin. On 31 May a French expeditionary

[17] A.N., X^{1a} 1554, fol. 1a–b.
[18] C. Porée, *Un parlementaire sous François Ier: Guillaume Poyet, 1473–1548* (Angers, 1898), pp. 107–24. See also A.N., U. 797, 798 (seventeenth-century copies of the trial proceedings). Also X^{1a} 1555, fols. 19b, 21a–b, 1556, fol. 309a–b.
[19] *L.P.*, xix (pt. 2), 382, 392, 455–6.

force landed in Scotland and, on 26 June, the Scots decided to raise an army for the invasion of northern England.[20] Francis, meanwhile, assembled an army of 30,000 men in Normandy and seven *compagnies d'ordonnances* in Picardy. He also assembled a fleet of more than 400 ships at Le Havre, including galleys of the Mediterranean fleet under baron de La Garde. On 27 June command of the fleet was given to Admiral Annebault, who, in spite of his title, had no experience of war at sea.[21]

Early in July the English admiral, Lord Lisle, planned to attack the French fleet in its anchorage, but was frustrated by bad weather. He was, however, able to frighten Francis as he surveyed his fleet from the clifftop at Sainte-Adresse. Cannon balls from Lisle's guns passed perilously close to the king's tent, but the only damage suffered by the French fleet was self-inflicted; on 12 July Annebault's flagship, *Le Philippe*, was destroyed by fire; next day his new flagship, the *Grande Maistresse* ran aground.

Yet the fleet sailed out of Le Havre on 16 July, and, a few days later entered the Solent as Henry VIII was dining on board his flagship, *Great Harry*. An engagement ensued during which the English ship, *Mary Rose* sank with the loss of 500 men, not as a result of French action, but after a breeze had sprung up, driving sea water through her gun ports. On 21 July the French landed on the Isle of Wight and burned a few villages before being driven back to their ships. Four days later they landed at Seaford, but again withdrew, this time to Dover. Annebault then crossed the strait and added his troops to the French camp outside Boulogne. On 15 August he came out to sea again and encountered the English fleet. A brief skirmish took place near Beachy Head, but Annebault, instead of taking advantage of his numerical superiority, retired to Le Havre.[22] Meanwhile, in the north, the Scots, after drawing close to the border, withdrew, leaving the way clear for a drive into the Lowlands by the Earl of Hertford.

By early September the war had reached stalemate; both sides looked to the German Protestants for help. The latter needed Anglo-French support against the Emperor, who was preparing to impose a religious settlement on them. The Schmalkaldic League, therefore, by way of mediation, offered to take Boulogne in trust, pending settlement of Francis's debts to Henry. But its efforts, which culminated in a conference near Calais in November, failed, largely because of mutual distrust between the English and the French. Both sides were negotiating with the Emperor, believing that the other was about to ally with him.

---

[20] *L.P.*, xx (pt. 1), p. xxxii, nos. 513, 767, 1049.
[21] L.-H. Labande (ed.) *Correspondance de Joachim de Matignon, lieutenant-général du roi en Normandie (1516–1548)* (Monaco, 1914), pp. 116–24; La Roncière, *La marine française*, pp. 412–17; *C.A.F.*, vii. 25203.
[22] La Roncière, pp. 417–28; J.J. Scarisbrick, *Henry VIII* (London, 1968), p. 455.

There was also much opposition within the French government, notably from Cardinal Tournon, to the Protestant mediators.[23]

Both sides now began to rearm, but without much enthusiasm. Henry merely wanted to cling to Boulogne, while Francis could not afford war on a large scale. Consequently peace talks were soon resumed. They began on 6 May, nearly broke down twice, but in the end reached agreement. Under the treaty of Ardres (7 June) France was to pay 2 million *écus* in 1554 in exchange for Boulogne. In the meantime Henry was to keep the town and the county and neither side was to undertake any fortification in the county. France also agreed to pay all the pensions she owed under past treaties. Henry's claim for 512,022 *écus*, which France had allegedly promised him in 1529, was to be submitted to commissioners within three months. England promised not to attack the Scots without cause.[24]

The peace, which was proclaimed on 13 June, was received with relief on both sides of the Channel, but failed to remove distrust. Lord Lisle, acting on Henry's verbal instructions, destroyed some French fortifications near Boulogne, yet Francis was conciliatory: he agreed to set up an enquiry and to pull down any fortification built since the treaty.[25] Another possible area of friction was Scotland, where, following the murder of Cardinal Beaton, a pro-English party was holding St Andrew's castle. Having agreed only with reluctance to the inclusion of the Scots in the treaty of Ardres, Henry now claimed that they had broken it. In the winter of 1546–47 Odet de Selve, the French ambassador in England, reported naval and military preparations in England. He believed they were aimed at the Scots, but could not be sure that the English were not planning an attack on Picardy or Normandy. On 26 November the Scots appealed to Francis for help, but what he sent them was insufficient to bring the pro-English faction to heel.[26]

Royal borrowing and fiscal reform

The war of 1542–46 was the most expensive conflict of the entire reign. As England entered the war, Francis was obliged to spend almost 2 million *livres* on his navy. He also decided to protect his kingdom from a repetition of the Anglo-imperial invasion of 1544 by fortifying its north-east frontier. This cost him another 706,000 *livres* in 1545–46. According to Cavalli, who wrote in 1546, the king was spending 250,000 *écus* per year on his new fortifications. In

[23] D. L. Potter, 'Diplomacy in the Mid-16th Century: England and France, 1536–1550' (unpublished Ph.D. thesis, Cambridge University, 1973), pp. 83–136; François, *François de Tournon*, p. 201.

[24] *L.P.*, xxi (pt. 1), 1014. The treaty is known also as the treaty of Camp.

[25] G. Lefèvre-Pontalis, *Correspondance politique de Odet de Selve* (1888), pp. 23, 27; *L.P.*, xxi (pt. 2), 117, 149, 254.

[26] *L.P.*, xxi (pt. 2), 451, 515; Lefèvre-Pontalis, pp. 63, 83.

the long-term such defences might prove more economical than raising an army, but each fortress needed a garrison which had to be paid and fed. In 1547, which was a peaceful year, the upkeep of garrisons in north-east France and Piedmont cost 180,000 *livres* per month. The overall cost of the war of 1542–46 has been estimated as in excess of 30 million *livres*. The maximum spent on the *extraordinaire des guerres* was 520,827 *livres* in 1544, which is not much higher than the 439,554 *livres* spent in 1537. But it was the cumulative cost over the four years which proved crippling: it was twice as heavy as in 1536–38 and 50 per cent more than in 1521–25. The proportion spent on the artillery and navy was also greater: 15 per cent in 1542–46 as against 6 per cent in 1536–38.[27]

Expenditure on such a scale necessitated a frantic search for money. The *taille* rose to 4,446,000 *livres* between 1542 and 1547, but corruption at the local level continued to erode its yield. Evidence produced at the trial of Admiral Chabot revealed that in Burgundy about twice as much tax was collected as actually reached the royal coffers. Indirect taxation rose to 9,000,000 *livres* in 1546. At the same time every known expedient was pushed to the limits. In 1543 the king seized specie and plate left by Jean de Laval, seigneur de Châteaubriant. And the clergy continued to be milked. Between 1542 and 1546 at least twenty tenths were levied by the crown, so that in effect the tenth became a regular tax on the church. The towns, too, were made to contribute. In 1543 they had to pay the *solde des 50,000 hommes de pied*. The substantial fiscal contribution made by the towns between 1542 and 1546 aggravated the social crisis caused by the grain famine of 1545. Yet their total contribution may not have been more than 5 million *livres*, less than that of the church.[28]

In the 1540s Francis was able to raise huge loans on the Lyons money market. William Paget, writing from Lyons on 9 August 1542, reported: 'great means is daily made for money. For whereas here, in Lyons, and in other places, men that have gotten any sum of money, likewise widows and orphans, use to put the same in bank, some for five, some for eight in the hundred, the King desireth to have all, and to give ten in the hundred.'[29] Loans raised with the bankers of Lyons were a major source of royal revenue in the last years of Francis's reign. Such loans had, of course, been raised before, but only exceptionally: as from 1542 they became regular and systematic. They were raised annually and renewed at each of Lyons's four fairs. The amount of interest paid was 4 per cent at each fair or 16 per cent over the year. This apparently satisfied the lenders, who no longer asked for personal guarantees from the

[27] G. Jacqueton, 'Le Trésor de l'Epargne sous François Ier, 1523–1547', *R.H.*, lvi (1894), 35; P. Hamon, 'L'argent du roi: finances et gens de finances en France au temps de François Ier' (unpublished doctoral thesis. University of Paris I. 1993), pp. 70–3, 77–83.

[28] *Ibid.*, pp. 103–15, 133–44, 246.   [29] *St. P.*, ix. 117.

royal intermediaries. Their confidence in the French crown had obviously been restored; they were even prepared to defer repayment and seemed no longer interested in short-term loans. Two possible explanations may be offered for their change of attitude: capital had become plentiful and profits from trade were falling. Consequently, investors were more interested in long-term speculation in government loans with a view to growth.

The method of borrowing was as follows. Commissioners were appointed by the king to contract loans with bankers or merchants. The first commission was appointed on 13 April 1543 and renewed at irregular intervals.[30] Then, as from 1545 a new commission, valid for one year, was appointed annually. The commissioners were mostly high-ranking members of the royal entourage, but there were also a number of local officials, who, being on the spot, were perhaps better able to negotiate loans. Astride of both categories was Cardinal Tournon, who was both a leading minister and governor of the south-east provinces. There is no truth, however, in Bodin's allegation that loans were first introduced in France by the cardinal in 1543 and that he planned to set up a royal bank in Lyons.[31] Another important negotiator of loans was Jean Cléberger, a German businessman who had settled in Lyons in 1530. As from 1543 he was constantly involved either as lender or intermediary between the French government and the German banks. In 1545 he raised a loan of 50,000 *écus* with help from the Welsers of Nüremberg and Weikmann of Ulm, and in 1546 raised another loan to which he himself contributed 13,500 *livres*.[32]

Loans raised by Francis at the end of his reign were large and mostly drawn on Italian, Swiss and German banks. The following details are known: in 1542 there was talk of a loan of 400,000 *livres* from four different sources (200,000 from the Florentines, 100,000 from the Luccans, 50,000 from the Welsers of Augsburg and 50,000 from French bankers). In 1543 100,000 *écus* were borrowed. In 1544 the same amount was lent to the king by Italians and 50,000 by Germans. These amounts, however, were only a small proportion of the total borrowed by him. The pace of borrowing then quickened: early in 1545 the Italian banks were asked for 100,000 *écus* and the Germans for 50,000. In 1546 a new loan of 300,000 *livres* was raised, and in September of that year negotiations took place with a view to raising cash for the Schmalkaldic League. In 1546 Francis owed the bankers of Lyons the colossal sum of 6,860,844 *livres*. Even after making peace with England in July, he continued to borrow. His war chests needed replenishment in anticipation of the next conflict.[33]

---

[30] C.A.F., vi. 22570.   [31] François, *François de Tournon*, pp. 192–3, 478–82.
[32] R. Doucet, 'Le Grand Parti de Lyon au XVIe siècle', *R.H.*, clxxi (1933), 474–82; A.N., X[1a] 1555, fol. 143a–b; M. Vial, *L'histoire et la légende de Jean Cléberger dit 'le bon Allemand' (1485?–1546)* (Lyons, 1914).
[33] Doucet, 'Le Grand Parti', pp. 478–80.

Not all the borrowed money was used: much found its way into the king's war-chests at the Louvre. According to Bodin they contained 500,000 *écus* 'and four times as much'.[34] But what, we may well ask, was the point of storing large sums of borrowed cash bearing an interest of 16 per cent per annum? Was Francis providing for contingencies or did he have another motive? According to Bodin, Tournon planned to attract foreign capital to France and thereby prevent France's enemies from raising loans themselves. The Habsburg-Valois wars were certainly fought not only on the battlefield but also on the money markets. Each government tried to starve its opponent of capital necessary to fight its wars. The traditional method of achieving this was to ban the export of precious metals, particularly specie. A ban might also be imposed on the use of letters of exchange. Currency was sometimes manipulated, notably by the Flemings who over-valued the *écu au soleil* so as to attract it out of France. In January 1543 a French sumptuary law forbade the purchase of luxury clothes from abroad so that money used for their purchase should not pass into enemy hands. Such measures, however, were counter-productive. If the Lyons merchants were asked for loans, they needed to be allowed a fair measure of commercial freedom. It is against this background of a fierce competition for capital that Francis's huge loans in the 1540s can be explained. Part of his strategy was undoubtedly to deprive Charles V of the cash needed to pay his armies. The king was thus able to help his Protestant friends in Germany without breaking his peace treaty with Charles. But he could not hope to soak up all the available capital. His policy was also risky and burdensome. It led to the *Grand Parti* under Henri II and the crown's eventual bankruptcy.[35]

The financial pressures resulting from the war of 1542–46 also led the king to continue reforming the fiscal administration. Until 1542 the old royal demesne was divided into four large fiscal districts or *généralités*: Languedoïl, Normandy, Languedoc and Outre-Seine-et-Yonne. In addition, there were four *recettes-générales*: Guyenne, Dauphiné, Provence and Burgundy. Now, under the edict of Cognac (7 December 1542) the *généralités* were subdivided into twelve smaller districts.[36] Languedoïl was split into four districts, Normandy into two, Outre-Seine-et-Yonne into three and Languedoc into three. The sixteen new districts were called *recettes-générales* and each was under a *receveur-général*, who was empowered to collect all regular revenues, including those from the demesne. This amounted to the fusion of what had once been the 'ordinary' and 'extraordinary' revenues. Since there was no longer any need for a special treasurer for domainal revenues, the post of *Changeur du Trésor* disappeared. The *receveur-général* was also directed to collect many of the

[34] J. Bodin, *Les six livres de la République* (1577), p. 681.
[35] Doucet, 'Le Grand Parti', p. 482; P. Hamon, 'L'argent du roi', pp. 207–19.
[36] Isambert, xii. 796–806.

deniers casuels, including clerical tenths, forced loans and other levies on towns.

Another change was the ending of the dual system created by the reforms of 1523–24. The *receveur-général des parties casuelles* was reduced to disbursing sums arising from the sale of offices. Jean Laguette protested at this diminution of his powers. He claimed responsibility for the collection of 'extraordinary' revenues, but an ordinance of January 1544 laid down that all revenues, both 'ordinary' and 'extraordinary', should in future be paid to the *Trésorier de l'Epargne*. This rule, however, was not strictly applied. In February 1544 Laguette was allowed to disburse cash out of receipts which had not been paid to the *Trésorier de l'Epargne*.

After 1542 Francis abandoned the idea of making all or most royal payments in cash and from Paris. The *recettes-générales* were authorized to make regular local payments, such as salaries and pensions, but only on the authority of warrants from the *Epargne*. They were also allowed to meet 'unforeseeable' obligations if these could not be met from Paris, but again they needed a warrant from the *Epargne*.

A consequence of these changes was the enhanced importance of the *Trésorier de l'Epargne*, who, in addition to being the head of all the *receveurs-généraux*, also had charge of locating emergency funds. Thus he shared the authority formerly exercised by the *gens de finances*, but was not allowed to tap the revenues of the *élections* and *bailliages*, or to control policy. This belonged to the king's council whose supremacy in fiscal matters is stressed by the contemporary legislation; the *Trésorier de l'Epargne* was simply its executive officer or cashier. In a list of February 1543, giving the names of those whom the king wished to admit to his council, the *Trésorier* appears, but right at the bottom, after the financial secretaries (*secrétaires des finances*), Bayard and Bochetel.

Historians disagree as to how far Francis I's fiscal reforms were premeditated. For Jacqueton, they represented the piecemeal application over a period of twenty years of a broadly conceived plan aimed at achieving greater centralization, uniformity and simplicity. But Philippe Hamon, the most recent authority, does not believe in the existence of a master-plan. In his judgment, the king and his ministers responded to each situation as it arose and were sometimes obliged to backtrack. However, the end result of their reforms probably served the king's needs more effectively than the old system handed down by Charles VII. Though the new fiscal administration was far from perfect, important guidelines for further improvement had been laid down.[37]

---

[37] Jacqueton, 'Le Trésor de l'Epargne', pp. 30–8; Hamon, pp. 311, 504–6.

The fight against heresy

On 30 August 1542 Francis admitted that, in spite of counter-measures so far taken, heresy was still growing. He urged the soverign courts to enquire 'diligently, secretly and thoroughly' into the 'assemblies, conventicles, intelligences and secret practices of the sectarians'. The ecclesiastical authorities were instructed to do likewise and to report their findings to the parlements within four months, but they resented any encroachment by the secular courts on their jurisdiction in heresy cases. On 23 July 1543 Francis decided that in future the power of search and arrest would be shared by the secular and ecclesiastical courts.[38] Thereafter royal decrees against heresy were issued almost without interruption till the end of the reign.

The Paris Faculty of Theology, meanwhile, produced clear doctrinal guidelines to assist the authorities, for there was much confusion about the church's teaching. Preachers often contradicted each other. All doctors and bachelors of the university were now required to subscribe to twenty-five articles. Any who refused were to be expelled for 'it is dangerous for wolves to be fed among one's flock'. The articles reaffirmed Catholic dogma, worship and organization. They urged the faithful to speak of Jesus Christ, not just 'Christ', and of St Paul and St Matthew, not just 'Paul' and 'Matthew'. Francis formally approved the articles on 23 July and ordered their publication throughout the kingdom. Anyone caught teaching a different doctrine was to be prosecuted.[39] The official adoption of the Faculty's confession of faith provided the campaign against heresy with a clearer sense of direction.

Books also came under fire in 1542. A public proclamation on 1 July called on every Parisian to surrender to the clerk of the Parlement within twenty-four hours, on pain of hanging, Calvin's *Institutes* and all other books banned by the court. This was followed by measures aimed at controlling the book trade. Every master printer had to have his own mark and was made personally responsible for misdeeds by his journeymen. Also in 1542 the Faculty of Theology began to compile an Index of forbidden books. When published in the following year, it listed sixty-five titles. Among them were works by Calvin, Luther, Melanchthon, Dolet and Marot and translations of Scripture published by Robert Estienne. Twenty-four booksellers complained about the Index, yet it was revised and enlarged in 1545 and 1546. Soon the search for banned books by the Parlement's commissioners in shops, colleges, religious houses and private homes began to yield results. On 14 January 1544 Calvin's *Institutes* and fourteen works published by Etienne Dolet were solemnly burnt

---

[38] Isambert, xii. 785–7, 818; A.N., X^1a 1549, fol. 440b; A.N., U. 2035, fol. 53a.
[39] Isambert, xii. 820–7.

outside Notre-Dame. Between 1541 and 1544 six Parisian booksellers or print-ers were brought to trial: one was tortured and two burnt at the stake.[40] In the provinces, too, members of the book trade suffered persecution. The most vulnerable were the *colporteurs* or book-pedlars. Whereas booksellers or printers sometimes saved themselves by invoking the protection of some influential patron, the *colporteurs* had no such recourse: if caught, they were burnt along with their wares.

Heresy was not, of course, restricted to the book trade. In the thirties and forties it made deep inroads in French society. It was particularly rife among the lower clergy, especially the mendicant friars, and the urban bourgeoisie and proletariat. The peasantry generally 'stood on the sidelines of religious division'. But, as yet, heresy could take a multiplicity of forms. The advent of Calvinism did not immediately impose order on the dissenters who may not have wanted or needed a coherent theology or vigorous discipline. 'Printing, evangelism, unorthodox preaching, could all serve to stimulate or strengthen heretical ideas, but they did not necessarily serve to draw together people with similar notions.'[41] The Affair of the Placards had revealed the existence of sacramentarianism among the French dissenters, but the extent of its influence is difficult to estimate. As a charge it became more prominent between 1538 and 1541, but it could be as vague as 'Lutheran'. It guaranteed the ultimate punishment in all its cruelty.

To what extent was the royal court now committed to defend the Catholic faith? In the past, as we have seen, the king was inclined to protect evangelical members of his entourage from persecution. How far had the situation changed by the 1540s? Several members of the court were described as 'Lutherans' by foreign observers. They included the duchesse d'Etampes and the king's younger son, Charles d'Orléans. Another was Jean du Bellay, cardinal-bishop of Paris. In September 1543 Orléans wrote to the Landgrave of Hesse, saying that he wished to see the Gospel preached in France and that only respect for his father and brother had restrained him from introducing it into his duchy. He intended, however, to do so in Luxemburg and for this reason asked to be admitted to the Schmalkaldic League.[42] But the duke may have been moved by political expediency rather than religious conviction: having just conquered Luxemburg, he was looking for the approval and support of the German Prot-estants.

The last seven years of Francis's reign saw a steep rise in the number of heresy prosecutions by the Parlement of Paris. A purge of the capital's religious

---

[40] N. Weiss, 'La Sorbonne, le Parlement de Paris et les livres hérétiques de 1542 à 1546', *B.S.H.P.F.*, xxxiv (1885) 19–28; A.N., U. 2035, fol. 60a; A.N., X[1a]1551, fol. 550b.

[41] D. J. Nicholls, 'The Nature of Popular Heresy in France, 1520–1542', *H.J.*, 26 (1983), p. 269.

[42] Herminjard, ix. no. 1278, pp. 23–5.

houses, especially the Augustinians, was undertaken, and the Parlement's prisons began to fill up.[43] Parisians, who had seen few burnings since May 1535, had to witness a new round of grisly spectacles. Foremost among the victims was the printer-publisher Etienne Dolet, who had already been arrested in Lyons, tried and pardoned. His unorthodox views had again attracted the notice of the authorities, and, on 3 August 1546, he was burned in the Place Maubert as a relapsed heretic.[44]

Outside Paris, yet within the Parlement's huge *ressort*, bishops were obliged to delegate their judicial powers to *parlementaires* charged with the prosecution of heretics. In 1545 five commissioners were assigned to specific areas with full powers of search and punishment. One of the most active was Nicole Sanguin, who arrested forty-seven men and seventeen women at Meaux on 8 September 1546. Of these, fourteen were tortured and burnt, four banished and the rest given various penalties; only four were released. The punishment of the Meaux heretics became 'one of the most celebrated events in the martyrology of sixteenth-century Protestantism'. Thousands of people came from the surrounding countryside to watch the show which lasted two days. For the execution itself, a relatively modest procession involved mainly local officials and notables, but on the following day a larger procession in honour of the Blessed Sacrament accompanied the public penance of the other heretics. Threethousand townspeople marched carrying torches, accompanied by the children of the town, clergy and urban notables.[45] The Parlement's commissioners were also very active in the Loire valley and along the Atlantic coast. At Orléans and Beaugency, Pierre Hotman threw so many people into prison for no apparent reason that the bishop's official and the *bailli* had to intervene and get them released. At La Rochelle, where the authorities feared a link-up of religious and political unrest, 118 people were arrested and twenty-five sentenced to death.[46]

Elsewhere, the actions of the parlements were uneven. In Dauphiné, only eleven cases of heresy were reported and light sentences given. Yet Protestant groups certainly existed in that province. In Normandy, the parlement was so lethargic that the king suspended it in 1540 and appointed commissioners to hold the *Grands Jours* at Bayeux, specifically to deal with heresy.[47] Even after the parlement had been reinstated, it remained feeble. In May 1542 it was the

[43] Imbart de La Tour, iv. 219–65; A.N., X^{1a} 1553, fols. 109b–110a, 274b–275a.

[44] J. Viénot, *Histoire de la réforme française des origines à l'Edit de Nantes* (1926), i. 158; R. C. Christie, *Etienne Dolet, the Martyr of the Renaissance* (London, 1880), p. 456. Cf. L. Febvre, *Le problème de l'incroyance au XVIe siècle: la religion de Rabelais* (1947), pp. 48–53. Herminjard, viii, 303 n. 22. D. R. Kelley, *The Beginning of Ideology: Consciousness and Society in the French Reformation* (Cambridge, 1981), pp. 215–20.

[45] H. Heller, *The Conquest of Poverty: The Calvinist Revolt in Sixteenth Century France* (Leiden, 1986), pp. 66–7.

[46] Imbart de La Tour, iv. 322–31; Weiss, 'La Sorbonne', p. 26.   [47] See below pp. 529–30.

scene of a remarkable squabble between the President and the archbishop's official, each blaming the other for a sharp rise in heresy in Rouen.[48] In Guyenne, too, the parlement was fairly easy-going. In 1542 it carried out a search and four years later repeated the exercise rather more energetically. Even so, the king suspended the court after the revolt at La Rochelle, transferring its powers to a special commission. But if four parlements were less than assiduous in hunting down heretics, the two where Roman law was applied fell over themselves to do their duty. The parlement of Toulouse waged a fierce campaign against dissenters in Languedoc. Prosecutions between 1540 and 1549 numbered 200 at least, and eighteen death sentences were passed. In Provence the parlement was more militant still: within fifteen months more than sixty people were arrested and sentenced. Persecution of the Vaudois was intensified.[49]

In May 1540 Francis empowered the parlement of Aix to prosecute the Vaudois, using torture if necessary, and to judge them in first instance.[50] On 18 November nineteen Vaudois from Mérindol, who had failed to answer a summons, were sentenced to be burned. Their families were to be arrested or banished from the kingdom, their property confiscated and their village destroyed. In December Francis ordered the decree, generally called the *arrêt de Mérindol*, to be carried out, but soon afterwards he received a report from Guillaume du Bellay, which showed the Vaudois to be hard-working, God-fearing and loyal subjects.[51] The king pardoned them in February 1541 provided they abjured within three months; but they refused to do so unless they could be shown to be in error by reference to Scripture.[52] In April, they petitioned the parlement, enclosing their confession of faith. They explained that they had disobeyed the parlement's summons, not out of rebelliousness, but because of harsh punishments meted out to them in the past, when they had obeyed the court. They begged to be allowed to live in peace.[53] The parlement, in reply, invited the Vaudois to come to Aix formally to abjure, but only one turned up with a demand for an unconditional pardon. Francis, after receiving a complaint from the parlement, ordered Grignan, the provincial governor, to wipe them out.[54] But an appeal from the German Protestants assembled at Regensburg led to a temporary stay of execution.[55] In March 1542 the par-

---

[48] Viénot, i. 151–3.   [49] Imbart de La Tour, iv. 331–6.
[50] V.-L. Bourrilly, *Guillaume du Bellay, seigneur de Langey* (1905), pp. 314–15.
[51] Herminjard, vii. 17 n. 15; Isambert, xii. 698; E. Arnaud, *Histoire des Protestants de Provence, du Comtat-Venaissin et de la principauté d'Orange* (1884), i. 22; C.A.F., iv. 11758; Bourrilly, *Guillaume du Bellay*, pp. 315–17. The original text of the report is missing, but it is summarized in J.-A. de Thou, *Histoire universelle* (London, 1734), i (bk. vi), 416–17. It is sometimes claimed to have been commissioned by Francis, but this is uncertain. Du Bellay may have acted on his own initiative or in response to the German Protestants.
[52] C.A.F., iv. 11826.   [53] Herminjard, vii. 80–2.   [54] Arnaud, i. 42.
[55] *Ibid.*, i. 43–5; Herminjard, vii. no. 983, pp. 126–8.

lement sent commissioners to Mérindol in an attempt to persuade the inhabitants to abjure, but the mission failed. Soon afterwards, the bishop of Cavaillon
led an armed force against the Vaudois of Cabrières. This provoked an intervention in their favour by the people of Mérindol and in March 1543 Francis
ordered the decree of November 1540 to be reactivated. Yet once again the
Vaudois were spared after they had complained to the king that their persecu-
tors were more interested in seizing their goods than in defending the faith.
Suspending the *arrêt*, Francis set up an enquiry. Meanwhile he forbade the
parlement to deal with the affair and evoked it to his own court.[56]

Vacillations in the king's policy towards the Vaudois are symptomatic of the
uncertainties, difficulties and pressures facing the authorities in their fight
against heresy. The persecution, even when conducted with vigour, was
unlikely to halt the advance of heresy. For judicial enquiries, especially in large
towns, were slow and tentative. A heretic could fairly easily escape notice by
going into hiding or simply keeping his mouth shut. Investigations tended to be
judicial rather than theological: magistrates would look for tangible offences
rather than ideas. Normally, they would use torture only if and when a suspect
refused to answer questions. Frequent clashes over jurisdiction occurred
between the secular and ecclesiastical courts, and parlements would revise or
quash sentences passed by local magistrates or ecclesiastical judges if they
detected some technical error or abuse.[57] Penalties for heresy were not uniform:
judges used a graduated scale that varied with the gravity of the offence and the
status of the accused. Many heretics were given light sentences, such as public
penance (*amende honorable*) or a fine. More serious offenders were flogged.
Only the incorrigible were normally banished or burnt. Before 1550 burnings
were relatively few. 'Executions of heretics were special events, meant to attract
particularly wide attention, and were never common.'[58] In 1543 the Parlement
of Paris judged forty-three cases of heresy, yet not one resulted in an execution;
fourteen ended in acquittal.[59] Neither the ecclesiastical nor the secular courts
wanted to create martyrs.

Given these facts and others, such as the immunity from prosecution enjoyed
by many foreign Protestants in France – German and Swiss mercenaries, university students and teachers, merchants and artisans – and the reluctance of
the more liberal prelates to apply the law harshly, it is not surprising that

---

[56] Arnaud, i. 45–54. See Francis's reply to the council of Basle (14 October 1543). Herminjard, ix.
no. 1293, pp. 68–70.
[57] On 1 August 1544 the Parlement of Paris forbade the *bailli* of Touraine to obstruct the *lieutenant-
criminel* of Anjou in his search for 'Lutherans' at Chinon on pain of a fine and loss of office. A.N.,
X^1a 1553, fols. 293b–294a.
[58] D. Nicholls, 'The Theatre of Martyrdom in the French Reformation', *Past and Present*, vol. 121
(1988), p. 50.
[59] E. de Moreau, P. Jourda and P. Janelle, *La crise religieuse du XVIe siècle* (1950), pp. 273–4.

heresy should have continued to thrive in France after 1538. Throughout the late thirties and forties 'Lutherans' (they were still called thus though their views were often different from and often more extreme than Luther's) continued to be reported from almost every part of the kingdom. In May 1542 the President of the parlement of Rouen claimed that the church had never been in so much danger since the days of the Arian heresy. Having contaminated the lower orders in Rouen, it had begun to win support among the 'chief families'. The archbishop's official pointed to a sharp drop in the number of communicants as evidence of a loss of confidence in the Sacrament.[60]

Now and again an incident made the king aware of the peril. In 1542, for example, disturbances occurred in Paris as a result of the heretical sermons of François Landry, *curé* of Sainte-Croix-de-la-Cité. Francis himself questioned the preacher, who was so terrified by the experience that he lapsed into complete silence. But others continued to preach in the same vein, notably François Perrucel, a Franciscan, at Saint-Germain-l'Auxerrois, provoking more disturbances, particularly now that heresy was officially regarded as a crime against the state.

On 20 September 1544 Charles de Milly informed the Parlement of the peace of Crépy. He added that Francis and the Emperor were determined to rid their dominions of heretics and that the king wanted those already in prison to be tried expeditiously. The First President, Lizet, promised that the Parlement would do its best to scatter the 'sectarians'.[61] When Cardinal Tournon returned from a mission to Flanders in November, he hoped that France's friendship with the Emperor was firm enough to allow more effective action to be taken in defence of the faith. But he may have felt the need for a demonstration of good intent by his master. This may explain the massacre of the Vaudois in April 1545 which historians have often regarded as an isolated episode in the French Reformation.[62] From Tournon's standpoint it could not have happened more opportunely, yet it seems that local circumstances rather than a decision of the central government precipitated the event.

The massacre of the Vaudois (April 1545)

Local pressure for renewed persecution of the Vaudois followed naturally from the appointment of Jean Maynier baron d'Oppède, as First President of the parlement of Provence.[63] His hatred of the Vaudois was not merely relig-

---

[60] Viénot, *Histoire de la réforme*, i. 151–2. See also D. Nicholls, 'Inertia and Reform in the Pre-Tridentine French Church: The Response to Protestantism in the Diocese of Rouen, 1520–1562', *Journal of Ecclesiastical History*, xxxii (1981), 185–97.

[61] A.N., X[1a] 1553, fols. 490b–491a.   [62] François, *François de Tournon*, pp. 214–16.

[63] Jean Maynier (or Meynier) became Second President of the parlement of Provence in November 1541 and First President in December 1543. C.A.F., vii. 24741, 25047.

ious: he had long coveted the lands of the dame de Cental who owned several Vaudois villages. Unfortunately for the Vaudois, Maynier d'Oppède's rise to power coincided with the disappearance of their protector, Guillaume du Bellay who had died in January 1543. During the winter of 1544–45 alarming reports of Vaudois activities, deliberately coloured by Oppède to suggest sedition on their part, began to reach the ears of the king and his ministers. At the same time the papacy, concerned by the presence of heretics in the Comtat-Venaissin, pressed Francis for joint action. On 31 January 1545 he ordered the *arrêt de Mérindol* to be carried out. In the absence of the provincial governor, Louis-Adhémar de Grignan, who had gone to Germany on embassy, responsibility for executing the edict fell on Oppède, who thus combined the supreme legislative and executive functions in Provence. After raising the *ban et arrière-ban* and the local *gendarmerie*, he enlisted the services, possibly with the king's approval, of the *vieilles bandes de Piémont*, veterans of the Italian Wars under the command of Antoine Escalin, baron de La Garde, alias Captain Polin, who were about to embark at Marseilles as an expeditionary force against England.[64] Oppède was also able to count on papal troops from the Comtat-Venaissin.

On 11 April Oppède and Captain Polin held a council of war at Marseilles, and a week later operations against the Vaudois began. As the royal and papal troops converged on Mérindol in battle formation 'with banners unfurled', the inhabitants fled. Whereupon the troops set fire to the houses and slaughtered stragglers. They then besieged and captured the fortified town of Cabrières. Regardless of whether or not it had offered resistance, the town was sacked. All the inhabitants regardless of age or sex were put to the sword, except for twelve who were taken to Avignon to serve as 'an example to the people'. Four of them – three men and one woman – were executed. Elsewhere, too, atrocities were committed. At Murs, twenty-five women and children took refuge in a cave. Soldiers tried to get them out by firing arquebuses into it. When this failed, they set fire to the cave's entrance, causing the fugitives to suffocate. The cave has been recently identified by archaeologists. Inside they have found the remains, dating back to the sixteenth century, of women, children and animals, thereby confirming the evidence of the contemporary lawyer, Jacques Aubéry.[65]

The massacre was followed by a wave of looting by peasants from other parts of Provence, regardless of the fact that property taken from heretics belonged to the crown. They were driven by greed rather than religious hatred. For Provence was no longer as prosperous as it had been at the time of the

---

[64] *C.S.P.Span.*, viii. no. 82, p. 148.
[65] G. Audisio, *Les vaudois du Luberon: une minorité en Provence (1460–1560)* (Mérindol, 1984), pp. 362–3; L. Beltrando and B. Ely, 'La grotte de la Bérigoule', *B.S.H.P.F.* (1972), pp. 349–53.

Vaudois immigration. There were too many mouths to feed for the amount of land under cultivation and poverty was increasing. The towns were groaning under the weight of taxation for the king's wars. The authorities also hoped to gain from the massacre and to recoup some of the cost of its preparation. Vaudois property was sold off by auction, but movables were more easily disposed of than land, which carried the risk of reprisals at a later date by former owners or their relatives. On 5 March 1545 Francis ordered the yield from such sales, as well from fines and confiscations, to be allocated to the upkeep of town fortifications for five years.[66]

The number of victims of the Vaudois massacre is not known exactly. Contemporary estimates vary widely: some say hundreds, others thousands. According to the Emperor, between 6,000 and 8,000 were killed, including 700 women, who were burnt in a church. A more reliable contemporary estimate put the number of dead at 2,700 and of survivors, sent to the galleys, at 600. It was partly to ease overcrowding in the prisons of Aix that some Vaudois were sent to the galleys at Marseilles. This was an unusual punishment for heretics whose offence was considered too serious for such a sentence. Yet service in the galleys was anything but a bed of roses and some Vaudois did not survive the experience. Those who did were released within a few months. Equally difficult to determine is the number of Vaudois who fled from the massacres. Several sought refuge in Geneva, but the timing of their arrival was inappropriate for the city was feeling the effects of famine and plague. Many Vaudois eventually returned to Provence and some managed to recover their property, though they sometimes had to wait for as long as fifteen years. But the legacy of the massacres was not easily forgotten or forgiven. An area, which had already suffered serious damage from the imperial invasion of 1536, the frequent passage of armies and a series of poor harvests, had been left badly scarred. Villages had been burnt to the ground, fields left untilled, orchards and vineyards neglected, and animals had all but vanished. At Lourmarin, eighteen months after the massacre, commissioners sent out by the *Chambre des Comptes* found nothing but destruction and despair. Orphans, too small to run property, were reduced to begging.[67]

The scale of the massacre may have been exaggerated by Protestant or imperial propagandists, yet it was a monstrous crime, particularly as the victims had never been tried. Indeed, some who were thrown into prison claimed not to be Vaudois at all. Many people at the time were shocked, but the king was not among them. He was thanked in April by the papal nuncio for his promptness in punishing the heretics in Provence and the Comtat-Venaissin. With evident pleasure Francis affirmed that he would never tire of

---

[66] Audisio, *Les vaudois du Luberon*, pp. 350–5, 368–71, 374–80.   [67] *Ibid.*, pp. 376–7, 386–98.

supporting respect for religion and for the service of the pope and his legate. On 18 August he congratulated Oppède for his efficient enforcement of the law, and in 1546 allowed him to become a papal count.[68]

Protestants abroad were appalled by the massacre. The council of Strassburg protested to the king, only to be sharply rebuked. He had never meddled with their subjects, he said, and was surprised that they should meddle with his and question the punishments he had decreed. The Vaudois, he continued, had interfered with the government of an important border province of his kingdom, and he could not see that this was sanctioned by the Gospel. Their views were such that no German prince or state would tolerate them. Finally, he warned the Strassburgers that he would answer them harshly if they dared to write to him again about his 'tyranny' and 'atrocious punishments'. A protest by the Swiss cantons received a similar reply.[69]

Under Henri II Maynier d'Oppède and his accomplices were brought to justice following a complaint from the dame de Cental, whose interests had been seriously damaged by the massacre. Oppède was imprisoned for more than two years. A special court (*Chambre de la reine*), set up at Melun, was soon dissolved and the case was transferred to the Parlement of Paris, where it opened on 18 September 1551. It became a *cause célèbre* and caused deep resentment in Provence where it was interpreted as a trial of the local parlement by its Parisian equivalent. The papacy put considerable pressure on the French crown in support of Oppède. Comparing himself to Saul to whom God had given the task of exterminating the Amalekites, he claimed that he had only carried out the king's orders. He denied responsibility for the massacre at Cabrières, since the town lay outside his jurisdiction, and accused the dame de Cental of bringing disaster on her vassals by stubbornly refusing to obey the parlement's decrees. In the end, he and all the accused, save one, were acquitted. The exception was the *avocat-général* Guérin, who was hanged for crimes not directly connected with the massacre. Captain Polin was pardoned and seven years later became captain and governor of Marseilles. As for Maynier d'Oppède, he was reinstated as First President of the parlement of Provence, and allowed to keep the titles of knight and count palatine given to him by the papacy. The trial, in short, must have seemed to the Vaudois like a 'whitewash'. In the words of the Protestant martyrologist, Jean Crespin, 'one might have expected some important judgments after such lengthy pleadings; instead, the high mountain produced but a puff of smoke'.[70]

---

[68] *Ibid.*, p. 400; Arnaud, i. 60–76; François, *François de Tournon*, p. 221 n. 2; P. Gaffarel, 'Les massacres de Cabrières et de Mérindol en 1545' *R.H.*, cvii (1911), 241–64.

[69] Arnaud, i. 82–4.

[70] Audisio, pp. 402–5; Gaffarel, pp. 264–71. Jacques Aubéry, whose evidence regarding the massacre is a major source, was Henri II's *procureur* at the trial.

Francis and the Schmalkaldic War (1545–47)

On 19 November 1544 Pope Paul III summoned the Council of Trent. For Charles V this was the long-awaited opportunity of resolving the religious problems of Germany. Having been frequently humiliated by the Protestant princes, he tried to negotiate with them at the diet of Worms in December, but soon lost all hope of a peaceful settlement. On 20 July 1545 Charles effectively declared war on the princes by issuing a ban against their two leaders, the Elector of Saxony and Philip, Landgrave of Hesse.[71]

At first the odds seemed to favour the Protestant side. By September, however, the imperial army had occupied several major towns in the Danube valley. The Protestants, who had begun to seek aid from England and France, stepped up their efforts, but Francis laid down absurd conditions. He required the election of a new Emperor, thinking of himself or the Dauphin as the obvious candidate. Even with a majority in the electoral college, it would have been difficult for the princes to depose Charles. What is more, Francis insisted on Henry VIII's participation in any alliance with them and on Boulogne being handed over to them as guarantors of the peace of Ardres.

Two explanations have been advanced for Francis's indecisiveness: first, his diplomats consistently underestimated the military threat faced by the Protestants; secondly, he was hampered by differences of opinion among his own advisers. While Madame d'Etampes, Marguerite de Navarre and Jean du Bellay favoured an anti-Habsburg policy, Tournon and Annebault were committed to upholding the peace of Crépy. Francis's credibility among the German Protestants had also been damaged by his persecution of their co-religionists in France and his alliance with the Turks. Furthermore, French policy beyond the Rhine was determined by Francis's insolvency. Five years of war had emptied his coffers, yet he needed a vast sum with which to redeem Boulogne. This had become his first priority; everything else, even his life-long obsession with Milan, was of lesser importance. How then could he have intervened effectively in the Schmalkaldic War? Yet Protestant appeals for French help did not go completely unanswered, for during the autumn of 1545 Piero Strozzi visited the Protestant camp at Donauwörth. According to Sleidan, Strozzi had been instructed by Francis to arrange for payment of a subsidy to the Protestants by the bankers of Lyons, but this was blocked by Tournon. It seems, however, that Strozzi's mission never had Francis's official backing. Furthermore, a large sum of money, estimated at 600,000 *écus*, did apparently reach the Protestants from the bankers of Lyons. Any financial help to the German Protestants needed to be carefully disguised, for Francis was anxious

---

[71] M. F. Alvarez, *Charles V Elected Emperor and Hereditary Ruler* (London, 1975), pp. 130–5.

to remain at peace with the Emperor so as to concentrate his efforts on the early recovery of Boulogne.

The situation in Germany at the start of the Schmalkaldic War was too finely balanced to justify open French support for the Protestants. In November, Annebault declared that the imperial alliance needed to be preserved at all cost, regardless of the Protestants. By January 1547, however, the military situation had become so ominous for the Protestants that Francis saw the need to strengthen their hand. He sent an envoy to the Elector of Saxony with instructions 'to find means to keep the war going in Germany against the Emperor'. While negotiating with Saxony and Hesse, Francis remained reluctant about committing himself to their cause until he had recovered Boulogne. The Protestants, therefore, failed to get the support which might have helped to avert their final defeat by Charles at Mühlberg on 24 April.[72]

---

[72] D.L. Potter, 'Foreign Policy in the Age of the Reformation: French Involvement in the Schmalkaldic War, 1544–1547', *H.J.*, xx (1977), 540–4; François, *François de Tournon*, pp. 197–200, 223–4.

Chapter twenty-six

An absolute monarch?

How absolute was the monarchy of Francis I? Two sharply contrasted schools of thought have existed on the question. 'Francis I and Henri II', according to Pagès, 'were as powerful as any other kings of France; it was at the beginning of the sixteenth century that the absolute monarchy triumphed.'[1] Imbart de La Tour believed that in 1519 'the whole nation abdicated into the king's hands'. In his view the destruction of provincial autonomy had begun under Louis XII and been completed by Francis.[2] For Doucet, it was under Francis that 'a new system of government' was set up, which, 'starting from the traditional and still feudal monarchy of Louis XII, foreshadowed the absolute and centralized monarchy of the following centuries'.[3] But Dognon has warned against confusing Francis's reign with that of Louis XIV, 'for the old traditions did not give way so easily to new rules'.[4] Prentout was more emphatic still: 'absolute monarchy', he wrote, 'if one must use this label, begins only with Louis XIV'. Historians, he suggested, who take it back to Francis and beyond, fail to distinguish between the absorption of the great fiefs into the royal demesne and monarchical centralization; the two processes were separated by several centuries, not merely forty years, as the partisans of an early absolutism imply. They fail to see 'how long the kings had been obliged to abstain from touching the form of the provinces, how long they had been forced to respect the privileges of each estate and *pays*'. Prentout thought a more suitable label for the monarchy between 1285 and 1589 would be 'contractual'.[5] More recently, J. Russell Major has described it as 'popular and consultative'. It stressed legitimacy because of its 'feudal-dynastic structure' and tolerated decentralization

---

[1] G. Pagès, *La monarchie d'ancien régime en France* (1946), p. 3.
[2] Imbart de la Tour, i. 199–205.
[3] Doucet, i. 3.
[4] P. Dognon, *Les institutions politiques et administratives du Pays de Languedoc du XIIIe siècle aux Guerres de Religion* (Toulouse, 1895), p. 491.
[5] H. Prentout, *Les Etats Provinciaux de Normandie* (Caen, 1925), ii. 469–74.

because of the limitations on its power. Ultimately it depended more on popular support than on military power and promoted the growth of representative institutions. Even under Francis, Major argues, 'the popular, consultative nature of the monarchy continued unmodified for the first third of the period and was only mildly altered thereafter'.[6] Writing in 1980, he compared the roles of the king and the estates to those of the President and Congress of the United States. 'Disagreements between the two', he explained, 'are frequent and at times one tries to dominate, but each accepts the existence of the other and makes no effort to destroy it.'[7]

The theory of absolutism

'Absolutism' is a neologism dating from the French Revolution, but the term 'absolute power' (*plenitudo potestatis*) was used in the Middle Ages and Early Modern period. As for the concept itself, it can be traced back to Antiquity, notably to Ulpian's third-century dictum: *quod principi placuit legis habet vigorem* ('what has pleased the prince has the force of law'). During the Middle Ages legists discussed at length the Roman maxim: *princeps legibus solutus (est)* ('the prince is freed from the laws').[8]

Absolutism, however, was seriously qualified in late mediaeval France by respect for the rights of the community in general and of the provinces in particular. As it tried to consolidate its authority following the Hundred Years War, the crown looked for support to the chartered towns, ecclesiastical corporations and lesser nobles. The price of that support was the king's willingness and ability to guarantee their privileges. Mutual obligations were often laid down in contractual agreements between him and the estates of a province that had been annexed to the royal demesne. Such agreements were usually confirmed at each royal accession. The king was expected to respect established law; his administration was reckoned to exist not only to enforce his will but also to ensure that he did not exercise it arbitrarily. By the fifteenth century the Parlement's right to remonstrate was well established.

Roman legal concepts, as elaborated by mediaeval commentators, were accepted in sixteenth-century France. Jurists identified the king with the Roman *princeps* and declared him to be emperor within his own kingdom. He was thus deemed to be independent of both the pope and the Holy Roman Emperor in temporal matters. The idea of his absolute authority was univer-

---

[6] J. Russell Major, *Representative Institutions in Renaissance France, 1421–1559* (Madison, WI, 1960), pp. 3–20, 126–44.

[7] J. Russell Major, *Representative Government in Early Modern France* (New Haven, CT and London, 1980), p. 179.

[8] R. Bonney, 'Absolutism: What's in a Name?' *F.H.*, i. (1987), 93–4; R. Bonney, *L'absolutisme* (1989), pp. 5–13.

sally accepted in French law. Yet the king was not expected to rule absolutely without the consent of his subjects as expressed through certain institutions, notably the Parlement of Paris, which was often regarded as the modern French equivalent of the ancient Roman Senate (both bodies having a nominal membership of one hundred). Jurists believed that the king could not invoke his absolute power to override or break a law that had been accepted by his people and confirmed by himself.[9]

The best-known statement of the constitutionalism that prevailed at the start of the sixteenth century is Claude de Seyssel's *La Monarchie de France*.[10] The author was rewarded with the see of Marseilles after long years of service to the crown as a councillor, administrator and diplomat. Before retiring there in 1515, he wrote his treatise for the new king, Francis I. Like Machiavelli, Seyssel was above all a realist: he treated politics as a science independent of morality and religion. Thus he abstained from pacifism, and tried to divert the young king from war by showing that it was easier to conquer a territory than to keep it. As an Aristotelian, he valued moderation in a constitution and admired the French monarchy, believing it to be tempered by aristocracy. This he identified not with the nobility but with the sovereign courts. The greatness of the kings of France, in Seyssel's opinion, stemmed from their willingness to accept three constraints (*freins*) on their power: religion, justice and *la police*. By acting as a devout son of the church, curbing judicial abuses and remembering his coronation oath, the king could prevent monarchy from lapsing into tyranny.

Two passages from *La Monarchie de France* exemplify Seyssel's constitutionalism. In the first, he defines justice as 'the various ordinances that have been made by the kings themselves and afterwards confirmed and approved from time to time, and which tend to the preservation of the kingdom as a whole and of its parts. These have been so well kept for so long a time that the princes do not derogate from them. And when they would have wished to do so, their commands were not obeyed. This is especially true when it comes to their demesne and royal patrimony which they cannot alienate except in circumstances of necessity and only if the alienation is examined and approved by the sovereign courts of the Parlement or by the *Chambre des Comptes*.' Regarding justice, Seyssel states that it is undoubtedly 'better authorized in France than in any country we know in all the world. This is especially owing to the Parlements, which have been instituted to put a bridle on the absolute power that our kings would have wished to use.'[11]

[9] J. H. Franklin, *Jean Bodin and the Rise of Absolutist Theory* (Cambridge, 1973), pp. 2–8.
[10] Claude de Seyssel, *La monarchie de France*, ed. J. Poujol (1961); Claude de Seyssel, *The Monarchy of France* ed. D. R. Kelley (New Haven, CT and London, 1981).
[11] Franklin, pp. 14–15; W. F. Church, *Constitutional Thought in Sixteenth-Century France* (Cambridge, MA, 1941), pp. 22–42; Q. Skinner, *The Foundations of Modern Political Thought* (Cam-

Another treatise, dedicated to Francis shortly after his accession, was Guill-aume Budé's *L'institution du prince* (1518). Its purpose was to bring the author to the king's notice by entertaining and instructing him. Like many of his con-temporaries, Budé believed that a knowledge of history was essential to poli-tical success. He tried to point Francis in the right direction by stringing together, sometimes rather clumsily, stories from Scripture and from ancient histories. While sharing Seyssel's high regard for monarchy, he was prepared to allow the nobility only privileges, not a share of authority. As for ordinary people, Budé dismissed them contemptuously as politically inept, citing the expulsion of Themistocles from Athens as evidence of their inability to recog-nize real worth. Because of his conviction that royal authority was vested in the king alone, Budé attached enormous importance to his education. He advised the king to listen to wise counsellors, to respect his predecessors' ordinances, to safeguard the freedom and prosperity of his subjects and to abstain from war. Budé admitted, however, that the king was free to reject this advice, the only limit on his absolute power being the judgment of posterity.[12]

Budé's acceptance of royal absolutism was characteristic of a strongly roya-list ideology which came into its own during Francis's reign. Its origin may be traced back to the time of Louis XII, when Jean Ferrault wrote a tract, called *Twenty Special Privileges of the Most Christian King*. This claimed almost unlimited powers for the French monarchy. Under Francis, the monarchy was exalted by jurists, such as Barthélemy de Chasseneuz and Charles de Grass-aille. The former in his *Catalogus gloriae mundi* (1529) lists 208 attributes of majesty culled from the *Corpus Juris* and various mediaeval sources. The flavour of Grassaille's *Regalium Franciae libri duo* (1538) is well conveyed by some of its chapter headings which describe the king of France as 'more glori-ous than any other king', 'like the morning star amidst the northern cloud', 'the vicar of Christ in his kingdom', 'the king of kings', 'a second sun on earth', and 'like a corporeal god'. Yet even such adulators of monarchy did not entirely abandon constitutional principles. Thus Chasseneuz, in a work on the customs of Burgundy, suggested that, having been collected by order of the king, approved by the provincial estates and confirmed by the crown, they could not be suspended or suffer derogation by means of a *non obstante* clause. Yet he could not deny that ultimately the king might use his absolute power. While believing that the king owed his authority to God, the jurists upheld the fundamental laws. Grassaille viewed the Salic Law as a custom that had been originally instituted by the king. While glorifying the monarch, Grassaille

bridge, 1978), ii. 260–7; N. O. Keohane, *Philosophy and the State in France: The Renaissance to the Enlightenment* (Princeton, NJ, 1980), pp. 32–42.
12 C. Bontems, L.-P. Raybaud and J. P. Brancourt (eds.), *Le prince dans la France des XVIe et XVIIe siècles* (1965), pp. 1–139; Keohane, pp. 58–61; Skinner, i. 205–16; ii. 354–5.

97. Francis I as Julius Caesar. One of a series of preparatory drawings by Francesco
Primaticcio for the panels of cupboards in the *Cabinet du roi* at Fontainebleau.

denied him any personal or hereditary right to his authority; he saw this as devolving upon the king through the fundamental law and divine sanction.[13]

A question much discussed by legists under Francis I was the nature of the authority exercised by the king's officials. Were they simply agents exercising his authority or did they have a proprietary right in the authority they exercised within their respective spheres of jurisdiction? Except for Rebuffi, all the legists ruled that governmental authority belonged to the king alone. All offices and dignities, in Chasseneuz's judgment, flowed from the king as from a fountain. Yet he did not relegate the Parlement of Paris to a subordinate position. He achieved this by making it a participant in the exercise of the prerogative, describing its magistrates as part of the royal person. Chasseneuz even argued that an offence against them was *lèse-majesté*.

Although the Roman law concept of *merum imperium* embodied two kinds of authority – judicial and legislative – the French legists of the early sixteenth century tended to emphasize the former. Thus Chasseneuz, while insisting that jurisdiction belonged to the king alone, was ready to concede legislative authority to others as well. Many legists regarded the law of the constitution as the embodiment, albeit imperfect, of God's law on earth. They consequently envisaged the king's legislative role as preservative rather than innovative. This left jurisdiction as his primary prerogative. While exalting him, the legists argued that he should consult his officers in important matters of state, such as lawmaking. But their assumption that he was divinely inspired and, therefore, could do no wrong inevitably reduced the significance of counsel to little else than facilitating the establishment of justice through the exercise of reason.[14]

The most systematic defender of royal supremacy was Charles Du Moulin, whose *Commentaries on the Customs of Paris* began to appear in 1539. This attacked the feudal vision of society as a stratified and harmoniously ordered whole. Du Moulin refutes the idea that vassalage, including the notion of personal service, originated in Roman law. In his view it was a Frankish invention of the sixth century. In other words, the system of vassalage and seigneurial rights which survived in France was a late, customary and illegal usurpation of the absolute *Imperium*, originally and rightfully possessed by the French monarchy. A fief, according to Du Moulin, was simply a form of land-holding; it implied no rights of personal service from the vassal. No legalized form of personal subjection could be owed by anyone to the king, for he alone was 'the source of all justice, holding all jurisdictions and enjoying full *Imperium*'. Since he had complete control over 'all temporal lords, whether secular or ecclesiastical', they were all equally subject to his absolute authority 'for the exercise of their jurisdictions and lordships'.

---

[13] Skinner, ii. 259–60; Church, pp. 43–73; Franklin, pp. 6–7, 13–14, 16.   [14] Church, pp. 52–60.

Du Moulin's critique of feudal relationships resulted in a new absolutist orthodoxy, which inevitably served to lessen Seyssel's three constraints on the ruler's exercise of power. This did not happen overnight. Yet legists began to argue that the king's judicial authority could not be lawfully challenged by the Parlement. True, Chasseneuz insisted that the king could not rescind any of the Parlement's acts 'out of his ordinary power', but he also held that the king's power was both 'ordinary' and 'absolute'. This implied that the king might use his 'absolute' power to override the Parlement's judgments. Du Moulin took this idea to its logical conclusion: since all authority flowed from the king, no court, however exalted, could legally check his powers. The officers of the Parlement, in his view, owed their authority to the king and remained dependent upon him. A decade later, Rebuffi noted that 'at one time the highest courts even controlled kings themselves' whereas kings no longer obeyed them. 'It is well known to everyone', he wrote, '[that] it is not lawful for the Parlements to make appeals, but only to supplicate their prince.'

Another of Seyssel's arguments to be dismantled by Francis I's legists was his notion that judges were irremovable, even by the king. If this were so, Du Moulin argued, they would have been granted *Imperium* as well as *jurisdictio*. This could not be, since only the king had *Imperium*. Any grant of *jurisdictio*, in his opinion, could be revoked. It was always open to the king to recover rights emanating from himself. This effectively disposed of Seyssel's ideal of a mixed constitution with an independent judiciary.[15]

The realities of power

From the beginning of his reign Francis showed a strongly authoritarian disposition. He seems not to have considered himself bound by tradition and to believe that he had the right to depart from existing ordinances, institutions and methods of government. The concept of the feudal state, comprising semi-autonomous elements, seems to have been absent from his political thinking, and on several occasions he rejected the parallel, which the Parlement liked to draw, between itself and the Roman Senate. The king was supported in his authoritarianism by Chancellor Duprat, who, as a former *parlementaire*, was well qualified to deal with resistance from this quarter. He denied that the court had any right to oppose the king's wishes. 'We owe obedience to the king', he declared in 1518, 'and it is not for us to question his commands.' All authority, he said, including the Parlement's, came from the king; otherwise the kingdom would be an aristocracy, not a monarchy.[16] His words anticipated the absolutist theory soon to be enunciated by Du Moulin rather than the constitutionalism of Seyssel.

---

[15] Skinner, ii. 265–7; Church, pp. 106–7, 180, 193–4.   [16] Doucet, i. 49.

Policy was decided by the king alone with the advice of his council. This was never so clearly demonstrated as in the matter of the Concordat of Bologna, which was imposed upon the French people in spite of the Parlement's bitter opposition. Likewise no attempt was made to test popular opinion in any shape or form before the king decided in May 1526 to repudiate the treaty of Madrid.[17]

A most important constitutional event in the reign was the king's return to Paris in April 1527 following his captivity in Spain. The Parlement, as we have seen, had taken advantage of his absence by challenging the authority of his mother, the Regent, over beneficial appointments and her use of *évocations* to the *Grand Conseil*. The Parlement was even preparing to indict the Chancellor when the king returned. Francis had undoubtedly suffered a serious diminution of prestige among his subjects by reason of his defeat at Pavia and subsequent imprisonment. His return was accompanied by a determined effort to reassert his authority which culminated in the *lit de justice* of 24 July 1527, when he appeared before the Parlement amidst a truly theatrical display of absolute power.[18] President Guillart, in a long speech that opened the proceedings, dared to criticize many aspects of royal policy, notably the evocation of lawsuits from the Parlement to the *Grand Conseil*. The true seat of royal justice, he claimed, was the Parlement which had originated as 'a public assembly like a convention of estates'. Justice, he continued, was indivisible: just as there was only one sun, so there was only one king of France and one justice. If two were allowed to exist, there would be division between nobles, communities and subjects 'which is the desolation of kingdoms'. Yet Guillart had to admit the vulnerability of his position. 'We do not wish to cast doubt on or to dispute your authority', he declared 'for this would be a kind of sacrilege and we know well that you are above the laws and that the laws and ordinances cannot constrain you and that no coactive authority binds you to them. But we wish to say that you do not or should not wish to do all that lies in your power, but only that which is good and equitable, which is nothing other than justice.' 'To rule absolutely', Guillart continued, 'pertains to a nature that is brutal rather than reasonable', yet he could not deny the king's right to exercise his will 'in any particular or singular case'. All he could do was to advise him to use his absolute power as little as possible or, better still, not at all. Towards the end of this speech, Guillart tried to soothe the king: the *parlementaires*, he said, rejoiced as much over his appearance in their midst as did the Apostles when Christ appeared before them at the Resurrection.[19]

---

[17] See above pp. 95–100; 253–4.   [18] See above pp. 264–6.

[19] A.N., X[1a] 1530, ff. 350b–357b. For a full transcript of Guillart's speech and a discussion of its significance see my 'Francis I and the *lit de justice*: a "legend" defended' *F.H.*, 7 (1993) pp. 53–83. This takes issue with the interpretation offered in S. Hanley, *The "Lit de Justice" of the Kings of France: Constitutional Ideology in Legend, Ritual and Discourse* (Princeton, NJ, 1983).

Francis was unmoved by Guillart's flattery. That afternoon he held a meeting of his council at which an edict was drawn up which effectively subordinated the Parlement to his supreme authority.[20] In particular, it was required to obtain each year his formal confirmation of its delegated authority. By ordering the Parlement to register the decree as it stood without imposing it by his presence, Francis manifested his authority more powerfully than if he had let the court shelter under the customary formula – *lecta et publicata de expresso mandato domini regis* – implying duress. Having re-asserted his authority, Francis was, it seems, content to allow the Parlement to resume its judicial and political functions. The court even continued to submit remonstrances on a variety of matters till the end of the reign. The king, however, did not abandon the principles laid down in the edict of 24 July 1527. He expected total obedience on certain matters, notably appointments to benefices. He did not easily forget the troubles of his captivity and resented the privilege of free election which certain churches, abbeys and priories had retained under the Concordat of Bologna. In 1531, therefore, he obtained a papal bull suspending the privilege during his reign. The Parlement, on being required to register the bull, waited six months before debating the matter. Although the *gens du roi* recommended registration, a majority of councillors opposed it. They sent a deputation to the king, who insisted on immediate registration. But another six months elapsed before Francis renewed his request, saying that his patience was exhausted. The Parlement, however, continued its delaying tactics and the bull was never registered. The king, it seems, managed without it.

In August 1539, as the Parlement decided to conduct a detailed examination of the ordinance of Villers-Cotterêts, Francis ordered its immediate registration. He expressed surprise that the court should be seeking legal advice after debating the ordinance for two and a half days. Chancellor Poyet wrote to the Parlement as impertinently as his predecessor, Duprat, would have done. Eventually, after more tergiversation, the Parlement agreed to register the ordinance while reserving the right to submit remonstrances at the earliest opportunity.

Sometimes the king and the Parlement worked together effectively. In 1540, for example, they discussed, point by point and at great length, a major ordinance on the kingdom's coinage. The *avocat-général* denounced various malpractices whereby the *généraux des monnaies* hoped to make large profits for themselves at the public expense. This was warmly received by the king and his council and a commission set up, including presidents and councillors of the Parlement, to devise a new ordinance, which was eventually published.

[20] A.N., X^{1a} 1530, f. 359. The edict is summarized in E. Maugis, *Histoire du Parlement de Paris* (1913), i. 582–3.

Overall it is not easy to decide who was the victor in the long tussle between crown and Parlement. Francis undoubtedly triumphed on 24 July 1527. The Parlement never again tried to fly in the face of his authority as it had done during the captivity. But, if Maugis is to be believed, the court emerged wiser and stronger from the experience. It had learnt to bend its head in the storm and gained a sense of what it could effectively achieve. At the same time, it earned the cautious respect of the king and his ministers by the bold stand it occasionally offered. For all his violent outbursts and displays of impatience, Francis learnt to live with the Parlement.[21]

Francis claimed absolute sovereignty over all the parlements: their role, he affirmed was to administer justice, not to question royal decisions. But members of the provincial parlements regarded themselves not only as supreme judges under the king, but also as defenders of provincial rights and privileges. They consequently opposed the creation of offices and the imposition of extra-ordinary taxes. They were more successful in opposing the crown than the Parlement of Paris because of their remoteness from the centre of government. This caused delays in the sending of *lettres de jussion* and made the holding of *lits de justice* difficult, if not impossible. Yet the king could make life difficult for a provincial parlement if he set his mind to it, as the parlement of Rouen discovered in 1540.

The magistrates of Rouen had an unsavoury reputation under Francis. It was said that they wore beards and dressed in a 'dissolute' manner, arrived late in court or suffering from hangovers, spent too much time playing tennis, cards or dice games, frequented bawdy houses, associated with people of low station, committed grave indiscretions, took bribes and allowed other improper con-siderations to affect their conduct as judges. The First President, Marcillac, complained in November 1539 that 'female suitors who lacked physical beauty were advised to bring with them beautiful girls or chambermaids when they called on magistrates concerned with their cases'. He warned his colleagues to mend their ways; otherwise, he said, 'the king, our sovereign lord, will be forced to intervene'.[22]

Having set up the parlement of Rouen, Francis was all the more aggrieved by reports of its disreputable activities. In 1527 he proposed that its councillors be distributed among other courts of the kingdom and replaced by members of other parlements. This was not followed up, though the parlement received a 'rough and strange' message from the king. No further action was taken till Chancellor Poyet clashed with the court over several matters, notably its oppo-sition to the ordinance of Villers-Cotterêts. Whereas in Paris the ordinance had

---

[21] *Ibid.*, i. 584–91.
[22] A. Floquet, *Histoire du parlement de Normandie* (Rouen, 1840), i. 505–22.

been registered within a month, at Rouen it encountered innumerable delays. Even more serious was the parlement's deliberate omission of sixteen clauses it found unpalatable, as the ordinance was registered on 16 June 1540.

Early in August the king forbade the parlement to go into recess, saying that he would be coming to Rouen with important things to tell the court. Fearing the worst, the parlement sent a deputation on 20 August to the Chancellor, who had preceded the king. After recalling that the sovereign courts had been created as 'an example and a light to others', Poyet castigated the magistrates. Marcillac begged him not to believe slanders and to placate the king. Six days later the parlement hastily registered the ordinance of Villers-Cotterêts in its entirety. It then sent a deputation to Francis at the palace of Saint-Ouen. 'I will go, Messieurs', he said, 'to see my parlement; worthy members (*gens de bien*) will be pleased and the rest displeased.' The parlement assembled next day expecting a *lit de justice*. Instead they were treated to a diatribe lasting four hours from the Chancellor. 'The king', he said, 'had planted a vineyard with choice plants; he had set up a winepress nearby in anticipation of the harvest; but the vines had produced only wild and sour grapes.' On 10 September the magistrates were called before the king. He informed them sternly that he was cancelling several of the parlement's recent decrees and closing it down till further notice. Later that day the court surrendered its seal to the king, and posters announcing its suspension were put up in Rouen.[23]

There was, however, too much crime in Normandy to allow a complete suspension of royal justice. Francis consequently commissioned some of the Rouen magistrates – presumably the *gens de bien* – to continue judging criminal cases in the town, and others to hold *Grands Jours* at Bayeux. *Grands Jours* were commissions of *parlementaires* sent out from time to time to various parts of the kingdom in order to buttress the administration of justice and relieve the parlements of part of their heavy load of work. They usually comprised a civil and a criminal chamber and their venue, which was chosen by the king, varied according to circumstances.[24] The magistrates who served at Bayeux in September 1540 had to deal with 'the unruly insolence of the nobility and the connivance of the local judges'. So critical was the situation that they had to invoke military help from the governor's lieutenant. Even so, their judicial impact was limited, as numerous criminals fled the area when the *Grands Jours* were announced. Many executions consequently had to be carried out in effigy: a life-size dummy of the condemned man, dressed in his own clothes, was hanged, beheaded or broken on the wheel. But the *Grands Jours* were not always so helpless: for example, they reformed religious houses in the Cotentin and Bessin, and punished many corrupt or negligent officers of the crown. Yet

---

[23] B.N., ms. Dupuy 17, f. 168b; Floquet, i. 522–35; ii. 1–15. [24] Doucet, *Institutions*, i. 217–20.

the effects of the *Grands Jours* were short-lived: by 1548, when they returned to Bayeux, Lower Normandy had reverted to a state of near anarchy.[25]

The two commissions issued by Francis in September 1540 enabled the Rouen *parlementaires* to redeem themselves. On 7 January 1541 they were told that he had decided to reopen their court. Nine councillors, however, were excluded from the reprieve, though eight were reinstated subsequently after they had been examined by a royal commission. The only exception, Antoine Le Marchant, was banished from the kingdom after a long imprisonment. The other magistrates were warned to perform their duties diligently and equitably, and to carry out the royal ordinances. They were forbidden to allow the proctor of the provincial estates to 'contradict, discuss, deduce or allege anything against verification of the edicts'. The king, they were told, would be watching them closely; defaulters would be punished and the rest exalted.[26]

The power to tax

At a practical level the degree of royal absolutism that existed in early sixteenth-century France may be measured by the amount of fiscal control exercised by the king. How far was he free to tax his subjects at will? Francis, as we have seen, had more control over the purses of his subjects than any of his fellow-monarchs in western Europe. Ever since the fifteenth century the *taille* had been raised each year without the consent of the people's representatives. Francis regarded the Estates General, the only national representative body in France, as useless and dangerous, and was never so weak as to be compelled to call them. The only time a meeting of the Estates General was seriously considered during the reign was in 1525 during the king's captivity.[27] It was discussed by the Parlement, but fear was expressed that the deputies might be tempted to wrest power from the regent or to control her actions too closely. The idea was, therefore, dropped, and the estates remained in abeyance till 1560, when religious unrest and royal bankruptcy forced Francis's grandson to call them. In the meantime, the *taille* increased from about 2.4 million *livres* in 1515 to 4.6 million in 1544–45.[28]

Taxation, however, was far more than the *taille*. As Francis became involved in costly wars, he found his traditional resources insufficient for his needs. Among expedients he was forced to use were the sale of crown lands and offices. Both were strongly resisted by the parlements. The sale of crown lands was in breach of the 'fundamental law' forbidding alienations of the royal demesne which the Parlement of Paris was committed to defend. It also had

[25] Floquet, ii. 16–42.   [26] *Ibid.*, ii. 42–80.   [27] Doucet, ii. 98–9; see above p. 227.
[28] P. Hamon, 'L'argent du roi', i. 103. M. Wolfe gives a figure of 5.3 million in 1547. *The Fiscal System of Renaissance France* (New Haven, CT and London, 1972), p. 99.

serious fiscal implications. When the king sold off parts of his patrimony, he was inevitably diminishing his 'ordinary' revenue, and was likely to try to recoup the loss by increasing taxation. The Parlement pointed to the adverse effect alienation would have on the king's 'poor subjects', but Francis was unmoved. In the end, his alienations were always registered, albeit under protest.[29] The sale of offices was another expedient much used by the king in spite of opposition by the parlements. As the Venetian ambassador wrote in 1546: 'offices are infinite in number and increase daily . . . half of which would suffice'.[30] Existing office-holders viewed with concern the multiplication of offices, which inevitably undermined their own status and income. They tried to limit the practice and sometimes obtained the suppression of a new office by buying it up themselves. Resistance to the creation of offices also took the form of dilatoriness by the parlements in registering the edicts of creation or in admitting the king's nominees. A particularly hard struggle was fought over the *Chambre du domaine*. Francis became very impatient at the Parlement's slowness in admitting councillors to the new court. He asked that it should be allowed to function below full strength and asked to be kept posted on failures in the examinations for admission. After more delay his displeasure became manifest: the *avocat-général* Rémon was received 'with such bitter words that his hair stood on end as he heard the king threaten the court with the last extremities'. He feared the worst, but for the grace of God. The Parlement accordingly speeded up the examination of the king's nominees. No sooner had this process been completed than he created twenty-one new councillors in the Parlement, including two presidents and twelve councillors in the *Grand' Chambre*, a move which again was resisted.[31]

The towns of France were often the target of fiscal exploitation by the crown. The *solde des 50,000 hommes de pied*, which was introduced in 1543, was not a new tax, as we have seen, but it was novel to the extent of being levied annually, even in peacetime.[32] Its impact on certain towns was far reaching. For example, Lyons's share of the *solde* was 60,000 *livres*. Strictly speaking,

---

[29] Doucet, i. 60–3; C.A.F., i. 102, 115, 379, 578, 648, 676, 742.

[30] R. Mousnier, *La vénalité des offices sous Henri IV et Louis XIII*, 2nd edn (1971), p. 41.

[31] A.N., X[1a] 1551, fols. 527a–528a; Maugis, i. 159–61. R. Descimon ('Modernité et archaisme de l'état monarchique: le Parlement de Paris saisi par la vénalité (XVI siècle)', in *Genèse de l'état moderne*, 1990) has drawn a useful distinction between two sorts of venality: 'customary venality', which had become established in the Middle Ages and related to offices serving the royal person, and 'legal venality', secured by the creation of the *parties casuelles* in 1522, which related to public offices, especially judicial ones. In his view: 'the innovation of 1522 played a decisive role in the processes whereby the French monarchical state was partially emancipated from its feudal and mystical foundations'.

[32] G. Zeller, *Les institutions de la France au XVIe siècle* (1948), p. 259; C.A.F., iii. 9783; iv. 13039; P. Benedict (ed.), *Cities and Social Change in Early Modern France* (London, 1989), p. 9; *Ordonnances*, ix. 74–81; B. Chevalier, *Les bonnes villes de France du XIVe au XVIe siècle* (1982), p. 40. See above p. 504.

it was a forced loan rather than a tax, since the king undertook to repay it over three years in four instalments, the debt being guaranteed against the revenues of Languedoc and the customs of Lyons. The money was raised by the municipal government or *Consulat* from the chief inhabitants, who offered no resistance, as they had been promised reimbursement. The king, however, broke his word: after two instalments the repayments ceased and the customs of Lyons were granted to two Italian bankers in settlement of other royal debts. In 1546, when the loan should have been cleared, the government still owed Lyons 33,000 *livres*. Such was the dissatisfaction among creditors that the *Consulat* was no longer able to call on them when the crown renewed its demand for the *solde* in 1544 and in succeeding years. It was forced to borrow from Italian bankers and reimburse itself by raising two indirect taxes: the *pied fourché*, a duty on cattle and meat imports, and in 1544, the *six derniers pour livre*, a duty on all imports other than foodstuffs. Indirect taxes of this kind were extremely unpopular, not only among the poor, who had to pay more for their food, clothing and fuel, but also among certain privileged groups, notably the clergy and foreign merchants. The clergy argued that they were being taxed twice, since they had already paid clerical tenths. Foreign merchants regarded the new taxes as in breach of the privileges given to them by the crown: they threatened to quit Lyons and disrupt its fairs. In the end, the *Consulat* had to give way: the *pied fourché* was abolished after three years and the *six deniers* after only thirteen months. As a result, Lyons failed to recoup its loans to the government; in 1547 it was left with a deficit of 107,000 *livres* and no revenues with which to clear it.[33]

In other towns, too, the *solde des 50,000 hommes* caused serious problems. Paris repeatedly asked the king to reduce its contribution, but to no avail; it was, therefore, obliged to resort to various foot-dragging procedures, which provoked royal threats of reprisal. In 1546 the *Bureau de la Ville* explained that the Parisians wanted to help the king, but could no longer do so because of the heavy burdens imposed on them in the past. Now, they were utterly wretched, crushed by taxes and debts and at grips with the plague. They implored the king to show them pity and treat them as part of his family. In March 1547 the *Bureau* reminded him of the privileges enjoyed by Paris in the past. 'The capital of Christendom', it said, 'had never been subject to taxation and had once enjoyed a reputation for freedom equalling, perhaps surpassing that of Rome or any other city, but it had now fallen into extreme poverty.'[34] Was Francis moved by this appeal? We cannot tell, for he died before replying. His successor,

---

[33] R. Doucet, *Finances municipales et crédit public à Lyon au XVIe siècle* (1937), pp. 24–8.

[34] *R.D.B.V.P.*, iii. 72, 74–5; P. Champion, *Paris au temps de la Renaissance: l'envers de la tapisserie* (1935), pp. 39–42. See also my 'Francis I and Paris', *History*, lxvi (1981), 18–33.

Henri II, reduced the *solde* in 1547, but did not abolish it. In 1555 he extended it, even to villages.

Representative assemblies

In the absence of the Estates General, the only national body remotely comparable to them which Francis summoned was a meeting held in the *Grand' Chambre* in December 1527. Historians have usually called it an Assembly of Notables. Sarah Hanley has called it a *lit de justice*.[35] It was described as such by Séraphin du Tillet, clerk of the Parlement, but this evidence is not conclusive. A clerk of the Parlement often allowed weeks, even months, to pass before writing up entries in the registers from his own minutes. This enabled him 'to be creative in his depiction of events if he chose to do so'.[36] Thus du Tillet may have been mistaken. The assembly of December 1527 contained far more notables than usually attended a *lit de justice*. The 200 delegates were drawn from the nobility, clergy, parlements and city of Paris. Yet the assembly was not fully representative, for, unlike the Estates General, it was not preceded by general elections.

Hanley has suggested that the meeting was intended to focus attention on the king's 'role as legislator and guardian of French public law', but its purpose was clearly different.[37] Its aims were first, to secure legal endorsement by the parlements of the decision already taken by the king and his council to break the treaty of Madrid, and secondly, to raise money from the king's subjects in order to pay a ransom for his sons or to wage war on the Emperor.[38] The semi-representative character of the assembly was determined by these objectives. Russell Major's view is eminently sensible: 'It seems useless to assign the name of a particular institution to the meeting; the king could summon whom he pleased to give advice, and this was the group he had chosen.'[39]

At the provincial level representative estates continued to exist in a large part of France. The principal *pays d'états* were Normandy, Languedoc, Dauphiné, Burgundy, Provence and Brittany. In most of them the three estates were represented, but they were not always chosen in the same way; nor was their role identical from one province to another. The clergy sat as landowners, not as representatives of the church, so as to avoid binding it to decisions taken by the estates. The nobles represented not only themselves but the rural population

---

[35] S. Hanley, *The "Lit de Justice" of the Kings of France*, p. 50.
[36] Mack P. Holt, 'The King in Parlement: The Problem of the *Lit de Justice* in Sixteenth-Century France', *H.J.*, 31 (1988), 507–23.
[37] S. Hanley, *The "Lit de Justice"*, p. 81.
[38] P. Hamon, 'Un après-guerre financier: la rançon de François premier', *Etudes champenoises* (1990), p. 12.
[39] J. Russell Major, *Representative Institutions*, p. 137.

generally. As for the third estate, it consisted of urban representatives only. There were numerous local variations. In Normandy, for example, a complicated electoral system gave the third estate a numerical preponderance in the general assembly; in Languedoc a high proportion of nobles and clergy failed to attend, while the third estate was made up of representatives of municipal oligarchies; in Brittany and Provence the nobility tended to dominate the estates, the upper clergy seldom attended and the third estate was again restricted to urban oligarchs. None of the estates was democratic: the majority of the people, both rural and urban, had no voice.[40]

The estates depended for their existence on the king. He called them, fixed the date and place of their meeting, appointed the president and determined their agenda. His commissioners put forward demands, negotiated with the delegates and met some of their requests. Usually the estates met once a year, but they could meet more often. In Normandy, for example, there were nearly always two meetings a year and sometimes three until 1528; thereafter there was only one each year except in 1544. The frequency of meetings was determined by the crown's fiscal needs.[41] In theory, the voting of a subsidy was conditional: this was the theory at least in Languedoc before 1538. The royal commissioners were supposed to attend to the estates' 'very humble supplications' before supply (octroi) was granted. But the estates expected little of the commissioners; they knew that the only decisions that mattered were those taken by the king and his council, which invariably followed a grant by several months. In 1538 Francis refused to accept even the theory; he ordered his commissioners at the estates of Albi not to reply to their doléances before octroi had been granted. The estates after protesting, accepted a compromise. They drafted their doléances on the eve of the vote and sent them direct to the king, by-passing his commissioners. In September 1541 the estates of Montpellier were forbidden to send a deputy to the king until they had agreed verbally to a subsidy. Even then, he rejected six demands out of seven.[42]

It has been argued that Francis, far from being absolute, treated the Norman estates 'in the same good-natured way as had his predecessors'.[43] It is true that he instructed his commissioners to ask them 'to grant freely' (libérallement octroier) the sum he wanted, but what did this freedom amount to? Certainly not freedom to refuse the taille or even to demand its reduction. The estates could only resist demands for supplementary taxes or crues, usually to no effect. In 1516 a delegate wanted a vote to be conditional on the abolition of all 'the innovations created since the start of the reign'. The 'innovations', however, remained, and each year the estates voted for ever larger crues. In

---

[40] Doucet, Institutions, i. 337–59.   [41] Prentout, Les Etats Provinciaux de Normandie, i. 256.
[42] Dognon, Institutions du Languedoc, pp. 574–5.   [43] Prentout, ii. 473.

Languedoc the situation was much the same. The estates sometimes delayed a *crue*, but they could never avoid it completely or reduce the amount. So predictable was their compliance that the king and *généraux des finances* often assigned funds on a *crue* still to be voted by the estates.[44]

In Dauphiné an extension of the administrative jurisdiction granted to the estates by Francis in 1537 and confirmed in 1542 did not result in a resurgence of provincial autonomy. As Van Doren has shown, 'the weight of the war levies during the 1540s and 1550s deepened divisions among and within the communities in ways that prevented the Estates from consolidating an effective defense of provincial liberties'.[45]

The estates frequently complained of the king's fiscal expedients, but seldom persuaded him to abandon them. In 1517, for example, Francis planned to extend the salt tax to the whole of Normandy. The estates protested, whereupon their spokesman was prosecuted for insulting the king. Francis dropped his proposal, but only for a time: in June 1546 the salt tax was restored. It also caused trouble in Languedoc, where the estates claimed that in 1488 they had been promised that no such tax would be imposed without their consent. Francis acknowledged their privilege but violated it at the same time. In 1537 the *crue* on salt became permanent in Languedoc. Its purpose was allegedly to pay the wages of the sovereign courts, but, as the estates pointed out, the *octroi* had already been voted for this purpose. Francis chose to ignore them.[46]

The creation of offices was a frequent source of trouble between the king and the estates. In 1543 Francis created a *Chambre des Comptes* at Rouen. The members were to buy their offices and receive their wages out of a local tax on goods. At the request of the people of Rouen, the king called a meeting of the estates – one of the rare instances when the initiative was theirs. On 5 April he offered to drop the new chamber in return for a composition of 220,000 *livres* (100,000 more thn he would have raised from the sale of the offices concerned). In the end, the estates paid 246,875 *livres* for the chamber's suppression. In Languedoc, too, the estates found that the only way of getting harmful offices abolished was to buy them up. They could not be sure, however, that the offices would not reappear in due course; they often did.[47]

It is a mistake to think that the king needed the consent of the inhabitants before raising taxes in a *pays d'états*. In Languedoc, the towns, clergy and nobility were all taxed regardless of the estates. Most towns were taxed like the countryside: only Carcassonne was totally exempt and Toulouse and Nar-

---

[44] *Ibid.*, i. 257; Dognon, p. 504.
[45] L. S. Van Doren, 'War Taxation, Institutional Change and Social Conflict in Provincial France – the Royal *Taille* in Dauphiné, 1494–1559', *Proceedings of the American Philosophical Society*, cxxi, 1 (February 1977), 94.
[46] Prentout, ii. 266–9; iii. 141–64; Dognon, pp. 519–20.
[47] Prentout, i. 275–8; Dognon, pp. 521–2.

bonne partially so. Francis none the less imposed the *solde des gens de pied* on them. When the estates claimed exemption, he recognized their privilege in return for a composition. Toulouse, however, was asked for a subsidy. Again the estates protested, claiming that it was not a *ville franche*. Francis, however, would not budge: 'Where there is a profit to be made in Languedoc', he said, 'the people of Toulouse are always there; but where there is an obligation, they declare themselves exempt.' The *solde*, in fact, became a heavy burden on the town. The church, too, was roughly handled by Francis. He raised a series of tenths without the consent of either the estates or assembly of the French church. Bishops were ordered to take the money directly off their clergy. As for the nobles, they had to suffer the *ban et arrière-ban*, sometimes four or five times in a year and were kept under arms at their own expense for months. The estates asked for the length of feudal service to be restricted to forty days: in January 1544 it was fixed at three months within France and forty days outside. Commoners owning noble fiefs, even very small ones, had to compound for military service.[48]

The burden of supporting military garrisons or troops passing through Languedoc was a standing grievance with the estates. In 1522 Francis promised to reimburse the province's expenditure on his army, but he did not keep his word. A year later, at the request of the estates, he fixed a tariff for supplies bought by his troops, but it was not enforced. The estates did obtain a reduction of the number of garrisons in Languedoc, but it rose again following Montmorency's fall from power. Attempts made by the estates to ensure a fair distribution of the military burden proved unworkable. Languedoc had to pay large sums in 1536 for the camp at Avignon and in 1542 for the siege of Perpignan. In neither case were the estates consulted.

The amount of taxes voted by the estates cannot be taken as a reliable estimate of the amount of cash actually raised by the king in a given province. The accounts of a single diocese in Languedoc show that two-fifths of the taxes raised there were unknown to the estates.[49]

Are we to conclude that the estates no longer had a significant role to play in the state? This would be a rash conclusion, for their petitions were not exclusively concerned with defending local privileges: they also dealt with administrative and economic matters about which no disagreement necessarily existed between them and the crown. It was to their mutual advantage, for example, to expose and punish corruption or negligence on the part of royal officials. The estates might also have some useful suggestions to make regarding economic matters, such as trade. The seriousness with which such suggestions were received by the crown is attested by comments such as 'reasonable', 'granted',

---

[48] *Ibid.*, pp. 524–32.   [49] *Ibid.*, pp. 534–44.

or 'they will have letters on this' to be found in the margins of the *doléances*. Yet the effectiveness of the estates under Francis was limited to matters of secondary importance to the crown; where its financial interest was at stake, they were virtually powerless.[50]

While conceding that Francis was a 'strong' monarch who occasionally imposed his will on the estates, particularly in fiscal matters, Russell Major has argued that the reign failed to check the revival of the estates which, in his view, spanned the late fifteenth and early sixteenth centuries. Francis, he writes, 'accepted the existence of the provincial and local estates, recognized their right to give consent to taxation and generally respected their privileges'.[51] This is strictly correct, but the king's official words were often belied by his deeds. His authoritarianism was widely recognized by contemporary observers. Thus Prince Philip, writing to his father the Emperor in January 1547, stated that Francis ruled like a despot rather than a natural overlord, following his whim rather than his reason, and that the French people were willing to put up with anything.[52]

'Limited absolutism'

Historians, who have attempted to label the monarchy of Francis I, may be divided into two camps: those whose standpoint has been the centre of the kingdom, looking outwards, and those who have approached it from the periphery. The first group have seen it as 'absolute'; the second as 'contractual' or 'popular and consultative'. Both views deserve serious consideration. Every contemporary theorist, as we have seen, believed that the king had an absolute authority given to him by God, but many believed that he should exercise it with moderation and always in the interest of his subjects. But Francis frequently acted in an authoritarian manner allowing no room for opposition or even criticism. His ruthless enforcement of the Concordat of Bologna in the face of bitter opposition by the Parlement and University of Paris hardly suggests a willingness to consult his subjects. When the estates of Languedoc claimed the right of exemption from the garrisoning of troops, Francis replied: 'this kingdom is one body and monarchy'. All his subjects, he explained, needed to be treated alike, since he esteemed and loved them all equally; if he exempted some, others would have to shoulder a proportionately heavier burden. This hardly suggests a desire to preserve local autonomy. On another occasion Francis declared: 'in times of necessity all privileges cease, and not only privileges but common laws as well, for necessity knows no law'. The

[50] *Ibid.*, pp. 577–80.
[51] J. Russell Major, *Representative Government in Early Modern France*, p. 55.
[52] C.S.P. *Span.*, viii. no. 384, p. 552.

estates certainly did not see him as a 'contractual' monarch: they complained in 1522 that he was treating them 'as if they had never had nor acquired the said privileges'.[53] True, he did sometimes bargain with them, but only over the means of raising a sum, not over the sum itself. He did not mind suppressing offices as long as he received as much money from their suppression as from their sale. In non-fiscal matters, he could be flexible: the estates might hope for a favourable reversal of royal policy, but in the long term it tried to undermine provincial autonomy. The king's philosophy was summed up by Poyet in 1540: 'The king is not asking for advice as to whether or not they [his laws] are to be observed; once the prince has decreed them one must proceed; no one has the right to interpret, adjust or diminish them.'[54] A monarchy holding such views cannot be deemed 'contractual' or 'popular and consultative'.

Francis liked to think of himself as 'absolute'. But was he so in practice as well as in theory? At a practical level it was possible for a ruler to be more or less 'absolute' according to circumstances. Francis was undoubtedly a strong monarch, but he could not ignore the foundations of mediaeval privilege on which his monarchy rested. Royal legislation was subject to ratification by the parlements, and, in the *pays d'états* at least, royal taxation was subject, in theory, to the consent of the people's representatives. The enforcement of the law depended on a willingness to obey not always evinced by local authorities. The testimony of the *Grands Jours* of Bayeux shows that even near Paris law and order had largely broken down by 1540. However ineffective the provincial estates may have been in resisting the crown's fiscal pressure, they nevertheless survived. All of this points to an absolutism that is far from complete.

David Parker has shown how vulnerable the French crown remained in the early sixteenth century.[55] Its recent advances, far from resolving the antagonism between centralizing and decentralizing forces within the body politic actually made it worse. The lack of institutional homogeneity stood revealed. In the absence of a national representative institution on the model of the English parliament, the French king had to contend with a multiplicity of local interests. Apart from the provincial estates, many towns retained substantial political and financial privileges. In spite of Francis's fiscal reforms, localism and particularism continued to make an impact on the revenue system. Taxation alone could not sustain the increasing burden of royal expenditure, particularly in wartime. The king had to fall back on fiscal expedients: while some increased his dependence on financiers, others served to buttress provincialism. The sale of offices, for instance, helped to reinforce local autonomy. Royal offices became the patrimony of well-to-do provincial families who used them

---

[53] Dognon, pp. 576–7.   [54] Floquet, ii. 9.
[55] D. Parker, *The Making of French Absolutism* (London, 1983), pp. 12–27.

to preserve their privileged status. Likewise, many nobles found opportunities for consolidating their position while serving in the provincial parlements. The constraints on monarchy were social, as well as institutional and legal. The nobles through their land ownership, domination of the peasantry and capacity to use force were the main obstacle in the path of an extension of royal power. Their loyalty to the crown could not be assumed: it had to be secured by concessions, the most important being tax exemption. This was 'a permanent impediment to the mobilization of the kingdom's wealth'.[56] The system of provincial governorships was a two-edged weapon: it could be used either to extend royal power or to preserve noble interests. Being a patrimonial, not a bureaucratic, form of administration, it conferred on the governors enormous powers of patronage that might be used against the crown. As captains in the *gendarmerie*, they could make or break the careers of the men who served in it. The *gendarmerie* has been described as 'the Renaissance monarchy's compromise with the indigenous patron-client networks in the provinces'.[57] Effective government depended on the crown's ability to manipulate personal and patrimonial ties.

Under Francis's strong rule the limits on monarchy were generally contained. With the exception of the Constable of Bourbon, the high nobility was loyal to the crown and even aided its centralizing efforts. The clergy and the towns may have complained about fiscal burdens imposed upon them by the king, but their obedience never wavered. The parlements and estates were also broadly submissive. And this situation continued to hold good till the accidental death of Henri II in 1559 deprived the ship of state of a strong hand on the tiller. The Wars of Religion, which broke out in 1562, exposed the structural weaknesses of the Valois monarchy. For almost a century its survival hung in the balance, but in the end, under Louis XIV it emerged stronger – more 'absolute' – than ever before.

As Denis Richet has shown, much needed to happen before absolutism, even in an imperfect form, could develop in France.[58] The doctrine of resistance evolved by the Huguenots in the late sixteenth century, the upheaval of the Fronde and the challenge of Cartesianism all prompted a hardening (*durcissement*) of the ideological and institutional fabric of monarchy. This process was accompanied by a huge increase in royal officialdom. One has only to compare the number of office-holders per head of population in 1515 with that in 1665 to see the distance that separated Francis's administration from that of Louis XIV. The total number of fiscal and judicial office-holders

---

[56] *Ibid.*, p. 26.
[57] R. R. Harding, *The Anatomy of a Power Elite. The Provincial Governors of Early Modern France*, (New Haven, CT, 1978), p. 25.
[58] D. Richet, *La France Moderne: l'esprit des institutions* (1973), pp. 37–40, 54–9.

under Francis has been estimated at 5,000: that is to say, one per 115 square kilometres or per 3,000 inhabitants (assuming a total population of 15 million). Louis XIV had eleven times as many servants to impose his will on his 20 million subjects.[59] It stands to reason that Francis was less able to be 'absolute' than Louis XIV. He could only point in the direction of the absolutism that developed under Richelieu and beyond. An 'absolutism' that is complete in theory yet imperfect in practice is best described as 'limited absolutism'.

[59] J. Jacquart, *François Ier* (1981), pp. 282–3. Rather different figures, based on an estimated total population of 18 million, are given by R. Mousnier, *Le conseil du roi de Louis XII à la révolution* (1970), pp. 17–20.

Chapter twenty-seven

Le roy est mort! Vive le roy!

News of Henry VIII's death on 28 January 1547 caused rejoicing at the French court. According to the imperial ambassador, Saint-Mauris, the duchesse d'Etampes ran to Queen Eleanor's bedchamber at an early hour, shouting at the top of her voice: 'News! News! We have lost our chief enemy, and the King has commanded me to come and tell you of it!' This greatly upset the queen, who began by thinking that her brother, the Emperor, had died. Doubtless the rejoicing would have been even wilder had this been so. Diplomatic forms, of course, concealed the realities. Thus Annebault told the English ambassador's servant of Francis's grief over the loss of his 'good and true friend', but the king was seen that same day 'laughing much and enjoying himself with his ladies'.[1] Soon afterwards, he allegedly received a message, sent by Henry from his death bed, reminding him that he too was mortal. He became depressed and fell into a fever.[2] In mid February, however, he left Saint-Germain and visited Villepreux, Dampierre and Limours. After hunting from a litter for three days at Rochefort-en-Yvelines, he set off for Paris, where he planned to attend a memorial service for Henry. But at the château of Rambouillet, home of Jacques d'Angennes, he became too ill to move.[3]

Among contemporary accounts of Francis's last days, one of the most informative was sent to the Parlement by Pierre du Chastel, bishop of Mâcon, the king's confessor. On 20 March, he tells us, Francis began to prepare for death: after hearing Mass, he made his confession and took communion. Then, after making a public confession, he admitted that he had broken God's commandments frequently and variously, but expressed confidence in His mercy.

---

[1] A. Castan, 'La mort de François Ier', *Mémoires de la Société d'émulation du Doubs*, 5th ser. iii (1878), 441–2; *C.S.P. Span.*, ix. 493.

[2] *Ibid.*, ix. 62–4.

[3] Castan, pp. 442–4; *C.A.F.*, viii. pp. 532–3; du Bellay, iv. 334–5. A memorial service for Henry VIII was celebrated at Notre-Dame on 21 March 1547. An orator praised his magnanimity, liberality and prudence, and certain books published in his name (*C.S.P.*, ix. 498–9).

98. Francis I in old age. This drawing by François Clouet may have been used to prepare the king's funeral effigy.

Turning to the Dauphin, Francis urged him to defend the kingdom, honour justice, and bear in mind the divine obligation incumbent on all monarchs to govern well. That afternoon, Princess Marguerite called on her father. 'Touchez-là', he said, holding out his hand, but he was so moved that he fell silent and turned on his side. On 29 March, he asked for extreme unction and, repeating his earlier admonitions to the Dauphin, said that, as far as justice was concerned, his conscience was clear: he could think of no one whom he had treated unjustly. Shortly before midnight he received the last sacrament, took communion and blessed his son. Francis spoke of visions from which he was being shielded by Christ and talked of religion. Next morning, he recognized some of his servants and thanked them for all they had done. He embraced and blessed the Dauphin. Then, after hearing Mass, he expressed confidence in the glory that awaits the children of God. That evening, the Dauphin received his father's blessing for the third time. During the night the king was disturbed by more visions and recited various passages from Scripture. On Thursday 31 March, after hearing Mass for the last time, Francis forgave his enemies and spoke of the heavenly crown he was about to receive. He asked to hear a homily by Chrysostom, but was given one by Origen instead. Noticing the error, he asked if Origen was not suspect. That afternoon, as his speech grew indistinct, he clasped and kissed a crucifix. Then, recalling God's forgiveness of the good thief, he said: '*In manus tuas, Domine, commendo spiritum meum.*' His last word was 'Jesus'. Finally, having lost speech and sight, he made the sign of the cross over his bed several times and breathed his last.[4]

Another account of the king's last moments, addressed to the regent of the Netherlands by Saint-Mauris, suggests that his conscience may not have been so clear. Francis, he writes, admitted to his son that he had harmed his subjects, especially by going to war on trifling pretexts. He expressed remorse for his 'great practices' against the good of Christendom (was he thinking of the Turks?) and urged the Dauphin to repair the injustices done to Charles III of Savoy, who had been deprived of his territories for eleven years. He also warned his son against being ruled by others, as he himself had been ruled by Madame d'Etampes. He asked Henri to settle certain debts he had contracted with merchants. Saint-Mauris provides some interesting details omitted by du Chastel. Thus Francis apparently recommended the duchesse d'Etampes to his son. 'She is a lady', he said. But he did not want her to witness his death: he waved her away as he was about to receive extreme unction. On the other hand, he asked Annebault, Tournon, Boisy and Sourdis to stay with him till the end 'lest he should lose his reason and be less able to take care of his

---

[4] R. Doucet, 'La mort de François Ier', *R.H.*, cxiii (1913), 309–16.

conscience'. During the night of 30 March the Dauphin fainted on his father's bed, and the king, half embracing him, would not release him. Finally, Saint-Mauris confirms the story of the mistaken homily (though he cites a different one from du Chastel's). Francis, he notes, in spotting the error, showed his 'great memory in that he could distinguish one from the other'. In another dispatch, written on 9 Apr., to Philip of Spain, the ambassador states that the king urged Henri to take care of his sister Marguerite and to marry her off fittingly. He advised him to defend the faith, to abstain from taxing his subjects needlessly and to protect Queen Eleanor, knowing how badly he himself had treated her.[5]

Two notable absentees from the king's bedside were his queen and sister. News of his illness was apparently kept from Eleanor in the daily expectation that he would recover. That at least was the excuse given to her by Henri after Francis's death.[6] As for Marguerite, she was on a retreat at a monastery in Navarre. She knew of her brother's illness and offered up prayers for his recovery. She was told of his death long after the event. Her *Chansons spirituelles* – perhaps the most deeply felt of her poems – eloquently express her anguish and the consolation she derived from religion:

> Je n'ay plus ny Père ny Mère
> Ny Soeur ny Frère
> Sinon Dieu seul auquel j'espère.[7]

Francis died between 1 and 2 pm on Thursday 31 March. He was fifty-two years old. The exact cause of his death is unknown. The record of the post-mortem has not survived, but two contemporary accounts suggest an extensive deterioration of his vital organs. The first, written by a Swiss doctor, indicates that the king's right lung was diseased.[8] The second, by Saint-Mauris, states that an 'aposthume' had been found in his stomach; his kidneys were wasted, his entrails decayed, his throat cankered and a lung affected.[9] For more than a century medical historians have argued for and against syphilis as the cause of the king's death. He had certainly been treated for the disease, but we cannot be sure that he died of it. Dr Cullerier, writing in 1856, argued that the king's symptoms did not point to syphilis. In his view, contemporaries would have identified any disorder of the genital organs with syphilis. He concluded that Francis's death was caused by a 'disease of the urinary ducts associated with an abscess in the region of the urethra'. Such a complaint could have had a vener-

[5] C. Paillard, 'La mort de François Ier et les premiers temps du règne de Henri II d'après les dépêches de Jean de Saint-Mauris (avril-juin 1547)', *R.H.*, v. (1877), 84–120.

[6] Castan, pp. 445–6.   [7] P. Jourda, *Marguerite d'Angoulême* (1930), i. 313–17.

[8] G. Dodu, 'Les amours et la mort de François Ier', *R.H.*, clxi (1929), 268, 273.

[9] Castan, p. 445; *C.S.P. Span.*, ix. 73.

eal origin without being syphilitic.[10] More recently, Dr Fraisse reached a similar conclusion: namely, that Francis died of a urinary infection. His abscess was probably the result of a stricture of the urethra, possibly caused by gonorrhea, which at the time would have been mistaken for syphilis.[11]

On 31 March the new king, Henri II, gave instructions for the triple funeral of his father and two brothers, the Dauphin François and Charles, duc d'Orléans, whose bodies had remained since their deaths at Tournon and Beauvais respectively. At the same time, the artist François Clouet travelled to Rambouillet from Paris to make Francis's death mask and to draw and take measurements for his funeral effigy. This took a fortnight to make. That night mendicant friars prayed and stood vigil over the king's body. On 1 April the royal physicians and surgeons carried out its examination. The king's heart and entrails were removed and placed in two caskets, while his body was embalmed and placed in a coffin. Next day this and the caskets were carried in procession to the priory of Haute-Bruyère, about six miles north of Rambouillet. For two days and nights the church bells rang continuously and services were held. On 6 April Francis's heart and entrails were buried in the priory church; five days later his body was taken to the palace of Saint-Cloud, belonging to the cardinal-bishop of Paris.

On 24 April the focus of the funeral ceremony shifted from the king's body to his effigy, which lay, hands clasped, on a bed of state at the end of the great hall at Saint-Cloud. This had been lavishly decorated with hangings of blue velvet and cloth of gold. The effigy had been made as lifelike as possible. It wore the state robes, the collar of St Michael around its neck and, on its head, the imperial crown. On either side, on pillows, lay the sceptre and hand of justice. There was a canopy over the bed and, at its foot, a crucifix and holy water stoop. Nearby were two stools, where heralds kept watch day and night, and offered the aspergillum to those who came to throw holy water on the effigy. Four candles provided the only illumination for the hall. Along the walls were benches for the nobles and clerics, who attended the religious services and the dead king's meals. These were the strangest part of the entire ceremonial. For eleven days they were served as if Francis were still alive: the table was laid and the courses brought in and sampled. The napkin used to wipe his hands was, as usual, presented by the steward to the most eminent person present, and wine was served to the king twice during each meal. At the end, grace was said by a cardinal with the addition of two psalms appropriate to a funeral.

On 4 May the last meal was served and the effigy removed. Overnight the

[10] Dr Cullerier, 'De quelle maladie est mort François Ier?', *Gazette hebdomadaire de médecine*, xlix (1856), 865–76.

[11] M. Fraisse, 'Sur la maladie et la mort de François Ier' (unpublished medical thesis, University of Paris, 1962). I am most grateful to R. Pillorget for help in connexion with this thesis.

salle d'honneur was turned into a *salle funèbre*, the blue and gold drapes were replaced by black ones. The king's coffin, which had been in an adjacent room, was now brought in and deposited in the centre of the hall. On it were the crown, sceptre and hand of justice. On 18 May Henri aspersed his father's body; this was his only official public appearance between Francis's death and his own coronation. Had he appeared while the effigy was still on display, the illusion of his predecessor still being alive would have been destroyed. The simultaneous exposure of two kings of France was held to be inadmissible.

On 21 May the king's coffin was taken on a waggon drawn by six horses to Notre-Dame-des-Champs and placed in the choir alongside the coffins of his two sons, François and Charles. That evening a requiem service was held, and all that night vigil was kept by Francis's officers and servants. Next morning, after Mass had been celebrated, the church was closed and the effigies of Francis and his sons were produced and attached to litters. The king's effigy now had a different pair of hands: instead of being clasped in prayer, one held the sceptre and the other, the hand of justice. When everything was ready, the church was opened to admit the members of the Parlement, who had come in solemn procession from Paris.

At about 2 pm the funeral cortège set out for Notre-Dame-de-Paris. Its order was as follows: the parish clergy, 500 poor carrying torches, the archers of the guard, and the town criers and watch. Marching on either side of the road were the mendicant orders, followed by the students of the university and other collegiate clergy. Then came a group of royal officers, followed by trumpeters and the last chariot bearing Francis's coffin. Immediately behind rode twelve pages and knights, carrying the king's gloves, helmet, shield and coat-of-arms. Thirty-three prelates, including Cardinal Jean du Bellay, came next; then the effigies of Francis's sons, each carried by gentlemen of their households, two knights carrying the king's spurs, his parade horse led by two grooms, and the Master of the Horse, the marquis de Boisy, holding the sword of France. He preceded the king's effigy, which was carried by the *hanouars* or salt-carriers of Paris. Only their feet, however, were visible, for the litter bearing the effigy was covered with a golden drape which trailed almost to the ground. Alongside marched eight gentlemen of Francis's household, who were attached to the litter by a kind of halter. Behind the effigy rode Admiral Annebault with the banner of France, four princes in deep mourning and, finally, the papal legate, a group of cardinals and ambassadors, and troops of the guard.

After a short service at Notre-Dame, the large company broke up, only to reassemble, the following day for the last rites. Each prince made an offering, and du Chastel delivered a long funeral oration. After a break for lunch, the company set off in the same order as before to the abbey of Saint-Denis, the traditional resting place of French kings. That evening vespers were celebrated,

99. Francis I in death. Detail of the marble *gisant* carved by Pierre Bontemps for the king's tomb in the basilica at Saint-Denis.

and next morning the last rites were repeated. The effigies were then removed and the coffins taken to a vault. The heralds deposited their coats-of-arms on a railing, the royal insignia were placed on the king's coffin, Boisy rested the point of the sword of France upon it, Francis's stewards threw their wands into the grave, and the Admiral, sitting near its edge, dipped the banner of France until its tip touched the coffin. 'Le Roy est mort!' cried Normandy herald three times, but the Admiral was too moved to shout 'Vive le Roy!', so the herald did so for him. Whereupon the sword and banner were raised and the various coats-of-arms retrieved. The company then retired to the refectory for supper, at the end of which Francis's chief steward, Mendoza, broke his wand to signify the dissolution of the late king's household. He told his fellow officials that they no longer had a master and must provide for themselves, but added tactfully that they could rest their hopes on the new king's kindness.[12]

Although Henri's relations with his father had not always been good, he performed his filial duty punctiliously by commissioning a splendid tomb for him. It was designed by Philibert de l'Orme on the model of a Roman

---

[12] R. E. Giesey, *The Royal Funeral Ceremony in Renaissance France* (Geneva, 1960), pp. 1–17, 193–5.

100. The tomb of Francis I and Claude de France in the basilica of Saint-Denis. The tomb, shaped like a triumphal arch, was designed by the great architect, Philibert de l'Orme. The *priants* of the king and queen are by François Carmoy and François Marchand; those of the Dauphin François, Princess Charlotte and Charles d'Orléans are by Pierre Bontemps, who also carved the *gisants* and the bas-reliefs depicting battle scenes.

triumphal arch, while at the same time conforming to the fifteenth-century convention of combining kneeling figures (*priants*) of the deceased and members of his family above the tomb with recumbent figures (*gisants*) on a sarcophagus in an arcaded enclosure below. The sculptor, Pierre Bontemps, who had worked under Primaticcio at Fontainebleau in 1536, was responsible for the *gisants* and the bas-reliefs depicting the battles of Marignano and Ceresole round the base of the tomb. The *priants*, apart from the king and Queen Claude, are of the Dauphin François, Princess Charlotte and Charles d'Orléans. Henri had intended that his sister, Louise, and his grandmother, Louise of Savoy, should also be represented, but their statues were never installed. The *priants* of the king and queen are the work of two lesser sculptors, François Carmoy and François Marchand.[13] Bontemps also worked under de l'Orme on a monument for the heart of Francis. This was set up at Haute-Bruyère in 1556, but is now at Saint-Denis. It is of white marble and consists of an urn and tall pedestal. The urn is decorated with bas-reliefs representing Architecture, Sculpture, Painting and Geometry, and the pedestal with others depicting Astronomy, Instrumental Music, Song and Lyric Poetry.[14] Another testimony to Henri II's filial devotion – a full-length statue of Francis wearing his state robes and holding the sceptre and hand of justice – was set up in the Palais de Justice in 1556, but was, alas, destroyed in a fire in March 1618.[15]

The palace revolution

The death of Francis was followed, as expected, by a palace revolution.[16] The forces of faction which had been gathering momentum during the last years of the reign, but which the king had managed to some extent to contain, were now allowed free rein. Henri II had not forgiven his father's mistress and ministers for the peace of Crépy. As the close friend of Anne de Montmorency, he was unwilling to tolerate the presence at court of the Constable's enemies. His character, so different in many respects from his father's, predisposed him to cleaning up the court. He began by curbing its entertainments so as to devote more time to 'grave and virtuous thoughts' and cashiered Francis's 'fair band' of ladies. Some of them sought refuge in the household of the long-suffering Queen Eleanor, but she would take only two – Madame de Massy and Françoise de Longwy, Admiral Chabot's widow. Madame de Canaples was expelled from the court and repudiated by her husband on the ground that

[13] A. Blunt, *Philibert de l'Orme* (London, 1958), pp. 69–70, 73; M. Roy, *Artistes et monuments de la Renaissance en France* (1929), pp. 157–92.
[14] P. S. Wingert, 'The Funerary Urn of Francis I', *Art Bulletin*, xxi (1939), 383–96.
[15] Roy, p. 170.
[16] Decrue, ii. 1–20; L. Romier, *Les origines politiques des Guerres de Religion* (1913–14), i. 34–57.

101. This monument for the heart of Francis I was carved by Pierre Bontemps and set up originally in the priory at Haute-Bruyère. The urn and pedestal are decorated with panels depicting various arts and sciences which the king had patronized.

she had been the late king's concubine. Henri also tried to get rid of the duchesse de Montpensier, but was prevented by his sister, Marguerite, who refused to go to court without her.

No one stood to lose as much from Francis's death as Madame d'Etampes, who had created so many enemies by her arrogance and nepotism. Saint-Mauris believed that, if she had appeared in public, she would have been stoned. Having retired to Limours shortly before Francis died, she tried early in April to reoccupy her apartment at Saint-Germain, but was informed by Henri that Queen Eleanor would determine its allocation. This was only the first of several humiliations for the duchess. She was forced to disgorge jewels given to her by Francis and was sued by her husband, who claimed that she had cheated him of certain revenues. For a time she was even imprisoned. Yet Madame d'Etampes was not ruined completely: she retired to one of her châteaux and devoted her last years to good works. As for her friend (and lover?) Nicolas de Bossut, comte de Longueval, he was tried for high treason, but saved his head by giving up an estate near Laon to the cardinal of Lorraine.[17]

Queen Eleanor, who had suffered so much indignity at the hands of Madame d'Etampes, was invited by Henri to remain in France, but she preferred to go to the Netherlands. In October 1555 she witnessed in Brussels the abdication of her brother, the Emperor, and soon afterwards returned to Spain. She died at Talaveruela in February 1558.[18]

The person who triumphed as a result of Madame d'Etampes's overthrow was her arch-enemy, Diane de Poitiers. As Henri's mistress, she now became the dominant woman at court and was soon receiving gifts and distributing favours to her favourites and kinsmen as unscrupulously as her predecessor had ever done.[19] In addition to Madame d'Etampes's jewels and lands, Henri gave her the *don de joyeux avènement* (money derived from his confirmation of offices and privileges) which Saint-Mauris estimated at 100,000 *écus*. On 14 April she received the revenues of Fougères, Bazouges, Rimoux and Antrain in place of others given to her daughter and son-in-law. Diane was also confirmed in her ownership of Nogent-le-Roi, Anet, Bréval and Montchauvet, lands which should have reverted to the royal demesne under an ordinance of 1532. In June 1547 Henri gave her the beautiful château of Chenonceaux.[20]

But the palace revolution of 1547 did not affect only the distaff side of the court. Its most significant feature was the return to power of the Constable, Anne de Montmorency. He had been living on his estates since his fall in 1541, but he had not lost his principal offices. He had simply ceased to exercise them or to draw their wages. The Dauphin, who was grateful to him for having freed

---

[17] Castan, p. 446; *C.S.P.Span.*, ix. 73–7; I. Cloulas, *Henri II* (1985), p. 143.
[18] K. Brandi, *The Emperor Charles V* (London, 1939), pp. 633, 641.
[19] Decrue, ii. 14–20.   [20] I. Cloulas, *Henri II*, pp. 143–4.

him from four and a half years as a hostage in Spain, had remained in close touch with him throughout his disgrace. Being relatively young and inexperienced, he could still learn much from Montmorency, who was fifty-four years old and had a vast experience of state affairs. Henri's first act on becoming king was to call the Constable to Saint-Germain. Here they talked in private for two hours, at the end of which Montmorency emerged as president of the king's council. On 12 April he took the oath of Constable to the new king and was confirmed as Grand Master and as captain of the fortresses of the Bastille, Vincennes, Saint-Malo and Nantes. His arrears of pay – amounting to 100,000 *écus* – were settled in addition to his normal salary of 25,000 *écus* per annum. He also recovered his governorship of Languedoc, while his brother, La Rochepot, was reapppointed governor of Paris and the Ile-de-France. In July 1551 Montmorency was created a duke and a peer, an unprecedented elevation for a mere baron, placing him on a par with the highest in the land.[21] His nephews, too, benefited from his elevation: the eldest, Odet de Châtillon, who was already cardinal-archbishop of Toulouse, was given additional benefices, including the see of Beauvais. His brother, Gaspard de Coligny became colonel-general of the infantry.

Montmorency's return to power led automatically to the disgrace of Admiral Annebault and Cardinal Tournon, who had run the government in Francis's last years. Annebault was allowed to remain Admiral, albeit without pay, but had to give up his marshalship to Jacques d'Albon de Saint-André. He was admitted to the king's council, but only to its less important section. The Admiral tried to link his fortunes to Montmorency's by suggesting a marriage between his son and one of the Constable's seven daughters, but nothing came of this. He never regained his former political importance, which was probably as well for the kingdom, since many people thought him a bonehead. 'I never talked in my life that I can remember', wrote Paget, 'with a man that should be wise and that hath so little reason.'[22]

Tournon's disgrace was, in the short term, more complete than the Admiral's. He tried to win the new king's trust by an extravagant display of grief over his late master's body, but this made no impression on Henri. Tournon's name was missing from the list of royal councillors published on 2 April. He was received coolly by the king at Saint-Germain, forbidden to reside at court and replaced as Chancellor of the order of St Michael by Charles de Lorraine. His nephews, Montrevel and Grignan, lost their governorships of Bresse and Provence respectively. After spending some time in his diocese of Auch, Tournon eventually went to Rome and participated in the conclave that

[21] *Ibid.*, ii. 2–7.
[22] E. Dermenghem, 'Un ministre de François Ier: la grandeur et la disgrace de l'amiral Claude d'Annebault', *Revue du XVIe siècle*, ix (1922), pp. 44–6; *L.P.*, xviii (pt. 1), 163.

elected Pope Julius III. This gave him an opportunity to assist in Franco-papal diplomacy, and in 1551 he became archbishop of Lyons. Two years later he and Montmorency were reconciled at Ecouen.[23]

The accession of Henri II was the signal for change not only at the highest ministerial level, but in other departments of state as well. Two secretaries of state, Bochetel and L'Aubespine, were retained, but Gilbert Bayard was dismissed, allegedly for making a disparaging remark about Diane de Poitiers's age and looks. He was imprisoned and died a year later without regaining his freedom. His office was filled by Cosme Closse, who had served the Dauphin. A fourth secretary was appointed in 1547 in the person of Jean du Thier.[24] Among new members of the king's council, two deserve particular notice: François, comte d'Aumale, and his brother, Charles, archbishop of Rheims. They were the sons of Claude, first duc de Guise, and the nephews of another royal councillor, Jean, Cardinal of Lorraine. Within the fiscal administration, Jean Duval was replaced as *Trésorier de l'Epargne* by André Blondet, one of Diane's creatures. Duval allegedly died of sorrow soon after his dismissal, while his lands were acquired by favourites of the new king. The *châtellenie* of Dampierre was sold to the cardinal of Lorraine in 1552.[25] Royal favours also took the form of sizeable sums in cash: for example, Montmorency, Aumale and Saint André shared 800,000 *livres* arising from two clerical tenths.

Historically, the most sinister aspect of the palace revolution of 1547 was the emergence of the house of Guise as a serious rival to those of Montmorency and Bourbon. A story to the effect that Francis, on his deathbed, had warned his son against its ambition is almost certainly an invention of historians inspired by subsequent events.[26] But the high favour enjoyed by the Guises at the start of Henri's reign is indisputable. Within a few months Charles of Lorraine had become a cardinal, and François d'Aumale, a duke. Both were in the flower of manhood, intelligent and immensely ambitious. They also had the backing of Diane, who needed a counterweight to the Constable's influence. She gave them property confiscated from her enemies, including Marchais, which had belonged to the comte de Longueval, and Meudon, previously the property of Cardinal Antoine Sanguin, Madame d'Etampes's uncle. Diane's daughter, Louise, married Claude, marquis de Mayenne, youngest son of Claude de Guise.[27]

As he rewarded his friends, Henri neglected important princes of the blood,

[23] M. François, *Le cardinal François de Tournon* (1951), pp. 228–35, 254, 276.
[24] P. Hamon, 'L'argent du roi: Finances et gens de finances au temps de François Ier'. (unpublished doctoral thesis, University of Paris I, 1993), p. 862; N. M. Sutherland, *The French Secretaries of State in the Age of Catherine de Medici* (London, 1962), pp. 17–19.
[25] Hamon, pp. 786, 791–2; Decrue, ii. 12–13.
[26] J.-A. de Thou, *Histoire universelle* (London, 1734), i (bk. iii), 183.
[27] Cloulas, pp. 140–41; J.-M. Constant, *Les Guise* (1984), p. 23.

especially the head of the house of Bourbon, Antoine duc de Vendôme and his three brothers, Jean comte d'Enghien, Charles the future cardinal, and Louis prince de Condé. The Albrets too were left in the cold. Henri, king of Navarre, hardly set foot at the new court, nor did his wife, Marguerite. Having been a close friend of Madame d'Etampes, she had no reason to feel welcome there. She spent the rest of her life mainly in Navarre. Her pension was continued by Henri, but she never regained any political influence. In September 1548 Marguerite witnessed the king's entry into Lyons, and, in October, was at Moulins for the marriage of her daughter, Jeanne, to Antoine de Bourbon. She died at the château of Odos, near Tarbes, on 21 December 1549.[28]

Thus the death of Francis was the signal for a struggle for power among the great nobles of France, which, capitalizing on the religious troubles of the age, would flare up violently in the French civil wars later in the century.

[28] Cloulas, p. 142; Jourda, i. 319–39.

Epilogue

In the mid sixteenth century Francis I was called 'le grand roy Françoys'. This had little to do with his physical appearance. 'He was called great', writes Brantôme, 'not so much because of his very tall stature and presence or his very regal majesty as on account of his virtues, valour, great deeds and high merits, as were once Alexander, Pompey and others.'[1] De Thou in his *Histoire univer-selle* writes of the 'eulogies deserved by that great prince'.[2] By the late seventeenth century, however, Francis's reputation had slumped. 'Francis I', writes Bayle in his *Dictionnaire historique et critique* (1697), 'was one of those great princes in whom great qualities were mixed with many faults.' Only the blind, he continues, can fail to see clearly in Francis's reign 'a long series of errors and rash actions'. Bayle credits Francis with courage and that 'frank and open generosity that is so rare among persons of his condition', but criticizes him for allowing himself to be ruled by women and unworthy favourites. The king's greatest mistake, in his judgment, was to admit women to his court. This, he concedes, did not lead to the overthrow of the Salic law, but 'one may say that, from that time until more or less the end of the sixteenth century, France was ruled by women'.[3]

Francis's reputation reached its nadir in 1832, when Victor Hugo's play, *Le roi s'amuse* received its première at the Comédie Française. It portrayed the king as a lecher who seduces the daughter of his fool, Triboulet, a hunchback. The latter hires an assassin to murder the king, only to be cruelly deceived. The story is better known to-day as the plot of Verdi's opera *Rigoletto*, which was originally called *Triboletto*. Only the location and identities have been changed in the opera to satisfy the Venetian censors. Why Verdi should have chosen in 1851 to turn an unsuccessful play into an opera is not our concern;

[1] Pierre de Bourdeille, abbé de Brantôme, *Oeuvres complètes*, ed. L. Lalanne (1864–82), iii. 82.
[2] J.-A. de Thou, *Histoire universelle* (London, 1734), i (bk iii), 180.
[3] P. Bayle, *Dictionnaire historique et critique* (1820), vi. 558, 560.

but the failure of *Le roi s'amuse* is of interest. The audience on the first night was shocked by its improbability and immorality; it was not revived till fifty years later.[4] Hugo's discomfiture, however, did not lead to the rehabilitation of Francis. His reputation suffered even worse damage at the hands of the great historian Jules Michelet, who, in 1840 to 1841, lectured at the Collège de France on the Renaissance and the Reformation. As a child of the French Revolution, Michelet viewed history as a long progression towards that supreme emancipation of the human spirit. For him, the Lutheran Reformation was an abortive attempt to achieve the same result two and a half centuries earlier. It failed in France because of the lack of understanding shown by the king and the persecution he initiated. For Michelet, Francis was anything but great: he was 'charm itself . . . a charming speaker, a fluent one, too fluent, for whom speech was not a serious matter'. The whole of Francis's upbringing, according to Michelet, can be summed up in two words: 'women' and 'war' – 'war to please women'. 'This dangerous object', he writes, 'who was to deceive everyone, was born, one might say, between two prostrate women, his mother and his sister, and thus they remained in this ecstasy of worship and devotion.'[5]

Perhaps the most savage condemnation of Francis is to be found in the lectures which Bishop Stubbs delivered at Oxford between 1860 and 1870. 'For want of faith', he said:

> for unparalleled selfishness in a ruler; for utter heartlessness as a man and a king; for incapacity as a ruler at home unredeemed by any brilliant successes in wars, which he never suffered to be interrupted by a sound peace; for a degree of *laches* incompatible with personal honour; with a reputation for the grossest ingratitude to his best servants, and for any unscrupulous tyranny exercised on behalf of the basest favourites, Francis occupies among the Kings of France a bad pre-eminence; deserves a condemnation which the splendour of his court, the magnificence of his buildings, the charm of his manner, the patronage of art for which he is famous, the general air of chivalry which, like our Edward III – a prince whom he strongly resembles in everything except power and success – he tried to throw over his dishonourable and abandoned life; not one of these nor all of them together, serves to do more than gild his infamy. All that is bad about him is too substantial and effective; all that seems good or noble is sham, and a sorry sham, a very ragged covering to the mismanagement, misrule, and tyranny that make him the fit representative, as he was the father, of the worst dynasty that ever reigned in Europe since the rotten empire of Rome fell to pieces . . .[6]

In 1885, thirty years after publication of Michelet's volumes on the Renaissance and Reformation in his *Histoire de France*, a serious attempt was made

---

[4] E. Biré, *Victor Hugo après 1830* (2 vols., 1891), i. 57–77; W. D. Pendell, *Victor Hugo's Acted Dramas and the Contemporary Press* (Baltimore, MD, 1947), pp. 61–71; J. Budden, *The Operas of Verdi*, i. 477–81.
[5] J. Michelet, *Histoire de France* (n.d.), ix. *La Renaissance*, pp. 344–6.
[6] W. Stubbs, *Lectures on European History*, ed. A. Hassall (London, 1904), p. 96.

by Paulin Paris to rehabilitate Francis. In a two-volume work edited posthumously by his son, he argued that most of the scabrous stories told about the king were the deliberate invention of three writers closely related to the house of Bourbon: namely, François Beaucaire, the sieur de Marillac and Antoine de Laval. All three had served the traitor Charles, duc de Bourbon. To these writers Paris adds the names of Brantôme, who could never resist a good story, particularly a dirty one; an obscure doctor of Uzerche called Guyon; and Varillas, who in 1686, published a two-volume history of Francis's reign containing many 'secret anecdotes'.[7]

The indictment drawn up by these authors either to vindicate Bourbon's treason or simply for effect is a long one. Francis had allegedly been dissolute since his earliest days; no beautiful woman had been safe from his lust. He had forced his attentions on Mary Tudor, Louis XII's widow, and only a warning that he might lose the throne to his own bastard had persuaded him to desist. He had contracted syphilis (invariably described as 'a shameful malady') in the arms of La Belle Ferronière and had passed it to his first wife, Claude de France, who had died of it. He had lured the beautiful comtesse de Châteaubriant to his court by means of a cheap trick, and she, after becoming his mistress, had used her influence to have her three incompetent brothers appointed to high military commands, with disastrous results. For purely selfish ends, she had allied with the king's mother and had forced treason on the duc de Bourbon. Having jilted Madame de Châteaubriant, who fell victim to her husband's cruel vengeance, Francis took as his mistress Anne de Pisseleu, one of his mother's ladies in waiting. But first he married her off to Jean de Brosse comte d'Etampes, one of Bourbon's accomplices, who complied with the king's wish in order to recover his own confiscated lands. Madame d'Etampes now became the supreme dispenser of favours and disfavours. She also deceived the king by having affairs with the comte de Brissac, the Constable of Montmorency, Admiral Chabot and the comte de Longueval. In 1539 she planned to take the Emperor prisoner during his visit to the French court, but he won her over by dropping a large diamond at her feet. Thereafter she was an imperialist, and during the war of 1544 she and Longueval tricked the heroic garrison of Saint-Dizier into capitulating to Charles V. Yet she retained her credit with Francis, although he was aware of her treasonable intrigues. Turning to Michelet, we find another allegation about Francis: namely, that his love for his sister, Marguerite, was incestuous.

According to Paulin Paris, this long catalogue of Francis's vices is nothing but a pack of lies for which no contemporary evidence exists. Alas, this is not strictly correct. Many of the stories can be disproved; others cannot be proved

---

[7] P. Paris, *Etudes sur François Premier* (1885), i. 1–25.

or disproved as they rest on hearsay only; others still, including the king's 'shameful malady', are almost certainly true. *Le roi s'amuse* may be a piece of republican propaganda, but its portrayal of the court of Francis is not so incredible; its morals left much to be desired. There are many contemporary references to the king's philandering. De Beatis, who visited France in 1517, wrote: 'The king . . . is a great womanizer and readily breaks into others' gardens and drinks at many sources.'[8] Nor did age temper Francis's licentiousness. Boisy wrote to Montmorency on 18 August 1543: 'our master's conduct is as you have always described it to me: the further he goes, the more he gets caught up with women, and he is quite shameless about it'. Pope Paul III, on learning of the king's death, compared his morals to those of Sardanapalus. Marshal Tavannes wrote in his memoirs: 'Alexander sees women when there is no business, Francis attends to business when there are no women.'[9] The king's taste in art, as we have seen, favoured the erotic. As for the influence exerted by Madame d'Etampes for good or ill on the politics of the last decade of the reign, it was certainly great; the reports of foreign ambassadors confirm this.

Francis had many faults and made many mistakes. He was wilful (some writers have compared him, rightly, to a spoilt child), impetuous, grasping, profligate, licentious and fickle; but he had qualities: intelligence, eloquence, physical bravery, and, by the standards of his age, humanity. Brantôme believed that Semblançay's execution was the king's only serious crime. Among his mistakes were his short-sighted provocation of the Emperor in 1521, his decision to campaign in the winter of 1524 and his handling of von Sickingen and Andrea Doria. He also did allow the duchesse d'Etampes too much influence. But the importance of his reign ought not to be judged simply in terms of the king's faults and errors. Nor should anachronistic criteria be applied. In the nineteenth century, for example, Francis's wars in Italy were deplored as a diversion of his subjects' energies away from their true destiny: the achievement of France's natural frontiers, especially in the east.[10] If territorial expansion is to be the only criterion, then Francis achieved little. He annexed parts of Savoy, but failed in his lifelong bid to extend his dominion beyond the Alps. His last years were overshadowed by the humiliation of losing Boulogne to the English. The king's main territorial success, apart from adding great fiefs to his demesne, was the purely negative one of holding on to Burgundy in the face of Charles V's determined efforts to recover the duchy.

A reign ought to be judged by its long-term impact on all aspects of national

---

[8] *The Travel Journal of Antonio De Beatis: Germany, Switzerland, the Low Countries, France and Italy, 1517–1518*, ed. J. R. Hale (London, 1979), p. 107.

[9] L. Romier, *Les origines politiques des Guerres de Religion* (1913–14), i. 22; *Collection complète des mémoires relatifs à l'histoire de France*, ed. C.B. Petitot (1819–26), xxiii. 217.

[10] G. Zeller, *La réunion de Metz à la France (1552–1648)*, i. *L'occupation* (1926), pp. 21–70.

life. From this standpoint, that of Francis was of great significance, since it witnessed and, in varying degrees, promoted or fostered fundamental changes in France's political structure, economy, society, religion and cultural life. The king's obsession with war, reprehensible as it is on moral grounds, stimulated administrative change. By entailing an expenditure far in excess of what the crown's traditional resources could provide, it obliged him to look for new sources of wealth, to reorganize the ramshackle fiscal system handed down by Charles VII and to promote administrative centralization wherever possible. But, of course, there were limits to the effectiveness of such changes. Francis never became as absolute as Louis XIV. To the end of his life, his kingdom contained many local privileges, exemptions and anomalies; his laws, even when registered by the parlements, were not always enforced. Yet, as Doucet noted, Francis's reign marked the beginning of a new, more 'absolute', system of government. France was more unified at the end of his reign than at the beginning. Among the king's fiscal expedients, the sale of offices, which he exploited more systematically than any of his predecessors, had far-reaching social and political consequences. Though remunerative in the short term, it was highly dangerous to the future of monarchy, for it created a sizeable class of royal officials, who, having bought their offices, quite naturally regarded them as their own property regardless of the public functions attached to them. Their loyalty or obedience had become so unreliable by the early seventeenth century that the crown had to by-pass them by sending out commissioners – the famous *intendants de la justice, police et finances* – who became the chief agents of Louis XIV's absolutism. It may not be too far-fetched to argue that Francis promoted centralization by creating a problem for his successors.

Economically, his reign saw the completion of the agricultural reconstruction that had followed the Hundred Years War. While the land was being reclaimed, the population grew, town life flourished and trade, both at home and abroad, expanded. Parochialism was still too strongly entrenched among the king's subjects for them to understand, let alone endorse, the far-reaching programme of economic reform proposed by Duprat in 1517, but the government did adhere to its principles in subsequent legislation. A national awareness, which economic historians have identified with the beginnings of Colbertism, certainly animated it, notably its reform of the customs system. New horizons were also opened up: the ports of the Atlantic coast were developed, the east coast of North America was mapped out and Canada was settled for the first time. All, however, was not well with the economy. The failure of food production to keep pace with the needs of a growing population caused grain prices to rise, while inflation depressed the living standards of many peasants and artisans. The growth of poverty under Francis led to a reappraisal by local authorities of existing methods of relief with results interesting for the future.

As the ruler who presided over the Renaissance and the Reformation in his kingdom, Francis has received a good deal of attention. Too much significance has perhaps been attached to the Concordat of Bologna, but it did clarify relations between the French crown and the Holy See, which the Pragmatic Sanction of Bourges had undermined, and, by tightening and extending the king's hold on ecclesiastical appointments, it helped remove a possible incentive to break with Rome. Francis's ambiguous attitude to religious dissent in the period before 1534 has often been seen as a lack of seriousness or a readiness to subordinate religious principle to diplomatic expediency. It may have been due rather to the ideological confusion of the age; but, whatever its cause, it did give the new faith a chance to strike root in France and grow into Calvinism. By the time sacramentarianism had alerted the king to the social and political dangers of Protestantism, it could no longer be eradicated. The burnings and massacres which disfigured the last years of his reign only served to inspire the dissenters by giving them martyrs. The French civil wars of the second half of the century have often been interpreted as aristocratic conflicts using religion as a cover, but they can only be fully understood if the deep religious divisions that originated under Francis are taken into account.

Francis's cultural patronage has generally been widely acclaimed. Why Stubbs should have dismissed it as a sham, is incomprehensible except in the context of his own narrow prejudices. The works of Budé, Marot and Rabelais, the handsome books printed by Robert Estienne, the portraits of Jean and François Clouet, the chansons of Sermisy and Janequin, and the châteaux built for Francis and his courtiers are all witnesses to the brilliant intellectual and artistic life of the court. Its impact on future generations is not easily measured, but few reigns have left a more notable or lasting cultural legacy. Francis's collection of works of art became the nucleus of the collection at the Louvre, and his library that of the Bibliothèque Nationale. By establishing the *lecteurs royaux* in 1530, he not only shattered the virtual monopoly of higher learning exercised by the 'Sorbonne', but also paved the way for the foundation of the Collège de France, where Michelet was to denigrate his memory in the 1840s. We should try to be fairer in 1994.

Manuscript Sources

This list contains only documents cited in the course of this book.
Chantilly: Musée Condé
  Ms. 899.
London: British Library
  Additional Ms. 28594
  Harley Ms. 3462.
London: Public Record Office
  State Papers 89
Paris: Archives Nationales
  J. 942
  K. 1483
  KK. 94, 98
  U. 797–8, 2035
  X^{1a} 1519–20, 1527–30, 1536, 1538, 1541, 1549–51, 1553–6, 8613
Paris: Bibliothèque Nationale
  mss. français 143, 2200, 2794, 2953, 2981, 2994, 3897, 4480, 4523, 5109, 5660, 5709, 5750, 5770, 7853, 10383, 10389, 10390, 10420, 10900, 11495, 13429, 14116, 15628–33, 17329
  mss. français, nouvelles acquisitions 8452
  mss. Dupuy 17, 211

Select Bibliography

This bibliography lists only works which I have found useful while working on this book. Unless otherwise indicated all books are published in Paris.

Primary works

Albèri, E. (ed.), *Relazioni degli ambasciatori veneti al Senato*, 14 vols. Florence, 1839–63

Auton, Jean d', *Chronique de Louis XII*, ed. R. de Maulde La Clavière, 4 vols. Société de l'Histoire de France, 1889–95

[Barrillon], *Journal de Jean Barrillon, secrétaire du chancelier Duprat, 1515–21*, ed. P. de Vaissière, 2 vols. 1897–99

Bèze, T. de, *Histoire ecclésiastique*. Lille, 1841

Bodin, J., *Les six livres de la République*. 1577

Bontems, C., Raybaud, L.-P., and Brancourt, J.-P. (eds.) *Le prince dans la France des XVIe et XVIIe siècles*. 1965

Brantôme, P. de Bourdeille, abbé de, *Oeuvres complètes*, ed. L. Lalanne, 11 vols. 1864–82

Briçonnet, G., and Marguerite d'Angoulême, *Correspondance (1521–24)*, ed. C. Martineau and M. Veissière, 2 vols. Geneva, 1975–79

Calendar of State Papers, Spanish, eds. G. Bergenroth, P. de Gayangos and M. A. S. Hume, 12 vols. London, 1862–95

Calendar of State Papers, Venetian, eds. R. Brown, C. Bentinck and H. Brown, 9 vols. London, 1864–98

Captivité du roi François Ier, ed. A. Champollion-Figeac, 1847

Castiglione, B., *The Book of the Courtier*, tr. G. Bull. Harmondsworth, Middlesex, 1967.

Catalogue des actes de François Ier, 10 vols. 1887–1910

[Catherine de' Medici], *Lettres de Catherine de Médicis*, ed. H. de La Ferrière-Percy, 10 vols. 1880–95

[Cellini], *The Life of Benvenuto Cellini Written by Himself*, tr. J. A. Symonds, ed. J. Pope-Hennessy. London, 1949

Champier, Symphorien, *Les gestes ensemble la vie du preulx Chevalier Bayard*, ed. D. Crouzet, 1992

[Charles V], *Correspondenz des Kaisers Karl V*, ed. K. Lanz, 2 vols. Leipzig, 1844–45

Charrière, E. (ed.), *Négociations de la France dans le Levant*, 4 vols. 1848–60

Cimber, L., and Danjou, F. (eds.), *Archives curieuses de l'histoire de France depuis Louis XI jusqu'à Louis XVIII*, 30 vols. 1834–49

Collection complète des mémoires relatifs à l'histoire de France, ed. C. B. Petitot, 52 vols. 1819–26

Collection of Documents Relating to Jacques Cartier and the Sieur de Roberval, A, ed. H. P. Biggar. Ottawa, 1930

Comptes de l'hôtel des rois de France aux XIVe et XVe siècles, ed. L. Douët-d'Arcq. 1865

Comptes de Louise de Savoie et de Marguerite d'Angoulême (1512–39), eds. A. Lefranc and J. Boulenger. 1905

Correspondance des nonces en France: Capodiffero, Dandino et Guidiccione, 1541–1546, ed. J. Lestocquoy. Rome, 1963

Correspondance des nonces . . . Carpi et Ferrerio, 1535–40, ed. J. Lestocquoy. Rome and Paris, 1961

Correspondance des réformateurs dans les pays de langue française, ed. A. Herminjard, 9 vols. Geneva, 1886–87

Correspondance politique de MM. de Castillon et de Marillac, ambassadeurs de France en Angleterre 1537–42, ed. J. Kaulek. 1885

Cronique du roy Françoys Premier de ce nom, ed. G. Guiffrey. 1860

De Beatis, A., *Voyage du cardinal d'Aragon (1517–18)*, tr. M. Havard de La Montagne. 1913

    The Travel Journal of Antonio De Beatis: Germany, Switzerland, the Low Countries, France and Italy, 1517–1518, tr. J. R. Hale and J. M. A. Lindon, ed. J. R. Hale. London, 1979

[du Bellay, Guillaume], *Fragments de la première Ogdoade de Guillaume du Bellay*, ed. V.-L. Bourrilly. 1905

    Mémoires de Martin et Guillaume du Bellay, eds. V.-L. Bourrilly and F. Vindry, 4 vols. 1908–19

du Bellay, Jean, *Ambassades en Angleterre. La première ambassade (sep. 1527–fév. 1529). Correspondance diplomatique*, eds. V.-L. Bourrilly and P. de Vaissière. 1905

    Correspondance du cardinal Jean du Bellay, ed. R. Scheurer, 2 vols. 1969–73.

Erasmus, D., *Opus epistolarum*, eds. P. S. Allen and H. M. Allen, 8 vols. Oxford, 1906–34

Estienne, C., *Le guide des chemins de France de 1553*, ed. J. Bonnerot, 2 vols. 1936

[Evelyn], *The Diary of John Evelyn*, ed. E. S. De Beer. London, 1959

Ferrante Gonzaga alla corte spagnola di Carlo V, ed. R. Tamalio. Mantua, 1991

[Florange], *Mémoires du maréchal de Florange dit le jeune adventureux*, eds. R. Goubaux and P. A. Lemoisne, 2 vols. 1913–24

Fontanon, A. (ed.), *Les édicts et ordonnnances des rois de France*, 3 vols. 1611

Fourquevaux, Sieur de, *Instructions sur le Faict de la Guerre*, ed. G. Dickinson. London, 1954

Fraikin, J. (ed.), *Nonciatures de France: Clément VII*, 2 vols. 1906

Français en Amérique pendant la première moitié du XVIe siècle, Les, eds. C.-A. Julien, R. Herval and T. Beauchesne. 1946

[Francis I], *Poésies de François Ier*, ed. A. Champollion Figeac. 1847
   Oeuvres poétiques, ed. J. E. Kane. Geneva, 1984

[Granvelle], *Papiers d'état du cardinal de Granvelle*, ed. C. Weiss, 9 vols. 1841–52

Guicciardini, F., *The History of Italy*, tr. A. P. Goddard, 10 vols. London 1763

Guiffrey, G., *Procès criminel de Jehan de Poytiers, seigneur de Saint-Vallier*. 1867

Hall, E., *Henry VIII*, ed. C. Whibley, 2 vols. London, 1904

Isambert, F.-A., *Recueil général des anciennes lois françaises*, 29 vols. 1827–33

Jacqueton, G., *Documents relatifs à l'administration financière en France de Charles VII à François Ier (1443–1523)*. 1891

Jourda, P., *Repertoire analytique et chronologique de la correspondance de Marguerite d'Angoulême*. 1930

Journal d'un bourgeois de Paris sous le règne de François Ier (1515–1536), Le, ed. V.-L. Bourrilly. 1910

Laborde, L. de, *Les comptes des bâtiments du roi (1528–71)*, 2 vols. 1878–80

Lefèvre-Pontalis, G., *Correspondance politique de Odet de Selve*. 1888

Le Glay, A. J. C., *Négociations diplomatiques entre la France et l'Autriche*, 2 vols. 1845

Letters and Papers, Foreign and Domestic of the Reign of Henry VIII, eds. J. S. Brewer, J. Gairdner and R. H. Brodie, 21 vols. London, 1862–1910

Louise de Savoie, *Journal* in S. Guichenon, *Histoire généalogique de la royale maison de Savoie* (Lyons, 1660), vol. ii, p. 457. Also in Michaud et Poujoulat

Loyal serviteur, Le, ed. J. Roman. 1878

Marguerite d'Angoulême, *Heptaméron*, ed. M. François. 1942
   Lettres de Marguerite d'Angoulême, ed. F. Génin. 1841
   Nouvelles lettres de Marguerite d'Angoulême, ed. F. Génin. 1842

Marot, C. *Les épîtres*. ed. C. A. Mayer. London, 1958

   Les épigrammes, ed. C. A. Mayer. London, 1970

[Matignon], *Correspondance de Joachim de Matignon, lieutenant-général du roi en Normandie (1516–1548)*, ed. L.-H. Labande. Monaco, 1914

Merval, S. de (ed.), *Documents relatifs à la fondation du Havre*. Rouen, 1875

Monluc, B. de, *Commentaires*, ed. P. Courteault, 3 vols. 1911–25

Négociations diplomatiques de la France avec la Toscane, ed. A. Desjardins, 6 vols. 1859–86

Ordonnances des rois de France: règne de François Ier, 9 vols. 1902–75

Paillard, C., 'Documents relatifs aux projets d'évasion de François Ier ainsi qu'à la situation intérieure de la France', *R.H.*, viii (1878), 297–367

Paradin, G., *Histoire de nostre temps*. Lyons, 1556

[Pellicier], *Correspondance politique de Guillaume Pellicier, ambassadeur de France à Venise, 1540–42*, ed. A. Tausserat-Radel, 2 vols. 1899

Picot, E., *Chants historiques français du XVIe siècle*. 1903

Procédures politiques du règne de Louis XII, ed. R. de Maulde La Clavière. 1885

Rabelais, F., *Pantagruel*, ed. V. L. Saulnier. Geneva, 1965

Registres des délibérations du Bureau de la Ville de Paris, i (1499–1526), ed. F. Bonnardot (1883); ii (1527–1539), ed. A. Tuetey (1886); iii (1539–1552), ed. P. Guérin (1886)

Relations des ambassadeurs vénitiens sur les affaires de France, ed. N. Tommaseo, 2 vols. 1838

Ribier, G., *Lettres et mémoires d'Estat des roys, princes, ambassadeurs et autres ministres sous les règnes de François Ier, Henri II et François II*, 2 vols. 1666

Ruble, A. de, 'La cour des enfants de France sous François Ier', *Notices et documents publiés pour la Société de l'Histoire de France*. 1884, pp. 323–30

Sanuto, M., *Diarii*, 58 vols. Venice, 1879–1903

Seyssel, C. de, *La monarchie de France*, ed. J. Poujol. 1961

   English tr. *The Monarchy of France*, by J. H. Hexter, ed. D. R. Kelley. New Haven, CT, 1981

Solmi, E. 'Documenti inediti sulla dimora di Leonardo da Vinci in Francia nel 1517 e 1518' in *Archivio Storico Lombardo*, IV, Ser. ii (1904), pp. 389–410

Spont, A., 'Documents relatifs à Jacques de Beaune-Semblançay' in *Bibliothèque de l'Ecole des Chartes*, lvi (1895), pp. 318–57

State Papers of Henry VIII, 11 vols. London, 1830–52

Sylvius, J. *Francisci Francorum Regis et Henrici Anglorum Colloquium*, eds. S. Bamforth and J. Dupèbe in *Renaissance Studies*, v (1991)

Teulet, A., *Relations politiques de la France et de l'Espagne avec l'Ecosse au XVI siècle*, 5 vols. 1862

[Tournon], *Correspondance du cardinal François de Tournon*, ed. M. François. 1946

Vasari, G., *Le vite de' più eccellenti pittori, scultori ed architettori*, ed. G. Milanesi, 9 vols. Florence, 1878–85

    Lives of the Painters, Sculptors and Architects, ed. W. Gaunt, 4 vols. London, 1963

[Versoris], *Livre de raison de Me Nicolas Versoris, avocat au Parlement de Paris, 1519–1530*, ed. G. Fagniez. 1885

Weiss, N., 'Documents inédits pour servir à l'histoire de la réforme sous François Ier, 1536–1537', *B.S.H.P.F.*, xxxiv (1885), 164–77

Secondary works

Adhémar, J., 'The Collection of Francis the First', *G.B.A.*, 6th ser., xxx (1946), 5–16

    'Aretino: Artistic Adviser to Francis I', *J.W.C.I.*, xvii (1954), 311–18

Alvarez, M. F., *Charles V: Elected Emperor and Hereditary Ruler*, London, 1975

Ambrière, F., *Le favori de François Ier, Gouffier de Bonnivet, amiral de France*. 1936

Anglo, S., *Spectacle, Pageantry and Early Tudor Policy*. Oxford, 1969

Armstrong E., *Robert Estienne, Royal Printer*. Cambridge, 1954. Revised edn 1986

    Before Copyright: the French Book-Privilege System, 1498–1526. Cambridge, 1990

Arnaud, E., *Histoire des Protestants de Provence, du Comtat-Venaissin et de la principauté d'Orange*, 2 vols. 1884

Aspects de la propagande religieuse, ed. G. Berthoud *et al*. Geneva, 1957

Aubenas, R. and Ricard, R., *L'église et la Renaissance, 1449–1517*. 1951

Audisio, G., *Les vaudois du Luberon: Une minorité en Provence (1460–1560)*. Mérindol, 1984

    Les 'vaudois'. Naissance, vie et mort d'une dissidence (XIIe–XVIe siècles). Turin, 1989

    Procès-Verbal d'un Massacre: Les vaudois du Luberon (avril 1545). Aix-en-Provence, 1992

Audisio, G. and E. Cameron, 'Les Vaudois des Alpes: débat sur un ouvrage récent', *Revue de l'histoire des religions*, cciii (1986), 395–409

Babelon, J.-P., *Paris au XVIe siècle*. 1986

    Châteaux de France au siècle de la Renaissance. 1989

Ballaguy, P., *Bayard, 1476–1524*. 1935

Bapst, E., *Les mariages de Jacques V*. 1889

Baratier, E., *La démographie provençale du XIIIe au XVIe siècle*. 1961

Baulant, M. and Meuvret, J., *Prix des céréales extraits de la mercuriale de Paris, 1520–1698*. 1960

Baumgartner, F. J., *Henry II*. Durham, NC, 1988

Baux, E., V.-L. Bourrilly and P. Mabilly, 'Le voyage des reines et de François Ier en Provence et dans la vallée du Rhône (Décembre 1515–Février 1516), *A. du M*, vol. 16 (1904), 31–64

Bayard, F. and P. Guignet, *L'Economie française aux XVIe, XVIIe et XVIIIe siècles* (1991)

Beaune, Colette, *Naissance de la nation française*, 1985. English tr. *The Birth of an Ideology: Myths and Symbols of Nation in Late-Medieval France*. Berkeley, CA, 1991

Bedos Rezak, B., *Anne de Montmorency Seigneur de la Renaissance*. 1990

Béguin, S., *L'Ecole de Fontainebleau: le maniérisme à la cour de France*. 1960
'Remarques sur la Chambre du Roi', *Actes du colloque international sur l'art de Fontainebleau*, ed. A. Chastel (1975), 199–230
'New evidence for Rosso in France', *Burlington Mag.*, cxxxi (1989), 828–38

Béguin S. *et al.*, *La Galerie François Ier au château de Fontainebleau* special no. 16–17, *Revue de l'art* (1972)

Béguin, S., J. Guillaume and A. Roy, *La galerie d'Ulysse à Fontainebleau*. 1985

Benedict, P., *Rouen during the Wars of Religion*. Cambridge, 1981

Benedict, P. (ed.), *Cities and Social Change in Early Modern France*. London, 1989

Berthoud, G., 'La "Confession" de Maître Noël Béda et le problème de son auteur', *B.H.R.*, xxix (1967), 373–97
Antoine Marcourt. Geneva, 1973

Bezard, Y., *La vie rurale dans le sud de la région parisienne de 1450 à 1560*. 1929

Biggar, H.P., *The Precursors of Jacques Cartier 1497–1534*. Ottawa, 1911

Bloch, J.-R., *L'anoblissement en France au temps de François Ier*. 1934

Bloch, M., *Les rois thaumaturges*. 1961. English tr. *The Royal Touch: Sacred Monarchy and Scrofula in England and France*. London, 1973
French Rural History. London, 1966

Blunt, A. *Art and Architecture in France, 1500–1700*. Harmondsworth, Middlesex, 1957
Philibert de l'Orme. London, 1958

Boissonnade, P., *Histoire de la réunion de la Navarre à la Castille*. 1893
'Le mouvement commercial entre la France et les îles britanniques au XVIe siècle', *R.H.*, cxxxiv (1920), 193–228; cxxxv (1920), 1–27

Bonney, R., 'Absolutism: What's in a Name?', *F.H.*, i (1987), 93–117
  L'absolutisme, 1989

Borély, A. E., 'Origines de la ville du Havre', *R.H.*, xiv (1880), 286–311

Bossuat, A., *Le bailliage royal de Montferrand, 1425–1556.* 1957

Bourrilly, V.-L., 'François Ier et Henri VIII; l'intervention de la France dans l'affaire du divorce', *Rev. d'hist. mod. et contemp.*, i (1899), 271–84

  'François Ier et les Protestants: les essais de concorde en 1535', *B.S.H.P.F.*, xlix (1900), 337–65, 477–95

  'La première ambassade d'Antonio Rincon en Orient, 1522–23', *Rev. d'hist. mod. et contemp.*, ii (1900–01), 23–44

  'L'ambassade de La Forest et de Marillac à Constantinople (1535–38)', *R.H.*, lxxvi (1901), 297–328

  'Le règne de François Ier: état des travaux et questions à traiter', *Rev. d'hist. mod. et contemp.*, iv (1902–03), 513–31, 585–603

  Guillaume du Bellay, seigneur de Langey. 1905

  Jacques Colin, abbé de Saint-Ambroise. 1905, repr. Geneva, 1970

  'Les diplomates de François Ier: Maraviglia à Milan (1532–1533)', *Bulletin italien*, vi (Bordeaux, 1906), 133–46

  'Le cardinal Jean du Bellay en Italie', *Revue des études rabelaisiennes*, v (1907), 246–53, 262–74

  'Antonio Rincon et la politique orientale de François Ier', *R.H.*, cxiii (1913), 64–83, 268–308

Bourrilly, V.-L. and Weiss, N., 'Jean du Bellay, les Protestants et la Sorbonne', *B.S.H.P.F.*, lii (1903), 97–127, 193–231, liii (1904), 97–143

Boutruche, R., *Bordeaux de 1453 à 1715.* Bordeaux, 1966

Bouwsma, W.J., *John Calvin: A Sixteenth-Century Portrait.* Oxford, 1988

Brandi, K., *The Emperor Charles V*, tr. C.V. Wedgwood. London, 1939

Braudel, F., *The Mediterranean and the Mediterranean World in the Age of Philip II*, tr. S. Reynolds, 2 vols. London, 1972–73

  Capitalism and Material Life, 1400–1800, tr. M. Kochan. London, 1973

  The Identity of France, tr. S. Reynolds. 2 vols. London, 1989–91

Breen, Q., *John Calvin: A Study in French Humanism.* Grand Rapids, MI, 1931

Brésard, M., *Les foires à Lyon au XVe et au XVIe siècles.* Lyons, 1914

Bridge, J. S. C., *History of France from the Death of Louis XI*, 5 vols. Oxford, 1921–36

Brown, H. M., *Music in the Renaissance.* Englewood Cliffs, NJ, 1976

Bryant, L. M., *The King and the City in the Parisian Royal Entry Ceremony: Politics, Ritual and Art in the Renaissance.* Geneva, 1986

Buisson, A., *Le chancelier Antoine Duprat.* 1935

Burns, J. H. (ed.), *The Cambridge History of Political Thought.* Cambridge, 1991

Cameron, E., *Reformation of the Heretics: The Waldenses of the Alps, 1480–1580*. Oxford, 1984

Carrière, V., 'Guillaume Farel propagandiste de la Réformation', *R.H.E.F.*, xx (1934), 37–78

Introduction aux études d'histoire ecclésiastique locales, 3 vols. 1934–40

Carroll, E. A., 'Rosso in France' in *Actes du colloque international sur l'art de Fontainebleau*, ed. A. Chastel. (1975), 17–28.

Rosso Fiorentino, Drawings, Prints and Decorative Arts. Washington, DC, 1987

Castan, A., 'La mort de François Ier', *Mémoires de la Société d'émulation du Doubs*, 5th ser., iii (1878), 420–54

Cauwès, P., 'Les commencements du crédit public en France: les rentes sur l'hôtel de ville au XVIe siècle', *Revue d'économie politique*, ix (1895), 97–123

Cazeaux, I., *French Music in the Fifteenth and Sixteenth Centuries*. Oxford, 1975

Champion, P., *Paris au temps de la Renaissance: l'envers de la tapisserie*. 1935

Paganisme et réforme. 1936

Chantérac, B. de, *Odet de Foix, vicomte de Lautrec*. 1930

Chartier, R., Chaussinand-Nogaret, G., Neveux, H., and Le Roy Ladurie, E., *La ville classique*, vol. 3 of *Histoire de la France urbaine*, ed. G. Duby. 1981

Chartrou, J., *Les entrées solennelles et triomphales à la Renaissance (1484–1551)*. 1928

Chastel, A., 'L'escalier de la Cour Ovale à Fontainebleau' in *Essays . . . to Rudolf Wittkower*, eds. D. Fraser, H. Hibbard and M. J. Lewine (London, 1967), pp. 74–80

'La demeure royale au XVI siècle et le nouveau Louvre' in *Studies in Renaissance and Baroque Art presented to Anthony Blunt* (London, 1967), pp. 78–82

The Sack of Rome, 1527, trs. B. Archer. Princeton NJ, 1983

Le cardinal Louis d'Aragon. 1986

Chatenet, M., *Le château de Madrid au Bois de Boulogne*. 1987

'Une demeure royale au milieu du XVIe siècle: La distribution des espaces au château de Saint-Germain-en-Laye', *Revue de l'Art*, 81 (1988), 20–30

'Le coût des travaux dans les résidences royales d'Ile-de-France entre 1528 et 1550', *Les Chantiers de la Renaissance*, eds. A. Chastel and J. Guillaume (1991), pp. 115–29

'Une nouvelle "Cheminée de Castille" à Madrid en France', *Revue de l'Art*, 91 (1991), 36–8

'Le logis de François Ier au Louvre', *Revue de l'Art*, 97 (1992), 72–4

Chaunu, P., and Gascon, R., *Histoire économique et sociale de la France*, i (1450–1660), pt. 1, *L'état et la ville*. 1977

Chevalier, B., *Tours ville royale, 1356–1520*. Chambray, 1983
   Les bonnes villes de France du XIVe au XVI siècle. 1982
Christie, R. C., *Etienne Dolet, the Martyr of the Renaissance*. London, 1880
Church, W. F., *Constitutional Thought in Sixteenth-Century France*. Cambridge, MA, 1941
Clamageran, J.-J., *Histoire de l'impôt en France*, 3 vols. 1867–76
Clément-Simon, G., 'Un conseiller du roi François Ier, Jean de Selve', *R.Q.H.*, lxxiii (1903), 45–120
Clough, C. H., 'Francis I and the Courtiers of Castiglione's *Courtier*', *E.S.R.*, viii (1978), 23–70
Cloulas, I., *Henri II*. 1985
Collier, R., and Billioud, J., *Histoire du commerce de Marseille*, iii (1480–1599). 1951
Constant, J.-M. *Les Guise*. 1984
   La vie quotidienne de la noblesse française aux XVIe–XVIIe siècles. 1985
Contamine, P., 'L'artillerie royale française à la veille des guerres d'Italie', *Annales de Bretagne*, lxxi (1964), 221–61
   Guerre, état et société à la fin du Moyen Age: Etude sur les armées des rois de France 1337–1494. 1972
   'Les industries de guerre dans la France de la Renaissance: l'exemple de l'artillerie', *R.H.*, 271 (1984), 249–80
Contamine, P. (ed.), *Histoire Militaire de la France: Vol. 1. Des origines à 1715*. 1992
Coornaert, E., 'La politique économique de la France au début du règne de François Ier', *Annales de l'Université de Paris*, viii (1933), 414–27
   Les Français et le commerce international à Anvers, 2 vols. 1961
   Les corporations en France avant 1789, 2nd edn. 1968
Courteault, P., *Blaise de Monluc historien*. 1908
Cox-Rearick, J., *La collection de François Ier*. 1972
Croix, A., *Nantes et le Pays nantais au XVIe siècle*. 1974
Crouzet, D., *Les guerriers de Dieu*. 2 vols. 1990
   'Désir de mort et puissance absolue de Charles VIII à Henri IV', *Revue de synthèse*, 4th ser. 3–4 (1991), 423–41
Crozet, R., 'Une ville neuve du XVIe siècle: Vitry-le-François', *La vie urbaine*, vols. 21–2 (1923), 291–309
   'Villes neuves du XVIe siècle: Vitry-le-François et Villefranche-sur-Meuse', *La vie urbaine* (1924–26), pp. 695–703
Cullerier, Dr, 'De quelle maladie est mort François Ier?', *Gazette hebdomadaire de médecine*, xlix (1856), 865–76
Cummins, J., *The Hound and the Hawk: The Art of Medieval Hunting*. London, 1988

Cuttler, S. H., *The Law of Treason and Treason Trials in Late Medieval France*. Cambridge, 1981

Davis, N. Z., 'A Trade Union in Sixteenth-Century France', *Econ. H.R.*, xix (1966), 48–69

Society and Culture in Early Modern France. London, 1975

Fiction in the Archives: Pardon Tales and their Tellers in Sixteenth-Century France. Oxford, 1988

Decrue, F., *De consilio regis Francisci I*. 1885

Anne de Montmorency, grand maître et connétable de France à la cour, aux armées et au conseil du roi François Ier. 1885

Anne de Montmorency, connétable et pair de France sous les rois Henri II, François Ier et Charles IX. 1889

Delaruelle, L., *Guillaume Budé*. 1907

Denieul-Cormier, A., *La France de la Renaissance (1488–1559)*. 1962

Dermenghem, E., 'Un ministre de François Ier: la grandeur et la disgrace de l'amiral Claude d'Annebault', *Revue du XVIe siècle*, ix (1922), 34–50

Descimon, R., 'Modernité et archaisme de l'état monarchique: le Parlement de Paris saisi par la vénalité (XVIe siècle)' in *Genèse de l'état moderne*. 1990

'La royauté française entre féodalité et sacerdoce: roi seigneur ou roi magistrat?', *Revue de synthèse*, 4th Ser. Nos. 3–4 (1991), 455–73

Desgardins, E., *Anne de Pisseleu duchesse d'Etampes et François Ier*. 1904

Des livres et des rois, eds. U. Baurmeister and M-P. Lafitte. 1992

De Tolnay, C., 'L'Hercule de Michel-Ange à Fontainebleau', *G.B.A.*, 6th ser. lxiv (1962), 125–40

Devèze, M., *La vie de la forêt française au XVIe siècle*, 2 vols. 1961

Dictionnaire de biographie française.

Diefendorf, B. B., *Beneath the Cross: Catholics and Huguenots in Sixteenth-Century Paris*. Oxford, 1991

Dimier, L., *Le Primatice*. 1900

Les portraits peints de François Ier. 1910

Histoire de la peinture française des origines au retour de Vouet 1300 à 1627. 1925

Di Stefano, G., 'L'Hellénisme en France à l'orée de la Renaissance' in *Humanism in France at the End of the Middle Ages and in the Early Renaissance*, ed. A. H. T. Levi. Manchester, 1970

Dodu, G., 'Les amours et la mort de François Ier', *R.H.*, clxi (1929), 237–77

Dognon, P., 'La taille en Languedoc de Charles VIII à François Ier', *A. du M.*, iii (1891), 340

Les institutions politiques et administratives du Pays de Languedoc du XIIIe siècle aux Guerres de Religion. Toulouse, 1895

Doucet, R., 'La mort de François Ier', *R.H.*, cxiii (1913), 309–16

'Pierre du Chastel, grand aumônier de France', *R.H.*, cxxxiii (1920), 212–57; cxxxiv (1920), 1–57

Etude sur le gouvernment de François Ier dans ses rapports avec le Parlement de Paris, 2 vols. 1921–26

L'état des finances de 1523. 1923

'Le Grand Parti de Lyon au XVIe siècle', *R.H.*, clxxi (1933), 474–82

Finances municipales et crédit public à Lyon au XVIe siècle. 1937

Les institutions de la France au XVIe siècle. 2 vols. 1948

'La banque en France au XVIe siècle', *Rev. d'hist. écon. et soc.*, xxix (1951), 115–23

du Boulay, C.-E., *Historia Universitatis Parisiensis*, 6 vols. 1665–73

Duby, G. and Wallon, A. (eds.), *Histoire de la France rurale*, ii. 1975

du Cerceau, J.-A., *Les plus excellents bastiments de France (1576–1607)*. Facsimile repr. Farnborough, 1972

Dupont-Ferrier, G., *Les officiers royaux des bailliages et sénéchaussées.* 1902

du Tillet, J., *Recueil des roys de France leurs couronne et maison*, 2 vols. 1602

Ecole de Fontainebleau, L'., Catalogue of exhibition at Grand Palais, Paris, 1972–73

Edelstein, M. M., 'The Social Origins of the Episcopacy in the Reign of Francis I', *F.H.S.*, viii (1974), 377–92

Ehrenberg, R., *Capital and Finance in the Age of the Renaissance*, tr. H. M. Lucas. New York, 1928. Reprint, Fairfield, NJ, 1985

Elam, Caroline, 'Art and Diplomacy in Renaissance Florence', *Royal Society of Arts Journal* (1988), 1–14

'Art in the service of liberty: Battista della Palla, art agent for Francis I', forthcoming in *I Tatti Studies – Essays in the Renaissance*, V, 1993

Emerit, M. E., 'Les capitulations de 1535 ne sont pas une légende', *Annales E.S.C.*, xix (1964), 362–3

Esmein, A., *A History of Continental Criminal Procedure*, tr. J. Simpson. London, 1914

Etchechoury, M., *Les maîtres des requêtes de l'hôtel du roi sous les derniers Valois.* 1991

Farge, J. K., *Biographical Register of Paris Doctors of Theology, 1500–1536.* Toronto, 1980

Orthodoxy and Reform in Early Reformation France: The Faculty of Theology of Paris, 1500–1543. Leiden, 1985

Febvre, L., *Autour de l'Heptaméron: amour sacré, amour profane.* 1944

'Dolet propagateur de l'évangile', *B.H.R.*, vi (1945), 98–170

Le problème de l'incroyance: la religion de Rabelais. 1947

Au coeur religieux du XVIe siècle. 1957

Febvre, L. and Martin, H.-J., *The Coming of the Book: The Impact of Printing.* London, 1976

Félibien, M., *Histoire de la ville de Paris*, 5 vols. 1725

Fêtes et cérémonies au temps de Charles-Quint, ed. J. Jacquot. 1960

Fleury, M. and Kruta, V., *Le château du Louvre.* 1990

Floquet, A., *Histoire du parlement de Normandie*, 7 vols. Rouen 1840

Fraisse, M., 'Sur la maladie et la mort de François Ier', unpublished medical thesis, University of Paris, 1962

François, M., *Le cardinal François de Tournon.* 1951
    'L'idée d'empire en France à l'époque de Charles-Quint', *Charles-Quint et son temps.* 1959

Franklin, A., *Précis de l'histoire de la Bibliothèque du Roi.* 2nd edn. 1875

Franklin, J. H., *Jean Bodin and the Rise of Absolutist Theory.* Cambridge, 1973

Freedberg, S. J., *Andrea del Sarto*, 2 vols. Cambridge, MA, 1963

Freedman, R., 'Paris and the French Court under Francis I', *The Renaissance*, ed. I. Fenlon. London, 1989

French Humanism, 1470–1600, ed. W. L. Gundersheimer. London, 1969

Freymond, J., *La politique de François Ier à l'égard de la Savoie.* Lausanne, 1939

Gachard, L.-P., *La captivité de François Ier et le traité de Madrid.* Brussels, 1860

Gaffarel, P., *Histoire du Brésil français au seizième siècle* 1878
    'Les massacres de Cabrières et de Mérindol en 1545', *R.H.*, cvii (1911), 241–71

Gaillard, G.-H. *Histoire de François premier*, 7 vols. 1766

Garrisson, J., *Royaume, Renaissance et Réforme, 1483–1559.* 1991

Gascon, R., *Grand commerce et vie urbaine au XVIe siècle: Lyon et ses marchands*, 2 vols. 1971

Gebelin, F., *Les châteaux de la Renaissance.* 1927

Giesey, R., *The Royal Funeral Ceremony in Renaissance France.* Geneva, 1960
    'State-Building in Early Modern France: The Role of Royal Officialdom', *J.M.H.*, 55 (1983), 191–207
    '*Cérémonie et puissance souveraine: France, XVe–XVIIe siècles.* 1987

Gigon, S.-C., *La révolte de la gabelle en Guyenne, 1548–49.* 1906

Giono, J., *Le désastre de Pavie.* 1963

Giry-Deloison, C., 'Money and Early Tudor Diplomacy. The English Pensioners of the French Kings (1475–1547)', *Medieval History* (forthcoming)

Godefroy, T., *Le cérémonial françois*, 2 vols. 1649

Golson, L., 'Serlio, Primaticcio and the Architectural Grotto', *G.B.A.*, lxxvii (1971), 95–108

Goubert, P., 'Recent Theories and Research on French Population between 1500–1700' in *Population in History*, eds. D. V. Glass and D. E. C. Eversley (London, 1965), pp. 456–73

Greengrass, M., *The French Reformation*. Oxford, 1987

'Property and Politics in Sixteenth-Century France: The Landed Fortune of Constable Anne de Montmorency', *F.H.*, ii (1988), 371–98

Guénée, B., *Tribunaux et gens de justice dans le bailliage de Senlis à la fin du Moyen Age*. Strasbourg, 1963

Guénée, B., and Lehoux, F., *Les entrées royales françaises de 1328 à 1515*. 1968

Guénin, E., *Ango et ses pilotes*. 1901

Guillaume Farel, 1489–1565: biographie nouvelle écrite d'après les documents originaux par un groupe d'historiens, professeurs et pasteurs de Suisse, de France et d'Italie. Neuchâtel, 1930

Guillaume, J., 'Léonard de Vinci, Dominique de Cortone et l'escalier du modèle en bois de Chambord', *G.B.A.*, i (1968), 93–108

'Léonard de Vinci et l'architecture française: 1. Le problème de Chambord', 2. La villa de Charles d'Amboise et le château de Romorantin: reflexion sur un livre de Carlo Pedretti', *Revue de l'Art*, 25 (1974), 71–91

'Fontainebleau 1530: le pavillon des Armes et sa porte égyptienne', *Bulletin monumental*, cxxxvii (1979), 225–40

'Léonard et l'architecture' in *Léonard de Vinci ingénieur et architecte*. Montreal, 1987

Guillaume, J. and Grodecki, C., 'Le jardin des Pins à Fontainebleau', *Bulletin de la sociéte de l'histoire de l'art français* (1978), 43–51

Gunn, S. J., 'The Duke of Suffolk's March on Paris in 1523', *E.H.R.*, 101 (1986), 596–634

Charles Brandon, Duke of Suffolk, c. 1484–1545. Oxford, 1988

Gutton, J. P., *La société et les pauvres: l'exemple de la généralité de Lyon, 1534–1789*. 1971

La société et les pauvres en Europe (XVI–XVIIe siècles). 1974

Guy, J., 'The French King's Council, 1483–1526' in *Kings and Nobles in the Later Middle Ages*, eds. R. A. Griffiths and J. Sherborne. (New York, 1986), pp. 274–94

Gwyn, P., 'Wolsey's Foreign Policy: The Conferences at Calais and Bruges Reconsidered', *H.J.*, 23 (1980), 755–72

Hale, J. R., 'Armies, Navies and the Art of War' in *The New Cambridge Modern History*, ii, *The Reformation*, ed. G. R. Elton. Cambridge, 1958

War and Society in Renaissance Europe, 1450–1620. London, 1985

Halkin, L. E. and Dansaert, G., *Charles de Lannoy*. Brussels, 1934

Hamon, P., 'Un après-guerre financier: la rançon de François Ier', *Etudes champenoises* (1990), 9–20

'L'argent du roi: Finances et gens de finances en France au temps de François Ier', unpublished doctoral thesis, University of Paris I. 1993

Hamy, le P., *Entrevue de François Ier avec Henri VIII à Boulogne-sur-Mer en 1532*. 1898

Entrevue de François Ier avec Clément VII à Marseille, 1533. 1900

Hanley, Sarah, *The 'Lit de Justice' of the Kings of France: Constitutional Ideology in Legend, Ritual and Discourse*. Princeton, NJ, 1983

Harding, R. R., *Anatomy of a Power Elite: The Provincial Governors of Early Modern France*. New Haven, CT and London, 1978

Hari, R., 'Les placards de 1534' in *Aspects de la propagande religieuse*, ed. G. Berthoud *et al*. Geneva, 1957

Hauser, H., 'Sur la date exacte de la mort de Louis XII et de l'avènement de François Ier', *Rev. d'hist. mod. et contemp.*, v (1903–4), 172–82

'Le journal de Louise de Savoie', *R.H.* 86 (1904), 280–303

Etudes sur la réforme française. 1909

Les sources de l'histoire de France au XVIe siècle: ii. François Ier et Henri II (1515–1559). 1909

'Le traité de Madrid et la cession de la Bourgogne à Charles-Quint', *Revue bourguignonne*, xxii (1912)

Les débuts du capitalisme. 1924

Ouvriers du temps passé. 1927

Heller, H., 'Marguerite of Navarre and the Reformers of Meaux', *B.H.R.*, 33 (1971), 271–310

'The Briçonnet Case Reconsidered' in *Journal of Medieval and Renaissance Studies*, 2 (1972), 223–58

'The Evangelicism of Lefèvre d'Etaples', *Studies in the Renaissance*, 19 (1972), 43–77

'Famine, Revolt and Heresy at Meaux, 1521–25', *A.R.*, 68 (1977), 133–57

The Conquest of Poverty: The Calvinist Revolt in Sixteenth-Century France. Leiden, 1986

Iron and Blood: Civil Wars in Sixteenth-Century France. Montreal and Kingston, 1991

Hempsall, D., 'The Languedoc 1520–1540: A Study of Pre-Calvinist Heresy in France', *A.R.*, lxii (1971), 225–44

'Martin Luther and the Sorbonne, 1519–21', *B.I.H.R.*, xlvi (1973), 28–40

'Measures to Suppress "La Peste Luthérienne" in France, 1521–2', *B.I.H.R.*, xlix (1976), 296–9

Herbet, F., *Le château de Fontainebleau*. 1937

Heubi, W., *François Ier et le mouvement intellectuel en France, 1515–1547*. Lausanne, 1913

Hexter, J. H., *The Vision of Politics on the Eve of the Reformation: More, Machiavelli and Seyssel*. London, 1973

Heydenreich, L. H., 'Leonardo da Vinci, Architect of Francis I', *Burlington Magazine*, xciv (Oct. 1952), 277–85

Higman, F. M., *Censorship and the Sorbonne*. Geneva, 1979

Hobson, A. *Great Libraries*. London, 1970
  Humanists and Bookbinders. Cambridge, 1989

Holt, M. P. (ed.), *Society and Institutions in Early Modern France*. Athens, GA, 1991

Hook, J. *The Sack of Rome*. London, 1972

Hughes, P. E., *Lefèvre: Pioneer of Ecclesiastical Renewal in France*. Grand Rapids, MI, 1984

Hyrvoix, A., 'François Ier et la première guerre de religion en Suisse, 1529–1531', *R.Q.H.*, lxxi (1902), 465–537
  'Noël Bédier, d'après des documents inédits', *R.Q.H.*, lxxii (1902), 578–91

Imbart de La Tour, P., *Les origines de la Réforme*, 4 vols. 1905–35

Ives, E. W., *Anne Boleyn*. Oxford, 1986

Jackson, R. A., *Vive le Roi! A History of the French Coronation from Charles V to Charles X*. Chapel Hill and London, 1984

Jacquart, J. *La crise rurale en Ile-de-France 1550–1670*. 1974
  François Ier. 1981
  Bayard. 1987
  Paris et l'Ile-de-France au temps des paysans (XVIe–XVIIe siècles). 1990

Jacqueton, G. *La politique extérieure de Louise de Savoie*. 1892
  'Le Trésor de l'Epargne sous François Ier, 1523–1547', *R.H.*, lv (1894), 1–43; lvi (1894), 1–38

Jedin, H., *A History of the Council of Trent*, tr. E. Graf, 2 vols. London, 1957–61

Joannides, P. 'Michelangelo's Lost Hercules', *Burlington Magazine*, cxix (1977), 550–5
  'A Supplement to Michelangelo's Lost Hercules', *Burlington Magazine*, cxxiii (1981), 20–3

Jouanna, Arlette, *Ordre social: mythes et hiérarchies dans la France du XVIe siècle*. 1977
  Le devoir de révolte: la noblesse française et la gestation de l'Etat moderne, 1559–1661. 1989

Joukovsky, F., 'L'Empire et les barbares dans la Galerie François Ier', *B.H.R.*, 50 (1988), 7–28

Jourda, P., *Marguerite d'Angoulême*, 2 vols. 1930

Julien, C. A., *Les voyages de découverte et les premiers établissements*. 1948

Kane, J. E., 'Sur un poème du roi François Ier', *B.H.R.*, 38 (1976), 89–92

Kast, P. 'Remarques sur la musique et les musiciens de la chapelle de François Ier au camp du drap d'or' in *Fêtes et cérémonies au temps de Charles-Quint*, ed. J. Jacquot (1960), pp. 135–46

Kelley, D. R., *The Beginning of Ideology: Consciousness and Society in the French Reformation*. Cambridge, 1981

Keohane, N. O., *Philosophy and the State in France: The Renaissance to the Enlightenment*. Princeton, NJ, 1980

Knecht, R. J., 'The Concordat of 1516: A Re-assessment', *University of Birmingham Historical Journal*, ix (1963), 16–32. Repr. in *Government in Reformation Europe*, ed. H. J. Cohn (London, 1971), pp. 91–112

'The Early Reformation in England and France: A Comparison', *History*, lvii (1972), 1–16

'The Court of Francis I', *E.S.R.*, viii (1978), 1–22

'Francis I and Paris', *History*, lxvi (1981), 18–33

'Francis I and the *lit de justice*: A "legend" defended', *F.H.*, 7 (1993), 53–83

Körner, M. *Solidarités financières suisses au XVIe siècle*. Lausanne, 1980

Kusenberg, K., *Le Rosso*. 1931

La Chapelle, Baron de, 'Jean Le Veneur et le Canada', *Nova Francia*, vi (1931), 341–3

La Coste-Messelière, M. G. de, 'Battista della Palla conspirateur, marchand ou homme de cour?', *L'oeil*, cxxix (1965), 19–24, 34

La Martinière, J. de, 'Les Etats de 1532 et l'Union de la Bretagne à la France', *Bulletin de la Société polymathique du Morbihan* (Vannes, 1911), 177–93

Langbein, J. H., *Prosecuting Crime in the Renaissance*. Cambridge, MA, 1974

La Roncière, C. de, *Histoire de la marine française*, 6 vols. 1899–1932

Lavedan, P., *Histoire de l'urbanisme*. 1941

Lebey, A., *Le connétable de Bourbon*. 1904

Le Clech-Charton, S., 'Les notaires et secrétaires du Roi et la commande artistique officielle: service du roi, des grands et de la ville', *Bibliothèque de l'Ecole des Chartes*, vol. 146 (1988), pp. 307–35

Chancellerie et culture au XVIe siècle. Les notaires et secrétaires du roi de 1515 à 1547. Toulouse, 1993

Lecoq, A.-M., 'La salamandre royale dans les entrées de François Ier' in *Les fêtes de la Renaissance*, iii, eds. J. Jacquot and E. Konigson (1975), pp. 93–104

'Un portrait "kabbalistique" du roi de France vers 1520', *Bulletin de la Société de l'Art français* (1981), 15–20

'La symbolique de l'Etat: les images de la monarchie des premiers Valois à Louis XIV' in *Les Lieux de Mémoire*, vol. II: *La nation*, ed. P. Nora (1986), pp. 145–92

François Ier imaginaire: Symbolique et politique à l'aube de la Renaissance française. 1987

'Une fête italienne à la Bastille en 1518' in *'Il se rendit en Italie'. Etudes offertes à André Chastel*, ed. G. Briganti (Rome, 1987), pp. 149–68

Lefranc, A., *Histoire du Collège de France*. 1893

La vie quotidienne au temps de la Renaissance. 1938

Le Goff, J. and R. Remond, *Histoire de la France Religieuse*, vol. II: *Du Christianisme flamboyant à l'aube des Lumières*, ed. F. Lebrun. 1988

Lemaitre, Nicole, *Le Rouergue flamboyant: le clergé et les fidèles du diocèse de Rodez, 1417–1563*. 1988

Lemonnier, H., *Les guerres d'Italie: la France sous Charles VIII, Louis XII et François Ier (1492–1547)*, vol. v of *Histoire de France*, ed. E. Lavisse. 1903

Léonard, E. G., *Le Protestant français*. 1953

Histoire générale du Protestantisme, 2 vols. 1961

Le Roy Ladurie, E., *Les paysans de Languedoc*, 2 vols. 1966

Carnival: A People's Uprising at Romans, 1579–80, tr. M. Feeney. London, 1980

L'Etat royal, 1460–1610. 1987

Le Roy Ladurie, E., and Morineau, M., *Histoire économique et sociale de la France*, i (1450–1660), pt. 2, *Paysannerie et croissance*. 1977

Lesueur, F., and Lesueur, P., *Le château de Blois*. 1914–21

Lesueur, P., *Dominique de Cortone, dit Le Boccador*. 1928

Levasseur, E., 'Mémoire sur les monnaies du règne de François Ier', in *Ordonnances*, i. pp. xi–ccxxxvii

Histoire du commerce de la France, 2 vols. 1911

Lewis, P. S., *Later Medieval France*, London, 1968

Lloyd, Howell A., *The State, France, and the Sixteenth Century*. London, 1983

Loirette, G., 'La première application à Bordeaux du Concordat de 1516: Gabriel et Charles de Grammont (1529–30)', *A. du M.*, lxviii (1956)

Lot, F., *Recherches sur les effectifs des armées françaises des guerres d'Italie aux Guerres de Religion, 1494–1562*. 1962

Loyseau, C., *Cinq livres du droit des offices*. 1610

McAllister Johnson, W., 'Once more the Galerie François Ier at Fontainebleau', *G.B.A.*, 6th ser., ciii (1984), 127–44

McFarlane, I. D., *A Literary History of France: Renaissance France, 1470–1589*. London, 1974

McNeil, D. O., *Guillaume Budé and Humanism in the Reign of Francis I*. Geneva, 1975

Major, J. Russell, *Representative Institutions in Renaissance France, 1421–1559*. Madison, WI, 1960

'The Crown and the Aristocracy in Renaissance France', *American Historical Review*, lxix (1964), 631–45

Representative Government in Early Modern France. New Haven, CT and London, 1980

'"Bastard Feudalism" and the Kiss: Changing Social Mores in Late Medieval and Early Modern France', *Journal of Interdisciplinary History*, xvii (1987), 509–35

The Monarchy, the Estates and the Aristocracy in Renaissance France. London, 1988

Mann, Margaret, *Erasme et les débuts de la réforme française, 1517–1536.* 1934

Margolin, J.-C., 'Humanism in France' in *The Impact of Humanism on Western Europe*, eds. A. Goodman and A. MacKay (London, 1990), pp. 164–201

Marias, F., 'De Madrid à Paris: François Ier et le Casa de Campo', *Revue de l'Art*, 91 (1991), 26–35

Mariotte, J.-Y., 'François Ier et la Ligue de Smalkalde', *Revue suisse d'histoire*, xvi (1966), 206–42

Martin, V., *Les origines du Gallicanisme*, 2 vols. 1939

Martineau, A., 'L'amiral Chabot, seigneur de Brion (1492?–1542)' in *Positions de thèses de l'Ecole des Chartes* (1883), pp. 77–83

Marx, J., *L'Inquisition en Dauphiné: étude sur le développement et la répression de l'hérésie et de la sorcellerie du XIVe siècle au début du règne de François Ier.* 1914

Masson, P. and M. Vergé-Franceschi (eds.), *La France et la Mer au siècle des grandes découvertes* (1993)

Maugis, E., *Histoire du Parlement de Paris*, 3 vols. 1913–16

Maulde La Clavière, R. de, *Louise de Savoie et François Ier: trente ans de jeunesse, 1485–1515.* 1895

Mayer, C. A., *La religion de Marot.* Geneva, 1960

'L'avocat du roi d'Espagne, Jean Bouchard, le Parlement de Paris, Guillaume Briçonnet et Clément Marot', *B.S.H.P.F.*, 137 (1991), 7–24

Mayer, C. A. and D. Bentley-Cranch, 'Florimond Robertet: Italianisme et Renaissance française', *Mélanges à la mémoire de Franco Simone*, vol. 4 (Geneva, 1983), pp. 136–49

Mellen, J., *Jean Clouet.* London, 1971

Merle, L., *La métairie et l'évolution agraire de la Gâtine poitevine de la fin du moyen âge à la Révolution.* 1958

Michaud, Hélène, *La Grande Chancellerie et les écritures royales au XVIe siècle (1515–89).* 1967

'Les institutions militaires des guerres d'Italie aux guerres de religion', *R.H.*, cclviii (1977), 219–43

Michelet, J. *Histoire de France*, ix, *La Renaissance*; x, *La Réforme.* Nd

Mignet, F., *La rivalité de François Ier et de Charles-Quint*, 2 vols. 1875

Molinier, H.-J., *Mellin de Saint-Gelays (1490?–1558)*. Toulouse, 1909

Moore, W. G., *La réforme allemande et la littérature française*. Strasbourg, 1930

Moreau, E. de, Jourda, P., and Janelle, P., *La crise religieuse du XVIe siècle*. 1950

Morgan, P., 'Un chroniqueur gallois à Calais', *Revue du Nord*, xlvii (1965), 195–202

Mousnier, R., *La vénalité des offices sous Henri IV et Louis XIII*, 2nd edn. 1971
    Le conseil du roi de Louis XII à la Révolution. 1970

Nicholls, D., 'Social Change and Early Protestantism in France: Normandy, 1520–62', *E.S.R.*, x (1980), 279–308
    'Inertia and Reform in the Pre-Tridentine French Church: The Response to Protestantism in the Diocese of Rouen, 1520–1562', *Journal of Ecclesiastical History*, xxxii (1981), 185–97
    'The Nature of Popular Heresy in France, 1520–1542', *H.J.*, 26 (1983), 261–75
    'The Theatre of Martyrdom in the French Reformation', *Past and Present*, 121 (Nov. 1988), pp. 49–73
    'France' in *The Early Reformation in Europe*, ed. A. Pettegree (Cambridge, 1992), pp. 120–41

Nordström, L., 'Albert de Rippe, joueur de luth du Roy', *Early Music*, vii (1979), 378–85

Orth, M., 'François Du Moulin and the Journal of Louise of Savoy', *The Sixteenth Century Journal*, vol. 3 (1982), 55–66

Pagès, G., *La monarchie d'Ancien Régime en France*. 1946

Paillard, C., 'La mort de François Ier et les premiers temps du règne de Henri II d'après les dépêches de Jean de Saint-Mauris (avril–juin 1547)', *R.H.*, v (1877), 84–120
    'Le voyage de Charles V en France', *R.Q.H.*, xxv (1879)
    L'invasion allemande en 1544. 1884

Panofsky, D., and Panofsky, E., 'The Iconography of the Galerie François Ier at Fontainebleau', *G.B.A.*, 6th ser., lii (1958), 113–90

Paris: fonctions d'une capitale, ed. G. Michaud. Colloques: Cahiers de civilisation, 1962

Paris, P., *Etudes sur François Ier*, 2 vols. 1885

Parker, D., *The Making of French Absolutism*. London, 1983

Parker, T.H.L., *John Calvin*. London, 1975

Pastor, L. von, *The History of the Popes*, trs. F. I. Antrobus and R. F. Kerr, 23 vols. London, 1891–1933

Pedretti, C., 'Leonardo da Vinci: Manuscripts and Drawings of the French Period, 1517–18', *G.B.A.*, 6th ser., lxxvi (1970), 285–318
    Leonardo da Vinci: The Royal Palace at Romorantin. Cambridge, MA, 1972

Penrose, B., *Travel and Discovery in the Renaissance, 1420–1620*. Cambridge, MA, 1952

Picot, E., 'Les italiens en France au XVIe siècle', *Bulletin italien*, i (Bordeaux, 1901), 92–137; iii (1903), 7–36

Pieri, P., *Il Rinascimento e la crisi militare italiana*. Turin, 1952

Pinvert, L., *Lazare de Baïf (1496?–1547)*. 1900

Plattard, J., *The Life of François Rabelais*. tr. L. P. Roche. London, 1963

Polizzatto, L., and C. Elam, 'La unione de' Gigli con Gigli: Two documents on Florence, France and the Savonarolan Millenarian Tradition', *Rinascimento*, 2nd ser. vol. xxxi (1991), 239–59

Pollard, A. F., *Henry VIII*. London, 1913

Pollet, J. V., *Martin Bucer*, 2 vols. 1962

Pope-Hennessy, J., *Cellini*. London, 1985

Porée, C., *Un parlementaire sous François Ier: Guillaume Poyet, 1473–1548*. Angers, 1898

Potter, D., *War and Government in the French Provinces: Picardy 1470–1560*. Cambridge, 1993

'Foreign Policy in the Age of the Reformation: French Involvement in the Schmalkaldic War, 1544–1547', *H.J.*, xx (1977), 525–44

Prentout, H., *Les Etats Provinciaux de Normandie*, 3 vols. Caen, 1925

Pressouyre, S., 'Les fontes de Primatice', *Bulletin monumental*, (1969), pp. 223–39

Procacci, G., 'La Provence à la veille des Guerres de Religion: une période décisive, 1535–45', *Rev. d'hist. mod. et contemp.*, v (1958), 249–50

Prunières, H., 'La musique de la chambre et de l'écurie sous le règne de François Ier, 1516–1547', *L'année musicale*, i (1911), 215–51

Quentin-Bauchart, E., *La bibliothèque de Fontainebleau, 1515–89*. 1891

Quilliet, B., *Louis XII*. 1986

Quinn, D. B., *North America from Earliest Discovery to First Settlements*. New York, 1978

Raveau, P., *La condition économique et l'état social du Poitou au XVIe siècle*. 1931

Reese, G., *Music in the Renaissance*, revised edn. New York, 1959

Renaudet, A., *Préréforme et humanisme à Paris pendant les premières guerres d'Italie, 1494–1517*. 1953

Humanisme et Renaissance. Geneva, 1958

Reumont, R., and Baschet, A., *La jeunesse de Catherine de Médicis*. 1866

Reymond, M., and Reymond, M.-R., 'Léonard de Vinci, architecte du château de Chambord', *G.B.A.*, i (1913), 337

Rice, E. F., 'Humanist Aristotelianism in France' in *Humanism in France at the End of the Middle Ages and in the Early Renaissance*, ed. A. H. T. Levi. Manchester, 1970

Richardson, W. C., *Mary Tudor, the White Queen*. London, 1970

Rodriguez-Salgado, M. J., *The Changing Face of Empire: Charles V, Philip II and Habsburg Authority, 1551–1559*. Cambridge, 1988

Roelker, N.L., *Queen of Navarre, Jeanne d'Albret*. Cambridge, MA, 1968

Rolland, R., 'Le dernier procès de Louis de Berquin' in *Mélanges d'archéologie et d'histoire*. Ecole française de Rome, vol. 12 (1892), 314–25

Romier, L., *Les origines politiques des Guerres de Religion*, 2 vols. 1913–14

Rott, E., *Histoire de la representation diplomatique de la France auprès des cantons suisses*, 10 vols. 1900–35

Roy, M., *Artistes et monuments de la Renaissance en France*. 1929

Rozet, A., and Lembey, J.-F., *L'invasion de la France et le siège de Saint-Dizier par Charles-Quint en 1544*. 1910

Ruble, A. de, *Le mariage de Jeanne d'Albret*. 1877

Russell, J. G., *The Field of Cloth of Gold*. London, 1969

'The Search for Universal Peace: The Conferences at Calais and Bruges in 1521', *B.I.H.R.*, xliv (1971), 162–93

Peacemaking in the Renaissance. London, 1986

Salles, G., 'Un traître au XVIe siècle: Clément Champion, valet de chambre de François Ier', *R.Q.H.*, n.s. xxiv (1900), 41–73

Saulnier, V.-L., 'La mort du Dauphin François et son tombeau poétique (1536)', *B.H.R.*, vi (1945), 50–97

Sauval, H., *Histoire et recherches des antiquités de la ville de Paris*, 2 vols. 1724

Scailliérez, Cécile, *François Ier et ses artistes dans les collections du Louvre*. 1992

Scarisbrick, J. J., *Henry VIII*. London, 1968

Schick, L., *Un grand homme d'affaires au début du XVIe siècle, Jacob Fugger*. 1957

Schmidt, C., *Gérard Roussel prédicateur de la reine Marguerite de Navarre*. Strasbourg, 1845

Schnapper, B., *Les rentes au XVIe siècle*. 1957

Schneebalg-Perelman, S., 'Richesses du garde-meuble parisien de François Ier: inventaires inédits de 1542 et 1551', *G.B.A.*, 6th ser. lxxviii (1971), 253–304

Screech, M. A., *Rabelais*. London, 1979

Seward, D., *Prince of the Renaissance: The Life of François I*. London, 1973

Shearman, J., *Andrea del Sarto*, 2 vols. Oxford, 1965

Mannerism. Harmondsworth, Middlesex, 1967

Shell, J., and Sironi, G., 'Salaì and Leonardo's legacy', *Burlington Magazine* (1991), 95–108

Shennan, J. H., *The Parlement of Paris*. London, 1968

Simone, F., *Il Rinascimento francese*. Turin, 1961. Partially tr. H. G. Hall as *The French Renaissance*. London, 1969

Skinner, Q., *The Foundations of Modern Political Thought*, 2 vols. Cambridge, 1978

Smith, M. H., 'La France et sa civilisation vues par les italiens au XVIe siècle', *Positions des thèses, Ecole des Chartes* (1988), 185–97

'François Ier, l'Italie et le château de Blois', *Bulletin monumental*, vol. 147 (1989), 307–23

Smith, P. M., *The Anti-Courtier Trend in Sixteenth-Century French Literature*. Geneva, 1966

Clément Marot, Poet of the French Renaissance. London, 1970

Solnon, J.-F., *La cour de France*. 1987

Spont, A., 'La taille en Languedoc, de 1450 à 1515', *A.du.M.*, ii (1890)

Semblançay (?–1527): la bourgeoisie financière au debut du XVIe siècle. 1895

'Marignan et l'organisation militaire sous François Ier', *R.Q.H.*, n.s. xxii (1899), 59–77

Spooner, F. C., *L'économie mondiale et les frappes monétaires en France, 1493–1680*. 1956

Starkey, D. (ed.), *Henry VIII: A European Court in England*. London, 1991

Stocker, C. W., 'The Politics of the Parlement of Paris in 1525', *F.H.S.*, viii (1973), 191–212

'Public and Private Enterprise in the Administration of a Renaissance Monarchy: The First Sales of Offices in the Parlement of Paris (1512–1524)', *The Sixteenth Century Journal*, ix (1978), 4–6

Stubbs, W., *Lectures on European History*, ed. A. H. Hassall. London, 1904

Sutherland, N. M., *The French Secretaries of State in the Age of Catherine de Medici*. London, 1962

The Huguenot Struggle for Recognition. New Haven, CT and London, 1980

Taylor, F. L., *The Art of War in Italy, 1494–1529*. Cambridge, 1921

Terrasse, C., *François Ier: le roi et le règne*, 3 vols. 1945–70

Tervarent, G., 'La pensée de Rosso', *Les énigmes de l'art: l'Art Savant* (Bruges, 1952), pp. 28ff

Thom, R., *Die Schlacht bei Pavia*. Berlin, 1907

Thomas, J., *Le Concordat de 1516: ses origines, son histoire au XVIe siècle*, 3 vols. 1910

Thomson, D., *Renaissance Paris: Architecture and Growth, 1475–1600*. London, 1984

Thou, J.-A. de, *Histoire universelle*, 16 vols. London, 1734

Tietze, H., 'Titian's Portrait of King Francis I', *Connoisseur*, cxxvi (Oct. 1950)

Toudouze, G.-G., *Françoise de Chateaubriant et François Ier*. 1948

Treccani degli Alfieri, G., *Storia di Milano*, 12 vols. and index. Milan, 1953–66

Trocmé, E., and Delafosse, M., *Le commerce rochelais de la fin du XVe siècle au début du XVIIe*. 1952

Ursu, J., *La politique orientale de François Ier*. 1908

Vaissière, P. de, *Charles de Marillac, ambassadeur et homme politique sous les règnes de François Ier, Henri II et François II (1510–1560)*. 1896

Valois, N., *Histoire de la Sanction Pragmatique de Bourges sous Charles VII*. 1906

Van Doren, L. Scott, 'War Taxation, Institutional Change and Social Conflict in Provincial France – the Royal *Taille* in Dauphiné, 1494–1559', *Proceedings of the American Philosophical Society*, cxxi (1977), 70–96

Varillas, A., *Histoire de François Ier*, 2 vols. 1685

Veissière, M., *L'évêque Guillaume Briçonnet (1470–1534)*. Provins, 1986
  'Guillaume Briçonnet évêque de Meaux et la réforme de son clergé', *Rev. d'hist. ecc.* (1989), 657–72

Vial, M., *L'histoire et la légende de Jean Cléberger dit 'le bon Allemand' (1485–1546)*. Lyons, 1914

Viénot, J., *Histoire de la réforme française des origines à l'Edit de Nantes*, 2 vols. 1926

Vigne, M., *La banque à Lyon du XVe au XVIIIe siècle*. Lyons, 1903

Viollet, P., *Le roi et ses ministres pendant les trois derniers siècles de la monarchie*. 1912

Weigert, R. A., *French Tapestry*. London, 1962

Weiss, N., 'La Sorbonne, le Parlement de Paris et les livres hérétiques de 1542 à 1546', *B.S.H.P.F.*, xxxiv (1885), 19–28
  La Chambre Ardente: étude sur la liberté de conscience sous François Ier et Henri II, 1540–1550. 1889
  'Les premières professions de foi des Protestants français, 1532–47', *B.S.H.P.F.*, xliii (1894), 57–74

Wendel, F., *Calvin*. London, 1965

Wingert, P. S., 'The Funerary Urn of Francis I', *Art Bulletin*, xxi (1939), 383–96

Wolfe, M., 'French Views on Wealth and Taxes from the Middle Ages to the Old Regime', *Journal of Economic History*, xxvi (1966), 466–83
  The Fiscal System of Renaissance France. New Haven, CT and London, 1972

Woodbrige, K., *Princely Gardens: The Origins and Development of the French Formal Style*. London, 1986

Wroth, L. C., *The Voyages of Giovanni da Verrazzano, 1524–1528*. New Haven, CT, 1970

Yates, F., *The Art of Memory*. London, 1966

Zeller, G., *La réunion de Metz à la France (1552–1648), i. L'occupation*. 1926
  'Les rois de France candidats à l'Empire', *R.H.*, clxxiii (1934), 273–311, 497–534

'Gouverneurs de provinces au XVIe siècle', *R.H.*, clxxxv (1939), 225–56

'L'administration monarchique avant les intendants: parlements et gouverneurs', *R.H.*, cxcvii (1947), 188–215

Les institutions de la France au XVIe siècle. 1948

'Une légende qui a la vie dure: les capitulations de 1535', *Rev. d'hist. mod. et contemp.*, ii (1955)

Zerner, H., *The School of Fontainebleau.* London, 1969

Index

Abbate, Niccolo dell', 418
Abbeville, 18
Abbiategrasso, 211
absolutism, 362, 519–26, 530–40
administration, royal, cost of, 43, 50
admiralty, 374–5
Adrian VI (Adrian of Utrecht), pope (1522–23), 182, 201, 211
Afonso V, king of Portugal (1438–81), 370
Agen, 357
Agnadello, battle of (1509), 43
Agramonte, Juan de, 371
agriculture, 24–5, 28, 354–5, 368, 559
Agrippa of Nettesheim, 150
aides, 58–9, 186, 195, 344, 362
Aigues-Mortes, 385–9, 395, 467
Ailly, Pierre d', 145
Aix-en-Provence, 26, 83, 155, 214–15, 323, 325, 335, 337, 339, 511 see also under parlements
Alamanni, Niccolò, 425
Alarçon, Fernando de, 226–7, 243, 248
Alba, Fadrique Alvarez de Toledo (d. 1531), second duke of, 15
Albany, John Stuart, duke of (1481–1536), 182, 195, 200–1, 216, 218, 227, 229, 244
Alberti, Leone Battista (1404–72), 423
Albi, 30, 534
Albizzi (Albisse), Roberto, banker, 188, 269
Albon, Jacques d' (d. 1562), seigneur de Saint-André, marshal of France, 522–3
Albret, Alain d' (d. 1522), regent of Navarre, 86
Albret, Catherine d', widow of Jean d'Albret, king of Navarre, 85–6
Albret, Henri d' (1503–55), king of Navarre, brother-in-law of Francis I, 86–7, 176, 224, 246, 250, 289, 309, 393, 396, 399, 452, 467, 554
Albret, house of, 19, 554
Albret, Jean d', king of Navarre, 84, 87
Albret, Jeanne d' (1528–72), queen of Navarre, 250, 394, 396, 487, 554
Alcalá de Henares, university of, 243
Aldine press, 147

Aleandro, Girolamo, 147
Alençon, 239, 261
Alençon, Charles, duc d' (d. 1525), brother-in-law of Francis I, 43, 75, 83, 107, 113–14, 203, 224, 372, 466
Alessandria, 212, 216, 219
Alexander VI (Rodrigo Borgia), pope (1492–1503), 93, 369, 375
Algiers, 330
Alvarotti, Ferrarese ambassador, 455
Alviano, Bartolomeo d', 73
Amboise, 12, 43, 71, 83, 107, 109n, 116, 140, 248–9, 315–16, 427–9
Amboise, Charles d', 140
Amboise, château of, 4, 112, 133–4, 137, 315, 318–19, 403, 448
Amboise, Georges d' (1460–1515), archbishop of Rouen, cardinal, 4, 11–14, 42, 133
Amboise, Georges d' (1488–1550), archbishop of Rouen (1510), cardinal, 513
Amboise, house of, 50
Amiens, 15, 23, 28, 180, 228, 249, 272–73, 281, 339, 351, 459
Amiens, treaty of (August 1527), 273
Amy, Pierre, 469
Amyot, Jacques (1513–93), 462
Ancona, cardinal of, 82n
Andrelini, Fausto, 146
Anet, château of, 454, 551
Angennes, Jacques d', 541
Angers, 11, 26, 30, 190, 436, 461
Ango, Jean (1480–1551), 370–1, 373–5, 393
Angoulême, 26, 43, 249, 493
Angoulême, Charles, comte d' (d. 1495), father of Francis I, 1, 3–4, 18, 468
Angoulême, house of, 1, 9, 18, 468
Angoulême, Jean d'Orléans (1404–67), comte d', Francis I's paternal grandfather, 1, 2, 11
Angoulême, Marguerite d', see Marguerite d'Angoulême
Angoumois, 4, 129, 289, 483
Anguillara, Virgilio Orsini, count of, 499
Anjou, 43, 129, 186, 275, 289; house of, 63

annates, 91, 94, 96, 98, 102
Anna, daughter of Ferdinand of Habsburg, King
   of the Romans, 340, 386, 493–4
Anne (1477–1514), duchess of Brittany
   (1488–1514), queen of France (as from
   1491), 9, 11–17, 42, 118, 192, 349, 459
Annebault, Claude d' (d. 1552), Admiral of
   France, 224, 340, 389, 396, 455, 480, 485,
   487, 497, 502, 517–18, 541, 543, 546–7, 552
Anne de France, *see* Bourbon, Anne de France,
   duchesse de
Anticosti (Canada), 377–9
Antwerp, 188, 253, 364, 366, 448, 494
Appian, 473
Apulia, 278–9, 340
Arabic, teaching of, 152
Aragon, 19, 84
Aragon, house of, 63
Aragon, Luigi, cardinal of, 428, 436
Arande, Michel d', almoner to Marguerite
   d'Angoulême, 161–2, 238, 239n
Arbresle, L', 116, 117n
Ardres, 140, 171, 174–5, 179
Ardres, treaty of (June 1520), 174; (June 1545),
   475, 503, 517
Aretino, Pietro Bacci (1492–1556), 432–3, 444–6,
   469
Argentan, 427n, 457
argenterie, 118, 344
Argouges, J. d', 207
Ariosto, Ludovico (1474–1533), 469
aristocracy, *see* nobility
Aristotle, 145–7
Arles, 83, 101, 336
Armagnac, Charlotte d', 4
Armagnac, Georges d', bishop of Rodez, 447, 472
army, *see also* artillery, *aventuriers*,
      ban-et-arrière-ban, *compagnies
      d'ordonnances*, *gendarmerie*, landsknechts,
      legions, mercenaries
Arran, James Hamilton (d. 1575), second earl of,
   486
Arras, 180, 240, 284
Ars, Louis d', 73, 75
Arthur, prince of Wales (1486–1502), 113
artillery, 28, 70, 75, 77, 130, 306, 336–7, 504
artisans, 34–6, 120, 358–9, 364, 512
Artois, 19, 66, 239, 246, 284, 339–40, 486
Assier, château of, 424
Asti, county of, 9, 12, 240, 256
Attaingnant, Pierre, music printer, 460
Attigny, 179
Aubenton, sack of (1521), 179
Aubert, Thomas, 370
Aubéry, Jacques, 514
Aubigny, Robert Stuart d' (d. 1544), marshal of
   France, 43
Audisio, G., historian, 325n
Aumale, comte d', *see* Guise, François de
Aumône-Générale, 358–60; *see also* poor
aune du roi, 361
Ausonius, 464

Austria, 85
Autun, 101
Autun, bishop of, *see* Hurault, Jacques
Auvergne, 22, 42, 53, 204, 208, 268, 289, 350
Auxonne, 255
Auxy-le-Château, 339
aventuriers, 69, 337
Avignon, 83, 215, 300, 302, 324–5, 335, 337–8,
   462, 480, 514, 536
Azay-le-Rideau, château of, 137, 140, 192

Babou, Philibert, *Trésorier de l'Epargne*, 193,
   198, 226, 419, 487
Bade, Josse, 36
Baden, diet of, 303
Badouin, Claude, 449
Bahia, 374
Baïf, Lazare de (1496–1547), 445
bailli(s), 31, 55–6, 69, 268, 275, 359, 510
bailliage(s), 26, 52, 54–6, 60, 195, 352–3, 507
Balbi, Girolamo, 146
Baltic states, 29
Balzac, Pierre de, seigneur d'Entragues, 418
Bandinelli, Baccio (1488–1560), 441, 447
Bandini, Giovanni, 443
ban-et-arrière-ban, 56, 69, 275, 481, 514, 536
banks, 29, 166–7, 187–9, 504–5; *see also* Lyons:
   banks and bankers; loans, royal
Bar, duchy of, 19
Barbarossa, Khair ad-Din (1467–1546), 299–300,
   329–30, 487, 489
Barcelona, 242, 330
Barcelona, treaty of (June 1529), 279
Bar-le-Duc, treaty of (January, 1534), 303
Barrillon, Jean, secretary to Chancellor Duprat,
   43, 85, 167, 361
Basle, 153n, 156, 307, 311, 326
Basle, council of (1431–49), 91, 96
Basoche, clerks of the, 18, 49
Bavaria, Ludwig, duke of, 295, 303
Bavaria, Wilhelm IV (b. 1493), duke of, 295, 303
Bayard, Gilbert, *secrétaire des finances*, 507, 553
Bayard, Pierre du Terrail, seigneur de
   (1473–1524), 77, 178, 211
Bayeux, 155, *See also Grands Jours*
Bayle, Pierre (1647–1706), 555
Baynton, Andrew, 315n
Bayonne, 15, 209, 248, 285–6, 391
Beatis, Antonio De, 105, 111, 113–14, 354, 428,
   471, 558
Beaton, David (1494–1546), archbishop of St
   Andrews, cardinal, 503
Beaucaire, 336
Beaucaire, François, 557
Beauce, 28, 31
Beaufort-en-Vallée, county of, 43
Beaugency, 510
Beaujeu, Anna de, *see* Bourbon, Anne de France,
   duchesse de
Beaujeu, Pierre de, *see* Bourbon, Pierre II, duc de
Beaujolais, county of, 204, 289
Beaune family, 192

Beaune, Guillaume de, *général des finances*, 192–3, 271, 348

Beaune, Jacques de (d. 1527), *général des finances*, baron de Semblançay, 189, 192–4, 196–7, 268–71, 348, 558

Beaune, Marie de, 271

Beaurain, Adrien de Croy (d. 1553), seigneur de, imperial chamberlain, 206, 211, 239–40

Beauvais, 277, 545

Beauvais, bishop of, 45, 552

Béda, Noël, (1470?–1537), principal of Collège de Montaigu; syndic of Sorbonne, 144, 146–7, 159, 161–2, 164, 239, 261, 293–4, 309, 312–13

Béguin, Sylvie, art historian, 432, 435

Bellarmato, Girolamo, Sienese engineer, 367–8

Belle Ferronière, La, 557

Belle Isle, Strait of, 375–6, 378

Belli, Valerio (1468–1546), 300–1, 439

Bellin, Niccolò, 417, 426

Benedict XIII, antipope (1394–1424), 91

Benisanó, 242

Berne, 73; council of, 326–7

Bernese, 332

Beroaldo, Filippo, 146

Berquin, Louis de (d. 1529), 163–4, 239, 260–1, 283

Berruyer, P., 232–3, 234

Berthelot family, 192

Berthelot, Gilles, seigneur d'Azay, 141, 192–3, 271, 348

Besnier, Etienne, 348

Bessan (Languedoc), 355

Beyries, monastery of, 286

Bèze, Théodore de, 318

Bibbiena, Bernardo Dovizi, cardinal and legate, 436, 438, 447

Bidassoa, river, 247–8, 278, 286

Bidoux, Prégent de, captain-general of the galleys, 83

births and deaths, registration of, 25, 352–3

Blois, 12, 17, 109, 114, 116, 201, 250, 308, 315, 318, 373, 425; château of, 4, 109, 134–8, 401, 423; king's library at, 109, 147, 260, 308, 468, 471–3

Blois, treaty of (August 1501), 12

Blondet, André, *Trésorier de l'Epargne*, 553

Blunt, Anthony, art historian, 137

Bochart, Jean, 232, 237

Bochetel, Guillaume (d. 1558), *secrétaire des finances*, 507, 553

Bodin, Jean (1530–96), 505–6

Bohemia, king of, 165–6

Bohier, Antoine, seigneur de Chenonceaux, 271

Bohier, Henri, 348

Bohier, Thomas (d. 1524), *général des finances*, 140, 192–3, 348–9, 392

Boileau, François, 264

Bois de Boulogne, 398, 400, 404

Boisy, cardinal de, *see* Gouffier, Adrien

Boisy, seigneur de, *see* Gouffier, Artus *and* Claude

Boleyn, Anne (1507?–36), queen of England, 297–9, 304

Boleyn, George (d. 1536), Viscount Rochford, 293, 298–9

Boleyn, Sir Thomas (1477–1539), earl of Wiltshire, 168

Bologna, 82, 103, 284–5, 298, 427, 436, 458, 468; *see also* Concordat of Bologna

Bomy, truce of (July, 1537), 340

Bonavista, Cape, 376

Boniface VIII, pope (1294–1303), 88, 90, 201

Bonner, Edmund (1500?–69), bishop of London, 122, 302

Bonneval, Jean de, 335

Bonnivet, Admiral, *see* Gouffier, Guillaume

Bontemps, Pierre (1506?–1570?), sculptor, 71, 549–50

bookbinding, 475–7

Book of Sentences, 144–5, 148–9

Bordeaux, 23, 26, 28, 30, 34, 131, 244, 249, 252, 294, 357, 361, 366–7, 369, 391, 445, 481; *see also under* parlements

Borgherini family, 441

Bossut, Nicolas de, *see* Longueval

Bouchage, Ymbert de Batarnay, seigneur du, 189

Bouchain, 180

Bouchard, Jean, 264

Boulogne, 209, 229, 501, 503, 517–18, 558; Anglo–French meeting at (1532), 297–8; siege of (1544), 491, 502–3

Boulonnais, 276, 486

Bourbon: demesne, 19; duchy of, 493; house of, 43, 112, 203, 553–4, 557

Bourbon, Anne de France (1460–1522), duchesse de, 1, 117n, 204

Bourbon, Antoine de (1518–62), duc de Vendôme (1537–62), king of Navarre (1555–62), 482, 486, 554

Bourbon, Charles de, cardinal, 101, 554

Bourbon, Charles de (1480–1537), comte then duc (1515) de Vendôme, governor of Paris then of Picardy, 37, 107, 179n, 200, 203, 209, 227, 235, 250, 275, 317, 337, 372

Bourbon, Charles III (1490–1527), duc de (1503–27), Constable of France, 16, 43, 46, 49, 72, 75, 77, 83, 107, 179n, 201–16, 226, 239–40, 242, 246–7, 250, 252, 256, 259–60, 267–8, 274, 284, 290, 335–7, 340, 373, 473, 539, 557

Bourbon, François de, vicomte then duc de Châtellerault (d. 1515), 43, 77n

Bourbon, François I de (1491–1545), comte de Saint-Pol, governor of Paris, 109, 211, 224, 231, 250, 279, 372, 487

Bourbon, François de (1519–46), comte d'Enghien, 487, 490

Bourbon, Jean I, duc de (d. 1434), 203

Bourbon, Louis de, cardinal, 101, 275

Bourbon, Louis de, prince de Condé, 554

Bourbon, Marguerite de, Francis I's maternal grandmother, 1

Bourbon, Pierre II, duc de (d. 1504), 1, 50, 203–4

Bourbon, Renée de, duchess of Lorraine, 208
Bourbon, Suzanne de (d. 1521), wife of the
    Constable of Bourbon, 203–4
Bourbonnais, 204, 289
Bourdichon, Jean (1457?–1521), 427
Bourg, 481
Bourg-en-Bresse, 332
Bourgeois de Paris, chronicler, 48, 190, 195, 210,
    264, 300, 404
bourgeoisie, 191, 245, 509
Bourges, 26, 91, 227, 361; archbishop of, 92;
    provincial synod, 275; Pragmatic Sanction
    of Bourges of (1438), 38, 82, 91–2, 94,
    96–100, 102, 263, 560
Bovelles, Charles de, 155
Boyvin, René, 432
Brabant, 66, 486
Braisne, Amé de Sarrebruck (1495–1525), comte
    de, 231
Bramante, Donato (1444–1514), 135
Brandenburg, bishop of, 168
Brandenburg, Joachim I, Margrave of
    (1499–1535), 165, 168
Brandon, Charles (d. 1545), first duke of Suffolk,
    67, 208–9, 297, 491
Brantôme, Pierre de Bourdeille (1540–1614),
    abbé de, 249n, 271n, 500, 555, 557–8
Braudel, F., historian, 22–3, 357
Brazil, 370–1, 373–6, 381
Bremgarten, treaty of (November 1531), 295n
Bresse, 129, 552
Bresse, Philip, count of, *see* Savoy, Philip of
Brest, 130
Brethren of the Common life, 145–6
Bretons, 349, 370–1, 374
Brézé, Louis de (d. 1531), *grand sénéchal* of
    Normandy, 201, 207, 210
Brice, Germain; *see also* Brie, Germain de
Briçonnet, Charlotte, 192
Briçonnet, Guillaume (1470–1534), bishop of
    Meaux, 101–2, 114, 155–6, 161–3, 237–9
Bricot, Thomas, 12
Brie, 28, 359
Brie, Germain de (1490?–1538), 153, 473
Brion, Bertrand Simon, alias, 211
Brienne, comtesse de, 500
Brissac, Charles de Cossé (1506–63), comte de,
    557
Brittany, 32, 39, 57, 129, 186, 190, 366, 483;
    estates of, 349, 350, 533–4; governor of 374,
    423; legion of 350–1
Brittany, duchy of, 9, 11, 19, 197, 493;
    annexation of, 349–50
Brittany, duke of, 17
Bronzino, Agnolo (1503–72), 445
Brosse, Jean de (1505?–65), seigneur de
    Penthièvre, comte then duc d'Etampes, 290,
    557
Browne, Sir Anthony (d. 1548), 249–50
Brück, Gregor (1484?–1557) chancellor of
    Saxony, 323
Bruges, 178

Bruges, treaty of (August 1521), 178–80
Brussels, 393, 448, 551
Bryan, Sir Francis (d. 1550), 289
Bucer, Martin (1491–1551), 304, 308, 322–3
Budé, Guillaume (1468–1540), 6, 147, 150–4,
    306, 311, 467, 469, 472–3, 522, 560
Bureau, Gaspard (d. 1469?), 70
Bureau, Jean (d. 1463), 70
Bureau des pauvres, 359–60
Burgundy, 22, 28–9, 32, 42, 57, 60, 129, 178n,
    231, 243, 254, 277, 355, 357, 504, 553;
    customs, 522; governor of, 253, 393; legion,
    350; *recette-générale*, 506
Burgundy, duchy of, 12, 66, 197, 239–40, 245–7,
    253–4, 256, 272, 274, 284, 333, 394, 493,
    558; duke(s) of, 117; house of, 19, 66; *see
    also* estates, provincial
Burgundy, Mary of (1457–82), 1
Busleiden, Jerome, 152
Bussy, Jacques d'Amboise, seigneur de, 77n

Cabala, 149–50
Cabrières, 324, 512, 514, 516
Caen, 26
Cahors, 26
Cajetan, Gaetano, cardinal, 156
Calabria, 279
Calais, 19, 175, 200, 209, 350, 486–7, 491;
    conference at (1521), 177–80; Anglo–French
    meeting (1532), 297; peace talks (1544), 501
Calicut, 361
Calvimont, Jean de, 257
Calvin, Jean (1509–64), 163, 311–12, 325–6, 467,
    508
Calvinism, 325, 509, 560
Cambrai, 283–4, 487
Cambrai, treaty of (March 1517), 85, 170;
    (August 1529) ('Peace of the Ladies'), 117,
    189, 268, 284–5, 291, 293, 295, 303, 305–6,
    331, 339, 343, 345, 395, 432–3, 445, 466
Cambrésis, 24
Cameron, E., historian, 325n
Camillo (Delminio), Giulio, 149
Camp, treaty of, *see* Ardres
Canada, 378, 382–3, 559
Canaples, Marie d'Acigné (1502–58), dame de,
    483, 549
Canossa, Lodovico di (1475?–1532), bishop of
    Tricarico (1511) and of Bayeux (1517), 93,
    155
Canossa (Paradis), Paul, *lecteur royal*, 307
Canova da Milano, Francesco, lutenist, 459
Capito, Wolfgang (1478–1541), 238, 261, 307
Capitulations (February 1536), 329, 476; *see also*
    Turks
Capidiferro (or Recenas), Jerome, papal nuncio,
    123
Caracciolo, Marino Ascanio (1469–1538),
    cardinal and legate, 334
Caraccioli family, 124
Carignano, siege of, 490
Carlat, 208: *vicomté* of, 204

Carlisle, 200
Carmoy, François, 548–9
Caroli, Pierre (d. 1550?), 156, 162, 238–9, 261, 317
Carré, Jean, 348
Cartier, Jacques (1491–1557), 375–84
Casa de Campo (Madrid), 404–5
Castiglione, Baldassare (1478–1529), 6, 8, 125, 473
Castile, 84, 176–7, 278, 370, 375, 401
Castillon, Louis du Perreau, seigneur de, 122
Catherine de' Medici (1519–89), wife of Henri, duc d'Orléans, later Henri II, king of France, 124–5, 297, 300–1, 305, 331, 338, 343, 399, 404, 411, 422, 439, 452, 475, 485n, 499
Catherine of Aragon (1485–1536), queen of England, aunt of the Emperor Charles V, 174–5, 272, 285, 291, 297, 299
Catholic Kings (Ferdinand of Aragon and Isabella of Castile), 369
Cavaillon, bishop of, 512
Cavalli, Marino (1500–73), Venetian ambassador, 25, 187, 354, 485, 497, 503
Cavriana, Emilio, 246
Cellini, Benvenuto (1500–71), 131, 133, 391, 431, 439, 444, 449–57, 498
censorship, 144, 159, 161, 163–4, 316, 320, 508–9
Cental, Mérite de Trivulce, dame de, 514, 516
Cercle de Meaux, 156, 162–3, 237–8, 260, 308, 313
Ceresole (Cérisoles), battle of (14 April 1544), 467, 490, 549
Ceri, Renzo da (1475–1536), 214, 448
Cervia, 279, 284
Chabannes, Antoine de, bishop of Le Puy, 206–7, 267
Chabannes, Jacques de (1465–1525), seigneur de Lapalisse, marshal of France, 43, 213, 224
Chabot, Charles, seigneur de Jarnac, mayor of Bordeaux, 481
Chabot, Philippe (1480–1543), seigneur de Brion, Admiral of France, 1, 284, 289, 297, 348, 379, 557; childhood companion of Francis, 1, 8; reassures Parisians, 209; defends Marseilles, 214; captured at Pavia, 224, 226; embassy to Spain, 243, 246; early career, 252–53; and Burgundy, 255; embassy to England, 304; chief minister, 331; invades Savoy, 332; recalled to France, 334; and Verrazzano, 373; and Portuguese, 374–5, 393; builds Pagny, 424; rivalry with Montmorency, 393, 484; fall, 348, 392–3; trial, 500, 504; rehabilitated, 484; and court faction, 484–5; death, 485
Chaleur Bay (Canada), 376
Challuau, château of, 407
Chalon, house of, 19
Châlons, 491–2
Chambéry, 83, 84n, 117n, 208, 332
Chambiges, Pierre (d. 1544), 405, 407
Chambord, château of, 112, 134, 137–40, 392, 401, 419, 423, 428

Chambre aux deniers, 120
Chambre de la reine, 516
Chambre de la Salle Verte, 231
Chambre(s) des Comptes, 42, 120, 191, 196, 269, 276, 346, 348, 515, 521
Chambre des monnaies, 363
Chambre du domaine, 531
Champagne, 28, 209, 337, 490, 492; legion of, 350–1, 385
Champier, Symphorien, 150, 358
Champion, Clément, 246
Chancellor of France, see also Duprat, Antoine; Poyet, Guillaume
Chancery, 39, 49, 52
Chanforan, synod of, 324–5
Changeur du Trésor, 61, 346, 507
Chantelle, 207–8
Chantilly, 105, 122, 286, 289, 398
Chantilly, château of, 331, 392, 423
Chapelle de musique, 458
Charles (1522–45), duc d'Angoulême then duc d'Orléans, third son of Francis I, 116, 132, 260, 297, 304, 317, 331, 333, 338, 340, 383, 386–7, 391, 394, 474, 480, 484, 493–4, 509, 545–9
Charles III, duke of Savoy (1504–53), 72–3, 299, 331–3, 386, 394, 543
Charles V, king of France (1364–80), 59, 89, 399
Charles V, Holy Roman Emperor (1519–58), king of Aragon, Castile and Naples (as Charles I, 1516–56), 9, 12, 104, 116–17, 129, 150, 153, 165, 175–6, 178, 180, 209, 253–5, 291, 296, 323, 331, 332–3, 341, 467, 478, 487, 507, 537; parentage and inheritance, 66; king of Spain, 84–6; signs treaty of Noyon, 84, 86; signs treaty of Cambrai, 85; and Leo X, 177; and Navarre, 86–7, 396; and tribute for Naples, 86, 185, 194; election to Holy Roman Empire, 166–8; and Henry VIII, 171, 175, 213, 486; contemporary reputation, 176; accuses Francis of starting war, 176; launches offensive against France's north-west frontier, 177–8; visits England, 200; and duc de Bourbon, 206–7, 214; insists on exchanging Milan for Burgundy, 211; his estimate of French losses, 212; and battle of Pavia, 226; cold-shoulders Henry VIII's plan to dismember France, 229; debts to Henry VIII, 239, 256, 259, 285; his peace terms, 239; welcomes Francis to Spain, 242; grants Montmorency's demands, 243; and duchy of Burgundy, 243, 245, 493; negotiates with Louise of Savoy, 243–6; and Clement VII, 257, 260, 278; visits Francis in Madrid, 245; listens to Lannoy, 247; invited to join League of Cognac, 255; his plans shattered by League of Cognac, 256; challenges Francis to a duel, 257, 278, 333–4; sent ultimatum by England and France, 256; refuses to release Francis's sons for ransom, 257, 278; orders their removal to Segovia,

278; and Andrea Doria, 279; and peace of Cambrai, 284; crowned Emperor in Bologna, 285; and German princes, 490, 517; and General Council, 517; mounts expedition against Barbarossa, 329–30; sends Nassau to France, 304; meets cardinal of Lorraine in Siena, 333; refuses papal mediation, 334; invades Provence, 326, 334; captures Aix, 337; accused of instigating Dauphin's murder, 338; retreats from Provence, 338; launches counter-offensive in northern France, 339; signs truce of Monzon, 340; opposes French overseas enterprise, 381–2; meets Queen Eleanor, 387; meets Francis at Aigues-Mortes, 385; accepts French proposals, 387; and Turks, 296, 386, 388, 391; suggests Franco-imperial embassy to Venice, 389; visits France, 343, 385, 389–92, 399, 403, 405, 411, 413, 435, 478, 495; crushes Ghent revolt, 394, 482; sends peace proposals to France, 394; and duchesse d'Etampes, 395; invests son with Milan, 395; and duke of Cleves, 396; satirised by Rabelais, 470; disclaims responsibility for murder of French diplomats, 479; calls off siege of Algiers, 479; Francis declares war on, 479; declares war on France, 486; seizes Cambrai, 487; besieges Saint-Dizier, 491; abandons march on Paris, 491, 493; signs peace of Crépy, 493, 513; favours mariage between his niece and duc d'Orléans, 494; and German Protestants, 502, 517; estimate of Vaudois losses, 515; abdicates, 551
Charles VII, king of France (1422–61), 22, 60, 91, 120, 197, 507, 559
Charles VIII, king of France (1483–98), 1, 3–4, 9, 22, 50, 56, 62–3, 112n, 118, 120–1, 123, 133–4, 204, 349–50, 369, 462
Charles IX, king of France (1560–74), 125, 268, 449
Charles-Bourg-Royal (Canada), 383
Charles the Bold, duke of Burgundy (1467–77), 239, 243
Charlotte (1516–24), daughter of Francis I, 86, 116, 178, 548–9
Charolais, 339, 394
Chartres, 29, 155, 249; county of, 274
Chasseneuz, Barthélemy de (1480–1541), president of the parlement of Aix, 522, 524
Chastel, A., art historian, 410
Châteaubriant, château of, 423
Châteaubriant, François de Foix, comtesse de, mistress of Francis I, 115–17, 557
Châteaubriant, Jean de Laval (1485–1543), seigneur de, 116, 423, 504
châteaux, royal, 132–40, 560; cost of, 418–19; use of space within 419–23; *see also* Amboise, Blois, Challuau, Chambord, Fontainebleau, La Muette, Madrid, Paris: Louvre, Saint-Germain-en-Laye, Villers-Cotterêts

Châtellerault, 203–4, 318n, 396, 461
Châtellerault, *vicomté* then duchy of, 43, 289, 493
Chatenet, Monique, historian, 403–4
Châtillon, Gaspard de Coligny (d. 1572), Admiral of France, 552
Châtillon, Louise de Montmorency, *maréchale* de, 277
Châtillon-sur-Marne, 492
Chenonceaux, château of, 140, 192, 349, 392, 551
Chevalier, B., historian, 23, 25n
Cheyney, Sir Thomas (1485–1558), 107, 122, 182, 254, 497
Chièvres, Guillaume de Croy (1458–1521), seigneur de, 66, 86–7
Chillou, Guyon Le Roy, seigneur du, 367
Chinon, 4
Christian (or evangelical) humanism, 6, 148, 161, 311
Cicero, 146, 306
Città di Castello, Gregorio da, 152
Claude de France (1499–1524), first queen of Francis I, 11, 45, 83, 112, 116, 134, 171, 201, 443, 472; birth, 9; character and physical appearance, 17, 114; betrothed, 12–14; marries Francis, 17; cedes claim to Milan, 71; her ladies, 109, 116, 117n, 120; her household, 120; gives Francis administration of Brittany, 349; at Field of Cloth of Gold, 174–5; and duc de Bourbon, 205; Raphael's *Holy Family* intended for, 436; death, 114, 134, 342, 349, 557; funeral, 116, 250; tomb, 547–9
Claudin, *see* Sermisy, Claude de
Cléberger, Jean, (Hans Kleberg), 188, 505
Clement VII (Giulio de' Medici) pope (1523–34), 100, 216, 258–9, 274–5, 291, 297, 305, 375, 439, 447; leader of imperial faction in Sacred College, 182; intercepts Cardinal Soderini's letters, 201; elected pope, 211; portrait, 217; signs treaty with Francis, 218; appoints *juges-délégués*, 237; negotiates with Louise of Savoy, 244; and trial of Berquin, 260, 283; and League of Cognac, 255–6, 259; anathematizes Colonna, 257; blames Francis for League's defeats, 257, 272; medal, 258; signs truce with Lannoy, 259; and sack of Rome, 260; escapes to Orvieto, 278; turns imperialist, 279; crowns Charles V Emperor in Bologna, 285; amends Concordat of Bologna, 100, 527; negotiates secretly with Francis, 298; fears General Council, 301; and Henry VIII's divorce, 282, 293–4, 298–9, 302; meets Francis at Marseilles, 132, 300–3, 331, 344, 470; his dowry to Catherine de' Medici, 343; gives Francis a casket, 300–1, 439; and a unicorn's horn, 439; issues bulls against French heretics, 301; death, 305
Clergy, 26, 31, 34, 37, 57, 142, 154–5, 282, 328, 349, 359, 539; and Assembly of Notables,

Clergy (*cont.*)
274–5, 282, 533; taxation of, 58, 186–7, 195, 344, 532, 535; clerical tenth(s), 82, 86, 168, 185, 187, 196, 198, 275, 300, 344, 504, 507, 532, 536, 553; and heresy, 509; and provincial estates, 533–4; *see also* episcopate
Clermont, county of, 204, 289
Clermont, Julien de, called Tallard, 497
Clermont, Robert de, 201
Cleves, William, duke of (1539–92), 388, 396, 486–7
Clichtove, Josse, 155, 159
Closse, Cosme (d. 1558), secretary of state, 553
cloth, *see under* industry, trade
Clouet, François (1520–72), 107n, 436, 496, 542, 545, 560
Clouet, Jean (1475?–1541), 44, 107, 122, 125, 435–6, 496, 560
Cloux, (Clos-Lucé) manor of, 140, 427, 431
Clovis, 45; legend of, 89, 131
Coblenz, 166
Cognac, 1, 3, 249, 253–4, 482
Cognac, edict of (7 December 1542), 506
Cognac, Holy League of (May 1526), 253, 255–9, 272, 274, 343
Coinage, *see* currency
Colbert, Jean-Baptiste (1619–83), 363
Colbertism, 559
Colet, John (1467?–1519), 149
Coligny, Odet de (1517–71), cardinal of Châtillon, 300, 552
Colin, Jacques, abbé of Saint-Ambroise (d. 1547), 473
Colines, Simon de, printer, 36, 423
Collège de Boncourt, 155
Collège de Montaigu, 35, 146–7, 149, 155
Collège de Navarre, 35, 155, 309
Collège de Sainte-Barbe, 35
Collège du Cardinal Lemoine, 35, 155
Cologne, archbishop of, 165
Colonna, Ascanio, Viceroy of Naples, 438
Colonna, Francesco (1433?–1527), 407
Colonna, Pompeo (1479–1532), cardinal, 211
Colonna, Prospero (1452–1523), 72, 84, 182–3, 208
Colonna family, 257–8
Commercy, 490
compagnies d'ordonnances, 54, 69, 123, 277, 342
Compiègne, 47, 120, 273, 499
Compiègne, treaty of (October 1538), 387
Comtat-Venaissin, 19, 324, 514
Comte, Jeanne, 3
Concordat (1472), 91; of Bologna (1516), 82, 94–100, 102–3, 155, 157, 187, 232, 234–5, 263–4, 470, 526–7, 537, 560
confraternities, 352–3
Coni, 334
conseil du roi (*conseil étroit, conseil privé, conseil secret*); composition and powers, 50–1, 120; and financial business, 61, 192–3, 199, 486; location of, 129; during Louise of Savoy's regencies, 192; advises Francis not

to fight in person, 334; attended more regularly by Francis, 395; and *gabelle* revolt, 482; Monluc's account of, 490; and Montmorency, 395, 552; and Parlement of Paris, 263, 266–7, 527; and peace of Madrid, 253–5; and peace of Cambrai, 284; and provincial estates, 54, 534
Constable of France, 42, 50, 203, 340; *see also* Bourbon, Charles III, duc de; Montmorency, Anne de
Constance, council of (1414–17), 91, 94, 96
Constantinople, 86, 245, 296, 329, 370, 436, 479
Cop, Guillaume, Francis I's physician, 150
Cop, Nicolas, rector of University of Paris, 309, 311–12, 319
Corbeny, priory of, 47
Cordier, Mathurin (1479–1564), 317
Corfu, 340, 472
Corion, Jean, Franciscan, 237, 239
Corneille de Lyon (d. c. 1574), artist, 498
coronation, 45–7, 89–90, 161
Corsica, 365
Cortés, Hernan (1485–1547), 370
Cortona, Domenico da, 138, 140, 400, 404
Costa, Lorenzo (1460–1535), 427, 436, 443
Cotereau, Jean, 192
Coucy, edict of (July 1535), 321–3, 325–7, 466
council, king's, *see conseil du roi*
court, 32, 61, 84, 105, 117, 170, 250, 252, 286, 290, 300, 340, 367, 371, 389, 391, 396, 398, 427, 431, 439, 467, 541; access to, 128; accommodation, 132–3; artistic life, 560; baggage, 132; ceremonial, 421; cost of, 122–3, 342; Budé's dislike of, 154, 469; criticism of, 125–6; daily life, 125; distribution of rooms at, 419–23; entertainments, 134, 176, 297, 458–9, 469; and *Epargne*, 346; faction at, 395, 483–5, 497, 549; Federico Gonzaga at, 425; feeding of, 118, 132; Homer in fashion at, 417; hunting, 111–12, 120, 123; intellectual life, 124; Italian influence on, 124–5; law and order at, 120; merchants and artisans attached to, 411; morals, 558; musicians at, 458; officials, 118, 122, 132; organization, 117–21
Cranmer, Thomas (1489–1556), archbishop of Canterbury, 298–9
Cremona, 180, 184, 226
Crépy-en-Laonnois, treaty of (September 1544), 493–4, 499, 506, 513, 517
Crespin, Jean, martyrologist, 318, 516
Cromwell, Thomas (1485?–1540), earl of Essex, 315n
crown lands, alienation of, 188, 190–1, 194–5, 197, 255, 530; *see also* demesne, royal
Croy, Adrien de, *see* Beaurain,
Croy, Guillaume de, *see* Chièvres
Cullerier, Dr, medical historian, 544
Curia, papal, *see* papacy
currency, xx–xxi, 286, 344, 362–3, 506, 527; devaluation of, 188; *see also* prices

Cusa, Nicholas of (1401–64), 147
customs duties, 362

Dacre, Thomas, Lord, Warden of the Marches, 200
Daillon, Jacques de, 141
Dampierre, 541, 553
Dandino, Girolamo (1509–59), cardinal and nuncio, 483, 485
Danès, Pierre, *lecteur royal*, 306
Daniray, 348
Danube, river, 296, 517
Dauphiné, 19, 57, 156, 239, 350, 362, 483, 510, 533, 535; governor of, 168n; *lieutenant-général*, 334; mint, 286; *recette-générale*, 506; taxation in, 186, 480
décime(s), *see* clergy, clerical tenth(s)
Delange, Etienne, 189
Della Palla, Battista, 114n, 439, 441, 443, 445
Della Robbia, Andrea, 403
Della Robbia, Girolamo (1488–1566), 403–4, 424
Della Robbia, Luca, 403
demesne (domain), royal, 46, 55–6, 58, 60, 166, 186, 255, 290, 346, 519
Demoulins (also called Rochefort), François, tutor to Francis I, 6, 89, 150, 152
Denys, Jean, 370
de Prie, Aymar, 206–7, 210, 213, 267
Descimon, R., historian, 531n
Désers, Louis des, 349
Desmond, James Fitzgerald (d. 1540), earl of, 200
Deux cents gentilshommes de l'hôtel, 120
De Vesc, Etienne, *sénéchal* of Beaucaire, 56
Devotio moderna, 145, 155
Dickens, A.G., historian, 318
Dieppe, 26, 371, 373
Dijon, 15, 63, 206, 231, 253, 255; *see also under* parlements
Dijon, treaty of (September 1513), 15, 63, 67
Dinteville, François de, bishop of Auxerre, 256n
Diodorus Siculus, 473–4
Dionysius of Halicarnassus, 477
Dionysius the Areopagite, 147
Diplomacy, costs of, 343
Disomme, Jacques, 112
Disque, François, 233
Divitis, Antonius (Antoine Le Riche) (*c.* 1470–*c.* 1534), 459–60
Dognon, Paul, historian, 519
Dolet, Etienne (1509–46), 467, 508, 510
Dom Agaya, 377–9
domestiques et commensaux du roi, 118
Donnaconna, 377–81
Doria, Andrea (1466–1560), Genoese admiral, 273, 279, 343, 365, 487, 558
Doria, Filippino, 279
Dorigny, Nicole, 95
Doucet, Roger, historian, 204, 559
droit(s) d'amortissement, 186, 195, 198
droit d'aubaine, 29, 58, 188
du Bellay, Guillaume (1491–1543), seigneur de

Langey, 122, 179–80, 221, 325, 492; captured at Pavia, 224; embassy to Italy, 257; contributes to royal ransom, 277; embassy to England, 285; portrait, 292; supports Henry VIII's divorce in 'Sorbonne' debate, 291, 293–4; at diet of Swabian League, 302–3; mission to Switzerland and Germany, 303–4; writes king's reply to Emperor's speech, 333n; king's lieutenant in Piedmont, 396; submits articles to Paris theologians, 322; mission to Schmalkaldic League, 323; sends 'articules' from Rome to Francis, 439; and Rabelais, 470–1; reports on Vaudois, 511; death, 514; memoirs, 87
du Bellay, Jean (1492–1560), bishop of Bayonne then of Paris, cardinal, 101, 292, 334; embassies to England, 294, 302; charged with heresy, 294; negligence in suppressing heresy denied, 312; sympathy for reform movement, 327, 509; in Paris procession, 317; embassy to Italy, 329–30; *lieutenant-général* of Paris and Ile-de-France, 337; advises king on foreign policy, 395; and Rabelais, 470–1; favours anti-Habsburg policy, 517; in Francis I's funeral procession, 546
du Bellay, René, 312
du Bois, Jacques, 174n
du Bois, Simon, 114, 317
du Bourg, Antoine, 269
du Bourg, Jean, 316
Du Cerceau, Jacques Androuet (1510?–85), 405–6
du Chastel, Pierre, bishop of Mâcon, *Grand Aumônier*, 359, 473, 541, 543–4, 546
Dudley, John (1502?–53), Viscount Lisle, 497, 502–3
du Fail, Noël, 40
Dugué, Jean, 264
Du Moulin, Charles (1500–66), 41, 524–5
Dunois, house of, 48
Dupaquier, J., historian, 23
Duprat, Antoine (1464–1535), Chancellor of France, archbishop of Sens, cardinal, 22, 51, 101–2, 163, 189, 252, 256, 261, 268–9, 277, 308, 527; early career, 42, 48; on royal authority, 49, 97, 525; takes Great Seal to Italy, 71; at Marignano, 75; Chancellor of Milan, 77; at king's meeting with Leo X in Bologna, 82n; and Concordat of Bologna, 93–5, 97–8; and imperial election, 168; at Calais conference, 178–80; rebukes Paris Faculty of Theology, 162; and treason of duc de Bourbon, 209, 212; assists the regent, Louise of Savoy, 227; archbishop of Sens and abbot of Saint-Benoît-sur-Loire, 232; bust of, 233; attacked by Parlement, 234–6, 249, 263–4, 526; vindicated by Francis, 263, 266–7; his unpopularity, 270; and Semblançay, 269–71; anti-heresy programme, 282–3; and Affair of the

Duprat, Antoine (*cont.*)
  Placards, 316, 318; on interest rates, 345; on
    Tour Carrée, 348; and annexation of
    Brittany, 349; captain of château of Madrid,
    400; economic programme, 95, 360–1, 363,
    559; on Portuguese spice trade, 369;
    portrait, 474
Duprat, Thomas, bishop of Clermont, 102
du Pré, Jean, 36
Durance, river, 323
du Restal, 6
Du Thier, Jean (d. 1560), seigneur de
    Beauregard, secretary of state, 553
du Tillet, Jean, 50
du Tillet, Séraphin, 533
Duval, Jean, *Trésorier de l'Epargne*, 553

échansonnerie, 118
Eck, John (1486–1543), 157
economy, *see* agriculture, currency, industry,
    prices, trade, wages
Ecouen, 250, 398, 553
Edward, prince (1537–53), son of Henry VIII,
    later Edward VI, king of England, 486
Egmont, count of, 226
Egypt, 86, 366, 369–70
Elam, Caroline, art historian, 412n
Elcano, Sebastiano (1476?–1526), 371
Eleanor (1498–1558), sister of the Emperor
    Charles V, successively queen of Portugal
    (1519–21) and of France (1530–47) as
    Francis I's second wife, 206, 254, 273, 284,
    297, 300, 317, 399, 432–3, 541, 549; her
    household, 125; marriage to Francis
    proposed, 246; Francis asks for her hand,
    240, 247; betrothed to Francis, 247, 259;
    introduced to Francis at Illescas, 247; upset
    by treatment of Francis's sons, 278; arrives
    in France, 286, 342, 466; marries Francis,
    117, 286–7, 433; coronation, 287;
    worshipped by Montmorency, 287; disliked
    by Francis, 289; her entry into Paris, 289;
    visits Charles V near Nice, 387; her
    emblem, 403; visits Brussels, 493; and court
    faction, 485; and duchesse d'Etampes,
    499–500, 551; absent from Francis's
    death-bed, 544; rescues ladies expelled from
    court, 549; witnesses Charles V's
    abdication, 551; death, 551
élection(s), 61, 507
Elizabeth, princess (1533–1603), daughter of
    Henry VIII, later Elizabeth I, queen of
    England, 304, 424
Elizabeth de France (1545–68), daughter of
    Henri II and Catherine de' Medici, later
    queen of Philip II of Spain, 449
Elizabeth of Austria, wife of King Charles IX,
    449
Ely, bishop of, *see* West, Nicolas
Emilio, Paolo, 146
Enghien, comte d', *see* Bourbon, François de
England, 19, 47, 178, 244, 254, 258, 283, 345,
    373, 387, 424, 486; declares war on France,
    195, 200; declares war on Emperor, 278;
    Emperor's visit to, 200; breach with Rome,
    282, 297; and peace of Cambrai, 284;
    French attack on, 371, 501, 514; French
    embassies to, 122, 170, 294, 302, 304;
    French trade with, 28–30, 361–2; and
    German princes, 517; international
    significance of, 170; treaties with, 174, 235,
    244, 254, 259, 264, 475, 503
entries, royal, 11, 47, 71, 82, 89, 104, 114, 121,
    129–31, 264, 289, 391, 427
Eparchos, Antonios, 474
Epargne, see *Trésor de l'Epargne*
Epernay, 492
episcopate, 100–2
Erasmus, Desiderius (1466–1536), 36, 147–9,
    152–3, 156, 161, 163, 260, 306, 311
Erfurt, university of, 157
Escars, François d', 206–7, 213, 267
Esguières, Antoine d', 210
Essomericq, 370
Estaing, François d', bishop of Rodez, 92, 101–2,
    155
estates, provincial, 22, 54, 57–8, 60, 244, 277,
    285, 520, 522, 533–9; Auxonne, 255;
    Brittany, 349–50, 533–4; Burgundy, 57,
    254–5, 533; Dauphiné, 57, 186, 533;
    Languedoc, 187, 331, 533–7; Normandy, 57,
    244, 530, 533–5; Provence, 57, 533–4
Estates General, (1484), 41, 92; (1577), 485n
Este, Alfonso I d', duke of Ferrara (1505–34), 82,
    250, 258, 274, 284
Este, Ercole II d', duke of Ferrara (1534–59),
    15n, 124, 250, 274, 330
Este, Ippolito d' (1509–72), cardinal of Ferrara
    (from 1539), 101, 448–50, 452, 457, 466, 482
Este, Isabella d', marchioness of Mantua
    (1474–1539), 113, 116n, 117n, 125, 242n,
    425, 427
Estienne, Charles, 23
Estienne, Henri (1531–98), 36
Estienne, Robert (1503–59), 475, 508, 560
Estimauville, Jacques d', 367
Etampes, Anne d'Heilly, dame de Pisseleu
    (1508–80), comtesse then duchesse d', 117,
    250, 393, 399, 452, 543, 557; meets Francis,
    249; early life and marriage, 290; Francis's
    constant companion, 289, 395, 483; political
    influence, 117, 290, 396, 498, 558; and
    Portuguese envoy, 381; husband, 290; and
    Montmorency, 395; favours anti-Habsburg
    policy, 395, 517; given Challuau by the
    king, 407; her apartment at Saint-Germain,
    421; flattered by Francis, 448; enmity for
    Cellini, 455–7; religious views, 484, 509;
    friends and enemies at court, 484–5, 497;
    and Chancellor Poyet, 484–5; and Claude
    d'Annebault, 497; and Cardinal Tournon,
    499; reports Henry VIII's death, 541; and
    Francis's death, 543; banished from court,
    549, 551; accused of treason, 557

Etampes, county, then duchy of, 290
Eugenius IV, pope (1431–47), 91
Eusebius Pamphili, 477
Evelyn, John, (1620–1706), 401, 404
évocations, 92, 162–3, 232, 235, 266, 512, 526
Evreux, 102
extraordinaire des guerres, 167, 194, 342, 347, 504
Ezquiros, battle of (30 June 1521), 177

fairs, 29, 56, 362, 491n
famine, 24, 34, 36, 355, 359–60, 504, 515
Fantuzzi, Antonio, 432
Farel, Guillaume (1489–1565), 156, 163, 307, 313, 315, 325
Farnese Alessandro (1520–89), cardinal, nephew of Pope Paul III, 305
fauconnerie, 111, 120, 123
Favier, Jacques, 231
Febvre, Lucien (1878–1956), historian, 161, 320
Fécamp, 374
Félibien, André (1619–95), architect and historian, 138
Ferdinand, archduke (1503–64), later King of the Romans (1531–58), brother of the Emperor Charles V, 224, 255, 294–6, 303, 321, 386, 393–4, 478–9
Ferdinand II, 'The Catholic', King of Aragon (1479–1516), V of Castile (1474–1504), 15, 17, 63, 66, 68, 72, 82, 84, 87, 178
Fère-en-Tardenois, 398
Feret, Guillaume, 315, 318
Ferrara, cardinal of, *see* Este, Ippolito d'
Ferrara, duchy of, 63; see of, 101
Ferrara, duke of, *see* Este, Alfonso I d' *and* Ercole II d'
Ferrault, Jean, 522
Ferrier, Geoffroy, *général des finances* for Milan, 194
Fichet, Guillaume (1433–80?), 146
Ficino, Marsilio (1433–99), 147
Field of Cloth of Gold, 105, 167n, 170–5, 185, 188, 259, 297–8, 343, 458, 460
Filhol, Antoine, archbishop of Aix, 102
Filhol, Pierre, archbishop of Aix, 155, 231
finances extraordinaires, 58, 198
finances ordinaires, 58, 198
Finé, Oronce, *lecteur royal*, 307
fiscal administration, 58, 60–1, 197–9, 345–9, 506–7, 559
fiscal expedients, 187, 344–5; *see also* crown lands, alienation of; offices, creation and sale of; loans, royal; *rentes sur l'Hôtel de Ville de Paris*
Fitzwilliam, Sir William (d. 1542), 111–12, 176n, 179, 203
Flanders, 19, 66, 129, 239, 253, 284, 337, 339, 345, 359, 361, 375, 448n, 466, 513
Fleury, Jean, 370
Florange, *see* La Marck, Robert III, seigneur de Florange

Florence, 30, 62–3, 68, 79, 82, 138, 146, 218, 253, 255, 259–60, 279, 284, 345, 403, 425, 431–2, 439, 441, 445
Florentines, 124, 177, 189, 194, 218, 371, 432, 505
Foix, André de (d. 1548), seigneur de Lesparre, 117, 177
Foix, Françoise de, *see* Châteaubriant, Françoise de Foix, comtesse de
Foix, Germaine, de (1488–1538), second wife of Ferdinand of Aragon, 84, 86
Foix, house of, 43
Foix, Odet de (1481?–1528), seigneur de Lautrec, marshal of France, *lieutenant-général* (governor) in Guyenne, 15, 55, 116–17, 132, 177, 250; marshal of France, 43; treats with Swiss, 73, 75; and hunting, 111; relieves Parma, 179; abandons Milan, 180; his portrait, 181; defeated at La Bicocca, 182–3; returns to France, 184; *lieutenant-général* in Milan, 203; escorts king back to France, 248; invades Italy, 273–4, 278; besieges Naples, 278–9; death, 279
Foix, Thomas de (d. 1525), seigneur de Lescun, 117, 177, 184, 222, 224
Fondulo, Girolamo, 472
Fontaine, Charles (1513–87), poet, 464
Fontaine, Simon, 318
Fontainebleau, 168, 381, 454, 475, 495
Fontainebleau, château of, 392, 398, 405, 407–19, 421, 423, 427, 432, 434–5, 441–2, 447–9, 452–3, 455, 523, 549; library at, 473, 475
Fontainebleau, edict of (1 June 1540), 328
Fontainebleau, School of, 435
Fontenay-le-Comte, 469
Fontevrault, 9n
Forez, county of, 204, 289
Fornovo, battle of (6 July 1495), 63
fortifications, 342, 345, 503, 515
Fossano, 334
Fournier, Martin, archbishop of Tours, 102
Fraisse, Dr, medical historian, 545
France, art of painting in, 427; communications, 23, 30, 318, 361; Erasmus on, 156; frontiers, 19; Gospel in, 308; harbours, 30, 365–9, 559; language, 19, 22, 352–3; legal system, 19, 22; population, 23–5, 28, 33, 355, 368, 559; prosperity, 354, 357, 368, 559; religious malaise, 141; society, 23, 38–40; surface area, 23; *see also* agriculture, bourgeoisie, clergy, currency, heresy, industry, law, nobility, peasantry, poor, prices, trade, wages
Franche-Comté, 66, 84, 165, 206, 209, 231, 255
Francis I (1494–1547), king of France (1515–47)
    absolutism, 255, 519, 526, 534, 537–40, 559
    accessibility, 128
    accession, 41, 89, 121
    accidents, 8, 109, 154, 176, 249
    armoury, 410
    authoritarianism, 49, 263, 497, 525, 537

baths, 412, 416, 418
building activities, 133–4, 398, 400, 405, 419
captivity, 129, 225–7, 238–43, 245–8, 260,
  263–4, 288, 345, 398, 404–5, 526
and Cellini, 450–7
chapel, 318, 421–2, 458, 460
character, 107, 112, 130, 153, 318, 322, 443, 558
châteaux, 132–40
children, 114, 116
collection of Greek manuscripts, 154, 472,
  476; *objets d'art*, 436, 439, 448–9; paintings,
  416, 425, 427, 429, 439, 445–7; statues, 443;
  tapestries, 448–9
companions, 8, 12, 43–4, 121–2, 129, 226;
and Constable of Bourbon, 203–8, 212–13,
  240, 267
coronation, 9, 45–6, 90, 161, 185, 437, 459
court, 117ff; *see also* court
daily routine, 118, 128
death, 443, 457, 541–5
debts, 194, 196, 198, 345, 505, 532, 543
economic policy, 360–4
education, 6, 8
emblem and motto, 10–11, 48
entries, 11, 47, 71, 77, 83, 104, 114n, 121,
  130–1, 264, 427
and episcopate, 100–2
and Erasmus, 152–3, 163
and Federico Gonzaga, 124, 134
and financial business, 193
foreign policy, 62, 84–5, 93, 176, 254–8, 272,
  274, 283–4, 291, 294–5, 297, 302–5, 331–3,
  385–96
funeral, 545–7
and General Council of the Church, 301
generalship, 225, 340–1, 493
health, 109, 112, 120, 129, 226, 245–7, 272,
  331, 389, 391, 457, 466, 471, 484, 495, 497
and heresy, 46, 163–4, 236, 238, 280, 282–3,
  301, 307–8, 312, 316–20, 324–7, 508,
  511–13, 515–16, 560
and humanism, 149, 161, 163
hunting, 8, 107, 111–12, 123, 129, 137, 247,
  249, 284, 400, 407–8, 483, 495, 497, 541
and Jewish studies, 149
and Leonardo da Vinci, 427–8, 431
letters, 107, 116, 226, 238, 241, 276, 309, 312,
  316
library, 260, 308, 409, 468, 471–7
love of Fontainebleau, 408; of letters, 149,
  154; of music, 458; of sport, 8, 107, 128
marriage to Claude de France, 12–14, 17; to
  Eleanor of Portugal, 117, 246, 286–7, 409,
  433
medals, 10, 15, 450
meetings with: Charles V, 245, 247, 385, 389,
  467, 478; Clement VII, 132, 298–302, 331,
  344, 470; Henry VIII, 170, 174–5, 259,
  297–8, 343, 458; Leo X, 82–3, 103, 427, 458;
  Mary of Hungary, 387; Paul III, 386, 459;
  Philip of Hesse, 303; Wolsey, 174, 272
menagerie, 131–2, 407

military campaigns, 71–3, 75, 77, 178–80, 192,
  203, 213, 215–25, 229, 273, 331, 334–5,
  339–41, 373, 487, 502
morals, 89, 112–13, 483, 558
Most Christian King, 88, 263, 282, 319
name, 153
'New Constantine', 103–4
and nobility, 155, 188, 191, 275
and overseas exploration, 371, 373, 380–1
and Paris, 37, 47, 129–30, 195, 212, 264, 276,
  398, 532
and Parlement of Paris, 94–96, 98, 164, 191,
  194, 212–13, 238, 260–1, 263–7, 527–9,
  531–2
and Parlement of Rouen, 528–30
patronage of artists, 430, 435, 456–7; of
  scholars, 149–54, 261, 283, 306, 320, 462,
  471
physical appearance, 8, 66, 89, 105–6, 452, 555
pilgrimages, 47, 83, 84n, 116
poetry, 107, 458, 461
portraits, 14, 16, 79, 105–8, 288, 336, 444, 496,
  542
power of healing, 47, 89, 242, 247
power over taxation, 187, 530–3
'privy (or fair) band of ladies', 249, 483, 549
progresses, 52–3, 126–30, 249, 398, 408
and provincial estates, 534
and Rabelais, 470–1
religion, 128, 161, 236, 249, 263, 281, 308, 323,
  380, 421, 543–4
reputation, 153, 321, 331, 555–8
and Semblançay, 196–7, 270–1
stables, 411, 422
taste for the erotic, 443; in reading, 473
tomb, 547–9
views on Charles of Spain, 165; force and
  corruption in public life, 166; interior
  decoration, 416; kingdom of France, 537;
  monks, 470–1; Paris's gift to Charles V,
  391; Parlement of Paris, 98; people of
  Toulouse, 536; rights of discovery, 375,
  381–2; Turks, 168, 300–1, 489
Francis of Paola, St, 3
Franciscans, 156, 237
François, Dauphin (1518–36), eldest son of
  Francis I, 170, 174, 246–7, 297, 317, 468,
  474; birth, 116, 203, 436; his marriage
  proposed, 240; hostage in Spain, 247–8,
  254–5, 259, 272, 278, 293, 308, 470; ransom,
  256–7, 274, 282, 286, 374, 533; released by
  peace of Cambrai, 284–6, 461, 466; duke of
  Brittany, 349–50; portrait, 431; death, 326,
  338, 399, 484; funeral, 545–7; tomb, 548–9
François, Dauphin (1544–60), son of Henri II
  and future King Francis II, 422, 467, 499,
  530
François, Gatien, master mason, 403
Frankfurt-am-Main, 167–8, 364
Frankfurt-am-Main, truce of (April 1539), 388
Fregosi family, 124
Fregoso, Cesare, 479

Fréjus, 338
French language, use in legal records, 22, 352–3
Fribourg, 73
Fribourg, 'perpetual peace' of (November 1516), 85, 185
Froben, John (1460–1527), printer, 156
fruiterie, 118
Frundsberg, Georg von (1473–1528), 221, 224, 258–9
Fuenterrabía, 179, 209, 247
Fugger, Jacob, 167
Fürstenberg, Count Wilhelm von (1491–1549), 327

gabelle(s), 58–60, 186–7, 195–6, 535, 480–1
Gadio, Stazio, 82n, 109n, 113, 116n, 117n, 134
Gadier, Pierre, 403
Gaguin, Robert (1433–1501), 19, 146, 149
Gaillon, château of, 133
Galiot, Guillaume, master of the plainchant chapel, 458
Gallarate, 73
Gallican liberties (Gallicanism), 91, 97, 99, 275
Garamond, Claude (d. 1561), 477
Garay, Pedro, de, 293–4
Gardiner, Stephen (1483?–1555), bishop of Winchester, 302
Garonne, river, 357
Garter, Order of the, 273, 297
Gascony, 70
Gattinara, Mercurino di (1465–1530), imperial chancellor, 177, 179, 243, 256
gendarmerie, 12, 55, 69, 75, 178n, 215, 222, 337, 346, 514, 539
General Council of the Church, 91, 94, 97–9, 273, 301–2, 305, 321, 323, 330, 334, 386, 493–4; *see also* Basle, Constance, Lateran
généralité(s), 61, 506
général(aux), des finances, 61, 191, 198–9, 346, 348
généraux des monnaies, 527
Geneva, 163, 325, 331, 467, 515
Geneva, treaty of (November 1515), 85
Génin, F., 112n
Genoa, 12, 30, 63, 67, 85, 124, 184, 214, 240, 242, 256, 273, 279, 304, 329, 339, 365, 387
Genouillac, Jacques de, called Galiot de (1465–1546), seigneur d'Assier, *sénéchal* of Armagnac, captain-general of the artillery, *Grand écuyer*, 77, 80, 174n, 221, 253, 424
gens de finances, 61, 189, 192–3, 196, 270, 347, 507
gens du roi 56, 159, 234, 500, 527
gentilshommes de la chambre, 121–3, 254, 292
German princes, 256, 291, 294, 322
German Protestants, 294–5, 300–1, 319, 322–3, 388, 493, 502, 506, 509, 511, 517–18
Germany, 30, 145, 165–8, 188, 271, 389, 395; anti-Habsburg opposition, 295, 303, 305, 396; and Charles V, 256, 493; Francis I's policy in, 291, 295, 297, 302–3, 315, 321, 343, 388, 478, 517–18; Francis's reputation in, 321; French diplomacy in, 302–3, 305,

322; French embassies to, 302–3, 322, 514, 518; Lutheran Reformation in, 159, 256, 279; trade with, 29–30
Gerson, Jean (1363–1429), 145
Ghent, 389, 482
Ghirlandaio, Ridolfo (1483–1561), 441
Giberti, Gian Matteo (1495–1543), bishop of Verona, 218
Gié, seigneur de, *see* Rohan, Pierre de
Gien-sur-Loire, 201
gilds, 56, 120, 364
Giocondo, Fra, 49
Giovio, Paolo, 448
Giustiniani, Agostino, 152
Giustiniani, Marino, 419
Glareanus, *see* Loriti, H.
Golein, Jean, 46
Gonneville, Paulmier de, 370
Gonzaga, Federico II, marquis (1519–30), then duke of Mantua (1530–40), 82n, 109, 113, 117n, 124–5, 134, 177, 412, 417, 425, 427
Gonzaga, Ferrante (1507–57), imperial governor of Milan, Viceroy of Sicily, 338, 490–1
Gonzaga, Francesco II (1466–1519), marquis of Mantua, 82n, 113, 117n, 124, 134, 425, 436, 443
Gouffier, Adrien (d. 1523), cardinal of Boisy, 82, 95
Gouffier, Artus (1475?–1519), seigneur de Boisy, Grand Master of France, 12, 43, 48, 86–7, 121, 141, 166, 168n, 189, 193
Gouffier, Aymar, abbot of Cluny, 100n
Gouffier, Claude, marquis de Boisy, *Grand écuyer*, 543, 546–7, 558
Gouffier, Guillaume (d. 1525), seigneur de Bonnivet, Admiral of France, 12, 43–4, 82, 166, 168, 170, 174, 179, 193, 208, 211–12, 215, 224, 252, 367, 372, 374
gouvernements, 54, 539
government, local, 54–8; *see also* Bailliage(s); *bailli(s)*; estates, provincial; governors, provincial; *sénéchal(aux)*; *sénéchaussée(s)*
governors, provincial, 54–5, 187, 397; *see also* individual provinces
grain, *see* agriculture, *and see under* trade
Gramont, Gabriel, bishop of Tarbes, cardinal, 297
Grand Aumônier (Grand Almoner), 118, 359, 375; *see also* du Chastel, Pierre; Le Veneur, Jean
Grand chambrier de France, 43
Grand chambellan, 118, 266
Grand Conseil, 4, 49, 52–3, 92, 98, 162–3, 189, 232–6, 263, 266–7, 294, 500, 526
Grand écuyer (Master of the Horse), 118; *see also* Genouillac, Jacques de; Gouffier, Claude; San Severino, Galeazzo da
Grande Rebeyne, 358, 365
Grand maître de France (Grand Master), 43, 50, 121–2, 193; *see also* Chabannes, Jacques de; Gouffier, Artus; Montmorency, Anne de; Savoy, René of

Grand Parti, 506
Grands Jours, of Bayeux, 510, 529–30, 538; of Rennes, (later Parlement), 57, 349
grands officiers de la couronne, 121, 245
Grandval, Marc de (1480–1520), 159
Grassaille, Charles de, 522
Grasse (Normandy), 367
Gravelines, 175
Greek: 157, 307; printing in, 147, 149, 477; teaching of, 146–7, 152, 306
Greengrass, Mark, historian, 320
Grenoble, 71, 327, 334, 459; parlement of 26, 53, 57
Grez-sur-Loing, 289
Gringore, Pierre, 48, 114n
Griffith, Ellis, 105
Grignan, Louis d'Adhémar, seigneur de, 511, 514, 552
Grimaldi, Augustin, bishop of Grasse, 101
Grisons (Graubunden), 219
Groote, Gerard or Gert (1340–84), 145
Groslot, Jacques, 232–4
Guadalajara, 243
Guelders, 70, 396
Guérin, Guillaume, 516
Guicciardini, Francesco (1483–1540), 70, 183, 189
Guidacerio, Agazio, *lecteur royal*, 306
Guillaume, Jean, art historian, 140, 411
Guillart, Charles, Fourth president of the Parlement of Paris, 166, 266, 526–7
Guimier, Cosme, jurist, 89
Guinea, 370–1, 375, 381
Guînes, 171, 174–5
Guise, 337
Guise, Charles de (1524–74), archbishop of Rheims, cardinal, 102, 553
Guise, Claude (1496–1550), comte, then first duc de, 209, 231, 250, 337, 553
Guise, Claude de (1526–73), marquis de Mayenne, 553
Guise, François (1519–63), comte d'Aumale, then second duc de Guise, 132, 393, 553
Guise, house of, 553
Guise, Jean de (1498–1550), cardinal of Lorraine, 101, 289, 333, 372, 393, 395, 435, 452, 461, 482, 485n, 551, 553
Guizot, François (1787–1874), historian, 6n
Guy, John, historian, 50
Guyenne, 15, 55, 70, 195, 482, 511; legion, 350–1; Lutherans in, 313n, *recette-générale*, 506
Guyon, Dr., 557

Habsburg, house of, 165, 295, 299, 302, 304–5, 321
Haetzer, Ludwig, 282
Hainault, 66, 179–80, 486
Hale, John, historian, 352
Hall, Edward (d. 1547), chronicler, 105
Hamon, Philippe, historian, 166n, 177n, 188, 199, 507

Hanley, Sarah, historian, 266n, 267n, 533
Harfleur, 375
Hauser, Henri, historian, 254n
Haute-Bruyère, priory of, 545, 549–50
Hebrew: 157; teaching of, 152, 306–7, 313; *see also* Jewish studies
Hedio, Caspar, 304, 322
Heilly, Anne d' *see* Etampes, Anne, duchesse d'
Heliodorus, 473
Heller, Henry, historian, 163n, 357
Hennequin, Nicole, 233–4
Henri, duc d'Orléans (1519–59), second son of Francis I, later Dauphin and Henri II, king of France (1547–59), 121, 128, 132, 259, 296–7, 317, 394, 399, 441, 452, 454, 466, 468, 474, 482, 483, 487, 490, 492, 497, 499, 501, 506, 516, 519, 533, 539; birth, 116; hostage in Spain, 247–8, 254–5, 259, 272, 278, 293, 308, 470, 552; ransom, 256–7, 274, 282, 286, 338, 374, 533; released by peace of Cambrai, 284–6, 461, 466; marries Catherine de' Medici, 124, 297, 299–301, 305, 439; and Milanese succession, 304, 331, 333, 338; and duchy of Brittany, 349, 493; and Emperor's visit to France, 389, 391; fails to capture Perpignan, 480, 484, 494; angered by peace of Crépy, 494, 549; campaign in Picardy, 501; rivalry with Charles d'Orléans, 484–5; and Montmorency, 392; and Francis's death and funeral, 543–6; continues work on New Louvre, 399; admitted to king's council, 494; and Diane de Poitiers, 499; distribution of rooms at Saint Germain under, 421–3; commissions Francis's tomb, 547–9; accession as Henri II, 553; 'cleans up' the court, 549; taxation under, 186; cost of his court, 123; his tomb, 404
Henri IV, king of France (1589–1610), 250
Henry VII, king of England (1485–1509), 113
Henry VIII, king of England (1509–47), 17, 68, 82, 93, 105, 111–13, 116, 167n, 178, 185, 249, 289, 291, 297, 305, 330, 335, 416, 447, 483, 497n, 502; invades Picardy, 15, 491; character, 67; jealous of Francis, 67, 85; and imperial election, 171n; his temporary palace at Guînes, 171; meets Francis at Field of Cloth of Gold, 174–5; offers his arbitration, 178; French pension to, 17, 174, 182, 343, 486, 503; plans invasion of France 200; and duc de Bourbon, 206–8, 213; makes treaty with Charles V, 178, 213; proposes dismemberment of France, 229; French claims, 229; makes peace with France, 244; and peace of Madrid, 254; Francis's gratitude to, 254; and League of Cognac, 259; allies with Francis, 259, 273–4; divorce, 272, 282, 285, 291, 293–4, 297–8, 301–2; declares war on Emperor, 278; Emperor's debts to, 239, 256, 259, 285; obtains Paris Faculty of Theology's approval of his divorce, 294; financial

concessions to Francis, 285, 297; and
German princes, 388; second meeting with
Francis at Boulogne, 297–8; fails to prevent
Francis meeting Clement VII, 299; angers
Francis by insulting pope, 302; treats with
Chabot, 304; fears Franco-imperial entente,
388, 392; allies with Emperor, 486, 490; and
Scotland, 486; declares war on France, 484;
and peace of Crépy, 494; captures
Boulogne, 493; makes peace with France,
503; death, 541
Heresy, 154, 156–64, 236–8, 260–1, 266, 280,
282–3, 301, 308–9, 312–21, 326–8, 358,
508–10, 512–13, 515; *see also* Calvinism,
censorship, Lutheranism,
sacramentarianism, Vaudois,
Waldensianism, Zwinglianism
Hermonymos, George, 147
Hertford, Edward Seymour (1506?–52), first earl
of, 490, 502
Hesdin, 200, 204, 239–40, 284, 339, 394
Hesse, 295, 478, 518
Hesse, Philip, Landgrave of (1509–67), 295, 303,
478, 509, 517
Hincmar, archbishop of Rheims (806–82), 45
Hochelaga (Canada), 378, 382
Holland, 66
Holy Roman Empire (Emperor), 19, 70, 88,
165–7, 382, 520; *see also* Charles V,
Maximilian I
Holy See, *see* papacy
Homer, 417
Honfleur, 253, 367, 370
Horace, 464, 469
hospitals, 359–60; *see also* poor
Hotman, Pierre, 510
Howard, Thomas (1473–1554), earl of Surrey,
third duke of Norfolk, 200, 289, 297, 299,
354, 491
Hudson, river, 372
Hugo, Victor (1802–85), 210n, 555–6
humanism, 144, 146, 154–5, 462; *see also*
Christian humanism
Humbercourt, Adrien de Brimeu, seigneur d',
77n
Humières, Jean de (1485?–1550),
lieutenant-général in Dauphiné, Savoy,
Piedmont, 334, 339–40
Hungary, 236, 296, 478–9
Hurault, Jacques (d. 1546), bishop of Autun,
207, 267
Hurault, Raoul, seigneur de Cheverny, *général
des finances*, 193, 271, 348
Husson, Louis de, bishop of Poitiers, 102
Hutten, Ulrich von (1488–1523), 163

Ibrahim Pasha, Ottoman Grand Vizier, 329
Ile-de-France, 28, 31, 355, 359, 398, 407;
governor of, 231, 552; nobles of, 275–6
Imbart de La Tour, P., historian, 519
Imperial election, cost of, 185
Indians, 370, 372–3, 376–81, 383–4

Indies, 370, 373, 381
industry, 26, 30, 368; cloth, 26, 30, 356, 359, 361;
metallurgy, 29; mining, 58; printing, 30–1,
35, 53, 146, 149, 306, 316, 364, 460, 473,
477, 509; salt, 29; silk, 26, 358, 364–5
Infantado, Diego Hurtado de Mendoza, third
duke of, 243
Innocent VIII, pope (1484–92), 324
Ireland, 200
Isabella of Portugal (1503–39), wife of the
Emperor Charles V, 247, 256
Issoire, 26, 42
Italians, 283; bankers, 92, 188, 194, 277, 365,
505, 532; bishops, 101; craftsmen, 133; at
French court, 124; humanists, 146; painters
in France, 427, 432; trading in France,
29–30, 365–6
Italy, 30, 62, 68, 70, 77, 85, 116, 146–7, 177,
179–80, 227, 239, 258, 284, 331, 337, 339,
389, 405, 456–67, 490; and Charles V, 176,
229, 256; Clement VII's policy in, 259;
Francis I aims to exclude Charles V from,
175–6; Francis's claims in, 240–6, 256, 284,
304, 445, 493; Francis and the League of
Cognac in, 256; Francis plans to invade,
340; Francis's policy in, 272, 297; Francis
seeks manuscripts in, 472; French defeats in,
180, 182–4, 200, 218–26; French invasions
of, 118, 273, 340, 460; influence on French
court, 125; League of Cognac's failure in,
257, 259; Louis XI's policies in, 91, Louis
XII and, 93; Louise of Savoy's policy in,
244; political structure of, 62–3; trade with,
29–30, 361, 364–5; and Turks, 296, 339,
487; *see also* Ferrara, Mantua, Milan,
Naples, Piedmont, Rome, Savoy, Urbino,
Venice

Jacquart, Jean, historian, 40, 252
Jacqueton, G., historian, 507
Jalons, 492
James V, king of Scotland (1513–42), 244, 339,
343, 367, 411, 486
Janequin, Clément (1475?–1560?), musician, 107,
460–1, 560
Jaques, Christovão, 374
Jativá, (Spain), castle of, 242n
Jeanne, half-sister of Francis I, 3
Jeanne de France (1464–1505), first queen of
Louis XII, 9
Jewish studies, 150, 157, 470
John, king of France (1350–64), 246
John III, king of Portugal (1521–57), 371, 374–5,
381, 393
Josquin des Prez (*c.* 1440–1521), 459–60
Juana 'La Loca' (The Mad) (1504–55), queen of
Castile, 10
Jud, Leo, 282
juges-délégués, 237–9, 261
Jülich, duchy of, 487
Julius II (Giuliano della Rovere), pope
(1503–13), 63, 92–3, 291

Julius III (Giovanni Maria del Monte), pope (1550–55), 553
justice, 31–2, 266–7, 271, 352
Justinus, 473

Karlstadt, Andrew Bodenstein of (1477–1541), 163, 282, 313
Kelley, D. R., historian, 320
Kempis, Thomas à, 145–6
king's council, *see conseil du roi*
Knight, Dr William (1476–1547), 206

L'Aubespine, Claude de, 552
La Barde, Jacques de, 235
La Barre, Jean de (d. 1534), comte d'Etampes, *bailli* then *prévôt de Paris*, 121–2, 226, 253, 260, 418, 472
La Bicocca, battle of (27 April 1522), 182–4, 225n
Labrador, 378
La Chambre, Philippe de, cardinal, 300
La Chapelle-Saint-Denis, 48
La Forêt, Jean de, 329, 370
La Garde, Antoine Escalin des Essars, baron de, (Called 'Captain Polin'), 479, 487, 489, 502, 514, 516
Lagarto, João, 380–1
La Garde, Josse de, 103
Lagny-sur-Marne, 492
Laguette, Jean, 507
La Goletta, 330
La Haye, Jean de, 95
Laisgre, Adam, king's librarian at Blois, 472
Lalande, Eustache de Bimont, called Captain, 491
Lallemant, Jean, Jr, 348
La Marck, Robert II (d. 1536), seigneur de Sedan, duc de Bouillon, 176–7, 179
La Marck, Robert III (1491?–1537), seigneur de Florange, marshal of France, 6, 8, 18, 42, 87n, 107, 175, 224–6, 253
La Marthonie, Mondot de, First president of Parlement of Paris, 93
La Mothe des Noyers, 224
La Muette, château of, 407, 419, 423
Lando, Ortesio, 125
Landrecies, 487
Landriano, battle of (21 June 1529), 279
Landry, François, 513
landsknechts, 70, 74–5, 77, 84, 206–7, 209, 221–2, 224, 339
Langart, 481
Langey, seigneur de, *see* du Bellay, Guillaume
Languedoc, 24–5, 28, 30, 43, 57–8, 60, 195, 209, 239, 271, 355, 365, 369, 382, 387, 483, 506, 533–7; *gabelle*, 59
governorship, 252, 552; legion, 350–1; nobility, 276; revenues, 532
Languedoïl, *généralité* of, 60, 192, 198, 506
Langres, bishop of, 38
Lannoy, Charles de (1482–1527), Viceroy of Naples, 211, 216, 222, 224–6, 239–42, 247, 254, 256, 258–9

Laon, 179n; bishop of, 45; cathedral, 195
Lapalisse, seigneur de, *see* Chabannes, Jacques de
La Renaudie, 484
La Rochefoucauld, château of, 423
La Rochelle, 26, 28–9, 366–7, 376, 383, 492, 510; *gabelle* revolt, 480–83, 511; governor, 481
La Rochepot, seigneur de, *see* Montmorency, François de
La Roche-sur-Yon, Louise, princesse de, 268
Lascaris, Anne, comtesse de Tende, mother-in-law of Montmorency, 277
Lascaris, Janus, 147, 153–4
La Spezia, 279, 300
Lateran council, fifth, 91–2, 94, 96–8
Latin: teaching of, 147, 307; use of, 22, 353
La Trémoïlle, Louis de (1460–1525), *lieutenant-général* in Dauphiné, chamberlain of Francis I, 15, 42, 63, 98–9
Lautrec, seigneur de, *see* Foix, Odet de,
Laval, Antoine de, 205, 557
Laval, Jean de, *see* Châteaubriant
law(s): canon, 46; codification, 22; customary, 22, 32; enforcement of royal, 538; fundamental, 255, 522, 530; Roman, 22, 46, 520, 524; Salic, 3, 41, 522, 555; *see also* heresy, justice
Le Breton, Gilles, 408, 410, 452
Le Breton, Guillaume, 407
Le Breton, Jacques, 407
Lebries, Jean, 449
Le Coincte, Nicolas, 189
lecteurs royaux, 306–7, 313, 470, 475, 560
Lefèvre d'Etaples, Jacques (1450–1536), 114, 147–8, 152, 154–6, 159, 161–4, 237–8, 239n, 260–1, 307–8, 472
Le Gendre, Pierre (d. 1524), 192
legions, provincial, 329, 331, 337, 350–2
Le Havre, 132, 182, 367, 502
Leipzig, 157
Le Lièvre, Jean, *avocat-général*, 99
Le Maçon, Antoine, 500
Le Lude, château of, 141
Lemaire de Belges (1473?–1524?), 464
Lemaitre, Nicole, historian, 154
Le Mans, 355
Le Marchant, Antoine, 530
Le Masson (Latomus), Barthélemy, *lecteur royal*, 307, 309
Lenoncourt, Robert de, archbishop of Rheims, 45–7
Leo III, pope, 103
Leo X (Giovanni de' Medici), pope (1513–21), 17, 68, 72, 79, 82, 84–6, 93–4, 97, 103, 152–3, 157, 168, 175, 177, 182, 187, 427, 436, 458
Leonardo da Vinci (1452–1519), 131, 138, 140, 171, 404, 427–31, 452
Leonbruno, 427
Le Picart, François, 309
Le Puy, 299, 358
Le Puy, bishop of, *see* Chabannes, Antoine de

Le Riche, Antoine, *see* Divitis, Antonius
Le Roy Ladurie, E., historian, 480
Lescot, Pierre (1510?–78), architect, 399
Lescun, seigneur de, *see* Foix, Thomas de
Leucate, 340
Leure, 367
Levant, 30, 329, 364, 369–70, 389, 475, 478
Le Veneur, Gabriel, bishop of Evreux, 102
Le Veneur, Jean, bishop of Lisieux, *Grand Aumônier*, cardinal, 207, 300, 375
Lévi, house of, 39
Leyva, Antonio de (1480?–1536), 216, 334, 338
Libourne, 481
lieutenant-général, 55–6; *see also* governors, provincial
Ligny-en-Barrois, 479–90
Ligurian coast, 30, 279, 365
Lille, 284
Lillers, 487
Limoges, 22–3, 361
Limours, 349, 541, 551
Limousin, 31
Lisieux, bishop of, *see* Le Veneur, Jean
Lisle, viscount, *see* Dudley, John
lit(s) de justice, 54, 129, 212, 264–5, 339, 526, 528–9, 533
Lizet, Pierre (d. 1554), First president of the Parlement of Paris, 162, 204, 212, 237, 293–4, 513
loans, royal, 37, 60, 187, 194, 337, 345, 363, 504–6, 532
Loches, 210, 391
Lodi, 73, 75, 183, 212, 216, 219, 256
Loire, river (Loire valley), 11, 29, 84, 98, 133, 248, 339, 361, 398, 409, 495, 510
Lombard, Peter (*c*. 1100–1164), 144
Lombardy, 93, 183, 273
London, bankers in, 166, 167n, 188, 269
London, treaty of (April 1515), 67; (October 1518), 170
Longland, John (1473–1547), bishop of Lincoln, 316n
Longueil (Longolius), Christophe de (1488–1522), 6, 152
Longueval, Antoine de, 460
Longueval, Nicolas de Bossut, seigneur de, 497, 551, 553, 557
Longueville, duc de, 48
Longwy, Claude de, cardinal, 300
Longwy, Françoise de, wife of Admiral Chabot, 253, 549
Lorges, Jacques de Montgommery, seigneur de, 179, 188n, 224, 492
Loriti, Heinrich (Glareanus), 153, 459
L'Orme, Philibert de (1505/10–1570), architect, 421, 547–9
Lorraine, 28, 166, 494
Lorraine, cardinal of, *see* Guise, Jean de
Lorraine, duchess of, *see* Bourbon, Renée de
Lorraine, duke of, 19, 236
Lorraine, François de, comte de Lambesc and marquis du Pont (d. 1525), 222, 224

Louis of Aragon, St, 83
Louis II Jagiello, king of Hungary (1516–26), 295
Louis IX, king of France (1226–70), 89, 203
Louis XI, king of France (1461–83), 1, 3, 28, 91–2, 243, 354, 362, 364–5, 369
Louis XII, king of France (1498–1515), previously Louis II, duc d'Orléans, 15, 57, 66–7, 87, 93, 111, 112n, 120–1, 123–4, 203, 244, 274, 362, 369, 458, 464, 519, 522; as duc d'Orléans, 3; claims guardianship of Francis and his sister, 4; becomes king, 4; marries Anne of Brittany, 9; concedes marriage of Francis and Claude, 12; marries Mary Tudor, 17; his death, 18; his funeral, 41, 458; his servants in Francis I's entry into Paris, 48, 121; and governors, 55; defeated in Italy, 63; cedes his claim to Naples, 84; calls council of Pisa, 92; and Parlement, 95; tries to marry off Marguerite d'Angoulême, 113; builds at Amboise, 134; leaves deficit, 185; taxation under, 186; and house of Bourbon, 204; stops crusade against Vaudois, 324; and duchy of Milan, 394; and Leonardo da Vinci, 427; court poetry under, 462
Louis XIV, king of France (1643–1715), 418, 435, 519, 539–40, 559
Louis XV, king of France (1715–74), 410
Louis XVI, king of France (1774–93), 85n
Louise (1515–17), daughter of Francis I, 84, 86, 116, 250, 549
Louise of Savoy (1476–1531), comtesse then duchesse d'Angoulême, mother of Francis I, 1, 10, 12–14, 17, 45, 83, 112–13, 134, 150, 160, 182, 200, 226, 228, 249–50, 252, 273, 372, 431, 443, 468, 549; her avarice, 289; parentage and marriage, 1–2; guardian of her children, 4; and Marshal Gié, 4, 6; educates her children, 5, 6; her *Journal*, 8, 15, 18, 83, 196; and Duprat, 42, 227, 232, 263; gifts from her son, 43, 204, 289; first regency, 71; influence, 113, 252; at Field of Cloth of Gold, 175; palace at Romorantin, 140, 428; health, 176, 248, 289; her council, 227, 235–6; and Semblançay, 192, 194, 196–7, 269; and heresy, 236–7, 260; second regency, 201, 205, 215, 227, 269, 530; and duc de Bourbon, 204–5, 208; and Wolsey, 113, 174, 278; tries to dissuade Francis from invading Italy, 215; and defence of kingdom, 229–31; and Parlement of Paris, 231–6, 248, 267, 526; rejects Charles V's peace terms, 240; foreign policy, 244–5; abandons Burgundy, 246; travels to Bayonne to meet son, 248; her actions endorsed by Francis, 263; complains of Charles V's inhumanity, 278; negotiates peace of Cambrai, 283–4; death, 289–90, 342, 409; her taste in art, 425; her inheritance, 289, 331, 500
Lourmarin, 515
Louvain, 306; trilingual college, 152–3

Louvre, *see under* Paris

Low Countries, *see* Netherlands

Loynes, François de (d. 1524), 96, 98

Lucca (Luccans), 30, 194, 505

Lugo, Alvares de, 286

Lumes, seigneur de, 351

Lurcy, Philibert de Saint-Romain, seigneur de, 206

Luther, Martin (1483–1546), 156–7, 159, 161, 163, 236, 256, 282, 303, 308, 311–12, 315, 508

'Lutheran', use of the word, 283, 313, 315n, 320, 509, 513

Lutheranism, 156, 159, 161, 201, 261, 263, 275, 279, 282, 313

Lutheran Reformation, 358

Lutherans, 236–7, 308, 312, 316–17, 322, 325, 513

Luxemburg, 66, 176–7, 432, 434–5, 480, 484, 487, 490, 509

Luxemburg, Charles of, *see* Charles V, Holy Roman Emperor

Lyonnais, 53, 350

Lyons (Lyon), 23, 26, 28–30, 36, 83, 101, 132, 190, 201, 207, 227, 231, 235, 239n, 248, 257, 312, 327, 331, 334, 338–40, 357, 362, 366, 373, 467, 470, 479–80, 510, 554; *aumône-générale*, 358–60; banks and bankers, 30, 92, 177, 188, 269, 339, 345, 504, 506, 517; Consulate (*Consulat*), 358, 364–5, 532; customs, 362, 532; fairs, 29, 365, 504; Florentine merchants, 189, 194, 345, 371; Francis I's entry, 71, 89, 131, 427; l'Ile-Barbe, abbey of, 358; nobility, 276; *pied-fourché*, 532; printers' strike (1539), 353; printing, 30; rise of, 364–5; silk industry, 358, 364–5; social structure, 34; taxation, 277; and infantry tax, 531; *deniers pour livre*, 532; *see also* Grande Rebeyne

Lyons, archbishop of, *see* Este, Ippolito d', and Tournon, François de

Lyra, Nicholas of (*c* 1270–1340), 145

Machiavelli, Niccolò (1469–1527), 521

Macon, Charles Hemart de Denonville, cardinal of, 395

Macrin, Salmon, 464, 470

Madeleine, half-sister of Francis I, 3

Madeleine (1520–37), queen of Scotland (1537), daughter of Francis I, 116, 290, 339, 343, 411

Madrid, 243, 246–7, 404; Alcázar, 404; Casa de Campo, 404–5

Madrid, château of, 392, 398, 400–5, 419, 423

Madrid, treaty of (January 1526), 246–7, 253–5, 272, 274–5, 284–5, 391, 394, 526, 533

Magdeleine, Jean de, abbot-elect of Cluny, 100n

Maigny, Charles de, 119

Maillart, Olivier, 142

Maillart, Gilles, *Lieutenant-criminel* of the Châtelet, 270

Maillezais, 469

Maine, county of, 43, 289

Mainz, Albert of Brandenburg, Elector and archbishop (1514–45), 167

Mainz, archbishop of, 165

Mair (Major), John (1467–1550), 147

maîtres des requêtes de l'hôtel, 50, 52, 120, 266

Major, J. Russell, historian, 519–20, 533, 537

Mameluk sultans, 366, 369;

Mangin, Nicole, 238

Mantegna, Andrea (d. 1506), 425

Mantua, 258, 323, 417, 432, 443, 459

Mantua, marquis and duke of, *see* Gonzaga, Federico, and Gonzaga, Francesco II

Manuel I, king of Portugal (1495–1521), 130

Manuzio (Manutius), Aldo (1450?–1515), Venetian printer-publisher, 472; Aldine press, 147

Maraviglia (Merveilles), Giovan-Alberto (d. 1533), 124

Marchand, François, sculptor, 548–9

Marchand, Jean, 48

Marche, county of, 204, 289

Marcillac, François de, First president of the parlement of Rouen, 528–9

Marcoul, St, 47

Marcourt, Antoine, 315–6

Marennes, 481

Margaret of Parma (1522–86), natural daughter of the Emperor Charles V, 282

Margaret of Savoy (1480–1530), regent of the Netherlands, aunt of the Emperor Charles V, 231, 255, 283–4

Marguerite d'Angoulême (1492–1549), duchesse d'Alençon, then (1527), queen of Navarre, sister of Francis I, 7, 83, 113, 160, 162, 179, 226, 250, 252, 308–9, 321, 372, 399, 452, 487, 557; medal, 10; birth and upbringing, 3, 113; her *Heptaméron*, 112n, 500; marries Charles d'Alençon, 113–14; interest in foreign affairs, 114; religious views, 114, 161, 321, 327; embassy to Spain, 238n, 242, 245–6; letters, 112n, 114, 161; marries Henri d' Albret, 114, 250; portrayed in masquerade, 236; protects Caroli, 239; meets Francis at Bayonne, 248; and Gérard Roussel, 261, 308; on Queen Eleanor, 289; lampooned in student play, 236, 309; prised by reformers, 308; her *Miroir de 'âme pécheresse* black-listed, 309; her portrait, 310; and Calvin, 312; and Francis's policy towards Navarre, 396; and daughter's marriage to duke of Cleves, 396; Raphael's *St Margaret* intended for her, 436; given works and portrait of Savonarola, 439; and Clément Marot, 466–7; and Rabelais, 471; her poetry, 464; favours anti-Habsburg policy, 517; and faction at court, 484–5, 499–500; mourns brother, 544; retirement and death, 554

Marguerite de France (1523–74), daughter of Francis I, later duchess of Savoy, 116, 290, 387, 394, 543–4, 551

Marignano, 73, 75, 85

Marignano, battle of (13–14 September 1515), 71, 74–9, 82, 84–5, 93, 103, 215, 549

Marignano campaign, cost of, 185

Marilhac, *avocat en Parlement*, 313

Marillac, Charles de (1510–50), 389

Marillac, Guillaume de, 205, 557

Marini, Girolamo, Italian military engineer, 491

Marot, Clément (1496–1544), 125, 270, 317, 448, 461, 464–8, 508, 560

Marot, Jean (d. 1526?), 464

Marseilles (Marseille), 23, 83, 107, 130, 242, 256, 300, 334–7, 339, 364, 369, 445, 487, 514–16; development, 365–6; Francis I meets Clement VII at, 132, 300–1; population, 365; see of, 155, 521; siege of, 214–15, 252; trade, 30

Martial, 464

Mary, daughter of the Emperor Charles V, 394

Mary of Portugal, niece of the Emperor Charles V, 240

Mary of France (1496–1533), sister of Henry VIII, queen of Louis XII, king of France (1514–15), then duchess of Suffolk, 17–18, 41, 48, 67, 112, 185, 244, 557

Mary of Hungary (1505–58), sister of the Emperor Charles V, regent of the Netherlands, 340, 387, 396, 493

Mary Stuart (1542–87), Queen of Scots, 486

Mary Tudor (1516–58), daughter of Henry VIII, later queen of England, 170, 174, 178, 259, 273, 304

Massa, Niccolò, 495

Massif Central, 355

Massy, Marie de Montchenu, dame de, 483, 549

Matignon, Jacques de, 207

Maugis, E., historian, 528

Maximilian I, Holy Roman Emperor (1493–1519), 9, 15, 66–8, 72, 82, 85–6, 93, 165–6, 185, 188, 203, 394, 479

Maximilian of Transylvania: *De Moluccis insulis*, 372

Maynier, Jean, baron d'Oppède, (1495–1585), 513–14, 516

Mazurier, Martial, 156, 162, 164n, 237, 239, 359

McFarlane, Ian, literary historian, 468

Meaux, 114, 162–3, 236–9, 359, 510; *articles de Meaux*, 162; diocese of, 102, 155–6; *see also Cercle de Meaux*

Medici, Alessandro de' (1510–37), first duke of Florence, 282, 284, 330

Medici, Catherine de' *see* Catherine de' Medici

Medici, Cosimo I, de', duke of Florence (1537–74), 457

Medici, Giovanni de', *see* Leo X

Medici, Giovanni de' ('delle Bande Nere') (1498–1526), 219, 227

Medici, Giuliano de' (1478–1516), brother of Pope Leo X, 82, 427–8

Medici, Giulio de' *see* Clement VII

Medici, house of, 62–3, 68, 79, 82, 182, 218, 260, 279, 284, 305, 439, 441, 445

Medici, Ippolito de', cardinal, 300

Medici, Lorenzo de', 'The Magnificent' (1448–92), 138

Medici, Lorenzo de' (1492–1519), duke of Urbino, nephew of Pope Leo X, father of Catherine de' Medici, 82, 124, 188, 436

Mehmet (Mohammed II), 'The Conqueror' (1451–81), Ottoman sultan, 86

Meigret, Lambert, 193, 348

Melanchthon, Philip (1497–1560), 159, 163, 303–4, 322–3, 508

Melun, 132, 516

Menant, Michel, 348

Mendoza, Diego de, alias Mandosse, 547

mercantilism, 363–4

mercenaries, 70, 79, 85, 339, 343, 352, 512

merchants, 29–30, 34, 39, 42, 85, 120, 264, 356, 362–3, 364–6, 370, 393, 512

Mérindol, 324, 511–12, 514

Merlin, Jacques, 264

Merveilles, *see* Maraviglia

metallurgy, *see under* industry

Metz, 471

Meudon, 553

Meuse, river, 19, 493

Mézières, 178–9

Michelangelo (1475–1564) 425, 432, 441–3, 445, 448

Michelet, Jules (1798–1874), historian, 112n, 175n, 556–7, 560

Midi, 55, 355

Milan, 30, 63, 72–3, 75, 77, 93, 124, 140, 176–7, 182, 208, 215–16, 219, 225, 256, 273, 300, 338, 341, 385, 427; castle, 77, 177, 184, 257; college of young Greeks, 153–4; duchy, 9, 12, 17, 62, 71, 85, 176, 182, 185, 201, 218, 240, 256, 284, 291, 304, 331, 333, 340, 386, 388–9, 394–5, 470, 517; merchants, 165n; see of, 101; senate of, 83

Milan, Pierre, 432, 454

Milly, Charles de, 513

Mini, Antonio, 432

mining, *see under* industry

mints, 286, 363; *see also* currency

Mirabello, 218

Modena, 82, 274, 279, 417

Mohács, battle of (29 August 1526), 295

Monaco, 214

Monluc, Blaise de (1499?–1577), marshal of France and memoirist, 224, 255n, 351, 490

Montbéliard, county of, 303, 343

Montbrison, 206

Montecuculli, Sebastiano de, 338

Montferrat, county of, 334, 340

Montholon, François de, Keeper of the Seals, 204, 482

Montjehan, René de, marshal of France, 340

Montmorency, Anne de (1493–1567), successively Grand Master and Constable of France, 117, 154, 193, 211, 241, 250, 252, 276–7, 279, 289, 293, 297, 304, 308, 341, 394, 399, 410, 421–2, 435, 466, 557–8; childhood companion of Francis I, 8;

Montmorency, Anne de (*cont.*)
  hostage in England, 170n; chases Bourbon out
    of Provence, 215; captured at Pavia, 224,
    226–7; negotiates with Charles V, 242–3;
    and peace of Madrid, 248; Grand Master
    and governor of Languedoc, 121, 252;
    portrait, 251; embassy to England, 273; and
    return of king's sons, 285–6; and Eleanor of
    Portugal, 117, 287, 289, 393; influence, 385;
    political ascendancy, 392–3, 398; retires
    from court, 331; returns to power, 334;
    lieutenant-général in the south, 334; defends
    Provence against Charles V, 335–8;
    lieutenant-général in the north, 339; invades
    Italy, 340; Constable of France, 340; builds
    Chantilly, 141, 423; his foreign policy, 117,
    385, 478; and Aigues-Mortes entente, 387–8;
    and Emperor's visit to France, 389–93; his
    diplomacy discredited, 395; fall, 395–7, 478,
    484–5, 536; loses governorship of
    Languedoc, 397; and Dauphin Henri,
    484–5, 549, 551–2; returns to power, 551–2;
    wealth, 252, 286
Montmorency, François de, seigneur de La
    Rochepot, (d. 1551), 224, 385, 552
Montmorency, Guillaume de (1452–1531), 193,
    286
Montmorency, house of, 553
Montmorency, Philippe de, bishop of Limoges,
    155
Montpellier, 26, 469, 480, 534
Montpellier, conference of (1519), 86–7
Montpellier, ordinance of (28 December 1537), 473
Montpensier, county of, 204, 268, 289
Montpensier, Louise de Bourbon, duchesse de, 551
Montreal, 383
Montreuil, 339, 491
Montrevel, Jean de La Baume, comte de, 552
Mont-Saint-Michel, 313, 375
Monzón, truce of (November 1537), 340
More, treaty of the (August, 1525), 235, 244,
    254, 264
Morelet de Museau, Jean, 348
Morette, Charles du Solier, seigneur de, 254n
Morin, Jean, *prévôt des marchands*, 231
Morlaix, 200
Morlaye, Guillaume, 459
Mortagne, 394
Moscoso, Alvaro de, 293
Moulins, 50, 203, 207, 340
Moulu, Pierre, 460
Mouton, Jean (1459–1522), composer, 459
Mouton, Pierre, canon of Notre Dame, 458
Mouzon, 178
Mühlberg, battle of (24 April 1547), 518
Muley Hassan, ruler of Tunis, 299
Murat, *vicomté* of, 204
Murs, 514

Nantes, 26, 29, 190, 264, 352–3, 366, 436, 552;
    population, 33, 355
Nantouillet, château of, 141

Naples, 63, 124, 240, 278–9, 409, 448
Naples, kingdom of, 9, 17, 63, 68, 82, 84–6, 93,
    133, 165, 177, 185, 194, 197, 216, 218, 256,
    259, 273, 278, 331, 333, 339, 365
Naples, Viceroy of, *see* Lannoy
Narbonne, 101, 187, 331, 340, 535–6
Nassaro, Matteo del, 448
Nassau, Henry, count of (1483–1538), 168,
    177–9, 335, 337–8
Naturelli, Philibert, 176
Naumburg, diet of (1540), 478
Navagero, Andrea, 25
Navarre, kingdom of, 15, 19, 84, 86–7, 176–7,
    246, 250, 393–4, 396
Navarre, Marguerite de, *see* Marguerite
    d'Angoulême
Navarro, Pedro, 70
navy, 83, 214–15, 240–1, 256, 279, 336, 342–3,
    367, 502–4
Nemours, duc de, *see,* Medici, Giuliano de';
    Rohan, Pierre de
Nemours, duchy of, 73, 82
Neoplatonism, 147
Nérac, 114, 308, 321, 500
Netherlands, 28–30, 84, 125, 145, 153, 165, 229,
    283, 285, 339, 366, 385, 387, 389, 391,
    393–5, 435, 493, 551
Netherlands, regent of, *see* Margaret of Savoy,
    Mary of Hungary
Neuchâtel, 315, 325
Neufville, Nicolas de, seigneur de Villeroy, 193,
    399, 418–19, 464
Nevers, Louis de Clèves, comte de, 224
Newfoundland, 370–1, 373, 375–6, 379, 383
Nice, 299, 331, 335, 386, 459, 487, 489
Nice, truce of (June 1538), 379, 381, 386
Nicholls, David, historian, 320
Nîmes, 327
Nivernais, legion of, 350
nobility, 22, 25, 28, 30–1, 34, 37–40, 43, 45, 48,
    55, 225, 244, 250, 275–6, 349, 387, 391,
    423–4, 521–2, 529, and *ban et arrière-ban*,
    69, 350, 536; and Assembly of Notables,
    274–5, 533; creation of, 188, 191; at court,
    39, 117–18, 123, 128, 132, 170, 252, 422;
    and king's council, 50–1; economic
    pressures on, 117; and episcopate, 100–1,
    155; exempt from tax, 58, 539; and *lit de
    justice*, 264; losses at Marignano, 77; losses
    at Pavia, 224; rising influence of, 252;
    power struggle among, 554; and provincial
    estates, 57, 533–4; and provincial governors,
    54–5; and provincial legions, 350; and royal
    authority, 539; taxation of, 535; and treason
    of duc de Bourbon, 206, 210–11; *see also
    seigneurie*
Noceto, Francesco di, 124
Nominalism, 145
Norfolk, duke of, *see* Howard, Thomas
Normandy, 43, 53, 57, 60, 70, 180, 196, 206, 229,
    276, 308, 313n, 502–3, 506, 510, 529–30,
    533–5; legion, 350–1

Notables, Assembly of (Tours, 1506), 12; (Paris, 1527), 274–5, 286, 533
Notre-Dame-de-Liesse, 47
Novara, battle of (June 1513), 15, 63
Noyon, 312
Noyon, treaty of (August 1516), 84, 86

Occam (or Ockham), William of (*c.* 1285–1347), 145
Odos, château of, 554
Odyssey, 417
Oecolampadius, Johann, (1482–1531), 307–8
office-holders, 32–4, 39, 101, 132, 187, 191, 198, 267, 277, 419, 422, 539
offices, 199, 252, 524; creation and sale of, 166, 188, 191, 198, 349, 500, 507, 528, 530–1, 535, 538, 559
Oiron, château of, 141
Oléron, Isle of, 481
Olivétan, *see* Robert, Pierre
Olivier, Jacques, First president of the Parlement of Paris, 87
Oppède, *see* Maynier, Jean, baron d'
Orange, Philibert de Chalon (1502–30), prince of, 209, 279
Orange, principality of, 19
ordinaire des guerres, 342
Orléans, 26, 28–9, 99, 168n, 244, 277, 315, 391, 509–10; population, 26
Orléans, Charles, duc d' (1395–1465), 1
Orléans, Charles, duc d' (1522–45), *see* Charles, duc d' Orléans
Orléans, Gaston, duc d' (1608–60), 134
Orléans, Henri, duc d', *see* Henri, duc d'Orléans
Orléans, house of, 9, 12, 63
Orléans, Louis I, duc d' (1372–1407), 1
Orléans, Louis II, duc d', *see* Louis XII
Orval, Jean d'Albret, seigneur d' (d. 1524), 166
Ottawa, river, 379, 383–4
Ottoman empire, *see* Turks
Outre-Seine-et-Yonne, *généralité* of, 60, 195, 506
Ovid, 3, 464, 466–7

Pace, Richard (1482?–1536), 167–8, 175, 214
Padua, 468
Pagès, Georges, historian, 519
Paget, William (1505–63), 483, 485–6, 504, 552
Pagny, château of, 424
Palamos, 242
Palatinate, 490
palatine, Elector-, 165
Pallavicini, Cristoforo, 180
Palmerio, Pierre, archbishop of Vienne, 102
Pampluna, 15
Pandolfo, 242n
Pannemaker, Pierre de, weaver, 448
Panofsky, D. and E., art historians, 413
papacy, 19, 100, 157, 165–6, 176, 182, 201, 254–7, 259, 297, 300, 303, 315, 343, 462, 520; appeals to, 94, 102; and appointments to benefices, 91, 94; authority in France, 90, 102; and conciliar movement, 92; and

Concordat of Bologna, 94, 96, 102; and ecclesiastical elections, 102; and French crown, 90–1, 93, 560; French policy towards, 94, 218, 297, 305; and General Council, 91–2; and Pragmatic Sanction of Bourges, 91; and taxation of French clergy, 187; and the Vaudois, 514, 516; *see also* individual popes
papal bulls, 53, 95, 312, 527; *Clericis laicos*, 90; *Divina providente gratia*, 94; *Inter Caetera*, 369, 381; *Pastor aeternus*, 94, 96; *Primitiva illa ecclesia*, 94; *Unam Sanctam*, 90, 96
Papal States, *see* States of the Church
Parajau, Jean, 348
Paris, 26, 28, 34–36, 53, 84, 95–6, 120, 132, 152, 156, 170, 189, 250, 269–70, 274–6, 286, 296, 303, 313, 315–17, 360, 401, 403, 432, 457, 460, 493, 510, 533; Bastille, 213, 269–70, 399, 484, 501, 552; Bibliothèque Nationale; 476, 560; bishop, *see* Poncher, E., Poncher, F. *and* du Bellay, Jean; book-trade, 36, 57, 159, 475, 508–9; bridges, 35, 49, 53; *Bureau de la Ville*, 37, 48, 227, 231, 250, 264, 276, 319, 360, 400, 462, 532; *Bureau des pauvres*, 360; Charles V's visit, 392, 395, 435; Châtelet, 35, 57, 194, 250, 264, 270; clergy, 99, 142; cloth industry, 30; Collège de France, 560; Conciergerie, 212–13, 239, 260; confraternities, 353; *échevins*, 37, 48; entries: (Francis I) 47–9, 114n, 121 (Claude de France), 114; (Eleanor of Portugal), 289; Charles V, 391, 403; Faubourg Saint-Honoré, 132; *faubourgs*, 34; Faculty of Arts, 35, 159; Faculty of Theology, 35, 156–7, 159, 161–3, 236–9; 249; 260–1, 263, 283, 291, 293–4, 308–9, 312–13, 316, 319–20, 322, 467, 470–1, 508; *Filles-Dieu*, 270; food supplies, 36, 53; fortification, 337; and Francis I, 129–30, 209, 212, 245, 276, 339, 398, 409, 492, 526; governor, 37, 231, 337, 400, 552; grain supplies, 55, 357; Grands Augustins, 282; Gros Tournois, 318n; *hanouars*, 546; heresy, 312, 315–17; Hôtel de Nesle, 154; Hôtel de Ville, 35, 140, 195, 212, 400, 419; Hôtel-Dieu, 35; hysteria in, 209, 315, 319; iconoclasm, 280; Ile-de-la Cité, 53; king's library moved to, 476; Louvre, 35, 260, 308, 315, 318, 346–7, 392, 398–400, 405, 421, 423, 452, 492, 506; luxury trades, 36; *Maison des Piliers*, 400; map, 143; Mathurins, 311; merchants, 36, 189; mint, 344; Musée du Louvre, 428, 430–1, 435, 445, 447n, 448, 452, 560; mystical tradition, 145; Notre-Dame, cathedral of, 35, 49, 94, 99, 163, 250, 289, 317, 435, 458, 509, 541n, 546; cloister of, 236; Notre-Dame-des-Champs, 546; *officialité*, 293; Pantin, 271; Palais de Justice, 35, 53, 392, 549; Petit Nesle, 452, 456–7; Place de Grève, 35–6, 210, 283, 400; Place Maubert, 510; poor relief, 360; population, 25–6; Porte de Nesle, 36; Porte

Paris (cont.)
Saint-Denis, 48; Pré aux Clercs, 36; preachers, 261, 308, 312, 513; *prévôt(é)*, 35, 37, 48, 56, 253, 266, 276–7, 309, 353; *prévôt des marchands*, 37, 48, 231, 275; prices, 356; printing, 30, 36, 146, 316, 509; procession, 316–17, 319; religious houses, 510; royal ransom, 276; Sainte-Catherine-des-Ecoliers, 271; Sainte-Chapelle, 317, 432, 460; Sainte-Croix-de-la Cité, 513; Saint-Germain-des-Prés, 34; Saint-Germain, fair of, 36; Saint-Germain-l'Auxerrois, 317, 513; Saint-Mathurin, 144; *Six-Corps*, 36; surface area, 35; taxation, 58, 129, 190, 195, 276–7, 337, 532; threatened by enemy invasion, 209, 490, 492; by disbanded troops, 229, 231; topography, 34; Tournelles, palace of, 18, 35; trade, 36, 364; trade gilds, 48 and treaty of the More, 244; treaty of (March 1515), 66; University of, 34–5, 57, 88, 94, 99, 144–7, 155–7, 261, 307, 309, 311, 469, 537; wages, 356; walls, 34; *see also* Collège de Boncourt, Collège de Montaigu, Collège de Navarre, Collège de Sainte-Barbe, Collège du Cardinal Lemoine, Parlement of Paris, Sorbonne
Paris, Paulin, historian, 557
Parisians, 130, 209, 212, 264, 276, 277n, 313, 337, 391, 398, 492, 508, 532
Paris region, 25; rural workers in, 356
Parker, David, historian, 538
parlements, 23, 26, 31, 42, 50–3, 57, 244, 274–5, 285, 320, 327–8, 385, 508, 521, 528, 531, 533, 538–9, 559; Aix-en-Provence, 22, 26, 53, 57, 511–13, 516; Bordeaux, 22, 26, 34, 53, 57, 213, 357, 482, 511; Chambéry, 385; Dijon, 26, 53, 57, 195; Grenoble, 26, 53, 57; Paris, 23, 35–7, 42, 48–9, 52–3, 245, 250, 318, 358, 393, 487n, 491n, 513, 533, 541, 546; and Affair of Placards, 316–19; and alienation of crown lands, 190–1, 530–1; appeals to, 56, 92, 162, 270–1, 283; and Louis de Berquin, 163, 239, 260, 283; and Charles, duc de Bourbon, 203–6, 212–13, 267; and Bourbon's accomplices, 209, 212–13, 267; and Suzanne de Bourbon's inheritance, 204; and Guillaume Briçonnet, 237–8; and censorship of books, 53, 237–8, 261, 308, 508; of plays, 245; and *Cercle de Meaux*, 163, 237–8, 260; *chambre du domaine*, 531; and Chancellor of France, 97; and Concordat of Bologna, 94–9, 232, 234–5, 249, 264, 470, 526–7, 537; and Cop's sermon, 312; councillors of, 54, 191, 194, 226; as court of peers, 243, 268; and peace of Crépy, 494; decrees (*arrêts de réglement*) of, 53–4, 56; and defence of northern France, 231; deputations to king, 260, 267, 492, 527; and Jean du Bellay, 194; and Antoine Duprat, 97, 232–6, 249, 263–4, 525–6; and Estates General, 235, 530; and *évocations*, 235, 266; First president, 54, 99,

212, 227; and Francis I, 94, 97, 232, 238, 260–1, 264, 526–7, 529; functions of, 53; and Gallican liberties, 91, 93, 97, 232; and *gens de finances*, 268; *Grand' Chambre*, 53–4, 264, 268, 274, 531; and *Grand Conseil*, 53, 232–3; headquarters of, 53; and heresy, 162, 232, 236–8, 260–1, 263, 309, 312, 321, 327–8, 510, 512; and king's council, 266; and sack of Lagny, 492; and Louise of Savoy, 204–5, 227, 231–6, 238, 263, 267, 526; and Lutheranism, 159; and Clément Marot, 466; and treaty of the More, 244, 264; and trial of Oppède, 516; and papal authority, 91, 93; and Paris, 318; powers of, 266–7; and Guillaume Poyet, 484, 500–1; and Pragmatic Sanction of Bourges, 91, 93–4, 96; presidents, 266; and reform of the coinage, 527; remonstrances of, 53, 97, 232, 266, 268, 520, 527; and René of Savoy, 95–6; *ressort* of, 53; and royal authority, 49, 54, 266; and royal legislation, 53; and sale of offices, 191, 530–1; and Semblançay, 270; and University of Paris, 100, 238; and ordinance of Villers-Cotterêts, 527–9; *see also Chambre de la Salle Verte, gens du roi, juges-délégués, lit(s) de justice*; Rennes, 26, 349; Rouen, 26, 53, 57, 213, 277, 510–11, 513, 528–30; Toulouse, 22, 26, 34, 42, 53, 57, 213, 327, 484, 494, 511
Parma, 68, 82, 179, 218, 273, 300
Parmigianino, Il, Francesco (1503–40), 417
Paul, Pierre, Italian architect, 404
Paul, St, 9, 148, 161
Paul III (Alessandro Farnese), pope (1534–49), 321n, 323, 330, 333, 380–1, 385–8, 459, 479, 487, 494, 517, 558
Pavia, 73, 75, 182, 216, 218, 224–6, 250, 479
Pavia, battle of (24 February 1525), 44, 193, 218–25, 229, 231, 244–5, 250, 252–6, 285, 466, 470, 526
pays d'états, 57, 60–1, 187, 533, 535, 538
peasantry, 25, 31, 33, 39, 58, 323–4, 335, 354–6, 359, 509, 514
Peasants' War, 229, 358
Pellicier, Guillaume, French ambassador in Venice, 472
Périgueux, 25
Périgord, 483
Pernambuco, 375
Pernes, 339
Péronne, 337–8
Perot, *see* Ruthie, Perrot de
Perpignan, 480, 484, 494, 536
Pérréal, Jean (1455?–1528?), artist, 427
Perrucel, François, 513
Persians, 299
Pescara, Ferdinando Francesco d'Avalos (1490–1525), marquis of, 216, 222
Petit, Guillaume (c. 1470–1536), bishop of Troyes then of Senlis, confessor of Francis I, 101, 150, 152, 161, 163, 294, 472
Petit, Jean, publisher, 36

Petrarch, 462, 469
Philip, archduke, 'The Fair' (1478–1506), king of Castile (1504–06), 9–10, 12, 66
Philip, prince of Spain (1527–98), son of the Emperor Charles V, later (1556–98) Philip II of Spain, 387, 394–5, 537, 544
Philip IV 'The Fair', king of France (1285–1314), 88, 90–1, 201
Piacenza, 68, 73, 82, 218–19, 300
Picardy, 15, 28, 70, 129, 180n, 200, 208, 215, 229, 231, 337, 354, 357n, 385, 490–1, 501–3; legion, 350–1
Pico della Mirandola, Giovanni (1463–94), 146–7
Piedmont, 72, 156, 323, 325, 332–5, 339–40, 345, 385, 471, 479–80, 490, 493, 504
Pigafetta, Antonio, 372
Pinerolo (Pigneroles), 334, 340
Pins, Jean de, bishop of Rieux, 468
Pio, Rodolfo, cardinal of Carpi, 386
Pisa, council of (1511), 92, 94, 156–7
Pisseleu, Anne de, *see* Etampes, Anne duchesse d'
Pitigliano, Gian-Francesco Orsini, count of, 490
Pizzighettone, 226, 240, 247
Placards, Affair of the (October 1534), 305, 313–21, 466, 509
Plato, 146, 306
Pléiade, the, 468
Plessis-lez-Tours, 3, 12, 14
Ploret, Roland de, 4, 6
Plotinus, 473n
Poggio a Caiano, Villa del, 138
Poitiers, 26, 102, 391, 468
Poitiers, battle of (September 1356), 246
Poitiers, Diane de (1499–1566), 210n, 392, 422, 454, 497, 551, 553
Poitiers, Jean de, seigneur de Saint-Vallier, 207, 209–10, 212, 267
Poitou, 129, 469, 481
Poland, 236
Poland, king of, 166
Pole, Reginald (1500–58), cardinal, 388
Pole, Richard de la (d. 1525), 200, 222, 224
Polignac, Anne de, 423
Polignac, Antoinette de, 3
Polignac, François de, 423
'Polin, Captain', *see* La Garde
Pollaiuolo, Antonio (1429–98), 441
Pompérant, seigneur, de, 224n
Poncher, Etienne, bishop of Paris (1503–19), archbishop of Sens (1519–25), 87, 101, 153, 155, 232n
Poncher family, 349
Poncher, François, bishop of Paris (1519–32), 163, 232n, 236, 261, 263–4
Poncher, Jean, *trésorier-général*, 271, 348
Poncher, Louis, 192
Pontbriant, Pierre de, 11
Pontormo, Jacopo da (1494–1557), 441
poor, 24, 33, 132, 356–9, 368, 532; relief of, 358–9, 559

Poor Men of Lyons, 323
Pope-Hennessy, J., art historian, 452
Popillon, Pierre, 213
population, *see* France
Portugal, 361, 369, 373–5, 382
Portugal, king of, *see* Afonso V, Manuel I, John III
Portuguese, 366, 370–1, 393
Postel, Guillaume (1510–81), orientalist, 471
Pot, Philippe, 41
Poyet, Guillaume (1473–1548), Chancellor of France, 204, 237, 332, 352, 392–3, 395–6, 484, 500–1, 527–9, 538
Praet, Louis de Flandre, seigneur de, 253
Pragmatic Sanction of Bourges, *see* Bourges, Pragmatic Sanction of
Pras, Honorat Puget, seigneur de, 214
Prentout, Henri, historian, 519
Preti, Federico de', 443
Preudhomme, Guillaume, *receveur-général*, 196, 347
Prévost, Jean, *commis à l'extraordinaire*, 196, 269
prices, 32, 53, 132, 344, 355–7, 368, 559
Primaticcio, Francesco (1504/5–70), 392, 410, 412, 417–18, 432, 435–6, 447–8, 455, 457, 498, 523, 549
princes of the blood, 45, 48, 50, 102, 120
printing, *see under* industry
Provence, 19, 24, 28, 156, 239, 323–4, 334–6, 341, 354, 365, 483, 489, 511, 514–16; agriculture, 25; annexation (1481), 30; estates, 57, 533–4; governor, 43, 552; invaded by duc de Bourbon, 214–15, 373; invaded by Charles V, 334–9, 515; legion, 350; mints, 286; *recette-générale*, 506; taxation, 58, 60; visited by Francis I, 129, 339; *see also* Marseilles, Vaudois, Waldensianism
Provence, counts of, 84
provinces, *see* individual provinces and estates, governors, legions, parlements
Puccini, Giovanni Battista, 431
Puteaux, 403
Pyrenees, 19, 256, 350

Quebec, 378

Raban Maur (776 or 784–856), 150
Rabelais, François, 292, 306, 467, 469–71, 560
Raemond, Florimond de, 318
Raimondi, Marcantonio, 436, 440
Rambouillet, château de, 541, 545
Ramus Pierre (1515–72), *lecteur royal*, 475
Ramusio, Giovanni, Battista, 384n
Raphael (1483–1520), 103, 427, 432, 436–8, 440
Raulin, Jean, 142, 155
Ravenna, 279, 284
Ravier, Jean, 269
Realism, 145
Rebuffi, Pierre, 524–5
recettes-générales, 346, 506–7

receveur-général des parties casuelles, 198, 507
receveurs-généraux des finances, 61, 346, 348
receveurs ordinaires, 60
régale, 92
Reggio nell'Emilia, 82, 274, 279
Rély, Jean de, 90
Rémon, Pierre, *avocat-général*, 531
Renée de France (1510–75), second daughter of
    King Louis XII, duchess of Ferrara, 15, 17,
    66, 84, 205, 250, 274, 330, 466
Rennes, 350; *see under* parlements
rentes sur l'Hôtel de Ville de Paris, 195–6
résignations, 191
Reuchlin, Johannes (1455–1522), 150, 157, 159
revenue, royal, *see* aides; clergy; clerical tenths;
    fiscal expedients; *gabelle*; *taille*
Rheims (Reims), 28, 45, 47, 102, 178, 203, 277,
    351, 487
Rhenanus, Beatus, (d. 1547), 147, 156
rhétoriqueurs, 150, 461–2, 464, 467–8
Rhine, river, 167
Rhodes, 30, 104, 182
Rhodes, Grand Master of, 369
Rhône, river, 19, 29, 84, 208, 336
Richet, Denis, historian, 539
Richmond, Henry Fitzroy, duke of (1519–36),
    297
Rieux, bishop of, 468; clergy of, 187
Riez, see of, 256n
Rincon, Antonio (d. 1541), 295–6, 389, 436,
    478–9
Robert, Pierre (alias Olivétan), 325
Robertet, Florimond (d. 1527), secretary of state,
    42, 192, 252, 267
Roberval, Jean-François de La Roque, seigneur
    de, 382–4
Rochefort, François de, *see* Demoulins, François
Rochford, Lord, *see* Boleyn, George
Rodez, see of, 92, 101–2, 155
Roger, François, *procureur général*, 234
Rohan, Charles de, comte de Guise, 42
Rohan, Pierre de (1451–1513), seigneur de Gié,
    duc de Nemours, marshal of France, 4, 8,
    11–12, 42
Roma, Jean de, inquisitor, 324
Romano, Giulio (1492–1546), 412, 417, 427, 432,
    436, 438, 448
Romano, Paolo, 457
Rome, 11, 62, 90, 103, 177, 236, 253, 282, 334,
    387, 425, 432, 439, 452; Belvedere, 411, 447;
    Charles V's speech in, 333; college of young
    Greeks in, 152–3; Greek manuscripts copied
    in, 472; Primaticcio's artistic mission to,
    417, 447; sack of (1527), 259–60, 272,
    279–80; *see also* papacy
Romorantin, 9, 109, 140, 176, 428
Roquefort-de-Marsan, 286
Rossi, Ruberto di, 447
Rosso, Giovanni Battista (1494–1540), 391–2,
    410–15, 432–5, 443, 454
Rouen, 29–30, 36, 104, 195, 244, 315, 351, 357,
    361, 364, 366, 370, 375, 482, 511, 513, 529,

535; *Chambre des Comptes*, 435;
    choir-school, 458; ordinance of (1532), 345;
    population, 26; procession, 317n; *see also*
    under parlements
Rouen, archbishop of, *see* Amboise, Georges I
    and II
Rouergue, 155
Roussel, Gérard (1480–1550), 156, 163, 238,
    239n, 260–1, 307–9, 470
Roussillon, 19
Rovere, Francesco Maria della (1491–1538),
    duke of Urbino, 82, 256
Rozone, Gian Stefano, 113n, 425
Rubens, Peter Paul (1577–1640), 441–2
Ruiz family, 366
Russell, Sir John (1486?–1555), 207, 214, 221,
    224
Rustici, Giovanni Francesco, sculptor, 447
Ruthie, Perrot de, 110, 111n
Ruzé family, 192
Ruzé, Jean, *receveur-général*, 231, 348
Ruzé, Jeanne, 271

Saalfeld, treaty of (October 1531), 295
sacramentarianism, 315, 320, 509, 560
sacramentarians, 313n, 320–1, 326
Sacred College, 86, 182, 201, 333
Sagredo, Diego de, 423
'Saguenay' (Canada), 378–84
Saint-André, marshal, *see* Albon, Jacques d'
Saint-Benoît-sur-Loire, abbey of, 232–4, 236,
    263, 266–7; abbot of, *see* Duprat, Antoine
Saint-Blancard, Bertrand d'Ornesan, baron de,
    336, 375
Saint-Bonnet, Hector d'Angeray, alias, 210
Saint-Claude, 208
Saint-Cloud, palace of, 545
Saint-Denis, 272n
Saint-Denis, abbey of, 41, 47, 71, 84, 84n, 114,
    201, 250, 287, 356, 546–9
Saint-Dizier, siege of, 491–3, 557
Sainte-Croix (Canada), 378–9, 383
Saint-Fort, 481
Saint-Gelais, Jean de, 3–4
Saint-Gelais, Mellin de (1491–1558), 464, 468–9,
    472
Saint-Gelais, Octovien de, bishop of Angoulême,
    3, 468
Saint-Gelais, Pierre de, 468
Saint-Germain-des-Prés, abbey of, 356
Saint-Germain-en-Laye, 12, 116, 250, 264, 276,
    401, 419–23, 431, 541, 552
Saint-Germain-en-Laye, château of, 132, 318n,
    398, 405–7, 551
Saint-Jean d'Angély, 481
Saint-Just, 481
Saint-Just (near Lyons), 226, 248
Saint-Macaire, 481
Saint-Malo, 376, 378–9, 383, 552
Saint-Marsault, François Green, seigneur de,
    193
Saint-Maur-des-Fossés, abbey of, 289

Saint-Mauris, Jean de, imperial ambassador in France, 188n, 313n, 541, 543–4, 551
Saint-Omer, 394
Saintonge, 3, 482–3
Saint-Pierre-le-Moûtier, 201
Saint-Pol, 339–40
Saint-Pol, comte de, *see* Bourbon, François I *and* II, de
Saint-Pol, county of, 339
Saint-Quentin, 337, 393, 459, 487
Saint-Rémi (Remigius), 45
Saint-Simon, Louis de Rouvroy (1675–1755), duc de, 243n
Saint-Vallier, *see* Poitiers, Jean de
Sala, Pierre, 112n
Salai, Giacomo, 431
salamander, 10–11, 48, 121, 131, 403, 414, 436
Salazar, Jean de, 232
Salet, Hughes, 472
Salic Law, 3, 41, 522, 555
Sallust, 146
Salon, 83
salt, *see under* industry, trade
salt tax, see *gabelle*
Saluzzo, bishop of, 111, 133
Saluzzo, Francis (Francesco), marquis of (from 1528), 334
Saluzzo, Michele-Antonio (1495–1528), marquis of, 279
Salviati, Francesco, 447
Sancerre, Louis de Beuil, comte de, 491
Sandrin, Pierre (*c.* 1490–d. after 1561), musician, 107
Sangallo, Aristotile da, 448
Sangallo, Giuliano da (1445–1516), 138
Sanguin, Antoine, cardinal, 553
Sanguin, Nicole, 510
San Sebastian, 15, 247
San Severini family, 124
San Severino, Galeazzo da (d. 1525), *Grand écuyer*, 124, 140, 224, 253
Sant'Angelo, Ferrante Castriot, marquis of, 222
Santi Quattro Coronati, cardinal, 82n
Saône, river, 19, 29, 206, 231
Sapin, Jean, 348
Sardinia, 279
Sarto, Andrea del (1486–1531), 430–2, 441
Sauval, Henri, historian, 399, 404
Savigliano, 340
Savona, 279
Savonarola, Girolamo (1452–98), 114n, 439
Savoy, duchy of, 29, 63, 72, 212, 323, 331–4, 385, 394, 467, 493, 558
Savoy, duke of, *see* Charles III, duke of Savoy
Savoy, Louise of, *see* Louise of Savoy
Savoy, Madeleine of (d. 1586), wife of Anne de Montmorency, 252
Savoy, Margaret of, *see* Margaret of Savoy
Savoy, Philip of (d. 1497), count of Bresse, Francis I's maternal grandfather, 1
Savoy, René of (d. 1525), called 'great bastard of Savoy', Grand Master of France, 43, 72–3, 93, 95, 96, 121, 193, 224, 252

Saxony, 295
Saxony, duke of, 165
Saxony, Frederick III 'The Wise', Elector of (1486–1525), 166, 168
Saxony, George, duke of (1500–39), 301
Saxony, John, 'The Constant', Elector of (1525–32), 295
Saxony, John Frederick, Elector of (1532–47), 322, 396, 478, 517–18
Scandinavia, 30
Scheldt, river, 19
Scheyern, treaty of (May 1532), 295, 297, 302
Schiner, Matthias (d. 1522), bishop of Sion, cardinal, 73–4, 85
Schmalkaldic League (1531), 295, 323, 388, 478, 505, 509
Schmalkaldic War, 517–18
scholasticism, 144, 147, 157
schoolmen, 149, 159
Scibec de Carpi, Francisque, 412
Scotland, 188n, 195, 200–1, 244, 343, 483, 486, 502–3
Scots, 125, 200, 244, 486, 490, 501–3
Scotus, John Duns (*c.* 1265–1308), 145
Screech, M. A., 470–1
seals, royal, 48, 51–2, 71, 253, 500
secrétaires des finances, 507
secretaries, royal, 39, 42, 52, 120, 128, 132, 422, 462, 553
Sedan, 177
Sedan, seigneur de, *see* La Marck, Robert II de
Segovia, 278
seigneur(s), seigneurie(s), 31–3, 38–9, 54, 356
Seine, river, 34–6, 357, 367, 401, 452, 455
Selim, 'The Grim', Ottoman sultan (1512–20), 86
Selve, Georges de, French ambassador in Venice, 466, 472
Selve, Jean de (1475–1529), First president of the Parlement of Paris, 77, 212, 227, 229, 243, 245, 269, 275
Selve, Odet de (d. 1563), 473n, 503
Semblançay, *see* Beaune, Jacques de
sénéchal(aux), sénéchaussée(s), 26, 52, 54–5, 60, 69, 268, 276
Senlis, bishop of, *see* Petit, Guillaume
Sens, archbishop of, *see* Duprat, Antoine; Poncher, Etienne
Sens, archbishopric of, 234, 236, 263, 266–7
Sens, cathedral, 51; chapter, 232; province, 282
Serlio, Sebastiano (1475–1554), architect, 410, 423, 447
Sermisy, Claude de (*c.* 1490–1562), musician, 107, 458, 460, 560
Serravalle, battle of (June 1544), 490
Sesia, battle of the river (30 April 1524), 211
Seyssel, Claude de (1450–1520), bishop of Marseilles, 28, 39–40, 83, 155, 521–2, 525
Sforza, Francesco (1495–1535), duke of Milan, 182, 255–7, 284, 304, 331
Sforza, house of, 62, 85
Sforza, Massimiliano (1491–1530), duke of Milan (to 1515), 63, 67–8, 72–3, 77, 99, 131, 188

Sicily, 30, 63, 330, 365, 487
Sickingen, Franz von (1481–1523), 165n, 558
Siena, 257, 333
Sigismund I, king of Poland (1506–48), 295
silk, *see under* industry, trade
Silveira, João da, 371
Sisteron, 83
Sixtus IV (Francesco della Rovere), pope (1471–84), 91–2
Sleidan, Johannes (d. 1556), 517
Soderini, Francesco, (1453–1524), cardinal, 201
Soissons, 492–3
Soissons, Mathieu de Longuejoue, bishop of, 395
solde des gens de pied, 26–7, 186, 195, 536
solde des 20,000 hommes de pied, 345
solde des 50,000 hommes de pied, 504, 531–2
Solothurn, 73
Solway Moss, battle of (25 November 1542), 486
Sorbonne, 35, 144–6, 156, 471, 560; *see also* Paris: Faculty of Theology
Sourdis, Jean d'Escoubleau, seigneur de, *valet de chambre* of Francis I, 543
Souveraine, half-sister of Francis I, 3
Spain, 31, 156, 165, 168, 179, 208, 248, 336, 386, 389, 391; Charles V's authority in, 86; Charles V's movements to and from, 256, 339; Queen Eleanor retires to, 551; Francis I's captivity in, 129, 241–3, 245–8, 401, 404, 495, 526; Francis's sons hostages in, 254–6, 293; Marguerite d'Angoulême in, 238n, 242, 245–6; and overseas enterprise, 369; trade with, 30, 243, 361; *see also* Aragon, Castile, Navarre
Spaniards, 125, 366
Speyer, diet of, 490
spices, *see under* trade
Spifame, Gaillard, 347–9
Spine (Spina), Pierre, banker, 188
Spont, Alfred, historian, 167n
Spurs, battle of the (16 August 1513), 15
St Lawrence river 377–9, 388, 552
St Petersburg, 107, 448
Stadacona (Canada), 378
Stafileo, John, bishop of Transylvania, 296
Standonck, John, 142, 146, 149
States of the Church, 62–3, 177, 218, 258, 365, 487
Stenay, 494
Strassburg (Strasbourg), 238–9, 322, 326, 516
Strozzi, Filippo (1489–1538), 330, 343, 441, 443
Strozzi, Leone (1515–54), prior of Capua, 489
Strozzi, Piero (d. 1556), 490, 517
Strozzi, Roberto, 443
Stubbs, W., historian, 556, 560
Sturm, Johannes (1507–89), 471
Suffolk, duke of, *see* Brandon, Charles
Suleiman 'The Magnificent', Ottoman sultan (1520–66), 245, 296, 299–300, 329, 366, 370, 389, 439, 478–9, 487, 489, 494
Surrey, earl of, *see* Howard, Thomas
survivances, 191
Suscinio, castle of, 349

Sussanée, Hubert, 470
Sutherland, N. M., historian, 320, 322
Swabian League, 165n, 168, 302–3
Swiss, 29, 43, 74, 82, 85, 93, 120, 125, 178n, 179–80, 182–3, 190, 208, 215, 218, 256, 505, 516; avarice of, 193; bear, 131; and Bonnivet's Italian campaign, 211–12; pensions to, 185, 188, 343; invade Burgundy, 15, 63; confederation (cantons), 29; and treaty of Dijon, 63, 67; envoys to France, 326–7; Francis I and, 72–3, 77, 79, 326–7; and 'perpetual peace' of Fribourg, 85; and Gallarate peace talks, 73, 93; at La Bicocca, 182–3; at Marignano, 73, 75, 77; mercenaries, 67, 70, 343, 350; defend Milanese, 72; at Pavia, 222, 225; reformers, 327 see also *Cent-suisses, Switzerland,* individual cantons
Switzerland, 303, 315, 389
Syria, 86, 369

Taignoagny, 377–8
taille, 32, 58–60, 186, 195, 229, 275, 344, 354, 504, 530, 534; collectors of, 286; *crue(s) de,* 58, 196, 229, 534–5; exemptions from, 34, 39, 189, 350–1, 367, 491n
Talaveruela, 551
Tallard, *see* Clermont, Julien de
Talmont, Charles de la Trémoïlle (1485–1515), prince de, 77n
Tarascon, 83, 336
Tarbes, bishop of, *see* Gramont, Gabriel
Tarragona, 242
Tavannes, Gaspard de Saulx (1509–73), marshal of France, 558
Tavel, François, 235
taxation, 19, 26–7, 54, 58–60, 186, 189–90, 344, 538; popular resistance to, 480; power to tax, 530; see also *aides,* clergy; clerical tenths, *gabelle, taille*
Taylor, Dr John (d. 1534), archdeacon of Berkshire, 131
Testard, Robinet, illuminator of manuscripts, 3
Thenaud, Jean, 104, 150
Thérouanne, 15–17, 239, 339–40, 486
third estate, 38–9, 57, 349, 534
Thizart, René, 348
Thomas Aquinas, St, 145
Thou, Jacques-Auguste de (1553–1617), historian, 555
Thucydides, 473
Ticino, river, 73, 216, 219, 222, 224
Ticquet, Jacques, 448
Tissard, François, 147
Tissart, Philibert, 348
Titian (Tiziano Vecellio) (1477–1576), 444–5
Tobia, Milanese goldsmith, 439
Toledo, 242, 246
tolls, 56, 58, 120, 361
Torrejon, 247
Tory, Geoffroy (c. 1480–c. 1533), 158, 423
Toulon, 215; Turkish occupation of, 489

Toulouse, 26, 30, 34, 36, 103, 190, 355, 367, 468, 535–6; population, 26; see of, 552; *see also under* parlements

Touraine, 403;

Tour Carrée, Commission de la, 268–9, 347–9

Tournai, 16–17, 67, 167n, 170, 179–80, 185, 239–40, 284, 394, 482

Tournon, Charles de (d. 1504), bishop of Rodez, 92

Tournon, François de (1489–1562), archbishop of Embrun then of Bourges, cardinal, 153n, 275, 365, 395, 399, 458, 466, 485, 492, 503, 517, 543, 553; embassy to Spain, 240, 243, 275; archbishop of Bourges, 253; cardinal, 285; supervises ransom for kings' sons, 285; embassy to Holy See, 297–9; *lieutenant-général* in south-east France, 339, 486; raises loans for king, 345, 365, 486, 499, 505–6; and duchesse d'Etampes, 499; supports peace of Crépy, 517; embassy to the Netherlands, 513; charged with dishonesty, 499; fall, 552

Tournus, 338

Tours, 12–13, 26, 30, 102, 171n, 244, 269, 315, 364, 403; shrine of St Martin, 116, 195

Toussain, Pierre, 114, 239

Toussaint, Jacques, *lecteur royal,* 306

towns, 12, 25–6, 28–31, 41, 55, 58, 95, 123, 130, 244, 356, 369, 391, 538–9, 559; death rate in, 33; and economic reform, 360–1; exploitation of countryside, 357; forced loans, 60, 187–9, 507; garrisons, 352; social structure, 33–4; taxation of, 186, 190, 195, 276–7, 344, 504, 515, 531, 535

trade, 26, 29–30, 34, 36, 356, 360–1, 366, 368–9, 505, 536, 559; cloth, 361, 364; grain, 28, 36, 356–7, 362; salt, 29, 36, 58–9, 366; silk, 36, 361, 364–5; spices, 36, 361, 364, 366–7, 369–70; wine, 28, 36, 361, 366–7

trade, royal control of, 362; *see also* customs duties

Trechsel, Jean, Lyons printer, 36

Tréguier, 101

Trent, 236, 517

Trésor de l'Epargne, 345, 507

Trésorier de l'Epargne, 198, 307, 346, 507; *see also* Babou, Philibert; Blondet, André; Duval, Jean

trésoriers de France, 60–1, 191–2, 198–9, 346, 348

Trésorier des parties casuelles, 198

Treviso, Girolamo da, 447

Tribolo, Niccolò, sculptor, 441

Triboulet, Francis I's fool, 555

Trier, Richard von Greiffenklau, archbishop and Elector of (1521–31), 165–8

Trier, see of, 167

Tripoli, 366

Trivulzi family, 124

Trivulzio, Agostino, cardinal, 334, 338

Trivulzio, Gian-Giacomo (1448–1518), marshal of France, 43, 72–3, 77, 124

Troyes, 26, 101, 190, 358

Tschudi, Pierre, 156

Tunis, 299, 330

Tunstal, Cuthbert (1474–1559), bishop of London then of Durham, 247, 475

Turin, 72, 155, 214, 332, 334, 340, 385, 467, 471

Turks, 62, 86, 103–4, 168, 182, 201, 229, 279, 291, 295, 297, 299–300, 305, 321, 329, 339–41, 366, 386–7, 393, 478–9, 489, 493, 517, 543; *see also* Barbarossa, *Capitulations,* Levant, individual sultans

Turquam, Thomas, 189

Turquet, Etienne, 365

Tuscany, 30, 365

Ulpian, 520

Urbino, 409

Urbino, duchy of, 331

Urbino, duke of, *see* Medici, Lorenzo de' and Rovere, Francesco Maria della

Valdés, Alonso de (1490?–1532), 255

Valence, 26, 337

Valencia, 242

Valencia, archbishop of, 479

Valenciennes, 180, 393

Valois, governor of, 253

Valois, house of, 1

Van Cleve, Joos, 107n

Van Doren, S. N., historian, 535

Vannes, 349

Var, river, 214, 335

Varazzo, 219

Varengeville, 371

Varènes, Alain de, 155

Varennes, Valéran de, 19

Varga, Francisco de, 404–5

Varillas, Antoine, historian, 249n, 557

Vasari, Giorgio (1511–74), 410, 412, 417, 427, 431, 435, 441, 443, 449

Vasto, Alfonso del Avalon (1500–46), marquis del, 219, 389, 490

Vatable, François, *lecteur royal,* 306

Vatican palace, 103, 135

Vaudois, 323–5, 511–12; massacre of (1545), 513–16

Vendôme, county then duchy of, 43

Vendôme, duc de, *see* Bourbon, Charles de; Bourbon, Antoine de

Vendôme, Marie de Luxembourg, duchesse de, 249–50, 285

vénerie, 111, 120, 123

Venetians, 43, 67, 73, 77, 86, 244, 256, 284, 369, 386, 389, 445

Venice, 30, 62–3, 85, 132, 154, 201, 244, 254–5, 343, 432, 439n, 445, 447, 466, 472, 479

Vérard, Antoine, 36

Verdi, Giuseppe (1813–1901), 210n, 555

Vergikios, Angelos, Cretan scribe, 472, 477

Verjus, André, 96, 98

Vernavola, river, 219

Versoris, Nicolas, chronicler, 195, 212

Verrazzano, Giovanni da (d. 1528), 371–4, 376, 384

Vexin, 28

Vienna, 296, 449, 452

Vienne, 208, 339

Vigne, André de la, 89

Vignola, Giacomo Barozzi da (1507–73), architect, 447

Villafranca, 72

Villefranche, 300, 386, 487

Villeneuve, 386

Villeroy, seigneur de, *see* Neufville, Nicolas de

Villers-Cotterêts, château of, 392, 398, 407, 419

Villers-Cotterêts, ordinance of (30 August 1539), 352–3, 500, 527–8

villes-franches, 58, 129, 198, 536

Villiers, Charles de, bishop of Limoges, 102

Vincennes, 250, 264, 393, 552

Vingle, Pierre de, 325

Virgil, 3, 146, 464, 467

Visconti, Filippo, 124

Visconti, house of, 62–3

Visconti, Valentina (d. 1408), 1, 62

Vitruvius, 423

Vitry-en-Perthois, 491

Vitry-le-François, 491n

Vives, Juan Luis (1492–1540), 359

Voré, Barnabé de, 322

wages, 53, 356–57, 368

Wain, Gervase (*c*. 1491–1554), 293, 295

Waldenses (Waldensians), *see* Vaudois, Waldensianism, 156

Wallop, Sir John (d. 1551), 416, 486–7

Warty, Perrot de (d. 1542), 207

weights and measures, 361

Weikmann, 505

Welsers, 505

West, Nicholas (1461–1533), bishop of Ely, 180

Westminster, treaty of (April 1527), 259

Wight, Isle of, 502

'Windsor indemnity', 285

wine, *see* agriculture *and under* trade

Wingfield, Sir Richard (1469?–1525), 109, 111

Wolfe, Martin, historian, 199

Wolsey, Thomas (1475?–1530), archbishop of York, cardinal, Chancellor of England, 67, 109, 113, 170–1, 174–5, 177–9, 214, 229, 258, 272, 278, 282, 297, 343

Worcester, Charles Somerset (1460?–1526), earl of, 170, 179

Worms, diet of (1521), 517

Wotton, Nicholas (1497?–1567), 497

Württemberg, Christopher, son of Ulrich, duke of, 302

Würtemberg, duchy of, 295, 302–3, 305

Würtemberg, Ulrich, duke of, 295, 303, 343

Wyatt, Sir Thomas (1503?–42), 392

Xaintois, 28

Zápolyai, John Sigismund (d. 1540), Voivode of Transylvania, 295–6, 478

Zeeland, 66

Zürich, 180, 282, 326–7

Zwingli, Huldrych (1484–1531), 261, 307, 313, 315

Zwinglianism, 315

Zwinglians, 308